# ROADS TO EXTINCTION:
# ESSAYS ON THE HOLOCAUST

CONFERENCE ON JEWISH SOCIAL STUDIES
THE JEWISH PUBLICATION SOCIETY OF AMERICA
*New York and Philadelphia   5740 · 1980*

# PHILIP FRIEDMAN

# ROADS TO EXTINCTION: ESSAYS ON THE HOLOCAUST

*edited by* ADA JUNE FRIEDMAN
*with an introduction by* SALO WITTMAYER BARON

*Library of Congress Cataloging in Publication Data
Friedman, Philip, 1901–1960. Roads to extinction.
  Includes bibliographical references and index.
1.  Holocaust, Jewish (1939–1945)—Addresses, essays,
lectures.  I.  Friedman, Ada June.  II.  Title.
D810.J4F739  1980     940.53'1503'924     79-89818
ISBN 0-8276-0170-0*

*Designed by Adrianne Onderdonk Dudden*

# CONTENTS

# FOREWORD

It has been a long-cherished hope of the board of directors of the Conference on Jewish Social Studies and the editors of its quarterly journal to publish a volume of the collected essays of Philip Friedman, "the father of the Jewish Holocaust literature." This, we felt, would constitute a significant service to the Jewish community. We are therefore pleased that such a volume is now a reality.

The late Philip Friedman was uniquely qualified for his task, combining, as he did, immediacy with sound historical methodology. He began his scholarly researches into the Holocaust just after World War II; himself a survivor of the catastrophe, he had the advantage of being personally acquainted with many of the persons involved in trying to keep the Polish Jewish communities alive during the Nazi occupation and could therefore obtain from them much important documentation as well as first-hand recollections. Later, when he served for two years as the educational director of the Displaced Persons camps in Germany, he had the opportunity to interview survivors and to elicit from them a great deal of oral and written information. Ultimately, an extensive archival collection he amassed was presented to the YIVO Institute for Jewish Research by his widow, Ada June Friedman, the editor of the present volume; there it has been used by numerous students of the great tragedy.

The results of some of his labors over the years are presented here in sober essays that appear to us as a much-needed corrective to predominantly emotional but often factually incorrect outpourings that mark so much Holocaust writing today.

Like the editor of this volume, we also are indebted to all those persons who have given of their time and effort to lend to these diverse essays, written under varying circumstances over a span of years, a sense of unity and continuity. We are also grateful to those individuals and organizations who have made this publication possible. We especially want to thank the Wurzweiler Foundation, Mr. Leon Jolson, the Memorial Foundation for Jewish Culture, Mr. Benjamin Cohen, the J. M. Kaplan Fund, Inc., and several Conference directors for their generous contributions.

Finally, we are happy to be able to publish this volume as a joint venture with The Jewish Publication Society of America.

*Jeannette M. Baron,* President
Conference on Jewish Social Studies

# PREFACE

The history of the Holocaust has now become a vital part of general and Jewish scholarship. Indeed, within recent years this relatively new historical discipline, of which the late Philip Friedman was a pioneer, has burgeoned, gaining the attention of an increasing number of researchers and the interest of a growing readership.

The present volume contains a selection of essays and studies on the subject of the Holocaust written by Philip Friedman over a period of fifteen years, from 1945 to 1960. In selecting the material for this collection, culled from approximately 200 bibliographical entries, the following criteria were considered: (1) to present those essays that are the most comprehensive and fundamental for the study of the Holocaust; (2) to include those which are of lasting value; (3) to show the author's approach to the problems of the Holocaust and indicate his method of work.

Many of the essays included in this volume are not readily accessible elsewhere. Only some were originally published in English. For the rest, they are to be found, in their original form, only in scattered journals and books in different parts of the world and published in various languages—Polish, Yiddish, and Hebrew. The present translations from Polish and Yiddish are my own. Considering that each language has its own idiom, the task for the translators was made doubly onerous as I tried, insofar as possible, to retain the original nuances. For the sake of uniformity, the translated material had to undergo a thorough stylistic revision. Much repetitious material was deleted, except in a few cases where comprehension of the essay as a whole would have suffered.

A constant problem in preparing the volume was the presentation of the footnotes. These, in some instances, are now dated in the sense that they were prepared at a time when research into the Holocaust was just beginning. Many documentary sources known today were not available to the author, and those existent were not yet published. I chose to reproduce the footnotes in their original form. However, many sources only fragmentarily cited can be supplemented easily by the data in *Guide to Jewish History Under Nazi Impact* by Jacob Robinson and Philip Friedman (New York, 1960) and in the Bibliographical Series published jointly by YIVO and Yad Vashem, as well as in other handbooks.

The idea to publish a collection of Philip Friedman's studies and essays on the Holocaust was put forward right after his death in 1960 by Salo Wittmayer Baron, the author's former teacher and lifelong friend. I am most grateful to Professor Baron for his unswerving belief in the importance of this project and for his efforts in bringing it to realization after so many years. I consider it a debt which can never be repaid. I am infinitely thankful to Jeannette M. Baron for her invaluable help and her personal dedication to the task of obtaining publication for the volume, as well as for her stimulating support and expert assistance in all the time-consuming stages of preparing the manuscript, including its final reading. I also wish to express my gratitude to the Board of Directors of the Conference on Jewish Social Studies for their contribution toward the publication of this volume.

I am truly obliged to the translators of the Hebrew essays. Theirs was a painstaking task requiring much familiarity with the subject matter and the linguistic subtleties of the original texts. I am grateful to Dalia Berman and Dr. Jane Gerber for their translations of essays 13 and 14; to Dr. Bertram Schwarzbach for the translation of essay 12 and for linguistic and stylistic corrections in essay 11; and to Dr. Amiel Ungar, who translated essay 10, the longest in the volume. I also wish to express my sincerest thanks to Henry Sachs, my friend and colleague, for his expert help in the translation of some complicated German texts that are quoted in various essays and for his knowledgeable advice; and to Dina Abramowicz, the librarian of YIVO, for her ungrudging assistance.

The copy editing and stylistic refinements are the work of Michelle M. Kamhi. I extend my deepest appreciation for her high degree of professional competence. Above all, she must be commended for involving herself with so much interest, understanding, and compassion in the myriad details that comprise the painful subject of this book.

*Ada June Friedman*

# ACKNOWLEDGMENTS

We are grateful to the publishers of the books, pamphlets, and periodicals listed below for their generosity in granting permission for the republication of the following essays:

American Academy of Jewish Research, essay 20
*Bitzaron,* The Hebrew Monthly of America, essays 13, 14
Central Commission for the Investigation of German Crimes in Poland, essay 9
Columbia University Press, essay 5
Conference on Jewish Social Studies, essays 3, 19, 21
*Davar,* Revista Literaria. Editado por la Sociedad Hebraica Argentina, essay 11
*Entsiklopedia shel galuyot,* Jerusalem, essay 10
*Historia Judaica,* essay 1
Jewish Book Council of America, essay 4
*Jewish Frontier,* essay 15
*Metsuda,* London (Ararat Publishing House), essay 12
Pergamon Press, Ltd., Oxford, England, essay 16
Rijksinstituut voor Oorlogsdokumentatie, Amsterdam, The Netherlands, Appendix
The Wiener Library, London, essay 7
*Yad Vashem Studies,* Jerusalem, essays 22, 23
*Yidisher Kemfer,* essays 6, 17
YIVO Institute for Jewish Research, essays 2, 8, 18

# ABBREVIATIONS

| | |
|---|---|
| *AJC Report* | American Jewish Committee Research Institute on Peace and Post-War Problems, "The Jews in Germany" (New York, July 1944) |
| Apenszlak, *Black Book* | Apenszlak, Jacob, ed., *The Black Book of Polish Jewry* (New York, 1943) |
| *BFG* | *Bleter far Geshikhte.* Quarterly of Jewish Historical Institute in Poland |
| *BGK* | *Biuletyn Głównej Komisji Badania Zbrodni Niemieckich w Polsce* |
| *Biuletyn* | *Biuletyn Żydowskiego Instytutu Historycznego w Polsce* |
| *Black Book* | *The Black Book: The Nazi Crime Against the Jewish People* (New York, 1946) |
| CDJC | Centre de Documentation Juive Contemporaine, Paris |
| CGQJ | Commissariat Général aux Questions Juives |
| CHC | Central Historical Commission |
| CJHC | Central Jewish Historical Commission in Poland |
| *CJHCA* | Archives of the CJHC |
| *CJR* | *Contemporary Jewish Record* |
| *Dapim* | *Dapim le-heker ha-sho'ah* |
| DP(s) | Displaced Person(s) |
| ERR | Einsatzstab Reichsleiter Rosenberg |
| FPO | Fareynikte partizaner organizatsye |

| | |
|---|---|
| GG | Government General |
| HIAS | Hebrew Sheltering and Immigrant Aid Society |
| *HJ* | *Historia Judaica* |
| *IMT* | International Military Tribunal. *Trial of the Major War Criminals Before the International Military Tribunal, Nuremberg* |
| *JBA* | *Jewish Book Annual* |
| *JF* | *Jewish Frontier* |
| JHI | Jewish Historical Institute, Warsaw |
| *JSS* | *Jewish Social Studies* |
| JTA *Bulletin* | Jewish Telegraphic Agency *Bulletin* |
| JUS | Jüdische Unterstützungsstelle |
| *MGWJ* | *Monatschrift für Geschichte und Wissenschaft des Judentums* |
| Monneray, *Est* | Monneray, Henri, ed., *La Persécution des Juifs dans le Pays de l'Est présentée à Nuremberg* (Paris, 1949) |
| Monneray, *Ouest* | Monneray, Henri, ed., *La Persécution des Juifs en France et dans les autres Pays de l'Ouest présentée par la France à Nuremberg* (Paris, 1947) |
| *NCA* | Office of United States Chief of Counsel for the Prosecution of Axis Criminality, *Nazi Conspiracy and Aggression* |
| *NMT* | Nuremberg Military Tribunals. *Trials of War Criminals Before the Nuremberg Military Tribunals Under Control Council Law No. 10* |
| *Notitsn* | Ringelblum, E., *Notitsn fun varshever geto* (Warsaw, 1952) |
| NSDAP | Nationalsozialistische Deutsche Arbeiter Partei |
| OUN | Organizatsia ukrainskikh natsionalistiw |
| *RGBL* | *Reichsgesetzblatt* |
| RMfdbO | Reichsministerium für die besetzten Ostgebiete |
| RSHA | Reichssicherheitshauptamt, Berlin |
| UGIF | Union Générale des Israélites de France |
| UNDO | Ukrainian National Democratic Union |
| UPA | Ukrainska Powstanska Armija |
| *Vestnik* | *Věstnik židovské nábozenské obce v Praze* |
| *WLB* | *Wiener Library Bulletin* |
| *YA* | *YIVO Annual of Jewish Social Science* |
| *YB* | *YIVO Bleter* |
| YIVO | YIVO Institute for Jewish Research |
| *YK* | *Yidisher Kemfer* |
| *YVS* | *Yad Vashem Studies on the European Jewish Catastrophe and Resistance* |
| ŻTOS | Żydowskie Towarzystwo Opieki Spolecznej |

ROADS TO EXTINCTION:
ESSAYS ON THE HOLOCAUST

# INTRODUCTION

*Salo Wittmayer Baron*

The author of this noteworthy collection of essays has often been called "the father of the Jewish Holocaust literature." A most energetic, imaginative, and careful historian, Philip Friedman, before the Nazi rise to power, devoted many years to the exploration of the modern history of the Jews in Eastern Europe. However, under the impact of the tragic experiences of the Second World War, which he miraculously survived under the Nazi occupation of Poland, he was induced to concentrate on the scholarly research into the history of that Catastrophe, the greatest in the blood-stained annals of Jewish history. He thus became the chief founder of a new discipline in Jewish studies and, since his demise on February 7, 1960, he has been greatly missed in the further shaping of this comparatively young area of investigation.

Friedman was born on April 27, 1901, in Lwów, Poland, then under Austrian domination.* Like other Galician youths of that period, he was

* The biographical data here included are largely reproduced from my obituary of Philip Friedman, published in the *Proceedings* of the American Academy for Jewish Research 29 (1960), 1–7.—S.W.B.

stimulated by the national Jewish renaissance, became an ardent Zionist, and combined in his early training the fruits of advanced Polish culture with good Hebraic knowledge and a zest for pioneering in the physical and intellectual reconstruction of his people. At the age of eighteen he arrived in Vienna, where he enrolled at both the Jewish *Paedagogium* and the University. From the outset he began specializing in Jewish history, especially under my direction at the *Paedagogium* and under Alfred Francis Pribram at the University. He received his doctorate in 1925 after preparing an archival study of *Die galizischen Juden im Kampfe um ihre Gleichberechtigung (1848–1868),* which was subsequently published in Frankfort in 1929 under the sponsorship of the Dr. A. S. Bettelheim Memorial Foundation established by George Alexander Kohut.

Upon the completion of his studies, Friedman returned to Poland, where he taught at a leading Hebrew secondary school in Lodz, the People's University of that city, the YIVO in Vilna (1935), and the prominent Jewish school of higher learning, the *Tahkemoni* of Warsaw (1938–1939). Although carrying a rather heavy teaching load, he untiringly devoted himself to research. The bibliography of his writings in the years from 1928 to 1939 shows an astonishing output of 144 items. While many of these publications were short articles or reviews in newspapers and magazines, they also included such a substantial work as his *Dzieje Żydów w Łodzi* (A History of the Jews in Lodz from the Beginnings of their Settlement to 1863) (Lodz, 1935); and comprehensive essays such as his "Wirtschaftliche Umschichtungsprozesse und Industrialisierung in der polnischen Judenschaft 1800–1870," *George Alexander Kohut Memorial Volume* (New York, 1935), pp. 178–247; and "Industrializatsye un proletarizatsye fun di Lodzer Yidn in di yorn 1860–1914," *Lodzer Visenshaftlekhe Schriftn,* 1 (1938), 63–132. Several other major studies appeared in Hebrew, Yiddish, Polish, and German.

From the outset, Friedman developed an intense interest in the modern history of the Jews of Poland. He felt that the primary scholarly task was to marshal the necessary evidence by careful bibliographic and archival research pertaining to important Polish regions. Even in his dissertation he had already (as I noted in my foreword to it)

succeeded in drawing . . . a comprehensive picture on the basis of many partially unpublished sources preserved in the various archival collections of the Viennese central authorities in control of Galician affairs. Of particular interest are the descriptions of events and developments originally found in documents which have since been destroyed in the fire of the Vienna Palace of Justice during the sanguinary clashes of July 15, 1927. Through this book alone they have been salvaged from total oblivion for use by scholarly investigators.

To round out this picture, Friedman published further documentary studies: "Die Judenfrage im galizischen Landtage, 1861–1868," *MGWJ,* 72 (1928), 379–90, 457–77; and "Joseph Perl vi a bildungstuer un zayn shul in Tarnopol" (Joseph Perl as a Protagonist of Enlightenment and His School in Tarnopol). Originally published by YIVO in 1940, this latter essay was destroyed by the Nazis along with the rest of the volume and had to be re-published in the *Yivo Bleter* in 1948 (vols. 31–32, pp. 131–90). His major work on Lodz was supplemented by many detailed investigations pertaining to the population, economic structure, and communal life of Lodz Jewry. Perhaps most important among these publications was a series of essays offering a history of the Lodz *Hebrah Qadisha,* biographies of the personalities buried in the Lodz cemetery, and annotated reproductions of the Hebrew tombstone inscriptions there. These detailed analyses appeared in the noteworthy volume *Stary cmentarz żydowski w Łodzi* (The Old Jewish Cemetery in Lodz) (Lodz, 1938), Polish section, pp. 37–111, 168–306; Hebrew section, pp. 5–115. In fact, this volume was prepared largely under his direction. He also wrote on other Polish communities and even succeeded in contributing something to the knowledge of Palestinian Jewry in the years 1815–1822 by publishing a series of Palestinian letters in *Zion,* 3 (1938), 267–74.

While being thus involved primarily in analytical studies, Friedman never lost sight of the need for broad historical syntheses. He not only wrote a brief and illuminating summary of the history of Galician Jewry from 1772 to 1914 which appeared in *Żydzi w Polsce odrodzonej* (Jews in Poland Reborn), I (Warsaw, 1933), 377–412, but conceived a major plan to write a comprehensive history of the Jews in Poland from the beginning to the twentieth century. This project, planned for three volumes, was sufficiently advanced by early summer 1939 for the author to send me a draft of Volume I, covering the period of prepartition Poland. Unfortunately I was so impressed by the quality of this work that I read it with dispatch and returned the manuscript with a number of suggestions to the author early in August 1939. With the author's other papers this manuscript was lost during the subsequent turmoil.

In all these writings Friedman combined great accuracy and attention to detail with awareness of the contemporary crisis of Polish Jewry. In his foreword to the work on Lodz, he emphasized:

The various transformations [of Jewish life in Poland] were faster and more intense in Lodz, that rapidly growing capital of Polish industry, than in any other Jewish community of the Kingdom of Poland. That is why Lodz Jewry served, so to say, as a sensitive seismograph signaling all economic and social changes which were to manifest themselves in various parts of the country many years later.

To these stimuli of a scholarly nature was added, in the course of the work, a social incentive. . . . It has become clear that it is the task of an historian to furnish to men of good will precise materials and as accurate a picture as possible of the economic activities of the Jews in the recent past. It is for him to show this development in the enormously important epoch of the rise and evolution of the capitalistic economy in Polish lands in a light divorced as much as possible from partisan politics, *sine ira et studio*.

Because of that social conscience Friedman joined many educational efforts to help Polish Jewish youth prepare itself for its hard struggle for survival. Possessing excellent organizational abilities, he organized several societies, some of which published scholarly magazines, trying to promote Jewish knowledge. He was also more keenly aware than most of his contemporaries of the need for greater cooperation among Jewish historians the world over; stimulated particularly by the sessions of the Jewish Section at the International Congress of Historians in Warsaw in 1933, he proposed a worldwide association of students in this field. This association was to sponsor a number of collaborative undertakings which, representing an urgent need in Jewish scholarship, transcended the capabilities of individual historians.

All these plans and projects were cut short by the German occupation of Poland and the subsequent Nazi attempt at the "Final Solution" of the Jewish question. In his personal reticence, Friedman rarely spoke of this great ordeal, during which he lost a wife and a daughter, and himself was hounded from one underground location to another. When he finally emerged from that self-imposed obscurity after the liberation of Poland in 1944, he was entrusted by the new Polish administration with the directorship of the Central Jewish Historical Commission which was to gather data concerning the Nazi war crimes. In this capacity he was not only the first to organize a detailed search for extant materials but also inspired the publication of a number of important studies which laid the foundation for all subsequent investigations in this field. His own contribution consisted of a comprehensive volume relating to Auschwitz, the most horrible of the concentration camps and the scene of the greatest mass murder in history. Published in Polish in Warsaw in 1945, it appeared in an abridged English version (from a Yiddish series in *Dos naye lebn*) by Joseph Leftwich, *This Is Oswiecim* (London, 1946). These volumes helped to awaken the conscience of mankind, incredulous at first because of the magnitude of the tragedy. When called to testify at Nuremberg during the great War Crimes Trials, he and his new wife, Dr. Ada June Eber, likewise a native of Lwów and a miraculous survivor of the Nazi terror, decided not to return to Poland but to devote themselves to the rebuilding of the morale of the other survivors then living in the new Displaced Persons camps in Germany.

After two years of service as director of the Educational Department of the Joint Distribution Committee in Germany during which time he also aided the Centre de Documentation Juive in Paris in setting up its vast documentary collections, Friedman came to the United States in 1948 at the invitation of Columbia University, at which he served first as research fellow and then, from 1951 to his death, as lecturer. From 1949 on, he also headed the Jewish Teachers Seminary, gave courses at the Herzliah Teachers Seminary, and lectured in various cities in the United States and Canada.

Preoccupied as he was with his teaching and administrative duties, as well as with the necessary adjustments to the new language and environment, he unrelentingly pursued his research, both substantive and bibliographical, in the history of the Holocaust. At first he found little response, even on the part of leading Jewish organizations, but obtained some assistance from Columbia University's Council for Research in the Social Sciences. With the establishment of the Conference of Jewish Material Claims against Germany, however, and the foundation of Yad Vashem in Jerusalem, a new opportunity was opened to him for concentrated work. Together with YIVO, Yad Vashem entrusted him with the major task of preparing comprehensive bibliographies for the history of the Jewish tragedy. The difficulties of this undertaking were stressed by him in his essay "European Jewish Research on the Holocaust" (see essay 20 below); he emphasized that "unlike earlier catastrophes in Jewish history, which for the most part were confined to one country, the Nazi Holocaust spread over continental Europe. The international character of the Holocaust is of tremendous import in the scientific study of the events." In fact, the available materials accumulated so rapidly that in 1953 he was able to publish in *Kirjath Sepher* (28, 410–15; 29, 162–71) a succinct bibliography of bibliographies pertaining to that period. But he realized that all this was merely a beginning and that the very methods of this research had to be greatly refined. For this purpose he published a brief analysis, "Preliminary and Methodological Aspects of Research on the Judenrat" (essay 22 below), and prepared, for his fellow workers as much as for himself, a comprehensive *Guide to Research in Jewish History, 1933–1945,* edited by him and Jacob Robinson. It formed the introductory volume to a series of bibliographies, of which Volume II, covering the publications in Hebrew books dealing with "The Jewish Catastrophe and Heroism in Europe" (edited solely by Friedman), and Volume III, covering similar books in Yiddish (compiled by him jointly with Joseph Gar), appeared posthumously in 1960 and 1962, respectively. The subsequent volumes of that large series, including Volume XII (prepared by Jacob Robinson with the assistance of Mrs. Philip Friedman, the editor of the present volume), have likewise borne the unmistakable imprint of Friedman's planning and personality.

Apart from his bibliographical work, Friedman endeavored to penetrate more deeply the social, cultural, and psychological manifestations of life inside the ghettos during the Nazi occupation. He published scores of articles in various journals in this country and abroad, each of which opened new vistas. One of these, "Aspects of the Jewish Communal Crisis in Germany, Austria, and Czechoslovakia During the Nazi Period," appears below (essay 5). His two books in English, addressed to the broader public, have been enthusiastically acclaimed by critics, both Jewish and non-Jewish. Entitled *Martyrs and Fighters: The Epic of the Warsaw Ghetto* (New York, 1954) and *Their Brothers' Keepers* (New York, 1957, 1978), these volumes describe, respectively, the famous uprising in the Warsaw ghetto and the help extended to Jews by humanitarian Christians, often at peril to their own lives. They had grown out of his earlier seminal articles. *Their Brothers' Keepers,* in particular, owed much to the two studies (essays 17 and 18 below) published in 1955.

With all this concentration on the most recent period, Friedman did not completely neglect his earlier interests. In a remarkable review essay on "Polish Jewish Historiography Between the Two Wars" (essay 19 below), he erected a monument not only to individual martyrs like Meir Balaban, Emanuel Ringelblum, Yitzhak (Ignacy) Schipper, and Moses Schorr but also pointed out the wide scope of their publications during the two decades 1919–1939. He also wrote analytical essays on the works of other historians of East European Jewry such as Simon Dubnow (Hebrew) and Jacob Shatsky (Yiddish), and contributed several articles to memorial volumes, in which he sketched the histories of various Jewish communities from their inception. One of his last essays to appear was the general survey "The First Millennium of Jewish Settlement in the Ukraine and in the Adjacent Areas," published in the *Annals* of the Ukrainian Academy of Arts and Sciences in the U.S., 8 (1959), 1483–1516. Even during the months of his last illness, he participated in the planning of a new collective work on the history of Polish Jewry from 1919 to 1939. At the same time he began extending his interest to the history of American Jewry, publishing for instance the survey "Political and Social Movements and Organizations" in *Jewish People Past and Present,* IV (New York, 1955), 142–86.

The following selection of Friedman's major essays in the field presents a vivid picture of the Nazi attempt at the "Final Solution" of the Jewish question. Written with considerable restraint—doubly remarkable on the part of a survivor of the Nazi atrocities—these chapters graphically describe what actually happened in both the historic reality and the psychological reaction thereto by the victims.

The first section is devoted to the analysis of the preliminary steps taken by the Nazi regime after the outbreak of World War II. It begins with the regime's unrelenting efforts to segregate the Jews from their neighbors and to weaken the physical and moral fibre of the prospective victims. Going beyond the medieval forms of discrimination, the Nazis placed Jews in separate quarters and even assigned a special Polish "reservation" to those forcibly brought from other lands. They also marked all Jewish individuals by special badges and thus succeeded in inflaming the anti-Jewish feelings, overt or latent, of the non-Jewish populations. At the same time they allotted ever diminishing food rations to the inhabitants of these ghettos and thereby systematically undermined their health. With these and other regulations the Nazis sought to stir up factional discord in the Jewish community and increasingly to deprive its youth of educational facilities.

All along the Nazis also nurtured in their victims the delusion that those were but temporary measures necessitated by the war, and that by meekly complying with the demands of the authorities, they would be "let alone." According to an official military report from the Russian front of July 1941, the German invaders themselves were amazed to note that "the Jews are strikingly ill informed about our attitude toward them and about the treatment Jews are receiving in Germany or in Warsaw."

Such tactics were also maintained during the final stages of the wholesale exterminations in 1941–1945. The second section of this volume describes not only the methods employed by the Germans in such localities as Friedman's native Lwów but also the criminal "scientific" experiments conducted on the Jewish prisoners in the extermination camps. We also learn a good deal about the reactions of the Jewish inhabitants of the ghettos, including those controlled by the Judenräte. These supposedly autonomous but in fact German-appointed "Jewish councils" were sometimes led by "pseudo-saviors" of the kind described below in three essays (12, 13, and 14). Many young Jews, however, escaped and joined the military resistance movement in both East and West.

From the outset, moreover, Friedman was conscious of the enormous difficulties confronting researchers of the Holocaust. The Nazis not only ordered the extermination of Jews but also systematically destroyed most records concerning their barbaric actions. In a series of studies (comprising the third section of this volume) Friedman tried to come to grips, therefore, with the grave methodological problems connected with the study of the great catastrophe. He also sought to offer surveys of the initial work done in this field in both Europe and America during the early postwar years and to warn serious students of the pitfalls confronting them in dealing with the ever growing literature of survivors (see essays 20, 21, 22, and 23).

In fact, almost immediately after the cessation of hostilities in Europe in 1945, Friedman prepared, primarily for his own use, a plan for the research to be conducted in the new field. He subsequently elaborated this program and submitted it to an International Conference in 1950. The plan was so carefully conceived that, even three decades later, it may still prove helpful in fostering some additional investigations. It is reprinted here as an Appendix.

In sum, even now, some two decades after his death, Philip Friedman's scholarly contributions to the study of this vital aspect of Jewish and European history in the years 1939–1945 rank among the significant achievements of contemporary Jewish historiography. The best the author's numerous admirers, coworkers, and successors can do to perpetuate his memory is to assist in the implementation of some of his as yet unrealized plans and in the continuation of the work so auspiciously begun by him.

# PART ONE

## 1939-1945 Segregation and Brutal Discrimination

# THE JEWISH BADGE AND
# THE YELLOW STAR IN THE NAZI ERA

Distinguishing signs intended to humiliate or restrict Jews (such as the Jewish hat, the yellow badge, and the Star of David) disappeared in Europe with the political emancipation of the Jews, or even before.[1] However, the revival of medieval forms of anti-Jewish legislation in the Nazi era brought to the fore the problem of special marks for Jews. The first suggestion that such marks be instituted probably came from Reinhard Heydrich, chief of the German Security Police, at the historic meeting in Hermann Göring's headquarters on November 12, 1938.[2] No action on this specific subject was decided upon at this meeting.

## Government General, Germany, and Protectorate of Bohemia-Moravia

It seems, however, that the idea of segregating and humiliating the Jews was already deeply rooted in the minds of some Germans, as a result of continuous Nazi propaganda. This may explain several instances from September 1939 on, of the imposition of the Jewish badge by individual German military and civilian authorities in occupied Poland. From the records of the chaotic days of the Nazi invasion of Poland which have come down to us, the Jewish badge was introduced almost simultaneously in Lodz (Litzmannstadt), Kalisz, Rzeszów (Reichshof), and Włocławek (Leslau). Since there was no uniform central legislation on Jewish affairs, the Jewish marks ordered by the local administrations showed great variety in design and scope. The Stadtkommissar of Włocławek, SS Oberführer Cramer, on October 24, 1939, ordered all Jews, without regard to age or sex, to wear on their backs a yellow triangle at least 15 centimeters high and 15 centimeters wide.[3] The Regierungspräsident of the province of Kalisz, Friedrich Übelhör, on November 14, 1939, commanded all Jews under his jurisdiction to wear a Jewish badge of "Jew-yellow color" (*von judengelber Farbe*) on the right arm.[4] A German scholar, Dr. Herbert Morgen, who made a trip through the "new German eastern areas" at the time, summed up this extravagant development in the following words:

As an external sign of belonging to their tribe the Jews carry—depending on the directive of the *Landrat*—a yellow Star of David or a yellow triangle or something like it on their breasts and back. The general impression one receives of this human mass is appalling. And one quietly arrives at the conclusion that one is dealing here with a completely degenerate, inferior part of human society.[5]

The humiliating intent of marking the Jews is clearly indicated by Morgen's statement. In some instances this intention expressed itself in bizarre forms. In Ozorków, near Lodz, the Germans assembled the entire Jewish population in a school building, ordered them to strip off their clothes, and sorted them into two groups: those fit and those unfit for labor. The fit were marked with a great *A* on their buttocks, the unfit with a *B*.[6]

The diversity of Jewish marks was eventually superseded by the decree of Hans Frank, the German chief executive of the Government General (GG), on November 23, 1939.[7] In his ordinance Frank directed every Jew of the GG above the age of ten years to wear on the right arm a white badge (at least 10 centimeters wide) with a Star of David, under penalty of fine and imprisonment. On the same date, he also ordered that Jewish business enterprises and stores be marked with a Star of David; he thereby overruled previously issued local regulations such as those of Cracow (September 8, 1939) and Rzeszów (September 13, 1939).

Two years after the introduction of the Jewish badge in the GG, the Reichsminister of the interior issued a police decree, on September 1, 1941, concerning the marking of Jews in Germany proper, in the incorporated former Polish provinces, and in the Protectorate of Bohemia and Moravia.[8] This decree differed substantially from the decree in the GG. It ordered the Jewish badges for all Jews above six years of age; the badge was defined as a yellow hexagram the size of a person's palm (*handtellergrosser Sechs-stern*), with the inscription *Jude* in black, to be worn visibly on the left side of the chest. Jewish stores were ordered to display a Star of David on the front.

It is not known whether the introduction of the Jewish badge in Germany and in the German-occupied Czech and Polish areas was preceded by discussions of dissent in Nazi ruling circles. In Western Europe, however, where the Germans could not act without regard for local political factors and conditions, the introduction of this discriminatory device was not so easy and involved the Nazis in protracted discussions and embarrassing situations.

## *"Battle of the Badge" in France*

As far as we know, France was the only Nazi-occupied country where anti-Jewish legislation on segregation paralleled similar anti-Negro legislation. On November 8, 1940, the German authorities in France issued several travel restrictions concerning Jews and Negroes. However, as was pointed out by Magny, prefect of police in the Seine district (Greater Paris), these regulations could be fully enforced only with respect to the Negroes, who could be distinguished by their physical appearance, and not among the Jews, who lacked distinguishing marks.[9]

In order to remedy this "lack of distinguishing marks," the head of the Jewish Department of the Gestapo in Berlin, Adolf Eichmann, suggested at a conference of experts on Jewish affairs, held in Berlin on March 4, 1942, that the Jewish badge be introduced in all occupied European countries. In compliance with this suggestion, and upon direct instruction from Himmler, Hellmuth Knochen, chief of the German Security Police in the Occupied Zone of France (Northern France) and in Belgium, on March 10, invited experts on the Jews in France, Belgium, and Holland to convene in Paris on March 14 to discuss the simultaneous introduction of the Jewish badge in all three countries.[10] Knochen intended to proceed with considerable speed, but he had to face unforeseen obstacles.

First, the German authorities also wanted to bring into line the French government in the Free Zone of France. The Germans even tried to put pressure on Vichy to publish the decree before the Germans did so in the occupied areas. But the Vichy government showed itself completely uncooperative on this point. The opposition of Xavier Vallat, Vichy's commissary for Jewish affairs, was particularly strong. Only a short time before (February 17, 1942) Vallat had shouted down the SS representative Captain Dannecker with the following words: "I am an anti-Semite of a much older vintage than you! I could be your father!"[11] It was with relief that the German ambassador to Vichy, Otto Abetz, reported, on March 31, that the uncooperative Xavier Vallat had been removed from his post. But the new commissary, Darquier de Pellepoix, did not budge from the negative Vichy attitude toward the Jewish badge. Before this duel between the Vichy government and the Germans came to an end, new opposition was signaled, this time from the German side. The chief of the German military administration of Belgium, Brigadier-General Eggert Reeder, announced his staunch opposition to the Jewish badge and was backed by the military governor of Belgium, General von Falkenhausen, a firm opponent of National Socialist extremism.

While the procedure in France and Belgium was thus stalled, the German authorities in Holland grew impatient, and published the decree on the Jewish badge on April 27, 1942, without regard to the other Western countries.[12] Eventually, on June 1, 1942, the German military commander in France published the ordinance (dated May 29) enjoining all Jews above six years of age to wear, on the left side of the chest, a yellow hexagram the size of a person's palm, with the inscription *Jude*.[13] Belgium followed. In the Free Zone of France, however, the Jewish badge was not enforced until after November 11, 1942, when southern France was occupied by the Germans.

In any case, the "battle of the badge" ended with only a half-victory for the Germans. In all three countries the decrees on the Jewish badge were loaded with exemptions. Moreover, many Jews not entitled to exemptions from the badge tried by every means to evade this form of discrimination, and frequently succeeded in doing so. In all Western countries a strong resentment against the branding of Jews spread among all strata of the population and manifested itself in various forms, as will be described below.

## The Jewish Badge in Other Occupied and Satellite Countries

In spite of the difficulties encountered in the West, the Germans insisted on the introduction of the Jewish badge in all other countries under their jurisdiction or influence. The results varied, from complete noncompliance to full implementation of the discriminatory policy. Total noncompliance was the case in Denmark. The Germans tried to prepare the Danish population for this measure through a propaganda campaign in semiofficial Nazi periodicals.[14] However, it failed to produce the desired effect, instead meeting the vigorous opposition of King Christian X, who declared that he would be the first to put on the Jewish badge. The Germans had to beat a retreat.[15]

Resistance was also encountered in Hungary. The Hungarian premier, Miklós Kállay, categorically rejected, in December 1942, German demands for several anti-Jewish injunctions, including that on the Jewish badge. After the Kállay cabinet was dismissed in March 1944, the newly appointed quisling cabinet, headed by General Dome Sztoyay, yielded to German pressure and introduced the Jewish badge.[16]

Bulgaria, too, tried, until the fall of 1942, to evade implementation of the badge. Finally, the Bulgarian cabinet adopted, on August 26, 1942, a resolution ordering the wearing of the badge. This injunction was only half-heartedly enforced by the Bulgarian authorities, however. According to Himmler's intelligence service, two and a half months after the law was introduced only one-fifth of the Jews in Sofia wore the badge. The manufacture of new badges, a thriving industry in some countries, ceased entirely in Bulgaria. The attitude of the Bulgarian population toward the anti-Jewish measures was absolutely negative. After the war, a confirmed anti-Semite, Professor Petko Stainow, who during World War II had written approving articles for Nazi law journals on Bulgarian anti-Jewish laws, found it necessary, in September 1944, in order to ingratiate himself again with the Bulgarian public, to write a jubilant article, "The Stars Are Falling!" (meaning the Jewish Stars of David).[17]

Rumania, in spite of that country's long anti-Semitic record, carried on a cautious policy to avoid antagonizing either their Nazi allies or the Western democracies. The anti-Jewish policies of the Rumanian government, though hard enough and cruel, were nevertheless more moderate than the Germans wanted. In general, the Rumanian anti-Jewish policy was much more severe in the occupied regions than in the old Rumanian provinces. Thus the yellow Star of David was introduced in the occupied provinces of Bessarabia and Bucovina in September 1941, for all Jews above twelve years of age.[18] In Transnistria, a new Rumanian province created from the former Soviet territories of Bessarabia and southwestern Ukraine, the Jewish star was introduced in July 1942. In some places Jewish dwellings had to be marked with a Star of David.[19] In the "old countries" the problem of marking the Jews was discussed from the autumn of 1941 on, but no action was taken until 1943. By then the chances of a German victory were already slim enough to discourage the Rumanian government from anti-Jewish measures. Significantly enough, the military commander of Czernovitz (Bucovina), Dragalina, abolished the Jewish badge in that city in October 1943.[20] Early in May 1944, however, yielding to incessant German propaganda, the ministry of the interior ordered the Jews of Moldavia to begin wearing the Star of David immediately, because this province had become "an area near the front."[21]

The Germans were very anxious to see the Jewish badge spread all over Europe. In May 1942, the SS officer Dannecker boasted in an official statement that the Jewish badge had already been introduced in Germany, Belgium, the Netherlands, the GG, the occupied Russian territories, Slovakia, Croatia, and Rumania.[22] In territories under German occupation the Jewish badge was introduced without too much discussion. In Serbia the German military commander ordered the Jews, on May 30, 1941, to start wearing the Jewish badge immediately.[23] After the Germans took over the Greek territories formerly occupied by the Italians, an ordinance of the SS commander of Thessalonica, on February 12, 1943, enjoined the Jews to wear on the left breast a yellow disk bearing, instead of the inscription *Jude,* the individual's registration number.[24]

In German-occupied Russian areas the Jewish badge was introduced immediately after the invasion. No general order was issued, however, and local varieties of the badge obtained in different places during the short span of time between the invasion and the total extermination of Russian Jewry.[25]

## Implementation of the Badge

The Germans did not introduce distinguishing marks only for Jews. In order to prevent the escape of foreign slave laborers, transported to Germany from the occupied countries, the Nazis ordered them to wear signs, too. Thus the Poles in forced labor in Germany had to wear on the right side of the chest a sign with the letter *P.*[26] In the concentration camps the Germans introduced a very elaborate system of marks for the diverse categories of camp prisoners.[27] But while only certain categories of the Gentile population were forced to wear the discriminatory marks, all the Jews were condemned to this stigmatization. The purpose of the measure was humiliation and degradation, isolation and segregation, of the Jews, as well as strict control of their movements and activities. This was frankly admitted in a rather cynical vein by Josef Goebbels. In an editorial of November 16, 1941, the German propaganda minister described the imposition of the Jewish star as "a very humane ordinance (*eine äusserst humane Vorschrift*), . . . a hygienic prophylactic in order to prevent the Jew from sneaking into our ranks without being recognized." And the minister continued: "Whoever wears a Jewish star is thus marked an enemy of the people."[28] In the Polish Jewish ghettos the rumor circulated that Goebbels used much more drastic language in one of his radio addresses, namely: "This is not a stigma—it's a death verdict." But no such statement is to be found in Goebbels' published speeches or editorials. However this may be, the introduction of the Jewish badge always signalized a change for the worse. In Germany the Jewish badge was introduced on September 1, 1941, and on September 16, deportation to the east began.

The implementation and consequences of the Jewish badge were not the same in all Nazi-dominated countries. Polish Jewry began to feel the impact of Nazi anti-Jewish policy in the first months of World War II. As noted above, the Jews of the GG were ordered to wear the Jewish badge in the autumn of 1939, while the Jews in the Polish areas incorporated into the Reich did not have to do so until as late as September 1941, and the Jews in the Russian and formerly Polish eastern areas not until the summer of 1941. The Jews of the GG and of the former Soviet Zone were compelled to wear on the right arm a white brassard with a Star of David, while the Jews of the incorporated areas were forced to wear a yellow Star of David on the chest. Overzealous officials tried to increase the imposition. Thus in Dinaburg (Dvinsk, or Daugavpils) in Latvia, Jewish women had to wear two yellow stars, one on the chest, another on the back. Jewish men had to wear a third star on the left knee. According to one eyewitness, the star was a pentagram, hinting at the Jewish relationship to Communism.[29]

A most dismal situation developed in the GG. Defiance of the order to wear the Jewish badge was threatened with imprisonment and an unlimited fine. The president of the province of Kalisz, Friedrich Übelhör, introduced the death penalty for transgressors. The German administration imposed even harsher penalties than were stipulated by the law. Jews caught on the street without a badge were often severely beaten.[30] There was a gradation of penalties: in Warsaw, fines, flogging, prison sentence of several months, deportation to a labor camp; in Częstochowa, beating, six-month prison sentence, shooting; in Cracow, fine, beating, torture, an eight-month prison sentence; in Bialystok, the penalties also included shooting.[31] In many cases a prison sentence or deportation to a labor camp actually meant a death sentence. A characteristic exchange of letters has been preserved. The Judenrat (Jewish council) of Sawin, on February 6, 1942, asked of the Judenrat of Lublin: "A man from Cracow, one Moses Shulman, was arrested in May 1941 in Biała Podlaska for not wearing the Jewish badge and was transferred to the prison in Lublin. Since December 1941 no letters have been received from him. Is he still alive?"[32] A Jew in Warsaw was arrested for the same crime and deported to Auschwitz. He never came back.[33] The Jewish historian Emanuel Ringelblum recorded as an exceptionally fortunate incident the case of the famous Polish Jewish educator and writer Janusz Korczak (pen name of Henryk Goldszmidt, a neurologist). Korczak refused to wear the Jewish badge and was arrested, but was later released from prison, thanks to the intercession of friends.[34] Rumors circulated in Warsaw that for every Jew without a badge brought to the Gestapo a reward of one hundred zlotys was paid.[35] In general, the German SS and policemen were very efficient in hunting down the Jewish badge "saboteurs" and in meting out severe punishment to them on the spot or dragging them off to jail. After the end of the war, former SS men brought to trial before German courts attempted to argue that "mere knowledge of the fact that the Jews were obliged to wear a Jewish star cannot be considered as a basis for condemnation."[36]

Jews were severely punished not only for failing to wear the Jewish badge but also for wearing a soiled or creased badge, for wearing the badge a centimeter lower or higher than the prescribed location, for pinning the badge to the garment with safety pins instead of sewing it firmly, and so on.[37] Frequently, these crimes were punished only with a fine, but sometimes heavier penalties were inflicted. One nineteen-year-old girl, an employee of the central association of the Jews in Germany, was seized during a Gestapo raid in Berlin because she had pinned the badge on her overcoat. She was immediately deported to a concentration camp, without even being permitted to say farewell to her mother. She never came back.[38] The practice of pinning the badge on instead of sewing it securely developed partly because of the scarcity of badges. One badge had to serve for several pieces of clothing, and was constantly shifted from one to another. In one place in eastern Poland the Jews pleaded that they could not obtain in time the necessary amount of yellow material for manufacture of the badge. In reprisal the Germans shot the head of the Jewish community.[39] In France only three badges per person were distributed, upon delivery of one ration coupon for textiles.[40]

But as time went on, the draconian German reprisals created a panicky atmosphere, and forced strict compliance with badge regulations. The Jews used all kinds of mnemonic devices to prevent dangerous oversights and other lapses. In Jewish apartment houses, on the walls and particularly on the inside of the entrance doors, large posters were placed with the following inscriptions: "The Badge!" "Remember the Badge!" "Attention, the Badge!" "Have you already put on the Badge?" "Before leaving the building, put on the Badge!" In some apartment houses a huge picture showing the armband, with the Star of David and a death's head, was hung on the wall.[41]

A new branch of the clothing industry developed—the manufacture of the Jewish badges. In Poland, production of the badges was not centralized but left to the individual initiative of private firms. Various fashions developed. Wealthy and esthetically minded persons preferred to wear badges with artistic, hand-embroidered stars, expensive armbands made of silk and satin instead of ordinary cotton. Celluloid and plastic bands enjoyed great popularity because they were washable and not easily crumpled. However, the privilege of wearing a celluloid badge was not granted to everybody; in Cracow, for example, only owners of a "dwelling license" were permitted to wear it.[42] Another thriving industry was the manufacture of protective cases, preferably of leather, for the badge. These cases prevented the badge from being soiled or wrinkled and had a celluloid window through which the Star of David could be seen. In smaller towns, the Jews contented themselves with simple homemade badges.

Since the production and distribution of the badges in Poland and Eastern Europe was not centralized, it is impossible to obtain exact figures about the volume of this industry. In Cracow, where members of the Jewish community were delegated to distribute the badges, 52,800 badges were handed out by September 30, 1940.[43] For a community with a Jewish population of about 70,000 this was a rather low figure.[44]

Some individuals were exempted from wearing the Jewish badge. Among them were foreign Jews, particularly citizens of neutral countries,[45] and a few Jewish personages whose activities seemed to be important to the Germans; certain members of the Judenrat, managers of great Jewish workshops, managers of the Jewish self-help organization, collaborators, and Gestapo agents. In general, these exemptions were much rarer in Eastern than in Western Europe. Ringelblum remarks that in Warsaw only three Jews were exempted from wearing the badge but later on adds to this list two Jewish Gestapo agents.[46]

Baptized Jews tried to get a general release from the badge restrictions and asked the Polish Central Council for Social Welfare (*Rada Główna Opiekuńcza,* or RGO) to intervene on their behalf. This intervention had fatal consequences for the converts. The Germans asked the RGO for a list of converts to be exempted and when it was presented to them, they used it to force the converts to move into the Jewish ghetto.[47] The converts still believed that they could claim a privileged status, but they were soon severely disillusioned. Members of one baptized family in Warsaw who did not wear the Jewish badge were punished, in October 1940, with a prison sentence of eight months.[48] But there were also different reactions. A group of baptized youths forced to live in the ghetto and put on the Jewish badge decided to make it a festive event. In April 1941 at 38 Sienna Street[49] in Warsaw, a celebration took place in which they put on the Star of David, and appropriate speeches were made.[50]

While total exemption from the Jewish badge was rare in Poland, a whole system of partial privileges developed. The German policy of "divide and rule" created an entire hierarchy of badge wearers. The Jewish badge was particularly dangerous because it exposed its bearer to the whim of every German passerby, soldier or civilian, who could dispose of the poor victim at will, drag him home or elsewhere for any kind of dirty or hard work, take him to a forced labor camp, order him to do humiliating exercises, and the like. The Germans therefore permitted certain privileged groups of Jews to wear an additional badge, which would allegedly protect them from that kind of treatment. For instance, Jews who were considered a valuable labor element were permitted to wear a badge with a large *A* (for *Arbeiter,* workman) and the registration number given them by the Labor Office. Jewish employees of the German Labor Office were identified by an additional, violet armband with the inscription *Arbeitsamt.* Employees in the armament industry wore green badges; the deaf and dumb, yellow badges; the Jewish police, a yellow badge with the letters *J.O.* (for *Jüdischer Ordnungsdienst*).[51]

In Warsaw, the mania for additional badges reached absurd dimensions. According to various sources, the Warsaw ghetto had the following additional badges:

A badge with the Red Cross, for Jewish physicians. This badge was later prohibited by a German ordinance of March 1940, however, and had to be changed for a new brassard with the inscription *Lekarz-Arzt* and a large Star of David.[52]

A green badge for collectors of old metal scrap and rags.

A white badge with the inscription "Patronate for Refugees," worn by the appropriate officials of the Judenrat.

A white badge with the inscription "Labor Battalion" (of the Judenrat).

A white badge with the inscription "Association of War Invalids of 1939."

A large dark blue badge for the executive members of the Judenrat.

A narrow dark blue badge for the employees of the Judenrat.

A yellow badge for the Technical Building Department of the Judenrat.

A yellow badge with the black inscription "Jewish Police" (*Służba Porządkowa*).

A yellow badge with the inscription "Transfer Place" (*Umschlagplatz*).

A yellow badge with a red inscription for the guards of the antiaircraft service.

A sea-green badge for the employees of the Transfer Office of the Jewish Social Self-Help.

A bright violet badge for officials of the Judenrat employed in transfer measures.

A dark violet badge for bus and truck drivers.

A bright green badge for employees of the Department of Trade and Commerce (Judenrat).

A white badge with a blue Star of David and the inscription *Prasa-Presse* (the press).

A white badge with red stars for the "Jewish Emergency Squad" (*Żydowskie Pogotowie Ratunkowe*).

A white-bordered black badge with a white inscription for employees of the funeral offices.

A gray badge with a black inscription for employees of the vocational schools of the Judenrat.

This list, observes its compiler, is by no means a complete one.[53] Ringelblum mentions in his diary another badge, with the inscription "Economically useful Jews" (*wirtschaftlich wertvoller Jude*)[54]—this type was used in other ghettos besides Warsaw.

The overexpansion of these identifications eventually resulted in confusion, and vitiated the protective value of the additional badges. The whole system was criticized by both its Jewish victims and its German initiators. An interesting criticism was voiced in the diary of a Jewish teacher and historian in Warsaw, Abraham Lewin:

Today [May 27, 1942] a new ordinance concerning the Jewish armband has been promulgated by the [Warsaw] ghetto commissioner Auerswald. . . . This ordinance orders the Jews to wear only the one compulsory badge. To more than this one, or to an alternate badge, are entitled only members of the Jewish police, who have, in addition to the ordinary Jewish badge, a special police badge. Until now all kinds of offices—e.g., the offices of the Jewish community and others, as well as some professions (physicians, dentists, etc.)—had their special badges with the indication of their occupation. This was supposed to be a kind of protection in the street against the German oppressors. [The protective badge] has to indicate: We are not common Jews, we are fulfilling important functions, therefore we have to be privileged. The new ordinance put an end to this. No longer are there various categories of Jews. There is only one large mass of outlawed, outcast, persecuted, tormented, spat on, kicked on, insulted and murdered Jews.[55]

Incidentally, even before the German administrator of the Warsaw ghetto issued his ordinance, the governor general, Hans Frank, had prohibited the issuance of the additional badges. His decree, dated November 13, 1941, stated: "Many offices and institutions (e.g., the railroad administration, the administration of the forests, the highway construction offices, the army, the department for guarding and protecting industrial plants, the auxiliary police) provide the Jews working for them with special badges in various colors. . . . Therefore, it is ordered that the Jews shall not be permitted to wear any other badge but the legally prescribed Jewish armband."[56] However, some of the additional Jewish badges survived the orders of both Frank and Auerswald.

Jews who could not obtain an exemption or a protective badge sometimes tried to camouflage the stigmatizing badge in various ways. In the summer Jewish men would wear white coats because the armband was not so conspicuous on this background. For the same reason women preferred white blouses, with short sleeves just the right length to cover the provocative badge. Briefcases, pocketbooks, flowers, and packages were carried in such a way as to serve the same purpose. Of course, all these devices were of short duration, meeting with the quick, often brutal reaction of the Germans.

An ironic situation developed in German-Polish relations. It is well known that the Germans never succeeded in creating a Polish quisling government. The activities of the Polish underground, and widespread sabotage by the Polish population, drove the Germans to savage measures, such as raids on the civilian Polish population, deportation of many thousands of Poles to forced labor camps and concentration camps, and public executions in the streets. It happened more than once that Poles used the Jewish badge for camouflage during the German round-ups. Characteristic episodes in Warsaw and Cracow were recorded by Ringelblum in his diaries. "A terrible day," wrote Ringelblum on May 8, 1940. "In all the streets they [the Germans] are rounding up the Poles. Jews are screened to see whether they are [camouflaged] Poles. . . . I heard that during the raid some Jews of Aryan appearance were asked to speak Yiddish in order to identify themselves as Jews."[57] A new trade developed. Many young Poles bought or borrowed a Jewish badge for the price of ten to fifty zlotys.[58] Poles who wanted to enter the ghetto in order to get in touch with the Jewish underground or for commercial purposes also put on the Jewish badge (entering the ghetto without a police permit was forbidden to Poles). "In the candy stores and cafés [of the ghetto]," wrote Ringelblum, "a new business has developed. A woman lends the Jewish badge to [Aryan] customers and gets for it ten to twenty groschen."[59] In January 1943 the Poles were jubilant over the German defeat at Stalingrad and did not hide these feelings from the Germans. In retaliation the Germans arranged one of the most gigantic raids in Warsaw. Many Poles used the Jewish badge to seek refuge in the ghetto.[60]

Less complicated was the situation in Germany. About 166,000 persons were compelled to wear the Jewish badge in compliance with the law of September 1, 1941. The deportations soon considerably reduced the number of Jews, however. On April 1, 1943, only 14,393 Jewish badge bearers were registered in Germany; 17,375 Jews of mixed marriages were exempt from this identification. Jews guilty of failing to wear the badge were sent to a detention camp (*Sammellager*) for fifty-six days. In the meantime their police records were minutely scrutinized, and if the smallest lapse could be found, such as a delay in paying taxes, this was used as a pretext for deporting the defendant to a concentration camp, from which there was no return. Curiously enough, the parsimonious German administration was extravagant in spite of the shortage of raw materials, in preparing about 1.5 million Jewish stars. This great reserve, however, was not distributed to the countries with a shortage of Jewish badges, but, on orders of the German Security Police, was carefully stored in 1943 in the cellars of the Central Association of Jews in Germany. A few months later, the Security Police suddenly ordered about ten thousand stars to be sent back to their headquarters in Kurfürstenstrasse. It was rumored that the Gestapo officials intended to use these stars for camouflage and to go underground if the Third Reich should collapse.[61]

In France, in the Nazi-occupied northern zone, 110,292 Jews above the age of six years were registered in November 1941. Of these, 100,455 were eligible for the Jewish badge: 61,864 French Jews and 38,591 foreign Jews (among them stateless Jews and citizens of Nazi-occupied and satellite countries). Exempt Jews, citizens of neutral and American countries and of Great Britain, numbered 9,837. Besides, individual exemptions were granted to the following persons: the widow of Professor Henri Bergson, the famous French writer Colette, the wife of the Vichy ambassador De Brinon, three protégés of Marshal Pétain, eight "economically useful Jews," and fourteen employees of the German and French police and espionage forces. These exemptions were criticized in the collaborationist press.[62]

For the 100,455 Jews eligible for the Jewish badge, private French firms prepared about 400,000 badges, using 5,000 meters of cotton material, of a total weight of 700 kilograms (about 1,680 pounds). The demand, however, was much smaller than anticipated. According to the reports of the French police (the police precincts were charged with the distribution of the badges), only 83,000 badges had been distributed by June 17, 1942. The German police tried to present this figure as practically equal to the number of actual Jewish badge wearers. We should bear in mind that every Jew was entitled to receive three badges, and it is reasonable to assume that the majority fully availed themselves of this small quota. Consequently, the figure of 83,000 distributed badges as against 110,455 eligible Jews indicates the failure of the German administration.[63] The hostile attitude of the French public toward German anti-Jewish legislation made it impossible to enforce strict observance of the law.

In Holland the list of exemptions included, among others, thirteen "old party members" (*sic!*), three art experts, a German Olympic champion of 1896, and the son-in-law of a former royal librarian.[64] Both in Holland and in Belgium it is impossible to tell how many Jews evaded the draconian regulations. In both countries the reaction of the non-Jewish population was very strong, perhaps even more vigorous than in France. It can therefore be assumed that in all the countries of Western Europe the Germans suffered a moral defeat in the "Battle of the Badge."

## Jewish Reaction

Jewish reaction to the badge was a strange mixture of conflicting emotions, ranging from shame to an elated sentiment of pride. The first reaction was in many cases a feeling of humiliation and depression. An underground Hebrew paper in Lodz, Poland, *Min ha-metzar,* dated July 8, 1941, reported that many Jews, particularly from the ranks of the intelligentsia, shunned the streets, preferring to stay for weeks in their homes in voluntary seclusion.[65] A similar reaction was reported in Warsaw: "For many weeks the Jewish intelligentsia retired to voluntary house arrest. Nobody dared to go out into the street with the stigma on his arm, and if compelled to do so, tried to sneak through without being noticed, in shame and in pain, with his eyes fixed to the ground."[66] The emotional reaction of a girl in Borysław (Eastern Galicia) was described by an eyewitness in this way: "Mother, I am afraid to walk in the street. Look, there is nobody in the street. People don't like to show up with the badge. . . . Where to hide myself? How to conceal the infamy?"[67] An old Jewish man in Paris wrote a letter of protest to Marshal Pétain calling the Jewish badge "une disposition humiliante."[68]

Reflection, however, gave birth to quite different attitudes. This curious emotional ambivalence has been rightly pointed out by a keen observer, himself a survivor and a historian of the Nazi catastrophe, who a few weeks after the liberation arranged an interesting interview with some French Jews. His first question was: "Did you feel disturbed on having to put on, for the first time in your life, a Jewish badge?" Most of them answered: "We are proud to wear it." The investigator suggests that these answers were imaginative conceptions, subconsciously constructed.[69]

The reaction of pride was particularly strong in Poland. I happened to see a prominent Jewish social worker, the late Dr. Cecilia Klaften, a few days after the introduction of the badge in Lwów. She told me how proud she felt to be marked as a Jew and that she intended to bear with her head erect this sign of her belonging to the Jewish fold. Ringelblum observes in his diaries that the Jewish badge became a touchstone and an internal moral test for the Jews because it stood for what he tersely calls Jewish solidarity and awareness of the common enemy.[70] Ringelblum also relates the following characteristic episode. The Nazis invited the chairman of the Judenrat in Lublin, Dr. Alten, to discuss the implementation of the Jewish badge. During the discussion the Germans used the expression "badge of infamy" (*Schandfleck*). Alten promptly replied that to him it was a "badge of honor" (*Ehrenzeichen*) and was penalized for his boldness with three days' imprisonment—a surprisingly mild punishment according to Nazi standards of "justice."[71] The underground paper *Min ha-metzar* published a Hebrew poem, "The Star of David," in which the author expressed his belief that the star would, in years to come, again be elevated to eminence as a symbol of freedom and salvation.[72]

It would be interesting to know the reactions of religious, particularly Orthodox, Jewry; but the pertinent sources are rather scant. In a story about a pious Jew called Leizer Yossels in a small town in Poland, the following details deserve attention. Leizer Yossels, it was told, managed to transform the Jewish badge, imposed by the Nazis for the sake of social debasement, into a symbol of sanctity and distinction. He was the first in the *shtetl* to put on the badge, and when he did so he said: "See what a sainted people we are! We have been marked with the Crown of Torah." He considered his traditional Jewish garb, the *kapote,* as endowed with distinction by the Star of David and as holy as, or even holier than, the prayer shawl. He therefore carried the star-marked *kapote* to religious services like a prayer shawl. Before passing away (he died a natural death in the ghetto, a fact considered in those times a sign of God's special grace), he asked to be buried in his holy *kapote* with the Star of David.[73] Historically, there is nothing surprising in this story. Jewish history knows of many instances where the wisdom of the Jewish people transformed originally vicious devices, intended for social degradation and humiliation (the Jewish hat, the special Jewish garb, and so forth), into sanctified institutions helping to maintain and protect Jewish identity and Jewish traditions.[74]

Psychological resilience in the face of humiliation also found expression in popular jokes.[75] Suffice it to give one example, then current in Warsaw: "Nalewki [the main street of the ghetto] is nowadays like Hollywood. Wherever you go you see nobody but stars!"[76]

There were other reactions, too. In Szczebrzeszyn and Kosów Poleski the Jews at first tried to ignore the injunction completely, but were soon brought to heel through brutal German reprisals.[77] It sometimes happened that individuals tried to express their protest in their own way, as in the incident with Janusz Korczak in Warsaw, mentioned above. In Paris the Jewish protest developed into public demonstrations. German Gestapo officials received secret intelligence that a Jewish protest march was expected on the Champs Élysées on June 7, 1942. We do not know what kind of precautions the Germans took to prevent the march. But another kind of demonstration took place that day. A number of Jewish war veterans of 1914–1918 put on all their war decorations just below their Jewish badges and paraded through the streets and boulevards of Paris. Other promenading groups put their Jewish stars on their backs or on their buttocks in order to ridicule the law. The French police smiled benignly at this *mascarade* (a term used in the pertinent German police record) and did not intervene. In conversations on the street, Jews declared that they were proud to wear the badge and to be the object of Nazi oppression.[78] On the other hand, as mentioned above, some Jews attempted to evade the order by various clever devices.[79]

## *Reaction of Non-Jews*

In some countries the reaction and resentment of non-Jews was even stronger than that of the Jews. This was particularly true in the Western countries. In France, after the publication of the decree, many French gentiles demonstrated their sympathy for the Jews in various ways: by publicly wearing yellow handkerchiefs in their coat pockets, by ostentatiously carrying yellow flowers and bouquets, by putting on yellow paper stars, and the like. For wearing a mark imitating or ridiculing the Jewish badge (*une insigne fantaisiste parodiant l'étoile juive*) many Frenchmen were arrested. A list of twenty people deported to the Drancy concentration camp (this was only a partial list of the total deportation) included Alice Couroble, who later published a book about this experience under the title *Amie des Juifs* (Paris, 1945). German police reports from the country confirmed that the feelings of the population there were the same as in Paris. "Large masses" in Bordeaux and "almost all classes of the population" in Nancy were reported as opposed to this German anti-Jewish legislation. However, some Nazi-controlled collaborationist newspapers vehemently supported the Germans, and small anti-Semitic groups (the largest of them is said in German reports to have been composed of a dozen individuals) tried to stage anti-Jewish demonstrations in Paris.[80]

Reaction was strong in the Low Countries. In Holland many non-Jews appeared on the streets with the Jewish star, and were punished with six weeks in jail. Particularly vigorous opposition developed in religious circles.[81] Popular feeling in Belgium is well characterized by the following episode: A Rexist, pro-Nazi newspaper in Brussels complained about Belgian teachers telling the Jewish children that the star was a mark of distinction. To corroborate this complaint, the newspaper related that a school teacher taking her children for an outing was overheard telling a little Jewish girl, "Nita, stand up straight. Show how proud you are to wear the pretty star."[82] It has been surmised that in order not to antagonize the Belgian population the German military administrators steadfastly opposed the introduction of the Jewish star.[83] Popular resentment and the king's opposition prevented the introduction of the Jewish star in Denmark.

The feelings of many Czechs were pointedly expressed in a public statement by Hubert Ripka, formerly long-time secretary of foreign affairs and during World War II a member of the Czechoslovak National Committee in London. On September 18, 1941, Ripka addressed the Jews of Czechoslovakia over the BBC in the following words:

Jews of Czechoslovakia, we think of you with profound sympathy in these days. . . . Today they [the Germans] wish to designate you publicly by a mark of shame. But the yellow Star of David is a mark of honor which all decent people will respect. . . . Jewish friends, do not hide your Jewish identity, be proud of it.[84]

In Bulgaria, where public resentment against the anti-Jewish legislation enacted under Nazi pressure was extremely high and led to many stormy demonstrations, the head of the Orthodox Church, Exarch Stephan, published in the official paper of the Church an order prohibiting the wearing of the Jewish star by baptized Jews, because "it is incompatible with wearing the Cross." In order fully to evaluate the importance of this statement, it must be noted that Christian priests in Bulgaria engaged in mass "mercy baptisms" to save the Jews from persecution.[85]

It is also interesting to realize that the Jewish badge was opposed by some Germans. A commander of the German Security Police in White Russia, SS-Obersturmbannführer Strauch, complained in a report of July 25, 1943, that a high official of the Generalkommissariat allowed a number of Jews to take off the Jewish star and had issued them identification cards as White Russians, based simply on their insistence that they were "one-quarter Jews."[86] Ringelblum relates, in a characteristic anecdote, that a Jew inadvertently lost his armband, and a German officer drew his attention to it in the following words: "Sie Jude, Sie haben das zwanzigste Jahrhundert verloren" ("You, Jew, you have just lost the twentieth century").[87] And last, but not least, was it consideration for the popular sentiment in Berlin that moved Goebbels to make an effort to eliminate the yellow stars from the streets of the capital?[88]

There is no record of Polish demonstration against, or opposition to, the Jewish badge. The underground paper *Min ha-metzar* reported a rumor that several members of the Polish Socialist Party (PPS) in Lodz planned to put on the Jewish badge as a token of solidarity with the Jews. There is no evidence that any action of this kind actually materialized, however. In any case, the situation in Poland was entirely different in many ways. As we have noted, the Poles sometimes used the Jewish badge for their own protection. This, of course, cannot be considered a pro-Jewish demonstration.

A bitter piece of historical irony occurred in Czechoslovakia after the war. The popular feeling of hatred against the Germans was so high that every person who was of German origin or who spoke German was compelled to wear a German mark of distinction. Thus, historical nemesis exacted retribution for the misdeeds of the occupation period. But in the first storm of indignation, officials did not bother to distinguish between the ethnic ("racial") Germans and the Jews (former Austrian and German citizens) who had been inmates of concentration camps and were liberated. Thus the victims of the Nazis were ordered to wear the "German badge" together with their oppressors. Only after many explanations and interventions (by the World Jewish Congress, for example) to "exclude all Jews from the group of Nazi traitors" were the law and the administrative practice changed and the Jews freed from the new badge.[89]

❡ This essay was first published in *Historia Judaica*, vol. 17, no. 1 (April 1955), 41–70.

## Notes

1. Guido Kisch, "The Yellow Badge in History," *HJ*, 4 (1942), 95–144. See also Raphael Straus, "The Jewish Hat as an Aspect of Social History," *JSS*, 4 (1942), 59–72.

2. *Trial of the Major War Criminals Before the International Military Tribunal* (Nuremberg, 1946–1949) (hereafter cited as *IMT*), IV, 499.

3. *Leslauer Bote, ABC dla Włocławka i Kujaw* (Guidelines for Włocławek and Kujawy), no. 15, October 25, 1939, as reproduced in *CJR*, 3 (1940), 42.

4. *Litzmannstädter Zeitung*, November 18, 1939.

5. *Zeitschrift für Geopolitik*, 18 (1941), 139; quoted from Max Weinreich, *Hitler's Professors* (New York, 1946), p. 94.

6. Shlomo Lipman, "In the Camps around Posen" (Yiddish), *Bleter fun payn un umkum* (Pages on Anguish and Extinction) (Melbourne, 1949), p. 87.

7. *Verordnungsblatt für das General-Gouvernement* (1939), p. 61. The Government General was created by the Germans in 1939 out of portions of occupied Poland. It comprised the four districts of Cracow, Radom, Lublin, and Warsaw. In August 1941 Eastern Galicia was added as the fifth district. The governor-general of this area was Hans Frank. Characteristic of the confusion concerning the Jewish badge is the fact that only two days before the decree of the governor-general was issued on November 23, 1939, the governor of the district of Cracow, Karl Otto Wächter, promulgated a decree compelling all Jews over twelve years of age in his district to wear the Jewish badge. *Krakauer Zeitung*, November 21, 1939.

8. After the invasion of Czechoslovakia on March 15, 1939, Hitler declared the provinces of Bohemia and Moravia a Protectorate, an autonomous part of the Reich. The former Czech head of state was given the title "state president," responsible to a Reich Protector, who was the actual ruler of the country. For the decree of September 1, 1941 regarding the Jewish badge, see *RGBL*, I (1941), 547; *Verordnungsblatt des Reichsprotektors in Böhmen und*

*Mähren* (1941), no. 44, p. 497. The full text of the decree is also found in Bruno Blau, "Der Judenstern der Nazis," *Judaica,* 9 (Zürich, 1953), 34–35. On the Jewish badge in Czechoslovakia, see also the following articles: "Zur Kennzeichnung der Juden: Die Ausfolgung der Kennzeichen," *Jüdisches Nachrichtenblatt,* no. 38 (Prague, 1941); "Die Ausgabe von Judensternen," *ibid.,* no. 16 (1942); also Jiři Weil, *Život s hvězdou* (Life with a Star) (Prague, 1949); L. Brod, "Magen David—the Emblem of Jewishness," *Věstnik židovské obce náboženské* (News Bulletin of the Jewish Religious Community, Prague), no. 24 (1950), 282.

9. Leon Poliakov, *L'Étoile Jaune* (Paris, 1949), pp. 54–55.

10. *Ibid.,* pp. 24–25; Gerald Reitlinger, *The Final Solution* (New York, 1953), p. 313.

11. Poliakov, p. 29.

12. *Ibid.,* p. 26; Goe, "Hollands Juden erhielten den Judenstern," *Die Judenfrage,* no. 10 (1942), 97–99.

13. Full text of the ordinance, in Poliakov, pp. 40–41.

14. See, for example, Ola Vinberg, "Jewish Stars," *Ragnarok,* 7 (1941), nos. 6–7, 214–15.

15. Poliakov, p. 70.

16. Reitlinger, pp. 416–23; the anonymous article "Die gelbe Armbände. Einsickernde Ostjuden. Abwehrmassnahmen gegen Parasiten," in *Deutsche Zeitung* (Budapest), March 27, 1943; David M. Gáspár, *A sárga csillag* (The Yellow Star) (Budapest, 1945).

17. Poliakov, pp. 38–39; Reitlinger, p. 380; Henri Monneray, ed., *La Persécution des Juifs dans les Pays de l'Est présentée à Nuremberg* (hereafter cited as Monneray, *Est*) (Paris, 1949), p. 249; Peter Meyer, "Bulgaria," in Peter Meyer et al., *The Jews in the Soviet Satellites* (Syracuse, N.Y., 1953), p. 624, n. 17; Peter Stainov, "Die neue Judengesetzgebung in Bulgarien," *Zeitschrift für osteuropäisches Recht,* vol. 7, nos. 11–12 (1941), pp. 553–58; vol. 9, nos. 1–3 (1942), pp. 51–59.

18. JTA *Bulletin* of September 21, 1941.

19. Matatias Carp, *Transnistria* (Buenos Aires, 1950), p. 249.

20. Reitlinger, p. 410.

21. Joseph Schechtman, "The Jews in Rumania during World War II" (typescript in the archives of YIVO Institute, New York), pp. 54–55.

22. Poliakov, p. 37.

23. Blau, *Judaica,* 9, pp. 40–41.

24. *In Memoriam: Hommage aux victimes juives des Nazis en Grèce,* II, prepared by Joseph Nehama, ed. by Michael Molho (Salonika, 1949), p. 19.

25. Records of various German local authorities quoted in Monneray, *Est,* p. 298, and Raul Hilberg, "The Role of the German Civil Service in the Destruction of the Jews" (Master's thesis, Columbia University, New York, 1950), p. 83.

26. *RGBL,* March 8, 1940.

27. A table of the various marks in the concentration camps (eighteen different patterns in eight colors) is reproduced in Eugen Kogon, *The Theory and Practice of Hell* (New York, n.d.), p. 297.

28. This editorial was published in *Das Reich* of November 16, 1941 under the title "Die Juden sind schuld!" (The Jews Are Guilty!) and was

reprinted in a volume of Goebbels's essays, *Das eherne Herz* (Munich, 1943), pp. 86–91.

29. Paula (Pessie) Frankel-Zaltzman, *Häftling Number 94771* (Montreal, 1949), p. 30. Conversely, another eyewitness states that the Jewish badge in Dvinsk was by no means different; that it was a hexagram as elsewhere. Jacob Rassin, *Mir viln lebn* (We Want to Live) (New York, 1949), p. 33. An interesting comment on the difference between the two symbols, the pentagram and the hexagram, was published in the collaborationist newspaper *Paris-Midi* of June 8, 1942. Completely overlooking the fact that the pentagram had become a Soviet symbol, the writer of the article, one R. Auberlain, declared: "No matter what, it would be advisable to explain here the difference between the two symbols, frequently confused: the hexagram, or 'the seal of Salomon,' and the pentagram, the star with five points instead of six, the emblem of all of Islam, of all the ancient lunar cults . . . an anti-Semitic symbol [*sic*]." Quoted from Poliakov, pp. 74–75.

30. A Jewish woman in Warsaw was cruelly beaten on Bielańska Street for this crime. Emanuel Ringelblum, "Notes from the Warsaw Ghetto" (Polish), *Biuletyn*, no. 2 (Warsaw, 1952), p. 92. Instances of the beating of Jews on the street for not wearing the badge are also recorded in Ludwik Hirszfeld, *Historia jednego życia* (The Story of One Life) (Warsaw, 1946), p. 188.

31. Michael Weichert's diary (typescript, in Polish, in the archives of the Jewish Historical Institute, Warsaw) p. 33; Shlomo Waga, *Hurbn Chenstokhov* (Destruction of Częstochowa) (Buenos Aires, 1949), pp. 37–38; Simon Segal, *The New Order in Poland* (New York, 1942), p. 217; B. Mark, *Der oyfshtand in Bialystoker geto* (The Uprising in the Ghetto of Bialystok) (Warsaw, 1950), pp. 63–64.

32. *Dos bukh fun Lublin* (Paris, 1952), p. 377.

33. Ringelblum, *Biuletyn*, p. 187.

34. *Ibid.*, pp. 160, 185.

35. *Ibid.*, p. 131.

36. A. W. Massow, "Der gelbe Stern," *Spruchgerichte*, II (Hamburg, May 1948), 136–37; Peters, "Genügt die Kenntnis eines Angehörigen der Waffen SS von der Pflicht der Juden zum Tragen des Judensterns zu seiner Verurteilung wegen organisierten Verbrechens?" *Spruchgerichte*, I (Hamburg, September 1947), 6–7.

37. *Dos bukh fun Lublin*, p. 386; Ringelblum, *Notitsn fun varshaver geto* (hereafter referred to as *Notitsn*) (Warsaw, 1952), p. 17.

38. Blau, *Judaica*, 9, p. 38; Abraham Lewin, "From the Ghetto Diary" (Yiddish), *BFG*, vol. 4, no. 4 (Warsaw, 1951), p. 54, relates the following episode under May 29, 1942: "Yesterday . . . I saw before the ghetto gate at Nalewki Street and the corner of Świętojerska Street a [German] policeman thrashing a young Jew for wearing a soiled badge . . . a barbarous scene."

39. *Pinkas kedoshey kehilath Kosów Poleski* (The Memorial Book of the Martyrs of the Community of Kosów Poleski) (Jerusalem, 1946), pp. 13–14.

40. Poliakov, p. 40.

41. I knew these devices from my own personal experiences. More information on these practices can be found in many published memoirs and narratives by the ghetto survivors, for example: Jonas Turkow, *Azoy iz es*

*geven* (Thus It Happened) (Buenos Aires, 1948), p. 131; also Leib Spizman, *Di yidn in nazi poyln* (Jews in Nazi Poland) (New York, 1942), pp. 74–75; and L. Brener, *Vidershtand un umkum in Chenstokhover geto* (Resistance and Extermination in the Ghetto of Częstochowa) (Warsaw, 1951), p. 16.

42. Spizman, p. 74.

43. "Bericht der jüdischen Gemeinde in Krakau in der Zeit von 13 September 1939 bis 30 September 1940," (Cracow, 1940) (mimeographed, in the archives of the JHI, Warsaw), p. 87.

44. *Ibid.* The official census of Jews registered with the Jewish community in the summer of 1940 gives the number as 68,482 persons.

45. Ringelblum, *Notitsn,* p. 23.

46. *Ibid.,* pp. 149, 189; Benjamin Orenstein, *Hurbn Otwock, Falenic, Karczew* (The Destruction of Otwock, Falenica, and Karczew) (Bamberg, 1948), p. 17.

47. Hirszfeld, pp. 188, 191.

48. Ringelblum, *Biuletyn,* p. 155.

49. Sienna Street was the "aristocratic" quarter of the Warsaw ghetto, where many wealthy converts lived.

50. Ringelblum, *Notitsn,* pp. 104–5, 112.

51. See essay 10 below, "The Destruction of the Jews of Lwów, 1941–1944."

52. Ringelblum, *Biuletyn,* p. 106.

53. The list of the various badges in Warsaw was recorded by a Mr. Janowski (the "Aryan" name of engineer Henryk Brisker) in his diaries (manuscript in the archives of the JHI, Warsaw, no. 90/ii). See also the diaries of Jan Mawult, pen name of the Warsaw lawyer Gombinski (manuscript in the archives of the JHI, Warsaw).

54. Ringelblum, *Notitsn,* p. 130.

55. Lewin (as cited above, note 38), p. 50.

56. *Rapporte des Generalgouverneurs. Hauptabteilung. Innere Verwaltung. Abteilung I. Allgemeine Stadtverwaltung,* I, 1330/41 (in the archives of JHI, Warsaw).

57. Ringelblum, *Notitsn,* pp. 22, 34; *Biuletyn,* pp. 104–6, 110, 130, 133, 197.

58. T. Walter, "The Jews under the German Occupation in Poland," *New Europe,* 1 (New York, December 1, 1940), 23; Jon Evans, *The Nazi New Order in Poland* (London, 1941), p. 127.

59. Ringelblum, *Notitsn,* p. 98 (entry of February 28, 1941). See also Bernard Goldstein, *The Stars Bear Witness* (New York, 1953), p. 79.

60. Władysław Szpilman, *Śmierć miasta* (Death of a City) (Warsaw, 1946), p. 136.

61. Blau, *Judaica,* 9, pp. 37–40.

62. A characteristic joke appeared in *Le Reveil du Peuple,* December 7, 1942: "Pourquoi une demie-étoile?—Parce que je suis demi-Juif . . ." ("Why a half star?—Because I am a half-Jew").

63. Poliakov, pp. 37, 40–42, 62–64; Reitlinger, pp. 313–14.

64. Reitlinger, p. 338.

65. Nos. 1–4 of *Min ha-metzar* have been reproduced in full in *Dapim l'heker ha-shoa ve-ha-mered* (Pages for the Research on the Catastrophe and

the Resistance) (Haifa, 1950), pp. 113–47. The facts referred to are quoted in *Dapim*, no. 1, p. 126.

66. Szpilman, p. 45.

67. Koppel Holcman, *Ziemia bez Boga* (The Earth Without God) (Wrocław, 1947), I, 215–17. See also Mark Dworzecki, *Yerushelayim delite in kamf un umkum* (The Jerusalem of Lithuania in Struggle and Destruction) (Paris, 1948), p. 28.

68. Poliakov, p. 45.

69. *Ibid.*, p. 43.

70. Ringelblum, *Biuletyn*, pp. 93–94.

71. *Ibid.*, p. 100.

72. *Dapim*, no. 1, p. 116. Since *Min ha-metzar* was a secret publication, contributions were not signed by the authors. According to B. Mark, *Umgekumene shraiber fun di getos un lagern* (The Perished Writers of the Ghettos and Camps) (Warsaw, 1954), p. 176, the author of this poem was Alter Shnur (pen name of Israel-Ber Itzinger).

73. A. Sarfi, "Leyzer Yossels in the ghetto" (Yiddish), *Undzer Veg* (New York), March 1954, p. 29.

74. See Guido Kisch (above, note 1), and Raphael Straus (above, note 1).

75. Ringelblum, *Notitsn*, p. 35.

76. Ringelblum, *Biuletyn*, p. 102.

77. Zygmunt Klukowski, "The Pain and Destruction of the Jews in Szczebrzeszyn: Pages from a Diary" (Yiddish), *BFG*, 4, no. 2 (Warsaw, 1951), 136; see also note 39.

78. Poliakov, pp. 46–48.

79. *Ibid.*, pp. 52, 72.

80. *Ibid.*, pp. 65–80, 87–91. The strong reaction of the French population against the Jewish badge is described by several French Jewish writers in *Yizkor-bukh tsum ondenk fun 14 umgekumene pariser yidishe shraiber* (Memorial Volume to Commemorate Fourteen Perished Jewish Writers of Paris), ed. by I. Spera et al. (Paris, 1946), pp. 17, 20, 196–97, 218. Of special interest are the pertinent reminiscences of the poet Moshe Shulstein: "I cannot forget the literary magazine *Di gele late* [The Yellow Badge], which A. Bekerman, M. Dzialowski, and I prepared for publication in June 1942, to coincide with the putting on of the Yellow Badge. . . . The material in this magazine was dedicated to this event . . . and included articles, accounts [reportages], songs, pictures, and letters by French writers to us about the yellow badge with expressions of sympathy and consolation. . . . On the very day when the yellow badge was introduced, French women kissed Jewish women, people in the subway trains offered seats to Jewish passengers, one shook hands with Jewish passers-by in the streets, and priests uncovered their heads on greeting them. Teachers leading their classes for a walk in the streets arranged that a Jewish child wearing a badge should always be paired arm in arm with a French [gentile] child." *Ibid.*, p. 20.

81. Poliakov, pp. 69–70.

82. Joseph L. Baron, *Stars and Sand* (Philadelphia, 1943), pp. 281–82; *Hitler's Ten-Year War on the Jews* (New York, 1943), pp. 253–54.

83. Reitlinger, pp. 342–43.

84. Baron, pp. 280–81.

85. *Donauzeitung,* November 22, 1942; quoted by P. Meyer, in *The Jews in the Soviet Satellites,* pp. 571, 622–23.

86. Nuremberg Trial documents quoted in Hilberg, p. 89 (see above, note 25). Another case of German reaction against the Jewish badge is reported in the published correspondence of a high officer of the German Wehrmacht, who wrote in one of his letters from Minsk, on the Eastern front, on November 19, 1941: "The transports of Jews from the Reich to Minsk . . . [are, like the imposition of] the Jewish star in Berlin, as I saw it there in September, not worthy of an alleged nation of culture. All that must bring revenge on us one day, and rightly so." "Ausgewählte Briefe von Generalmajor Hellmuth Stieff," *Vierteljahrshefte für Zeitgeschichte,* 2 (1954), 302–3.

87. Ringelblum, *Notitsn,* p. 97.

88. See the following entry, dated April 18, 1943, in his diaries: "I gave orders to investigate all Jews still left in Berlin. I do not want to see Jews with the Star of David running about the capital. Either the Star must be taken from them and they be classed as privileged, or they must be evacuated altogether from the capital of the Reich." *The Goebbels Diaries 1942–1943,* ed. by Louis P. Lochner (New York, 1948), p. 335. Of course, evacuation meant extermination.

89. P. Meyer, "Czechoslovakia," in *The Jews in the Soviet Satellites,* p. 79. Judah Nadich, chaplain of the United States Army in Europe during World War II, and after August 1945 adviser on Jewish affairs to General Eisenhower, wrote thus about the yellow badge of the Germans: "The next morning [October 12, 1945] I drove across . . . the Sudentenland. . . . One is only human and I must confess to having felt some measure of satisfaction at seeing the same *Sudeten* Germans now walking the streets of the town and villages of this part of Czechoslovakia with yellow bands on their sleeves. They were thus set aside from the rest of the Czech population prior to their deportation to Germany." Judah Nadich, *Eisenhower and the Jews* (New York, 1953), p. 201.

During the original typesetting of this essay for publication, an article containing supplementary material appeared: "The Yellow Badge: A Shibboleth in Nazi Europe," *WLB,* 8 (1954), 40, 42.

# 2

# THE LUBLIN RESERVATION AND THE MADAGASCAR PLAN: TWO ASPECTS OF NAZI JEWISH POLICY DURING THE SECOND WORLD WAR

## *The Lublin Reservation*

From the very beginning of their occupation of Poland the Nazis used the district of Lublin, in the southeastern part of the Government General,[1] as their favorite area for experimenting with various projects of population transfer. As soon as Poland was occupied they began to set up a reservation for Jews in Lublin. In February 1940 the Nazis devised the plan to transfer the 30,000 Germans who had been living in the Lublin district since 1865 back to their "German homeland." They began to carry out this plan in September 1940. The Lublin Germans were settled in Warthegau[2]—one step in a policy to Germanize that province—and the Poles of that region were brought to Lublin. On June 15, 1941, however, before the start of German-Soviet hostilities, Odilo Globocnik, the chief of the SS and the police in the district of Lublin, surprised the representatives of the German press with an announcement which amounted to a complete reversal of this transfer policy. He announced that a "purely German community" was now to be formed in the Lublin territory, for German colonists from Bulgaria, Yugoslavia, Bessarabia, and other countries where they lived as a minority. In order to make room for the Germans, the Nazis began to deport the Poles of the Zamość region (in the southeastern part of the Lublin district). About 110,000 Poles (from 297 communities), constituting 31 percent of the Polish population of the Zamość region, were deported between November 1941 and August 1943.[3]

These population transfers were only part of an extensive policy practiced by the totalitarian regimes of Soviet Russia and Nazi Germany. The method of exchanging populations in order to solve knotty minority problems had been applied after World War I (by Greece and Turkey, 1923; by Greece and Bulgaria, 1919–1932).[4] But not until World War II, when the Soviet Union and Nazi Germany began to "solve" complex nationality problems by shifting entire nations and tribes, were population transfers carried out on such a gigantic scale and in such a brutal, inhuman fashion. It is hard to tell in this case who set the model for whom. Soviet transfers still go on, embracing millions of people and constituting a menace to the surviving Jews in the Soviet Union and in the satellite states. These maneuvers resemble the gigantic and inhuman population transfers planned and carried out by the Nazis. Hitler began in South Tyrol (through a treaty with Mussolini) and in the occupied zones of Poland (through a treaty with Stalin). He had much more ambitious projects, such as ejecting the Czechs from the Protectorate of Bohemia-Moravia, and the French from Alsace, transferring the South Tyroleans to Crimea, transplanting tens of millions of East European ethnic groups to Siberia, etc.[5] Amidst all these projects for population transfers the deportation of Jews could easily pass as a part of the general plan. There was therefore little suspicion, at first, that behind this innocent mask of "resettlement" a scheme was in preparation of a quite different nature—nothing less than the total extermination of the Jews.

Execution of all the population transfers in the Lublin district was in the hands of the chief of the SS and the police, Globocnik. This Austrian SS leader gained a reputation among the Nazis as "the man with the iron hand." He was an organizer of the Nazi terror in Austria and of the assassination of Chancellor Dollfuss. He was appointed chief of the SS and the police in the district of Lublin in November 1939. As soon as Globocnik arrived in Lublin, the governor, Schmidt, entrusted him with the "systematic organization of all matters pertaining to the Jews of the district of Lublin." Globocnik immediately set up a special Division for Jewish Affairs, headed by Dr. Hofbauer. The Division prepared a plan for forced Jewish labor and for settling Jewish refugees in the Lublin region, and began to put the plan into effect. Soon a sharp conflict developed between Globocnik and the German civil authorities. Governor Zörner, who succeeded Schmidt, and Richard Türk, Zörner's consultant on Jewish affairs and head of the department for *Bevölkerungswesen und Fürsorge* (Population and Relief), constantly complained to their superiors that Globocnik was interfering with their work and usurping their jurisdiction in connection with the Jewish question. To this Globocnik replied that Governor Schmidt had authorized him to concentrate all Jewish matters in his hands and that Governor Zörner had agreed to the arrangement.[6] The conflict between the SS and police, on the one hand, and the civil administration, on the other, grew in intensity. To be sure, it was not a conflict over basic principles, but over prestige and authority. Both Zörner and Globocnik were at one on the basic policy of Jewish extermination. The first bloody actions in the Lublin district (especially the action of March through April 1942 in the city of Lublin) were carried out by Zörner himself with the greatest brutality.

In the end, Globocnik won out in this struggle for prestige. Zörner was forced to resign, and Globocnik's authority increased. Early in 1942 he was given new, wide powers for dealing with the Jews. He began organizing Jewish labor camps and, later, Jewish extermination camps. He was named head of all the extermination camps in the GG (Treblinka, and the three camps which he had founded in the Lublin district: Bełżec, Majdanek, and Sobibór) and was entrusted with the task of annihilating the Jews of the whole GG (Operation Reinhard). Late in the summer of 1943, after the fall of Mussolini, Globocnik was dispatched to carry out the important mission of "pacifying" the provinces of northern Italy.[7] This was the man charged with the task of setting up the Lublin reservation.

The plan for such a reservation originated in the days before World War II. On July 8, 1938, Alfred Rosenberg posed the question "Whither the Jews?"[8] On February 7, 1939, in an address to foreign diplomats and journalists, Rosenberg declared:

Palestine, as an area for compact Jewish concentration, is out of the question. . . . The area must be capable of absorbing about 15 million Jews. . . . And since the two projects, Madagascar and British Guiana, have already been taken up officially, the whole problem must be concentrated around these two territories. . . . If the millions of Jews are to be resettled, it would be a consideration of elementary humanity toward the Jews not to leave them alone among themselves, but to hand over those colonies into the hands of administrators experienced in policing. The question is not of creating a Jewish state, but a Jewish reservation.[9]

Rosenberg's words make it quite clear that the Nazis drew a distinction between a Jewish state and a Jewish reservation.

A short time after the start of German-Polish hostilities in 1939, the head of the Jewish section of the Gestapo, Adolf Eichmann, called to his office a group of Jewish representatives from Berlin, Vienna, Prague, and other cities.[10] He informed them that an autonomous Jewish territory was about to be created in the district of Lublin, and he requested that they submit lists of Jewish volunteers for "immigration." It appears that only the Vienna representatives agreed to comply with this request.[11]

The Germans made no secret of the Lublin reservation. On the contrary, the German propaganda machine sought to publicize the plan as widely as possible in the foreign press—giving, of course, its own interpretation. As early as September 19, 1939, the plan was discussed in the Belgrade newspaper *Vreme*. Soon the whole European press began to devote space to the Lublin reservation in connection with Hitler's address in the Reichstag on October 6, 1939, in which he hinted at the need for "putting in order and regulating the Jewish problem." At the same time the Germans launched a propaganda campaign for the plan among the Polish Jews. Shmuel Zygelbojm mentions in his diary[12] that on the very day they invaded Warsaw the Germans began spreading rumors about the Lublin reservation. In Częstochowa the officer for Jewish affairs in the Gestapo stated to a Jewish delegation which appeared before him on September 16, 1939: "All of the Lublin district will be cleared of non-Jews, and Jews will be transferred there from all occupied countries. A Jewish state will be set up there."[13]

German newspapermen and German officials naturally gave their enthusiastic support to the project sponsored by their government. The well-known political commentator Hermann Erich Seifert wrote:

From time to time there is talk of a Jewish settlement area in the district of Lublin, a sort of a Jewish reservation, in which the Jews would live among themselves and, for the first time in their existence, would have to organize their lives in every detail. . . . Since February 1940 they began tackling the Jewish question, especially in Lublin, not with the "humanitarian" nonsense you find in the democracies, or with soulful appeals, but according to new methods, with order and work.[14]

Seifert was evidently favorably impressed by Globocnik's "new methods."

General Jürgen Stroop, who was later in command of the German troops during the uprising in the Warsaw ghetto, mentions in his well-known report the attempts to create a Jewish reservation in the district of Lublin: "At the same time [spring 1940] a plan was considered to declare the District of Lublin the collecting area for all Jews within the GG especially for the evacuated or fugitive Jews arriving from the Reich."[15]

The broader objectives of the Lublin reservation were discussed in retrospect by Peter-Heinz Seraphim:

It is well known that . . . such a reservation for the Jews in the eastern portion of the present Government General was often under consideration, the intention being for that area to admit the Jews of the Greater Reich and of the rest of the Government General and, in time, also of the rest of Europe.[16]

On November 17, 1939, Arthur Seyss-Inquart, then deputy of Hans Frank, left Cracow on a tour of inspection of the whole GG. He visited Lublin, where he conferred with Governor Schmidt and the higher SS officers Hasselberger and Globocnik. It was then decided to set up in the Lublin region a reception center for "destructive elements" (Jews, as well as Poles, from the Polish provinces incorporated into the Reich). The plan was even submitted for approval to Governor-General Frank.[17] Evidently, they did not have to wait long for Frank's consent. In October 1939, even before Frank's official approval of the project, transports of Jews from the Reich, from Austria, and from Warthegau began to arrive in the GG.

In the meantime, the project for the Lublin reservation received the blessing of the highest Nazi political authorities. At a conference in Berlin on February 12, 1940, under the chairmanship of Marshal Hermann Göring, and attended by Heinrich Himmler, Hans Frank, the Gauleiters Forster and Arthur Greiser, and other cabinet ministers and state secretaries, it was decided to shift 30,000 Germans from the Lublin district, which was to be set aside for a Jewish reservation.[18] One would expect that a project of such dimensions would have been preceded by careful preparation. Nothing of the kind took place. Nothing was done to prepare for the reception of this mass of humanity, consisting mainly of Jews, but also including Poles and Gypsies.

In a letter of February 13, 1940,[19] Globocnik mentions the fact that in December 1939 his consultant on Jewish affairs, Dr. Hofbauer, had sent out a questionnaire to the local authorities in the Lublin district to find out where the transports of Jews could be placed. It is not known what replies Globocnik received to his queries. In any case his questionnaire was belated, since tens of thousands of Jewish refugees had already arrived in the Lublin district and Globocnik expected the immediate arrival of another 162,000 Jews.

In setting up the Lublin reservation no account was taken of the numerous complexities involved. During a vehement discussion in Globocnik's office on April 22, 1940, Türk, the consultant on Jewish affairs for the civil administration, roundly berated Globocnik for the whole business of the transfer. He pointed out that the Ukrainians in the southeastern part of the Lublin district had been promised that they would not be made to live with Poles, and he added that certainly "they ought not to be blessed with numerous—rather too numerous—additions of Jews." To this Hofbauer, consultant on Jews in Globocnik's office, replied that there was no intention of settling the transported Jews in areas populated by Ukrainians.

In general, he said, there was no thought of allowing the Gypsies or the Jews to settle permanently, or even semipermanently. This was to be only a temporary arrangement, and they would soon be shipped off to various labor camps.[20] It is clear that from the very beginning the object was to exterminate the Jewish refugees, and all the talk about "colonization" was merely a device to keep the Jews calm in order to effect a smooth transfer. The implementation of the transfer showed that such was the real objective.

As already mentioned, the transfers began with Jews from Vienna. In October 1939, the Jewish community in Vienna sent out a number of mimeographed announcements under the caption "Memorandum on Resettlement in the Polish Province" in which the recipients were requested to report within two or three days for transport to Poland for "colonization work." On October 20, the first shipment of Jews from Vienna left for Poland. The Jewish community in Vienna is said to have been ordered to supply a thousand Jews weekly. During the month of October, 1,672 Jews arrived from Vienna in the Lublin reservation.[21]

At the same time large shipments kept on arriving from the Protectorate (Bohemia-Moravia). The first transport, of 600 Czech Jews, left on October 26, 1939. The transports came from Prague, Brno, Mährisch-Ostrau (Moravska Ostrava), Pilsen, Cieszyn (Teschen), Bohumin, and other Czech towns. According to Czech sources, ten to twenty thousand Jews were sent out from Moravska Ostrava alone. These figures seem grossly exaggerated. The journey was very difficult. Transports which left at the end of October did not arrive in the Lublin district until about November 26.[22] Large transports of Jews also arrived from the Polish provinces that had been incorporated into the Third Reich. From October 1939 to July 1940 more than fifty Jewish communities of the Warthegau were broken up and uprooted and their members sent to Poland, mainly to Lublin.[23] Transports also arrived from the German Reich itself, such as the one from Stettin and other cities in Pomerania, which came early in February 1940 with 1,200 Jews.[24] Besides that, thousands of Jewish war prisoners from the Polish army were brought to Lublin. Globocnik assigned them to a special camp in Lublin (at 7 Lipowa Street), and later to one in Majdanek.[25]

The number of Jews "colonized" in the Lublin reservation kept growing. At a conference in the Berlin office of Reinhard Heydrich, the chief of the SS and the police, on January 30, 1940, it was reported that 78,000 Jews had already been shipped and that plans called for the transfer of 400,000 more Jews during the following months.[26]

The German administration in the GG protested sharply against the deportation of such large numbers of Jews to Poland. In a memorandum entitled "German War Economy in Poland," the administration complained to Berlin about these "unbridled deportations," which were cause for so many headaches:

These evacuations, without any plan, render it extremely difficult to take any census, to collect any statistical data, or to make any methodical use of Jewish labor, and have crowded all the ghettos with an impoverished proletariat. The continuation of such transports will endanger the social and economic future of the whole province.[27]

In another report (March 28, 1940), the language used is even more outspoken:

Despite the protests of [the administration of] the Government General against the hasty and chaotic deportations of German Jews to eastern Poland, those deportations are still carried on at the order of the SS. . . . The governor [of Lublin, Zörner] refuses to bear any responsibility for these steps or for their consequences. Marshal Göring has been informed of it.[28]

Among all the arguments used to protest the deportations one argument is wholly absent—the humanitarian argument regarding the cruel sufferings of the victims. Such an argument was, of course, unthinkable for a Nazi official. The most characteristic feature of the struggle was the keen competition between the civil and military authorities, on the one hand, and the Nazi party and SS, on the other. The conflict became more pronounced when Governor-General Frank sent a sharp protest to Berlin, in which he underscored that he was the highest German authority in the GG and that the SS must obey his orders.[29] As we now know, these protests availed little in Berlin. The heads of the SS (Friedrich Wilhelm Krüger in Cracow, and Globocnik in Lublin) acted more and more on their own and managed in time to oust the civil administration from all influence in the Jewish question.[30] Four years later the arrogant Hans Frank was still smarting from his defeat. At a conference with higher officials in Cracow, on May 16, 1944, he bitterly criticized Globocnik's policies, although Globocnik had left Lublin long ago and was then in Italy.[31]

On arriving in Lublin, the deported Jews were placed in dilapidated buildings, in empty barracks, warehouses, stables, synagogues, and schools. When there was no more room in such places, they were simply left in the open fields, in areas fenced off by barbed wire. The sufferings of the deportees filled the Polish Jews with horror. The truth of what was going on in the Lublin reservation soon reached the outside world, and the foreign press published alarming reports. Jews who escaped from Poland brought shocking details. A. Hartglas, former deputy of the Polish Sejm, reported that the refugees lived mostly in tents.[32] A refugee who had passed through Lublin described the plight of the thousands of Jews who were lying in the streets, falling victim to death by starvation and pestilence. He gave an exaggerated estimate of the number of Jews in the city of Lublin as 200,000 to 250,000 Jews (including the 40,000 Jewish residents of the city). American and West European journalists estimated the number of Jews transferred to Lublin at between 30,000 and 60,000. A prominent American newspaperman, Oswald G. Villard, wrote: "It is impossible to conceive of any more barbarous cruelty, and it is deliberately calculated."[33] S. McCrea Cavett, general secretary of the Federal Council of Churches in America, wrote in a similar vein.[34] The Jewish press in America was especially loud in its condemnation of these Nazi brutalities.[35]

There is no evidence in the official correspondence or the numerous printed documents of the Nazi regime that foreign public opinion had any effect on the Nazi rulers. Nevertheless, the transport of Jews to the Lublin reservation was suddenly stopped. Göring, who on February 12 had presided over a meeting at which further steps for creating the Jewish reservation were determined, issued an order on March 23, 1940, to discontinue transfers. Heinrich Himmler, too, immediately issued an order strictly forbidding any more "deportation of Jews" to the east. The chief of the SS and police for the GG Krüger issued a directive in April 1940 in which he indicated that the plan to set up a Jewish reservation in the Lublin district was no longer being considered.[36]

What brought about this sudden reversal of policy? We can only conjecture, since the available documents fail to explain why the previous policy was altered. A number of factors may have been involved. First, as a result of the overcrowded, unsanitary living conditions, a typhus epidemic developed in the area. Second, the Germans needed all their means of transportation for the invasion of Norway and Western Europe which they were now preparing; they could not, therefore, undertake any large-scale transport of Jews. Third, the invasion of the Soviet Union (Operation Barbarossa) was already in its preparatory stages, and the Nazis may have wanted to avoid creating a mass of Jews on the Russian-Polish border. Finally, the sharp conflicts between Globocnik and the civil authorities may have influenced the decision.

The abandonment of the plan for the Lublin reservation did not mean the end of Jewish deportations to Poland, however. The final decision in this matter stemmed from the Führer himself. On October 2, 1940, Hitler entertained some of his closest collaborators, including Martin Bormann, Hans Frank, Baldur von Schirach (then Gauleiter of Vienna), Erich Koch (then Gauleiter of East Prussia), and others. After dinner they started a discussion of the Polish and Jewish problems. Hans Frank boasted that he had confined the Jews of the GG in ghettos and that soon the capital city, Cracow, would be completely cleared of Jews. Von Schirach then remarked that he still had 50,000 Jews in Vienna whom he wanted Frank to take from him. Koch said that he too would have to transport all the Jews and Poles of the Ciechocinek district to Frank in the GG. Frank replied that he had no facilities for receiving more people. As usual, Hitler had the last word. His verdict was that the evacuation of the Jews to Poland must go on.[37]

In March 1940 Dr. Gottong[38] was appointed consultant on Jewish affairs for the GG. Immediately after his appointment, he was informed that, beginning on May 1, 1940, there would arrive in Poland 400,000 Jews, for whom he would have to find a place. Gottong did not even think of placing them in the Lublin reservation, but looked for a new solution. In his circular of April 6, 1940, to all the district chiefs in the GG,[39] he proposed a plan of his own. First of all he wanted to effect a strict isolation of the Jews from the Poles. In time all Jewish settlements would be concentrated in one area, where they would have an autonomous community under the supervision of the Reich. In the meantime he asked all district chiefs to let him know of any territory under their jurisdiction which might be suitable for "exclusively Jewish colonization."

Gottong was apparently a naïve bureaucrat who lacked an understanding of the real objectives pursued by his government, and who busied himself with paper plans. At the same time, Globocnik, after a series of pointed discussions and vehement sessions, put through his plan. Under Globocnik's leadership the Lublin reservation went through a remarkable metamorphosis. Out of the reservation for Jewish settlement grew labor camps, where Jews were slowly tortured to death, and out of the labor camps slowly grew extermination camps, with a highly developed, accelerated technique for mass killings. Naturally, Globocnik did it all with the knowledge and consent of the highest authorities in Berlin, who were later to designate him officially for this mission. At a session on April 22, 1940, Globocnik proposed the plan for labor camps for Jews. Men and women were to be isolated from each other. They were to be set at digging trenches and other fortifications on the Polish-Russian border. Globocnik reported that he had already registered about 50,000 Jews for that purpose.

The first camps were set up early in the summer of 1940. In July of that year there were more than thirty camps with 10,000 Jews.[40] In a detailed report prepared for the Warsaw ghetto archives by officials of the Jewish community of Warsaw early in 1941 the names and places of fifty-one labor camps in the district of Lublin were listed: forty-one of them at that time contained about 17,000 Jews; as for the others, no statistical data were available.[41] The largest camp was in Bełżec, established in July 1940. Globocnik brought specialists from Germany to help him set up his camps. Among them was Major Dolf, one of Hitler's oldest friends and comrades in the Nazi party. Globocnik named him commandant of the camp for war prisoners in Lublin (January 1940) and, later, commandant of the camp at Bełżec. Dolf soon acquired notoriety as one of the worst sadists and tormentors.[42]

In connection with the camps, there was a renewal of the bitter rivalry between Globocnik and the civil administration. We have a record of a telephone inquiry made by the Department of Interior Administration, Population, and Relief of the GG in Cracow to the Lublin administration, about the camp at Bełżec, which was to be abolished. The answer came from Türk, in an acrimonious letter dated October 21, 1940, saying that he had no knowledge of the matter, although the subject of Jewish labor was under his administration. But, he said, the administration of the labor department had no idea of what was going on, "on account of the poor cooperation of the SS-Brigadeführer Globocnik."[43] He went on to complain that it was "no longer possible in practice to attain the right kind of cooperation on the part of the SS and the police." He cited an example of the calamitous effects of the situation: two trainloads of Jewish laborers, containing approximately 920 persons, left for Hrubieszów, but only 500 arrived. Nobody knew what had happened to the other 400. It did not stand to reason, Türk argued, that 400 persons had been shot. Something much worse, in his opinion, must have taken place. "I have heard it rumored," he said, "that they were most probably released as a result of bribes." On another occasion Globocnik complained that the civil administration had sent to Chełm a whole transport of Jews intended for Bełżec. The outcome of the quarrels we know: Globocnik was the victor, and the Lublin reservation became a center for extermination camps under his supervision.

The rapid end of the Lublin reservation did not destroy allusions to its continued existence. On July 10, 1940, the chief of the department of resettlement in the Warsaw district, Waldemar Schön, inquired of the chief of the department dealing with resettlement in the district of Lublin, Türk, if he could send 10,000 Jews to Lublin from the Warsaw district. Schön was especially eager to send Türk Jews from Żyrardów, which had to be cleared of Jews, or from Łowicz. To this Türk replied with a categoric "No."[44] In 1942 there were still rumors circulating among the Jews of Warsaw that the Germans were seeking to create a Jewish reservation in Eastern Europe.[45] The Germans wished to perpetuate the idea, and used it even in the latter part of 1942 to mask their real objectives with regard to the Jews. At that time the German foreign office addressed a request to the Hungarian government, with a plan to deport a number of Jews from Hungary to Poland. The German undersecretary of state, Martin Luther, assured Premier Kállay of Hungary that the Jews would be employed in building roads, after which they would be settled in the Jewish reservation.[46] By that time, as is well known, there was not a trace left of the reservation.

## The Madagascar Plan

The island of Madagascar, a French colony since 1896, has an area of 228,000 square miles, and had a population, in 1936, of 3.8 million natives and 36,000 Europeans, mostly French. In 1926 the Polish government considered a plan to send a number of impoverished Polish peasants to that island, but the plan was soon abandoned. The first proposal to colonize Jews in Madagascar came from the pen of a German publicist, probably a Nazi, in 1931, who wrote that "the entire Jewish nation sooner or later must be confined to an island. This would afford the possibility of control and minimize the danger of infection." On the cover of the pamphlet was a map of the island of Madagascar.[47] The name of the author was apparently fictitious. The pamphlet was probably published in Nazi circles close to Himmler. At any rate, Himmler told his personal physician, Felix Kersten, that he had suggested to Hitler in 1934 that the Jews be settled in Madagascar.[48] Other high-placed Nazis, in their testimony after the war, also mentioned Himmler as the initiator of this plan.[49]

In 1937 the Polish government again took up the Madagascar project. This time, however, it was intended not for peasants but for Jews.[50] The Polish government sent a commission to Madagascar to investigate the situation. The commission consisted of Major Mieczyslaw Lepecki, representing the ruling political party (Sanacja); a well-known Jewish agriculturist from Tel Aviv, Shlomo Dyk; and Leon Alter, director of the Jewish Emigration Association (JEAS) in Warsaw. The commission could not agree on a unanimous report. Lepecki thought it possible to settle about 40,000 to 60,000 persons immediately, half of them farm workers and half merchants. Alter saw possibilities for only 400 families. Dyk had doubts even about that number. Both the Polish and the French government thought Lepecki far too optimistic. The local population in Madagascar demonstrated its strong opposition to the whole project. *La Dépêche,* the most influential newspaper in Madagascar, also voiced violent opposition.[51]

The Jewish press in Poland naturally opposed the plan and treated the whole idea with irony.[52] Despite all the protests, the Polish foreign minister, Józef Beck, endeavored to secure the consent of the French government and, according to reports in the Nazi press, carried on negotiations regarding the matter with the French prime minister, Léon Blum.[53] Studies were made by the French colonial office, and materials were gathered. Later on, after France was invaded, the Nazis got hold of the materials and used them in developing their own Madagascar plan. During the years immediately before the war, the Madagascar plan became popular in certain Polish circles, as a means of getting rid of the Jews. A Polish novel was published revolving around the theme of Jewish emigration to Madagascar. The author of this utopian novel envisaged a situation in which only 100,000 thoroughly assimilated Jews would remain in Poland.[54]

In 1938 the Nazis again revived the Madagascar plan, this time on a broad international scale. This was probably intended as an answer to the discussions at the Evian conference (July 1938), which dealt with the problem of the refugees from Nazi Germany. The Nazis wished to present their own plan, as against the various plans for colonization suggested by the Western powers. Mention has already been made of Alfred Rosenberg's reaction to the Evian conference, particularly to the Guiana and Madagascar projects. At a German cabinet meeting on November 12, 1938, Hermann Göring declared that Hitler was preparing a new proposal on the Jewish question, and that he would suggest to the Western powers that the Jewish question be solved by the creation of a Jewish territory in Madagascar.[55] Germany initiated talks in London with the British government and with the Intergovernmental Committee for Refugees set up after the Evian conference. The negotiations were carried on by Hjalmar Schacht during his visit to London, and they were continued by the German ambassador in London, Herbert von Dirksen, the Austrian finance minister, Fischböck, and others.[56] Schacht's plan called for securing an international loan for Germany to finance the emigration, which would bolster German exports. (The Jews would be allowed to take out a portion of their possessions from Germany, but only in German goods.) The Madagascar plan became a subject of international politics. According to some sources, Hitler took up the matter personally with the French ambassador in Berlin, André François-Poncet.[57] The defense minister of South Africa, Oswald Pirow, played an active role in those negotiations. Pirow was an admirer of Hitler and a self-confessed "outspoken anti-Semite." In an editorial in the first issue of his periodical *Neuwe Orde* (October 4, 1945), Pirow described his journey to Europe in 1938 and his negotiations. At first Pirow discussed the plan with the British prime minister, Neville Chamberlain, and with a Jewish member of Parliament (whose name is not given). Then he went to Berlin. Here he suggested to Hitler that Jews be allowed to emigrate to one of the following three countries: former German East Africa, British Guiana, or Madagascar. Hitler selected Madagascar, stating that he was ready to offer France compensation for the island. This could only mean that the Jewish "homeland" was to be placed under a German protectorate. From Berlin Pirow was to go to Paris to negotiate with the French government, but the sudden outbreak of the general strike and the cabinet crisis in France forced him to postpone his visit.[58]

The Italian government also supported the Madagascar plan. Italy, preparing to displace Great Britain in the Middle East, was interested in hampering the development of the Jewish National Home in Palestine and in winning the friendship of the Arabs. The Madagascar plan served both of these purposes. *Informazione Diplomatica,* the organ of the Italian foreign ministry, in its issue of February 16, 1938, wrote that the only answer to the Jewish question was to create a Jewish state, but not in Palestine. The Italian foreign minister, Count Galeazzo Ciano, in his diary, mentioned a conversation with Mussolini and the U.S. ambassador, William Phillips, on January 3, 1939. Phillips presented a message of President Roosevelt suggesting that Ethiopia be opened to Jewish immigration. Roosevelt's proposal was based on the fact that the Fascist Grand Council had approved, on October 6, 1938, a resolution "permitting controlled emigration of European Jews into some parts of Ethiopia, in order, among other things, to divert Jewish emigration from Palestine." Mussolini, in this January conversation, rejected the plan of a Jewish settlement in Ethiopia, but declared himself favorable to the creation of an independent Jewish state.[59] (Of course, Palestine was excluded.) As we have already noted, Alfred Rosenberg discussed, on February 7, 1939, at a press conference in Berlin, the plan to settle 15 million Jews in Guiana or in Madagascar.[60]

After Rosenberg's fantastic project, the discussion of the matter suddenly subsided. Pirow explains it by the continuous attacks on Hitler by Churchill and "the Labor party politicians," which made friendly negotiations impossible. In his pro-Nazi explanations, Pirow left out one factor, however: in March 1939 Hitler, by his attack on Czechoslovakia, had aroused the indignation of the whole free world. The pressure of an aroused public opinion most probably made the governments of the Western powers discontinue their negotiations with Germany. Not long afterward, World War II erupted.

The Madagascar plan again became an issue when the Nazis, after the war broke out, decided to use it in a new diplomatic game in a new setting. In December 1939 the German foreign minister, Joachim von Ribbentrop, submitted a peace proposal to the pope, which contained, among other items, a plan for the emigration of all German Jews, to Palestine, Ethiopia, and Madagascar.[61]

Military operations soon caused a complete change in the Jewish policy of the Nazis, however. They now had a large portion of European Jewry under their rule, and they were in a position directly to determine the fate of the Jews. They were able to use this power to press their plans with the Western powers. Their victories in Poland and in Western Europe strengthened the belief of the Nazis in their ultimate victory, and held forth the prospect of forcing the defeated French to cede the island of Madagascar. Diplomatic talks were now of secondary significance. First in importance were the practical preparations for carrying out the colonization of the island. The matter was now primarily in the hands of the German police and the SS rather than the foreign ministry.

On May 15, 1940, Himmler, after the official collapse of the Lublin reservation project, prepared a detailed memorandum entitled "Some Thoughts on the Treatment of Non-Germans in the East," in which he devoted only one sentence to the Jews: "I hope that, thanks to the possibility of a large emigration of all Jews to Africa or some other colony, I shall live to see the day when the concept of Jew will have completely disappeared from Europe." Himmler wrote those words in his official capacity as "Reichskommissar for the consolidation of German *Volkstum* in the East," and he submitted his plan to Hitler on May 20, 1940. Hitler designated Himmler's proposals as "very good and correct," and ordered a few copies of this strictly confidential document to be distributed among his Reichsleiters in Eastern Europe (Erich Koch, Albert Forster, Arthur Greiser, and Hans Frank).[62]

Frank, seeing this decision, was overjoyed. He had long been complaining against the incessant transport of Jews to the GG. Frank himself, his deputy Dr. Josef Bühler, and the expert on Jewish affairs, Peter-Heinz Seraphim, used every occasion to point out that there were too many Jews in the GG, and that any further increase in their number would be an unbearable burden.[63] On June 10, 1940, Frank gleefully told his associates that the Jews of the GG were going to be shipped overseas. On July 12, 1940, he discussed the whole plan at a meeting of his department and district chiefs in Cracow:

The Führer's decision, which came at my suggestion, is of the utmost importance. No more transports of Jews to the Government General are to take place. It is now planned to transfer the whole Jewish tribe from the Reich, the Government General and the Protectorate, within the shortest possible time after the conclusion of peace, to some African or American colony. There is talk about the island of Madagascar, which France will have to yield for this purpose. An area of 500,000 square kilometers ought to suffice for several million Jews. I tried also to win for the Jews of the Government General the privilege to build their own life anew on new soil. That has been accepted. Thus, we may expect that within the very near future we shall be tremendously relieved.

Speaking before a larger party meeting in Cracow, Frank related the news in a jovial tone:

As soon as sea communications permit the shipment of the Jews [laughter in the audience], they shall be shipped, piece by piece, man by man, woman by woman, girl by girl. I hope, gentlemen, you will not complain on that account [merriment in the hall]. I believe, therefore, that we are already, as they say, out of the morass.[64]

It appears that for a short time even the highest authorities in Germany took the Madagascar plan quite seriously. Hitler's official interpreter, Paul

Schmidt, related in his memoirs that on June 18, 1940, when Hitler and Mussolini talked about the disposition of French colonies, Hitler said, "A Jewish state could be created on Madagascar."[65] Also Ciano mentioned in his diaries, under the dates of June 18 and 19, 1940, that the German Madagascar plan was communicated to him by Ribbentrop. Soon thereafter, on July 18, 1940, the semiofficial *La Stampa* of Turin wrote about the Madagascar plan as an officially adopted project. At the same time an Italian racist periodical ran an article about Madagascar as a place for Jewish settlement.[66]

Preparation for the implementation of the Madagascar plan started during the early months of the war. The Berlin Gestapo called in representatives of the German Jews and told them to speed up Jewish emigration. After some lengthy negotiations and after hearing several proposals by the Jews, the Gestapo announced its own plan: to ship 5 million Jews to the island of Madagascar, with the financial assistance of the Jewish Agency for Palestine and Jewish organizations in America.[67] Von Ribbentrop charged the chief of the Jewish division in the foreign office, the ambitious young jurist Franz Rademacher, with the preparation of a detailed plan from the point of view of international law. On July 3, 1940, Rademacher submitted a memorandum entitled "The Jewish Question in the Peace Treaty," with the slogan "All Jews Out of Europe."[68]

Rademacher's plan was as follows: France was to cede Madagascar to the German government for the purpose of solving the Jewish question. The 25,000 Frenchmen living on the island would have to leave so that the Jews might be cut off from any contact with white Europeans. Germany was to be given a mandate over Madagascar, with the right to install naval and air bases. The parts of the island not occupied by German military bases or by the native population would be set aside for Jewish colonization. Jewish immigration was not to be voluntary, but based on forced deportations. With this in mind, Germany was to include in every peace treaty with European nations a clause calling for the evacuation of all Jews from Europe. The Jews of Madagascar were to serve as hostages in German hands for the "good behavior of the people of their race in America" toward Germany. The Jews in Madagascar were to enjoy local autonomy, have their own mayors, their own postal service, railway service, and so forth. But the island was to be administered by a German police governor, who would take his orders from the central German police authorities. Money derived from confiscated Jewish possessions in Europe would be used to set up a bank in Europe to purchase land in Madagascar for Jewish colonization and to buy and import the necessary goods.

The plan was soon endorsed by Ribbentrop and was enthusiastically received by the Reich Security Main Office (SS, Police, and Gestapo).

Heydrich instructed his official Theo Dannecker (later the hangman of French and south-European Jews) to work out a plan for emigration and for transportation to Madagascar. Dannecker submitted his plan on August 15, 1940. It called for the creation of a special fleet of ships of the North German Lloyd and Hamburg-American lines to carry the emigrants. The Jews were to pay their own passage. The transports were to begin after the end of the war. Four million Jews from Europe (evidently the Jews of Soviet Russia were not yet included) were to be transported to Madagascar. First to go would be the pioneers who would prepare the land for colonization.[69]

The Nazis, in formulating their Madagascar plan, employed some of the terminology of Zionists and Territorialists and proposed to use some of their methods. But the Nazi concepts of international trusteeship, Jewish territorial autonomy, an international Jewish colonization bank, and pioneer vanguards, emerge as travesties of the Jewish formulations. The basic idea becomes apparent in the decision to appoint a police governor over the Jewish territory and to isolate the Jews from every contact with the surrounding world, especially with the white race. In other words, Madagascar was to become a vast prison for the Jews, or, as the foreign press put it, a "super-ghetto" or concentration camp. The Nazi rulers were also well aware that there was no room on the island for millions of new immigrants, particularly when they were to be relegated to the poorest land not settled by the natives and not reserved for the German military installations. In short, like the Lublin reservation, Madagascar was conceived as a gigantic concentration for slow death.

For a brief period, even the Reich Security Main Office, especially the Jewish affairs division under Adolf Eichmann, saw in the Madagascar plan a possibility for the "final solution of the Jewish question."[70] There was even a candidate for the office of police governor; it was the chief of Hitler's private chancellery, Philip Bouhler.[71] Hitler himself endorsed the project. In a statement on May 29, 1942, he let the cat out of the bag as to why Madagascar had been selected of all places. He declared that Jews must not be exiled to Siberia, where the rigorous climate might toughen them and endow them with new vitality. They must be sent to Africa, where climatic conditions have a debilitating effect on the human organism and lower its resistance.[72] This was as telling a revelation of the motives behind the Madagascar plan as one could expect.

After Rademacher and Dannecker had submitted their memoranda, the subject of Madagascar became very confused and was set aside, like its twin project, the Lublin reservation. The new turn in the situation came in August or September of 1940. On September 20, 1940, Hitler ordered his general staff to prepare a plan of action for the invasion of the Soviet

Union. This meant the prolongation of the war. But it also involved a new policy toward the Jews. The under-secretary for foreign affairs, Martin Luther, was told by Heydrich that the Jewish question could no longer be solved by emigration. At the outbreak of German-Soviet hostilities, Luther declared that owing to political developments, the Madagascar plan was no longer practicable. Somewhat later Rademacher wrote to his friend Ambassador Bielfeld that the Führer himself had decided that the Jews were to be transported not to the island of Madagascar but to Eastern Europe.[73]

Notwithstanding all this, the Madagascar affair was kept alive as a means to befuddle the public: Hitler, Goebbels, Rosenberg, and others continued to speak of the plan in 1942 and 1943. Hitler brought up the subject several times in talks with his close associates. On July 24, 1942, he remarked: "After the war the Jews will emigrate to Madagascar or to another Jewish national state." Since the extermination of European Jewry had already been decided at a conference at Wannsee on January 20, 1942, this statement was nothing but cynical hypocrisy. In 1941 the Madagascar plan was mentioned by Admiral Darlan of France.[74] The plan was likewise submitted by Alfred Rosenberg in his paper at a session of the Institute for the Study of the Jewish Question at Frankfurt on March 28, 1941.[75] The Nazi news agency *Der Weltdienst,* on April 28, 1941, published the following report: "Rumors are circulating here that a secret clause in the Franco-German armistice calls for the French government to permit all European Jews to come to Madagascar." The following day the Jewish Telegraphic Agency cabled from Stockholm: "Jewish personages from the Reich, Austria, Nazi-occupied Poland, and the Protectorate have been convened by the Nazi government to Berlin to confer on a plan for evacuating all Jews from Europe to Madagascar." No such conference took place: the JTA fell for a Nazi propaganda trick. The Jewish public abroad never took the plan very seriously. Responsible Jewish leaders in the United States took a negative attitude.[76] Polish Jews knew about the plan in 1940, but there are not enough materials to enable us to evaluate their reaction.[77]

In the meantime the Nazi press kept writing about the project. It was given the greatest publicity by H. E. Seifert, who insisted, in all his writings, that the ghettos were not the final solution but only a "transitional solution" of the Jewish problem.[78] It is not enough to segregate the Jews, he argued. They must be completely isolated. The Lublin reservation was also not "a final solution." Any such ultimate solution must be based on the principle that "the Jew does not belong to the community of white peoples, but to the area of habitation of the colored peoples." The final habitation of 10 million European Jews must be located as far as possible from the white race and must be strictly guarded. Seifert recalled that at the International

Congress of Anti-Semites in Budapest in 1926 "influential German quarters" had offered suggestions which sounded fantastic at the time but were now capable of execution. Seifert did not mention the island of Madagascar by name, nor did he designate any territory for his colonial "colored" Jewish reservation. The plan was revived again, this time as a means for anti-Jewish incitement, when the British forces occupied Madagascar in May 1942. The Nazi and collaborationist press in France wrote that the perfidious British had been scheming since 1937 to hand over to the Jews this island, "with its ideal climate" [*sic!*] and "with all its numerous natives to slave for them."[79] Thus, the Madagascar plan became, in the Nazi press, a Jewish contrivance!

It is interesting to note that Goebbels, after studying the plan for the extermination of European Jewry, as evolved at the conference at Wannsee, still toyed with the idea of Jewish emigration to Madagascar.[80] He used the Madagascar plan for propaganda purposes as late as 1943. At a conference for the foreign press in Berlin on March 14, 1943, Goebbels hinted that "that international poison," the Jews, could be removed in a humanitarian fashion through the creation of a state "entirely reserved for European Jews." The collaborationist press in France seized on this idea and gave it a great deal of publicity.[81] Goebbels was clever enough not to mention the name Madagascar, which by that time had already been exposed as a fraud of German propaganda. He evidently had appraised the whole project from the beginning as a swindle. In his diaries (May 7 and 8, 1942), Goebbels discusses the occupation of the island by the British, but makes no mention at all of the plan for Jewish colonization.[82] All his talk about creating a Jewish state for millions of Jews, at a time when most of the Jews in Europe had already been murdered, was nothing but a smoke screen.

As a characteristic detail it is worth mentioning that the Nazi plans for a Jewish reservation in Europe (Lublin) or Africa did not fail to have some effect among Allied statesmen. In the spring of 1942 Zygmunt Kaczyński, a highly placed Polish cleric who was a member of the Polish National Council and vice-minister for information in the Polish government-in-exile in London, came to the United States. He brought with him a plan for settling the Jews after the war in some reservation in eastern Poland or in Bessarabia (with the approval of the Rumanian government). Apparently the plan had the support of the Polish underground in Warsaw.[83] At the Bermuda Conference (April 19–30, 1943), during the discussion of the refugee problem, somebody let a remark drop about asking the French government to open Madagascar to the refugees. Although the intention of the proposal was totally different from that of the Nazi Madagascar plan, it was, from a purely psychological point of view, a false move. "This was especially deplorable," a Jewish historian comments, "in view of the unsavory reputation the Madagascar venture had earned in connection with plans of the pre-1939 Polish government and the Nazi government to ship European Jews there."[84]

❰ This essay was first published in *Yivo Annual of Jewish Social Science,* 8 (1953), 151–77. It also appeared in Yiddish in *Yivo Bleter,* 38 (1953), 5–36.

## Notes

1. See above, "The Jewish Badge and the Yellow Star," note 7.

2. Portions of western Poland were incorporated by the Germans in 1939 into the German Reich. Parts of these areas, especially in the regions of Posen, Kalisz, and Lodz, were constituted as the Reichsgau Warthegau and were placed under the administration of Arthur Greiser.

3. See Z. Klukowski, ed., *Teror niemiecki w Zamojszczyźnie 1939–1944* (German Terror in the Zamość Region 1939–1944), 2 vols. (Zamość, 1945–1946); *Akt oskarzenia przeciwko Dr. Józefowi Bühlerowi: Prokuratura Najwyższego Trybunału Narodowego* (Act of Indictment against Dr. Josef Bühler: Office of the Prosecution of the Supreme National Tribunal) (Cracow, May 31, 1948. Mimeographed, in my archives.) See also *Gazeta Żydowska* (Cracow, September 27, 1940); Joseph B. Schechtman, *European Population Transfers, 1939–1945* (New York, 1946), pp. 214–23.

Himmler showed great interest in the expulsion of the Poles from Zamość and dreamt of establishing a closed German colonization area in that section. On July 21, 1941, Himmler visited Zamość. According to Gerald Reitlinger, a *Führerhof* (a school for the Nazi élite) was established in Zamość on that occasion, and the name of the city was changed to Himmlerstadt. *The Final Solution* (London, 1953), p. 45. According to Polish sources, these projects were never implemented.

4. See Marc Vishniak, *Dos transferirn bafelkerungen* (The Population Transfers) (New York, 1942).

5. See *Hitler's Secret Conversations, 1941–1944,* ed. by H. R. Trevor-Roper (New York, 1953); "Hitler's plan of removal of 50 million Slavs" (Polish), *BGK,* V (1949), 209–42.

One of Himmler's weird dreams was to transfer the Dutch to Russia and the British—after Germany's victory, of course—to the Baltic states. Up to August 1943 the Germans transferred to the Greater Reich (including the incorporated Polish provinces) 546,000 *Volksdeutsche* (ethnic Germans) from Eastern Europe after the expulsion of 1.2 million Poles and 300,000 Jews from the incorporated Polish provinces (see Reitlinger, pp. 36, 40).

6. Letter from Globocnik to Zörner, February 13, 1940, in the archives of the JHI, Warsaw, Lublin documents.

7. On Globocnik's part in the liquidation of Polish Jewry, see S. Piotrowski's *Misja Odyla Globocnika* (The Mission of Odilo Globocnik) (Warsaw, 1949).

Many documents dealing with the conflicts between Globocnik and Zörner are found in the Lublin archives of the Jewish Historical Institute of Warsaw. Among these is an interesting account by Simkhe Turteltaub (a Jewish forced laborer in the office of the Lublin governor) of the German discussions which he overheard regarding these conflicts. The differences between Zörner and Globocnik pertained not only to the Jews but also to the Poles. Goebbels, in his diary entry May 25, 1943, tells of a visit from Zörner, who came to explain his resignation as governor of Lublin. Globocnik's brutal policy of forced transfer of the Polish population led many Poles to join the partisan bands in the forests. Zörner opposed the deportations, and was supported by Hans Frank. But Frank did not have sufficient authority to overrule the SS leader. Piotrowski, pp. 8, 25–26, 93–94.

8. *Völkischer Beobachter,* July 8, 1938.

9. *Ibid.,* February 8, 1939. An abridged version of Rosenberg's speech is found in Hebrew translation in Moshe Prager's *Hurban Yisrael beeropa* (The Destruction of the Jews in Europe) (Ein Harod, 5708 [1948]), pp. 269–70.

10. It is possible that Moses Merin, head of the united Jewish communities of Upper Silesia, also participated in this conference. See Ka-tzetnik, *Salamandra* (Tel Aviv, 1946), p. 124; P. Wiederman, *Płowa bestia* (The Blond Beast) (Munich, 1948), pp. 85–88; E. Ringelblum, "Notes from the Ghetto" (Polish), *Biuletyn,* 2 (1951), 125–27.

11. Marie Syrkin, *Blessed Is the Match* (Philadelphia, 1947), pp. 66–67.

12. S. J. Hertz, ed., *Zygelbojm-bukh* (New York, 1947), pp. 188–89.

13. L. Brener, *Vidershtand un umkum in tshenstokhover geto* (Resistance and Destruction of the Częstochowa Ghetto) (Warsaw, 1950), p. 11.

14. Hermann Erich Seifert, *Der Jude an der Ostgrenze* (Berlin, 1941), pp. 86, 88.

15. *NCA,* III, 719–20, Doc. PS–1061.

16. "Bevölkerungs-und wirtschaftliche Probleme einer europäischen Gesamtlösung der Judenfrage," *Weltkampf,* 1 (1941), 43–51. This speech was delivered on March 26, 1941, at the opening session of the Frankfurt Institut zur Erforschung der Judenfrage.

17. *IMT,* Document PS–2278.

18. *Ibid.,* Document EC–305.

19. See above, note 6.

20. Archives of the JHI in Warsaw, Lublin documents. Minutes of the session of April 22, 1940, with the chief of the SS and police in the Lublin district.

21. *YB,* 15 (1940), 154–57. A facsimile of another announcement is published in *CJR,* 3 (1940), 78–79; and in *The Black Book,* pp. 130–31. See also T. Brustin-Bernstein, "The Expulsions as a phase in the German policy of extermination of the Jewish population" (Yiddish), *BFG,* 3 (Warsaw, 1950), 52–53; Winfried, "Tagebuch für Ruth," *Wiener Revue,* Sonderheft (1946).

22. Simon Segal, *The New Order in Poland* (New York, 1942), p. 233; *The Black Book,* p. 134; *Czechoslovakia Fights Back* (Washington, 1943), pp. 110–11.

Before the first transports departed for the Lublin reservation, several transports were sent to Nisko, on the San, in Western Galicia, among them a transport from Moravska Ostrava (October 12, 1939) and one from Vienna (October 20, 1939). See Reitlinger, pp. 43, 44.

23. Isaiah Trunk, "Contribution to the History of the Jews in the 'Wartheland,' during the Holocaust Period, 1939–1944" (Yiddish), *BFG,* 2 (1949), 77–78.

24. Minutes of the Lublin Judenrat session of February 17, 1940, Archives of the JHI, Warsaw, Lublin documents. More details regarding the transports from Stettin and other parts of Pomerania are found in the unpublished doctoral dissertation of Hans Lamm, "Über die innere und äussere Entwicklung des deutschen Judentums im Dritten Reich," available in the YIVO Library.

25. In the archives of YIVO and of the Jewish Historical Institute in Warsaw there are many documents regarding the Lublin camp for war prisoners. Jewish war prisoners were permitted to write brief letters to their families. Thousands of such letters that were never mailed were found after liberation in the Nazi archives in Lublin, and are at present in the archives of the JHI in Warsaw. See also *Dokumenty i Materiały,* I, *Obozy* (Camps), ed. by Nachman Blumental (Lodz, 1946), pp. 127–28.

26. *IMT,* Document ND–5322.

27. *Ibid.,* EC–344.

28. *Ibid.,* NG–2490.

29. Leon Poliakov, *Bréviare de la haine* (Paris, 1951), p. 42.

30. On the conflicts between the Nazi party and SS, on the one hand, and the civil administration, the economic authorities, and the Wehrmacht, on the other, see Hannah Arendt, *The Origins of Totalitarianism* (New York, 1951), pp. 381 ff.

31. "Diary of Hans Frank, Governor General of GG. Excerpts." *IMT,* XXIX, PS–2233.

32. The report of Hartglas is published in *Sefer hazevaot* (Book of Horrors), ed. by J. Klausner and B. Mintz (Jerusalem, 5705), pp. 1–8. On the reservation, see *ibid.,* pp. 20–22, 106–8. See also *Luxemburger Wort,* October 21, 1939; *Neue Zeitung,* November 1, 1939; S. Moldawer, "The Road to Lublin," *CJR,* 3 (1940), 119–33; M. Mandelbaum, "The Road to Lublin," *The Nation,* October 10, 1942; *Hitler's Ten-Year War on the Jews* (New York, 1943), p. 140; Segal, pp. 233–35; Israel Cohen, *The Jews in the War* (London, 1943), p. 30. Even the commander-in-chief of the German army, Field Marshal Johannes Blaskowitz, complained, in his report of December 1939, that Jewish children arrived in the transport trains frozen to death, and that those who survived perished of starvation in the villages where they were settled. See Reitlinger, p. 44.

33. "The Latest Anti-Jewish Horror," *The Nation,* December 30, 1939. Some Polish émigrés in London also reacted vigorously. A Polish writer spoke of the Lublin reservation as a "fiendish German plot"; Francis Aldor, *Germany's "Death Space"* (London, 1940), p. 162.

34. "The Jewish Reservation," *Religion* (February, 1940).

35. *CJR,* 2 (1939), 5, 35–36.

36. Trunk, pp. 82, 90. General Stroop's report in *NCA,* III, 720.

37. The full text of this conversation, as reported by Martin Bormann, is published in *Der Ruf,* Munich, July 1, 1947.

38. This is most likely the same person who published articles on racial policy in the GG. See H. Gottong, "Zwei rassenkundliche Untersuchungen im General Gouvernement," *Volk und Rasse* (1943); *idem,* "Die Judenfrage und die Anfänge ihrer Lösung im General-Gouvernement," *Der Deutsche im Osten,* vol. 4, no. 2 (1941), pp. 92–100; *idem,* "Stand der anthropologischen Forschung im früheren Polen," *Deutsche Forschung im Osten,* vol. 1, no. 4 (1941), pp. 11–17.

39. Archives of the JHI, Warsaw, city documents, no. 40, pp. 87–90.

40. *Gazeta Żydowska,* June 8, 1940.

41. "Materyaln vegn arbet-lagern in lubliner gegnt" (Documents on labor camps in the Lublin area). A manuscript from the Ringelblum archives published in *BFG,* 2 (1949), 242–72.

42. On August 14, 1940, the Bełżec camp had about 10,000 Jews who worked at six different sites. See the archives of the JHI, Warsaw, documents of the Lublin Judenrat; see also the testimony of Simkhe Turtletaub and Blumental, *Obozy,* pp. 217–24.

43. Archives of the JHI in Warsaw, Lublin documents. The original text of the letter is published in Blumental, pp. 220–21.

44. Archives of the JHI in Warsaw, Documents.

45. Bernard Goldstein, *Finf yor varshever geto* (Five Years in the Warsaw Ghetto) (New York, 1947), p. 240.

46. *IMT,* Document NG–1800.

47. Egon von Wingheue, *Arische Rasse, christliche Kultur und das Juden-problem,* cited in E. Hevesi, "Hitler's Plan for Madagascar," *CJR,* 4 (1941), 381–95.

48. *The Memoirs of Dr. Felix Kersten* (New York, 1947), pp. 213–35.

49. I. Kastner, "The Weeks in Which the Verdict Was Sealed" (Hebrew), *Molad,* 1 (1948), 121, 124. Julius Streicher also boasted of the fact that he was one of the first initiators of the Madagascar plan. In an editorial published in the *Stürmer,* January 1, 1938, he wrote: "Several years ago, when the *Stürmer* suggested that the transfer of the Jews to the French colonial island of Madagascar offered a possibility for a solution of the Jewish problem, we were ridiculed by the Jews and their friends and declared inhuman" (*IMT,* XLI, 556–57).

50. The Polish Peasant Party was violently opposed to a peasant emigration to Madagascar, but was not averse to sending Jews there. See Joel Cang, "The Opposition Parties in Poland and Their Attitude towards the Jews and the Jewish Problem," *JSS,* 1 (1939), 250.

51. M. B. Lepecki, *Madagaskar, kraj, ludzie, kolonizacja* (Madagascar, country, people, colonization) (Warsaw, 1938); "Projects for Jewish Mass Colonization," *Jewish Affairs* (November, 1941), pp. 1–15; Hevesi, see above, note 47.

52. Białoskórski, "The Hell of Madagascar" (Polish), *Chwila Poranna,* Lwów, January 18, 1938; Gen, "Madagaskariada," *ibid.,* March 11, 1938; "The Madagascar Legend Has Vanished into Thin Air," *ibid.,* March 12, 1938; "Let Them Go to Madagascar, There They Will Be Destroyed by the Plague and Typhoid" (Polish), *Chwila Wieczorna,* Lwów, March 5, 1938, and other articles in the issues of January 10 and February 26, 1938.

53. *Danziger Neueste Nachrichten,* January 20, 1937, cited in Heinz-Peter Seraphim, *Das Judentum im osteuropäischen Raum* (Essen, 1938), p. 672.

The *Stürmer,* nos. 1 and 20 (January and May 1938), reported that the Polish government was about to conclude an agreement with the French government for the transfer of 30,000 Polish Jews to Madagascar. A regular line of communication between Gdynia (a Polish port) and Madagascar was considered. The Polish-French negotiations were conducted during the visit of the French foreign minister Delbos to Warsaw. The *Stürmer* refers to a report in the Italian daily, *Il Tevere,* of January 18 and 19, 1938 (see *IMT,* XLI, 557–58). No other documents confirming Streicher's information are known at present.

54. See M. Mazor, "La cité engloutie," *Le Monde Juif,* 5 (1950), 2.

55. *IMT,* XXVIII, 538–39.

56. Herbert von Dirksen, *Moskau, Tokio, London* (Stuttgart, 1951); M. Glazer, "The Jewish Problem and the United States," a confidential mimeographed document in my private archives. Schacht negotiated with Lord Bearsted, Lord Winterton, and George Rublee, of the Evian Committee. He left London in December 1938, and as early as January 2, 1939, he had a lengthy conversation with Hitler in Berchtesgaden. Three days after this conversation Hitler appointed Schacht as "special deputy for Jewish emigration." At the Nuremberg trial Schacht declared that as late as December 1939 Hitler backed his emigration plans for the Jews (see Reitlinger, p. 20).

57. *Staatsanwaltschaft bei dem Landgericht Nürnberg-Fürth,* AZ:3 c Js 1321–24/49. *Anklageschrift gegen Franz Rademacher und Dr. Karl Klingenfuss* (1949); *Das Schwurgericht bei dem Landgericht Nürnberg-Fürth,* 85 KS, 4/50. *Urteil* [against Franz Rademacher]. Mimeographed, in my private archives.

58. Materials are found in the following South African newspapers: *Die Vaterland,* March 8, 1941, June 1, 1942, December 12, 14, 1942; *New Letter,* May 2, 1945; *Die Neuwe Orde,* October 4, 1945, January 16, February 21, September 12, October 4 and 18, December 13, 1946; *The Star,* March 12, 1943; *Dagbreek en Sondagnuus,* February 22, 1948; *The Naval Mercury,* March 17, 1937, April 13, 1948; *Rand Daily Mail,* April 15 and 30, 1938, December 13, 1947; *The Friend,* March 23, 1940.

Hitler's valet, Kurt Wilhelm Krause, reported that he accidentally overheard this conversation between Hitler and Chamberlain during the latter's visit to Berchtesgaden on September 15, 1938. Chamberlain asked: "How do you propose to solve the Jewish problem, Herr Reichskanzler?" To which Hitler replied: "The British Empire has plenty of islands. Set aside one of them. There all the Jews of the world can gather . . . above all, a place where there are quarries. We [Germans] shall supply the food, and the Jews the marble." Krause, *Zehn Jahre Kammerdiener* (Hamburg, n.d.), p. 367. If the report is authentic, Hitler then discussed with Chamberlain the problem of Jewish emigration to the colonies.

59. Joshua Starr, "Italy's Anti-Semites," *JSS,* 1 (1939), 117.

60. *Ciano's Diaries, 1939–1943* (Toronto, 1947), p. 4; C. M. Cianfarra, *The Vatican and the War* (New York, 1944), pp. 145–46.

61. Cianfarra, p. 209.

62. A Polish translation of the documents is found in *BGK,* IV, 117–25.

63. Peter-Heinz Seraphim, "Die Judenfrage im General-Gouvernement," *Die Burg,* I (1940), 56–63; "Das deutsche General-Gouvernement, Raum, Bevölkerung, Landschaft," *Deutsche Monatshefte* (1940), 169–84; *Die Wir-*

*schaftsstruktur des General-Gouvernements* (Cracow, 1941); "Bevölkerungs- und wirtschaftliche Probleme einer europäischen Gesamtlösung der Juden- frage," *Weltkampf* (1941), 43–51.

64. *Frank's Diaries;* T. Brustin-Bernstein, *BFG,* 3 (1950), 54; S. Szroit, "Hitler's Occupation of Poland as Reflected in the 'Diary' of Hans Frank and the Minutes of Government of GG" (Polish), *BGK,* II (1947), 9–41; E. Ośmiańczyk, "The Gallows of Hans Frank" (Polish), *Rzeczpospolita,* March 12, 1946.

65. "Behind the Brown Curtain," *New York Times,* August 25, 1950; *Ciano's Diaries,* p. 267.

66. C. Barduzzi, "The Solution of the Jewish Question, Madagascar," *La Difesa della Razza,* Rome, July 20, 1940.

67. Cf. M. Nussbaum, "Life in Wartime Germany," *CJR,* 3 (1940), 577–86.

68. Nuremberg Document NG–2586–B.

69. The original draft of Dannecker's plan is lost. The documents of the *IMT* contain only the notes of under-secretary Luther.

It is significant that the new French governor-general of Madagascar, Armand Annet, appointed by the Vichy government in December 1940, appar- ently knew nothing of the plan for Jewish colonization. At any rate, there is no mention of it in his memoirs, *Aux heures troublées de l'Afrique française* (Paris, 1952). He does mention, however, that he found in Madagascar a "very small number of Israelites," who had resided there for a long time. The wife of the director of the cabinet was Jewish. This proved to be a great em- barrassment, "since it was a time when the Jews were eliminated from public life." Annet finds it necessary to emphasize the fact that after he discovered the great secret, his relations with the director remained unchanged, and the friendly relations between the households continued exactly as heretofore.

70. According to the testimony of Dieter Wisliceny, *IMT,* IV, 395.

71. According to the testimony of Victor Brack in the *NMT,* case no. 1: Medical Case trials. See also Poliakov, pp. 51–52.

72. *Hitler's Tischgespräche,* ed. by H. Picker (Bonn, 1951), pp. 118, 311.

73. My chief sources on the Madagascar plan are chiefly the following: *NMT,* Documents, NG–2586, NG–5764; case no. 11: Ministries Case; *Franz Rademacher Prozess, Anklageschrift und Urteil; Le Monde Juif* (1949), pp. 16 ff.; Anatole Goldstein, *From Discrimination to Annihilation* (New York, 1952), pp. 14–16.

I wish to express my thanks to Public Prosecutor Gitler of the Land- gericht of Nürnberg-Fürth and to Dr. Schnelvogel, archivist of the Nuremberg public archives, for material and data regarding the Rademacher trial and the Madagascar plan. (See note 57.)

74. See CDJC *Bulletin* (November 1945), 2–3.

75. "Die Judenfrage als Weltproblem," *Weltkampf* (1941), 64–72.

76. "Sending the Jewish masses . . . to Madagascar . . . would mean sending them to their grave. . . . The forced deportation . . . *en masse* . . . must be resisted by decent people of whatever origin or mentality [; it] is an outrage. No pogrom in history would equal the slaughter. . . ." (Hevesi, p. 394). "It appears that Madagascar may be destined, if Hitler has his way,

to become a Devil's Island for the Jews of Europe" (*Jewish Affairs,* November 1941). See also Aryeh Tartakover, "Damaging Speculations" (Yiddish), *YK,* November 29, 1940, in which he opposes negotiations with Germany and Italy about the settlement of European Jews in tropical countries.

77. The head of the population section of the GG, Dr. Arlt, told a delegation of Jews who came to him in Cracow to ask for repeal of the Warsaw ghetto order: "The Führer will solve the Jewish question after the war by creating a fatherland for the Jews" (see Ringelblum, *Biuletyn,* p. 110. There are three allusions to Madagascar in Ringelblum's diary, but without comments; *ibid.,* pp. 110, 155, 156). Hillel Seidman relates that Alfred Nossig worked on a German plan for Jewish emigration from Poland. Nossig once took Seidman with him to a conference in the Warsaw Gestapo office, in February 1940, and they discussed various plans for emigration. Considerable attention was given to the Madagascar plan, but no mention was made of emigration to Palestine. See Seidman's *Togbukh fun varshever geto* (Diary from the Warsaw ghetto) (Buenos Aires, 1947), pp. 246–48.

78. *Der Jude an der Ostgrenze,* pp. 85, 88; *Der Jude zwischen den Fronten der Rassen, der Völker, der Kulturen* (Berlin, 1942), pp. 150–58.

79. Claude Wacogne, "Les Juifs et Madagascar," *L'Appel,* May 28, 1942; Jean Boissel, "Madagascar aux Juifs," *Le Reveil du Peuple,* September 1, 1942 (these articles are available in the YIVO archives).

80. "I read a detailed report from the SD and police regarding a final solution of the Jewish question. Any final solution involves a tremendous number of new viewpoints. The Jewish question must be solved within a pan-European frame. There are 11 million Jews still in Europe. They will have to be concentrated later, to begin with, in the east; possibly an island, such as Madagascar, can be assigned to them after the war. In any case there can be no peace in Europe until the last Jews are eliminated from the continent" (*Goebbels Diaries,* pp. 115–16).

81. *Pariser Zeitung,* March 13, 1943; "Y aura-t-il un État Juif?" *Le Nouvelliste,* Lyon, March 17, 1943.

82. *Goebbels Diaries,* pp. 207–9.

83. See Izhak Schwartzbart in *Folk un Velt* (New York, February 1952), pp. 16–19, in which he refers to a secret document sent from Warsaw to the Polish government-in-exile in London.

Adolf Berman, in his article "Jews on the Aryan side" in the *Entziklopedia shel galuyot, Varshe* (Encyclopedia of the Dispersion: Warsaw), I (Jerusalem–Tel Aviv, 1953), relates the following: In the spring of 1944 the Jewish organizations in Warsaw discovered that the Warsaw director of the foreign department of the Polish government-in-exile in London wrote an article stating that even after the great Jewish catastrophe there would still remain too many Jews in Poland and that it would be necessary to assign to them a closed territory somewhere in the east. Berman does not indicate the name of the writer or the publication in which the article appeared.

84. Marc Wischnitzer, *To Dwell in Safety* (Philadelphia, 1948), p. 247.

# 3

# THE JEWISH GHETTOS OF THE NAZI ERA

This essay deals with Nazi policy of confining the Jews to ghettos, as a preliminary step toward genocide. Ghettoization, it must be noted, preceded the isolation of Jews in concentration camps. The many sociological aspects of the ghettos, their internal life, institutions such as the Judenrat and the Jewish police, the reactions of the inhabitants, their social and economic activities and moral climate, are not dealt with here. It is my present intention merely to examine the public actions and legal factors that led to the establishment of the ghettos and to the development of their outward forms.

## Heydrich's Dispatch and the "Ultimate Goal" in the Solution of the Jewish Question

On September 21, 1939, three weeks after the invasion of Poland, a conference in Berlin, apparently under the chairmanship of Reinhard Heydrich, chief of the German Security Police, took up the question of the occupied Polish territory. On the same day, Heydrich sent out a secret dispatch—addressed to the chiefs of all Einsatzgruppen (special detachments) of the Security Police and containing precise instructions about the Jews—which referred to the conference. No other record of the conference is known. No minutes have been found of that fateful gathering, which sealed the doom of East European Jewry. It is probable that the participants in the conference included, in addition to the chiefs of the Security Police, representatives of the army and of various government departments, for Heydrich sent copies of his dispatch to the high command of the Wehrmacht, to the deputy representative of Hermann Göring (as the "plenipotentiary of the Four-Year Plan"), to the ministry of food and economics, and to the heads of the civil administration in the occupied area.[1]

Heydrich distinguished two stages in his proposed "solution of the Jewish question," namely: planned comprehensive measures (*die geplanten Gesamtmassnahmen*) leading to the "ultimate goal," which was to be kept in strict secrecy; and short-term stages (*Abschnitte*), capable of immediate implementation. His instructions dealt only with the "short-term stages," the first of which called for concentrating the Jews in the larger cities. Heydrich ordered that in the incorporated zones[2] efforts ought to be made to eliminate the Jews altogether, or at least to create only a few urban Jewish concentrations. He suggested that a fairly large number of cities of concentration might be set up in the Government General[3]; that, as a general rule, all Jews living in cities with fewer than 500 Jewish inhabitants must be shipped to the nearest cities of concentration; and that wherever possible the concentration points be set up at a railway junction, or at least near a railway line. In carrying out this directive, the Security Police was ordered to work in close cooperation and understanding with the civil administration and the military authorities.

Many points of Heydrich's dispatch are not clear. Much of its vague phrasing may have been deliberate. For instance, there is no direct indication of the meaning of the expression "ultimate goal." It is quite possible that a plan for physical annihilation of the Jews had already been spelled out. Or perhaps an alternate plan, for their deportation from Europe, was being considered. The order to concentrate all Jews near the railway lines could have well fitted either plan, by facilitating transportation.

The well-known sinister threat uttered by Hitler in his Reichstag address of January 30, 1939,[4] can be viewed as a clear indication that he was then considering total annihilation. It is not clear, however, whether at that time concrete plans had already been developed in accordance with the Führer's intent. General Erwin Lahousen, chief of section II of the bureau of foreign intelligence of the German army under Admiral Wilhelm Canaris, stated at the Nuremberg trial that directives for the annihilation of the Jews and the Poles in the occupied zones had been discussed in Hitler's parlor train on September 12, 1939.[5] In addresses by Hans Frank on August 4, 1940, in Cracow[6] and by Hitler at the Berlin Sport Palast on

January 30, 1941,[7] the "ultimate goal" was referred to in such diplomatic doubletalk[8] that it could be interpreted to mean either annihilation or deportation.

Heydrich's instructions concerning the concentration of the Jews are equally vague. There is nothing explicit in his dispatch about segregating the Jews from non-Jews after their concentration in the larger cities. The circular read (part 2, par. 5):

Concentration of the Jews in the cities will likely lead, on the grounds of police security, to ordinances in these cities to the effect that certain city areas will be entirely prohibited to Jews; that, for instance, except for economic necessities, they will never be permitted to leave the ghettos [or] to go out after specified hours in the evening, and so on.

These ambiguities left much room for local administrative interpretation and whim, just as they are now open to different interpretations. It is possible that such was the intention, so that blame could be laid to the "limited subordinate intelligence" of lower officials. Other factors may have been involved as well. It is possible that the top Nazis had ready a complete plan for attaining an "ultimate goal" of annihilation but that they preferred to keep it secret, even from their own lower officials. Perhaps they wanted to accustom their people to the plan by degrees, fearing that a sudden revelation of the brutality involved might produce too violent a reaction. Or it may be that two different conceptions of the "ultimate goal"—emigration and annihilation—were still being debated, and that the final decision of Hitler and his coterie had not yet crystalized. Finally, it may be that more precise instructions were given at the Berlin conference, by word of mouth.

There is indirect evidence, however, that Heydrich's "concentration" of the Jews was intended as the first step toward gradual extermination—perhaps partial extermination, as originally conceived, by hunger, cold, disease, epidemics, forced labor, and finally by the murder operations (called "actions" [*Aktionen*] by the Germans).

Perusal of the Nazi press, of Nazi "scientific" studies, and of the statements and speeches of Nazi leaders leads to the decisive conclusion that the methods employed in carrying out the genocide policy were not of a spontaneous or accidental nature, but were rather part and parcel of an unfolding plan, which began with the concentration and isolation of the Jews. It must not be forgotten that in the totalitarian Nazi state all expressions of "public opinion" were products of the gigantic official propaganda machine, which conveyed only the opinions of the ruling circles. Examination of "public" discussions of the Jewish question, therefore, will reveal the true intentions of the German government, which itself inspired and guided the discussions.

## Lebensraum *for the Germans and* Todesraum *for the Jews*

The German *Lebensraum* theory is well known.[9] Karl Haushofer's geo-political theory was modified by Hitler and his disciples mainly in that they sought expansion first on the European continent, rather than in overseas colonies.[10] This policy was discussed at a conference of military and civil leaders held at Hitler's Berlin headquarters on November 5, 1937, at which were present, in addition to the Führer, the minister of war, Field Marshal Werner von Blomberg; General Werner von Fritsch, then commander-in-chief of the German army; Grand Admiral Erich Raeder; Field Marshal Hermann Göring; Foreign Minister Baron Constantin von Neurath; and General Friedrich Hossbach (adjutant to Hitler), who wrote up the minutes. The so-called Hossbach Protocols reveal that the discussion turned to the "scarcity of space" (*Raumnot*) for the German people—the continual Nazi complaint. Hitler then formulated three tenets for the conquest of *Lebensraum*: (1) Space must be sought in Europe only; (2) the new areas must be contiguous with the German Reich; and (3) the resistance of the settled populations must be broken.[11] These tenets were generally in accordance with Hitler's earlier views voiced in *Mein Kampf* and expounded in some of his addresses and articles.[12]

Hitler's view of the process of "breaking the resistance of the settled populations" appears in the testimony of Ernst Kaltenbrunner (chief of the Reich Security Main Office since 1943) at the Nuremberg trial and in various memoranda submitted by his consultants and by Heinrich Himmler, the special "Reichskommissar for the Strengthening of Germandom (*Deutschtum*) in the East." These plans envisaged the annihilation of many millions of Slavs (according to some testimony, 30 million); the forced transfer of entire peoples and tribes; their forced Germanization, sterilization, and annihilation by hunger, forced labor, and other means.[13] Karl R. W. Best,[14] the German expert on *Grosslebensraum,* stated in 1942: "Historical experience teaches that the annihilation of an alien people is not contrary to the laws of life, provided the annihilation is complete."[15]

A hint of the antithesis of *Lebensraum* for the Germans and *Todesraum* for the Jews is found in the writings of Alfred Rosenberg, who stated that any territorially confined "living space" for the Jews should be at best a "living space in the opposite direction," namely, leading to death and not to life.[16] Governor General Hans Frank, who fancied himself a learned jurist and philosopher, published a bombastic article entitled "Die Epoche des Ostens" in the Cracow "scientific" quarterly *Die Burg,* in which he sought to prove that a new era in the history of Europe would begin the moment the eastern area merged completely with the German Reich as its *Lebensraum.*[17] The Nazis were so intoxicated with geopolitics that they failed to take into account the possibility of the resistance of millions of Slavs. Naturally, they paid no heed to the fate of weak minorities such as Jews and Gypsies.[18]

## Crystalization of the Segregation Policy

Propaganda Minister Josef Goebbels set the tone for the agitation in favor of isolating the Jews. Following an inspection trip in October and November 1939 to the occupied Polish territory, particularly Warsaw and Lodz, Goebbels's unidentified companion stated over the Berlin radio: "That people must be isolated completely, otherwise all of Europe will be poisoned."[19] Goebbels himself expressed much the same idea two years later: "The Jews must be segregated from the German national community, as they imperil our national cohesion."[20] Hans Frank gave the idea an even sharper formulation, urging hermetic isolation.[21] The "scientific" argument was provided by Professor Peter-Heinz Seraphim, the "expert" on Jewish problems, who argued that the 1.7 million Jews in the GG, including 330,000 deported from the incorporated territory of West Prussia and Warthegau, according to Heydrich's order, presented a difficult economic and political problem, as well as a problem of "cultural hyperalienation" (*Überfremdung*). "For the duration that question requires a definite solution," wrote Seraphim, who saw as the "ultimate goal" the "clearing of that area [the GG] of the Jews."[22] Without advancing a clear proposal, he advocated segregation for the time being.

At first, the *Krakauer Zeitung* and *Warschauer Zeitung* were not too clear on the ghetto problem. In an article entitled "German Order Enters the Ghetto," one observer wrote: ". . . to be sure, we do not like the Jews. . . . But not a single German will be found who would wish to solve the Jewish problem through pogroms. . . . The German administration has introduced order in the ghetto, which is the best proof that we do not seek a solution to the Jewish problem by pogroms."[23] The writer expressed his satisfaction with the special insignia (the Star of David) and with the establishment of the Judenrat. Obviously, he viewed the ghetto in its prewar, nonsegregative light. There was, in fact, confusion about the meaning of the term "ghetto." In the early days, the Germans often preferred to employ terms such as "Jewish residential section" or "closed quarantined section."[24] However, the Germans did not intend to reintroduce the medieval ghetto.[25] They understood that their own "twentieth-century ghettos" were different. This subject was even treated in dissertations for academic degrees in the German universities.[26] Seraphim emphasized the difference in a paper read at the festive opening of the

Institut zur Erforschung der Judenfrage, in Frankfurt a.M., March 26–28, 1941:

> The ghetto of the Middle Ages was largely a Jewish privilege rather than a forced measure. . . . It was a residential community; in addition to which it by no means excluded business contacts between Jews and non-Jews. . . . The ghetto of today must be different from the medieval ghetto; it must be a compulsory ghetto . . . without contact or possibility of contact with non-Jews.

Seraphim opined that ghettos would be created only in Eastern Europe: "For most towns in Central, Western, and Southern Europe, and in the towns of Eastern Europe where the Jewish population is small in numbers, the Jews cannot be ghettoized; they are too few."[27] As a matter of fact, it was only in Eastern Europe, or more precisely in the Polish and Lithuanian territories, that ghettoization was carried out on a large scale. In all other countries, such attempts were sporadic and short-lived.

## "Ghettoization" Attempts in Western, Southern, and Central Europe

As early as 1922, Hans Blüher, German philosopher, youth leader, and object of the unbounded admiration of the extreme nationalists, expounded the theory that the Jews must be sent back to the ghettos.[28] The first Nazi demand for a ghetto was expressed in 1935 in a remark in *Deutsche Justiz,* the official Nazi law periodical, that in the Middle Ages "segregation was a wise and honest institution, the abolition of which brought harm to all nations."[29] However, it was not until 1938 that ghettoization began to be seriously considered in German government circles. At the October 14, 1938, conference of the Reich Committee for the Four-Year Plan, chairman Göring declared: "If necessary, we shall introduce ghettos for the Jews in the large cities."[30] A further direct stimulus for these discussions came in consequence of the assassination, on November 7, 1938, of Ernst vom Rath, the third secretary of the German embassy in Paris, by the seventeen-year-old Jewish boy from Poland, Herschel Grynszpan. Vom Rath's death provoked the tragic Kristallnacht of November 9–10 and a pogrom in which Nazis set fire to or destroyed some 190 synagogues and arrested some 20,000 Jews all over Germany. At a conference on the Jewish question held at Göring's office on November 12, 1938, ghettoization was given much consideration. Heydrich voiced his objections to a plan for a *Judenghetto,* because of the difficulties in police control over it.[31] Heydrich's views prevailed, but news of the discussion leaked out. When some foreign correspondents asked Goebbels at a press conference, "How will the Jews live in such a world?" his jocular reply was, "They can live on their investments."[32] Influential Nazi newspapers came out with demands for ghettos, particularly in Berlin.[33] Nevertheless, no ghettos were established in Germany. Decrees were promulgated, however, excluding Jews from various municipal districts, hotels, restaurants, and German cultural institutions. Jews were also ordered to live in specially assigned apartment houses and to avoid residing in buildings inhabited by non-Jews.[34]

In Austria, where 90 percent of the Jews lived in Vienna, similar restrictions were imposed on residence and travel. Over 50 percent of Vienna's Jews managed to escape abroad in the great panic of the German invasion. As early as October 1939 the Nazis began to deport the remaining Viennese Jews to Poland. The Nazi Gauleiter Baldur von Schirach preferred the speediest possible transfer of Vienna's Jews to Poland to a ghetto.[35] Similarly, immediately after Czechoslovakia's occupation, the Germans began to force the Jews to concentrate in one place—a policy strongly reminiscent of Heydrich's September 1939 directives. Thus the inhabitants of 123 of the 131 Jewish communities in the Protectorate of Bohemia-Moravia were ordered to move to Prague in preparation for forced emigration. When emigration was no longer feasible, after the outbreak of the war, the Nazis began to search for other solutions. One of these called for the establishment of a "model ghetto" in the medieval Czech fortress town of Theresienstadt (Terezin). The first forced transport of 342 Jews arrived there from Prague late in November 1941. By the end of 1942, some 109,000 Jews had been transported to Terezin. By the end of the war (May 1945), almost 140,000 had been sent there, including 73,600 Czech, 15,230 Austrian, 42,830 German, 4,900 Dutch, 466 Danish, and 1,500 Slovak Jews. There were never more than 40,000 to 50,000 Jews in Theresienstadt at any time. The place was primarily a "transit ghetto," and in time became a transit camp from which Jews were sent on to Auschwitz and other extermination centers; only 17,320 Jews remained there at the moment of liberation.[36] The Jews of several Moravian towns were concentrated in Uhersky Brod (Moravska Ostrava).[37] According to some reports, the Jews of Bratislava (Pressburg), satellite Slovakia's capital, had already been forced into the ghetto by the middle of May 1938.[38] In other Slovak towns, ghettos were set up mostly in the latter part of 1942.[39] Slovakia's president, Monsignor Josef Tiso, followed most eagerly the Nazi example of persecuting the Jews.

Other satellite states were less enthusiastic. Italy failed to introduce any ghettos. Hungary, an anti-Semitic country of long standing, resisted the full execution of the Nazi racist program because of internal reasons and diplomatic considerations, and therefore resisted ghettoization. It was only after the March coup of 1944 that the new Nazi Magyar government embarked, under strong German pressure, upon such a policy, setting up ghettos in thirty-four towns.[40] Nazi pressure also succeeded in forcing the introduction of ghettos in several surrounding countries. The Ghettos were established in April and May 1944 in Transylvania (Siebenbürgen) and other Rumanian provinces. Czernowitz in Bucovina had a ghetto as early as the fall of 1941. In the satellite state of Croatia, ghettos were introduced in 1944. On May 4, 1944, Edmund Veesenmayer, the German ambassador in Budapest, reported that the 200,000 Jews of Carpatho-Russia were confined to ten ghettos, and that the ghettoization of 110,000 Jews had already begun in Transylvania. He also reported that ghettoization would be extended to Croatia and Serbia and would be "crowned" by ghettos in the interior Hungarian provinces and, finally, in Budapest.[41] These ghettos lasted for very brief periods, as their inhabitants were transferred to extermination camps after a few weeks or months.

Ghettoization began in certain parts of Yugoslavia (outside of satellite Croatia) in October 1941. The haphazard manner in which it was carried out failed to save the Jews from speedy and total extermination. The Germans placed some 20,000 Serb Jewish women and children, after the massacre of their menfolk, in the Gypsy quarter in Belgrade, together with 1,500 Gypsy widows and orphans. They were later deported to a camp in the Serbian town of Zemun (Sajmiste or Semlin) on the Danube, where many were killed. The survivors were deported to an extermination camp in the east (probably to Auschwitz) and were annihilated in the summer of 1942. Dalmatian Jews were placed in ghettos on several Adriatic islands.[42]

No ghettos were established in Bulgaria; instead, a special status for the Jews was declared, following the German model. In 1943, however, the Bulgarian government expelled all Jews from Sofia and from several other cities and settled them in rural districts and internment camps.[43] There were no ghettos in the Italian occupation zone in Greece. The 50,000 Jews of Salonika were ghettoized in February 1943, several weeks before their deportation to Poland.[44] No ghettos were introduced on the mainland of Greece. According to some writers, the Germans had to take into account the opposition of non-Jews, particularly of Greek Orthodox churchmen.[45]

Non-Jewish opposition was also a decisive factor in the Scandinavian countries. No ghettos were set up in Denmark or Norway, despite the demands of the Quisling government.[46] Since the Jewish population in these areas was small, the Nazis did not take the risk of antagonizing many non-Jews. In France, too, the Germans met with considerable hostility when they introduced the yellow badge. No ghettos were established, therefore; but the policy of isolating alien Jews in internment camps was adopted under German pressure.[47] In Belgium, the Jews were not ghettoized, but were restricted to the four cities of Antwerp, Brussels, Liège, and Charleroi, which they were not allowed to leave.[48] In the Netherlands, the Germans restricted the movement of Jews early in 1941. In March of that year, they concentrated some Jews from the provinces in three wards in Amsterdam.[49]

The Germans wished to see the establishment of a Jewish ghetto even in Shanghai, though they refrained from exerting direct pressure on the proud Nipponese. Not until after Hitler's personal appeal did the Japanese establish a ghetto, for stateless Jews only, in February 1943.[50]

Thus it can be seen that the Nazi attempts to establish ghettos in Western, Central, and Southern Europe failed for the most part. They did manage to confine the Jews in ghettos in some countries, but not before 1943 or 1944, when the liquidation of European Jewry was already under way. When the Nazi leadership decided on mass deportation of the remaining Jews from these countries into Poland and other East European territories, the problem of segregation became even more complicated in the East. Moreover, the Nazi propaganda machine still needed time to present to the outside world its justification for isolation of the Jews. In addition, the leaders also faced the problem of working out the actual technique of management of the ghettos. Decisions had to be made whether they were to be open, half-open, or hermetically sealed areas of segregation.

## German Rationale for Segregation

At first, German propaganda tried to justify the establishment of the ghettos by arguing that they would protect the health of the non-Jewish population. Typhus, tuberculosis, and other contagious ailments were alleged to be prevalent in districts inhabited by Jews. Posters depicting a Jew with a large louse on his garments were widely displayed at all Nazi exhibits, together with similar pictures. Even before the introduction of the ghettos, the Nazis used to display in many Jewish districts the inscription "Beware, Danger of Epidemic!" (*Seuchengefahr*). The Germans claimed that the Jews, who supposedly enjoyed relative immunity from typhus, were its most dangerous carriers. This was backed by citing mortality figures, for that disease, of 8–10 percent among the Jews, 20–40 percent among the Poles, and 50–80 percent among the Germans.[51] German newspapers described the Jewish streets as breeding places of filth and disease. An article in *Krakauer Zeitung* of November 15, 1939, entitled "Ghetto, a World of Decay," stressed that "the Cracow ghetto is one of the many [ghettos] of former Poland, where Jews are crowded by the tens of thousands in filth, in unsanitary conditions, in tatters, where the most dangerous germs are bred . . . in refuse pits . . . in miserable dwell-ings." Another German journalist wrote about the Lublin ghetto: "Here dwells the Jewish people in its encrusted filth. . . ."[52] Another German "war correspondent" employed biting sarcasm to depict the filth of the ghetto, ending with the words: "Let them suffocate in their own filth!"[53] Inadequate sanitation was used to justify the liquidation of the rural Jewish communities. According to the Nazis, these were "not subject to any super-vision by the health authorities—which is a cause of epidemics." The rural Jews were transferred to the overcrowded city ghettos.[54] The propagandists also pointed to "the proverbial criminality of the Jew." Hitler's close asso-ciate Robert Ley stressed "racial ethics" in his argument that "a lower race requires less space, less food, and less culture than a higher race; the German cannot live under the same conditions as a Pole or a Jew."[55]

A good deal of space was devoted by Nazi theoreticians to the eco-nomic aspect. They argued that the German economic machinery could not function smoothly as long as Jews were in contact with non-Jews, especially with peasants. Jews were accused of carrying on "black market" activities and "speculation."[56] There was also a political rationalization. The Jews were accused of sabotaging German decrees and regulations, of carrying on political propaganda, and of spreading rumors. They supposedly incited the Poles against the Germans, and thus stood in the way of the Slavs' "peaceful" germanization.[57]

## True Reasons for Ghettoization

The true reasons for setting up the ghettos emerge from allusions made by high officials in private conversations or in conferences held by the Nazi party. Some of those party secrets leaked through in the Nazi press. Although the "ultimate goal," according to Heydrich's instructions, was to be kept in strict secrecy, hints concerning it appeared on various occasions. Thus when the Lodz ghetto was formed, the *Litzmannstädter Zeitung* of June 9, 1940, gave it extensive pictorial coverage under the telling title "The Litzmannstadt[58] Ghetto—A Necessary Transitional Solu-tion of the Jewish Question" (note the word "transitional"). When Friedrich Übelhör, the Nazi district chief (Regierungspräsident) of Kalisz, first came forward on December 10, 1939, with a plan for a ghetto in Lodz, he concluded his elaborate, strictly secret presentation with the words: "The creation of the ghetto is not, of course, any more than a transitional measure (*eine Übergangsmassnahme*), and I reserve the deci-sion as to when and by what means the city of Lodz is to be cleansed of the Jews. The ultimate goal, must, at any rate, be the ceaseless burning of that plague–boil (*diese Pestbeule restlos ausbrennen*)."[59] Dr. Joseph Bühler, secretary general of the GG, stated in an address in Cracow on October 26, 1940, that "the dejudaization of Zakopane[60] and Cracow, and other means to force the Jews out, are not sufficient. Comprehensive plans are simultaneously being developed for the total solution of the Jewish question."[61] An official publication sponsored by Dr. Ludwig Fischer, governor of the Warsaw district, declared even more clearly: "All measures of today are merely of a provisional character. After the war the Jewish question will receive a uniform solution in all of Europe. Until then the ghettos must fulfill their aim."[62]

The purpose of the ghettos became apparent from the manner of their formation. From the very beginning, Nazi policy called for the impoverishment of the Jews. They were given little time to move to the ghettos. Sometimes they were not even permitted to take their furniture there. In many cases they were allowed to carry with them only their personal belongings. Usually their business places outside the ghetto had to be abandoned entirely; this was the case in Warsaw, and in Lodz, where they were taken over by German trustees and commissars. That was the first economic blow. In the ghetto itself the Jews were compressed in crowded quarters, located for the most part in the poorest sections of the town, without parks or squares. The food supply was strictly and precisely controlled, and the earning capacities of the inhabitants were reduced to a minimum. These harsh physical and economic conditions served to raise the rate of mortality. The ghettos were designed to serve the Nazis as laboratories for testing the methods of slow and "peaceful" destruction of whole groups of human beings. Goebbels aptly characterized the ghettos as *Todeskisten* (death caskets).[63] The governor of Warsaw, Ludwig Fischer, was reported (in January 1942) to have made the following remark, giving away the secret of ghettoization: "The Jews must adjust themselves to all conditions, but we shall endeavor to create such conditions for them as will make the adjustment difficult." On another occasion, Fischer is reported to have said: "The Jews will disappear because of hunger and need, and nothing will remain of the Jewish question but a cemetery."[64]

It is likely that at first the Germans were quite content with the results. Thus the *Kölnische Zeitung* wrote on April 5, 1941: "Although the ghetto in Lodz was first conceived merely as an experiment, as an introduction to the solution of the Jewish question, it has shown itself to be the best and fullest solution of the problem at this time." However, soon after the invasion of Russia, the slow pace of death in the ghettos no longer satisfied the Nazis. On April 1, 1942, Governor-General Frank declared in an address in Lwów: "That we have sentenced 1.2 million Jews to die of hunger should be noted only marginally. It is clear that, if the Jews do not starve to death, this will result in the speeding up of anti-Jewish measures."[65]


## *The First Ghettos*

Some historians divide the segregation of the Jews into three distinct stages: (1) the Lublin reservation project; (2) the Madagascar transfer plan; and (3) the ghettos after the failure of the earlier plans.[66] This view fails to take into account the Nazi intentions. The three plans were actually simultaneous procedures leading to the "final solution." True enough, the Germans sought to mislead the world by claiming that they had selected the most suitable of several possible plans. The GG *Korrespondenz Antisemitische Aktion* stated that the Nazis, faced with the choice between ghetto and reservation, decided on the latter as the more feasible.[67] The facts, however, are quite different. As early as October 7, 1939, Fischer, the governor of Warsaw, declared at a meeting in Cracow that ghettos must be established. Soon after, Governor-General Frank corroborated this opinion.[68] As we have already seen, on December 10, 1939, Friedrich Übelhör posed a detailed plan for a ghetto in Lodz.[69] After consultations, the decision was made to set it up by February 9, 1940. The Lodz chief of police, SS-Brigadeführer Schäfer, was commissioned to carry the plan out. Subsequently, the highest German officials continued to discuss at meetings the future of Lodz Jewry in terms of expulsion or ghettoization. On February 12, 1940, in a meeting at Göring's residence, Frank stated that he would admit the Lodz Jews into the GG. Arthur Greiser, Gauleiter of the Wartheland, to which Lodz belonged, strongly supported the expulsion plan. A second *Hauptbesprechung* (general discussion), held in Berlin on April 1, 1940, confirmed the decision to establish the ghetto, stressing again its "provisional character." The ghetto was finally closed off on May 1, 1940, housing 163,776 persons, according to official estimates. The remainder of the Jews of Lodz were expelled by the Germans, or were moved to Warsaw, Cracow, Częstochowa, and other places in the GG. The Lodz ghetto was located in Bałuty, the city's poorest section, with narrow, unpaved streets and wooden houses, some of which were unfit for human habitation.[70]

In Warsaw, where the Jews constituted at least 38 percent of the population, the Gestapo, early in November 1939, ordered the Judenrat to set up a ghetto within three days. The order was countermanded, however, by General Neumann-Neurode, military commander of Warsaw, following a visit by a delegation of the Judenrat. Apparently the Gestapo and the military authorities disagreed on this matter.[71] The military commander ordered the Judenrat to put signs on the Jewish streets with the inscription *Seuchensperrgebiet* (epidemic zone). The Jews refrained from leaving these streets, fearing attacks by German or Polish ruffians.[72] But the ghetto project continued to be discussed. In February and March 1940, the Germans planned to locate the ghetto in the Praga suburb, but its Polish municipal council prevailed upon the Nazis to give up the plan. In the spring of 1940, the Germans planned to establish two or more ghettos on the city's outskirts. In the summer after the campaign in France, the Germans began to concentrate troops in the Warsaw district and intensified preparations for the ghetto. On August 7, 1940, Ludwig Leist, Stadthauptmann of Warsaw and plenipotentiary of the Warsaw governor, decreed that Jewish newcomers to Warsaw or Warsaw Jews who moved from their homes would be permitted to settle only in a designated area, to be separated by a wall (*Aussperrmauer*), and he ordered that such walls be built by the Jews in a number of streets.[73] This may be considered the first step in the establishment of the ghetto. About 140,000 Jews who lived in other sections were not yet ordered to move, possibly because the administration had not yet mastered the technique of establishing a ghetto of this size. Finally, on October 16, 1940, after consultation with Hans Biebow, chief of the Lodz ghetto administration,[74] a decree was issued establishing the ghetto, to comprise 4.6 percent of the city's residential area and 1,692 of its 24,632 houses, with 27,000 residential units or apartments totaling about 67,000 rooms, apart from industrial and commercial establishments and uninhabitable quarters, such as kitchens, alcoves, and attics. This area became the "living space" of 420,000 to 500,000 Jews. By May 1941, it was reported that the average number of inhabitants of a residential unit was 39.3, with fourteen persons occupying a single room. Jews were moved out of and into different streets. Walls were built, pulled down, and built again.[75] This deliberate chaos further aggravated the overcrowding, and hastened economic decline. People were forever in search of housing, even of a temporary kind; some were forced to live in the streets. The irrepressible humor of the Jews found material even in that tragedy. The musical comedy *Libe zukht a dire* (Love Is Looking for an Apartment) by Jerzy Jurandot enjoyed great success in a ghetto theatre.[76]

The establishment of ghettos was not always the result of discussions and preparations. In the absence of a general directive, a different course was followed in every local administrative unit. There were, as a result, all kinds of ghettos: open, closed, and half-closed. In many places, particularly in the smaller towns, no ghettos were established. For instance, it was found to be "technically impossible" to segregate the seven hundred Jews of Sieradz, near Lodz. Szydłowiec, nearly 100 percent Jewish, was declared to be a "Jewish town." The five or six thousand Jews of Bełchatów were free to live anywhere in the town, however in separate buildings. Radków had no ghetto, but late in 1940 signs were put up on the main highway announcing that the Jews were prohibited to leave the town, on pain of death.[77]

The first ghetto in the province of Wartheland was established in Tuliszków, Turek county, in December 1939 or January 1940. By the spring and summer of 1940 nearly all the towns of Wartheland had ghettos established—Pabianice, in February 1940; Brzeziny (renamed by the Germans Löwenstadt), on April 28, 1940; Kutno, on June 16, 1940.[78]

The first "experimental" ghetto in the GG was set up in October or November 1939 in Piotrków, but this attempt was subsequently given up. The establishment of a regular ghetto was not decreed until March 1, 1942.[79] In Staszów, the ghetto was established on February 15, 1940; in Bochnia, on March 15, 1940. The confusion of the officials is seen in Max du Prel's statement, in his semi-official book, that the former Łowicz county was the first to introduce Jewish residential zones in the GG. "As far back as May 1940," stated du Prel, "15,000 Jews were settled in compact quarters in five towns." General Jürgen Stroop repeated the same error. He stated that in the spring of 1940 many Jews from Wartheland illegally entered the GG, especially Łowicz county. In order to limit their freedom of movement, ghettos were created in Łowicz, Główno, Bolimów, Kernozia, and Łyszkowice. The last three were small ghettos, with an average of 500 to 650 residents.[80] During 1940, ghettos were established in Krasnystaw (in July); in Mława (on September 6); in Przedbórz, Łęczna, and Kazimerz (in December); in Skierniewice (on December 15); and in Rejowiec, Radom, and Chrzanów. [81] There may have been others, but no records of them are known.

The Germans desired to hasten ghettoization in the GG. The head of the resettlement department of the Warsaw district told a session of the German county chiefs (Kreishauptmänner) late in 1940 that the ghettoization of the Warsaw district would soon be completed.[82] The pace was accelerated in 1941 with the creation of dozens of new ghettos. Their precise number cannot be ascertained. Since no general decree for the establishment of ghettos was issued, systematic official statistics were most probably not collected. After the war, the International Research Bureau of the International Refugee Organization listed in its register 134 ghettos in western and central Poland, and seventeen ghettos in the Soviet-incorporated, former eastern Polish, provinces. This list is far from complete; the names of many ghettos mentioned in other documents are not included in it.[83]

A brief review of information about some of the larger ghettos in the GG is in order. At first the Germans intended to expel the Jews from

Cracow. Governor-General Hans Frank declared, in an address on April 2, 1940, that the capital city must be free of Jews (*judenfrei*). He reiterated the same point on October 15.[84] The number of Jews in Cracow at that time was 70,000. At first they did not take seriously the decree of May 18, 1940, ordering them to leave the city. However, the German pogroms of December 1940 and the forced resettlement reduced their number to 15,000 or 17,000. For the remaining Jews, the order of March 3, 1941, established a ghetto in the poorest and dirtiest alleys of the suburb of Podgórze. About two square meters of space were allotted, on the average, to a person, or one window for three persons. The ghetto had about 320 houses. Subsequently its area was reduced twice.[85]

The Lublin ghetto, housing 40,000 Jews, was decreed on March 24, 1941. But the Germans viewed that half-closed ghetto as too roomy. At the second meeting devoted to this subject (October 17, 1941), it was declared that the ghetto was temporary and that only the complete deportation of the Jews would constitute the definitive solution. After the horrible action of March and April 1942, in which most of the Jews of Lublin were murdered, a ghetto was set up for the 4,000 survivors in Majdan Tatarski on April 16, 1942.[86]

At the very beginning of the occupation the Germans began to drive the Jews out from various streets of Częstochowa, where over 40,000 lived in 1939. Early in 1940, Jews were permitted to live in eighty-four out of some 400 streets. Later the number was reduced to twenty-eight. On March 29, 1941, the Governor of Radom, Dr. Karl Lasch, called a meeting on the ghettoization of his district, where Częstochowa was located. On April 9, 1941, Dr. Wendler, Stadthauptmann of Częstochowa, issued the decree establishing the ghetto. The Częstochowa ghetto was known for its relative "liberalism." Its area was fairly large; its inhabitants were allowed to bring in their belongings; and there were no German pogroms during the period of moving as there were in many other Polish towns. Nor was the ghetto fenced off. It was merely marked by signs reading *Jüdischer Wohnbezirk* (Jewish residential district). In August 1941, when the chief of police proposed the addition of thirty signs, the city captain agreed, but on the condition that the words "Danger of Epidemics" be added. Moreover, as late as the first half of 1942, a number of skilled Jewish workers and specialists lived outside the ghetto, where even the offices of the Judenrat were located for some time. Understandably, Jews from other parts of the GG made attempts to settle there. This idyllic picture was abruptly changed, however, with the bloody action in September-October 1942.[87]

In some towns the ghettos were set up very late—for example, Dąbrowa, Sosnowiec, Będzin (late in 1942 and early in 1943), Lubaczów (October 1942), and Tarnów (June 1942).[88]

## Types of Ghettos

The Radom ghetto, where 25,000 Jews lived in 1939, was not fenced off, but, like that of Częstochowa, was merely marked by signs on its border streets. The Radom ghetto even contained some "Aryan" enclaves.[89] Chełm, with a Jewish population of 14,000 in 1939, also had an "open" ghetto, as did Kielce, with 21,000 Jews. Also open were the ghettos of Łask, Ozorków, Dąbie near Koło, Kalisz, Włocławek, and Zduńska Wola. In the last town, the ghetto, marked by a high pole with a sign displaying a blue Star of David, consisted of four streets in the Old City. In Rejowiec, the ghetto was open at first and only later fenced off with barbed wire, as in the early stages of the Warsaw ghetto.[90] There were also barbed wire and wooden fences in Lodz, Lwów, Kielce, Biała Podlaska, Gniewoszów near Dęblin, Lublin, Sandomierz (there the fence was only two feet high), Złoczów, Grodno, Dubno, Łachwa (in Polesie), Czernowitz (in Bucovina), among others. In Lublin, a plan was considered to change the barbed wire enclosure for a wall three meters high. The Skierniewice and Cracow ghettos were segregated behind brick walls. The wall of the Cracow ghetto was built in the form of Jewish tombstones, as if to remind its denizens that they were buried alive.[91] The ghettos of Lodz and Kutno were hermetically closed, the latter after a typhus epidemic. There were also other closed ghettos.[92]

In their effort to ruin the Jews economically and morally, the Germans applied a strategy of changing ghetto boundaries. For instance, in Rzeszów, the location of the ghetto was changed constantly. With each resettlement the Jews lost some of their property, and were given worse quarters. The same happened in Warsaw, Cracow, and many other places. The Germans frankly designed this policy "to give the Jews a shaking" or "to comb them out" (*durchschütteln* or *durchkämmen*). The ghettos were located in the dirtiest and poorest sections of the remoter suburbs, as in the case of Lodz (Bałuty), Radom, Sosnowiec, and Cracow, cited above; also Kalisz and Kutno, where the ruins of the paper factory Konstancja, with its broken windows and doors and without sanitary facilities, were assigned to the Jews. The ghetto of Włocławek was located in the suburb of Rakówek, formerly inhabited by the town's underworld. It remained unpaved and without electricity. The ghetto of Żychlin was established in the suburb of Pabianówka, a breeding place for disease, without even a well. The ghetto of Dąbrowica was located in the ruins of an old brick factory; that of Lwów, in the dirtiest part of the suburb of Zamarstynów. The ghetto of Główno was shifted to Stary Warchałow, a summer resort, where the Jews lived in wooden cabins.[93]

Kielce's 16,000 Jews, together with several thousand refugees and expellees, mostly from Vienna, were driven, on April 7, 1941, into a narrow ghetto, planned as early as 1940. It was declared a contagious zone (*Ansteckungsgebiet*). Significantly, a problem which concerned Stadthauptmann Drechsel was the renaming of streets of the ghetto. He compiled a list, dated August 17, 1940, replacing the old names with derisive or ironic German and Polish ones.[94] The list appears in the table below.

As was mentioned earlier, in a number of towns the Germans established two or sometimes even three ghettos. Usually a "Ghetto A" was set up for "productive" Jews, while a "Ghetto B" was assigned to the unemployed or unemployable, the aged and the sick. Ghetto B was usually destroyed or "transported" before Ghetto A. Soon the nature of the division

*Street Names in the Ghetto of Kielce*[95]

| | New Names | |
| Old Names | GERMAN | POLISH |
| --- | --- | --- |
| Ulica (Ul.) Okrzei | Jerusalemgasse, Goldsteingasse, or Mojschegasse | Jerozolimska (Jerusalem St.) |
| Ul. Silniczna | Galileergasse, Silbensteingasse, or Jojnegasse | Srebrnego Kamienia (Silver Stone St.) |
| Staro-Warszawskie Przedmieście | Synagogenstrasse, Maselgasse, Kupfersteingasse, or Arongasse | Szczęśliwa (Happy St.) |
| Ul. Jasna | Betlehemgasse, Grünspangasse, or Isackgasse | Zaśniedziała (Tarnished St.) |
| Ul. Krzywa | Ziongasse, Pomeranzenduftgasse, or Abrahamgasse | Abraham (Abraham's St.) |
| Ul. Wązka | Rabbinnergasse, Ritualgasse, or Salomongasse | Rabinów (Rabbis' St.) |
| Ul. Stolarska | Palästinergasse, Koschergasse, or Davidgasse | Dawida (David's St.) |
| Pocieszka | Lewitengasse, Treifegasse, or Samsongasse | Trefna (Non-Kosher [Treyfa] St.) |
| Ul. Lipowa | Makkabäergasse, Süsskindgasse, or Judasgasse | — — — — — — |
| Ul. Cicha | Pharisäergasse, Feingoldgasse, or Kajphasgasse | Kruszcowa (Metal Ore St.) |
| Nowy Świat | Hassydergasse, Cymesgasse (Tsimes St.), or Ruchlagasse (Rachel St.) | Arona (Aaron's St.) |
| Ul. Przechodnia | Heddergasse, Schamesgasse or Saragasse | Ul. Sary (Sara's St.) |
| Ul. Targowa | Schabesgasse, Hasergasse, Isak, or Schlamagasse | Ul. Izaka (Isaac St.) |
| Ul. Szydłowska | Talmudgasse, Knoblauchgasse, or Ruthgasse | Czosnkową (Garlic St.) |
| Ul. Dąbrowska | Hohepriestergasse, Feigenblattgasse, or Maselgasse | Ul. Figowego Liścia (Fig Leaf St.) |
| Przecznica | — — — — — — — — — — | Ul. Jojnego (Jonah's St.) |

became apparent, and transfer from Ghetto A to Ghetto B was viewed as a calamity. Two ghettos were established in Warsaw (the "large" and the "small" ghetto),[96] Radom, Lublin, Bochnia, Tarnów, Cracow, Częstochowa, Piotrków, Przemyśl, Łachwa, Kowel, Vilna, Lwów, Riga (Latvia), Borysław, Grodno, Kaunas, (Kovno, Lithuania), Minsk (White Russia), and other towns; Otwock had three ghettos. In most cases, special passes were required for passage between the ghettos, as in Radom, Lublin, and Nowy Sącz. Sometimes peculiar arrangements were devised to make life more miserable for the Jews. For instance, the town of Piaski had two ghettos, housing 5,000 persons; but the soup kitchens, the hospital, the only well, and the outhouses were all located in one ghetto, to which the inhabitants of the other had access for only one hour in the morning and one hour in the evening.[97]

After the outbreak of Russo-German hostilities, the Germans set up ghettos in various places in the newly conquered areas, including Vilna (with a Jewish population of about 65,000 in 1939), Kovno (30,000), Grodno (22,000), Szawle, Lida, Bialystok (60,000), Minsk (80,000–90,000), Mogilev (34,000), Smolensk, Vitebsk (37,000), Riga (32,000), Dinaburg (Dvinsk or Daugavpils, 15,000 to 18,000), Liepaja (Libau), Lwów (Lemberg, 160,000), Stanisławów (27,000), Kołomyja (16,000), Drohobycz and Borysław (together 27,000), Równe (25,000), Dubno (7,000), Zhitomir (35,000), Umań, Berdichev (35,000), Radomyśl, Suceava (Bucovina), Czernowitz (Cernauti, 62,000), Kishinev (Chisinau, 80,000), Tulchin (Transnistria), among others. In Kharkov (150,000), Kiev (175,000), Odessa (180,000) and elsewhere, extermination proceeded so fast that ghettos were not needed. Even where ghettos were established, their life was very short and filled with incessant tragic deportations and actions.[98] In several towns of Eastern Galicia, the Ukrainians urged the Germans to establish ghettos. Such was the case in Złoczów and in Żołkiew.[99]

In July 1942, Friedrich Wilhelm Krüger, the higher SS and police chief in the GG, received an order from Himmler (dated Lublin, July 19, 1942) to have all Jews in the GG concentrated in five camps before December 31, 1942.[100] This order was never carried out. After a few months it was superseded by two strange decrees (dated October 10 and 28, 1942), the only all-embracing orders for ghettoization in the GG. They ordered the establishment of fifty-five ghettos: six, eight, four, five, and thirty-two ghettos respectively in the districts of Warsaw, Lublin, Radom, Cracow, and Galicia.[101] Oddly, the decrees were issued after the mass murder, under the direction of the very persons who had issued them, of most of the Jews. Thus no permanent ghettos were established on the basis of these decrees.

The contradiction between the orders of July and October 1942 can be viewed as a sham, in line with the discrepancy between the "legislation" and the real situation. In fact, the decrees were intended to conceal from the Jews and from the outside world the tragic truth of genocide. One theory also has it that the October decrees were intended to entice back to the ghettos, for ultimate annihilation, those Jews who were hiding in non-Jewish homes or who were on forged "Aryan" papers, by holding before them the illusion of secure conditions of life in the ghetto. As a matter of fact, many Jews who had lost their money or could no longer endure the constant fear and tension, the blackmail and denunciations by their paid "Aryan protectors," returned voluntarily to the ghetto. As is generally known, the last remaining ghettos were annihilated by the Nazis in 1943 and 1944.

❆ This essay was first published in *Jewish Social Studies,* 16 (January 1954), 61–88.

## Notes

1. Reinhard Heydrich's *Schnellbrief* appeared in English translation as Document PS–3363 in the U.S. government publication *Nazi Conspiracy and Aggression* (Washington, 1946–1947), VI, 97–101. The original German text was published under the title "The German Death Sentence against the Jewish People," in *YB,* 30 (1947), 163–68. See also Itzhak Lewin, *Nokhn hurbn* (After the Holocaust) (New York, 1950), pp. 149–56.

2. Incorporated into the Third Reich were a part of Polish Silesia; the province of Poznań and a part of the province of Lodz, renamed Reichsgau Wartheland under Gauleiter Arthur Greiser; and parts of Polish Pomorze (Pomerania), the Danzig area, and the Polish Corridor (Reichsgau Danzig-Westpreussen).

3. See essay 1 above, "The Jewish Badge and the Yellow Star in the Nazi Era," note 7.

4. Hitler stated as follows: "Today I want to be a prophet once more: If the international Jewish financiers inside and outside Europe once more succeed in plunging nations into another world war, the result will be not the bolshevization of the world and thereby the victory of Jewry, but the annihilation of the Jewish race in Europe." Translated from Gerhard Brendel, *Der Führer über die Juden* (Munich, 1943), p. 82.

5. Cf. Lahousen's affidavit at the Nuremberg hearing of January 21, 1946, in *NCA,* VIII, 589–90.

6. Frank closed this address at a Nazi party rally with the words: "The Jews must disappear from all of Europe" (see *Krakauer Zeitung,* August 16, 1940).

7. Hitler's address was published in *Der Grossdeutsche Freiheitskampf: Reden Adolf Hitlers von 1. September 1939 bis 10 März 1940,* II (Berlin, 1942), 222.

8. Leon Poliakov explains Hitler's doubletalk in his *Bréviaire de la*

*haine* (Paris, 1951), p. 36. Hitler had already at that time crystalized in his mind two alternate plans. The first plan called for permitting the Jews to survive in some isolated area, should he become the ruler of the world. In case of the world's unwillingness to capitulate before him, the Führer's second plan called for the punishment of the Jews for this failure by their total annihilation. Poliakov offers no proofs for his conjecture, which seems to be pure speculation. He tends to simplify the tangled web of political, ideological, and tactical reasons, substituting instead the single psychological motive of revenge as the decisive factor behind Hitler's policy of genocide.

9. The Jewish implications of the *Lebensraum* theory have been treated by Max Weinreich in his *Hitler's Professors* (New York, 1947), pp. 67–74. The book also contains a selected bibliography on the subject.

10. In an intimate conversation with his tablemates, Hitler made clear his ideas about this problem: "Colonies are a problematic possession. This continent [Europe] is a safe property for us. What India was for England in the East, [East Europe] has to be for us." Henry Picker, *Hitler's Tischgespräche im Führerhauptquartier* (Bonn, 1951). See also my review of the volume in *JSS,* 15 (1953), 38–85.

11. Friedrich Hossbach, *Zwischen Wehrmacht und Hitler* (Wolfenbüttel, 1949), pp. 207–20, appendixes ii and iii. See also Hermann Förtsch, *Schuld und Verhängniss: Die Fritschkrise im Frühjahr 1938* (Stuttgart, 1951), pp. 75–82. The full text of the Hossbach Protocols was also published in *Die Wandlung* (Heidelberg, 1945–1946), I, 347–65.

12. *Mein Kampf,* 10th ed. (Munich, 1932), pp. 143–44, 151–56, 731–41. A characteristic example of indoctrination in the *Lebensraum* theory is Hitler's Berlin address of May 1, 1939. See *Schulungsbrief, das zentrale Monatsblatt der NSDAP,* 5–6 (1941) and "Der Führer als Schutzherr des deutschen Lebensraumes," *Schulungshefte für den Unterricht über national-sozialistische Weltanschauung, Herausgegeben vom Oberkommando der Wehrmacht,* no. 2 (1939), 15–21.

13. *IMT,* IV, 494; VII, 192. Important documents concerning the policy of biological warfare against the Poles and the Jews appeared in Polish translation in Jan Sehn, "The Hitlerite Plan of Biological Warfare against the Polish Nation" (Polish), *BGK,* 4 (Warsaw, 1948), 109–71.

14. The high Gestapo official Karl Rudolf Werner Best, SS-Brigadeführer, was appointed chief of the administrative office of the German military commander (Militärbefehlshaber) in France during World War II, and, later, Germany's minister plenipotentiary in Copenhagen, Denmark.

15. Werner Best, "Grossraumordnung und Grossraumverwaltung," *Zeitschrift für Politik* (June 1942), quoted in Hayim Greenberg, "The Plan of Destruction," *The Massacre of a People* (New York, 1943), p. 17.

16. *Berliner Börsenzeitung* (October 15, 1939) quoted in *Les Massacres des Juifs en Pologne* (Paris, 1945), p. 7. See also Francis Aldor, *Germany's "Death Space": The Polish Tragedy* (London, 1940). Its subtitle reads as follows: *Nazi Theory Has Evolved the Concept of "Lebensraum" (Living Space)— Nazi Practice Has Realized the Part of "Todesraum" (Death Space).*

17. *Die Burg,* vol. IV, no. 1 (January 1943), pp. 7–16. This article was written in Frank's capacity as president of *Das Institut für deutsche Ostarbeit.*

18. About 500,000 Gypsies were killed by the Nazis. See below, essay 15; also my essay in *Kiyoum* (Paris, 1950), 1661–67; Dora E. Yates, "Hitler and the Gypsies," *Commentary*, 8 (1949), 455–59; Macfie Scott, "Gypsy Persecutions," *Journal of the Gypsy Lore Society*, ser. 3, vol. 22 (1943), 65–78; Frédéric Marx, "Le sort des tziganes dans les prisons et les camps de concentration de l'Allemagne hitlerienne," *ibid.*, 25 (1946), 23–34; Vanya Kochanowski, "Some Notes on the Gypsies of Latvia by One of the Survivors," *ibid.*, 34–38, 112–16; Mateo Maximoff, "Germany and the Gypsies," *ibid.*, 104–8; Jan Molitor, "The Fate of a German Gypsy," *ibid.*, 26 (1947), 48–52.

19. *Manchester Guardian* (November 3, 1939), cited in Simon Segal, *The New Order in Poland* (New York, 1942), p. 236.

20. *Das Reich* (November 16, 1941); also reprinted in Josef Goebbels, *Das eherne Herz*, p. 88.

21. The *Reichsdeutsche* and *Volksdeutsche* in the GG, said Frank, have to live in "economic segregation" (*fachliche Trennung*) from the Poles and in "hermetic isolation" (*hermetische Abschliessung*) from the Jews. An abstract of Frank's address was published by Günther Bergman, "Das deutsche Leben in Krakau," *Krakauer Zeitung* (August 14, 1940), no. 195, special supplement, p. 7.

22. Peter-Heinz Seraphim, "Die Judenfrage im General Gouvernement als Bevölkerungsproblem," *Die Burg*, vol. 1, no. 1 (October, 1940), pp. 61–64.

23. Dietrich Redeker, "Deutsche Ordnung kehrt ins Ghetto ein," *Krakauer Zeitung*, March 21, 1940.

24. *Jüdischer Wohnbezirk, Jüdisches Wohngebiet, Seuchen-Sperrgebiet*. See N. Blumental, *Słówka niewinne* (Innocent Little Words) (Lodz, 1946), pp. 225–26. However, the German authorities in Lodz used the term ghetto from the very beginning. See *Dokumenty i Materjały, III. Getto Łódzkie* (Ghetto Lodz), edited by A. Eisenbach, pp. 26–31; and *Krakauer Zeitung* (as cited above, note 23).

25. In a radio speech delivered after his visit to Lodz, Goebbels was reported to have given assurance that "we have no intention of instituting the medieval ghettos in Poland. There could be no greater nonsense"; Israel Tabaksblatt, *Hurban Lodz* (Buenos Aires, 1946), p. 34. Tabaksblatt quotes a long citation from Goebbel's address, but does not refer to any printed source. In all probability his quotation is based on his or other listeners' reminiscences of the broadcasts. We could not find a transcript of the address in any of the collections of Goebbels's speeches or in his published articles. It must be assumed, however, that the demoniacal minister of propaganda was well aware that those "Jewish dwelling quarters" were merely transitional measures toward the "ultimate goal."

26. See Ottmar Katz, "Gettos des zwanzigsten Jahrhunderts," *Brüsseler Zeitung* (April 12, 1941). The following dissertation was listed in a survey of German doctoral theses of 1942: Kurt Hönig, *Die Entwicklung der Rechtseinheit des Gettos in Rahmen des Judenrechts des deutschen Mittelalters* (Munich, 1942). See also Hans Praesent, "Neuere deutsche Doktorarbeiten über das Judentum," *Die Judenfrage*, 7 (1943), 351–53; and *idem*, in *Der Weltkampf*, 4 (1944), 103–5.

27. "Bevölkerungs- und wirtschaftliche Probleme einer europäischen Gesamtlösung der Judenfrage," *Der Weltkampf*, 1 (1941), 43–44.

28. Hugo Valentin, *Antisemitism, Historically and Critically Examined* (London, 1936), p. 249.

29. *Deutsche Justiz,* August 2, 1935; cited in Marvin Lowenthal, *The Jews in Germany* (Philadelphia, 1936), p. 403.

30. Document PS–1301 in *IMT, XXVII,* 163–64.

31. Document PS–1816, in *IMT, XXVIII,* 499.

32. Abraham L. Sachar, *Sufferance Is the Badge: The Jews in the Contemporary World* (New York, 1939), p. 66.

33. *Völkerischer Beobachter* (Berlin), December 6, 1938.

34. *RGBL,* 1 (November 28, 1938), 1678; *Völkerischer Beobachter,* December 5, 1938. The pertinent German legislation was collected and commented on by Bernard Dov Weinryb in his *Jewish Emancipation under Attack* (New York, 1942), and by Bruno Blau in his comprehensive compilation *Das Ausnahmerecht für die Juden in den europäischen Ländern, 1933–1945, I. Teil. Deutschland* (New York, 1952) (photo offset).

35. Von Schirach proudly boasted of this policy in an address before the European Youth Congress (Vienna, September 14, 1942), in which he declared: "Every Jew who exerts influence in Europe is a danger to European culture. If anyone reproaches me with having driven from this city [Vienna], which was once the European metropolis of Jewry, tens of thousands upon tens of thousands of Jews into the ghetto of the east, I feel myself compelled to reply: 'I view this as an action contributing to European culture.'" See *Völkerischer Beobachter* (Vienna), September 15, 1942, p. 2.

36. Mirko Tuma, *Ghetto nasich dni* (The Ghetto of Our Days) (Prague, 1946), p. 13; Zdenek Lederer, *Ghetto Theresienstadt* (London, 1953), pp. 14, 33, 247–48. Theresienstadt was officially transformed into a ghetto by Heydrich's order of July 1, 1942, which forced all non-Jews to leave the town. The administrative functions had been delegated earlier to a Judenrat appointed by the Germans.

37. American Jewish Committee, Research Institute on Peace and Post-War Problems, "The Jews of Czechoslovakia" (mimeographed report) (New York, 1944), p. 27. Simultaneously, the Germans started the mass deportation of Jews from Moravska Ostrava to Poland. See Lederer, pp. 203–4.

38. Sachar, p. 131.

39. Frederic Steiner, ed., *The Tragedy of the Slovak Jewry* (Bratislava, 1949), pp. 74–75; International Tracing Service, *Catalogue of Camps and Prisons in Germany and German-Occupied Territories* (hereafter cited as ITS, *Catalogue*), 2 vols. (Arolsen, 1949–1950) and *Catalogue Supplement* (Arolsen, 1951). The *Supplement* lists (pp. 13–14) Jewish ghettos in Slovakia and Carpatho-Ruthenia. This list seems to be incomplete, however. On March 7, 1942, the Slovak minister of the interior, Sano Mach, published a decree confining all Jews to their quarters until the completion of the "transfer to the east" of the Jewish communities. See *The Black Book,* p. 138. Most likely, the order had not been carried out.

40. On March 22, 1944, the Hungarian premier Dome Sztoyay told his cabinet that the head of the Reich Security Main Office, Ernst Kaltenbrunner (Heydrich's successor), insisted on the establishment of ghettos for Hungarian Jews. See Gerald Reitlinger, *The Final Solution* (New York, 1953), p. 420.

For a full list of the ghettos see Jekutiel Yehuda (Leopold) Greenwald, *Toyznt yor yidish lebn in Ungarn* (One Thousand Years of Jewish Life in Hungary) (New York, 1945), p. 9; that list includes some areas incorporated by Hungary from 1939 on (for example, Carpatho-Russia). ITS, *Supplement* (pp. 50–51), lists only twenty-two ghettos in ethnic Hungarian territory; moreover, it states that some ghettos had already been established before 1944—namely, in Miskolcz in 1940; in Kistarcza and Budapest in 1942; and in Nyiregyhaza in 1943. It is likely that the editors of the ITS, *Catalogue* confused the establishment of ghettos with that of labor camps. More detailed information is available about Budapest. On June 15, 1944, its 63,000 Jewish inhabitants with no foreign protection were forced to move into 2,681 specially assigned "Star Houses." No ghetto was established, because BBC broadcasts induced fear in the town council that formation of a ghetto would invite retaliatory bombing by the Allies. On the other hand, Budapest's 33,000 "protected Jews," who had been granted special status by the consulates of Switzerland, Sweden, Spain, and Portugal, respectively, moved into "Red Cross Houses." After November 29, 1944, the unprotected Jews were moved into an enclosed ghetto, which contained 162 apartment houses (Reitlinger, pp. 431, 446). The communal leader, Rezsö Kasztner, a reliable authority, states that the Budapest ghetto was set up in the last week of November 1944. It housed about 100,000 Jews in 6,000 to 7,000 rooms made available for them in the seventh district of the city. See Kasztner, *Bericht des Jüdischen Rettungskommitees aus Budapest 1942–1945 (Streng vertraulich)* (Budapest, 1946), p. 131 (mimeographed). On living conditions in the Hungarian ghettos, see Vilmos Tarjan, *A bedezkázott riporter* (The Reporter behind the Barbed Wire) (Budapest, 1945). See also Eugene Duschinsky, "Hungary," *The Jews in the Soviet Satellites* (New York, Syracuse, 1953), pp. 388, 398.

41. Henri Monneray, ed., *La Persécution des Juifs dans les Pays de l'Est présentée à Nuremberg* (Paris, 1949), pp. 234–35, 219–20, 273 (hereafter cited as Monneray, *Est*). In general, the establishment of ghettos in the old Rumanian provinces of Moldavia and Walachia progressed slowly and chaotically. The *New York Times* reported, on November 10, 1941, that the Bucharest Jews had been segregated in the Dudesti-Vacaresti area, an old Jewish quarter. This plan was only partially carried out, however. Other reports mentioned a ghetto for the unemployed Bucharest Jews in the suburb of Zhighnitz. As late as June 1944, the Bucharest chief of police ordered the establishment of a ghetto for the entire Jewish population. According to the JTA *Bulletin* of December 24, 1941, and January 7, 1942, ghettos were planned or established in Giurgiu, Constanza, and Ploesti, as well as in some other Moldavian localities. See Joseph Schechtman, *The Jews in Rumania during World War II* (typescript in the archives of the YIVO Institute).

42. Zdenko Levental, ed., *Zlocini fasistickih okupatora i njihovih pomagáca protiv Jevreja u Jugoslaviji* (The Crimes of the Fascist Occupants and Their Collaborators against the Jews in Yugoslavia) (Belgrade, 1952), pp. 17–25; ITS, *Catalogue,* I, 361; Monneray, *Est*, pp. 239, 243; Staatsanwaltschaft bei dem Landgericht Nürnberg-Fürth, Anklageschrift [gegen] *Rademacher, Franz und Dr. Klingenfuss, Karl* (1949); and *Urteil . . . in der Strafsache gegen Rademacher, Franz* (1950), pp. 52 ff., 76 (mimeographed).

I am indebted to Herr Güttler, Staatsanwalt at the Landgericht Nürnberg-Fürth, for the transcripts of the Rademacher trial.

43. See *Les Juifs en Europe, 1939–1945* (Paris, 1949), p. 124; American Jewish Committee, "Report on the Jews in Bulgaria" (mimeographed; New York, 1944), p. 8.

44. On the very short-lived ghetto in Salonika, see I. A. Matarasso . . . *Ki homos holoi tous den pethanan: He catastrophe ton hellenohebraion* (However, Not All Had Been Killed: The Catastrophe of the Greek Jews) (Athens, 1948), pp. 31–39; *In Memoriam*, ed. by Michael Molho, II (Salonika, 1949), 19; Monneray, *Est*, p. 245; my essay "The Jews in Greece During the Second World War," in *The Joshua Starr Memorial Volume* (New York, 1953), pp. 241–48. According to Reitlinger, p. 371, there were three ghettos in Salonika; one of them was located in the Baron Hirsch quarter.

45. *In Memoriam*, pp. 22–23; Dorothy Macardle, *Children of Europe* (Boston, 1951), p. 84.

46. *Les Juifs en Europe*, p. 131.

47. See Henri Monneray, ed., *La Persécution des Juifs en France et dans les autres Pays de l'Ouest présentée à Nuremberg* (Paris, 1947), p. 120 (hereafter cited as Monneray, *Ouest*); Leon Poliakov, *L'étoile jaune* (Paris, 1949), pp. 49–58.

48. Monneray, *Ouest*, pp. 202–16. See also the articles in the *Brüsseler Zeitung:* Heinrich Tötter, "Der Weg ins Ghetto," December 7, 1941; and W[alter] F[reund], "Das Judenviertel in Antwerpen," April 20, 1941.

49. See Monneray, *Ouest*, pp. 231 ff.; Poliakov, p. 65.

50. Felix Gruenberger, "The Jewish Refugees in Shanghai," *JSS*, 12 (1950), 342; Robert M. W. Kempner, "Nazis errichteten das Shanghai Ghetto," *Aufbau* (New York), January 16, 1953.

51. Michael Weichert's diaries, "Żydowska samopomoc społeczna" (Jewish Social Self-Help); typescript, in my private archives, p. 122.

52. Hermann Erich Seifert, *Der Jude an der Ostgrenze* (Berlin, 1941), p. 12.

53. Walter Dörig, "Blick in ein Judenghetto," *Die Deutsche Polizei*, no. 16 (August 1941).

54. This was done ostensibly "to improve the sanitary conditions," according to an official report of the county chief (*Kreishauptmann*) of Grójec, quoted in T. Brustin-Berenstein, "Resettlements in the Warsaw District" (Yiddish), *BFG*, 1 (1948), 139.

55. Cited in Macardle, p. 71.

56. See *Krakauer Zeitung*, January 23, 1941, November 17, 1941; *Ostdeutscher Beobachter* (Posen), March 29, 1941; and an official publication of the office of the Warsaw governor, *Zwei Jahre Aufbauarbeit im Distrikt Warschau* (Warsaw, 1941), pp. 71 ff.

57. A typical example of this charge is the article about the Lodz ghetto by the Lodz chief of police, SS-Brigadeführer Dr. Albert, in *Die deutsche Polizei*, reprinted in abbreviated form in *Deutschland im Kampf*, nos. 35–36 (February 1941), p. 131. See also below, note 70.

58. Lodz was renamed Litzmannstadt by the Germans.

59. The full original text of Übelhör's memorandum of December 10, 1939 was published in A. Eisenbach, *Getto Łódzkie* (Lodz, 1946), pp. 26–31. Übelhör's opinion about the transitory character of the ghetto was shared

by many German officials. The same opinion was voiced by Hermann Erich Seifert, a reporter and feature columnist for *Der Angriff* (one of the most influential Nazi newspapers), who wrote: "If today, for instance, it turns out that in several states and in some cities the Jews are again being concentrated in their ghettos, this is only a transitory measure, which does not signify a permanent situation." Translated from his *Der Jude zwischen den Fronten der Rassen, der Völker, der Kulturen* (Berlin, 1942), p. 150.

60. Zakopane is a famous resort in the Carpathian Mountains, south of Cracow.

61. *Prokuratura Najwyższego Trybunału Narodowego: Akt oskarzenia przeciwko Dr. Józefowi Bühlerowi* (Polish Supreme National Tribunal: Act of Indictment against Dr. Josef Bühler) (Warsaw, 1948), pp. 88–99 (mimeographed; in my private archives).

62. *Zwei Jahre . . . Distrikt Warschau* (as cited in note 56), p. 76.

63. Act of Indictment against Bühler (see above, note 61), pp. 194 ff.

64. Quoted in Jacob Apenszlak, ed., *The Black Book of Polish Jewry* (New York, 1943), pp. 178–80; see also Leib Spizman, *Di yidn in natsi poyln* (The Jews in Nazi Poland) (New York, 1942), pp. 110, 125; *Davar* (Tel Aviv), January 21, 1942.

65. See his *Diaries* in *IMT*, XXXIX, 580. See also Eugeniusz Szrojt, "The German Occupation in Poland in the Light of the Diaries of Hans Frank and the Minutes of the Meetings of the Government General" (Polish), *BGK*, II (1947), 9–41, esp. p. 33.

66. Monneray, *Est*, p. 175; on the Lublin reservation and the Madagascar plan, see essay 2 above, "The Lublin Reservation and the Madagascar Plan."

67. Cited in *New Yorker Staatszeitung*, September 12, 1940.

68. Edmund J. Osmańczyk, "The Diaries of Hans Frank" (Polish), *Dokumenty pruskie* (Warsaw, 1947), pp. 54–115.

69. For the full texts of Übelhör's memo and the various ordinances, regulations, and minutes of the conferences about the ghetto of Lodz, see Eisenbach, *Getto Łódzkie*, pp. 25–71, 81–87, 165–69.

70. Some important publications on the Lodz ghetto are Israel Tabaksblatt, *Hurban Lodz* (Buenos Aires, 1946); B. Hershkovitz, "Ghetto Litzmannstadt" (Yiddish), *YB*, 30 (1947), 21–58; I. Nirnberg, "The History of the Ghetto in Lodz" (Yiddish), *In di yorn fun yidishn hurbn* (In the Years of the Jewish Catastrophe) (New York, 1948), pp. 211–94. See also the following Nazi publications: Sturmbannführer Dr. Zirpius, "Das Ghetto in Lodz kriminalpolizeilich gesehen," *Kriminalistik*, no. 9 (Berlin, 1941), pp. 27 ff., reprinted in *Deutsche Polizei*, nos. 21, 22, 23 (1941); Dr. Albert, "Unser Kampf gegen das Chaos," *ibid*, no. 2 (January 1941). The establishment of the ghetto in Lodz greatly depressed the Jews of Warsaw; see entry of February 9–14, 1940, in the diary of the noted historian and martyr Emanuel Ringelblum, *Notitsn fun varshever geto* (Warsaw, 1952), p. 17; *Notes from the Warsaw Ghetto: The Journal of Emanuel Ringelblum*, ed. and trans. by Jacob Sloan (New York, 1958), p. 19.

71. The episode is described in the memoirs of Shmuel Zygelboim in *Zygelboim bukh*, pp. 126–36; and in Benjamin Mintz and Israel Klausner, eds., *Sepher hazevaoth* (Book of Horrors) (Jerusalem, 1945), pp. 10, 14–17.

72. Mary Berg, *The Warsaw Ghetto: A Diary* (New York, 1945), entry for July 16, 1940.

73. *Gazeta Żydowska,* no. 7, August 14, 1940.

74. See communication from Marder, the mayor of Lodz, to the Lodz chief of police, October 1, 1940, in the Archives of the CJHC.

75. Of course, the Jewish community had to pay the cost of erecting the walls. The wall on the corner of Złota and Próżna Street alone cost the Judenrat 250,000 zlotys (see Ringelblum, p. 32). The entire ghetto wall was about eleven miles long and ten feet high, with a depth of two bricks. The cost was very high because of several changes in the ghetto borders, which necessitated the removal and reconstruction of various sections of the wall. See Jonas Turkow, *Azoy iz es geven* (Thus It Happened) (Buenos Aires, 1948), pp. 104–6. The ever-ready *galgenhumor* of the Warsaw Jews dubbed the wall "the continuation of the Siegfried line" (Ringelblum, *Notitsn,* p. 130). Ringelblum reported the following characteristic incident: "I heard of a Jew who moved in and out seven times because of the continual changes in the ghetto borders. Another one moved four times. After he was expelled from Hoża Street, he moved to Freta Street, later to Grzybowska no. 68, and finally he had to move for the fourth time" (*ibid.,* p. 68).

76. The German military authorities and the civilian administration objected to the establishment of the ghetto as an impediment to the production of war material; this view was expressed in the memorandum *Deutsche Rüstungswirtschaft in Polen,* submitted by the *Feldwirtschaftsamt* to the central authorities in Berlin. To cite: "According to the report of the war industry management in Warsaw of January 29, 1941, the establishment of the ghetto in the center of the city crudely fragmented the unity of economically important installations. Two thousand Aryan enterprises were evacuated from the ghetto area and four thousand Jewish enterprises were transferred into the ghetto." Quoted from the file "Deutsche Kriegswirtschaft in Polen, 1939–1940," containing materials for 1941 as well; only a small portion of this document was published in *IMT,* XXXVI, 327–31, which does not include the above-quoted passage, available in the full mimeographed text of document USA 297–EC 344, in the Columbia University Library, New York.

The bibliography of publications on the Warsaw ghetto is so extensive that it is impossible to enumerate even the more important studies here. For details, see my "Bibliography of the Warsaw Ghetto," *Jewish Book Annual,* 11 (New York, 1952–1953), 121–29; and "The Destruction of Warsaw in the Literature" (Yiddish), *Kultur un Dertsiung,* vol. XX, nos. 4 and 5 (New York, 1950), pp. 9–12, 61–63.

77. Eyewitness record no. 55 in CJHC archives; Abraham Finkler, "Shidlovtze" [Szydłowiec] (Yiddish), *Fun Letstn Hurbn,* no. 10 (1948), pp. 106 ff.; Mark Turkow, *Malke Ovshany dertsaylt* (Malke Ovsheny Tells the Story) (Buenos Aires, 1945), p. 21; *Litzmannstädter Zeitung,* June 23, 1940; my "Contribution to the History of the Jews in Bełchatów" (Yiddish) in *Belchatov yizkor bukh* (Buenos Aires, 1951), pp. 40–60.

78. Isaiah Trunk, "A Contribution to the History of the Jews in Wartheland in the Era of Extermination, 1933–1944" (Yiddish), *BFG,* 2 (1949), 82, 98; *Litzmannstädter Zeitung,* April 28, 1940.

79. J. Kurtz, *Sepher Eduth* (Tel Aviv, 1944); S. Pudłowski, "The Fate

of the Jews of Piotrków" (Yiddish), *Dos naye Lebn,* no. 24 (Lodz, 1945); Lilke, "Out of Past Days" (Yiddish), *Undzer Tsayt,* nos. 11–12 (New York, 1947), pp. 147–50; Trunk, in *BFG,* 2, 98; Mintz-Klausner, p. 119.

80. See the report of Jürgen Stroop on the battle of the Warsaw ghetto, in *NCA,* III, 270; Nuremberg Doc. PS–1061; eyewitness record no. 263 in the CJHC archives; Brustin-Berenstein, p. 135; *Gazeta Żydowska,* September 21, and December 10, 1940; Max du Prel, *Das General Gouvernement,* 2nd ed. (Würzburg, 1942), p. 357. Max du Prel was a high official in the Nazi ministry of propaganda. He was appointed by Goebbels in 1939 as liaison officer to the administration of the GG. In 1940 he returned to Berlin and resumed his work in the Reich press office.

81. Eyewitness records nos. 1427, 1445, 1448, in *CJHCA;* Jacob Shatzky, ed., *Pinkas Mlave* (Memorial book Mława) (New York, 1950), p. 401; A. Stunzeiger, *Yizkor tsum ondenk fun di kedoyshey Krasnystaw* (A Memorial for the Martyrs from Krasnystaw) (Regensburg-Munich, 1949), p. 26; S. Drelichman, ed., *Shtil vi in Ravyets* (Quiet as in Rawicz) (Bergen Belsen, 1947), pp. 18–42; *Der Weltkampf,* 18 (January 1941), 36.

82. *Gazeta Żydowska,* December 10, 1940.

83. ITS, *Catalogue, Supplement,* pp. 82–89, 97–98, 103–4.

84. In the presence of Baldur von Schirach, Gauleiter Erich Koch, Martin Bormann, and others, at an after-dinner talk in Hitler's residence on October 2, 1940, Hans Frank reported to Hitler that the Jews of Warsaw and other towns in the GG had already been ghettoized and that the capital, Cracow, would soon be *judenrein.* See Martin Bormann's note in Jan Sehn, "Hitler's Biological Warfare against the Polish Nation" (Polish), *BGK,* 4 (1948), 128.

85. Frank's *Diaries* (entry dated April 12, 1940), in Szrojt, p. 36; eyewitness record no. 832 in *CJHCA,* Weichert's *Diaries* (see n. 48), p. 41; *Krakauer Zeitung, Sonderbeilage,* July 14, 1940; Gazeta Żydowska, August 18, 1940; *Bericht über die Tätigkeit der jüdischen Gemeinde in Krakau,* pp. 26, 86; Tadeusz Pankiewicz, *Apteka w getcie krakowskim* (A Pharmacy in the Cracow Ghetto) (Cracow, 1947), pp. 5–10; *W trzecią rocznicę zagłady getta krakowskiego* (On the Third Anniversary of the Destruction of the Cracow Ghetto) (Cracow, 1946), pp. 26–27, 33–35, 60, 105, 109, 112–20; Abraham Melezin, *Przyczynek do znajomości stosunków demograficznych wśród ludności żydowskiej w Łodzi, Krakowie i Lublinie podczas okupacji niemieckiej* (A Contribution to the Knowledge of the Demographic Situation among the Jewish Population in Lodz, Cracow, and Lublin during the German Occupation) (Lodz, 1946), pp. 26 ff.; and the official Nazi publication, *Ein Jahr Aufarbeit im Distrikt Krakau* (Cracow and Warsaw, 1940), pp. 101–2.

86. Eyewitness record of S. Turteltaub, in *CJHCA*; M. J. Feigenbaum, *Podlasie in umkum* (The Destruction of the Jews in Podlasie) (Munich, 1948), pp. 18–19; Melezin, pp. 34 ff.; *Krakauer Zeitung,* March 30, 1941; *Amtsblatt des Gouverneurs des Distrikts Lublin,* no. 12 (December 31, 1941), nos. 2 and 4 (1942).

87. L. Brener, *Vidershtand un umkum in Czenstokhover geto* (Resistance and Destruction of Częstochowa Ghetto) (Warsaw, 1950), pp. 9, 20–25; Weichert's *Diaries,* pp. 121, 215; eyewitness record no. 32 of I. Majerowicz in CJHC archives; Raphael Mahler, ed., *Czenstokhover yidn* (Jews of Często-

chowa) (New York, 1948), pp. 236 ff.; Benjamin Orenstein, *Hurbn Czenstokhov* (Destruction of Częstochowa) (Munich, 1948), p. 209; S. Waga, *Hurbn Czenstokhov* (Destruction of Częstochowa) (Buenos Aires, 1949), pp. 100–8, 179–81; W. Gliksman, "In the Ghetto of Częstochowa" (Yiddish), *Fun Letstn Hurbn,* no. 2 (1946), pp. 51–55; *Rada Starszych w Częstochowie* (The Council of Elders in Częstochowa), *Drugi Rocznik Statystyczny,* 1940 (Second Statistical Annual, 1940) (Polish) (mimeographed). In the archives of the city council of Częstochowa.

88. Eyewitness records nos. 436 and 818 in CJHC archives (about Tarnów); Trunk, p. 95; *Gazeta Żydowska,* August 21, 1940; Natan E. Szternfinkel, *Zagłada Żydow sosnowieckich* (The Extermination of the Jews in Sosnowiec) (Lodz, 1946), pp. 45–50; P. Wiederman, *Płowa Bestia* (The Blond Beast) (Munich, 1948), pp. 202, 278, 303–9; and see essay 10, "The Destruction of the Jews of Lwów, 1941–1944."

89. Weichert's *Diaries,* p. 209; J. Rottenberg, ed., *Dos yidishe Radom in hurves* (Jewish Radom in Destruction) (Stuttgart, 1948).

90. Eyewitness records, nos. 1445 and 1448 in *CJHCA;* Trunk, pp. 94–95.

91. Weichert's *Diaries,* p. 111; Frank's *Diaries,* entry of October 17, 1941, in *IMT,* XXIX, 494; eyewitness record no. 1447 in CJHC archives (about Gniewoszów); I[srael] K[aplan], Schworin, Chaim Shklar, and Abraham Feinberg, "Lachwa," in *Fun Letstn Hurbn,* no. 3 (Munich, 1947), pp. 4–10; Moshe Weisberg, "Life and Death of Dubno Ghetto," *ibid.,* no. 2 (1946), pp. 14–27; A. Silberschein, ed., *L'Éxtermination des Juifs en Pologne,* ser. 5 (Geneva, 1945), p. 42; and Mintz-Klausner, p. 16. Photographs of the Cracow ghetto wall and gate are reproduced in *W trzecią rocznicę* (Polish), p. 105. The form of the wall is mentioned in the memoirs of T. Pankiewicz, p. 8.

92. Trunk, pp. 96–97; Weichert's *Diaries,* p. 110; eyewitness record no. 303 in *CJHCA* (on Kutno).

93. Trunk, pp. 94–98.

94. Eyewitness records nos. 65 and 68, and the folder on Kielce, in *CJHCA;* Weichert, pp. 207–8; Ringelblum, p. 168. A similar episode in Lwów was described by Tadeusz Zaderecki in "How the Germans Invented 'National' Street Names for the Jews," *Nasza Opinia,* no. 11 (Warsaw), January 31, 1947. The Germans assigned this task to one "Oskar," a renegade Jew. However, soon after they killed him for unknown reasons. The streets of Lwów were not renamed.

95. Cf. note 94. Some names were underlined in the original memo, apparently because they were preferred or accepted. In all probability this curious project was carried out since some of the street names have been recorded in Ringelblum's diaries in September 1941 (p. 168). These allusions prove how quickly the news traveled from Kielce to Warsaw.

96. The two parts of the Warsaw ghetto were divided by the "Polish Corridor." Both parts were governed by one Judenrat. After the great extermination in the summer of 1942, the ghetto was divided into several separate areas, each fenced in, and without a common administration. The area between Gęsia, Smocza, and Bonifraterska streets was commonly called "The Ghetto," while the small triangle between Twarda, Żelazna, and Prosta (according to other sources, Ceglana) streets was named "The Small Ghetto."

97. Aron Eisenbach, "The Genocide Policy of German Imperialism in the Period of the Crisis on the Eastern Battle Front" (Yiddish), *BFG,* vol. III, no. 3–4 (1950), p. 26; Weichert, pp. 106, 125, 209; Benjamin Orenstein, *Hurbn Otwock, Falenits un Karchev* (The Destruction of Otwock, Falenica, and Karczew) (Regensburg, 1948), p. 25 (including a map of the three ghettos in Otwock); eyewitness records, nos. 678, 691, 1427 in CJHC (on Rzeszów and Przemyśl); eyewitness record of Dr. Abraham Kondracki in CJHC (about Sambor); Josef Gar, *Der umkum fun der yidisher Kovne* (The Destruction of Jewish Kovno) (Munich, 1948), pp. 46–48; Shmerke Kaczerginski, *Hurbn Vilna* (Destruction of Vilna) (New York, 1947); Mark Dworzecki, *Yerushelayim delite in kamf un umkum* (The Jerusalem of Lithuania in Struggle and Destruction) (Paris, 1948); *Dokumenty zbrodni i męczeństwa* (Documents of Crime and Martyrdom) (Cracow, 1946), p. 28; M. Kaufmann, *Hurbn Lettland* (Munich, 1948), pp. 91, 96, 128, 274–76; Nachman Blumental, "Aperçu sur les ghettos en Pologne," *Les Juifs en Europe,* pp. 202–9; Pankiewicz, pp. 90–91; *W trzecią rocznicę,* p. 134; *Gazeta Żydowska,* November 19, 1940 (on Otwock); *Amtsblatt des Gouverneurs des Distrikt Lublin* (February 28, 1942); Polish Underground Report, No. 1638 of February 19, 1942 (about Będzin) in the archives of the Instytut Historji Najnowszej (Institute of Contemporary History) in Warsaw; *The Black Book,* p. 347 (about Grodno); and essay 10 below, "The Destruction of the Jews of Lwów, 1941–1944."

98. The figures in parentheses refer to the statistics of Jewish population at the beginning of the German invasion. Of course, evacuation, deportations, and extermination actions reduced the Jewish population before the ghettoization pogroms. As in all the Eastern occupied territories, the ghettos in Bessarabia and Bucovina were soon superseded by an almost wholesale deportation to Transnistria. Of the 80,000 to 100,000 Bucovinian Jews, only 16,000 were left in Czernowitz (Cernauti) and subsequently confined in a ghetto in the fall of 1941. Ghettos were also established in other places, as for instance, in Kishinev (Chisinau), Balta, Bershad, Mohilev, Sharogrod, and others. See Schechtman, note 41; Matatias Carp, *Transnistria* (Buenos Aires, 1950), pp. 94, 110–13, 196, 231, 277, 278, 286–88, 306, 325 ff.; Jacob Ungar, "Czernovitz" (Yiddish), *Fun Letsn Hurbn,* 4 (1947), 30–41 (with a map of the ghetto); Reitlinger, pp. 222, 232, 402.

99. Shloime Mayer, *Der untergang fun Złoczów* (The Destruction of Złoczów) (Munich, 1947), p. 23 ff.; Gerszon Taffet, *Zagłada Żydów Żółkiewskich* (The Extermination of the Jews of Żółkiew) (Lodz, 1946), p. 16.

100. Doc. NO–5574 in Monneray, *Est,* pp. 177–78.

101. The decrees were issued by the Chief of the SS and Security Police in GG, Krüger, and were dated October 10, 1942, for the districts of Radom, Cracow, and Galicia and October 28, 1942, for the districts of Warsaw and Lublin. *Verordnungsblatt für das General Gouvernement,* No. 94 (1942), pp. 665 and 683.

# 4

# THE FATE OF THE JEWISH BOOK

Jewish books have often shared the persecutions inflicted upon the Jews, the "People of the Book." The first recorded persecution of the Jewish book probably occurred more than two millennia ago, in the time of Antiochus IV, king of Syria. In his zeal to Hellenize the Jews, Antiochus ordered the Torah scrolls to be torn to pieces and set on fire (1 Macc. 1:56). Later, during the destruction of the Second Temple, Torah scrolls and other Hebrew manuscripts were destroyed. The same happened during the Bar Kochba uprising.

In the Middle Ages, the burning of Jewish books often preceded the extermination of Jewish "heretics." In 1242, twenty-four cartloads of talmudic manuscripts were publicly burned in Paris; in 1288 ten Jewish martyrs and their books were burned in Troyes. Jewish books were publicly burned in Spain on various occasions; for example, in 1263, in Barcelona. Christian kings and ecclesiastical authorities in several countries ordered the burning of the Talmud and other Hebrew books. Pope Clement IV issued a bull decreeing the confiscation and destruction of the Talmud. In 1299, Jewish books were destroyed in England; and in 1415, after the famous dispute in Tortosa, Pope Benedict XIII condemned copies of the Talmud. A condemnatory order including the books of the Kabbalah and other Hebrew works was issued by the emperor Maximilian I in 1510. The last large-scale suppression of Jewish books prior to the Nazi period occurred about two hundred years ago. After a disputation between the Jews and the adherents of Jacob Frank, Dembowski, the Catholic bishop of Kamenets Podolski (Ukraine), ordered the confiscation and destruction of all copies of the Talmud in his diocese.

None of the recorded confiscations and destruction of the Jewish book attained the gigantic dimensions of the Nazi campaign, however. In order to appreciate the magnitude of this greatest book pogrom in Jewish history, we must take stock of the Jewish books in public libraries and private collections in Nazi-occupied Europe. Jewish libraries existed in almost every European country before 1939. They were founded and maintained by institutes of higher learning, rabbinical seminaries, educational and research institutes, synagogues, youth organizations, and the like. Jewish bookstores, publishing houses, scholars, bibliophiles, and private families were the proud possessors of large collections or of innumerable small libraries. Valuable collections were also to be found in many non-Jewish municipal, state, university, and ecclesiastical libraries, as well as in the possession of individual Gentiles.

A complete computation of so vast a wealth of printed treasure is patently impossible, but I have made a checklist of Jewish book collections in twenty European countries occupied or controlled by the Nazis, or exposed to Nazi bombing. My calculation included only Jewish and a few large non-Jewish collections like the Rosenthaliana and the Simonsensiana housed in the universities of Amsterdam and Copenhagen. Only libraries containing at least a thousand volumes were included in this survey.

There were 469 such libraries, with a total of more than 3.3 million volumes. The largest collections were in Poland (251 libraries, 1.65 million books), Germany (55 libraries, 422,000 books), the Nazi-occupied sections of the Soviet Union (7; 332,000), France (16; 146,000), Austria (19; 126,000), Hungary (5; 76,000), the Netherlands (17; 74,000), Rumania (25; 69,000), Lithuania (19; 67,000), and Czechoslovakia (8; 58,000). If the numerous small libraries and private collections could be added, the figures would probably total 5 million or more books. It may be assumed that nearly all of the approximately 1.5 million Jewish families comprising the 6 million Jews killed during the Nazi period treasured at least a few books, religious or profane, in Hebrew, Yiddish, or other languages. There is no way of making an accurate estimate of those stupendous cultural losses, however.

The diabolical forms of destruction inflicted by the Nazis were diverse. During the first phase of their domination in 1933–1938, the Nazis were bent on outright destruction of Jewish books, preferably by spectacular autos-da-fé. After they had seized power in January 1933 they initiated a savage campaign calling for the burning of all "non-German books." This included books by liberal, democratic, and leftist authors and, of course, all books written by Jews. The campaign culminated in raucous and barbarous celebrations which drew widespread attention in the free world and evoked severe condemnation in the press (*The New York Times*, June 11, 1933).[1] Hayyim Nahman Bialik articulated his lament in a touching poem entitled "How Does One Fear the Fire?"[2]

The merciless war against the Jewish book entered a new phase in 1938 when several synagogues were wrecked in Munich, Nuremberg, and Dortmund. These hostile acts were the precursors of the ominous Kristallnacht of November 9–10, when one of the worst pogroms in modern history was carried out by SA and SS troops in every part of Germany. In retaliation for the assassination, by Herschel Grynszpan, of Ernst vom Rath, third assistant in the Nazi embassy in Paris, numerous synagogues, with thousands of books, Torah scrolls, and manuscripts, were put to the torch and completely destroyed. Reinhard Heydrich, head of the Reich Security Chief Office, reported at a meeting of German ministers on November 12, 1938 that 101 synagogues had been destroyed by fire, and 76 wrecked. Many more synagogues were seized between November 1938 and September 1939, and were converted into German schools, Hitler youth houses, sport clubs, and the like. Synagogues were bombed and burned in Austria, Sudentenland, and Danzig, too, although these areas had not yet been incorporated into the Reich. A contemporaneous Jewish estimate put the number of destroyed religious edifices as between 413 and 520.

This policy of destruction was continued during World War II. According to an authoritative estimate,[3] there were approximately 1,300 synagogues in Germany at the beginning of 1938. Only a few of this number were still in existence in 1945. It is impossible to speculate on the number of books consigned to a fiery doom. In only a few instances were Jewish religious objects and books salvaged by courageous non-Jewish Germans. The commendable efforts of Cardinal Michael Faulhaber in 1938, on behalf of the Great Synagogue in Munich, are a noteworthy example.

After the outbreak of World War II and the invasion of Poland in September 1939, the German armies embarked upon a wild spree of destruction, mainly of synagogues. German newspapers described these acts of vandalism with utter callousness. The *Krakauer Zeitung* of November 29, 1939, stated: "A few nights ago the synagogue and prayer-house in Tomaszów . . . went up in flames. The fire brigade succeeded in preventing the fire from spreading to neighboring buildings." The

*Litzmannstädter Zeitung* of November 16, 1939, reported: "The synagogue on the Kościuszko Alley went up in flames yesterday morning. The first and third fire brigades prevented the flames from spreading to adjoining buildings." At times, the Nazi correspondents shamelessly vented their joy in reporting the barbarous acts. Thus the destruction of the famous library of the Lublin Yeshiva in 1939 elicited this arrogant statement:

For us it was a matter of special pride to destroy the Talmudic Academy, which was known as the greatest in Poland. . . . We threw the huge talmudic library out of the building and carried the books to the market place, where we set fire to them. The fire lasted twenty hours. The Lublin Jews assembled around and wept bitterly, almost silencing us with their cries. We summoned the military band, and with joyful shouts the soldiers drowned out the sounds of the Jewish cries.[4]

In several Polish cities, notably in Będzin and Poznań, special German *Brenn-Kommandos* (arson squads) were assigned to burn synagogues and Jewish books. Jews attempting to save Torah scrolls or books from the burning buildings were shot or thrown into the flames. Similar brutalities were reported in other countries, especially Holland and France, after their occupation by the Nazis. In the Nazi-occupied Soviet territories, 532 synagogues and 258 other buildings belonging to religious institutions whose denomination is not specified were "burned, looted, destroyed, and desecrated," according to General R. H. Rudenko, chief prosecutor for the U.S.S.R., before the Nuremberg International Military Tribunal.[5] Inasmuch as Jewish religious buildings had long since been nationalized in the Soviet Union proper, the Soviet prosecutor listed only the synagogues destroyed in the former Polish areas of the Soviet Union. The Nazis put the torch not only to Jewish books but also, in a limited degree, to non-Jewish books. The Yiddish poet Abraham Sutzkever asserts that Johannes Pohl, a high German official, ordered the burning of the books in the medical library of the Vilna University Hospital.[6] Other non-Jewish libraries are also known to have been pillaged, but such attacks never attained the force directed against Jewish institutions.

At the same time that the Nazis were engaging in a mass destruction of Jewish books, they inaugurated a policy of saving a small number of rare and precious volumes for commercial and scholarly purposes. Those looted items were offered for sale by agents in various European countries. The well-known Jewish historian Cecil Roth stated in an address in April 1943:

More than once in pre-war days I was offered, through reputable agencies in this country [England], objects of art of German-Jewish provenance, sold by order of the Nazi Government; and in 1939 even the contents of the Jewish Museum in Berlin were hawked about the art world on the instruction of the

Reich Minister of Finance. . . . After the German occupation of Lithuania, new copies of the much-reviled Talmud, from the famous Rom Press in Vilna, were offered for sale in Amsterdam, in return for ready money.

Copies of rare Jewish books and manuscripts were also offered for sale, according to unconfirmed reports, by Nazi agents in Switzerland.

A few "intellectuals" among the Nazi leaders came to realize that the captured Jewish books might serve to found specialized research libraries on the Jewish question. Upon the seizure of the Sudentenland in the autumn of 1938, Alfred Rosenberg, the top Nazi theoretician, requested the Reich commissioner for the Sudeten area, Konrad Henlein, to confiscate all religious and secular Jewish literature. Henlein promptly delegated this undertaking to one of his aides, Dr. Suchy. In November 1938 the chief of the Security Police, Reinhard Heydrich, included with his directives for the Kristallnacht pogroms this injunction: "The archives of the Jewish communities are to be confiscated by the police, so that they will not be destroyed [in the planned anti-Jewish riots]. Important in this respect is the historically valuable material."[7] The following dispatch, sent on November 15, 1938, by local SS and police leaders from Graz, Austria, reveals how Heydrich's orders were observed: "By order of the Security Police the valuable library of the Rabbi [D. Herzog] was placed under the seal of the Gestapo during the night of November 10th, [also] . . . large portions of the archives and the library [of the synagogue] were removed by the Security Police from the burning office building to safe custody." The same line of action is indicated in a letter written by a high SS officer in Munich on March 18, 1939: "The Security Police . . . is designated as the official agency for the processing of the Jewish archives [and books] taken into custody during the *Judenaktion.*"

Alfred Rosenberg, whom Hitler had charged with the Nazi indoctrination of the German people, was given the additional assignment of waging the "ideological and spiritual war against Jews and Judaism." This program included the establishment of a *Hohe Schule* (advanced training institute) of the NSDAP in Frankfurt to study the "ideological enemies of Nazism," particularly the Jews. On January 20, 1940, Hitler authorized Rosenberg to continue preparations for the *Hohe Schule,* and to procure for its library all necessary items from Jewish libraries and collections. Rosenberg was also authorized to set up an adequate staff for the acquisition of Jewish property. Thus the infamous *Einsatzstab Reichsleiter Rosenberg* (Rosenberg task force, hereafter referred to as ERR) was created. The ERR engaged well-trained German librarians familiar with Jewish books, archives, museums, and art collections. Johannes Pohl, author of several viciously anti-Semitic books, was one of the chief collectors for the

ERR. In 1933 he was sent by the Nazis to study in Palestine, and is purported to have attended the Hebrew University until 1936. On March 1, 1941, he became chief of the Hebraica collection in the library of the Institut zur Erforschung der Judenfrage (Institute for the Study of the Jewish Question), founded by Alfred Rosenberg in Frankfurt-am-Main. Another German expert on Judaica, Peter-Heinz Seraphim, compiled a bulky volume on East European Jewry (published in Essen in 1938), with the help of a staff from the Ost Europa Institute in Königsberg. Seraphim made several research trips to Eastern Europe and also visited the YIVO library in Vilna in 1936. Volkmar Eichstädt, another Nazi expert on bibliography, compiled a survey of the literature in German libraries on the Jewish question.[8] The Nazis established the Institut für deutsche Ostarbeit in Cracow, for the occupied Polish areas. Its Jewish department was headed by Dr. Joseph Sommerfeldt, who was conversant with East European Jewish history and bibliography.[9] The Hungarian Nazi, Mihail Kolozvary-Borcza, published a comprehensive bibliography of Jewish literature in Hungary. Also associated with Rosenberg's institute was Wilhelm Grau, a Nazi specialist in Jewish history. He was succeeded in 1942 by Otto Paul; Paul died in 1944 and was succeeded by Klaus Schickert, author of a lengthy volume on the "Jewish Question in Rumania."

The ERR became active without delay. In July 1940 its representatives arranged with the SS and police in France and Belgium for joint examination of the Jewish libraries in those countries. August Schirmer, a former staff member of the anti-Semitic news agency *Der Weltdienst,* became the ERR representative in Amsterdam. Up to March 1, 1942, the ERR had established offices in Paris, Amsterdam, Brussels, Belgrade, Riga, Minsk, Vilna, Kaunas, Dorpat, Liepaja, Bialystok, Kiev, Dniepropetrovsk, Kherson, Simferopol, Kharkov, Rostov, Lodz, Vitebsk, Smolensk, Mohilev, Orel, Stalino, and Krasnodar. According to a postwar estimate by a high United States official, Colonel Seymour J. Pomerenze,[10] the Germans screened and looted, in Eastern Europe alone, 375 archives, 957 libraries, 531 research and educational institutes, and 402 museums. The widespread spoliation of Jewish libraries and collections in France was described and carefully documented by Jacques Sabille.[11] The jurisdiction of the ERR was not limited to Nazi-occupied areas. On March 21, 1942, it was extended to the territory of the whole Reich.

Among the confiscated collections incorporated in Rosenberg's Frankfurt Institute were the libraries of the Berlin Jewish community, of the rabbinical seminary in Breslau, and of the Jewish community and the rabbinical seminary in Vienna. Also seized were the Hebraica and Judaica departments of the Frankfurt Municipal Library, which had survived the bombings of March 1941, and the library of the Collegio Rabbinico in

Rome (part of the loot, approximately 6,600 books, was identified and returned after the war). The report of August Schirmer, ERR leader in the Netherlands, reveals the enormous extent of the confiscations in that area. The libraries and archives of various Masonic lodges were packed in 470 cases and transferred to Germany. The libraries of the Societas Spinoziana in The Hague and the Spinoza Home in Rijnburg were packed in eighteen cases, and the libraries of the publishing houses Querido, Pegazus, Fischer-Berman, and others, in seventeen cases. The library of the International Institute of Social History in Amsterdam (staffed mainly by refugee Jewish scholars from Germany) was packed in 776 cases. Also "acquired" in Amsterdam were the libraries of Beth Hamidrash Etz Hayim (4,000 volumes), the Israelitic seminary (6,300 volumes), the Portuguese Israelitic seminary (25,000 volumes, and 600 incunabula), and the Rosenthaliana (25,000 catalogued books, but actually, according to Schirmer, 100,000 volumes and 300 manuscripts). An ERR group headed by Dr. Pohl went to Salonika in 1941. After sealing off the collections of various yeshivas, they proceeded to Volo to seize the library of Rabbi Moshe Pessah. Most of the Greek loot was never transferred to Germany, however, probably for lack of adequate transportation facilities.

Vilna, with its famous Jewish libraries, became an important hunting ground for the Nazi "book lovers." The Germans began in August 1941 with the Strashun library. Two Gestapo prisoners—Noah Prylucki, the great Jewish scholar, Yiddish philologist, and civic leader; and A. Y. Goldschmidt, writer and librarian of the Historic-Ethnographic Society—were conscripted for the task. Strashun, grandson of the founder of the library, committed suicide when ordered to assist in the cataloguing project.

In January 1942 Pohl arrived in Vilna, accompanied by four assistants: Dr. Miller, Dr. Wulf, Sparkett, and Gimpel. Pohl ordered all the important Jewish book collections to be concentrated in the YIVO building at 18 Wiwulski Street. He demanded twenty workers from the Judenrat of Vilna, five of them experts on Judaica, for the task of selecting, cataloguing, and shipping the books. The number of Jewish workers in this ERR enterprise was later increased to about forty. They included the great scholar and executive member of the YIVO, Zelig Kalmanovitch;[12] the writer and civic leader Herman Kruk;[13] the poets Abraham Sutzkever[14] and Shmerke Kaczerginski;[15] and the teacher Rachel Pupko-Kryński.[16] New books arrived from Kovno, Shavli, Mariampol, Volozhyn, and many other localities. Books were also assembled from at least three hundred synagogues and from various private collections. During his short stay, Pohl made the first selection of books suitable for transport to Germany. Out of 100,000 books he selected 20,000 for shipping, and ordered the rest to be sold for pulp to a paper mill, for 19 reichsmarks per ton of paper. He disposed of the copper plates of the famous Rom publishing house in a similar commercial deal. Pohl's assistants were even more unscrupulous in their transactions. One of them, Sparkett, dumped five cases of rare books and manuscripts from a transport prepared for shipment to Berlin—in order to make room for a black-market shipment of hogs.

The Jewish employees of the ERR, some of them connected with the Vilna underground, tried to save as many manuscripts and books as possible. Risking their lives, they concealed the most valuable items and smuggled them, one by one, out of the closely watched YIVO building. Many of the salvaged cultural treasures were buried in safe hideouts in the ghetto. After the war some were restored to the Jewish museum in Vilna, and others were sent to Jewish institutions the world over.

Many libraries were destroyed and looted in Kovno, too. Soon after the German invasion, the books of the famous Mapu Library were publicly burned. The ceremony was witnessed by high German officials, while a military band played and storm troopers danced around the fire. The vandalism of those early days, however, gave way to a lucrative business pattern. Dr. Gotthardt, aided by Giselher Wirsing and other experts, took charge of the ERR in Kovno and proclaimed a Jewish "book action" in February 1942. The most valuable books were transported to Germany, and the remainder was turned over for pulp to a paper mill.

These exploits did not sate the avarice of the ERR. In May 1941 Wilhelm Grau suggested in a memorandum to Alfred Rosenberg that the ERR's activities ought to be extended to Spain, Italy, Rumania, Hungary, and Slovakia. Three years later, after Hungary had come under the heel of the Nazis, Dr. Gerhard Utikal, ERR chief of staff and author of the slanderous *Der jüdische Ritualmord,* dispatched a special unit (Sonderkommando), headed by Dr. Zeiss, to confiscate Jewish books, archives, and art treasures in Hungary. The Jewish libraries suffered not only from these roving pillagers but also from domestic Hungarian Nazi rogues and from periodic bombing. The Nazi-sponsored Institut zur Erforschung der Judenfrage in Budapest amassed a considerable library from books looted from Transnistria, the Carpathian Ukraine, and Budapest (among them the collection of Jehiel M. Gutman). The institute was bombed during the siege of Budapest, and most of its books were destroyed. The library of the rabbinical seminary was also hit, with a loss of half of its 40,000 volumes. Little was left of the libraries of the synagogues or the *batei-midrashim,* in Budapest or in the country. Among others, the library of the late Rabbi Emanuel Löw in Szeged was confiscated.

In June 1944 Gerhard Utikal sent SS-Standartenführer H. W. Eberling to carry out the seizure of Jewish books in Denmark and in Norway.

The libraries in occupied Poland were hard hit. The great library of the synagogue and of the institute for Jewish studies on Tłómackie Street in Warsaw was carried away to Berlin by a special commando unit headed by the SS-Untersturmführer Professor Paulsen. Other Jewish libraries in Warsaw were removed to Vienna. What remained of the huge library of the Lublin yeshiva after the auto-da-fé of 1939 was catalogued (about 24,000 volumes) and prepared for transportation, together with 10,000 volumes from private collections.[17] Approximately 70 percent of all the libraries (Jewish and non-Jewish) were looted and destroyed. The percentage in Czechoslovakia was somewhat lower—about 50 percent. A considerable portion of the Jewish books from Bohemia and Moravia was concentrated in Theresienstadt, where the Nazis had transferred part of the Berlin research library. In addition, a "central ghetto library" was established for residents of the ghetto. At least 200,000 Jewish books in Hebrew, Yiddish, and other languages were assembled for this purpose. Both collections survived the end of World War II.

Another sizable collection was established in Poznań (Posen), where the Germans founded a chair for Jewish history and languages. Some 400,000 books were confiscated from various Jewish libraries for this venture. The hastily gathered books were deposited in temporary storages— in churches, in damaged and abandoned buildings, and the like. Unfortunately, only a fraction of these carelessly scattered treasures could be recovered after World War II. Other Nazi institutions were also equipped with looted Jewish books, notably the Jewish department of the Reichsinstitut für Geschichte des Neuen Deutschland (Reich Institute for the History of the New Germany) in Munich. (Later, after the books had been recovered from the institute and restored to the library of the Central Committee of the Liberated Jews in Germany, I saw in Munich part of the library of Professor Moses Schorr of Warsaw.)

When the ERR selected books for shipment to Germany, the rejected books were usually destroyed on the spot. The following directives were issued, in February 1943, by Dr. Cruse, of the section for acquisition and examination: Books in Hebrew script (Hebrew or Yiddish) of recent date, later than the year 1800, may be turned to pulp; this applies also to prayer books, *Memorbücher,* and other religious works in the German language. On the other hand, all writings which deal with the history, culture, and nature of Judaism, as well as books written by Jewish authors in languages other than Hebrew and Yiddish, must be shipped to Frankfurt.

The Frankfurt institute apparently had no interest in acquiring Torah scrolls. One ERR official suggested: "Perhaps the leather can be put to use for bookbinding." Many scrolls were in fact used in Nazi-occupied areas for binding books and for manufacturing shoes, pocketbooks, belts, and other leather products.

The coveted goal of establishing a great Judaic library for the Frankfurt institute was nearing achievement. A comprehensive report stated that, as of April 1, 1943, more than a half-million valuable Jewish volumes had already been assembled there, and many additional thousands were awaiting transportation from various points.

A serious competitor of the ERR in the collection of books was the Reich Security Main Office in Berlin. Its first chief was the notorious Franz Alfred Six. Prolific writer, SS-Obergruppenführer, and head of the department of foreign studies in the University of Berlin, Six had been in charge of one of the murderous Einsatzgruppen (Nazi extermination squads) in Eastern Europe in 1941. SS-Sturmführer Dr. Günther was head librarian, and Dr. Kellner, a defrocked priest, controlled the Jewish collection. The library "collected" more than 2 million books in the fields of religion, Marxism, Freemasonry, and Jewish studies. In the fall of 1941, the Reich Security Office ordered the Reichsvereinigung der Juden in Deutschland (Association of Jews in Germany) to produce eight scholars qualified to deal with the Jewish books. Headed by Dr. Ernst Grumach, this staff was eventually increased to twenty-five (all of whom survived). When the evacuation of Berlin was ordered in August 1944, many of the books were transported to castles in Czechoslovakia; some 60,000 Hebrew and Yiddish books were sent to Theresienstadt. Here a group of Jewish ghetto inmates, led by Dr. Benjamin Murmelstein, the *Judenältester* of the ghetto, was put in charge of cataloguing the collection. The principal contents of the Security Office library, however, including the library of the Hochschule für Wissenschaft des Judentums (Berlin), and collections brought from Vienna and Warsaw, were left behind in Berlin and were largely destroyed by bombings.

After Germany's defeat in the spring of 1945, the Jewish collection at Frankfurt passed into the custody of the American authorities. A great cache of books, manuscripts, and art treasures (about 100,000 items) was subsequently discovered in a cave near Hungen, thirty-two miles from Frankfurt. The Rothschild library in Frankfurt was designated by the United States Army as the assembling point for Jewish cultural treasures recovered in the U.S. Zone of Occupation. Up to November 1946, 2.3 million volumes were assembled in Frankfurt. This massive gathering contained approximately 400 collections from Poland, a like number from Lithuania, 582 from Germany, 141 from Latvia, 50 from Austria, 15 from Czechoslovakia, and smaller numbers from other countries. Eventually the collections were transferred to a large depot in Offenbach, where they were processed and returned to their legitimate owners. Since a number of institutions had gone out of existence, and many former owners were no longer alive, the ownerless property was distributed, by the Jewish Cultural Reconstruction Inc. of New York, headed by Salo W. Baron, to Jewish libraries and other institutions the world over.

Semiofficial libraries and the private collections of German scholars and experts on the Jewish question had also been equipped with Jewish books. For instance, Julius Streicher, the infamous editor of *Der Stürmer,* acquired several thousand Hebrew books from every part of Europe and employed a Hebraist of little competence to organize the library and indicate the importance of each book. The retributive pattern of history seems to have been vindicated by the ironic fate that overtook Streicher. After the liberation his villa, together with his farm and its valuable experimental agricultural equipment, was assigned by the U.S. military authorities to the members of Kibbutz Nili (an acronym for the Hebrew verse *netzah Yisrael lo yeshaker,* "the Glory of Israel does not deceive" [1 Sam. 15:29])— youthful survivors of the Nazi Holocaust who were preparing for settlement on the land in Israel. Thus the treasures collected by the rapacious and ruthless *Judenfresser* eventually came to serve a noble purpose, the training of his victims for emigration to Israel. This presage of a brighter tomorrow is a happy augury for the "People of the Book." It cannot obliterate the tragic past, but it will surely inspire a deeper rededication by the whole Jewish people to the spiritual and intellectual tasks that must be woven into the fabric of the Jewish future.

❧ This essay was first published in *Jewish Book Annual,* 15 (1957/ 1958), 3–13. It was reprinted in Philip Goodman, comp., *Essays on Jewish Booklore* (New York: Jewish Book Council of America, 1971), pp. 112–22.

## Notes

1. *New York Times,* June 11, 1933.
2. "Ekha eyra et ha-esh" (Hebrew), in *Kol kitve H. N. Bialik* (Collected Writings of H. N. Bialik) (Tel Aviv, 1947), p. 379.
3. *Former Jewish Communal Property in Germany* (New York, 1947).
4. *Frankfurter Zeitung,* March 28, 1941.
5. *IMT,* VII, 189.
6. Abraham Sutzkever, *Vilner Geto* (Paris, 1945).
7. *IMT,* XXXI, 515–19, PS–3051.
8. *Forschungen zur Judenfrage,* 6 (1941), 253–64.
9. See his article on Jewish historiography in Eastern Europe published in the quarterly, *Die Burg* (Cracow, 1940).
10. " 'Operation Offenbach.' The Rescue of Jewish Cultural Treasures Robbed by the Germans" (Yiddish), *YB,* 29 (1947), 282–85.
11. Jacques Sabille, *Le Pillage par les Allemands des oeuvres d'art et des bibliothèques* (Paris, 1947).

12. Kalmanovitch describes his ERR work in his diary, posthumously published in *YA*, 8 (1953), 9–81.

13. Kruk, "Diary of the Vilna Ghetto," *YA*, 13 (1965), 9–78.

14. As in note 6.

15. Shmerke Kaczerginski, *Partizaner geyen* (Partisans on the Move) (Buenos Aires, 1947). Mentions his work in ERR in the Vilna ghetto.

16. "My Work in the Yivo under Nazi Supervision" (Yiddish), *YB*, 30 (1947), 214–22.

17. *Nowy Czas*, Vol. 5, No. 81, July 14, 1943.

# 5

# ASPECTS OF THE JEWISH COMMUNAL CRISIS IN GERMANY, AUSTRIA, AND CZECHOSLOVAKIA DURING THE NAZI PERIOD

In his paper "Aspects of the Jewish Communal Crisis in 1848," Salo Wittmayer Baron thus epitomizes the effects of that crisis:[1]

1. Decline in membership and in revenue of the Jewish communities.
2. Undermining of communal control and weakening of communal authority.
3. Growing indifference of several peripheral groups to the Jewish community, leading to aloofness, desertion, and even hostility.
4. Democratization of communal leadership.
5. Rapprochement between Jews and non-Jews, increased good will and fraternization leading to intermarriage and assimilation.
6. Intensification of the issue of religious reform.
7. Acceleration of free Jewish migratory movements.
8. Reorganization and regeneration of Jewish communal life.

Almost a hundred years later, under the Nazi regime, another communal crisis affected Jewish life, with effects diametrically opposed to those in the period of the "Spring of Nations." The results of the communal crisis of the Nazi era can be described as follows:

1. Increased membership in the Jewish community, brought about by a forced concentration, in ghettos of all Jews—or rather all persons, converts included, considered by the Nazis to be "racial Jews."

2. Immensely enhanced communal control and authority, with the power to decide even over individual life and death.

3. Instead of centrifugal tendencies, a strong centripetal trend, imposed from outside on the diffuse and previously scattered Jewish residents; even totally estranged elements were prompted, despite themselves, to participate actively in the social and cultural life of the ghetto.

4. Instead of democratization, an entirely undemocratic communal leadership, developing in many cases into outright tyranny and dictatorship.

5. Instead of rapprochement, strict isolation of Jewish life from the outer world.

6. Instead of religious reform, the prime issues in the community were primordial: survival, food, and shelter; self-defense against cold, disease, physical force, and brutality.

7. Instead of free migratory movements, repeated forced deportations and expulsions and forced or voluntary introduction of destitute expellees, deportees, and refugees into the crowded ghettos.

8. Finally and tragically, instead of regeneration and reorganization, disintegration and extermination.

In this essay only certain aspects of these tragic developments may be traced. I have had to limit my research to a few areas of Central Europe; namely, to Germany, the Protectorate Bohemia-Moravia, and Austria, where the Nazi regime began its attack on the Jewish community even before the outbreak of World War II. The experience gathered by the Nazis in these areas probably became the pattern for their later policy in the occupied countries of Western and Eastern Europe, and also had an impact on the situation of the Jewish communities in the Axis and satellite countries.

The first Jewish communities to be affected by the Nazi seizure of power were those in Germany. In 1933, the first year of the Nazi regime, there were 1,611 Jewish communities in Germany. By October 1938 these had been reduced, by emigration and persecution, to 1,208.[2]

In the period of the Weimar Republic the Jewish communities of some of the seventeen member republics of the Reich were united into state associations (*Landesverbände* or *Landesversammlungen*). As late as 1928 a "working committee" of the Jewish state associations in the German Empire was established. With the Nazi seizure of power, and the "urgent needs" of that situation, a permanent body, the Reichsvertretung der jüdischen Landesverbände Deutschlands (National Representation of Jewish German State Associations), was created in the summer of 1933. This body was succeeded, in September 1933, by the Reichsvertretung der deutschen Juden (National Representation of German Jews), which was later renamed, under Nazi pressure, the Reichsvertretung der Juden in Deutschland (National Representation of Jews in Germany).

The Reichsvertretung was not a mere continuation of the former working committee of the state associations. It was based on a broader representation of the various Jewish organizations in Germany—the Zionist organizations, Orthodox Jewish organizations, the Centralverein, the Council of Jewish Women, the National Council of the Jewish youth organizations, the Landesverbände, and the larger Jewish communities.[3]

Curiously enough, the new Nazi rulers, who pelted the Jewish community with a veritable hailstorm of humiliating, restricting, and discriminatory decrees, did not concern themselves at first with this field of inner Jewish life. In his survey of Nazi anti-Jewish legislation, Bruno Blau listed no fewer than 132 anti-Jewish laws and decrees between April 1933 and March 1938, when the first Nazi law concerning the Jewish communities per se was promulgated.[4] The "Gesetz über die Reichsverhältnisse der jüdischen Kultusvereinigungen" of March 28, 1938 (*RGBL,* I, 338), divested the Jewish communities and associations of their position as public bodies, and deprived their employees of the status of public employees. A second decree, of March 29, 1938, denied the Jewish communities the privilege of property tax exemptions.[5]

Neither the law of March 28, 1938, nor the supplement issued the next day defined the responsibilities and activities of the Jewish community, however. Nor did the law actually mention the de facto existence of the Reichsvertretung, which continued to operate as a central agency for Jewish welfare, religious, and cultural activities. Yet new and onerous responsibilities were imposed, de facto, upon the Jewish communal bodies and their organizational superstructure, the Reichsvertretung.

At first the executive members of the Reichsvertretung[6] had a rather too optimistic vision of its legal and political possibilities. As early as the summer of 1933, the Reichsvertretung der jüdischen Landesverbände published a statement against "placing the blame for any system" on the Jews (the Nazis had accused the Jews of supporting the democratic Weimar Republic, or the so-called *Systemzeit*). In the same statement, the Reichsvertretung asked for "dignity, work, freedom," a free dialogue on the "basis of justice, legality, and honesty." In the summer of 1934 the Reichsvertretung intervened with the Reichsminister of internal affairs against the ritual slander campaign of *Der Stürmer*. After the promulgation of the Nuremberg Racial Laws in 1935, the Reichsvertretung again protested, asking that an end be made to the defamation and economic boycott of the Jews.[7]

The next years of the Nazi regime prompted the Reichsvertretung to view its naïve hopes and meager abilities more realistically. The program of the Reichsvertretung was now directed to meeting the desperate needs of the hour—to hastening Jewish emigration from Germany and facilitating it by means of vocational training and assistance to emigrants, to supporting the increasing number of people ruined by restrictions and persecutions, and to meeting the educational and religious needs of the Jewish population.[8] This program of activities is clearly reflected in the budget of the Reichsvertretung for 1937, the last normal budgetary year before the vicissitudes of the year 1938. The requirements for 1937 amounted to 4,054,000 reichsmarks. Significantly enough, the once-rich Jewish community in Germany was able to meet only one-third of its budget itself; only 1,591,000 RM were drawn from internal income sources, while 2,463,000 RM were contributed from abroad, chiefly by the American Jewish Joint Distribution Committee. Of this total, 1,415,000 RM were spent on economic assistance, 1,150,000 on emigration, 719,000 on education, 447,000 on social welfare, and only minor sums on other communal needs and administration. The number of Jewish schools supported by the Reichsvertretung was 135 in 1935 and 160 in 1936. In 1936, 22,000 Jewish children received their education in these schools, 18,000 of them on the primary level, 4,000 on the secondary.[9]

The leadership of German Jewry must have realized the fruitlessness of negotiating with the Nazi government to protect Jewish life and the rights of Jews. In the words of one German Jewish leader:

The leaders of the Reichsvertretung could [not] have cherished any illusions in the long run. They realized more clearly and quickly than the Jewish masses the impossibility of negotiating anything with this [Nazi] government. . . . Of course, attempts were made to temper the impact of the onslaught against the Jews, and some results may have been achieved in several individual cases . . . for example, the comparatively undisturbed . . . autonomy of the internal Jewish life, at least until 1938. They succeeded in getting permission for the transfer of money—thus facilitating emigration to Palestine—and in getting allowances for children who were sent abroad for education.[10]

In reaction against increased restrictions and persecution, Jewish emigration from Germany increased, several communities were dissolved, and the economic and moral strength of the remaining communities was seriously affected. This rapid disintegration cast a gloom, discernible in the Reichsvertretung's New Year's message to the German Jews in 1937: "The process of disintegration of German Jewry is going on. Many are now facing the problem of their emigration, and many others have to follow." There is also sadness but no despair in the message issued on the eve of the Jewish High Holydays in 1938: "Heavier than in previous years has been the burden of [recent] events. Nobody in our midst has been spared. . . . But we Jews are a kind of people who know where hope lies. Our perseverance is our force. We must keep alive in our hearts our faith, the faith of our Jewishness."[11]

Events that followed this wistful New Year's message surpassed the most pessimistic forebodings. After the Kristallnacht of November 9–10, 1938, a collective fine of 1 billion reichsmarks was imposed on the German Jews, and a new series of anti-Jewish decrees was promulgated.[12]

With these events, which definitely marked the transition from a Nazi cold war against the Jews into a hot war, a rearrangement of the status of the central Jewish communal body was in order. As a matter of fact, the Reichsvertretung as a democratic representative body did not fit well into the fabric of the Nazi Reich. In the totalitarian Nazi state the *Führer-prinzip* had to be applied to the Jewish community as well. By the "Tenth Decree supplementing the Reich Law on Citizenship," of July 4, 1939 (*RGBL,* I, 1097 f.), an association (Reichsvereinigung) of Jews in Germany was organized, with its main office in Berlin and local branches (communities) throughout the Reich. The chief function of the new Reichsvereinigung was defined as being "to further emigration." Additional functions were maintaining schools for Jewish children (all these schools were considered private schools) and furnishing relief for Jews. Membership in the Reichsvereinigung was compulsory for all "racial" Jews residing in the Reich, both German subjects and stateless Jews, and optional for foreign Jews and Jews married to "Aryans." Contrary to the constitution of the Reichsvertretung, the laws and by-laws of the Reichsvereinigung provided no regulations about a general assembly or the protection of the rights of the constituency to check the activities of the organization. The executive board of the Reichsvereinigung therefore owed no responsibility to the members.[13]

The institution of the Reichsvereinigung was considered by the Nazis an important step toward the liquidation of German Jewry. The official party organ, *Völkischer Beobachter,* found it appropriate to comment on this event on its front page, on July 7, 1939, in the following words:

The tenth supplementary decree to the Reich Citizen Law carries forward the solution of the Jewish question in a decisive manner. . . . Its paragraphs have but one meaning and they do not allow the slightest doubt as to the national-socialist point of view, that the Jewish problem will be considered as a definitely solved question when there will be no more Jews in Germany. . . . The most important thing is to get rid of them, all and sundry, and that as quickly as possible.[14]

The new Reichsvereinigung replaced the former Reichsvertretung, whose assets were automatically transferred to it. The executive board of the new association was partially drawn from the former executive members of the Reichsvertretung. Rabbi Leo Baeck was again appointed chairman. The other members were as follows: vice chairman, Heinrich Stahl;

managing executive director, Otto Hirsch; and members, Dr. Paul Eppstein, Moritz Henschel, Philip Kozower, Dr. Arthur Lilienthal, and Dr. Julius L. Seligsohn.[15]

In the beginning of 1940 the Reichsvereinigung still had 142 primary and secondary Jewish schools under its supervision, as well as a number of vocational and preparatory courses. There were then more than 15,000 Jewish children under the age of fifteen in Germany, and 300–400 teachers were employed in their education. The Reichsvereinigung also operated 90 homes for the aged, 26 children's houses, 14 Jewish hospitals, 16 residential homes for boys and girls, 6 homes for the sick and invalid, and 2 special homes. Early in 1942 the Jewish community in Berlin was still operating 17 soup kitchens for the poor.[16]

The Reichsvereinigung issued its official weekly *Jüdisches Nachrichtenblatt,* the only Jewish periodical left after the storm of 1938. The paper, edited by Leo Kreindler, and renamed *Mitteilungsblatt* in 1941, ceased publication in 1943. Contrary to administrative practice in the Nazi-occupied countries, no Jewish police force was created in Germany with the Reichsvereinigung. Only in December 1942 was an auxiliary Jewish force (*Ordnertrupp*) established to help the Germans in searching thoroughly (*Durchkämmung*) Jewish homes for deportation.[17]

The positive role of the Reichsvereinigung was very limited, and was gradually reduced. Eventually the Reichsvereinigung served the Reich Security Office—the central agency of the SS and police—as an instrument to control the Jewish population, enforce emigration, and exact the heavy taxes imposed upon the Jews (particularly the onerous emigration tax, amounting to 10–60 percent of total assets). In the final stage of Jewish history in Germany, the Reichsvereinigung was forced to assist anti-Jewish authorities in the liquidation of German Jewry. The majority of Jewish leaders believed that, by assisting the Nazis, they would save not only their own lives but also some of their coreligionists.[18] This assumption proved to be entirely wrong. Of the 318,200 persons in Germany classified as Jews according to the Nuremberg laws in 1939, only 31,807 were left by April 1, 1943. Of these, only 14,000 were *Volljuden*; the rest were *Mischlinge* of various gradations.

In February 1940 the first deportations to the "Lublin reservation" started. Later there followed transports to France (particularly to the Gurs concentration camp); to Lodz, Warsaw, Lublin, Riga, and Minsk; and to the concentration camps of Theresienstadt and Auschwitz. (Only a few thousand individuals managed to survive and return after the war.[19]) The activities of the Reichsvereinigung were gradually narrowed. On June 20, 1942, the Reichsminister for internal affairs ordered the Reichsvereinigung to close all Jewish schools in Germany, "in light of the recent development in the deportation of the Jews."[20]

Both the executive board and the employees of the Reichsvereinigung shared the fate of their coreligionists. Their official capacity, far from protecting them, seems, on the contrary, to have exposed them to the Nazis. As early as December 1940, Seligsohn was arrested, allegedly because he suggested the observance of a fast day on behalf of the deported Jews of Baden. After several months in jail, he was sent to the Sachsenhausen concentration camp, where he died in 1942. Dr. Otto Hirsch, arrested in the spring of 1941, was sent to the Mauthausen concentration camp, where he was immediately killed. Dr. Conrad Cohn, head of the relief department, was arrested in the summer of 1941 and sent to Mauthausen, where he died. In June 1942, a number of employees of the Reichsvereinigung, among them Dr. Arthur Lilienthal, Dr. Cora Berliner (head of the emigration department), Ilse Cohn and Paula Fuerst (both of the education department), were deported somewhere to the east, probably to some place near Bialystok, and never came back. Heinrich Stahl (in summer 1942), Dr. Paul Eppstein (in February 1943), Moritz Henschel, Philip Kozower, Martin Gerson, and Dr. Leo Baeck were deported to Theresienstadt. Of them all, only Henschel and Baeck survived.[21]

On October 20, 1942, large numbers of officials of the Reichsvereinigung and of the Jewish community in Berlin (according to some accounts, about 600 persons) were designated for deportation. Some of them failed to report, however, while others committed suicide. Enraged by this "lack of discipline," the Nazis arrested four leading officials of the Berlin Jewish community and four of the Reichsvereinigung and executed them on December 2.[22] Leo Baeck, chairman of the Reichsvereinigung, was arrested five times, and was eventually deported to Theresienstadt, on January 27, 1943. Dr. Max Wiener, a colleague of Leo Baeck, observed of his work during the Nazi years: "No historian will ever be able to do justice to the fearlessness, outstanding humanity, and dignity with which Baeck on many an occasion moderated and delayed measures of persecution. His efforts gained precious time during which many individuals were enabled to reach havens of refuge."[23] As a matter of fact, during the Nazi period Leo Baeck received many invitations to leave Germany (including a call to the Rockdale Temple in Cincinnati), but turned them all down, insisting that it was his duty to stay with German Jewry to the end. Until 1939, he accompanied transports of Jewish children from Germany to England, but always returned. In an interview with Erich Boehm after the war, Baeck said of the leaders of the Reichsvereinigung: "[They] applied themselves tirelessly and selflessly to their difficult tasks, often turning down opportunities for emigration because of their duty. . . . Persons in such exposed positions were of course arrested often and on the slightest pretext." About the sore problem of cooperation with the Germans in preparing the deportations, Baeck observed:

I made it a principle to accept no appointments from the Nazis and to do nothing which might help them. But later, when the question arose, whether Jewish orderlies should help pick up Jews for deportation, I took the position that it would be better for them to do it, because they could at least be more gentle and helpful than the Gestapo and make the ordeal easier. It was scarcely in our power to oppose the order effectively.[24]

Actually, by the spring of 1943 almost all the leaders of the Reichsvereinigung and the Berlin Jewish community had been arrested, deported, or executed, and only a small skeleton organization was left, under Dr. Walter Lustig, to take care of the survivors—Jews in mixed marriages and their children.[25] The Reichsvereinigung ceased to function early in March 1943. On June 10, 1943, the assets of the Reichsvereinigung and of the affiliated Jewish communities and organizations were confiscated and transferred to the office of the Oberfinanzpräsident Berlin-Brandenburg. The inventories made on this occasion showed an assessed property value of the Reichsvereinigung and its affiliated branches throughout the country of 144 million reichsmarks and of the property of the Berlin Jewish community of over 22.5 million reichsmarks.[26]

The short history of the Jewish community of Austria under the Nazi regime was one of rapid decline. When the Nazis marched into Vienna on March 12, 1938, there were approximately 185,000 Jews in Austria, 170,000 of them in Vienna, the rest in Graz, Linz, Mödling, Baden, Wiener-Neustadt, Krems, Innsbruck, and some towns in Burgenland. As early as March 26, 1938, Hermann Göring announced at a mass meeting that Vienna must be free of Jews within four years. Under terrible Nazi pressure, the exodus of the Jewish population was of necessity very rapid. Between March 1938 and November 1941, about 128,000 Jews voluntarily left Austria. This emigration overlapped the deportation of Austrian Jews to the east, begun by the Nazis as early as October 1939. Both movements contributed to a rapid depopulation. By December 1939, only 55,000 Jews remained in Austria; in the first months of 1942, 30,000; at the end of that year, according to a Jewish source, 12,000 to 15,000 (according to official Nazi statistics, only 8,102). In June 1944, no more than a thousand Jews were reported to remain.[27]

The Nazis, whose plans for wholesale Jewish emigration from Austria were executed at such a formidable rate, did not bother to rearrange Jewish community life there according to the patterns already developed in Germany.

The community even retained its traditional name, Israelitische Kultusgemeinde, until December 1942, when the Jewish religious community was dissolved and its functions transferred to a council of elders (Ältestenrat).[28] Since the smaller Jewish communities had practically ceased to exist soon after the *Anschluss,* all Jewish communal life was concentrated in Vienna. Even after incorporation into the Reich, the Jewish community of Vienna was not affiliated with the Reich association of German Jews. At that time the Jewish community council of Vienna was ruled by a Zionist majority, with the well-known Zionist leaders Dr. Desider Friedmann as chairman and Robert Stricker as vice chairman.[29]

Soon after the Nazis entered Vienna, they sent the chairman of the Jewish community and several of its members to the Dachau concentration camp, allegedly because the community council had failed to collect the subscription of 800,000 schillings demanded by the Nazis. Not until February 1940 was Dr. Friedmann released from the concentration camp, and the required amount remitted. From the beginning the new authorities required the Jewish community to cooperate actively in the "resettlement" of the Jews in the east. The lists of eligible persons, the circular letters, the arrangements for assembly points, had to be prepared by the Jewish community. At that time the community itself employed about 375 persons, approximately twenty-five of them in the welfare department. The number of employees in the welfare department soon had to be increased to 100.[30] In 1942, between June and October, thirteen transports of about 14,000 Viennese Jews were directed to Theresienstadt. Among the deported were these leaders of the Jewish community: Desider Friedmann, Robert Stricker, Dr. Joseph Löwenherz (director of the community), and his deputy, Dr. Benjamin (Bernard) Murmelstein.[31] Of them, only Löwenherz and Murmelstein survived. In Vienna, a skeleton staff of 180 persons was still operating, headed by Dr. Löwenherz, who apparently came back from Theresienstadt; Dr. Tuchman; and two other members of the former executive board, Ernst Felberg and Weiger. In March 1943, Adolf Eichmann wanted to deport this poor remnant as well, but his order was rescinded through the intervention of the deputy commander of the Security Police in Vienna, Dr. Adolf Ebner, who asked that this group be spared in order to look after the interests of some 6,000 Jews in mixed marriages, and their children.[32]

On March 15, 1939, the German troops crossed the Czechoslovak borders. The president of Czechoslovakia was forced to sign an agreement creating the so-called Protectorate of Bohemia and Moravia. Statistics compiled by the Nazis showed, as of March 15, 1939, 118,310 "racial" Jews in the Protectorate, among them 14,350 persons of "other than Jewish faith." Emigration continued in the first month after the invasion, reducing the total to 90,147 professing Jews by October 1, 1939.[33] The Jewish communities of Bohemia-Moravia were in a state of confusion and depression. They were immediately placed under the supervision of the Gestapo, with its rule of terror and oppression. German policy toward the Jews was the same here as in Austria—that is, to promote Jewish emigration. For this purpose, the Zentralstelle für jüdische Auswanderung (Central Office for Jewish Emigration) had been organized in Vienna in April 1938; it was headed by a former Gestapo spy in Austria, Adolf Eichmann. After the annexation of Czechoslovakia, Eichmann, who had by then been promoted to the rank of SS-Hauptsturmführer, also established an office in Prague. The SS-Hauptsturmführer (later Sturmbannführer) Rolf Günther, nicknamed "the smiling hangman," served as Eichmann's second in command.[34]

The Prague office was later renamed the Zentralamt für die Regelung der Judenfrage in Böhmen und Mähren. By a decree of March 5, 1940, the Reich protector for Bohemia and Moravia granted "the Central Office" supervisory power over all Jewish communities and all Jews in Bohemia-Moravia, including those of "non-Mosaic faith." The functions of the Jewish communities were described in this decree and several subsequent ordinances as follows: (1) to collect fees imposed upon Jews; (2) to provide relief for poor Jews; (3) to collect statistical data about Jews; (4) to foster Jewish emigration; (5) to assemble persons for forced labor and for evacuation.[35] Thus, in the Protectorate, as in Germany and Austria, the Nazi seizure of power brought radical changes in the basic structure and activities of the Jewish community. Kurt Wehle, one of the surviving leaders of the community, thus epitomized these changes:

The Jewish religious community in Prague was transformed from a large denominational institution into a large autonomous body, with great powers and enlarged responsibilities in fields of activity entirely unknown to them until then; its competence was extended to so-called racial Jews and to the entire area of the Protectorate.[36]

The Germans centralized the Jewish communities by ordering several district communities (*Kreisgemeinden*) to supervise the work of the smaller communities in their respective areas.[37] The Jewish congregations of Greater Prague were united into one central community empowered to issue directives (*Weisungsrecht*) to other communities in the country. Besides this, the registration services of all communities were concentrated in one central registration office in the Prague community.[38] Gradually, with the progressive evacuation of provincial Jewry, the provincial communities disappeared, and the pitiful remnants were taken care of by the branches of the Prague community. Later on, the central community in Prague became, aside from the Ältestenrat in Theresienstadt, the only representative body of the Jews in Bohemia-Moravia. In 1943, the Jüdische Kultusgemeinde Prag was renamed the Ältestenrat (Council of Elders), but its area of competence was not affected.[39] A list for December 1941 shows that the Jewish religious community in Prague had departments for each of the following: the provincial communities; economics, finance, and statistics; the central registration office (*Zentralmatrik*); social welfare; emigration; hospitalization; the chief rabbinate;[40] education; the judiciary; non-Mosaic Jews; housing; publishing of the *Jüdisches Nachrichtenblatt*; and so on.[41] But, as in all other Jewish communities under the Nazi regime, this apparently favorable image of teeming activities was a mere sham. Under constant pressure of German police terror, the community was called upon to cooperate with the Gestapo in matters of emigration, forced labor, deportation, registration of Jewish property, etc. The slightest "lack of discipline" was severely punished. For example, in the fall of 1941, 1,000 Jews were ordered to report for "emigration" to the east. Only 500 reported. Günther's deputy in the Zentralstelle, Karl Rahm, regarded this as an act of sabotage on the part of the Jewish communal leaders. Consequently, he arrested the chiefs of the emigration department, Dr. Hanus Bonn and Dr. (Erich) Kafka, and sent them to the Mauthausen concentration camp. A fortnight later the Jewish community was advised that they had both died in Mauthausen.[42]

In this unequal fight the Jewish leadership tried to use tactics of delay. Kurt Wehle summarized the bitter experience of this period in the following words:

What could the Jewish community do, confronted by the overwhelming enemy? It could only postpone, drag on, soften, sabotage, win concessions in little things, try to protect a part of its assets, such as the historical relics, the museum, etc. But the community could not prevent the Germans from reaching their main objective: the extermination of the Jews. This was the saddest chapter in the history of this ancient Jewish community, and the saddest destiny was to serve as an instrument in enemy hands. . . . Until 1942 the main function of the community was relief and social welfare; after 1943 it was forced to cooperate in the liquidation.[43]

Thus the policy of appeasement, of placating the enemy by partial sacrifices in order to save the rest—so characteristic of the Reichsvereinigung in Germany—was considered to be the most feasible policy by the leaders of Prague's Jewish community as well.

In the hour of mortal danger a kind of political truce came about between the two main camps, the assimilationist Czech Jews' party and the nationalistic Zionists. Significantly, their bipartisan policy was jointly represented by Dr. Frantisek Weidman and Jakub Edelstein. Weidman—a leading personality among the Czech-Jewish patriots, and secretary general of the Prague Jewish community before the outbreak of the war—had been involved in many heated political controversies with the Zionists in the 1930s. In October 1939, he was appointed leader of the community by the

German authorities.[44] Weidman's political opponent but, since the German occupation, close collaborator in communal affairs was Jakub Edelstein, scion of a Polish-Jewish Hasidic family and a Socialist-Zionist.[45] The developments in the first two years of German occupation seemed to justify the appeasement policy. On October 17, 1939, 1,200 young Jews of Moravska-Ostrava and environs were mobilized and sent to occupied Poland in order to prepare a Jewish camp in the neighborhood of Nisko (in the district of Cracow on the river San). Plans for a large-scale deportation of Jews from Czechoslovakia and Austria to the Nisko area were under consideration. Several representatives of the Jewish communities of Prague and Vienna were brought to Nisko, among them Jakub Edelstein and Benjamin Murmelstein, and were ordered to prepare a plan for this settlement. After submitting the project, they were sent home.[46] More transports were sent to Nisko from Vienna, Teschen, Bielsko, and Kattowitz, but none from Prague or other towns of Bohemia-Moravia. Beginning with September 1939, there was talk in the Nazi press about the Lublin reservation. In October 1939, the first transports of Jews left for the Lublin reservation from Vienna and from the Protectorate. But in 1940, while the transports of Jews from Austria and the incorporated Polish provinces to Lublin continued, the transports from the Protectorate were stopped for a number of months. Not until October 1941 did the first five transports leave Prague for Lodz, while another transport, bound for Minsk in White Russia, was suddenly stopped.[47]

There were several reasons for this German policy, but the biographers of Weidman and Edelstein give the credit for this development to the combined efforts of these two community leaders. According to these sources, Weidman and Edelstein persuaded the Germans of the usefulness of distributing the Jewish forced labor squads from Bohemia-Moravia within the borders of the Protectorate.[48] This was considered an important achievement by the Jewish leadership. It proved also to be a remarkable advantage in the negotiations over the ghettoization of Czech Jewry that soon followed. At a meeting of the top Nazi officials in Berlin on October 4, 1941, the establishment of ghettos in Bohemia-Moravia was decided upon.[49] The Jewish community in Prague was ordered to submit a plan to the Zentralstelle. Such a plan was submitted as early as October 9,.1941; it envisaged the ghettoization of the 88,000 Jews of the Protectorate within the borders of Bohemia-Moravia. The initial German plan to build wooden barracks to accommodate all Czech Jews was soon abandoned, after a memorandum of the Jewish community pointed out the extraordinary costs of building the necessary 1,300 barracks (at a cost of 125 million kronen) and the enormous amount of wood and other scarce materials necessary for this purpose. Then a plan emerged to accommodate the Jewish ghetto in one of the existing towns of the Protectorate. It was not easy to find such a place; SS-Hauptsturmführer Günther, in his letter of October 11, 1941, excluded a considerable number of towns. Eventually, Theresienstadt (in Czech, Terezin), a garrison town with an old fortress and military barracks, was suggested to the Jewish communal leaders as the suitable place. The Jewish community tried to fight against this choice. In a memorandum of October 19, 1941, the Jewish community suggested the creation of three Jewish ghettos in the suburbs of Prague, Moravska-Ostrava, and Brno. The memorandum pointed out that Theresienstadt was already overcrowded. These objections were not considered, however.

On November 10, 1941, the Germans ordered the Jewish community to send a group of pioneer workers (342 young men, most of them skilled craftsmen) to Theresienstadt, where they were scheduled to arrive on November 24 and immediately start work as *Aufbaukommando* no. 1 (AK1).[50] Thus the dangerous illusion of the "model ghetto," Theresienstadt, came into being. The pioneer group of AK1 was accompanied by several officials of the Prague community, headed by Jakub Edelstein and engineer Otto Zucker, former head of the Palestine Office in Prague and chairman of the Jewish community in Brünn (Brno, in Moravia). On December 4 a second *Aufbaukommando* of 1,000 men arrived, and the first Ältestenrat was appointed by the SS inspector of the camp. Edelstein was nominated Judenältester, and Zucker was appointed his deputy. They were made responsible for the construction of a ghetto in which, according to German plans, 70,000 Jews were to be housed.[51]

The two leaders of the Ältestenrat were men of different type. While Edelstein liked the limelight, Zucker was retiring and modest. Both, however, were devoted to their work and looked upon it as a way to rescue the Czech Jews from deportation and annihilation. Edelstein was the "soul of the whole," "the father of everything." He invested a tremendous amount of energy, enthusiasm, and travail in the scheme of rebuilding the decrepit and dilapidated houses and barracks into a suitable housing project for many thousands. After all, the small garrison town which in 1940 was barely able to serve as living quarters for 3,500 soldiers and 3,700 civilians had to become the home of all the Czech Jews and many others. Into Thereseinstadt, from November 1941 to May 1945, were brought about 140,000 Jews from the Protectorate, Austria, Germany, Holland, Denmark, and Slovakia. Many stayed for only a few months until further deportation. The average Jewish population at any one time was between 35,000 and 40,000; the peak was reached in September 1942, when the ghetto harbored 53,000 souls. There was not enough housing, not enough building material to add new housing units; there was a dearth of food, of medical and sanitary supplies, of everything. The German SS administration, cruel and brutal, established a full set of regulations and restrictions which continually imposed on the Ältestenrat the onerous task of selecting some individuals for forced labor, others for deportation, and still other "undisciplined" persons for "exemplary execution."

The old conflict between the Zionists and the assimilationists also affected the social life of Theresienstadt. The Zionists were the most influential and active group in the ghetto and had a strong hold on the Ältestenrat. On the other hand, the rank and file of the first transports were rather indifferent, or even hostile, to Zionist ideology. The non-Zionists interpreted the motive of Edelstein and Zucker, in zealously building up and developing the ghetto, as seeking to transform the ghetto into a kind of preparatory training camp, *hakhshara,* for future emigration to Palestine.[52] Besides these two groups there were others, such as the "racial" Jews, persons of Jewish descent who were now members of the Catholic or other Christian churches, who had no feelings of solidarity, through either national or religious bonds, with the ghetto population. For the "racial" Jews, numbering about 9,000 souls in 1943, Theresienstadt was a forced commune, united only by outside compulsion.[53] Another group in the ghetto, of rather little influence, were the Communists.

The young Elder of the Jews, Edelstein, was, according to several eyewitness accounts, a man of forceful personality. He has been described by his ghetto inmates as of ready wit, a clever person, a bit of a demagogue though a modest man, and an able negotiator with the Germans—always ready to outwit them and to help his coreligionists. Though he was rather unpopular at the beginning, he soon learned to win the sympathies of the population. His brief experience in the camp of Nisko in 1939 stood him in good stead for his first steps in the administration of Theresienstadt. But he lost much of his popularity after the Germans delegated to the Ältestenrat the responsibility for selecting those to be deported to the east. Edelstein clearly had the strength of character needed for leadership. In January and February 1942, for example, the German ghetto administration set the death penalty for nine Jews arrested for having attempted to smuggle letters out of the ghetto to relatives still at large. For this offense they had been sentenced to be hanged publicly, and the members and officials of the council of elders had been ordered to watch the execution. Edelstein refused to attend, and submitted his resignation, which was not accepted by the SS command of the ghetto.[54]

The job of administering Theresienstadt was in some ways different from the activities carried on by the Jewish councils of Germany, Austria, and Prague. By an order of the SS of July 1, 1942, the entire non-Jewish population was evacuated from Theresienstadt. From that time on, therefore, the population was entirely Jewish, and a full-fledged territorial administration was assigned to the Ältestenrat. The Ältestenrat thus had to assume the full responsibilities of a normal city council, in addition to its own many special functions. The ghetto had its building and construction department, particularly active after December 1943, when the Germans embarked upon their program of "embellishing" Theresienstadt.

The technical department, the economic department, the department of internal administration (with a legal section, a housing section, a registry, a section for religious services, and a postal service), the labor department, and the health department were also very active. A ghetto police, wearing special armbands and headgear, was established at the very beginning, and numbered approximately 200 persons until its reorganization in September 1942, when its number was considerably increased.[55] To enlarge the illusion of autonomy, the Germans, in April 1942, ordered the issue of a special currency for Theresienstadt by the Bank der jüdischen Selbstverwaltung (Jewish-managed bank). The notes of the bank, utterly worthless and never to be circulated outside the ghetto, bore the effigy of Moses holding the tablets of the law, and were signed by Jakub Edelstein.[56] The Nazis even issued a postage stamp depicting a lovely panorama of Theresienstadt.[57] They did everything to give the impression that Theresienstadt was a ghetto for privileged Jews, for protected prominent personages, and an *Altersghetto* for the aged. In addition to the Czech Jews, after June 1942 many transports of German and Austrian Jews began to pour in: in April 1943, Jews from Holland; in October 1942, from Denmark; in December 1944, from Slovakia. While the transports from other countries never reached the dimensions of the Czech transports (73,608), the German and the Austrian Jews were numerous enough (42,832 and 15,254, respectively) to influence the life of Theresienstadt.

The influx of so many new and varied elements, among them many leading Jewish personalities, necessitated a reshuffling of the ghetto administration. In the period between October 1, 1942, and January 31, 1943, the Ältestenrat was reorganized three times. The first reorganization order, of October 1942, took notice of the population changes and introduced a number of German Jews into the council. Edelstein was reappointed Elder, and Heinrich Stahl, of the Reichsvereinigung der Juden in Deutschland, was named deputy-elder. Six of the former Czech members of the Ältestenrat were retained, and five new members—representing Austrian (Dr. Desider Friedmann and Robert Stricker) and German Jews (Dr. Leopold Neuhaus of Frankfurt-am-Main, Karl Stahl, and Dr. Hermann Strauss)—were added.

By order of Adolf Eichmann on January 27, 1943, the preceding arrangement was superseded by a more centralized body, the "Board of Three" (*Die Leitung*), consisting of Dr. Paul Eppstein (of the Reichsvereinigung), Dr. Löwenherz (of Vienna), and Jakub Edelstein. Eppstein was appointed head of the board; and this, according to Zdenek Lederer, immediately provoked Edelstein to resign his post. His resignation was not accepted, but a reshuffling took place four days later, Löwenherz being replaced by Benjamin Murmelstein. The "Board of Three" had to run the ghetto, with the help of the department chiefs (Ältestenrat), who were also reshuffled, with Austrian and German Jews being assigned to some of the offices.[58] These changes were not ordered with the goal of bringing more cooperation and harmony into the ghetto; on the contrary, the Germans incited the national groups against each other, and tension and competition were increased by the new arrangement.

As a matter of fact, the strains and intrigues preceding the creation of the new trinational board were problem enough to prompt an attempt to set up a kind of military dictatorship in the ghetto. In September 1942, when the ghetto guard was reorganized, an elderly newcomer, Dr. Karl Löwenstein, was appointed commander of the police force. Löwenstein was a colorful personality; in World War I he had been a high-ranking German officer and (according to Lederer) aide-de-camp to the German crown prince. He came to Theresienstadt from Minsk, where he had been deported from Germany. He had direct access to the German headquarters, and this gave him a position rather independent of the Ältestenrat. He organized the four hundred men of his guard along military lines, and received special privileges for them; he then started to organize military parades with his men in the streets of Theresienstadt, and began to interfere with the affairs of the Ältestenrat. Löwenstein's frequent clashes with the ghetto administration, and his growing influence, eventually led to his downfall. German authorities in Berlin were not pleased to learn that a paramilitary formation had been organized in the ghetto. Simultaneously, the Ältestenrat discovered some minor offenses in the conduct of the police commander. Löwenstein was put in prison, and his special guard was disbanded in September 1943.[59]

In the meantime, the members of the ghetto triumvirate were in conflict. The head of the "Board of Three," Eppstein, was considered by some ghetto inmates "the weakest personage among these men. . . . He seemed to lack courage and merely complied with all orders from [SS] Headquarters. . . . Not only was he disliked by most of the prisoners, but his prospects at the hands of the Germans were grim."[60] A former lecturer in sociology at the universities of Bonn and Heidelberg, Eppstein was a

lawyer, philosopher, sociologist, piano virtuoso, and poet, trying to appear as a socialist, a rather poor negotiator, and, in certain inexplicable instances, enormously ambitious. Among the German Jews he had the reputation of being a courageous and energetic man.[61] Why the SS men entrusted the leadership [of the ghetto] to him is inexplicable. He was a wiseacre, wrapped in a strange pretense of sentimentality, an amateur of fantastic paintings, of Debussy, and of atmospheric storms. . . . He did not like the Czechs but concealed his Germanism by [his] Zionism. . . . He was much more unpopular than his predecessor [Edelstein].[62]

Before long, Eppstein's first deputy and former elder of the Jews, Edelstein, fell victim to Nazi suspicion. In November 1943 he was arrested, together with some of his closest coworkers, and indicted for having aided and abetted the escape of fifty-five ghetto inhabitants evading a transport destined for Auschwitz. In December, Edelstein was sent to Auschwitz with his family, and was shot there, on Himmler's order, in June 1944.[63]

The next to be liquidated was Eppstein. After February-March 1944, when the Austrian SS-Hauptsturmführer Karel Rahm (until then in Prague) took over command of the camp, Eppstein's position was undermined. Rahm disliked Germans (*Grossdeutschen*) with the peculiar hatred of a stalwart *Österreicher,* and a German Jew was a rather easy target for hatred. One day, soon after Rahm's arrival, Eppstein returned from his usual visit to SS headquarters with a black eye. This was the beginning of the end. In September 1944, Eppstein was ordered to headquarters, where he was humilated and killed. A few days later a purge of the German and Czech members and officials of the Ältestenrat began. All those who had been friends of Edelstein, Zucker (deported in September 1944), and Eppstein were sent to the east.[64]

During those trying months, when the stars of Edelstein and Eppstein kept fading, the star of Benjamin Murmelstein, Eppstein's second in command, steadily rose. Soon after Eppstein's arrest, the Council of Elders was disbanded, and all executive power transferred to Murmelstein. Before World War II, Murmelstein had served as rabbi in one of Vienna's suburbs. He was a lecturer at the Jewish theological seminary in Vienna and (according to Lederer and Tuma) also at the University of Vienna. He was the author of several popular books and pamphlets on Jewish history and the Talmud.[65] In 1937 he became a member of the executive board of the Kultusgemeinde in Vienna and remained on that board during the Nazi occupation. He was deported, on January 19, 1943, to Theresienstadt and, in the same month, was appointed second deputy to Eppstein. After Edelstein's fall he actually became the most influential member of the Ältestenrat. In the beginning of December 1943, the Germans entrusted the important responsibility for the "embellishment" program to Murmelstein. Visits by international committees were expected in Theresienstadt, and the Nazis wanted to show off with a perfect Potemkin facade, as it were, of a "model ghetto." This assignment seemed to be Murmelstein's main contribution to the administrative activities of the Ältestenrat before the arrest of Eppstein. At first, there were no great changes after Murmelstein's appointment. The deportations from Theresienstadt continued under his administration for a full month (from September 28 to October 28), reached a very high number, and then suddenly stopped.

In all, 86,934 people were deported to the east from Theresienstadt. Thirty-five transports totaling 44,000 people in 1942; eight transports of 12,000 in 1943 until Edelstein's arrest (November 1943); ten transports of 12,500 until Eppstein's arrest; eleven transports of 18,500 during Murmelstein's administration.[66] No conclusions about the diplomatic negotiating power of the Ältestenrat can be drawn from these figures. Various factors entirely beyond the influence of the Jewish communal leaders affected German decisions on deportations. In the last months of 1944 the strategic situation of Germany and the shortcomings of the transportation system substantially hampered the implementation of the deportation program.

In general, Murmelstein continued the policy of political expediency pursued by his predecessors. Lederer believes that this was the only possible policy, since any attempt at open defiance would have prompted the liquidation of the ghetto. He considers Murmelstein's policy particularly clever. According to Lederer, Murmelstein was

an extraordinary man. . . . Besides being a man of scholarly attainments and great organizing abilities, he was also extremely ambitious. Though highstrung, he knew how to conceal and control his emotions. . . . It is certainly more than a mere coincidence that his favorite characters were Herod the Idumaean and Flavius Josephus. . . . It appears that he saw himself as another Flavius Josephus who, undeterred by the vociferous contempt of his people, worked for its salvation.[67]

A dissident view has been given by another inmate of Theresienstadt, Mirko Tuma:

a man weighing no less than 100 kg. [220 pounds], with an enormous head, a sunken nose, small eyes, and puffed up lips. He used to tell everybody around him that the Righteous God (in whom he had no personal faith at all) called upon him to sacrifice himself for the sake of the persecuted Jews, and, if necessary, to dishonor his own reputation in order to protect them.[68]

There were, however, also other, entirely different opinions.

After the deportations of October 1944, the Germans embarked upon a policy of stabilization. No more transports were sent out from Theresienstadt. On the other hand, transports (totaling more than 8,000 persons) continued to arrive in Theresienstadt from Germany, Prague, Vienna, and Slovakia until April 1945. Two transports left Theresienstadt for freedom:

in February 1945 a transport of 1,200 left for Switzerland, and in April of that year about 350 Danish Jews were "repatriated" to their country. Of course, the Jewish leadership in Theresienstadt had no influence whatsoever on these two unusual acts of Nazi generosity which were due to the changing international situation and the endeavor of the Nazi henchmen of Theresienstadt to create extenuating "alibis" for themselves.

In those last months of "stabilization," from November 1944 until the liberation in May 1945, the Ältestenrat was reorganized. To Murmelstein, who remained chief, four other executives were added, representing the four main nationalities of Theresienstadt: Rabbi Leo Baeck for the German Jews; Dr. Albert Meissner, a former member of the Austrian parliament, and minister of justice (1920–1929) and social welfare (1934) in Czechoslovakia; Dr. Edward Maurice Meijers, famous Dutch lawyer, substitute councilor at the high court of justice in The Hague, and professor of civil and international law at the University of Leyden; and Heinrich Klang, authority on civil law and university professor at Vienna.[69] A few days after the departure of the Germans early in May 1945, Murmelstein resigned, and Theresienstadt was then run by the "Council of Four." On May 12, 1945, Jiři Vogel, a Czech Jew and member of the first Ältestenrat, was appointed head of the community by general consent of representatives from all the groups of the ghetto.

As in other liberated countries, heated discussions about the role of the Judenrat and its alleged or real collaboration with the Germans immediately began here. In October 1945, the Jewish community of Prague established a civil "court of honor" (*Ehrengericht*) to investigate charges and complaints against the former executives and employees of the Jewish communal administration during the Nazi regime.[70] Murmelstein, the only surviving high executive of the Theresienstadt ghetto, was arraigned by Czechoslovak authorities but then freed.[71] He was again arraigned in Rome by a civil court of the Organization of the Jewish Displaced Persons in Italy in August 1948, but the case was dismissed.[72] On the other hand, the staunch defenders of the Ältestenrat and its policy of expediency pointed to the fact that Theresienstadt was the only ghetto with almost 19,000 survivors (17,320 on the day of liberation in Theresienstadt, the rest rescued via Switzerland and Denmark during the early months of 1945), more than any other ghetto. It still remains to be decided how much credit for this can be given to the Ältestenrat and how much was merely the result of international developments and of internal differences among the Nazis. It may be that final judgment on this very complicated question will never be possible.

¶ This study first appeared in *Essays on Jewish Life and Thought, presented in honor of Salo Wittmayer Baron,* edited by Joseph L. Blau, Arthur Hertzberg, Philip Friedman, and Isaac Mendelsohn (New York, 1959), pp. 199–230. It was intended to be part of a larger study on Jewish communal organization in the Axis-controlled countries during the years 1933–1945, which unfortunately was never completed.

## Notes

1. Salo W. Baron, "Aspects of the Jewish Communal Crisis in 1848," *JSS,* 14 (1952), 99–144.
2. Hilde Ottenheimer, "The Disappearance of Jewish Communities in Germany, 1900–1938," *JSS,* 3 (1941), 189–206.
3. Jacob Marcus, *The Rise and Destiny of the German Jew* (Cincinnati, 1934), pp. 193–95, 197, 328; Hans Lamm, "Über die innere und äussere Entwicklung des deutschen Judentums in Dritten Reich" (inaugural dissertation, University of Erlangen, 1951; mimeographed copy in the library of YIVO Institute, New York), pp. 98–101, 105.
4. Bruno Blau, *Das Ausnahmerecht für die Juden in den europäischen Ländern, 1933–1945,* vol. I: *Deutschland* (New York, 1952), pp. 15–40.
5. *Ibid.,* pp. 40–41.
6. In a meeting on September 17, 1933, the following executive members of the Reichsvertretung had been elected: Rabbi Leo Baeck, president; Otto Hirsch, chairman; Siegfried Moses, vice chairman; Rabbi Hoffmann, Landsberger, Franz Meyer, J. L. Seligsohn, Heinrich Stahl. Lamm, pp. 99–100.
7. *Ibid.,* pp. 98, 105.
8. In a message to the German Jews in November 1936, the Reichsvertretung described its program in the following words: "Welfare, economic help, school and education, vocational retraining, preparation for emigration to all countries." Kurt Alexander, "Die Reichsvertretung der deutschen Juden," in *Festschrift zum 80 Gerburtstag von Leo Baeck* (London, 1953), p. 79.

Before long the problem of emigration became the central issue. In July 1938, the Reichsvertretung sent the executive director, Otto Hirsch, as its representative to the International Conference in Evian (on the border of Switzerland and France) dealing with the problem of refugee immigration. The negotiations of the Reichsvertretung also helped to bring about a considerable relaxation of the strict British anti-immigration policy, thus enabling many German Jews to emigrate to Great Britain after the terrible events of November 1938. Kurt Alexander, p. 83. Marc Wischnitzer, "Jewish Emigration from Germany 1933–1938," *JSS,* 2 (1940), 23–44.

9. On March 1, 1937, there were 167 Jewish schools in 144 communities in Germany, with a total of 23,670 pupils; Lamm, pp. 80–81.
10. However, adds the writer quickly with respect to the "autonomy of Jewish life," almost every meeting of the Reichsvertretung was watched by an official of the Gestapo, and the Jewish leaders had to justify everything they undertook, large or small, to the Gestapo; Alexander, pp. 78–79.
11. Lamm, pp. 112, 116–17.

12. Gerald Reitlinger, *The Final Solution* (New York, 1953), pp. 14–16; chaps. 3 and 4.

13. The text of the decree of July 4, 1939, quoted in *The Black Book: The Nazi Crime Against the Jewish People* (New York, 1946), pp. 508–9; and in Blau, *Das Ausnahmerecht*, I, 71–74.

14. *Völkischer Beobachter*, Süddeutsche Ausgabe, no. 188, as quoted by Hans Erich Fabian, "Die letzte Etappe," in *Festschrift . . . Leo Baeck*, p. 85.

15. Lamm, p. 125.

16. *AJC Report* (New York, July 1944), pp. 30, 32, 40.

17. *AJC Report*, p. 24; Lamm, pp. 305–6; Reitlinger, p. 160; *Hitler's Ten-Year War on the Jews* (New York, Institute for Jewish Affairs, 1943), p. 29.

18. Lamm, p. 120. Artur Eisenbach in his *Hitlerowska polityka eksterminacji Żydów* (Hitler's Policy of Exterminating the Jews) (Warsaw, 1953), p. 168, has blamed the Reichvereinigung for being an "instrument of the Gestapo" and has sought to support this judgment with a quotation from the statistical report on the "Final Solution of the Jewish Problem in Europe" (mimeographed copy in the YIVO archives), prepared on March 23, 1943 by Richard Korherr, the inspector for statistics in the office of the Reichsführer-SS. Eisenbach quotes Korherr's statement as follows: "This institution [the Reichsvereinigung] works under the control of the Reich Security Main Office and for its purposes. Whatever was the initial doubtful attitude of the Jews, it seems that the Reichsvereinigung is doing an honest job."

A careful analysis of the Korherr document indicates that Korherr was concerned only with statistical aspects of the Jewish question, however, and was not giving any overall evaluation of the work and the policies of the Reichsvereinigung. The context is crucial here. Korherr was appraising the statistical data collected by the Jewish autonomous bodies, and that alone. I quote his full statement in a translation from the German: "The following data on the statistical development of the Jews in Germany . . . have . . . been provided primarily by the Reichsvereinigung der Juden in Deutschland and by the communities in Vienna and Prague, which have been using census figures, record cards for the population movement, . . . and also calculations and estimates. These Jewish agencies function under the control and for the aims of the Reich Security Main Office. . . . Apart from the questionable initial number of Jews, the Reichsvereinigung der Juden in Deutschland seems to work reliably."

The Korherr report has been published, in abbreviated form, in Leon Poliakov and Josef Wulf, *Das Dritte Reich und die Juden: Dokumente und Aufsätze* (Berlin, 1955), pp. 239–48.

19. Bruno Blau, "The Last Days of Germany Jewry in the Third Reich," *YA*, 8 (1953), 197–98, 200; see also Blau, "Der Judenstern der Nazis," *Judaica*, 9 (Zurich, 1953), 36; and Reitlinger, pp. 42–43, 212–14.

20. Blau, *Das Ausnahmerecht*, I, 103.

21. Lamm, "Über die innere und äussere Entwicklung," pp. 127–29; *AJC Report*, p. 51; Fabian, in *Festschrift . . . Leo Baeck*, pp. 90, 93. See also the biography of Otto Hirsch, in *Allgemeine Wochenzeitung der Juden in Deutschland* (Düsseldorf, January 7, 1955), p. 8, "Porträt der Woche," by E. G. Löwenthal.

In an unpublished report, entitled "Contribution towards the History of the Jews in Holland from 10 May 1940 to June 1944," Gertrud Van Tijn, representative of the American Joint Distribution Committee in the Netherlands, wrote of her visit to the Reichsvereinigung in Berlin in 1939 (p. 36): "The last time I was in Berlin in the beginning of September 1939 . . . I was appalled. . . . Hirsch, Seligsohn, and Brasch were in a concentration camp and Paul Eppstein, who was in charge, was so harassed that he was only a shadow of his former self." Copies of the extensive report by Mrs. Van Tijn (129 pp.) were submitted to the chairman of the AJDC in New York by J. L. Magnes, president of Hebrew University, with an accompanying letter dated Jerusalem, November 23, 1944.

According to Else R. Behrend-Rosenfeld, *Ich stand nicht allein: Erlebnisse einer Jüdin in Deutschland 1933–1944* (Hamburg, 1945), it was not Seligsohn but Hirsch who was held responsible by the Nazis for the idea of a fast day in behalf of the deported Jews in Baden; Behrend-Rosenfeld writes in her memoirs under the date November 10, 1940 (pp. 106–107): "To commemorate this terrible new blow, the Reichsvereinigung had suggested that all members of the community should fast on a certain day. We gladly followed this suggestion. But to our horror Mr. Rat informed us yesterday that Ministerial-Councillor Hirsch, alleged to be the author of the suggestion, was arrested and taken to a concentration camp. A suggestion such as this was considered sabotage of a government directive."

22. Bruno Blau, "Der Geiselmord vom 2. December 1942," *Aufbau*, December 19, 1952; Lamm, p. 305.

23. Erich H. Boehm, ed., *We Survived* (New Haven, 1949), p. 283. About Rabbi Baeck's refusal to leave Germany in 1938, there is another interesting record by the Scottish intelligence agent Sir Michael Bruce in his book *Tramp Royal* (London, 1954). Sir Michael was sent by a group of British Jewish leaders to Germany in mid-November 1938 to aid secret rescue operations. In a meeting with German Jewish leaders in Berlin, a suggestion was made to bring Rabbi Baeck to safety in Great Britain. To which Baeck replied, "I will go when I am the last Jew alive in Germany." And Wilfred Israel, owner of a famous department store in Berlin, added: "I will go when the Rabbi goes" (Bruce, p. 242). There are almost no materials about the fate of the local Jewish community leaders. Noteworthy is the case of Eugene Isaac Neter, chairman of the Jewish community in Mannheim. Since his wife was a pure "Aryan," he could be exempted from deportation, but he decided to join his community when the deportation was decreed. He left his wife in Mannheim, however, because she was not strong enough to bear the hardships of exile (Behrend-Rosenfeld, p. 105). Miraculously, Neter survived all the traumas of deportation and a concentration camp, and went, after the war, to Israel, to Kibbutz Dagania, where he was interviewed by a German journalist, Gerhard Seger, in 1955 ("Von Damaskus bis Beersheba," *Aufbau*, March 18, 1955, pp. 19–20).

24. Leo Baeck, "A People Stands before Its God," in Boehm, pp. 285, 288. In his personal narrative *Hast Du es schon vergessen? Erlebnisbericht aus der Zeit der Verfolgung* (Frankfurt-am-Main, 1954), Siegmund Weltinger, a German Jewish communal leader, wrote thus of the tensions, dangers, and moral dilemmas involved in the activities of the Jewish leadership under the Nazi

regime (p. 22): "It was by no means a simple matter to be active in a responsible position in the Jewish community. One was always in great danger for oneself and one's family, always subject to interrogations, threats, and blackmail by the Gestapo. In addition, one missed most probably all chances at emigration. But above all one had to ask oneself if it was better to cooperate with the Gestapo than simply to offer passive resistance, if not altogether to leave the full responsibility for the carrying out of many measures to the controlling authority. In long talks with Director Stahl, I discussed the pros and cons at that time. We both became convinced that it was better to hold out to the end and that it would after all be to the advantage of the Jewish public if the execution of difficult directives, such as the "evacuations," were undertaken by the community itself. Through skillful negotiations one could often alleviate things, and could obtain postponements in urgent cases; and, above all, there was still hope that someday the system would break down and that much could be gained by postponements. It was a race with time, which, alas, was lost by the Jews. But one could not know that at the time, and it is very easy to say today that nothing would have helped anyway. This is certainly not correct. One thinks only of the brief period during which the notorious Brunner from Vienna and his men at his own will snatched away people from the streets and out of buildings and no preparation could be made. One should never forget how many personal sacrifices were involved for the leaders in holding out at their post."

25. Reitlinger, p. 165; Lamm, p. 130; Fabian, in *Festschrift . . . Leo Baeck,* p. 93. According to Blau, "The Last Days of German Jewry," *YA,* 8, p. 198, there were in Germany on September 1, 1944, 14,574 Jews, including both *Volljuden* and *Mischlinge.*

26. Fabian, p. 92. Lamm, p. 15, quotes the statistical survey made in 1944 by the Federation of Jews from Central Europe. According to this estimate, the property of the Jewish communities and organizations amounted, on November 9, 1938 (i.e., before the Kristallnacht), to 236.5 million reichsmarks. Lamm finds this figure too low; he estimates the total Jewish communal assets in Germany in 1933 at no less than 300 million reichsmarks.

27. *The Black Book,* pp. 129–33; *Hitler's Ten-Year War,* pp. 46–50; Wilhelm Krell, "La Communauté Culture Israélite de Vienne," in *Les Juifs en Europe,* pp. 190–94. Korherr's report to the Reichsführer SS of March 23, 1943, p. 4, mentions only 8,102 Jews and the same figure is repeated in Korherr's second report, of April 19, 1943, p. 2.

28. *Jüdisches Nachrichtenblatt,* Vienna edition, no. 51 (December 18, 1942); in the issues of December 18 and 25, two editorials commented on this important change in the Jewish community. Both editorials pointed out in a wistful tone the great changes in the life of the Jewish community of Vienna since 1938: "In 1938 the community had to develop vast relief activities for hundreds of thousands of people. . . . Every month about 10,000 emigrants, about 50,000 people in vocational training, about 38,000 patrons of people's kitchens, and about 3,000 children and aged persons in special homes had to be cared for. . . . The successive reduction [of activities] followed the gradually diminishing number of Jews . . . and after the emigration [deportation] was completed it was not an easy job to rebuild the organizational structure thoroughly. . . . It is a hard job to reduce [the community] in such a way that

the still surviving remnants should be able to become a harmonic entity capable of living. . . . The [new] Ältestenrat will look ahead to a hard task . . . , particularly because for the first time a Jewish community is bound to embrace everybody who is a Jew according to his descent, while until now the Jewish faith alone used to be the basis of a Jewish communal bond." The statute of the Ältestenrat (published in no. 51 of the *Jüdisches Nachrichtenblatt*) made it compulsory for every "racial Jew to belong to the Ältestenrat" (this name being used in the *Satzungen* not only for the executive board but for the entire body politic of the Jews). An earlier decree of March 25, 1942, retroactive to September 1, 1941, made secession from the Jewish community dependent on a special permit from the minister of internal affairs (*Jüdisches Nachrichtenblatt*, Vienna edition, no. 16, April 17, 1942).

29. Oskar Karbach, "The Liquidation of the Jewish Community of Vienna," *JSS*, 2 (1940), 255–78.

30. *AJC Report*, on Austria, pp. 27–28.

31. *Ibid.*, p. 28; Zdenek Lederer, *Ghetto Theresienstadt* (London, 1953), pp. 42–43, 249.

32. Reitlinger, p. 165.

The last Jewish visitor to call on the Vienna Jewish community before the end of the Nazi regime probably was Rudolf (Rezsö) Kasztner of the Jewish relief and rescue committee (Vaad Ezra Ve-hatzala) in Budapest. Dr. Kasztner was in Vienna on January 4–15, 1945, and again on April 2, 1945. According to his information, the head of the Ältestenrat was again Löwenherz, who had probably been sent back from Theresienstadt. The Jewish administration was located in an old, almost empty, and derelict building of the former Kultusgemeinde at no. 4 Seitenstättengasse, where there were also short religious services on Saturdays. A small "synagogue" had also been established by the efforts of Dr. Tuchman, chief of the Jewish health department, in an air-raid shelter on 7 Malzgasse. Besides these two Jewish community officials Kasztner still found in Vienna the following Jewish figures: Arnold Raschkes, the former president and staff physician of the Jewish Kultusgemeinde and later director of the Jewish hospital; Max Bienenstein, director of the home for the aged; and Dr. Mathias Reich, chief surgeon of the Jewish hospital.

Besides these Viennese Jews, Kasztner met in Vienna a large colony of Hungarian Jews who had been deported to Austria in compliance with the agreement of July 1944 between Adolf Eichmann and the Jewish rescue committee of Budapest. About half of these 17,500 to 18,000 Jews had been brought to Vienna as factory hands, and lived in special labor camps under SS supervision. Their only connection with the Jewish Ältestenrat in Vienna consisted in getting burial rights in the Jewish cemetery for their dead, and medical treatment for their sick in the Jewish hospital. Rezsö Kasztner, "Der Bericht des jüdischen Rettungskomitees aus Budapest, 1942–1945" (n.p., n.d.), mimeographed and marked *Vertraulich* (available in the YIVO library, New York), pp. 49–50, 154–56, 171.

33. Korherr's report (see above, note 18), p. 4; Peter Meyer, "Czechoslovakia," in Peter Meyer et al., *Jews in the Satellite Countries* (Syracuse, N.Y., 1953), pp. 60–61; Gerhard Jacoby, *Racial State* (New York, 1944), pp. 5–19.

34. Reitlinger, pp. 26, 153, 509; Lederer, pp. 80–81.

35. *Jüdisches Nachrichtenblatt-Zidovske listy,* Prague, March 15, 1940, and April 4, 1941; Jacoby, pp. 233–34.

36. Kurt Wehle, "The Jewish Religious Community during the Occupation and after the Liberation of Czechoslovakia" (Czech), *Věstnik židovske náboženské obce v Praze* (hereafter cited as *Věstnik*), Prague, VII, no. 1 (September 1, 1945), 2–4. At a congress held in Prague in September 1945, Wehle, a Zionist leader, was elected secretary general of the council of Jewish religious communities in Bohemia and Moravia, and he kept this office till March 1948 when he left Czechoslovakia. Meyer, pp. 114, 121, 123.

37. In an announcement of the Jüdische Arbeitszentrale in Prague, July 1941, the following *Kreisgemeinden* were mentioned: Brno, Kladno, Hradec, Kralove, Kolin, Pardubice, Pizen, Pisek, Protejov, Tabor, Trebic, Uherske Hradiste, and Prague. *Jüdisches Nachrichtenblatt-Zidovske listy,* July 4, 1941. In various issues of the *Jüdisches Nachrichtenblatt* of 1941, the following communities were still mentioned: Moravska Ostrava, Budejovice, Klattau, Bensov, Zlin, Milevsko, Ledec, Vodnanu, Luza, Olomouc, Pelhrinov, Trest, Litomysl, Lipnik, Dobruska.

38. *Jüdisches Nachrichtenblatt-Zidovske listy,* October 17, 1941; H. G. Adler in his *Theresienstadt 1941–1945: Das Antlitz einer Zwangsgemeinschaft* (Tübingen, 1955), p. 683, sets March 15, 1940, as the date when the provincial communities were put under the control of the Prague community.

39. Wehle in *Věstnik,* September 1, 1945, p. 3; Meyer, p. 113. The last Judenältester in Prague was the well-known Zionist Frantisek Friedmann, who belonged, owing to his marriage with a gentile Englishwoman, to the privileged group of members of mixed marriages. Kasztner, "Der Bericht," p. 36. See also note below.

40. The following members of the rabbinate are mentioned in *Jüdisches Nachrichtenblatt,* September 19, 1941: chief rabbi Aladar Deutsch and the rabbis Otokar Kraus and Arpad Hirschberger.

41. *Jüdisches Nachrichtenblatt,* December 5, 1941.

42. Karl Rahm trial, as reported in *Věstnik,* nos. 12 and 17 (1947), 168 and 253. The trial of Rahm, Günther's deputy in Prague and later commander of the Theresienstadt ghetto, was reported in detail in *Věstnik* in twelve installments in 1947, in nos. 10–26. The verdict of death was reported in *Věstnik,* no. 18 (April 30, 1948), 211.

43. Wehle in *Věstnik,* September 1, 1945, p. 3.

44. Frantisek Fuchs, "Dr. Frantisek Weidman" (Czech), *Věstnik,* no. 12 (October 28, 1946), 107; Lederer, p. 157.

45. E. Orensteinova, "Remembering Jacob Edelstein" (Czech), *Věstnik,* no. 3 (October 28, 1945), 19; Tresler, "Remembering a Great Man and a Great Human Being" (Czech), *Věstnik,* no. 7 (July 10, 1946), 60 (with a black-and-white photograph of J. Edelstein).

46. The Nisko experiment, entirely abandoned by the Nazis after six months, was described in detail in the memoirs of J. Zehngut, "Nisko: Experiment in Primary Deportation of the Jews from the Protectorate" (Czech), *Věstnik,* vol. 11 (1949), nos. 8, 9, 10, 11, 13, 26–27; T. Guttman, *Dokumentenwerke über die jüdische Geschichte in der Zeit des Nazismus,* I (Jerusalem, 1943), 62–66; Reitlinger, pp. 43–44; Lederer, pp. 203–4. Murmelstein later summarized his experience in the Nisko experiment thus in his "Geschicht-

licher Überblick" (p. 1): "There is no doubt that the authors of this project were thinking of the Jewish settlements in the Crimea or in Birobidjan when they started to carry out the plan. The goal here, however, was not construction but rather destruction, and events developed accordingly. The execution was desultory, incompetent, and cruel, all at the same time. Thus they had to come to a dead end, in the fullest sense of the word—over rows of dead bodies. To a large extent, the plan also failed because of the resistance of the military and the newly established civilian administration." The "Geschichtlicher Überblick," an attempt at an impersonal historical account of the Theresienstadt ghetto from its establishment to its termination in May 1945, was most likely written down immediately after the liberation, sometime in the summer or fall of 1945, and was submitted soon thereafter to the Wiener Library in London. A copy, of sixty-nine typewritten pages, was prepared by the courtesy of the Wiener Library for the YIVO archives in New York. I am very much indebted to the Wiener Library for making this relevant source available to me.

47. See essay 2 above, "The Lublin Reservation and the Madagascar Plan"; also Lederer, pp. 13, 204.

48. Fuchs, in *Věstnik,* October 28, 1946; Orensteinova, in *Věstnik,* October 28, 1945.

49. Frantisek Kraus, "K 4 Rijnu" (Czech), *Věstnik,* no. 38 (1949), 429.

50. Rudolf Iltis, "How the Ghetto in Theresienstadt Was Established" (Czech), *Věstnik,* no. 48 (1948), 532; Mirko Tuma, *Ghetto nasich dnu* (The Ghetto of our Days) (Czech) (Prague, 1946), pp. 14–16, tells of 342 men; Lederer, pp. 12–14. The negotiations and preparations which preceded the establishment of the camp-ghetto of Theresienstadt are extensively described in Adler, *Theresienstadt,* pp. 16–36.

51. Lederer, pp. 15–20. The first Ältestenrat consisted of thirteen members; the other members of the council, in addition to Edelstein and Zucker, were Rudolf Bergman, Leo Hess, Dr. Erich Munk, Erwin Elbert, Leo Janowitz, Egon Popper, Julius Grünberger, Erich Klapp, Karel Schliesser, and Jiři Vogel (one name is missing). The former head of the Prague Jewish community, Dr. K. Weidmann, never had any official position in Theresienstadt. He was nevertheless active in the social life in the ghetto and was known for several courageous public speeches on various occasions. He was deported to Auschwitz on October 28, 1944, and died there. Fuchs, in *Věstnik,* October 28, 1946; Lederer, p. 157.

52. Tuma, p. 16; Lederer, pp. 27, 41, 123–24, 132.

53. Heinrich Liebrecht, "Therefore Will I Deliver Him," in Boehm, *We Survived,* pp. 230 ff.; Lederer, pp. 123–24. About the conflicts between Zionists and assimilationists, as well as about the various nationalities and the converts in the camp, see Adler, *Theresienstadt,* pp. 292–315.

54. Tuma, pp. 32–33, 37; Liebrecht, "Therefore Will I Deliver Him," in Boehm, *We Survived,* p. 230; Lederer, pp. 41, 44; Orensteinova, in *Věstnik,* October 28, 1945; Tresler, in *Věstnik,* July 10, 1946; Fuchs, in *Věstnik,* October 28, 1946. (Lederer, pp. 20–22, does not mention Edelstein's resignation in January 1942, but tells of a second attempt by Edelstein to resign, on January 27, 1943, after the Ältestenrat had been reshuffled by order of SS-Obersturmbannführer Adolf Eichmann. This request was also turned down by the Ger-

mans; Lederer, pp. 42–43.) A detailed description of the January–February 1942 incident is in Adler, pp. 83–86. The execution of the nine offenders was carried out in installments; two of them were hanged on January 10; the remaining seven, on February 24.

55. Lederer, pp. 20, 59–60, 72. On December 31, 1943, the number of persons employed in the police and security department was 964. An impression of great funds allegedly available for the "development" of Theresienstadt was temporarily created by the Nazis. Part of this money was channeled, by various channels and excuses, into the Reich treasury, however, while another part was frozen and was never utilized for the benefit of the ghetto. To quote Murmelstein's "Überblick," p. 6: "In 1942 and 1943, the assets of the disbanded Jewish organizations in Vienna and Berlin were likewise transferred to Prague, since in the meantime Jews from both these centers had come to Theresienstadt. Shortly before the ghetto was dissolved, there was a total of 95 million Reichsmarks but in April 1946 about half of this sum was used for the purchase of Reich Treasury Notes (Reichsschatzscheinen)."

56. Lederer, pp. 62–63, 88. Photostats of Theresienstadt banknotes have been published in many books: e.g., *The Black Book*, p. 291; Moshe Prager, *Hurban Yisrael beeropa* (Destruction of the Jews in Europe) (Ein-Harod, 1948), illustrated appendix (unpaged); K. E. Loret, "Paper Money Issued in the Concentration Camp of Theresienstadt," *The Numismatist,* 9 (June 1947), 422–23.

The Jewish leadership was forced to cooperate with the Nazis in this deceptive farce. A characteristic episode occurred in 1944. In spring 1944, the Jewish relief committee of Budapest managed to send a sum of $10,000 for the Theresienstadt ghetto inmates. The money was sent to Dr. Frantisek Friedmann in Prague, who forwarded it to Theresienstadt. Afterward, Rudolf (Rezsö) Kasztner, the representative of the Jewish relief committee in Budapest, received two letters: one of May 24, 1944, from Friedmann in Prague; and another, of May 23, 1944, from Theresienstadt, signed by Franz Kahn, Dr. Paul Eppstein, Dr. Erich Österreicher, Dr. Erich Munk, Otto Zucker, and Gert Körbel. In both letters, life in Theresienstadt was praised, and depicted as a sheer idyll, in a time when almost 70,000 Jews had been deported from Theresienstadt to the extermination camps in the east.

The letter from Theresienstadt reads as follows: "Dear Chawer . . . In Theresienstadt a veritable Jewish city has come to exist, in which all work is done by Jews; from street cleaning to a modern health system with a large staff of nursing personnel; from all kinds of technical work to the feeding in public kitchens; from its own police and fire department to special court, postal, and transportation systems; from a bank with its own settlement money and stores for food, clothing, and housewares to recreation with regular lectures, theatrical plays, and concerts. The children, who are the object of special attention, are taken care of in child and youth centers; the old people who are unable to work are accommodated in old-age and nursing homes, under medical supervision and care. Those fit to work are specially assigned to work in the administration. There are eminent specialists from all fields. This benefits not only the necessary professional work in technological, hygienic, and administrative spheres; in the recreational sphere, too, a rich cultural life, Jewish as well as general, has been able to develop. A library with nearly 50,000 volumes and with several reading rooms, a coffee house with regular musical offerings provide recreation, especially for the older people. A central bath and a central laundry promote the public hygiene, which naturally is especially valued. Thus, once one has accomplished the external and internal resettlement and readjustment, one can feel quite well here. You can see a picture of the town on the letterhead. . . ."

Dr. Friedmann wrote in his letter: ". . . All are working in their particular fields and have become very accomplished in their skills. Erich Munk is head of the health care system in Theresienstadt. Erich Österreicher directs the labor assignment there. Kahn is active in recreation. Schuster dedicates his time primarily to his little daughter. The rest are mainly active in youth work, which is exemplary in Theresienstadt and has excellent results in its achievements. They have created a rich Jewish life, are proud of their exceedingly rich library, a large theater with opera performances, the daily open-air concerts, a coffee house, town band, and the daily lectures of a very high level. That the region is unusually beautiful, you probably know, to which I should add that especially tasteful park grounds were established. . . . With heartfelt shalom, yours Dr. Friedmann." Facsimiles of both letters in the original German are reprinted in Rezsö Kasztner, *Der Bericht*, appendix, pp. 5–6. According to Adler, p. 121, the first banknotes were put into circulation as late as May 1943.

57. A facsimile of the stamp was published on p. 15 of the catalogue of *A Century of Jewish History* (New York, 1950), a philatelic exhibit prepared by Emil Weitz and sponsored by the American Section of the Jewish Agency.

58. A photo of a staff meeting of the Ältestenrat with Dr. Eppstein as chairman and about sixteen other persons participating, was published in *Věstnik*, vol. 9, no. 12 (1947), p. 168. According to H. G. Adler (see below, n. 59), "the Ältestenrat was of considerably less importance than the *Leitung* consisting of the Judenältester [and his two deputies—P.F.] with the staff of the *Zentralsekretariat* and his entourage." According to Sulamith Cholewa, "Danish Jews in Theresienstadt" (Yiddish), *YB*, 30 (1947), 311, M. Friediger, the chief rabbi of the Danish Jews, was also a member of the Ältestenrat. The maximum number of members of the Ältestenrat was twenty-seven. A detailed description of the composition, the members, and the agenda of the Ältestenrat can be found in Adler, pp. 193–94, 248–54.

59. Lederer, pp. 60, 94. Another version of the Löwenstein episode is given by H. G. Adler, a Theresienstadt survivor who, at the time of this writing, was preparing his comprehensive psychological and sociological study on Theresienstadt (see n. 38). On December 10, 1954, Dr. Adler wrote me: "Dr. Löwenstein, an old German naval officer of half-Jewish origin, was installed as chief of the security department. Löwenstein's influence with the SS was relatively large, but the three internal camp leaders disliked his struggle against corruption and were frightened by his strong and stubborn personality which unfortunately was not understood by them. In this originated a fight of all these four men [Eppstein, Edelstein, Murmelstein, and Löwenstein] and I must say that the role of the three leaders [Eppstein, Edelstein, Murmelstein] was at least imprudent and irresponsible. Löwenstein was eliminated late in summer 1943 by means which had a tremendously bad effect on the future of the camp."

Löwenstein's biography, his rigid personality, and his sincere efforts to reform and improve the management of Theresienstadt were extensively described in Adler's *Theresienstadt,* pp. 135–36 and *passim* (see index). Karl Löwenstein himself published an interesting personal narrative: "Minsk: Im Lager der deutschen Juden." *Aus Politik und Zeitgeschichte,* Beilage zur Wochenzeitung *Das Parlament,* XXXXV, 56 (Bonn, November 1956); this paper seems to be a fragment of a larger memoir of the author's experiences in Minsk and Theresienstadt, in the years 1941–1945 (see Adler, p. 723).

60. Lederer, pp. 43–44. Lederer's opinion of Eppstein concurs with the view of Adler (in his letter to me of December 10, 1954), who described Eppstein as a "weak character."

61. This opinion, contradictory to Lederer's and Adler's evaluation, has been shared by another Theresienstadt survivor, the German Catholic (formerly Protestant) lawyer of Jewish descent, Heinrich Liebrecht: "Eppstein . . . was endowed with tremendous energy and was always fair and honest." Liebrecht, "Therefore Will I Deliver Him," in Boehm, p. 230.

62. Tuma, pp. 32–33. The moral climate of the Lilliputian ghetto empire, its dictatorial elite, and the personality of its leader, Dr. Eppstein, changed and twisted by the powers granted to him, have been pointedly analyzed by Emil Utitz in his book *Psychologie des Lebens im Konzentrationslager Theresienstadt* (Vienna, 1948). Dr. Utitz, former professor of philosophy and psychology at the universities of Halle and Prague, spent more than three years in Theresienstadt, and made the following observations (pp. 68–69): "In the delusion of the prisoners, the camp just became a kind of midget state in which reactionary tendencies mingled with progressive ones in the most intense fashion. . . . Thus, a truly scurrilous kind of parody of an idyllic state developed, especially in 1944. The Elder of the Jews surrounded himself with a complete court. It was hardly possible to get through to him. The granting of a brief audience seemed a special favor. His oracular words were meant to give in their obscurity the impression of the deepest profundity. Addresses to the people were festive occasions. Ceremonies were very popular. It is true, there were no monuments to be unveiled, but there were openings of institutions and such, during which the substantive content counted less than the formal facade. Art and science were most graciously cultivated. There was even a kind of court theater for the pleasure of the highest-ranking dignitaries. Their presence was considered a special honor, their praise an invisible laurel wreath. Ambitious and plotting mistresses crowded around His Serene Highness. He was, of course, not popular; only a small number of servile flunkies paid homage to him; over them gleamed the beams of his benevolence, toward them the strictness of the ruler softened. At that, this man was a gifted, cultured, university graduate, with a first-rate scientific training, an artist of taste and understanding. Circumstances were stronger than he. Vanity, ambition, incipient megalomania broke him. And in the end: the SS leadership—he was so proud of his ability to deal with them—arrested him, took him away, and murdered him."

63. Utitz, p. 37; Lederer, pp. 102–3; Orensteinova, in *Věstnik,* October 28, 1945. From the time of Edelstein's arrest until his deportation in September 1944, Otto Zucker represented the Czech Jews in the *Leitung.* An interesting sidelight on Edelstein's personality is shed by the report of Gertrude Van Tijn

("Contribution towards the History of the Jews in Holland," pp. 34–35): "In March 1941 we received a visit of two Jews from Prague—Edelstein and Friedmann—who told us that they had been delegated to visit us by the Zentralstelle für Jüdische Auswanderung in Prague, which was dealing with the whole Jewish problem in Czecho-Slovakia. They told us that a similar S.S. office would be opened in Amsterdam, that the emigration forms which were to be used in Holland would be modeled on those in use in Czecho-Slovakia and that their orders were to make us acquainted with the contents of these questionnaires as well as with the general procedure. . . . Any feelings of misgivings I might have had about Edelstein and Friedmann—Jews visiting us at the orders of the Gestapo—soon gave place to a feeling of appreciation, particularly for Edelstein. I do not know what estimation Czecho-Slovakian Jewry has of him and his activities but I can only say that when he initiated me into this new work he mainly taught me how to obstruct and delay. . . . Whereas my dealings with Edelstein and Friedmann concerned mainly the future emigration of Jews, they had many talks with Prof. Cohen in his capacity as President of the 'J.R.' [Joodsche Raad; Judenrat in Amsterdam], warning him as to the task which lay ahead of him. In Czecho-Slovakia the notorious Eichmann was in charge of the Jewish question and he, a close associate of Himmler and at the same time an expert of the Jewish question, was a particularly vicious specimen of the S.S. Although it was probable that those who would be put in charge in Holland might not be quite as bad, still Edelstein did not seem to have many illusions on this subject. I think it was he who told Prof. Cohen that he would probably be made the mouthpiece of such dreadful news concerning the Jews that he would become hated and despised by his own people. This was said at a time, it must be remembered, when actual deportation had not taken place."

The report of Gertrude Van Tijn has been supplemented by another contemporaneous document, the diary of Menahem Pinkhof, a leader of the Jewish Halutz underground in Holland, published in *Yediot bet lohamey hagetaot* (Bulletin of the Ghetto Fighters' House), no. 1 (Haifa, January 1956). Pinkhof wrote in his diary (p. 18): "Edelstein, at that time head of the Judenrat in Theresienstadt, visited Holland in the beginning of 1941, in order to give advice on the organization of the Judenrat. Besides this assignment, he made a short visit to our institute [the Halutzim farm] in Lundstrecht. In the serene rural atmosphere of our farm, with only two or three of our *haverim* [closest friends] attending the meeting, he expressed his absolutely pessimistic views as to the fate of European Jewry, if the war would not end soon—'and there is no hope for it.' "

More about Edelstein's arrest and his death in Auschwitz is in Adler, pp. 155–56, and 730.

64. Rahm trial, *Věstnik*, 9 (1947), 168–69; Lederer, pp. 148–55; Tuma, pp. 43–46. It is worthwhile to add here the explanation given by Adler: "Eppstein saw himself almost as the emperor of the camp—though not in Rumkowski's [dictator of the Lodz ghetto] fashion—and in consequence, he made disastrous mistakes. This was the true reason for his imprisonment, under a flimsy pretext, in the early autumn of 1944 and of his execution a few days later."

65. For example, Murmelstein had published, in 1935, the polemic booklet *Einige Fragen an Prof. P. Severin Grill, Verfasser der theologischen*

*Studie: Der Talmud und Schulchan Aruch,* Foreword by chief rabbi David Feuchtwang, published by the Union der Österreichischen Juden. Probably one of his last prewar publications was his *Geschichte der Juden: Des Volkes Weltwandern* (Vienna, 1938).

66. These figures are based on statistics published in Lederer, pp. 205–51.

67. *Ibid.,* pp. 58, 159, 167.

68. Tuma, pp. 43–44. Adler drew the following economical but sharp sketch of Murmelstein: "Among all the internal leaders, he was the most intelligent and cautious, but also the coldest and most unscrupulous, fighting mainly for his personal survival. His behavior against the inmates was far from human, and in his fits he did not even restrain [*sic*] from beating people."

69. Lederer, p. 191; Tuma, p. 48; Baeck, in Boehm, *We Survived,* pp. 292, 296; *Festschrift . . . Leo Baeck,* p. 97; see also the moving postmortem about H. Klang by Guido Kisch in his review of *Österreichische Rechts- und Stattswissenschaft der Gegenwart in Selbstdarstellungen,* ed. by Nikolaus Grass in *HJ,* 16, (1954), 134–35. The last person to visit the camp before its liberation was Kasztner of the Jewish rescue committee of Budapest. He was in Theresienstadt on April 16, 1945, and had a talk with Murmelstein, then still chief of the administration, and with Leo Baeck. Kasztner, "Der Bericht," pp. 178–80.

70. *Věstnik,* no. 2 (October 28, 1945), 15.

71. Lederer, p. 166, n. 2. Among other unpublished sources, Lederer (see p. 267) utilized for his book Murmelstein's "Geschichtlicher Überblick" (see above, note 46).

72. Report on the trial published in *Baderekh,* Rome (September 3, 1948), p. 3.

# 6

# SOCIAL CONFLICTS IN THE GHETTO

One of the subjects insufficiently treated in the Holocaust literature is the social upheaval in the ghetto under Nazi rule. Some of the writers who have dealt with this subject (for instance, Bernard Mark[1] and Raphael Mahler[2]) have done so with a one-sided approach and have brought too much controversy into the discussion. It is impossible to approach this subject in terms of a social philosophy. We must keep in mind, above all, that a free play of social forces was entirely impossible in the closed, Nazi-dominated ghettos. It is one thing for us to collect, analyze, and interpret the facts to try to draw certain conclusions from them; it is quite another to come to the subject with a ready-made doctrine and seek a confirmation for it through interpretation of selected facts. My aim here is to avoid, as far as possible, that aprioristic method of selection and interpretation. I am aware that this attempt, probably the first on this subject in the literature of the Holocaust, is not exhaustive, and I shall be very glad if it stimulates other writers to do research in this area.

In the short period of the Nazi regime, European Jewry underwent the most radical and most rapid social revolution in human history. This revolution did not result from internal developments or factors in Jewish society. It was rather the force of the powerful political and social changes in the areas occupied by the Soviets, and the terrifying persecutions in the areas taken over by the Nazis, which shattered with lightning speed the whole economic and social structure of European Jewry. We have to keep in mind that the Jewish economy and society had already been considerably damaged by the developments from 1914 to 1939. But the economic and social revolution of the years 1939–1943, followed by the exterminations, soon overshadowed the catastrophes of the past.

That a tremendous social revolution was taking place in Jewish life was intuited by several writers during the disastrous period in the ghettos. With a keen sense of observation and a comprehensive understanding of historical processes, the well-known physician Israel Milejkowski wrote:

All of Jewish society in the ghetto is precisely as if it has been thrown into a huge kettle of boiling water standing on a fire—the fire of our suffering. In the boiling water one can distinguish two layers: . . . the upper layer boils and seethes, and on its surface appear large bubbles; the lower layer is also boiling, but quietly, more calmly. The most visible is the first layer, although far from being the most numerous or important, only [appearing so] because it is most agitated.[3]

Approximately the same view was expressed by Abraham Lewin, historian and teacher in Warsaw, in his diary (May 21, 1942):

This is one of the . . . results of the war. . . . "The top people are on the bottom, and the vulgar are on the top" . . . the disaster of incompetent leaders. . . . It has been proven that such has always been the case for us. . . . In the era of Czar Nicolas I, notes the writer Josef Rabinowicz, the top positions in the Jewish *kehillah* could have been occupied either by righteous men ready to sacrifice their lives for the community or by scoundrels. The virtuous men withdrew—the outcasts remained. . . . And now the situation is the same.[4]

## Destruction and Degradation of the Intellectuals

One of the leading social groups in any community is that of the professional intellectuals. Under the Nazi regime, that group was crushed by two almost simultaneous processes: systematic extermination on the one hand, and social degradation on the other. The Nazis adopted a policy of destroying the intellectual class in all the countries they conquered. But with non-Jews they carefully weighed the political consequences of their destruction program, and proceeded very cautiously; while their annihilation of Jewish intellectuals was open and massive. Immediately after the invasion of Poland in 1939, the Germans began to exterminate the Jewish intellectuals there, as well as other leading Jewish personalities. The same policy was later applied in the territory occupied by the Soviets. There are eyewitness reports on the actions carried out against Jewish intellectuals in many cities and villages—for instance, Warsaw, Lodz, Częstochowa, Międzyrzec, Rzeszów, and Tomaszow. A characteristic incident occurred in Częstochowa after an extermination action in 1942. The Germans had agreed to admit a number of Jews as workers in a metallurgy factory—a position that would grant them literally a temporary "leave for life." At the gate before the entrance to the factory, however, a German guard excluded any Jew who looked like an intellectual. Similarly, in Eastern Europe, though the Germans were in great need of medical personnel, right after they entered Łuniniec (Volhynia) they killed all the Jewish doctors. After the outbreak of German-Soviet hostilities, the Germans carried out actions against Jewish intellectuals in Równe, Bialystok, Lwów, Stanisławów, Brody, Czortków, Prużana, Bielsk Podlaski, Kishinev (Bessarabia), and in numerous other cities.

The remaining Jewish intellectuals were being destroyed economically and morally. Almost all of the Jewish white-collar employees, jurists, directors, engineers, and other professionals lost their jobs and their livelihood. Jewish doctors had to limit themselves only to Jewish patients. This hopeless situation led to many suicides—a phenomenon rather rare among other strata of Eastern European Jewry (especially before the major extermination of 1942–1943). Ringelblum wrote in his diary: "Some among the Jewish intellectuals, aware that the outlook for the future is hopeless, that they do not have the money to pay the hundred zlotys for a loaf of bread, and seeing that the danger of being caught and taken to the *Umschlagplatz* [gathering place for deportation] is imminent, have taken the step ahead and met death themselves by committing suicide. According to statistics, there have been hundreds of suicide cases and the majority have been from the ranks of the intelligentsia."[5]

## Pauperization and Equalization

The impoverishment of the Jewish population under the Nazi regime was also improbably swift. In their first ordinances, the Germans confiscated all Jewish bank accounts; they ordered that all money (except for a small sum), jewelry, gold, and silver be surrendered to them. In addition, in almost all the cities, they imposed a huge contribution on the Jews (in many places, such imposts were repeated several times). In this manner they extorted a substantial total of the Jews' movable assets—the more so as few were clever or courageous enough to risk withholding. The next step was "Aryanization"; that is, the confiscation of Jewish real estate, shops, stores, and warehouses. Only in rare cases, as in Częstochowa, were factory- and shopowners granted monthly payments of two hundred zlotys (for this sum one could buy two or four small loaves of bread on the black market). But soon even this payment was stopped. It was then much better to be employed as an ordinary worker or night watchman in the factory one had formerly owned. The Jewish bourgeoisie had lived in well-furnished modern houses, in the new fashionable parts of the cities. But these were just the districts chosen by the Germans for themselves. The well-to-do Jews were thrown out of their homes at the very onset of the German occupation, and had to leave everything behind, while the population of the poorer Jewish sections were not required to move as yet. Later, many of the ghettos were established in the districts inhabited by the poorer Jews; thus even they suffered less displacement than their wealthier brethren.

In addition, the more affluent classes were the victims of robbery and blackmail. The Nazis and their eager collaborators blackmailed them until they were drained of all their resources, and finally they were annihilated. Not to yield to blackmail was tantamount to death. A characteristic case, in Western Europe, involved the Amsterdam banker Baron Gutman. A personal friend of the Italian foreign minister Count Ciano, he had received, after tedious efforts, a permit to go to Italy, but Arthur Seyss-Inquart, the Nazi governor of the Netherlands, demanded that Gutman transfer all his property to the Third Reich before his departure. Gutman refused and was punished by being sent to Theresienstadt, where he was tortured to death. His wife was deported to Auschwitz and was killed there.[6]

From the few cases of wealthy Jews (in Holland, France, Estonia, Hungary, and Poland, among others) who succeeded in bribing the Gestapo to obtain release from the Nazi hell, the historian Gerald Reitlinger concluded that only poor Jews were truly threatened with extinction by the Nazis and that the richer always had a chance to be saved.[7] This is false reasoning; for Reitlinger generalizes from rare cases that occurred only in the early period of the Nazi occupation. In the later years, many attempts at self-preservation by such means ended in blackmail and death; some cases were simply set up by the Gestapo and by various swindlers to pull rich Jews into a trap. Soon, even the affluent had no means left to pay ransoms or bribes. A number of wealthy Jews had the courage not to report their assets, or they converted their real properties into ready money or exchanged them for jewelry or foreign currency, which was easier to conceal. But this did not always help. Many lost their hidden treasures through betrayal by informers or through speculation. Emanuel Ringelblum noted in his diary (October 23, 1940): "A number of well-to-do Jews have lost all their money. For instance, diamonds bought for 100,000 zlotys are now worth 5,000 zlotys. U.S. dollars, previously [exchanged at the rate of] 250 zlotys for one dollar, now are only 30 zlotys."[8]

When the Jewish population was forced into the ghettos, the process of pauperization accelerated, and expanded to affect all classes of the society. Generally, those entering the ghetto were not allowed by the Germans to bring anything more than a few necessities from their former home; sometimes, on short notice, they were permitted to pack a small bundle that could be carried on the back. Very seldom were they permitted to transport all their possessions into the ghetto (as for instance in Częstochowa). Moreover, in many cities the ghettos were rearranged several times, and moving from one place to another involved abandoning more of one's possessions. This process was called by the Germans "sifting out" or "shaking out" the Jews. Ringelblum tells of one Jew who had to change his residence four times, and of another who had to do so seven times.

How the process of pauperization contributed to social upheaval is indicated by this comment by Mark Dworzecki in his diary: "Jews could enter the ghetto [after the action of September 6, 1941, in Vilna] with a bag on their shoulders and with 300 rubles. Gold and valuables had to be surrendered earlier. Merchants and intellectuals were afraid to take a risk. The underworld characters and 'tough guys' did take a chance."[9] The Kovno chronicler Josef Gar describes the process of pauperization from still another viewpoint: "Looting thoroughly carried out by the Germans had already created, in September 1941, thousands of newly poor people. After the big action [late October 1941] an intense mood of depression followed in the ghetto; people did not even care about food anymore, they simply waited for death."[10] It is understandable that in such a mood of depression and fatality, one could not think of saving possessions.

In various ghettos social equalization went even farther. Because so many families were decimated, the habitual pattern of individual households had to be abandoned, and a communal system of cooking and eating was adopted. This occurred in the Theresienstadt ghetto, for example, and in some ghettos in Poland. Solomon Waga wrote of Częstochowa: "The day after the second action (late September 1942) people did not have anything to eat. In many houses they collected the foodstuffs from all the inhabitants and cooked in a common kettle. The well-to-do, who did not want to participate, were forced into the partnership by the poor people."[11] In several larger ghettos (Theresienstadt, Vilna, Lodz, Sosnowiec, among others), paradoxical as it may seem, a half-communist system of managing the domestic economy gradually developed; the entire juridical and administrative apparatus for the production and distribution of foodstuffs and other life necessities was centralized in the Judenrat or the ghetto dictator.

Many of the branches of production were monopolized. Theresienstadt and Lodz even had their own currency, circulated only inside the ghetto.

Social equalization found its expression in the folklore of the ghettos. The Warsaw ghetto jester, the half-mad Rubinstein, popularized the phrase "Everybody equal," which soon became a catchword in the ghetto and even served as the theme for a satirical show in one of the ghetto theaters.[12] "Everybody equal" was only half-true. Notwithstanding the forces tending toward equalization, all were not equal. A new Jewish *lumpenbourgeoisie,* as it were, worked its way up in the ghetto—as we shall see below— while the vast masses of the Jewish population were precipitated to the very depths of human existence, compared to which even the few possessions of the déclassés seemed an unfulfillable dream.

## Lumpenproletariat

While the déclassé elements in the ghetto had some roofs over their heads, something to sell in their homes, some underpaid job, some aid from the social self-help, there were other individuals who had no resources whatever. These were the masses of street beggars, who lived under the most horrible conditions. Above all, there were large numbers of homeless, orphaned, wild beggar children. Shocking reports about the ghetto beggars, the bread-snatchers, and other neglected human beings are found in many memoirs, especially that of Rachel Auerbach,[13] who was in charge of a public kitchen in the Warsaw ghetto.

Even worse than in Poland were the conditions of the refugees in Rumania and the southern Ukraine. Immediately after the outbreak of Soviet-German hostilities, the Rumanians occupied Bessarabia and the southern Ukraine and created a new province, Transnistria, which served as a reservation for deported Jews, much like the Lublin reservation in Poland. Tens of thousands of Jews from Bucovina and the old Rumanian provinces were deported to Transnistria and were "accommodated" in the ghettos of Kishinev, Beltsy, Sharogrod, Mohilev, Berschad, and elsewhere. The chaos and hardship of life among the refugees exceeded the worst suffering of the Jews in Poland. As an example, let us note the report given by the president of the Jewish community in Mohilev after his visit to several refugee points in 1941 or 1942. On that occasion he discovered in a long, dark granary in a field in Kantokawice in the Sharogrod region— a group of seventy half-naked emaciated creatures. They were beggars. Their leader was a former banker from Dorobin Zhudic, in the Dorohoi region.

In the settlements of Grobiwic and Halczyniec were people who sustained themselves by eating the flesh of horses, buried by the authorities in ditches two meters deep and sprinkled with carbolic acid.

## Lumpenbourgeoisie

Notwithstanding all the difficulties of life in the ghetto, a new social group emerged which not only managed to make a living but even began to accumulate wealth—at least until the big extermination actions in 1942 and 1943. This group was the so-called *lumpenbourgeoisie,* which presented the strongest contrast with the *lumpenproletariat.* Some of these entrepreneurs were merchants who extended their prewar businesses or developed new enterprises, especially in the field of highest priority—food of all kinds, including baked goods and candy, and food services such as cafés and restaurants. Then there were those who were granted concessions to manufacture certain products (for instance, brushes) and those who were given exclusive monopoly of ghetto transportation (for example, Kon and Heller, who operated the streetcars in the Warsaw ghetto).

There also came to life a new type of war speculator, who made huge profits from the abnormal economy in the ghettos. There were large-scale smugglers, go-betweens in all sorts of transactions, "profiteers," dealers in foreign currency, and subcontractors of German firms. The big speculators were notorious in the ghettos because of the boldness of their transactions, their shrewd schemes, their enormous profits, and their flamboyant, profligate way of life—all of which have been vividly described by Ringelblum,[14] Bernard Goldstein,[15] and others. This decayed class of *lumpenbourgeoisie* brought into the ghetto the most ruthless corruption. In some ghettos, a number of members of the Judenrat and of the Jewish police either belonged to this group or were associated with it.

Around the war profiteers gathered individuals from the working class, as well as from the middle class. In addition to the agents, go-betweens, managers, and profiteers, and the owners of cafés, night clubs, and restaurants, there were a number of ordinary people, such as the vehicle drivers and porters, who because of the character of their work were directly connected with the smuggling and black market operations. A substantial income was made by the hundred carriage drivers in the Bialystok ghetto, for instance; they had German passes to leave the ghetto and had built into their coaches secret compartments for smuggled goods. The porters were often partners in smuggling or in blackmail. Ringelblum wrote (October 2, 1940): "Heard today that the majority of the porters are informers. They follow the merchants who carry packages and they inform on them. And those who do not inform are dying from starvation."

Thus the harsh conditions of ghetto life led directly to corruption. Moreover, the "smart ones" (*di voyle,* as they were called in Warsaw) and the "strong ones" (*di shtarke,* as they were known in Vilna) did not content themselves with economic profit but had a far bigger ambition— to gain power in the ghetto by force. Ringelblum wrote about this in veiled language (about December 20, 1940): "The 'smart ones' have said to the Germans: 'We are sure that we will find the money of the rich Jews. Then we can split it.' Lesz-13 [the Jewish Gestapo agency of Abraham Gancwajch, at 13 Leszno Street] is acting in a similar manner . . . they want to be the second council and to take care of the whole community, not forgetting about themselves. There are among them many shady characters."[16] What Gancwajch wanted to achieve in the Warsaw ghetto was tried by other unscrupulous individuals and collaborators in Kaunas, Bialystok, Bełchatow, Lodz, Lublin, and other cities. In most cases the Judenrat succeeded, after a hard battle filled with intrigues and incriminations, in retaining authority (more on this below).

The *lumpenbourgeoisie* allowed itself to enjoy life without thinking of tomorrow. In any case, tomorrow would bring death to everybody. Abraham Lewin describes in his diary a typical fate of a war profiteer: "Tonight, again, several people were shot to death . . . among others, Szymonowicz, who recently made a fortune, about four million zlotys, on brush production. Last week he made a wedding for his daughter. The cost of the reception was allegedly about 25,000 zlotys. The Nazis treat their helpers . . . according to an old German saying: 'The Moor has done his duty, the Moor can go. . . .' "[17]

Even in prison, this new "ghetto elite" tried to drive away concern for the morrow, through entertainment and merrymaking. Jonas Turkow, who by chance was thrown into a cell with smugglers and thieves, tells about their behavior:

Day and night they sang. They exhausted almost the entire repertory of the Yiddish theater. . . . They were brought the best food: roast geese, chicken, chicken soup with noodles, white bread, and vodka in beer bottles. It was the first time in my life that I had seen such an excess of food as was brought in for them. One could forget that one was in the ghetto, where people were starving to death. They, the gang of thieves, could be considered among the ghetto élite along with the police, the "Thirteen," and the rest of the "high-boot people."[18]

In the Warsaw ghetto, many luxurious places of entertainment came into being: night clubs, locals, cafés, and restaurants.[19] There were similar places in the Częstochowa[20] and Cracow ghettos as well. People from outside the ghetto went there to eat and for entertainment. Among the Aryan profiteers on the outside, this phrase became quite popular: "One amuses oneself as in the ghetto." The Cracow ghetto was called "Fun City" (*wesołe miasteczko*) by the Poles.

## Social Stratification

Not all ghetto historians share this view that a radical social revolution took place in the ghetto. Zdenek Lederer has written: "Generally speaking, the moral and social code which prevailed in the normal *kehillah* [before the war] remained unchanged."[21] Raphael Mahler maintains that the "social differences in the Nazi-created ghettos were *a heritage of the social classes before the war* [italics mine]," but adds "—a heritage that in most cases was tending to break down and shatter to pieces."[22]

In reality, the situation in Eastern Europe was quite different from that in Western and Central Europe. In Western and Central Europe (with few exceptions) there were no closed ghettos, and the economic and social catastrophe of the Jewish masses unfolded at a slower pace than in the east. Jewish life was more stable and to a large extent was a continuation of prewar conditions, at least until the mass deportations of 1942–1943 (in Hungary, 1944). But in Eastern Europe, the upheaval occurred immediately after the outbreak of the war, with a revolutionary impetus. The German excesses were far more extreme and cruel in the east, the isolation of the Jews from the surrounding population far more rapid and complete. In the territories occupied by the Soviets from 1939 to 1941, the social revolution was more thorough and profound, because social equalization was already far advanced there when the Germans took over.

In the east the German abuses and atrocities followed one upon another so rapidly that no new social order could be established. It was not only a radical but a continual revolution, which maintained a constant state of flux in the society. For instance, there were times when money was the most significant factor in saving one's life, particularly in the first years of the German occupation (until about the end of summer 1942). From this period of relative stability originated the popular Yiddish song, "Moes, oy moes": "Money, money, money is the most important thing; if you do not have it, you are in big trouble." But in the later period of continuous "actions" and deportations, money lost its previous power. "On our black market," wrote a young ghetto fighter in May 1943, "the best 'currency' is a revolver, its equivalent in price is 10 kilos of pork-fat, one hundred cigarettes, or a half a liter of vodka. In the second place are cigarettes. One cigarette is worth one kilo of *kasha* [grits].[23] Money and jewelry have no value at all on our market."

After the mass deportations and the liquidations of most of the ghettos—in the period of the few remaining ghettos, enclosed work shops, "blocks" (self-sustaining working and living areas), and *Judenlager*—the money aristocracy was less important than the worker aristocracy of skilled craftsmen and of supervisors, *Oberjuden,* and members of working brigades. Social position was no longer determined by money, only by more immediately useful things such as provisions, clothing, and a good bunker. The owner of a secure bunker was held in greater esteem than a millionaire without a bunker. In general, in the later period the social dividing line ran between "those who shall live and those who shall die." The holders of *Lebensscheinen* (lit., "life certificates"; good working papers) were unquestionably more respected than the "wild ones" or "illegals" (unemployed persons), who were considered superfluous and whom any German had the right—or rather the duty—to shoot down without further reason. New social distinctions arose between the "yellows" and the "whites" (bearers of yellow or white certificates in Vilna); between *A*-Jews (the letter *A* on the Jewish armband stood for *Arbeiter,* worker, and meant a degree of security) and ordinary Jews (*Schmelz,* "junk," in the vicious slang of the SS men); between the owners of "hard" or "soft" certificates ("hard" papers indicated a permanent job; "soft" papers, a temporary job, which meant an earlier death).

In the early period of the ghettos, it was considered a privilege to be employed in the Judenrat or the Jewish police. But eventually this privilege became a death sentence. In various cities, the Germans treated the members and employees of the Judenrat as hostages, and arrested or killed them on the slightest provocation. Following the massive actions, when the Germans no longer needed many Jewish policemen, a number of them were sent to concentration camps, the rest were murdered on the spot. After these occurrences, moreover, resentment of the Jewish police intensified because of their role in the actions. In Warsaw, following the action of summer 1942, hatred of the Jewish police was so intense that they did not dare show their faces on the ghetto streets. In several cities (for instance, Bialystok, Grodno, and Zbaraż) a number of Jewish policemen abandoned their posts or simply ran away.

There were times when wealth was dangerous because it provoked blackmail. But there were also times when poverty meant death and one had to pretend to be well off in order to stay alive. When the Germans were deporting poor people, persons receiving assistance from the social help organizations tried to have their names removed from the lists of indigents, insisting that they did not need to be supported any longer. One report from Częstochowa (spring 1942) stated: "Enormous waiting lines before the Judenrat, thousands of old skeletons wrapped in rags are trying to persuade the officials that they have been affluent for a long time and that they do not need further social assistance, that they are able to work and, as a productive element, should remain in Częstochowa."

Most ghetto inmates changed both occupation and social class, and lost social and class status. There was not even enough time for their new class identification to become firmly established. It is therefore not surprising that a prominent social leader in the Vilna ghetto, the engineer Markus, put forth the theory that there was only one class in the ghetto—the "ghetto class." The entire ghetto economy, according to Markus, should become a collective enterprise. Everybody should give up his money and his possessions to the one and only ghetto organization, which would apportion it to all Jews.[24] Though Mark Dworzecki has called this plan utopian and unrealistic, a partly collectivized economy had been developed in the Vilna ghetto and elsewhere, as we have already mentioned. As a class the artisans and workers had the highest degree of social stability. The artisans and the foremen of work groups, especially in the areas away from the front lines, were very important to the German war industry. Skilled workers—particularly tailors, shoemakers, furriers, and the like—also served the German civilians in the occupied areas, and thereby maintained a semi-privileged position. The best Jewish tailors and shoemakers in Częstochowa, for example, were put up in a nice house right at the entrance to the ghetto, and had other privileges as well.

The most valued, best-protected occupation was brushmaking. It employed thousands of skilled craftsmen, especially in Warsaw and Międzyrzec. Brushes were in great demand among the Germans—obsessed as they were with cleanliness—for use on the frontline or in the "filthy" Jewish apartments they occupied in Eastern Europe. In general, artisans and skilled workers were less likely to be abused or deported. Their morale was therefore higher than that of other ghetto groups.

There was a strong impetus toward industriousness. Jacob Gens, in Vilna, advised Jews to find the hardest kind of work and try to be very useful, so that the Germans would need them and not liquidate them. "Work as a means of rescue" became the guiding principle of life. In a German shop in Warsaw, leading personalities—heads of yeshivas, rabbis, scholars, and pious Jews—mended shoes while they analyzed, from memory, a page from the Talmud or a difficult portion from Maimonides, or immersed themselves in a discussion of Jewish law.

Since these novice artisans and craftsmen were inexperienced and rather incompetent, they were very dependent on their skilled masters, the professional shoemakers, tailors, carpenters, brushmakers, and so on. And since success in the new occupation was literally a matter of life or death, the authority of the experienced craftsmen rose very high. In a short period, the prestige of skilled craftsmen became so great that they were considered authorities even in matters unrelated to their crafts. A new attitude developed toward them—one of exaggerated submissiveness, humility, and flattery. The author of the *House of Dolls,* Ka-tzetnik, observed this psychological process with a keen eye:

In Będzin, the German labor commissar ordered the Judenrat to establish a shoe factory. But no shoemakers were available anymore, because the Judenrat had long before delivered all the poor cobblers to the Germans "as a ransom for the rich Jews." Hence, in a big rush, they collected doctors, lawyers, cantors, merchants, etc. Only one shoemaker was found in the ghetto, Vevke; he was put in charge of the shop. At the narrow, low workbenches sat the famous doctors, noted lawyers, and rabbis, trying with all their might to appear like real shoemakers in the eyes of the German simpleton. Vevke moved around, angry. Silently he instructed them in the art ["Torah"] of shoemaking, and here and there he had to lend a hand to fix the poor, clumsy work. From all sides he could hear reverential calls of "Herr Direktor! Herr Direktor!" When the German supervisor left, the atmosphere became less tense. Vevke sat down, relaxed, at one of the workbenches. The intelligent apprentices considered it a great honor that Vevke had chosen their table. A noted doctor had just finished a report on the latest radio news. Now for the sake of the honored guest, he repeated the entire report, while Vevke half-listened with an air of benevolence.[25]

This episode is a perfect example of the upheaval in social values that was taking place in the ghetto.

When the Germans began to collect all kinds of junk, rags, scrap, iron, metal, and so forth to use as raw material for their war production, thousands of Jews found work in this *Werterfassung* (appropriation of goods). After the huge deportations, the Germans used a great many Jews as *Aufräumungskommandos* ("cleaning-up commandos") to empty out the apartments of the deported Jews. The *Werterfassung* and *Aufräumungskommandos* mostly employed former Jewish merchants, professionals, and intellectuals. The supervisors of the commandos were former porters or truckmen. These overseers let their subordinates know that they were the bosses. But no price was too high to pay for the position of rag-collector, whom others, themselves wrapped in rags, envied enormously.

## Women and Children

From the very beginning of the occupation the Nazis attempted either to send the majority of Jewish men off to forced labor camps or to kill them outright. In the pogroms in Bialystok in June and July 1941, for example, about 4,000 Jewish men were killed. In the Lithuanian village of Telsiai, a ghetto was established in December 1941 for 600 young women whose husbands had been killed. In Szczuczyn, immediately after the Germans entered, almost all the Jewish men were shot; when a ghetto was established, some time later, only women and children were left to inhabit it. In Łuniniec the German invaders immediately carried off all but thirty-six (who managed to save themselves) of the Jewish males of twelve years or older, none of whom ever returned. In Jaworów, almost all the men were taken away to the labor camps, leaving only women and children behind. In Międzyrzec, 2,295 men, nearly all the males fourteen to sixty-two years old, were sent to the labor camps in June 1940. Many died there, and those who returned were either sick or crippled. With the influx of about 6,000 refugees to Międzyrzec, the offset in balance between women and men came to a halt.

As a result of the mass murder of Jewish men, the proportion of men and women in the ghetto changed. In Warsaw at the beginning of 1942 the ratio was 132 females for every 100 males (for the twenty to thirty age group alone, 182 women for every 100 men). In Kaunas, after the summer action of 1941, the ratio was 130:100. In the Greater German Reich, according to the census of April 17, 1939, there were 1,366 Jewish women for every 1,000 Jewish men. Because of the merciless arrests and slaughter, Jewish men, especially those without work, shunned the streets. Women, in less danger of being taken, were often the breadwinners. Husbands remained at home and did the chores, while their wives went out to work. Numerous women were active in buying and selling goods, or bartering; others did physical labor. The Nazis, particularly in the later period, forced women to perform even the most demanding physical labor. In several ghettos, because of the shortage of men, women assumed important communal responsibilities. For instance, in Warsaw the executives of many house committees were women. In Wieliczka, the Judenrat was composed of five women and two men, and was headed by a woman. Such conditions altogether changed the relations between the two sexes, especially the position of women in the family.

In numerous families half-grown children, sometimes no more than seven or eight years old, took over the function of breadwinner, mostly by begging or smuggling. There is this account by a nine-year-old youngster from Warsaw:

In our family Daddy, my Mama, and my little sister all became sick at the same time. My brothers and I took care of them. But soon our small supply of provisions ran out, because none of us was earning any money. Then my brother and I got the last couple of zlotys from our parents and sneaked out from the ghetto to buy something. In the ghetto prices were 50 percent higher than those on the "other side."[26]

There are numerous songs and a large literature about child beggars and child smugglers during the Nazi era—proof that this was a mass phenomenon. Beggar children and child smugglers were common not only among the Jews but also among other peoples under the German occupation.

This most complicated picture of the social differentiation in the ghetto becomes therefore even more intricate. Women's and children's work, the disintegration of family life, the social and moral effects on the new reality, still have to be investigated more thoroughly.

## Antagonisms and Conflicts

In keeping with their basic strategy of "divide and rule," the Germans did all they could to exacerbate the tension and friction between groups and to create hostility between the different classes in the ghetto. Waldemar Machol, a high Gestapo official in the Bialystok ghetto who was caught after the war and brought before a Polish court in Bialystok, gave a clear insight into the strategic importance of this policy. When asked whether the Germans had not feared an uprising in the ghetto, Machol replied: "The Germans never considered the question of what to do should the Jews attempt an armed revolt. It was well known to them that *it would never come to such unity and harmony* among the Jews."[27] Disunity, in the Nazi view, kept the Jews weak.

Everywhere, the Germans created privileged and imperiled groups and pitted them against each other. In Belgium and France, for instance, they treated "native" Jews differently from "foreign" Jews (immigrants and refugees). In the Theresienstadt ghetto, the Nazis systematically instigated the "native" Czech Jews against the "foreign" German and Austrian refugees, and vice versa. In Holland, they created several categories of privileged Jews, who were registered on *blocked* lists (of persons not to be deported). Another privileged category in all the occupied countries were the *Mischlinge* (children of mixed marriages, or persons married to "Aryans"); also Sephardic Jews, certain groups of oriental Jews and Jewish citizens of neutral countries. In all the larger ghettos there were small groups of Jews who were "valuable for the German war economy" (*Wirtschaftlich wertvolle*), who also enjoyed special privileges.

As another means of increasing tension, the Germans put converts in a number of ghettos, many of whom had not had any association with Jews for a long time and in some measure disliked Jews. In the Warsaw ghetto, there were six thousand converts and several churches, with priests who themselves were converts. Among the converts were the well-known anti-Semitic Polish writer Zuzanna (Susan) Rabska and Josef Szeryński, also an anti-Semite and a former Polish police officer, who became chief of the Jewish ghetto police. The converts held many administrative posts. In general, their economic position was better than that of the other Jews, because they received assistance from the powerful Catholic organization Caritas and from their non-Jewish relatives and friends. The Jewish population related to them with mixed feelings, as can be judged from these words of Hillel Zeitlin: "The Jews now have pity for the converts . . . they are in a privileged position . . . they have their own public kitchen cared for by ŻTOS [Jewish Society for Social Welfare] with better meals. . . . the council is favoring the converts and provides them with better jobs. . . ."[28] Another "wedge" driven into several ghettos (such as Warsaw and Siedlce) were the Gypsies. In the Lodz ghetto, the Germans ordered that several streets be emptied for a special Gypsy quarter, and that the Judenrat arrange for food supplies and sanitary help for the 5,000 Gypsies. Several Jewish physicians died from typhoid, fighting an epidemic in the Gypsy ghetto.

## Class Struggle and the Social Policy of the Judenrat

While social differences and conflicts in the ghetto were, as we have seen, the direct or indirect result of German repressions, there is still the question of the Jews' own role in the social turmoil of the ghetto. In particular, did the Jewish self-governing body do anything to lessen the misery or ease the social conflicts? What was the social policy of the Judenrat? I must limit myself here to certain general observations, as background for the present discussion. The composition of the Judenräte was far from uniform. In numerous ghettos, the Germans approved the old *kehillah* administration, if the members had remained after the German invasion. These Jewish communal bodies were not democratically elected. In prewar Poland, ruled by the political party Sanacja, the council members of the *kehilloth* were chosen mostly under pressure from the government and were boycotted by the majority of workers and by Zionist-oriented voters. Therefore, they represented a minority of nonpartisan merchants and assimilated elements with conservative or reactionary sympathies. In a number of *kehilloth,* administrative commissions were put in charge by the Polish authorities. This had proved to be the best solution. But in many communities the invading Germans could find none of the Jewish councilmen, who had either escaped or gone into hiding; as a result, they appointed whoever was available.

In the territory formerly occupied by the Soviets, there were no Jewish communal bodies left when the Germans took over, and all the

Jewish councils were newly nominated. In fact, the local German admin-istration controlled the "autonomous" Jewish community; at will, the Nazis appointed Jewish councils, removed Jewish councils, meddled in their internal affairs, and built the Judenrat into an instrument of their own policy. In general, the responsible Jewish leaders avoided becoming members of the Judenrat, and the "authority" fell into inexperienced, often irresponsi-ble, hands. The German administration changed the composition of many Jewish councils seven, eight, or more times in a period of two or three years. The former members were often shot or were sent to concentration camps. With each changeover, the makeup of the Judenrat usually became worse. Many of the skilled communal leaders had left before the German invasion, many were arrested on Soviet territory and were deported to Siberia; many intellectuals and leaders, the reader will recall, were killed by the Germans immediately after their entry. As a result only rarely could one find individuals politically or morally equipped for the dreadful new tasks that lay before them, unlike anything yet experienced. In the political underground, especially in the youth organizations, strong new personalities began to develop, but they did not yet make their presence felt in public life.

Given the dearth of Jewish leaders, it is not surprising that in various cities men of despotic inclination pushed themselves to the top of the Judenräte and tried to gain exclusive power for themselves or for a small clique. Those "dictators," like all other dictators, carried out a policy leading to self-destruction, although they made themselves believe that they were saving as many people as possible. (Among them were Moses Merin in Sosnowiec, Mordechai Chaim Rumkowski in Lodz, Jacob Gens in Vilna, Efroim Barasz in Bialystok.[29])

Only in the relatively stable first period can we assume that the Jewish councils had a certain uniformity and represented the prewar class of merchants and industrialists with their conservative tendencies and in-clinations toward political opportunism. The Jewish masses, with their vast political movements ranging from the right to the extreme left, did not participate directly in the councils; workers and organized youth also shunned the Judenrat. German atrocities and treachery eventually drove even the conservative elements away from the councils. The Judenrat then became a haven for adventurers, worthless persons, marginal individuals who had no definite economic or social position and who hovered on the boundary between acceptable society and the underworld.

The social policy of the Jewish councils evoked much criticism. In his memoirs, Michel Mazor[30] described in detail Warsaw society's censure of the local Judenrat for its indifference to the indescribable misery of the refugees and for its failure to help the Jewish workers in German labor camps (as compared with the Jewish councils of Częstochowa and Lublin, which showed great concern for their laborers in the camps and gave as much help to them as was within their power). In 1942 (May 30) Ringelblum evaluated the problem much more deeply and touched upon the crucial dilemma, for which he had no ready answer:

Social help does not solve the problem. It sustains people for a short time only. But they have to die in the end anyway. It prolongs the situation, it does not bring any salvation; for, in order to accomplish anything, the relief organization would need millions of zlotys monthly at its disposal, and it does not have them. . . . Therefore, one may ask, "Would it be more rational to allot the available money to a selected few—to those who are socially active, to the intellectual élite and the like?" . . . Thus there remains the tragic dilemma: What to do— give everyone a spoonful and nobody will survive, or give with full hands, and there will barely be enough for a handful [to survive].[31]

Another Jewish writer, Abraham Einhorn, expressed an even soberer, more hopeless view: "Notwithstanding our negative attitude toward this organization, one has to emphasize that the *kehillah* can hardly do anything to ease the misery of the Jews; if it really were in a position to achieve something, and if it had the means to obtain the necessary resources, the 'decision-making factor' [i.e., the Germans] would never allow it to happen but would rob them of those resources without delay."[32]

The Jewish population, especially in the larger cities, established self-help organizations, for instance, the social-help committee in Vilna, which criticized the Jewish Council or even entered into open conflict with it (such as the house committees in Warsaw). A glorious chapter in the history of the Częstochowa ghetto was written by the labor council, established in May 1940, which openly criticized the Judenrat, organized a conference of workers' organizations in Częstochowa in December 1940, and carried out demonstrations in the spring and summer of 1941. In May 1942, the Germans arrested the most active leaders of the labor council and deported them to the death camp at Auschwitz.

The moral dilemma of whether to sacrifice a part of the population in order to save the more valuable, younger, stronger individuals or to require all to perish together was the ultimate question. In some of the ghettos, the Judenrat turned to a rabbinical court for advice. In many cities, the discussion centered around the famous ruling of Maimonides, which was interpreted to mean that one should not deliver for destruction even one Jewish soul, not even to save the whole community.[33]

The Jewish masses in numerous ghettos openly protested against the policies of the Judenräte. They mounted demonstrations or strikes. In the summer of 1941, in such cities as Szczebrzeszyn, Kutno, Poddębice, Lodz,

Bialystok, Vilna, Bełchatów, Sosnowiec, and Częstochowa, and even in Paris, demonstrations—one with 5,000 participants—were staged against the Jewish coordinating committee. In the summer of 1940, meager food rations led to violent demonstrations by the workers of Lodz, and Rumkowski, the dictatorial chairman of the Lodz Judenrat, had to give in; but soon after, he retracted. He dissolved the workers' representation and arrested some of its members. Protest activity shifted for a time to the new underground movement. Buildings in the ghetto were plastered with handwritten proclamations against Rumkowski and the Judenrat. In February and May 1941, further demonstrations and strikes provoked a clash with the Jewish police. In May 1942, demonstrations by children and youth who worked in the "resorts" (ghetto factories and shops) took place.

Conspicuously, the Germans, who generally were merciless in punishing even the smallest infringement of their regulations, adopted a "liberal" policy of nonintervention in regard to the demonstrations in the ghetto. Their "tolerance," considered a novelty by some of the ghetto writers, was only part of the calculated "divide-and-rule" policy. A classic example is the dramatic conflict that took place in the Vilna ghetto between the dictator Jacob Gens and the United Jewish Partisan Organization (FPO).[34] The Germans ordered the surrender of Yitzhak Wittenberg, commander of the FPO. Gens deceitfully invited Wittenberg to a meeting with him, and ordered the ghetto police to arrest Wittenberg and deliver him to the Gestapo. The FPO immediately issued a call to their fighting groups, who succeeded in liberating Wittenberg. Now Gens began a campaign against the Fareynikte Partizaner Organizatsye (FPO). He incited the masses and the underworld (the "strong ones") by warning them that, if Wittenberg were not surrendered to the Germans, the entire ghetto would be destroyed. The situation became extremely tense, and open combat between Jews in the ghetto was imminent. In order to avert the bloodbath that would ensue, Wittenberg gave himself up to the Gestapo, and perished in one of their dungeons. Gens had won, and became the sole "ruler" in the ghetto. The FPO had disbanded its fighting groups and executive body during the violent days of the Wittenberg crisis; it had lost its prestige, and its power was broken.

Vilna was not the only place where ghetto "dictators," or collaborators with dictatorial ambitions, tried to gain power for their own sake with the help of the mob and the underworld, or to win over the poorest masses of the population by passing themselves off as protectors and benefactors. Abraham Gancwajch, chief of the "Thirteen" in the Warsaw ghetto, tried to seize power from the Judenrat and win popularity among the masses and intellectuals alike by handing out free bread, delivering imflammatory and demagogic speeches, leading an illusory "fight against the speculators in the ghetto," and becoming a patron of hungry writers and artists. But he did not win the contest, and when he was of no more use to the Germans, they shot him. In the Kaunas ghetto, the Gestapo agent Kaspi-Srebrowicz and Beno Lipcer, overseer of the work brigade and later chief of the ghetto police, tried to advance themselves by similar means, but in the end the Judenrat suppressed them. In Lodz, David Gertler, commander of the Jewish *Sonderdienst* (office for "special service"), tried to take advantage of the demonstrations and the grievances against Rumkowski to seize the dictator's place for himself. But he failed. In Bialystok a group of opportunists associated with the Gestapo ("the little fives"), and their helpers ("the little hundreds"), attempted to snatch power from the Judenrat, but they lost the risky game, which was played without conscience by both parties. In Theresienstadt, Dr. Karl Löwenstein, the chief of the ghetto security department, a convert and former high German officer, tried to form a paramilitary youth organization (a new sort of ghetto police) and attempted to seize power. Eventually the Germans dismissed his "élite guard," because a Jewish military organization was not convenient for them; Löwenstein was removed from office in September 1943, and put in prison.[35]

In none of the larger ghettos did the collaborators and underworld figures manage to seize power. But in a number of smaller cities, especially in the later period of the war, collaborators became, almost without opposition, the sole "rulers" in the ghettos, because the conservative Jews, the main supporters of the Judenräte, were too weak, and the people's terror of the Germans was too strong to resist them. The Germans tried to destroy organized resistance in the ghetto by infiltrating the Jewish underground organizations with informers and provocateurs, or by creating new "fighting organizations" led by their own intelligence men (in Warsaw, for instance, such an organization was formed by Captain Lontsky [or Łącki], and a similar attempt was later made by Abraham Gancwajch). Thus the Jewish Fighting Organization had to struggle with great effort against informers and traitors, and even executed a number of them. After the action in Bialystok, numerous informers were lynched on the streets by the Jewish populace.

Interesting but rather little known are the relations between the underground and the underworld. In general, the Germans tried to exploit the underworld by inciting its members against the underground, but they were not always successful. A passionate struggle between the underground and the underworld took place in the concentration camps. Although this conflict was most intense between non-Jewish inmates, it affected Jews to some extent as well. Germany did not have sufficient army personnel or SS men to keep guard over the thousands of concentration camps, with millions of inmates. They were therefore forced to delegate certain functions, even police duties, to the inmates themselves, to the *Kapos,* "block-elders," and camp elders. The candidates for these positions were chosen from the ranks of the professional criminals (the "greens," that is, those wearing a green patch). But as the "greens" were mostly crude illiterates, the Germans had to give assignments requiring some intelligence (such as office work and hospital duties) to the political prisoners (the "reds," those wearing a red patch). In time, the "reds" took over more and more positions and gained prestige and authority in the self-government of such camps as Auschwitz. The camp commanders, however, favored the "greens" and often incited them against the "reds." At Buchenwald, the "greens" caused great sufferings to the other inmates, and were especially cruel to the political prisoners in the camp. When the underground organization decided to make an end to that situation, there was an open clash between the "greens" and the "reds"—in which the "greens" left hundreds of dead bodies on the battlefield. From that time on, the political inmates had the upper hand.

Though the Jewish Fighting Organization in Warsaw established a degree of authority among the underworld figures and was treated by them with great respect, there were other places, as we have seen, where the ghetto "dictators" or other influential collaborators tried to mobilize the underworld against the Jewish underground.

## Conclusions

We have seen that the ghetto community was not a direct continuation of the prewar Jewish society, with its class differences and interrelations. Under the tremendous pressure of the Nazi persecutions, a social revolution took place, which swiftly and radically shattered the whole prewar order. On the ruin of the old social system followed a chaos of continually changing conditions, which prevented the establishment of a new social order of any permanence. Instead, Jewish society was kept in a perpetual state of flux. Class distinctions in the ghetto were based less on the prewar criteria of monetary wealth and professional or intellectual achievement than on factors related directly to survival under the new conditions: shrewdness, audacity, indifference to the plight of others, physical strength, manual dexterity, and the external factors such as access to the German authorities. In the jungle, money and scholarship do not count for much— only strong teeth and nails—and the ghetto created by the Nazis was a jungle, in which group was pitted against group in a struggle for survival against impossible odds, a struggle carefully orchestrated by the Nazis to undermine communal solidarity and foster the growth of a corrupt, manipulable underworld.

On the other hand, we must emphasize that nowhere did the Germans succeed in obliterating the ethical and moral values, the conscience, of Jewish society. All the ghetto chroniclers and memoirists cite numerous examples of highly ethical behavior, of communal solidarity, of self-sacrifice for the good of the community. Worker and youth organizations, the few remaining intellectuals, and public leaders as well as the religious leaders and pious Jews, all contributed to uplifting the morale of the ghetto.

The conflicts and antagonisms in the ghetto may be compared to a struggle among people aboard a sinking ship, each vying for a place to jump into the sea, yet aware that their chances for survival in the water were very slim.

One has to try to perceive these most complicated, entangled, and fluctuating processes of the social existence in the ghetto to understand the complexity, and not to oversimplify it by resorting to conventional formulas. Otherwise, one draws a false picture with false interpretations and a false conclusion.

❏ This essay was first published in Yiddish under the title "Sotsyale Konflikten in Geto" in *Yidisher Kemfer,* Passover issue, 5714 (1954), pp. 77–83, and April 30, 1954, pp. 13–14.

## Notes

1. Bernard Mark, "Problems of Research on Resistance in the Ghettos" (Polish), *Biuletyn* (November 1950), 1–3; also in Yiddish, *Yediot,* 2 (Warsaw, November 1950), 1–3. *Idem,* "Polemics about the Research on the Warsaw Ghetto Uprising" (Yiddish), *Dos naye lebn* (The New Life), Lodz, July 11, 1947, p. 3.

2. Raphael Mahler, "The Research on the Last Jewish Martyrology Takes a New Direction" (Yiddish), *Yidishe Kultur,* 11 (February 1949), 1–8; *idem,* "What Should Be the Moral of the Present Jewish Catastrophe" (Yiddish), *ibid.,* 11 (April 1949), 34–42.

3. Reply to a questionnaire of the "Oneg Shabbat" (code name for the secret ghetto archives in Warsaw), *BFG,* I, 2 (1948).

4. Abraham Lewin, "From the Ghetto-Diary" (Yiddish), *BFG,* V, 4 (1952), 41–42.

5. *Notitsn,* p. 294.

6. Lederer, *Ghetto Theresienstadt,* pp. 38–39.

7. Reitlinger, *The Final Solution,* p. 4.

8. *Notitsn,* p. 64.

9. Mark Dworzecki, *Yerushelayim delite in kamf un umkum* (The Jerusalem of Lithuania in Struggle and in Destruction) (Paris, 1948).

10. Josef Gar, *Umkum fun yidish Kovne* (The Destruction of Jewish Kowno) (Munich, 1948).

11. Solomon Waga, *Hurbn Czenstokhov,* p. 155.

12. Jonas Turkow, *Azoy iz es geven* (Thus it Happened) (Buenos Aires, 1948), p. 123.

13. Rachel Auerbach, *Behutsot Varshah, 1939–1943* (In the Streets of Warsaw, 1939–1943) (Tel Aviv, 1953).

14. *Notitsn,* pp. 205, 227, 228.

15. Bernard Goldstein, *Finf yor in varshever geto* (Five Years in the Warsaw Ghetto) (New York, 1948); also in an English translation, *The Stars Bear Witness* (New York, 1949; London, 1950).

16. *Notitsn,* p. 31.

17. Abraham Lewin, *BFG,* V (October–December 1952), 45.

18. Turkow, pp. 180–85. High boots, the symbol of power, were worn in the ghetto by some individuals to imitate the fashion of the Germans, Polish agents, and the like.

19. Turkow, pp. 196–98.

20. Waga, pp. 129–30.

21. Lederer, *Ghetto Theresienstadt.*

22. Raphael Mahler. See note 2.

23. Leon Najberg ("Marjan") in *Dokumenty i Materjały,* II, *"Akcje" i wysiedlenia* ("Actions" and Deportations), ed. by Josef Kermisz (Lodz, 1946), p. 344.

24. Dworzecki, p. 158.

25. Ka-tzetnik 135633, *The House of Dolls* (New York, 1955), pp. 6–7.

26. Mietek Eichel, in L. W. Schwarz, ed., *The Root and the Bough: The Epic of an Enduring People* (New York, 1949), p. 285.

27. Szymon Datner, "Materials on Machol-Friedel: A Contribution to the Historical Research on 'Bezirk Bialystok' " (Yiddish), *BFG,* III, 3–4 (1950), 63–103.

28. Answers by Jewish writers and scholars in the Warsaw ghetto to questionnaires of the "Oneg Shabbat" (Yiddish), *BFG,* I, 2 (1948), 111–12.

29. See essays 12, 13, and 14 below.

30. Michel Mazor, *La Cité Engloutie: Souvenir du Ghetto de Varsovie* (Paris, 1955), pp. 39, 43–45; also in *Le Monde Juif,* 36 (1950), 8–10.

31. *Notitsn,* pp. 231–32.

32. Answers by Jewish writers and scholars in the Warsaw Ghetto to questionnaires of the "Oneg Shabbat" (Yiddish), *BFG,* I, 2 (1948), 120.

33. *Hilkhot Yesodei Hatorah,* chapter 5, par. 5. Also see essays 12, 13, and 14 below.

34. See essay 14 below, on Jacob Gens.

35. See essay 5 above, "Aspects of the Jewish Communal Crisis in Germany, Austria, and Czechoslovakia During the Nazi Period."

# THE KARAITES UNDER NAZI RULE

The Karaites are the only schismatic Jewish sect other than the Samaritans to have survived to date. Both sects have dwindled to insignificant minority groups, and neither has been considered by the Jews or the governments of their countries of residence to be part of the Jewish community. In the early Middle Ages the main centers of Karaism were in Egypt and Palestine; later Karaites also settled in Byzantium (particularly in Constantinople) and—under Khazar rule in Eastern Europe, from the eighth to the tenth century—in the southern parts of Russia and the Ukraine (particularly the Crimea). There is not sufficient evidence to corroborate the theory of Karaite scholars that the Karaites of Eastern Europe are descendants of the Khazars or of other Turko-Mongol groups converted to this brand of Judaism by the Karaite scholar Itzhak Singari.[1] This theory, rejected by various Jewish and non-Jewish scholars alike, has been firmly sustained by Karaite writers and leaders, and played a great role in deciding the fate of the Karaites under the Nazi regime.

During the fourteenth century a number of Karaites from the Ukraine and the Crimea settled in Lithuania (Troki) and in Red Ruthenia[2] (Halicz) and later founded several other settlements in Poland, entirely isolated from the Jewish communities in that country. This isolation continued after the partitions of Poland, under Austrian rule in Galicia and under Russian rule in Lithuania, Volhynia, and the Crimea. The Russian government was especially sympathetic to the endeavors of the Karaites to dissociate themselves from the Jews. In 1840 the Karaites were recognized as a separate religious community; their status was further improved in 1863; and by decrees on November 5, 1881, and February 8, 1893, they were exempted from the discriminatory anti-Jewish laws and put on a par with the Christian citizens of Russia.[3] During World War I, approximately 700 Karaites served in the czarist army, about 500 of them in officer's rank. Many Karaites participated in the military operations against the Bolsheviks in the Crimea during the Civil War. During the evacuation of the Crimea by the White Russians, in 1920, many Karaites, particularly officers and soldiers, fled to the West and thus a new small Karaite diaspora developed. In France, which had had only two Karaite residents before 1914, the number grew to 250 or 270 by World War II.[4] About a hundred Karaite families immigrated to the United States, mostly from Lithuania and the Crimea, among them former officers and soldiers of the armies of Denikin and Wrangel. Before World War II several thousand Karaites lived in Turkey and Egypt. About 9,000 to 10,000 lived in the Soviet Union, a large proportion of them in Crimea. Less numerous was the Karaite community in Poland, estimated between 700 and 1,300. The largest communities were Troki (300), Vilna (300?), Halicz (150), and Lutsk (50). Scattered families lived in Lithuania (Ponevezhis), Latvia (Riga), and Byelorussia.[5]

During World War II almost all the Karaite communities in Europe came under Nazi rule. Unwarranted, fantastic rumors about their fate were circulated both during the war and after. In 1942 reports were published that the Karaites were regarded as Jews by the Nazis and were being treated accordingly.[6] Details about the extermination of the Karaites appeared in an American Jewish journal in 1950.[7] These reports have proved to be inaccurate. The small Karaite community succeeded in escaping the Nazi's genocidal drive. But how this was achieved has not yet been fully recorded. A Karaite scholar, for instance, in a recent thirty-page study on the Karaites, included only a brief note about this historical episode.[8]

I had the opportunity to observe, in Galicia in 1942, some stages of the German occupation authorities' investigation of the Karaite problem, and also to obtain first-hand contemporary reports on the Karaites of Halicz. This personal experience and the scarce eyewitness records published in the postwar era by survivors have been supplemented by official documentation in the archives of YIVO and the Centre de Documentation Juive Contemporaine (CDJC). In the light of all these materials a first attempt at a history of the Karaites during the Nazi regime can be presented.

## Karaites in Germany and Italy Before World War II

In all of Germany in 1941 there were only eighteen Karaites, most of them former officers of General Wrangel's army.[9] It seems that this small group started to intervene quite early with the government of the Third Reich to avoid being identified as Jews. In the early years of the Nazi regime the noted Orientalist Paul E. Kahle, at that time head of the Deutsche Morgenländische Gesellschaft, was sent to Leningrad to examine the rich Oriental collections available there in order to determine the status of the Karaites. As a result of his research, Kahle agreed with the position of the former czarist regime, that the Karaites should be treated as an independent religious group unconnected with the Jews.[10] This definition, though sufficient to secure the Karaites a privileged status in czarist Russia, could not have the same implications in the Third Reich, where racial criteria were decisive. The Karaites had, therefore, to continue their efforts, which were intensified in 1938, in all probability because the situation of the Jews was rapidly deteriorating. In reply to two applications submitted by the Karaites to the Reichsministerium des Innern on September 5 and October 10, 1938, the minister decreed, on December 22, 1938:

In accordance with the first regulation of the Reich Citizenship Law, para. 2, art. 2, the sect of the Karaites is not to be regarded as a Jewish religious community. The statement that the Karaites are as a group of kindred blood, can still not be made, because the racial classification of a person cannot be determined solely by one's belonging to a particular people but should always be defined by one's personal descent and racial-biological characteristics.[11]

This decree was brought to the attention of the Karaites' representative, S. de Douvan,[12] in a letter dated January 9, 1939, from the head of the Reichsstelle für Sippenforschung (Reich Office for Racial Research). Later this letter was frequently referred to as the "decree of 9 January 1939."

As can be seen, the Reichsminister's decree only confirmed the recognition of the Karaites as a separate religious community. On the racial question, the decree was evasive. Apparently, the German government had reached no definite conclusion as yet on the racial background of the Karaites. Its indecision was reflected in the works of two German scholars whom the Nazis regarded as experts on East European Jewry.[13] In administrative practice, however, the tiny Karaite group was exempted from anti-Jewish laws and measures. With regard to later developments, particularly in Nazi-occupied France and Eastern Europe, the decree of 9 January 1939 became extremely important. In the absence of any other legislation concerning the Karaites, it became a kind of Magna Carta on which their rights and exemptions from the harsh anti-Jewish laws were based until new instructions were eventually issued. In all the countries under Nazi occupation the decree of 9 January 1939 was interpreted by the Germans in favor of the Karaites in a much broader sense than the letter of the text indicated.

Germany's ally, Italy, also harbored a small group of Karaites (the exact number is not known). In 1934, well before the Reich's racial policy toward the Jews was adopted in Italy, an Italian anthropological expedition headed by Professor Gini was dispatched to Eastern Europe, and examined about 130 Karaites in Galicia. The conclusion arrived at by this research group was that the Karaites examined were of Armenoid descent, with a Mongolian strain. Gini published a paper on his observations in the ethnographic journal *Genus,* in Rome in 1936, while another member of the expedition, M. Magnino, published his views in the racist *La Difesa della Razza* (Vol. II, Rome, 1939–1940).[14] Consequently, the Karaites in Italy were exempted from Italian anti-Jewish legislation and were permitted to enjoy their civil rights as before.

## The Karaite Problem During World War II in France

Thus far, the Karaite problem in Germany and Italy was confined to an infinitesimally small group of people, and attracted little attention in government circles. After the German occupation of Western and Eastern Europe, however, the dimensions of the problem broadened; it was now a question of how to handle several hundred people in the West and several thousand in the East. That question arose first in France, in 1940–1941. According to a list submitted to the French police on February 19, 1941, by the Association des Caraïmes en France, about 200 Karaites then lived in Paris and its environs, while about forty to fifty lived in the nonoccupied zone of France in Marseilles, Nice, St. Girons in the subdepartment of Arièges, in Montedon, and elsewhere. Only a small percentage of them— thirty-three persons—had already acquired French citizenship. One hundred and thirty-three persons were defined as Russian refugees. Turkish citizens were also comparatively numerous (twenty-seven persons), while the remainder were divided among these nationalities: Polish (seven), Iranian (eight), Estonian (five), Dutch (four), Spanish (three), Czechoslovak (two), Rumanian (two), Bulgarian (two), Georgian (two), and one each from Yugoslavia, Armenia, and Latvia. Two declared themselves as Soviet citizens, five were listed as of "undetermined nationality."[15]

Trouble started for the Karaites after the Vichy government published the second *Statut des Juifs,* of June 2, 1941. The French definition of who was a Jew was based on a mixture of racial and religious criteria. Everybody who belonged to the Jewish faith or had at least three grandparents of Jewish denomination was considered a Jew.[16] In accordance with this view, the Commissariat Général aux Questions Juives (CGQJ) asked the Karaites to register as Jews, and subjected them to the *Statut des Juifs*. Karaites in the nonoccupied zone[17] refused to register, claiming that they were non-Jewish. Regional offices of the CGQJ became confused,[18] and raised the question with their headquarters. The answer was clear and left no doubt about the official attitude of the Vichy government; replying on August 14, 1941, to the regional director in Toulouse, the CGQJ headquarters emphasized that the Karaites "ought to be likened to the Jews in regard to the law [of 2 June 1941]."[19] In his letter of February 25, 1942, to the regional director in Marseilles, the director of the Statut des Personnes, a department of the CGQJ dealing with the main problems of racial classification and with the implementation of the registration of Jews, stated: "I have the honor of informing you that the Karaites, being merely a dissident sect, ought to be considered Jews under the terms of the law of 2 June 1941."[20] As late as September 1942 the regional office in Lyons received the same answer.[21] This attitude seems to have been common even among the highest authorities of the CGQJ. In January 1942, at the request of the Karaites in Paris, an influential French priest, Léon Robert, superior-general of the Societé des Missions Étrangères in Paris, tried to intervene with the head of the CGQJ, Xavier Vallat, pleading that the Karaites should not be designated as Jews. Vallat replied curtly but firmly, on January 17, 1942, that he had referred this problem to experts for examination and that in their opinion, the Karaites must be regarded as Jews. The only differences between Jews and Karaites, he added, were in certain matters of religion.[22]

During December 1942 and the early months of 1943, there was a complete change in the attitude of Vichy CGQJ in this matter—a dramatic turnabout due to the developments in Paris. In the occupied zone the problem of the Jews and the Karaites was the common responsibility of the German occupation authorities and of the CGQJ; contrary to the attitude of the CGQJ, the German authorities in France regarded the Karaites as non-Jewish. In a letter dated October 30, 1941, the police prefect of Paris advised the directorship of the Statut des Personnes: "Since the occupying authorities do not consider individuals of Karaite extraction to be Jews, the persons concerned have been exempted, since last month, from the measures imposed on Jews."[23]

Was this the result of an action which the Karaites had undertaken in the meantime? There is some evidence to support this view. In February 1941 the Association des Caraïmes in Paris submitted to the police and to the CGQJ lists of its members in Paris and the nonoccupied zone, with carefully collected personal data, including the address and occupation of each member. It may be assumed that the preparation of those lists, and also the negotiations with the appropriate authorities for that matter, had started at least a few months earlier. The association also submitted copies of its *Statut* and the modifications resolved at its general assembly in Paris on June 29, 1941, with a *Note Explicative*. These modified laws tightened the rules on membership and made any infiltration by "undesirable elements" practically impossible by the following provision: "Only *the offspring of two Karaite parents are considered Karaites, and no exception is allowed.*"[24] Moreover, in a letter to the CGQJ dated September 23, 1941, the president of the association, Simon Kasas,[25] emphatically stated: "With the object of avoiding the possibility of infiltration into our midst by any undesirable element, we have put ourselves at the disposal of the prefecture of police for the review of each claim of Karaite extraction."[26]

On September 26, 1941, three representatives of the association, Messrs. Kasas, Alivaz, and Bakay, personally called on the CGQJ in Paris to present their case. They also submitted several documents, books, and scholarly papers to prove that the Karaites had never been considered Jews in Russia, Rumania, or Hungary.[27] The CGQJ, however, was apparently not impressed, either by the attitude of the German occupation authorities or by the representatives of the Karaites, and stuck to its own interpretation. To the above-mentioned letter from the Paris police prefect on October 30, 1941, the director of the Statut des Personnes in Paris, Jacques Ditte,[28] replied: ". . . no special measures can be taken in favor of the sect of the Karaites, who practice moreover certain rites of the Jewish religion."[29] After this letter the police prefect, J. François, could do no other than advise the president of the association (in a letter of November 26, 1941): ". . . The members of the Association des Caraïmes of Paris are considered Jews—with regard to the law of 2 June 1941, bearing the *Statut des Juifs*—by Monsieur the Commissaire Général aux Questions Juives." Consequently he invited the Karaites to come to his office and register as Jews.[30]

The decision of the CGQJ and the subsequent letters of the police prefect struck the Karaites like a thunderbolt. In a letter to Xavier Vallat dated November 29, 1941, the president of the association explained how deeply shocked all Karaites were by this development. He asked the Commissaire to revise his decision, and outlined eleven points distinguishing Karaites as a religious and ethnic group different from the Jews. Of these points, the following deserve special attention: The Karaite religion is independent and autonomous (§1). The Karaites have never accepted Jews into their community (§7) and have never mixed with them (§8). The Karaites are not Semites, but of Tauro-Cimmerian origin (§8). There is violent antagonism between the Karaites and the Jews and "this antagonism has created a certain anti-Semitism among the Karaites" (§9). The

Karaites have an entirely different mentality from the Jews. They were never in prison except in Soviet Russia for political reasons (§10). A memorandum of twelve pages and twenty-five appendices was attached to the letter.[31]

Thus, the respective attitudes were determined and a militant debate was begun between the Karaites and the CGQJ, in which the Karaites skillfully advanced ever-new and better arguments. They produced a statement by the archbishop of Paris that their religion "is considered by the Catholic Church . . . to be completely autonomous and closer to Islam than to the Jewish religion."[32] Similar statements were issued by the metropolitans Euloge and Seraphin of the Russian Orthodox Church in Western Europe.[33] With particular pride, the Karaites adduced the opinion of the rabid anti-Semite George Montandon, who during the Nazi occupation was raised to a high position as the director of the Nazi-sponsored Institut d'Études des Questions Juives et Ethnoraciales, and as the racial expert of the CGQJ. In an article on the Karaites in *L'Ethnie Française* of January 1943, the "learned professor" developed original pseudoscientific theories of his own. He distinguished between "biological race," based on physical hereditary elements, and "ethnicity," based on what he called "all the human characteristics (physical, moral, mental)," and arrived at the conclusion that the Karaites are in the ethnoracial sense "Irano-Tatarofinno-Slavs," probably descended from Khazars. In addition, there was another reason why he personally could not consider them Jews: they did not have the "Jewish mentality."[34]

The Jewish community in France also became involved in the heated debate. In the *Bulletin de l'Union Générale des Israélites de France* (Vol. I, nos. 30, 31, 32, dated August 7, 14, and 21, 1941) there appeared a series of articles on the Karaites, followed by another series on the Khazars. The attitude taken by the writers of the *Bulletin* was that the Karaites were a Jewish sect, and that they were not descendants of the Khazars. The reaction of the Karaites and their allies was brisk and vehement. In two statements in September 1942 the Office des Émigrés Russes en France, the mother organization of the Karaites, placed itself "unreservedly" behind the Karaite thesis, and concluded that the attitude of the Jews was motivated by

the ardent desire . . . to see the little colony of Karaites—who have dared to refuse to become the accomplices of a few Jews in their fraud [sic]—to see this colony submitted to the same restrictions as the Jews.

The *Bulletin* articles were repudiated in the same aggressive vein in the memoranda of Colonel Bogdanovitch, a Karaite, in September 1942. It is noteworthy that Bogdanovitch's knowledge of Jewish religion and culture was based primarily on the slanderous book by August Rohling (in French translation: *Le Juif selon le Talmud*), from which he quoted profusely.[35]

The Karaites tried to get support from the German authorities and organizations, even though some of them were only remotely familiar with the problem. For instance, on the request of a Karaite resident in the department of Savoie, a local bureau of the Verbindungsstelle Frankreich der Organisation der deutschen Wirtschaft in Lyons issued a statement, on November 3, 1942, apparently based on a misunderstanding or misinterpretation of the 9 January 1939 decree. In the interpretation of the Verbindungsstelle, this decree classified the Karaites as an "Aryan ethnic group" having nothing in common with the Jews.[36]

On the other hand, the statements and decisions made after the autumn of 1941 on the Karaite question, by the officials of the Reichsministerium für die besetzten Ostgebiete [RMfdbO (Reich Ministry for the Occupied Eastern Territories)] might have influenced the decisions of the CGQJ. In any case, the official correspondence of the RMfdbO on this problem was studied by the French authorities, and was included in the Karaite files in the CGQJ.

The Karaites finally won their dogged battle. The CGQJ completely retreated from its former position, and adopted the German racial line. The first sign of this change was hinted at in Jacques Ditte's letter to the police prefect of Paris, on August 17, 1942, in which Ditte expressed an opinion contrary to the attitude hitherto maintained by the entire CGQJ, including himself. Why, asked Ditte innocently, should the anti-Jewish laws issued upon recent German instructions affect the very people who are non-Jewish according to the German point of view? Owing to a certain interpretation of the *Statut des Juifs* of June 2, 1941, Ditte continued, the CGQJ had considered the Karaites Jews, but this official French interpretation had recently been repudiated by French courts of appeal and tribunals. It was most illogical and quite unjust, Ditte maintained, to apply a very rigorous German law against Jews to people who, according to the same German law, are non-Jewish. The French interpretation was wrong—and this, added Ditte cleverly, he had already pointed out eight months earlier.[37]

This about-face was definitely conceded in the comprehensive summary, dated February 8, 1943, prepared by the Statut des Personnes. In this memorandum, Ditte went even further in rewriting recent history. He contended that although he had signed the letter of November 11, 1941, to the police prefect, denying the Karaites the right to be considered non-Jews, he was personally "of a contrary opinion." He concluded with the suggestion that the French interpretation, unfavorable to the Karaites, be repealed and that they be exempted from the anti-Jewish legislation.

While the bureaucratic machine still continued to chew over the issue, some practical steps in favor of the Karaites were taken in January 1943. On the request of the regional offices of the CGQJ in Lyons and Nice, the Vichy headquarters of the CGQJ explained, in its replies of January 13 and 22, 1943, that according to a recent agreement the Karaites were no longer to be considered Jews.[38] Thus the tiny Karaite community of France was saved from the predicament of the French Jews. Moreover, the discussions and decisions in France on that matter were helpful in the formulation of the attitude of the German occupation authorities in Eastern Europe toward the Karaite question.

## The Karaite Problem in Nazi-Occupied Eastern Europe

The Karaite problem in Eastern Europe became acute only after the outbreak of Soviet-German hostilities and the subsequent German occupation of Eastern Galicia, Volhynia, Lithuania, and the Crimea—where there were many more Karaite residents than in Western Europe. The so-called 9 January 1939 decree concerning the Karaites in Germany and the discussion on the Karaite problem in France at that time, were known to the German administration in the occupied East European areas and influenced their dealings with the Karaites.

The problem had to be dealt with by the German authorities on two different levels. First, it had to be decided whether the Karaites were to be included in the program for the total extermination of the Jewish population in Eastern Europe. The heads of the Einsatzgruppen charged with this assignment did not know whether to include the Karaites in the extermination program or to exempt them as a separate, non-Jewish community. An inquiry was sent to Berlin and the instruction came back to spare the Karaites. This was revealed during the trial of the Einsatzgruppen commanders before the Nuremberg Military Tribunal, particularly during the cross-examination of Otto Ohlendorf, chief of Einsatzgruppe D, which operated in southern Ukraine and the Crimea. Ohlendorf stated that "the Karaites had the Jewish religion, but they could not be killed because they did not belong to the Jewish race." Ohlendorf also mentioned that simultaneously with the Karaite problem, another question arose—the fate of the Krimchaks (the small group of Tatar-speaking Jews in the Crimea, distinct from the Ashkenazic Jews). Again an inquiry was sent to Berlin, and the answer came that the Krimchaks were to be regarded as Jews. The difference between them and the Karaites, explained Ohlendorf, was just "in the blood." The result: from November 16 to December 15, 1941, a total of 17,765 Jews and 2,504 Krimchaks were killed in western Crimea (Simferopol, Eupatoria, and other towns), while the Karaites were spared.[39] Ohlendorf did not mention the names of the superiors who gave these orders, and we can only guess that they were issued by Reinhard Heydrich or Heinrich Himmler, and that they were probably issued to the other Einsatzgruppen commands (A, B, and C) as well, because the Karaites of Galicia, Volhynia, and Lithuania were spared too. No written instructions of the Berlin SS headquarters with regard to Karaites and Krimchaks were presented at the Nuremberg trials, and, as far as I know, none have been discovered.

Thus, the Karaites were saved from the SS extermination operations. But this did not solve the problem of their status under the German civilian administration in the occupied areas in the East. Intensive negotiations in this direction started at the very beginning of the German occupation. As early as August 31, 1941, three high officials of the Generalkommissariat Kauen (Lithuania), Hauptabteilungsleiter Dr. Essen, Oberregierungsrat Dexheimer, and Regierungsrat Baumgürtel, came to New Troki to interview the head (*hakham*) of the Karaite community, Hadzhi Seraja Khan Szapszal, and his deputy, Szymon Firkowicz. This very friendly conversation was carried on in Russian, because the Karaites did not understand German. The three German officials prepared a favorable report (dated September 1, 1941) on this visit, and reached the following conclusions:

The Karaites . . . are, by the Turks as well as by the Soviets, included among the Turkish people and not among the Jews. . . . Neither in their gestures nor in their appearance do they make a Jewish impression. . . . Their religion is very mixed. . . . Christ and Muhammad are recognized [by them] as prophets. . . . The leadership of the Karaites derives from their spiritual head in Troki . . . so the treatment of the Karaites here, as well as in the Crimea and in the remaining Orient, is significant.

To this report the German officials attached a copy of the 9 January 1939 decree and a copy of the Polish pamphlet by Szymon Firkowicz, *O Karaimach w Polsce,* published in 1938 in Troki. On the very same day, September 1, 1941, the Generalkommissar of Lithuania, Theodor Adrian von Renteln, sent this report to the three Gebietskommissare of his province, in Kaunas, Vilna, and Siauliai, with the following instruction: "According to the above statement, the Karaites are not to be equalized with the Jews."

On September 25, a similar instruction was issued for the entire Ostland territory by the Reichskommissar for the East. Finally, on October 1, 1941, a letter signed by Georg Leibbrandt, chief of the political division of the RMfdbO, gave official approval to the "viewpoint that the Karaites are not members of the Jewish religious community," but added the following reservation:

Nevertheless, I advise you, in further dealing with this question, to pay attention to the fact that an intermingling between individual Karaites and Jews has occurred. Such cases are to be known from Lutsk and Halicz. Therefore, I ask you, first of all, not to make a general resolution regarding the classification of the Karaites which would go beyond the separation of the Karaites from the Jewish religious community.

A second instruction issued by the Reichskommissar on October 14, 1941, tightened up the rules concerning the "impure" Karaites:

In general [the Karaites] are keeping themselves strictly separate from the Jews. Nevertheless, in individual cases they have intermingled with them. If in such cases the Karaite partner in marriage explicitly adheres to the Jewish religion, he should be recognized as belonging to the Jewish religious community, and should be treated as a Jew.

Karaites in mixed marriages with Jewish spouses are also to be treated as Jews, even without an explicit confession of adherence to the Jewish religion. The same applies to the offspring of such mixed marriages. They too are subject to the guidelines regarding the treatment of Jews.

In November 1941, the Karaite *hakham* in Troki asked the RMfdbO to extend the ruling of 9 January 1939 to the Karaites in the Crimea and other parts of southern Russia. It took some time, however, before this request was granted in the instruction of the RMfdbO, of October 6, 1942, to the Reichskommissar of the Ukraine.[40]

Thus far, only the religious separation of the Karaites from the Jews had been recognized in the instructions of the RMfdbO. What the Karaites, and their friends in the ranks of the German administration, were driving at went much further: namely, to prove the non-Jewish racial origins of the Karaites. Only this could give them permanent security. The search for evidence of racial distinction went on, therefore, with a great drive and in many directions. All the literature on the Karaites and the Khazars was dug up and diligently studied. Opinions and elaborate statements on the subject were sought from various German and non-German experts on race and linguistics.[41] Karaite, and even Jewish, scholars were consulted.

The Nazis' consultation of Jewish scholars deserves closer examination. In Vilna, the Germans approached Zelig Kalmanovitch, a prominent Jewish scholar and one of the prewar leaders of YIVO. During the Nazi occupation, Kalmanovitch was employed, together with a number of other Jews, by the so-called ERR, which confiscated Jewish art treasures, libraries, archives, and other cultural assets all over Europe. A branch of the ERR had its headquarters in Vilna, in the confiscated YIVO building, and concentrated the looted Jewish books there. The material was classified with the help of Jewish experts working under forced labor conditions;

the more valuable books were shipped to Germany, while the rest, deemed less valuable by the Nazi supervisors, were distributed as raw material to German industrial plants, particularly in the paper industry.[42]

The leader of the ERR group in Vilna asked Kalmanovitch to collect material concerning the Karaites and to translate some of it into German. It took Kalmanovitch and his assistants several months to complete this assignment.[43] In his diary, Kalmanovitch noted under the date of August 9, 1942: "It is necessary to make a survey of the literature about the Karaites, to write the history of the Karaites and of their present condition."[44] Another assignment given to Kalmanovitch was to translate a Russian book by the Karaite *hakham* (the nature of the book is not indicated; probably it dealt with the ethnic origins and the religion of the Karaites). Kalmanovitch was not greatly impressed with the *hakham*'s scholarship.[45] Meanwhile he was still busy preparing a bibliography on the Karaites.[46] Another interesting development was the debate which the Nazis arranged between the *hakham,* Seraja Szapszal, and Kalmanovitch. The date of this debate, which was mentioned in the memoirs of certain Vilna ghetto survivors, is not known. Nor is it known whether the debate was public. It can rather be assumed that the audience was limited to a small group of experts and German officials interested in the Karaite question. The result was that Kalmanovitch, in spite of his superb scholarship, let himself be "defeated" by the Karaite *hakham,* and conceded the thesis that the Karaites were neither affiliated with the Jewish religious community nor related to the Semitic race.[47]

In Warsaw, the German authorities asked the outstanding Jewish historians Meir S. Bałaban and Dr. Itzhak Schipper to prepare two separate papers on the Karaite question. Bałaban was also asked to prepare other studies on the history of Polish Jewry by Peter-Heinz Seraphim, then on the staff of the recently created Nazi Institut für deutsche Ostarbeit in Cracow.[48] According to Michał Weichert (then head of the Jewish Social Self-Help in the GG), who submitted the papers of Bałaban and Schipper to the department *Bevölkerung und Fürsorge* of the Governor-General in Cracow, both writers concluded that the Karaites are not of Jewish origin in order to save the small Karaite community from the tragic fate of the Jews.[49]

Since the only considerable concentration of Karaites in the territory of the Government General was in Halicz in Eastern Galicia (*Distrikt Galizien*), the German officials attempted to obtain the opinions of Jewish historians in that part of the country, particularly in Lwów (Lemberg), on the Karaite question. At the beginning of 1942, when I was in Lwów, I was asked by Dr. Leib Landau, a well-known lawyer and director of the Jewish Social Self-Help in the Galicia District, to prepare a study of the origins of the Karaites in Poland. The study had been ordered by Colonel Bisanz, a high official of the German administration in Lwów. Both Landau and I saw clearly that a completely objective and scholarly study, indicating the probability of the Karaites' Jewish origin, might endanger their lives. Besides, everything in me revolted against writing a memorandum for the use of the Nazis, and I asked Landau to give the assignment to another historian of Polish Jewry, Jacob Schall. He agreed, and Dr. Schall prepared a memorandum which I went over carefully, together with Landau. The memorandum was so drafted as to indicate that the origin of the Karaites was the subject of heated controversy, and great emphasis was laid on those scholars who adhered to the theory of the Karaites' Turko-Mongol extraction.[50]

In any case, the opinions of Jewish scholars did not carry much weight with Nazi officials, not only because of their negative attitude toward Jews on principle, but also because they considered the Jews a party to the issue and, therefore, not qualified to give an impartial opinion.[51] In particular, the attitude of the German administration in the Galicia District (and in the Government General, for that matter) remained extremely cautious, and they tended not to treat the Karaites as a group, but to consider each case individually, on its own merits.[52]

In their search for Karaites, German officials "discovered" some even in a remote township in the district of Bialystok. After a thorough examination it appeared that this small group, about 440 persons, was probably a splinter group of early fourteenth-century Mohammedan immigrants, long since completely Polonized. It seems that after this discovery the group was no longer bothered by German suspicions or racial investigations into their origins.[53]

Similar investigations regarding the Karaites were also made in the Ukraine.[54] In February 1943, two officials of the RMfdbO (*Hauptabteilung I, Sonderdezernat* Ie [*Rassenpolitik*]), Regierungsrat Dr. Firgau and Regierungsrat Dr. Gallmeier, were sent to the Reichskommissariat Ukraine, to Równe, and one of their assignments was "a clarification of the Karaite question beyond its present stage."[55]

The material obtained in all these investigations was concentrated in Berlin, in the RMfdbO, and decisions on this question were made in permanent consultation with the Reichskommissariat Ostland and its subdivision, the Generalkommissariat Lithuania. On the other hand, the Karaites made frantic efforts to influence the German decisions, their most important efforts being concentrated in Vilna and Troki, where the head of the Karaite community in Eastern Europe, the *hakham* Seraja Szapszal, had his residence.

The *Sonderdezernat* Ie (*Rassenpolitik*) in the *Hauptabteilung* I/i was headed by Amtsgerichtsrat Erhard Wetzel, an ambitious and ruthless careerist.[56] He is known as the author of various memoranda on the treatment of non-German minorities in Eastern Europe, in which drastic steps were recommended to reduce the Slavonic populations of those areas and completely "eliminate" the Jewish population.[57] Wetzel assigned the task of formulating a "temporary position on the Karaite question" to a member of his staff, Holtz. In an undated memorandum (probably June 1942), Holtz, after a thorough discussion of the various theories about the racial origin of the Karaites, concluded that they were not of Jewish origin, especially because of the "racial psychological characteristics." The Karaites, he contended, have a long military tradition, and "it is inconceivable to see a Jewish populace as bearers of a distinct military tradition. This is a strong evidence that the Karaites are not of Jewish but of Turkic-Tatar origins." Finally, Holtz added these considerations:

It is also politically propitious with regard to the Ottoman Turks . . . and the Tatars of the Soviet Union—who may perhaps be of greater service to us in the future—to consider the Karaites as non-Jews, yet of racially alien blood. Their legal position should be similar to that of the rest of the Turkic-Tatars of the Soviet Union.

A similar "provisional report" was also prepared by F. Steiniger, an official dealing with political-racial matters in the Reichskommissariat Ostland.[58] Both reports were sent, with Dr. Wetzel's endorsement, to the head of the *Hauptabteilung* I of the RMfdbO, Dr. Georg Leibbrandt, and to the head of the *Hauptabteilung* I/i, Dr. Otto Bräutigam. Dr. Holtz and Dr. Steiniger also carried out a series of anthropological examinations of the Karaites, in the late fall of 1942, in Vilna, Troki, and Riga.[59]

During the period when these investigations were being made, a number of articles sympathetic to the Karaite cause appeared in German periodicals. In addition to articles by Steiniger (see above, note 58), an article by the war correspondent Herbert Gaskers (in *Mitteldeutsche Nationalzeitung,* April 24, 1942) contended that the Karaites, being descendants of the Khazars, were determined enemies of the Jews.[60] In the *Wilnär Zeitung,* June 26, 1942, an article appeared entitled "The Destiny of a Small Nation, From the Crimea to Vilna," which even Holtz, who was friendly to the Karaites, characterized as "gilding the lily for the benefit of the Karaites." An article "Vilna—Rome of the Karaites" by a Mr. Bergmann, in the *Deutsche Allgemeine Zeitung (DAZ),* no. 239 of 1942, inspired an irate response from another German writer, a certain Mara (Dagmar) Krüger (née Brandt)—referred to in the official German correspondence as a "renowned authoress"[61]—who was very upset not only by the pro-Karaite article in the *DAZ* but also by rumors which had reached her about the forthcoming decision to exempt the Karaites from anti-Jewish legislation. She wrote a strong rebuttal to Bergmann's article, as well as a letter to the editor of the *DAZ* asking that her article be published. In her letter, dated May 19, 1943, she did not mince words:

In our total war with Jewry, we certainly cannot allow ourselves to absorb additional Jewish pockets of resistance and, as if this were not enough, to glorify them as a group—simple fools that we are and always will be! . . . The Karaites . . . are the most fanatical Jews in the world. . . . I have sacrificed eight years of my life for this study [of the Jews and Karaites in Russia]. While writing my book, which took me two years, . . . I was having one frightening thought—and I was working myself to death in order to finally publish it—the thought that it should not be too late. . . . The Karaites should not again succeed in embezzling "special rights" for themselves. . . . My book is in print.

In the article she sent for publication, Krüger-Brandt developed the following ideas:

The Karaites are Jews. Uncontested, pure, fanatical Jews. The Karaites are Israelites [descendants of the Ten Lost Tribes of Israel]. . . . The ten tribes came to the Caucasus. They were called Khazars. The Jewish government and the upper classes of the Khazars—the analogy with the Soviet Union is depressing—have enslaved seventy-three nations. Today the Karaites play-act as anti-Semites, but this is only their hatred toward Talmudic Jewry. . . . They have the same plans for conquering the world and the same messianic dreams as the Jews.[62]

Even the Nazi press, thoroughly imbued with Jew-hatred, refused to print this pseudo-scientific nonsense (her book was published a few months later, however), and on May 11, 1943, Krüger-Brandt appealed, in a pathetic letter, to the Führer himself:

My Führer:
     This letter must—must!—reach you personally. . . . I want nothing, absolutely nothing, for myself. For my idea, however, . . . I expect everything. . . . By chance, it became known to me, that what I have feared most has actually happened. . . . The Karaites . . . have not been placed under the Jewish Law. . . . After days of absolute perplexity and frustrated rage, I have sat down to write this letter to you. . . . If it would not sound too dramatic, I should like to be allowed to say that my heart is bleeding in horror when I think of it, that this people has again and again—as has happened innumerable times in Russian history—managed, through fraud and secret manipulations, to destroy the power of the German sword. . . . No Mercy should be granted here. . . . And now, my Führer, I beg you: investigate the matter yourself.[63]

The chancellery of the Führer sent the letter to the *Sonderdezernat Rassenpolitik* of the RMfdbO, and received a reply dated May 31, 1943: "Frau Krüger's conclusions are neither racially nor scholarly substantiated." The Krüger episode was like the retarding moment in a classical drama: just when everything had been set for a favorable decision on the Karaites, Krüger attempted, though unsuccessfully, to reverse all the progress in the matter. As we have seen, the officials of RMfdbO simply ignored her tirades. On May 13, 1943, Wetzel prepared a draft of an "Enactment about the Karaites." His draft, with a few small alterations, was adopted by the RMfdbO and was submitted, on June 12, 1943, in the form of a confidential express letter to the following offices: Parteikanzlei, Munich; Reichminister des Innern; Reichssicherheitshauptamt; Oberkommando der Wehrmacht, with a request for their opinion and in the form of an advisory to the two Reichskommissariate (Ostland and Ukraine), to the Reichssippenamt and to the Arbeitsbereich Osten of the NSDAP.

In this draft, after a long historical and racial discourse, Leibbrandt arrived at the following conclusion:

The identification of the Karaites with the Jews is thus out of the question. In my judgment, they are to be treated as the other Turkic-Tatar people. Because of their inherent racial strains, they are to be classified as of alien blood. The intermixture of Germans with Karaites is therefore to be rejected on racial grounds.

The answers received by Leibbrandt were not included in the archival files at my disposal. Apparently they were in agreement with the draft, for on July 31, 1943, the RMfdbO sent the following instruction, signed by Otto Bräutigam, to the Reichskommissar for Ostland and Ukraine:

The Karaites are not to be treated as Jews; rather the same measures must be applied toward them as toward other Turkic-Tatar peoples. All unnecessary severity toward them is to be avoided, especially as the manner of their treatment may have an impact in the Orient.[64]

The most puzzling aspect of the protracted battle waged and finally won by the Karaites in France and Eastern Europe is that the decision on their fate was effectively made in Berlin long before the issue of their racial origin and religious identity was decided on paper. While the written instructions of the French and German authorities, granting the Karaites a de jure status distinct from that of the Jews, were handed down as late as January and June 1943, respectively, the Karaites had, from the very beginning, experienced a favored status and de facto preferential treatment compared to the Jews—not only under the German occupation authorities but at the hands of the SS and the Einsatzgruppen as well. In day-to-day life this treatment found expression in many different ways. For example, the Karaites in Vilna enjoyed the same rights as other non-Jewish ethnic groups, and were not hindered in their occupations or in the exercise of their religion. Some of them held important positions of trust: Simon Szyszman was reputedly the director of the Daiwa chemical factory in Malostefańska Street; another Karaite was appointed director of a plywood factory;[65] in Lutsk and Halicz, too, some Karaites were interpreters for the German authorities, and others continued their prewar occupations as farmers, merchants, craftsmen, and professionals.[66] To prevent any Jewish infiltration, it may be assumed that the Germans ordered the Karaite leaders to keep lists of members, with addresses, ready for police examination at any time, as in France (no such lists in Eastern Europe have been found, however, in the files at my disposal). In the Vilna ghetto, rumors were widespread that several hundred Jews who attempted to establish themselves in the "Aryan" quarters of the city on the basis of forged Karaite papers were caught and executed in Ponary by the German police. Only a few cases are known where Jews succeeded in passing as Karaites without being discovered.[67]

While the Karaites were in a privileged position in comparison with the Jews, they were not exempted from the hardships to which the non-German ethnic groups were subjected during the Nazi occupation. For instance, a landed estate of 180 hectares (Sarklü-Sala, between Vilna and Kaunas) which belonged to their religious congregation was confiscated, and the payment of salaries to the Karaite religious ministers was discontinued. Regierungsrat Baumgürtel, a faithful friend of the Karaites, intervened many times with Wetzel in a futile attempt to remove such hardships. Wetzel's attitude was cold and intransigent, as can be seen in his memorandum to Dr. Bräutigam, of July 6, 1942:

Even if they [the Karaites] are not to be regarded as Jews, they nevertheless are to be considered of alien stock. It is not in our slightest interest to have people not of kindred blood living next to German-settled territory. . . . One day, we will face the dilemma . . . to transfer [the Karaites] to places where their kindred people live. If their situation in Lithuania at present is not satisfactory, then the question of transfer into other regions in the future will cause fewer difficulties.

In another memorandum, of September 1, 1942, Wetzel added this argument:

The Karaites are politically too insignificant to make much fuss about them. . . . Only I would have difficulty if the Karaites were equated with the Jews, because then other people could again draw certain inferences from this.[68]

This statement illuminates the Nazis' *ultima ratio* for their treatment of the Karaites. Their decisions on behalf of the Karaites were influenced not by humanitarian considerations but by cold political calculations. Political calculations also set limits to the "freedom" granted to the Karaites, and laid down the ultimate goal of their deportation in the years to come.

But matters developed quite differently from what the Nazis had calculated. Instead of evacuating East European groups from their native soil to remote places beyond the future colonization areas, the Nazis had to start their own evacuation from Eastern Europe. Within the framework of this evacuation, the German authorities also contemplated transferring the Karaites to Germany, in particular to Upper Styria. (Whether this plan was devised at the request of the Karaite leaders or without their knowledge or participation, we do not know.) However, in a letter dated July 20, 1942, a German official of the Führungsstab Politik, F. Weiss, who apparently was assigned to this job, expressed objections to the plan. One of his reasons was fear of an unfavorable reaction from the German public, as a result of the recently published book by the aforementioned Krüger-Brandt, in which "the theory of the Karaites' Jewish origins is being strongly defended." Weiss suggested that the Karaites be assigned a refuge in the GG, "particularly because in Warsaw, indeed, a few Karaites exist." Further meetings and discussions followed, and it was finally decided to wait until there was a sizable flight of Karaites from Eastern Europe into the Reich.[69]

How many, if any, Karaites voluntarily fled with the retreating German armies, or were evacuated, is not known. According to one Karaite scholar, a number of Karaites emigrated from the Soviet Union after World War II, particularly during the exchange of populations between the USSR and Poland. Some of these émigrés settled in Poland, particularly in Warsaw, in Silesia (Wrocław and Opole), and Pomerania, while others traveled farther, to settle in Western Europe and Israel.[70]

℃ This essay was first published in *On the Track of Tyranny, Essays Presented by the Wiener Library to Leonard G. Montefiore, O.B.E. on the Occasion of His Seventieth Birthday*, edited by Max Beloff, London, 1960, pp. 97–123.

## Notes

1. This theory was particularly developed by Abraham Firkovich in his *Avnei Zikkaron* (Stones of Memory) (Vilna, 1872). See also the works of other Karaite scholars: Simon Szyszman, *Osadownictwo karaimskie na ziemiach Wielkiego Ksiestwa Litewskiego* (The Settlement of the Karaites on the Territories of the Grand Duchy of Lithuania) (Vilna, 1936); Szymon Firkowicz,

*O Karaitach w Polsce* (About the Karaites in Poland) (Troki, 1938); Ananjasz Zajączkowski, *Ze studjów nad zagadnieniem chazarskiem* (Studies on the Problem of the Khasars) (Crakow, 1947); Simon Szyszman, "Die Karaer in Ost- und Mitteleuropa," *Zeitschrift für Ostforschung,* Marburg, 6 (1957), 24–54. On the other hand, see essay 19 below, "Polish Jewish Historiography Between the Two Wars"; and D. M. Dunlop, *The History of the Jewish Khazars* (Princeton, 1954).

2. In the fourteenth century, Eastern Galicia was called Red Ruthenia or Red Stronghold (Ruś Czerwona, or Grody Czerwiénskie).

3. Reinhart Maurach, "Die Karaimer in der russischen Gesetzgebung," *Zeitschrift für Rassenkunde,* Stuttgart, 10, nos. 2–3, (1939), 163–75.

4. The facts about Karaite participation in World War I and in the Revolution in Russia, as well as about their immigration to France, were recorded in several memoranda submitted by the Association des Caraïmes in France, in the years 1941–1943, to French authorities. This material is available in the archives of the CDJC in Paris. I am greatly indebted to the CDJC for this valuable documentation. See also the essay by Leon Poliakov in the volume *On the Track of Tyranny, Essays Presented . . . to Leonard G. Montefiore . . .* , Max Beloff, ed. (London, 1960), pp. 174 ff.

The reader will note that the name of the sect has many variant spellings: in French documents, Karaimes, Caraïmes; in German documents, Karaimen, Karaim, Karaer, Karaiten; and so on.

5. Statistical data concerning the Karaites are contradictory. See *Encyclopaedia Judaica* [German ed.], IX, 951–54; *Universal Jewish Encyclopedia,* VI, 319; Itzhak Ben–Zvi, *The Exiled and the Redeemed* (Philadelphia, 1957), pp. 154–63; *idem,* "About the Karaites in the Soviet Union" (Hebrew), *Davar* (Tel Aviv), January 1, 1950. There are, for instance, great discrepancies over the number of Karaites in Vilna; while the *Encyclopaedia Judaica* recorded 150 Karaites in 1911, Israel Cohen, who visited Vilna after 1923, found forty Karaite families; see his *Travels in Jewry* (New York, 1953), pp. 153–58. In 1941 the German authorities reported about 300 Karaites in Vilna and 300 in Troki (see the *Vermerk* of September 1, 1941, in the archives of YIVO, Occ $E_3$ b.α–100). The Karaites in the Crimea, according to the Soviet census of 1925, numbered 4,213 with 3,928 in urban and 285 in rural areas. From 1925 to 1939, the general population of the Crimea increased by over 55 percent. It can therefore be assumed that the number of Karaites in the Crimea grew to about 6,500. See "Vorläufige Angaben über die Krim (Stand vom 15. Dezember 1941)," pp. 11, 28, 29, in YIVO, Occ $E_4$–18; this mimeographed brochure was prepared by the Reichskommissariat für die Festigung des deutschen Volkstums, Stabshauptamt, Hauptabteilung Planung und Boden.

6. *Nasza Trybuna* (a Polish-language periodical) (New York), vol. III, no. 3, March 2, 1942, reprinted an article by Gisela Weinfeld from the London *Observer,* January 23, 1942, stating that the Germans considered and treated the Karaites as Jews. In another issue, *Nasza Trybuna* (IV, 4) published a statement—by a Polish soldier of the Karaite sect, who was evacuated from Russia to the Middle East—to the effect that the Nazis had killed about 1,500 Karaites, chiefly in the district of Vilna. The Yiddish daily *Morgn-Zhurnal* (New York), February 6, 1942, reporting on the extermination of the Jews in Troki, also mentioned Nazi persecution of the Karaites.

7. *The American Hebrew,* July 28, 1950, p. 7, reported from Vienna:

"A group of thirty-seven Karaite families arrived here on their way from Poland to Israel. There were a thousand Karaite families in the vicinity of Vilna, but they were mostly killed off by the Nazis. The present thirty-seven families are the remnant." In 1953, Israel Cohen (see note 5 above), p. 158, stated: "The Nazis . . . recognized no distinction between Orthodox Jews and the Karaites; they exterminated them alike."

8. In his essay (cited in note 1) Simon Szyszman noted (pp. 50–51): "The Second World War affected the situation of the Karaite population of Poland and Lithuania severely; several times the war fronts passed over them; new state borders separated the communities from each other. The legal rulings of the German legislation turned out to be favorable and that thanks to the endeavors of a small group of Karaites who had settled in Western Europe following the First World War."

9. These data are quoted from the *Vermerk* of September 1, 1941 (see note 5).

10. The Kahle expedition was referred to in a memorandum of the Association des Caraïmes in Paris, November 29, 1941; CDJC, XXXII–106.

Kahle's trip to Russia must have been accomplished sometime before November 1938, because after that he and his family fell into disgrace with the Nazis on account of their sympathy shown to Jews during the November 1938 pogrom. Kahle left Germany secretly in March 1939. In his pamphlet, *Bonn University in Pre-Nazi and Nazi Times (1923–1939): Experiences of a German Professor* (London, 1945), Kahle does not mention his mission to Russia for Karaite research.

11. YIVO, Occ $E_3$ b.$\alpha$–100; CDJC, CCXVI–8.

12. It has not been definitely ascertained whether the addressee of the January 9, 1939 letter, S. de Douvan, was identical with Serge de Douvan, listed in the February 19, 1945, roster of the Karaites in France (CDJC, XXX–92 and XXXII–106) as former chairman of the county council (*ziemstwo*) of Eupatoria and mayor of that Crimean city until the early 1920s.

13. Peter-Heinz Seraphim, *Das Judentum im osteuropäischen Raum* (Essen, 1938), p. 281, n. 1: "As a special exception another group must be mentioned which is very small in numbers and consists of persons who belong to the mosaic religion but who, in terms of race, are probably not or not purely of Jewish origin, namely the Karaites, that small ethnic group of the mosaic faith which is probably of Tatar-Khazar-Jewish origin." Reinhart Maurach, *Russiche Judenpolitik* (Berlin, 1939), pp. 103–4: "Still, the Jewish origin of the Karaites has been in doubt as long as since the middle of the nineteenth century. There is agreement that at least the physical type of the Crimean Karaites has nothing whatever in common with the Eastern Jewish type. . . . In addition—the author identifies with these findings because of his personal knowledge of numerous Crimean Karaite families—the social life, attitudes and character of the Karaites are so different from the Crimean Jews that an unbiased observer is forced to exclude the possibility of a racial kinship between both groups. Perhaps that assumption is justified which sees the Karaites as descendants of the Khazars."

14. See the memorandum by Dr. Holtz (sometimes spelled Holz), of June 1942, YIVO archives, Occ $E_3$ b.$\alpha$.–100; and the memorandum submitted by the Association des Caraïmes, Paris, to the Commissariat Général aux Questions Juives on November 29, 1941, CDJC, XXXII–106. It is noteworthy that

one of the members of Gini's expedition was a young Jewish scholar named Freilichman-Gil, later deputy director of the statistics department in the government of Israel. See Itzhak Ben-Zvi, "About the Immigration of the Karaites," *Davar* (Tel Aviv), February 23, 1950.

15. The lists were submitted to the French police on February 19, 1941, and were supplemented on July 11, 1941. Full text of the lists are in CDJC, XXXII–99.

16. Joseph Billig, *Le Commissariat Général aux Questions Juives* (Paris, 1957), II, pp. 158–64.

17. For example, the seven Karaites of the small community in St. Girons, Department of Arièges, cf. text in CDJC, XXXII–101.

18. For example, the regional offices in Toulouse, Marseilles, Lyons, and Nice. CDJC, XXXII–15 and XXXII–96.

19. CDJC, XXXII–96.

20. CDJC, LXXIII–8.

21. CDJC, XXXII–15.

22. CDJC, XXXII–109.

23. CDJC, XXXII–101, 103; CCVI–8; also Billig, II, 191.

24. CDJC, XXXII–133 and 134–36. The italicized words in the translation correspond to words underlined in the original French text.

25. In the documents submitted by the Karaites, the name of their president is alternatively spelled Kasa or Kazas.

26. CDJC, XXXIII–98.

27. CDJC, XXXII–99.

28. The director of the Status des Personnes in Vichy was Boutmy. Ditte was his associate director for the occupied zone.

29. CDJC, XXXII–104; also Billig, II, 191.

30. CDJC, XXXII–105.

31. CDJC, XXXII–106.

32. CDJC, XXXII–108.

33. CDJC, XXXII–106; Statements of November 5 and 10, 1941.

34. CDJC, CCXVI–8. Memo of the Statut des Personnes, February 8, 1943.

35. CDJC, XXXII–116–17. Included are two versions of Bogdanovitch's memo; a six-page typescript dated September 5, 1942, and a nine-page typescript, undated.

36. CDJC, XXXII–119.

37. CDJC, CXX–63; also Billig, II, 192–93.

38. CDJC, XXXII–119 and 121–22; also Billig, II, 193.

39. *NMT*, IV, 185–86, 275, 478. See also Rudolf Löwenthal, "The Extinction of the Krimchacks in World War II," *The American Slavic and East European Review*, 10 (1941), 130–36.

40. YIVO, Occ $E_3$ b.α–100. The Firkowicz brochure was translated into German and published in mimeographed form, by the Publikationsstelle Berlin-Dahlem, for the internal use of German officials in the occupied Eastern territories.

41. German scholars frequently consulted were Gerhard von Mende— lecturer (after 1936) and associate professor for Russian political science (after 1940) at the University of Berlin, and during World War II, chief of the

Abteilung I₅ (Kaukasus) in the RMfdbO—and Professor Kuhn, a Semiticist, in Stuttgart.

42. For a more detailed description of the activities of the ERR, particularly in Vilna, see essay 4 above, "The Fate of the Jewish Book." The ERR in Vilna employed about twenty, and later about forty, Jewish workers.

43. The assistants were Jacob Gordon, Dina Yaffe, and I. Lamm. E. Gershater, "Beyond the Ghetto Walls" (Yiddish), *Bleter vegen Vilne* (Lodz, 1947), pp. 44–45.

44. Zelig Kalmanovitch, "A Diary of the Nazi Ghetto in Vilna," *YA,* 8 (1953), 23; and the same in Yiddish translation in *YB,* 35 (1951), 31. The original text of the diary (in Hebrew) has not yet been published.

45. Kalmanovitch wrote in his diary on November 15, 1942: "I am translating the *hakham*'s book. How limited is his horizon! He is proud of his Turkish-Tatar descent. He has a better understanding of horses and arms than of religion" (p. 37; Yiddish ed., p. 45). Kalmanovitch started the translation on October 11, 1942 (p. 29) and finished it sometime in the spring of 1943 (pp. 52–54).

46. Kalmanovitch, p. 50.

47. E. Gershater, pp. 44–45; Mark Dworzecki, *Yerushelayim delite in kamf un umkum* (The Jerusalem of Lithuania in Struggle and in Destruction) (Paris, 1950), p. 332.

48. Emanuel Ringelblum, "From the Last Notes" (Yiddish), *BFG,* 11 (1958), 17.

49. Michał Weichert, Żydowska Samopomoc Społeczna (1939–1945) (Jewish Social Self-Help [1939–1945]) (Polish), typescript in my archives, p. 142.

50. See also essay 19 below, "Polish Jewish Historiography Between the Two Wars."

51. Holtz's memo of June 1942: "Jewish research has always advocated the thesis that the Karaites are descendants of Jews. Of course, Jewish research was partisan as far as the Karaite question is concerned." CDJC, CXLV a–76.

52. Walter Föhl, "Die Bevölkerung des Generalgouvernements," *Das General-Gouvernement,* ed. by Josef Bühler, then deputy to the governor-general, Cracow, 1943, p. 48. In this official publication Föhl, a member of the German civilian administration, wrote about the Karaites: "The members of this Turk-Tatar ethnic group . . . adhere to the Mosaic faith. There is no doubt that many of their members . . . had married Jews; thus, in spite of the claim that there had merely been premarital intermingling, each individual Karaite is to be scrutinized closely."

53. *Landesstelle Ostpreussen für Nachkriegsgeschichte,* Bericht Nr. 8 (Regional Office East Prussia for Postwar History, Report No. 8). The ethnic conditions in the Bialystok district and their historical development: I. The district of Bialystok, undated (YIVO, Occ E₁ −28), p. 4, makes the following report on the "Moslem Karaites": "As a special case the few non-polonized adherents of the Moslem persuasion should be mentioned. They are descendants of Tatar settlers from the Black Sea and Crimea, whom Grand-Duke Witold . . . settled in his territory at the end of the 14th century. The main centers of this splinter group are Troki, Vilna, Lutsk, and Halicz. . . . In 1921, a total of 441 people of Moslem faith was counted in the district of Bialystok, mainly residents of Sokolka county."

54. The brochure "Vorläufige Angaben über die Krim" (note 5) makes the following statement: "An ethnic character of their own can be granted to the Karaites. . . . The Karaites . . . show apparently strong Turkic consanguinity. The language . . . Tataric with many archaisms, a fact which seems to allow [for] the conclusion that they were living in the Crimea prior to the Tatar invasion. . . . The principal center of the Karaites is Yevpatoriya."

55. YIVO, Occ E₄–13.

56. Wetzel was raised to the rank of Regierungsrat in 1942, and to the rank of Ministerialrat in 1944. For more biographical details on Wetzel, particularly on his part in planning the extermination of the Jews and other ethnic groups in Eastern Europe, see Helmut Heiber's introduction to "Generalplan Ost," *Vierteljahrshefte für Zeitgeschichte*, 6 (1958), 286–88.

57. See document no. 2 in "Der Generalplan Ost," pp. 297–324; and the document "Die Frage der Behandlung der Bevölkerung der ehemaligen polnischen Gebiete nach rassenpolitischen Gesichtspunkten," in Polish translation in the *BGK*, 4 (Warsaw, 1948), 135–71.

58. Steiniger published the following articles about the Karaites: "Die Karaimen," *Deutsche Zeitung in Ostland*, no. 314, November 15, 1942; and "Bilder von Karaimen und Tataren in Ostland," *Natur und Volk*, 1–2 (1944). In the first article (for which I am indebted to Shaul Esh, Jerusalem), Steiniger came to the following conclusion. "In terms of race, the Karaites in Latvia, Lithuania, and in the Government General are quite closely related to the Mohammedans living in the same territory. . . . The majority of the Karaites belong to the Turanian race, although there are Near Eastern, Oriental strains in their racial makeup as in that of the Jews. But those racial influences are not stronger than among the present-day Turks in general. To deduce from that proof of the possible Jewish origin of the Karaites is, therefore, misleading."

59. CDJC, CXLV a–76.

60. Quoted from the French translation in CDJC, XXXII–134–36.

61. CDJC, CXLV 2–76.

62. The reference is, of course, to the Karaites, whom Mara Krüger called by such names as "die Karaimjuden" and "die Unholde."

63. The dots are in the original letter.

64. YIVO, Occ E₃ b.α–100.

65. YIVO, "Eyewitness Account of Joseph Foxman." See also the column "Fun eybikn kval" (From the Eternal Source) by Menashe Unger, *Der Tog*, New York, August 27, 1954.

66. Jacob Eilbirt in M. Unger's column, *Der Tog*, October 26, 1954. Also see essay 19 below, "Polish Jewish Historiography Between the Two Wars."

67. Mark Dworzecki, "The Karaites and the Jews in the Days of Trial" (Hebrew), *Hadoar*, New York, 30 (April 14, 1950), 628–29. Also the above-mentioned (n. 65) eyewitness account by Joseph Foxman; E. Gershater (n. 43), M. Chersztajn, *Geopfertes Volk* (Stuttgart, 1946), pp. 27–28; Hayka Grosman, *Anshey hamahteret* (People of the Underground) (Merhavia, 1950), p. 49; Aleksandra Sołowiejczyk, "Nine Months Under German Rule in Vilna" (Yiddish), *YB*, 30 (1947), 91–92.

68. CDJC, CXXXVII–12.

69. CDJC, CXXXVII–12.

70. According to S. Szyszman, note 1, pp. 50–51, no exact figures on this emigration are available.

# 8

# UKRAINIAN-JEWISH RELATIONS
# DURING THE NAZI OCCUPATION

Comparatively little Jewish research has been published on Ukrainian-Jewish relations under the Nazi occupation. In 1939, there were some 36–40 million Ukrainians in the territories which would be occupied during World War II by the Germans or their allies (about 29 million in the Soviet Ukraine; 5.6 million in the Polish area of Galicia, Volhynia, Polesie, and the district of Chełm; 630,000 in the Carpatho-Ukraine, first under Czech and later under Hungarian rule; 1.2 million in Bessarabia; 320,000 in Bucovina, under Rumanian rule). In this ethnically Ukrainian territory lived about 3.1 million Jews: in the Soviet Ukraine some 1.6 million, in Poland 1 million, in Carpatho-Ukraine 110,000, in Bessarabia 300,000, and in Bucovina 100,000. Besides Ukrainians and Jews, there lived in this territory a considerable population of other nationalities—large numbers of Poles and Russians, and smaller numbers of Germans, White Russians, Czechs, and Gypsies.[1] In the past, Ukrainian-Jewish relations had been marked by social tension and conflicts. Although both peoples were oppressed by the ruling nations, there did not arise a sense of solidarity against their oppressors.

From around the sixteenth century on, some Jews had served as managers or lessees of the estates of Polish owners. This function had repeatedly brought down upon them the wrath of the Ukrainian peasants and Cossacks, and frightful pogroms occurred in 1648–1649 (led by Bogdan Chmielnicki); in 1768 (incited by the Haidamacks); and in 1918–1921 (the period of Semyon Petlura). Such events had a powerful effect upon Ukrainian-Jewish relations in the Nazi period, which were exacerbated by the assassination of Petlura (whom the Jews held responsible for the pogroms of 1918–1921) in Paris, on May 25, 1926, by a Ukrainian Jew, Sholem Schwarzbart. Ukrainians, extreme nationalists as well as democrats and liberals, regarded Petlura as a national hero and martyr, and totally denied his complicity in the pogroms.[2]

On the other hand, there were also good moments in Ukrainian-Jewish relations. Although contacts between Jewish and Ukrainian intellectuals were rare, relations between the Ukrainian and Jewish masses—with the above-noted exceptions—were generally friendly. This amicable rapport is reflected in the mutual influences on folklore, folksongs, and music, and on that great Jewish movement of the eighteenth and nineteenth centuries, Hasidism.[3] Toward the end of the nineteenth century and in the early years of the twentieth, a number of Jews rose to prominence in the Ukrainian national movement and in the Ukrainian literary renaissance: George Rafalovitch, M. Hechter, Arnold D. Margolin, L. Pervomayskyj, A. Kopstein, A. Katzenelson, L. Smilanskyj, A. Rybak, and Joseph Hermayze, among others. There were even instances of successful political collaboration—in the 1870s in Galicia, and in the bloc of national minorities in the elections to the second Polish Sejm in 1922.[4] In the two Ukrainian republican states (Eastern Ukraine, with Kiev as its capital; and Western Ukraine, with Stanislav as its capital) which arose after the collapse of the Russian and Austro-Hungarian monarchies, the Jews were granted national-cultural autonomy, and a special ministry of Jewish affairs was created. Several Jews occupied important positions in the government and civil service of those states. But these were sporadic, short-lived episodes. The strongest Ukrainian party in Poland, the Ukrainian National Democratic Union (UNDO), established in 1925, was a typical party of the center, with democratic watchwords but a strong Uniate clerical orientation. Although the officially proclaimed goal was the establishment of an independent, united, and democratic Ukraine, the party followed a realistic political course, and conducted negotiations with the Polish government about "normalization" of relations (a kind of Ukrainian-Polish agreement). UNDO was not anti-Semitic. Some of its representatives in the Sejm (e.g., Vasyl Mudryj and Milena Rudnytska) frequently cooperated in political matters with Jewish representatives. In the 1930s, when a wave of aggressive anti-Semitism spread over Poland, leading to clashes in several universities and to pogroms in a number of cities, moderate Ukrainian politicians

—as well as the influential Ukrainian newspaper *Dilo,* in Lwów—raised their voices in protest against the excesses.[5]

But the influence of UNDO on the Ukrainian population was constantly declining, and the illegal Organization of Ukrainian Nationalists (OUN), founded in 1929, was in the ascendant. The Ukrainians were then in a mood of utter despair and disillusionment. The two Ukrainian republics, established in 1918–1919, soon collapsed under the blows of the Soviet and Polish armies, and no one in the outside world raised a finger on behalf of them. The Soviets persecuted and liquidated not merely the Ukrainian nationalists but also Ukrainian Communist leaders, who were accused of "nationalist deviation." The Ukrainian peasantry was exceedingly embittered by forced collectivization of the farms. In Poland the Ukrainians saw themselves threatened by military colonization by Polish settlers in their territory, and "pacification" actions by the police in the 1930s aggravated matters. The Ukrainian radical-nationalist circles increasingly pinned their hopes on Germany, which, like themselves, was displeased with the Treaty of Versailles and demanded revisions. The German government supported the Ukrainian revisionist aspirations. While the OUN carried on its activities in Poland as an underground organization, its military arm, Prowid Ukrainskikh Nationalistiw (Leadership of the Ukrainian Nationalists)—headed by Colonel Andrew Melnyk of the Ukrainian military organization Sichovy Striltsy, who was a prominent Ukrainian political figure in Kiev and Lwów—had its seat in Germany, where it worked in close cooperation with the *Wehrmacht* and particularly with the counterintelligence service of the German army (*Abwehr*), headed by Admiral Canaris. Within the Nazi party, Alfred Rosenberg was an ardent champion of a great semi-independent Ukraine, under German protectorate.[6] This trend in Nazi thinking did not abate with Hitler's accession to power. Formally, the Third Reich concluded in January 1934 a nonaggression treaty with Poland, with a promise to curtail the activities of the Ukrainian nationalist organizations in Germany. Several leaders of the Ukrainian underground movement, including Mykola Lebed, were even extradited from Germany to Poland by the Gestapo. But Germany pursued a policy of double-dealing with regard to Poland. Professing amity, it strove in every possible way to undermine the stability of the Polish state by fomenting unrest among its national minorities and by organizing a German fifth column. In effect, the central offices of the Ukrainian organizations were moved from Germany to Switzerland, but they continued their close contact with the *Wehrmacht* and the German foreign office. Meanwhile the OUN in Poland had recourse to terrorist measures: they assassinated the Polish statesman Tadeusz Hołówko and the minister of the interior, Bronisław Pieracki (June 1934). Two Ukrainians, Mykola Lebed and

Stepan Bandera, son of a Ukrainian priest and leader of the OUN in Galicia, were charged by the Polish government with organizing the assassination of Pieracki. Bandera was sent to jail in Warsaw, whence he was freed by the Germans in 1939.[7]

After the outbreak of World War II, the Germans constantly favored the OUN, at the expense of more moderate Ukrainian groups. The extremist Ukrainian nationalist groups then launched a campaign of vilification against moderate leaders, accusing them of various misdeeds. Among the charges leveled at them was that they were of Jewish descent. Conflicts also developed within the ranks of the OUN. These brought about an open split between the more moderate wing, under the leadership of Melnyk, and the extremist group of Bandera. The Germans strongly supported Bandera.[8]

In preparation for their attack on Soviet Russia, the Germans began to recruit young Ukrainian men, fugitives from the Carpatho-Ukraine or Soviet Russia as well as Ukrainians from the GG. To avoid open provocation of Soviet Russia, with which Germany at that time still officially maintained friendly relations, these Ukrainian divisions were called "labor service" or "labor divisions." In reality, however, they received full military training. When the Germans invaded Eastern Galicia, in June 1941, they brought with them the Ukrainian military formations "Roland" and "Nachtigall," led by Bandera's adherents under the supervision of the German *Abwehr*.[9] As early as the spring of 1940, a central Ukrainian committee was organized in Cracow under the chairmanship of Volodimir Kubiovitch, for aid and relief to the Ukrainian population. On June 22, 1941, a new political organization was established in Cracow, the National Ukrainian Committee, consisting of "representatives of all Ukrainian nationalist groups, with the exception of the Melnyk group."[10] Shortly before the outbreak of Russo-German hostilities, the Germans, through Colonel Erwin Stolze, of the *Abwehr,* conducted negotiations with both OUN leaders, Melnyk and Bandera, requesting that they engage in underground activities in the rear of the Soviet armies in the Ukraine.[11] There is no documentary evidence that Stolze's negotiations with them touched upon the Nazi policy of exterminating the Jews. There are documents which, however, make it amply clear that in adopting the Nazi political platform with regard to Eastern Europe, the two leaders had to accept, or at least tolerate, the anti-Jewish policy, so integral a part of the Nazi program. Prior to Russo-German hostilities, the second general congress of the OUN (Bandera's followers), which met in Cracow in April 1941, adopted the following resolution:

The Jews in the USSR constitute the most faithful support of the ruling Bolshevik regime, and the vanguard of Muscovite imperialism in the Ukraine. The

Muscovite-Bolshevik government exploits the anti-Jewish sentiments of the Ukrainian masses to divert their attention from the true cause of their misfortune and to channel them in time of frustration into pogroms on Jews. The OUN combats the Jews as the prop of the Muscovite-Bolshevik regime and simultaneously it renders the masses conscious of the fact that the principal foe is Moscow.[12]

Thus this resolution adopted the classic Nazi anti-Jewish equation of "Jew-Bolsheviks." At the same time, the resolution was against pogroms on Jews, since such actions only played into the hands of Moscow.

But in the implementation of its program with reference to the Jewish problem, the Bandera group complied with the wishes of their Nazi protectors to a much greater extent than in theory. A German police report tells that, in the beginning of the war, the Bandera group organized, with German consent, expeditionary forces (*Marschketten*), who marched from the Government General and from Lwów eastward. The task of these groups was to appoint Ukrainian mayors, create a Ukrainian militia, and "combat Jews and Communists." The report goes on to state that "under the guise of these tasks the Bandera groups have everywhere organized underground political organizations.[13] Thus, as early as October 1941, the Germans voiced their disappointment in the activities of the *Marschketten,* and their apprehension of the ambitions cherished by these groups. Altogether there were six such groups: three consisted of Bandera adherents, and the other three of Melnyk adherents. The Bandera group was the first to break with the Germans to turn to underground activity. The Melnyk groups followed suit considerably later. The first open conflict took place immediately after the German invasion of Eastern Galicia and Volhynia. On June 30, 1941, the OUN in Galicia "under the leadership of Stepan Bandera" proclaimed "the reestablishing of the Western Ukrainian state," headed by Jaroslav Stetsko. Similar provisional governments were proclaimed in October 1941 in Rovno, Volhynia, and in Kiev (the Kiev organization was in the hands of the Melnyk group). The German reaction was swift and drastic. On July 12, 1941, Stetsko and one of his ministers, Roman Ilnytzkyj, were arrested and taken to Germany. In September of the same year, the Gestapo arrested several leaders of the Bandera group, and closed their offices. Finally, Bandera was arrested on September 15, 1941, and was later sent to the concentration camp in Sachsenhausen. The blow to the Melnyk group came two months later, toward the end of November 1941. It had organized a large conference to commemorate the anti-Soviet Ukrainian partisans killed by the Bolsheviks in the last months of the civil war in the Ukraine. The Germans utilized the occasion to arrest twenty-odd organizers of that conference, who were executed in Zhitomir. At the same time the Germans broke up the organizations of the Melnyk groups in Kiev, Poltava, and Kamenets-Podolsk. Much later (January 1944), Melnyk himself was arrested, and was sent to the same concentration camp where his rival Bandera was. The Ukrainian military formations "Roland" and "Nachtigall" were removed from the Ukraine and sent to fight the partisans in the White Russian forests. The Ukrainian militia, consisting of local volunteers, was placed in charge of the SS. Several weeks later the militia was disbanded, and in its place was organized the Ukrainian auxiliary police under German direction.[14]

The Ukrainians saw themselves still more deceived when the Ukrainian territories were distributed among the occupants. Eastern Galicia was incorporated in the Government General; Bucovina, Bessarabia, and Transnistria were ceded to Rumania. Carpatho-Ukraine was ceded by Hitler, as far back as 1939, to Hungary. Widening rifts developed within Ukrainian society because of these developments. Some elements continued their collaboration with the Germans, among them were the Ukrainian auxiliary police, municipal and rural administrations, the Ukrainian central committee in Cracow, the Ukrainian regional committee in Lwów (under the chairmanship of the attorney Kost Pankiwsky), and other organizations. Several moderate groups altogether withdrew from political activity. The followers of Bandera and Melnyk and a few smaller groups went underground. In October 1941 the German secret service in Lwów received a letter signed by the Bandera group, stating that Hitler had deceived the Ukrainians, and demanding the release of the imprisoned Ukrainian nationalists. The letter proclaimed the following watchword: "Long live greater independent Ukraine without Jews, Poles, and Germans. Poles behind the San, Germans to Berlin, Jews to the gallows."[15] Whether the letter was authentic or changes were introduced into the text by the German police or SS, who reported it to Berlin, is unknown.

There was no ease in the ranks of the OUN. All efforts on the part of Ukrainian politicians to bring about a reconciliation between the Bandera and Melnyk groups were in vain. In September 1941 two prominent members of the Melnyk group were assassinated in Zhitomir. Ukrainian public opinion blamed this outrage on the Bandera followers.[16] By this time the Ukrainian nationalists had organized several partisan groups. The oldest was undoubtedly the Bulba group, organized by Chief Borovets, who called himself Taras Bulba, after the hero of Gogol's novel. Bulba-Borovets, a native of Ludwipol (Volhynia), placed his partisans, the Poliśka Sič, at the service of the Germans, and started guerrilla activities against the Red Army in Polesie as early as 1940, before the beginning of Soviet-German hostilities. They operated in the vicinity of Ludwipol, Sarny, and Kostopol, in Volhynia. According to Ukrainian sources, this formation consisted of a maximum of 330 men. This formation was the first one to use the name

UPA, the initials of the Ukrainska Powstanska Armija (the Ukrainian insurgent army).

The Melnyk partisans were concentrated in Volhynia, in the vicinity of Kremenets and Vladimir Volynski. The largest formations were organized by Bandera followers, who operated in Polesie, Volhynia, and Eastern Galicia. Early in 1943 attempts to reconcile these groups were renewed, again without results; however, a unified military command was established, under General Taras Chuprynka (formerly a high officer in the "Nachtigall" formation). The Bulba and Melnyk groups were subordinated to the Bandera group. Outside the UPA were "wild" Ukrainian groups, as well as Red partisans, who were part of the general Soviet partisan movement.[17]

Sometime in the winter of 1942–1943 the various Ukrainian partisan groups began an intense fight against all non-Ukrainians. Jews who escaped from the ghettos were seized on the highways, in villages, or in the forests, and were put to death (more details on this subject will be found below). Soviet prisoners of war, whom the Germans had liberated on the condition that they report to the police and work in the fields on the large estates, were also put to death, with the result that other prisoners began to escape to the forests to join the Soviet partisans. The Bandera adherents disapproved of the Ukrainian clergy in Volhynia and the Soviet Ukraine, not only because the church there was Greek Orthodox and the services were conducted in Old Slavic rather than Ukrainian, but also because a number of the clergy collaborated with the Germans. In this fratricidal war several high dignitaries of the Greek Orthodox Church lost their lives.[18] In the summer of 1942 a campaign against the Poles began. Many isolated Polish watchmen in the forests were killed. Later, entire Polish colonies were attacked and destroyed. Responsibility for this bloody Ukrainian-Polish conflict is hard to fix and is beyond the scope of this paper. Polish historians put the blame on the Ukrainians, while Ukrainian writers contend that the UPA merely retaliated against acts of terror perpetrated by Polish armed units upon the Ukrainian population.[19] In April 1943 the UPA partisans controlled practically all of Volhynia (with the exception of the large cities with strong German garrisons) and a considerable part of Polesie. The climax of the campaign against the Germans was reached in May 1943, with the killing of the SS general, Victor Lutze. From July to September 1943 the Germans, under the command of General von dem Bach-Zelewski, carried on a major campaign against the UPA, in which the Germans lost 3,000 men and the Ukrainians lost over 6,000 men. Sometime after this campaign a sort of unofficial armistice was declared between the two warring factions.[20] The Soviet armies began to oust the Germans from the Ukraine, and UPA shifted its major effort to the struggle against the Soviets. In their leaflets the Ukrainian partisans declared: "The

Germans are our temporary enemies. . . . They came and they will leave." The Bandera groups launched a fierce attack on the Soviet partisan groups, including the division of General Sydor Kovpak.[21]

Thus relations between the Nazis and the UPA became somewhat less tense. In 1944 Bandera and other Ukrainian leaders were released from concentration camps, presumably with the proviso that their partisan formations combat the Soviets. Several Ukrainian observers attended the conference of pro-Nazi Russian leaders, called in November 1944 by General Vlasov, in Prague.[22] None of them represented the official leadership of the OUN, however. Moreover, leaders of the Ukrainian nationalist organizations voiced their protest against General Vlasov's plan of integrating the Ukraine into the restored Russian empire that he contemplated.

## Attitude of Collaborationists Toward the Jews

In the early days of the German occupation, pro-Nazi collaborators came to the fore in the Ukrainian community. They took over the subordinate positions in the civil service, municipal and state administration, and formed the nucleus of the Ukrainian militia (later the auxiliary police). These elements sought to curry favor with the Germans through anti-Semitic activities. Thus to the traditional anti-Semitism and to the anti-Semitism "on principle" there was added a new brand—a kind of circumstantial anti-Semitism. Many Ukrainians who had never before manifested anti-Semitic attitudes, and had even maintained friendly relations, were now eager to demonstrate their anti-Semitism, since this was a quick means of acquiring wealth, prestige, and power in the new political constellation.

These collaborationists wanted to out-Herod Herod—a goal easily achieved where the Jews were concerned. They stressed the argument of "Judeo-Bolshevism," which was the central theme of Nazi anti-Jewish propaganda. They also repeated the Nazi canard that Jews had occupied the most important administrative positions in Soviet-occupied Galicia and Volhynia[23]—though these positions, particularly in the realm of education and culture, had in fact been given by the Soviets almost exclusively to Ukrainians. Another widespread allegation against the Jews was that they had denounced Ukrainian anti-Soviet underground fighters to the NKVD and had aided in their arrest (Ukrainian fighters and leaders were killed in prison by the Bolsheviks before their retreat[24]). This groundless libel not only was repeated orally but was published in Ukrainian newspapers and even in proclamations to the people issued by local Ukrainian committees.[25] In several cities, such as Lwów, Tarnopol, Sambor, and Żółkiew, the Germans opened the prisons and allowed Ukrainians—and, to a lesser extent, Poles—to identify relatives among the dead victims. The aroused mob seized Jews, dragged them to the prisons, and compelled them to wash the corpses. These Jews were murderously beaten; some of them were killed outright. The tortures and slayings in the prisons were under the direction of German officers and soldiers. Occasionally, the Germans themselves executed the Jews. Thousands of Jews lost their lives in the various cities and towns.[26] In the eastern Ukraine (former Soviet territory) another libel was spread—that the Jews, together with the Bolsheviks, had systematically razed the most beautiful streets in Kiev, especially the famous Kreshchatik, by pouring gasoline on many houses and setting fire to them. The Germans made use of this libel to justify the slaying of thousands of Kiev Jews in Babi Yar.[27]

From the very beginning of their occupation, the Germans flooded the Ukrainian areas with anti-Jewish propaganda. Posters with anti-Semitic slogans and caricatures were seen everywhere. The collaborationist Ukrainian press in the occupied territories, Germany, and Bohemia published anti-Semitic articles.

There is a remarkable dearth of data from non-Jewish sources—Ukrainian, Polish, or German—on Ukrainian-Jewish relations during the Nazi occupation. Conceivably, the picture which emerges from the numerous Jewish eyewitness testimonies, records, and diaries may be somewhat one-sided. The accounts in Jewish sources may have been tinged with emotion. Most of the chroniclers of these events were not trained historians. But they did not fabricate the events. To be sure, the sheer quantity of reports is in itself no earnest of their veracity; however, the concurrence in detail of so many of the reports, written independently and under diverse circumstances, is ample warranty for their evidential admissibility.

Pogroms took place in the very first weeks of the occupation. They were mainly wild, spontaneous outbursts of the urban or rural populace. Bands were organized in the villages, which held up passing Jews, robbed and mistreated them.[28] Many Ukrainian peasants, generally very poor, were goaded by greed for Jewish possessions. They would come with carts to the towns of Eastern Galicia and Volhynia for the purpose of plunder. Their adventures were not confined to plunder, however, and frequently ended in bloodshed.[29] In some instances, the pogroms were directed by the local intelligentsia,[30] and attempts were even made to involve school children in various anti-Jewish activities.[31] In several places the Ukrainian population, on its own initiative, established concentration camps for Jews.[32]

A number of Ukrainians turned over to the Germans Jews who had escaped from ghettos into the forests and villages or who possessed "Aryan" papers. In many instances Ukrainian peasants promised to conceal Jewish acquaintances but later delivered them to the Germans.[33] The peasants were greedy for the reward the Germans had promised for the delivery of Jews.[34]

The aforementioned anti-Jewish activities were mainly the work of an inflamed populace. But anti-Jewish moves were also made by Ukrainian organizations. Report no. 23 of the Einsatzgruppen (July 15, 1941) has reference to a telegram sent to Hitler by the Ukrainians of Lwów on July 10, which contained "a pledge of most faithful attachment [to the Führer] in the building of a Europe liberated from the bloody Judeo-Bolshevist rule and plutocratic oppression."[35] The report does not mention the name of the organization that sent the cable. The municipal administrations, which were largely taken over by pro-Nazi elements, assumed a hostile attitude toward Jews. In Ratno the municipality issued an antifraternization order, forbidding any conversation with Jews.[36] In some cities the Ukrainian officials in charge of Jewish affairs issued anti-Jewish ordinances.[37] In Tarnopol the Germans called a session of the Ukrainian committee in order to prepare a joint plan for a "Jewish campaign."[38] The Ukrainian committees of Kosów Huculski, and Gliniany applied to the Germans for permission to launch a campaign against the Jews.[39] The Ukrainian leaders in Złoczów and in Żółkiew[40] requested the establishment of ghettos in their cities.[41] Two Ukrainian physicians in Buczacz requested that the Germans eliminate the Jews in order to guard against epidemics.[42] In several places the Ukrainians prepared lists of "suspected" Jews and turned them over to the Germans.[43]

Not all Ukrainian organizations and committees were hostile toward the Jews, however. In the central Ukrainian committees, particularly in Lwów and Cracow, moderate Ukrainian elements were also represented. These elements, as a rule, did not engage in Jew-baiting. At the initiative of the Ukrainian relief committee in Lwów, a coordinating body was created, comprising Poles and Jews, for the purpose "of aiding the imprisoned." The coordinated committee was headed by Kost Pankiwsky; his associates were Mrs. Bartel, widow of the Polish prime minister Kazimierz Bartel, who had been killed by the Nazis; and Dr. Max Schaff, of the Jewish relief committee. The committee saw to it that those held in German prisons received additional food, medicaments, and underwear. In November 1941 the Germans announced their intention of establishing a ghetto for the Jews of Lwów. The members of the coordinating committee then submitted a memorandum to the Germans opposing the establishment of a ghetto. The memorandum was handed to the governor of Galicia and the SD commandant by the head of the coordinating committee.[44]

The principal collaboration with the Germans was through the Ukrainian semimilitary and police formations. The Ukrainian auxiliary police, organized throughout the Ukrainian ethnic area, including the Galicia District, was in effect subordinate to the Germans. One of its functions was to assist the German police and the SS in their anti-Jewish campaigns. At first "assistance" was confined to seizing and arresting Jews and delivering them to the German authorities, or to participating in raids by the German police. But this "assistance" did not satisfy the Germans. In the early days of the occupation, the Germans sought to create the impression that massacres of Jews were a purely Ukrainian activity—so that they might acquit themselves of responsibility. Such was the so-called Operation Petlura, carried out in late July and early August 1941, by the Ukrainian police, under the slogan: "Revenge for the assassination of *atamàn* Petlura."[45] Gradually, the functions of the Ukrainian police were being extended. They kept watch over the ghetto during the anti-Jewish campaigns, convoyed transports to the extermination camps, and directly participated in the extermination of the Jews.[46]

The Ukrainian auxiliary police was active in non-Ukrainian areas as well. The Germans dispatched them to Warsaw and to other Polish and Lithuanian ghettos. They were also used as guards and to carry out the work of extermination, in various concentration camps: Sasów, Ostrów, Grochów, Poniatów, Płaszów, the Janowska Street camp in Lwów, and the death camps of Sobibor, Treblinka, among others. Further, Ukrainian policemen were used to guard prisons that held Jews, such as the notorious Pawiak prison in Warsaw.[47]

I have already referred to the Ukrainian paramilitary organizations that collaborated with the Germans—the military battalions "Roland," "Nachtigall," the Sič, and Bulba groups and several battalions of HiWi (*Hilfswillige,* "Eager to Help"), a Ukrainian auxiliary formation in black uniforms. At the initiative of the governor of Galicia, K. Otto Wächter, the first Ukrainian SS division was organized in the spring of 1943. The Germans expressly forbade the name "Ukrainian division," however, and the official name was "fourteenth grenadier division of the SS Halichina [Galicia]." In July 1943 the division numbered 28,000 volunteers. In late 1943 and early 1944, it already fought on the eastern front.[48] Toward the end of 1944, when the military situation of the Germans became critical, they began negotiations with Ukrainian public leaders and military men for the organization of a second Ukrainian SS division.[49] Reliable Ukrainian sources put the number of Ukrainians fighting on the German side in October 1944 at 220,000.[50] Presumably, the Ukrainian auxiliary police was included in this number.

Ukrainian historians maintain that the Ukrainian SS divisions were engaged in purely military tasks and had no part in the anti-Jewish operations. They point out that the SS divisions were organized toward the end of 1943 and in 1944, when the major extermination operations against the Jews had already been completed. But even in 1943 and 1944 executions of individuals and groups found in hiding were still going on. These numerous, little-known executions were performed by various German and other military and police formations who stumbled across their quarry; we may assume that some of the units were Ukrainian military groups. At any rate, the official Polish investigation of German crimes in Poland, conducted in 1945, listed a number of executions of Poles and Jews by the Ukrainian SS,[51] but it is possible that witnesses confused the Ukrainian auxiliary police and HiWi with the Ukrainian SS.[52]

How large was the number of the Ukrainians who collaborated with the Germans? No complete answer to this question is possible as yet. The Germans were everywhere received enthusiastically by the Ukrainian population.[53] But the enthusiasm cooled considerably after the bitter political disenchantment of the Ukrainians. Moreover, the Ukrainian peasants soon began to feel the heavy burden of the German administration, which set over three million Ukrainians at compulsory labor, crippled the Ukrainian economy, and emptied its food reserves. Toward the end of the German occupation, the sympathies of the Ukrainian population were mostly on the side of the Ukrainian nationalist fighters or, to a lesser degree, on the side of the Soviet partisans.

The active pro-Nazi collaborationists included elements that would probably not have attained a position of power in Ukrainian society in normal times. The Ukrainian police was recruited mainly from among the rabble and criminals. However, the large number of pro-Nazi fellow travelers, particularly in the first years of the Russo-German hostilities, when the military prestige of the Germans was very high, added weight to the collaborationists. And it was precisely in those years that the most extensive anti-Jewish operations took place. Apparently the pro-Nazi elements deliberately exploited the "Jewish problem," tempted by the prospect of getting rich quickly from Jewish plunder or appointment to positions vacated by Jews, or simply seeking compensation for an inferiority complex. Among the 35–40 million Ukrainians were many who remained indifferent to the catastrophic events. A handful secretly sympathized with the hunted Jews, and discreetly expressed that sympathy. A still smaller group had the courage to risk life and limb in the attempt to rescue Jews (more on this below).

## The Ukrainian Underground Movement

As previously stated, the most powerful Ukrainian underground organization was under the leadership of Stepan Bandera or his lieutenants (during his imprisonment in Sachsenhausen). His followers aimed at liberating the Ukraine from "foreign elements," and many of his fanatical adherents in the local underground and partisan groups included also Ukrainian Jews among these "foreign elements" and harried them. This is reported by many Jewish witnesses, who also speak of persecutions by other partisan units such as the Melnyk and Bulba groups. There are many such reports.[54] It is, of course, quite possible that some witnesses mistook the "wild" independent gangs for UPA detachments or Bandera groups, since the name "Bandera groups" became very popular and, among those not initiated into the internal Ukrainian political alignment, easily came to stand for any armed Ukrainian group. On the other hand some witnesses, the numerous writers of memoirs, were thoroughly familiar with the military and political developments among the Ukrainians and were of sound judgment, and their reports are reliable. The attempts on the part of Ukrainian writers to refute these reports cannot be taken seriously.

It is hard to determine whether the leadership of the OUN issued any instructions to its followers concerning the Jews. No proofs other than the aforementioned proclamation and manifestoes are known to me. Nor are there any documents showing that the leadership made an effort to stop the persecution of the Jews by the local partisan groups in the first two years of the German occupation.[55] In the second half of 1943, when the rift with the Germans ripened into full-fledged warfare, the new development was reflected in a shift of emphasis in regard to the Jewish question. The third general congress of the OUN, which met in August 1943, no longer included the anti-Jewish resolution of the second congress, cited above. Instead, a resolution was adopted which, by stating that in an independent Ukraine all citizens regardless of creed or nationality would enjoy equal rights, repudiated the concept of an ethnic Ukraine. Even more articulate on the Jewish question was the official organ of the OUN leadership, *Idea i Chin* (Thought and Action), Vol. II, No. 2, 1943. In an article containing instructions to the "march groups," the third paragraph urges the men "to liquidate the manifestations of harmful foreign influence, particularly the German racist concepts and practices."[56]

Ukrainian writers maintain that the Bandera groups adopted several hundred, or even thousand, Jews—mostly physicians, dentists, hospital attendants, and artisans. The Bandera groups were badly in need of physicians and technicians, and sought to obtain them from the Galician and Volhynian ghettos. Jewish physicians were at first suspicious of these offers, for the news of persecution of Jews in the villages and forests had already reached the ghettos. When the extermination operations began in the ghettos, however, many Jews took the risk and escaped to the Bandera groups. Ukrainian partisans opened courses for medical personnel. One such course, of six months' duration, is said to have had one Ukrainian and two Jewish instructors and twelve students, eight of whom were physicians; but the source of this information is unreliable.[57]

Ukrainian sources speak of a considerable number of Jewish physicians, dentists, and hospital attendants who served in the ranks of the UPA.[58] The question is: Why did only a small number of them remain alive?[59] The Bandera groups also utilized other Jewish skilled workers. According to Lew Shankowsky, practically every UPA group had a Jewish physician or pharmacist, as well as Jewish tailors, shoemakers, barbers, and the like.[60] Again the question arises: What happened to these hundreds of thousands of Jewish professionals and skilled workers? Betty Eisenstein states that in the spring of 1943 the Bandera groups began to imitate the German tactic of "selection." Only the skilled workers were left alive, and they were concentrated in special camps, where they worked at their trades or on the farms. One such camp, established in April 1943 near Poryck, Volhynia, contained more than 100 Jews. A second camp, which had some 400 Jews, was located in Kudrynki, nearly 20 miles from Tuczyn, Volhynia. Eisenstein reports that at the approach of the Soviet army the Bandera groups liquidated the Jews of the camps.[61].

There were also some Jews in the left-wing Ukrainian partisan groups. A Jewish underground youth group in and around Brody, Galicia, was affiliated with the Ukrainian communist movement and received from it arms, instructions, and even military reinforcements.[62] Babij, a Ukrainian Communist of Dolina, Eastern Galicia, organized (in the fall of 1943) a partisan unit consisting almost exclusively of Jews. They began military operations at once. In the winter of 1943–1944 many members of this unit lost their lives in fierce battle with the Germans.[63] Several Ukrainian Communists in Volhynia helped Jews escape from the ghetto and established partisan groups in the forests, mostly under Soviet leadership.[64] But conditions in the Soviet partisan groups, too, were far from ideal. In the last years of the war the Ukrainian auxiliary police began to look for means of escaping the Germans and disappearing before the reentry of the Soviet army. In several places they mutinied against their German superiors and joined the partisans, not only the nationalist groups but, to a lesser extent, also the Soviet groups.[65] At any rate, the Soviet partisan groups were also pervaded by anti-Jewish elements and an anti-Semitic mood.[66]

In addition to the UPA and the Soviet partisan groups there roamed through the forests various other groups, known as "wild partisans." These were generally bands of robbers who committed pillage and murder in the villages and forests under the guise of partisan activity.[67] Needless to say, their first victims were the Jews.

## Ukrainians Friendly to Jews

How many Ukrainians helped Jews during the Nazi era, or went so far as to risk their lives to rescue Jews? In all probability we shall never have exact statistics on these "good gentiles" (as they were known in popular parlance). A fair idea about them may be gained from the official German publications of the SS and the police of the Galicia District, from October 1943 to June 1944. On the basis of a German law "to combat anti-German activities" promulgated October 2, 1943, no fewer than 1,541 Ukrainians were sentenced to death for various political offenses, such as membership in proscribed Ukrainian organizations or in various armed bands, economic and industrial sabotage, and the like. Included in the condemned group were some hundred Ukrainians executed for helping or concealing Jews (*Judenbegünstigung*).[68] This is a substantial number when we take into consideration the following: (1) only a fraction of the Ukrainians who helped Jews were apprehended and executed; many were never apprehended, and some of those apprehended were given lighter sentences; (2) in many instances those guilty of this "offense" were executed on the spot and do not figure in the official statistics; (3) the death sentences cover only the period between October 1943 and June 1944, the date of the Russian takeover of the territory; (4) this number covers only a part of the Ukrainian territory, the Galicia District.

We learn of many similar instances in incidental sources. A well-known Ukrainian leader, on the basis of testimonies gathered by the Yiddish writer Joseph Schwarz, lists eleven Ukrainians who rescued Jews, among them an engineer, Alexander Kryvoiaza of Sambor, Eastern Galicia, who employed fifty-eight Jews in his factory and helped conceal them during an anti-Jewish operation. The forester Lew Kobilnitsky and his brother-in-law rescued twenty-three Jews in Zawałów, Eastern Galicia.[69] Another Ukrainian, a former forester in the district of Przemyślany, Eastern Galicia, reported the following: The district contained five towns and thirty-six villages. The population was 70 percent Ukrainian. Among the foresters were thirty-five Ukrainians and five Poles. With the help of the foresters, 1,700 Jews were concealed in the forests. Some Jews were concealed in the monastery of the Ukrainian order of the Studites, which was located in the woods.[70]

In addition, many individual, frequently dramatic, accounts of Jews rescued by Ukrainians of various classes are extant.[71] In some instances the rescuers were former domestics, other employees, or ordinary peasants. Occasionally they were of the Ukrainian middle class or intelligentsia. There are also records of sympathy meetings and even demonstrations by Ukrainians on behalf of the Jews.[72]

An interesting chapter is the attitude of the Ukrainian church toward the persecution of Jews. In Galicia the Ukrainian church was Uniate; in Volhynia and Eastern Ukraine, Greek Orthodox. At the head of the Uniate Church in Galicia was the Metropolitan Andreas Sheptitsky (b.

1865). In poor health and half paralyzed, he was one of the leading Ukrainian statesmen and scholars and the highest moral authority among his people.[73] His attitude toward the Jews was always friendly. He knew Hebrew and even corresponded in Hebrew with Jewish communities.[74] When the Nazis began their anti-Jewish operations with the help of the Ukrainian auxiliary police, Sheptitsky, in February 1942, addressed a letter to Reichsminister Heinrich Himmler, protesting against these operations and particularly against involving the Ukrainian auxiliary police in them. Himmler's office sent that letter back to Lwów to the German security police. The leaders of the security police in Lwów did not want to resort to drastic means in dealing with the old and highly respected divine, but retaliated in another way. They closed the office of the Ukrainian national council in Lwów, of which Sheptitsky was honorary chairman.[75] In November 1942, Sheptitsky published, in the official organ of the Galician Uniate Church, a pastoral letter entitled "Thou Shalt Not Murder," in which he stressed the importance of this commandment and threatened all offenders with excommunication. Undoubtedly because of German censorship, no concrete facts are mentioned in the letter. But since the letter was published in the fall of 1942, when the extermination operations peaked, its relevance is clear. Only the last paragraph referred to the fratricidal wars among the Ukrainians (an allusion to the fight between the Bandera and Melnyk followers).[76] The effect of the metropolitan's letter on the Ukrainian community cannot be determined. Later, on many occasions, the metropolitan fearlessly spoke his mind to the Germans. In September 1943 a certain Dr. Frederic visited the metropolitan on a mission for the German foreign ministry. Sheptitsky boldly reproached his visitor for the Germans' inhuman attitude toward Jews. In Lwów alone they had killed 100,000 Jews, and in the rest of the Ukraine millions. A Ukrainian youth, he said, confessed to him that he had single-handedly slain seventy-five Jews in Lwów in one night. The extermination of the Jews was intolerable, the metropolitan concluded.[77]

Sheptitsky was not content with mere words. He actually took part in rescue activities. On August 14, 1942, two rabbis who were employed in the religious department of the Judenrat, David Kahane[78] and Dr. Chameides (rabbi in Katowice before the war), visited Sheptitsky. They asked him to conceal the scrolls of the Law in the Jewish community's building, as the scrolls were in danger of being destroyed by the Germans in the extermination operations in Lwów, which had begun on August 10. They also asked the metropolitan if he would conceal several Jewish children. The metropolitan summoned his brother, Father Superior Clement Sheptitsky, who was the archimandrite of the Studite monasteries, and gave the two rabbis a recommendation to his sister, Sister Josepha, mother superior of the nunneries. The result of these conversations with the Sheptitskys was that some 150 Jews, mostly small boys and girls, were admitted to the various Studite monasteries and were thus saved. Although some 550 Studite monks and nuns knew the secret, none of the concealed Jews was betrayed to the Germans. In addition, Sheptitsky concealed in his own residence in Lwów fifteen Jews, among them Rabbi Kahane.[79]

Jewish survivors also tell of other Ukranian priests—Uniate or Greek Orthodox—who rescued Jews or helped them.[80] Noteworthy are the rescue activities of a Greek Catholic priest in France. Father Valentin Bakst, who had a parish of Ukrainian dock workers in Marseilles, concealed Jews in his church and provided them with forged Aryan papers. Probably he was aided in this work by some of his parishioners. When the Germans got wind of his rescue activities he fled. He was placed in charge of a children's colony, in which most of the children were disguised Jews, in the Haute-Savoie department, close to the Swiss border. Apparently, some of the children were successfully smuggled into Switzerland.[81]

Interesting, too, is the fact that Ukrainian Baptists in Volhynia and Seventh-Day Adventists in Galicia showed great sympathy to the persecuted Jews, helped them, and even concealed them.[82]

## Conclusion

As previously noted, over 3 million Jews lived among 40 million Ukrainians prior to the Nazi invasion. The history of Ukrainian Jewry should therefore be an essential part of modern Jewish historiography. However, insufficient research has been done in this field. There is a particular dearth of information and documentation on the fate of Ukrainian Jewry and on Ukrainian-Jewish relations in the crucial period of World War II. Moreover, the scant documentation available to me mainly covers events in the western Ukraine, that is, Eastern Galicia, Volhynia, and Polesie. Very little material is available on the fate of the Jews or on Ukrainian-Jewish relations in the Soviet Ukraine, Bucovina, Bessarabia, and Carpatho-Ukraine. The little that is available is of inferior quality. The German documents, particularly the reports of the Einsatzgruppen and the Gestapo, are not always trustworthy. Practically no Soviet or Polish documentary material has been made available. The bulk of the evidence at my disposal is of a rather subjective character—personal or anecdotal accounts from Jewish or Ukrainian sources, which cannot furnish a conclusive picture. This material has not been subjected to thorough scholarly examination nor has it been supplemented by other findings. Again, the memoirists on both sides of the fence saw the events from different standpoints. Jewish writers described the sufferings inflicted upon the Jews by the Nazi occupants, and frequently pointed out the collaborationist role of Ukrainians. To be sure, they also mentioned, although to a lesser extent, any aid and comfort given to Jews by other Ukrainian elements, religious and political groups. On the other hand, Ukrainian writers are somewhat reticent and evasive on the Jewish question, and mention the terrible predicament of Ukrainian Jews only in passing. The Ukrainian press in America and in Western Europe has striven to prove that many Ukrainians helped, even rescued, persecuted Jews, and that the majority of the Ukrainian population did not cooperate with the Nazi program for the extermination of the Jews. Leo E. Dobransky, a prominent Ukrainian scholar, wrote an article vigorously protesting against "the revived myth" of Ukrainian anti-Semitism.[83] Unfortunately, the documentation to substantiate his thesis is very scant. Another Ukrainian writer has stated: "It is the duty of Ukrainian students to investigate most thoroughly this matter [the alleged persecution of the Jews by the UPA formations], even if such an investigation incriminates us. . . . It is time for us, Ukrainians, to prepare a scholarly publication on Ukrainian-Jewish relations."[84]

¶ This essay was first published in Yiddish in *YIVO Bleter,* XLI (1957/ 58), 230–63, and in *YIVO Annual of Jewish Social Sciences,* XII (1958/ 59), 259–96.

## Notes

1. These data are culled from various sources, partly contradictory. I have attempted to extract from them the most reliable information. The sources are Clarence Manning, *Twentieth-Century Ukraine* (New York, 1951); *idem, Ukraine under the Soviets* (New York, 1953); *Slavonic Encyclopedia,* ed. by Joseph S. Roucek (New York, 1949); Ihor Kamenetsky, *Hitler's Occupation of the Ukraine, 1941–1944* (Milwaukee, 1956); Solomon M. Schwarz, *The Jews in the Soviet Union* (Syracuse, 1951); Peter Meyer, et al., *The Jews in the Soviet Satellites* (Syracuse, 1953); Simon Segal, *The New Poland and the Jews* (New York, 1938); Arthur Ruppin, "The Jewish Population in the World," *The Jewish People Past and Present* (New York, 1956), I, 348–60.
2. John S. Reshetar, *The Ukrainian Revolution, 1917–1920* (Princeton, 1952); *Material concerning Ukrainian Jewish Relations during the Years of the Revolution, 1917–1921* (Munich, 1956); Sholem Goldelman, *In goles bay di ukrainer* (In Exile among the Ukrainians) (Vienna, 1921); and my "The Jews and the Ukrainians," *YK* (June 13, 1952).
3. C. Chajes, "Baal Shem Tov among the Christians" (Polish), *Miesięcznik Żydowski,* 4, nos. 5 and 6 (Warsaw, 1934), 440–59, 550–65; Ustym Karmaluk, *Sbornik Dokumentov* (Collection of Documents) (Kiev, 1948); S. Ansky (Shloyme Zanvel Rapoport), "Mutual Cultural Influences," *Gezamlte Shriftn* (Collected Studies) (Yiddish) (New York, 1925), XV, 257–58.

4. Philip Friedman, *Die Galizische Juden im Kampfe um ihre Gleichberechtigung, 1848–1868* (Frankfurt am Main, 1929), p. 186; Segal, pp. 29, 34; A. Hafftka, in *Żydzi w Polsce odrodzonej* (Jews in Reborn Poland) (Warsaw, 1934), II, 292–95.

5. Segal, pp, 162–67; Manning, *Twentieth-Century*, pp. 105–11; Roman Ilnytzkyj, *Deutschland und die Ukraine, 1934–1945* (Munich 1955), I, 72–73; Kost Pankiwsky, *Wid derzhawi do komitetu* (From Statehood to a Committee) (New York, 1957), pp. 18–19.

6. Myroslav Prokop, "Ukraine in Germany's World War II Plans," *Ukrainian Quarterly*, 11 (1955), 134–44; Alexander Dallin, *German Rule in Russia, 1941–1945* (New York, 1957), pp. 114–16, 123–62.

7. Ilnytzkyj, pp. 64–71, 75, 277 ff.; Kamenetsky, pp. 9, 13 ff.; Segal, p. 164; Pankiwsky, pp. 19–20, 32–33; "Ukrainian Nationalists: The Galician SS Division," *WLB*, 4 (1950), 35; John A. Armstrong, *Ukrainian Nationalism, 1939–1945* (New York, 1955); Lew Shankowsky, review of John A. Armstrong's *Ukrainian Nationalism, 1939–1945, Ukrainian Quarterly*, 11 (1955), 183–86.

8. The rift in the ranks of the OUN widened after the conference of OUN leaders in Cracow, in 1940. Thereafter, there were in effect two organizations, OUN solidarists (the Melnyk group) and OUN revolutionaries (the Bandera group). Following the second congress of the OUN, which took place in Cracow in 1941 without the Melnyk group's participation, the Bandera group took over virtual control of the entire OUN apparatus. This congress adopted several strongly worded resolutions against the Melnyk group, and ousted Melnyk from the party. With the help of the Germans, another Ukrainian nationalist organization, the "Ukrainian government-in-exile," was also liquidated. Several of the leading members of that government were arrested by the Germans in Warsaw and Paris. There was a third Ukrainian nationalist movement, the Greek Orthodox "Hetman Organization" (with Hetman Pavlo Skoropadsky at the head), which continued to be tolerated by the Germans, but lost its political influence. In May 1940, when Hetman Skoropadsky wanted to pay an official visit to the Reich Protector of Bohemia and Moravia, in Prague, the German foreign ministry declined this request, on the ground that "the Hetman movement has lately declined in comparison with the OUN, which is favored by the higher German authorities." Cf. U.S. Department of State, *Nazi-Soviet Relations, 1939–1941* (Washington, 1948), p. 145; Ilnytzkyj, pp. 79–82, 220, 272–78; Kamenetsky, p. 54; Pankiwsky, p. 100; Fedir Dudko, "Let Us Not Whitewash Ourselves" (Ukrainian), *Swoboda* (New York, January 18, 1952), p. 2, particularly on the accusation of Jewish descent hurled by some Ukrainian leaders at their political opponents.

9. Ukrainian sources maintain that in 1941 (before the outbreak of Russo-German hostilities) there were 700,000 Ukrainians in the Government General. This total was augmented by 20,000 refugees from the Soviet Western Ukraine and Carpatho-Russia. Beginning with 1941 the Germans conducted negotiations with the Bandera group about the formation of a Ukrainian legion. The results of these negotiations were the two military units designated as "Roland" and "Nachtigall," which numbered 700 men. The "Nachtigall" battalion entered Lwów alongside the Germans on June 30, 1941. Cf. Ilnytzkyj, I, 251; II, 142–43; Kamenetzky, I, 55; Pankiwsky, p. 53; S. Piotrowski, *Dziennik*

*Hansa Franka* (Hans Frank's Diary) (Warsaw, 1956), pp. 121–42; Walter Schellenberg, *The Labyrinth* (New York, 1950), p. 202; Basil Dmytryshyn, "The Nazis and the SS Volunteer Division, Galicia," *The American Slavic and East European Review*, 15 (1956), 3–4.

As early as 1939, German officials thought of using the Ukrainian units against the Jews. Suffice it to quote the following note Admiral Canaris made in his diary entry of September 12, 1939: "I would have to make appropriate preparations with the Ukrainians so that, should this alternative become real, the Melnyk organization (OUN) can produce an uprising which would aim at the annihilation of the Jews and Poles" (Dallin, p. 115). How much German pressure in this direction was put on the Ukrainian nationalists, and how far they were able to withstand this pressure, is not known.

10. Ilnytzkyj, pp. 146–47; Pankiwsky, pp. 39–40.

11. On Stolze's negotiations with the leaders of the OUN, see *IMT*, VII, 272–73. See also Otto Heilbrunn, *The Soviet Secret Service* (New York, 1956), pp. 157–59. Following the arrest of Jaroslav Stetsko and Roman Ilnytskyj, Stolze was also used by the Germans as liaison officer for Ukrainian affairs. See Ilnytskyj, II, 187.

12. Paragraph 17 of the resolution of the congress. See *Postanowy II. welikoho zboru organizatsii ukrainskikh natsionalistiw* (Resolutions of the Second General Congress of the Ukrainian Nationalist Organization) (Stryj, 1941), p. 14.

13. "The strongest group advocating an independent Ukraine is now as before the Bandera group, whose followers are extremely active and whose fanaticism is borne in part by personal emotions and in part by deep nationalistic feelings.

"At the beginning of the campaign, Bandera's followers were organized in small groups in Lemberg [Lwów] and Sanok, and received a brief training. They also were provided with money and propaganda material. Under the cover of the performance of such tasks as the installation of mayors, formation of militia, and fight against Jews and Communists, they did political work." (Sixth Activity and Situation Report of the Einsatzgruppen in the Soviet Union from October 1–31, 1941, translated from Ilnytzkyj, II, 144.) For a comprehensive study of the *Marschketten,* see Lew Shankowsky, *Pokhidni grupi OUN* (Expeditionary groups of the OUN) (Munich, 1958).

14. Ilnytzkyj, II, 94, 144, 195–99; Kamenetsky, I, 53–54; Pankiwsky, pp. 15, 20, 45, 48–49, 61, 72–73, 113–19; Gerald Reitlinger, *The Final Solution* (New York, 1953), p. 230; *Ukrainska Disnist* (Berlin), July 15, 1941, p. 1; September 1, 1941, p. 1.

Kost Pankiwsky tells that at first the deported members of the Bandera and Melnyk groups lived in comparative freedom in Berlin under a kind of "house arrest"; only later were they sent to Sachsenhausen. See Pankiwsky, "The Years of the German Occupation," *Listi do priyateliw* (Letters to Friends) (Newark, 1958), V, 12–14. Another Ukrainian writer, a member of the Bandera group, tells how he and other members of the group were arrested in Lwów and sent to Auschwitz, and later to other concentration camps. He names some 200 members of the Bandera group who were in Auschwitz. See Petro Mirchuk, *W nimetskikh mlinakh smerti . . . 1941–1945* (In the German Mills of Death . . . 1941–1945) (New York, 1957), pp. 17, 21, 22, 65–69, 119.

15. This document is cited in the Ereignismeldung no. 126 of the Einsatzgruppen and in the "Political Review" of the German SP and SD, Berlin, October 29, 1941, Nuremberg document no. 4134: "The Commander of Security Police and SD in Lemberg (Lwów) reports: 'In a letter signed by the OUN addressed to the Gestapo in Lemberg, the Bandera group again advocated political autonomy and independence for the Ukraine.' "

The letter stated that Hitler has deceived the Ukraine and that America, England, and Russia would establish an independent Ukraine from the San River to the Black Sea. The letter also expressed doubt of an ultimate German victory and declared that without the Ukraine Germany could not win the war. Additionally, the OUN demanded the release of the arrested Ukrainians.

The report was published, in the original German, by Ilnytzkyj, II, 216, with the omission of the phrase relating to the Jews, Poles, and Germans. Ilnytzkyj also tells (II, 219) that the anti-German proclamations of the Bandera group were severely criticized at the sessions of the Ukrainian national council in Lwów, and a call was issued to the group to deny the authorship of these proclamations. After the arrests in July 1941, the OUN revolutionaries decided to form an insurgent army, "not linked to German or Soviet imperialism." After Bandera's arrest, the virtual leader of the OUN movement was Mykola Lebed (Maxim Ruban). A joint leadership was agreed upon only in August 1943, with General Taras Chuprynka (Roman Shukhevitch) at the head. In the beginning of 1944, Chuprynka became commander-in-chief of the UPA (Ukrainska Powstanska Armija [Ukrainian Insurgent Army]). See Ilnytzkyj, I, 282–302; II, 90–91, 193; Lew Shankowsky, "Ukrainian Insurgent Army" (Ukrainian) in *Istoria ukrainskoho wiska* (The History of the Ukrainian Army) (Winnipeg, 1953), p. 704.

16. Pankiwsky, pp. 72, 73, 95; Kamenetsky, pp. 55, 69–70; A. Dolinets, "The Irony of Fate" (Ukrainian), *Ukrainska Disnist* (October 1, 1941), p. 2.

17. Shankowsky, *Istoria,* pp. 658–60, 662 ff.; Ilnytzkyj, II, 201–2; Kamenetsky, pp. 69–70; Moyshe Kaganovitch, *Di milkhome fun di yidishe partizaners in mizrekh-eyrope* (The War of the Jewish Partisans in Western Europe) (Buenos Aires, 1956), II, 117–23; Manning, *Twentieth-Century,* pp. 131–50; *idem, Ukraine under the Soviets,* pp. 159–74; *Ukrainian Resistance: the Story of the Ukrainian National Liberation Movement in Modern Times,* published by the Ukrainian Congress Committee of America (New York, 1949); Mykola Lebed, *UPA, Ukrainska powstanska armija* (UPA, Ukrainian Insurgent Army) (1946), pp. 40–42.

The German police in Lwów estimated the number of men in the UPA, in Galicia alone, in 1944, at 80,000 (Ilnytzkyj, II, 79).

18. In May 1943, the Greek Orthodox metropolitan Alexis, was killed, together with his escorts, on the way from Kremenetz to Dubno. They were traveling in the automobile of the German district commissar Müller, and struck a mine planted by the UPA. Lebed (p. 41) says that Alexis was killed for his collaboration with the Germans. On the other hand, Shankowsky, *Istoria* (p. 665), maintains that the Ukrainian partisans wanted to kill Müller, and had not realized that the metropolitan was traveling in his car. Betty Eisenstein-Keshev, in her study "The Jews in Volhynia 1939–1944" (Yiddish), *Fun noentn ovar* (New York, 1957), III, 42, states that the partisans killed, in the summer of 1942, the Greek Orthodox Archbishop Simon of Kremenetz and his retinue; she apparently confused Archbishop Simon, who had been executed in

a Soviet prison in June 1941 (Ilnytzkyj, II, 173), with the metropolitan Alexis. The negative attitude of the Ukrainian nationalists toward the Greek Orthodox Church is clearly formulated in this statement of the Ukrainian Congress Committee of America: "The Orthodox Church organization in the Ukraine was entirely under the aegis of the Nazi occupation authorities and served their purposes. The Russian elements in the Orthodox Church openly combatted the Ukrainian Liberation Movement" (*Ukrainian Resistance*, p. 56).

19. The fierce fight between Poles and Ukrainians is described by many writers, among them Eisenstein-Keshev (pp. 36–40); Yehoshua Shiloni, *Ehad shenimlat* (One Who Escaped) (Tel Aviv, 1955), pp. 54, 108, 110–14; Lebed, pp. 52–53, 76–79; Shankowsky, *Istoria*, pp. 690–703; *Ukrainian Resistance*, pp. 72–76; Meylekh Bakalchuk, *Zikhroynes fun a yidishn partizan* (Memoirs of a Jewish Partisan) (Buenos Aires, 1958), pp. 136, 220–22.

Lebed (pp. 25–53, 76–79) states that the aim of the UPA was "to clear the forests and the surrounding areas of foreign elements." Presumably the "foreign elements" included not only Poles but also Jews and Russian partisans.

20. On the "unofficial armistice" between the Ukrainian nationalists and the Germans, see Kaganovitch, II, 121; Gad Rosenblat, *Esh ahaza bayaar* (A Fire Consumed the Forest) (1957), p. 289.

The policy of a truce with the Ukrainian nationalists was strongly recommended by several high officials of the Ministry for the Occupied Eastern Territory, such as by SS-Obergruppenführer Gottlob Berger, chief of section "Politics." See "Notice" dated Berlin, October 21, 1943: "Under the impact of the approaching front, these [Ukrainian nationalists] seem to be inclined to stop fighting the Germans so Germany should not lose the war against Bolshevism. . . . If we only succeeded in concluding an armistice with the nationalists, we would also free a substantial number of troops for immediate front assignment. . . . One should immediately make an attempt to negotiate with some [Ukrainian] partisan groups if only to divide them and play them off against each other." (*YA*, Occ. E₄–1, pp. 19–20).

21. Shankowsky, *Pokhidni*, pp. 104–10; *idem*, "Ten Years of the UPA Struggle, (1942–1952)," in *The Ukrainian Insurgent Army in the Fight for Freedom* (New York, 1954), pp. 32–34. Though the UPA concentrated on fighting the Soviet partisans, the OUN and UPA leadership instructed commanders of field units to refrain from military cooperation with the Germans. Nevertheless, some leaders of the Ukrainian insurgents—for example, Taras Bulba-Borovets—did cooperate with the Germans. Early in 1944 the UPA court-martialed two commanders of UPA field units for military cooperation with Germans. One of them had carried out a successful joint military operation with the Germans, and had afterwards celebrated with them (Shankowsky, *Istoria*, pp. 662, 667).

22. Gerald Reitlinger, *The SS: Alibi of a Nation, 1922–1945* (New York, 1957), p. 204. According to Reitlinger, Bandera took an active part in the Prague conference. On the other hand, Ukrainian sources maintain not only that Bandera stayed away from this conference but that he strongly protested against it. See Pawlo Shandruk, "This Is How it Was" (Ukrainian), *Rozbudowa Derzhawi* (Cleveland, 1954), 3, pp. 33–45. Shandruk states, however, that Bulba-Borovets made peace with the Germans and in April 1945 headed a Ukrainian brigade for "special tasks" under the Germans.

23. These lies were repeated in countless articles in the Ukrainian

collaborationist press and in the memoirs of various writers. See H. Eisenbeis, "Moscow's Kremlin—a New Zion" (Ukrainian), *Ukrainska Disnist,* August 15, 1941, p. 2; Iwan Kalinowitch, "The Ukrainian People and the Jewry" (Ukrainian), *ibid.,* August 1, 1941, p. 1; Wsewolod Harmaniw, "Under Jewish Rule" (Ukrainian), *ibid.,* September 1, 1941, p. 2. Even the conservative leader Iwan Nimchuk, former editor-in-chief of *Dilo,* could not free himself from being stereotyped as a "Judeo-Communist." See Iwan Nimchuk, *595 dniw yak sowietski wiazen* (595 Days as a Soviet Prisoner) (Toronto, 1950), p. 21.

24. Among the political prisoners in the Soviet prisons who were killed prior to the retreat of the Soviet armies, there were also Jewish political prisoners—Zionist and Labor Bundist leaders, members of Jewish youth groups, and others. German propaganda suppressed this fact. On the whole the bodies were in such a condition that identification was impossible. Where the corpses were not so strongly disfigured as to preclude identification, the police removed the Jewish corpses before visitors were admitted. See Koppel Holcman, *Ziemia bez Boga* (The Earth without God) (Wrocław, 1947), I, 112 ff.; this book appeared in a Hebrew translation, *B'ein Elohim* (Without God) (Tel Aviv, 1956). The number of victims in the various cities is given by Ilnytzkyj, on the basis of reports by German correspondents. See Ilnytzkyj, II, 171–73. One German correspondent unwarily admitted that "To give an exact number is not possible because . . . in the cellar . . . gasoline was poured over the bodies and ignited. For sanitary political reasons it is no longer possible to determine the number of the murdered retrospectively." "The Bloodhell in Lemberg," *Völkerischer Beobachter,* Munich edition, July 6, 1941. Soon, however, the Nazi press made a "correction" and "established" that not a single Jew was among the victims. See Valenti Schuster, "Inhuman Scenes of Horror in the Cellars of the GPU: On the Tracks of the Lemberg Mass Murder," *Völkerischer Beobachter,* Munich edition, July 9, 1941.

25. SS-Hauptsturmführer Hans Joachim Bayer, a close collaborator of the German commandant in Lwów, gave an interview, to the Ukrainian publication in Cracow, *Krakiwski Wisti,* on July 6, 1941, which was reprinted in Germany in the *Ukrainska Disnist,* on July 15, 1941, and in the *Ukrainski Wistnik,* July 16, 1941. In the interview, Bayer said that "the Jews had a large share [in these killings], for they had turned over to the NKVD suspected Ukrainians." See also Szloyme Mayer, *Der untergang fun zlotchev* (The Destruction of Złoczów) (Munich, 1947), p. 7; he states that the Ukrainian committee in Złoczów issued a proclamation charging the Jews with the death of the Ukrainian prisoners.

26. See essay 10 below, "The Destruction of the Jews of Lwów, 1941–1944"; Izhak Lewin, *Aliti mi-spezia* (I Left Spezzia) (Tel Aviv, 1946), p. 61 (on Lwów; the author estimates that 2,000 Jews perished "in the process of washing the corpses"); Avraham Oks, "Tarnopol in the Era of World War II" (Hebrew), *Entsiklopedia shel galuyot,* 3 (Jerusalem, 1955), 385; Holcman, I, 112–89 (on Borysław).

27. Dokia Humenna, *Khreshtchati yar* (*Kiiw, 1941–1943*) (The Khreshtchati Ravine: Kiev, 1941–1943) (New York, 1946), pp. 174–75, 194–96; report no. 6 of the Einsatzguppen for October 1–31, 1941, Nuremberg Doc. R–102, American Jewish Conference, *Nazi Germany in War against the Jews* (New York, 1947), pt. III, p. 586; Schwarz, p. 314.

28. There are many accounts of such attacks on Jews. See H. Halpern, ed., *Megilas gline* (The Story of Glina) (New York, 1950), p. 261; *Sefer hazikaron likdoshe bolehov* (Memorial Book of Bolechów) (Haifa, 1957), p. 309 (on anti-Jewish posters and propaganda).

29. Eisenstein-Keshev, pp. 43–46, 56; *Yizkor-bukh ratne* (Memorial Book of Ratne) (Buenos Aires, 1954), pp. 493, 604; *Sefer hosht* (Memorial Book of Huszcza) (Tel Aviv, 1957), p. 46; Bunye Nayman, *Der Tog,* New York, October 24, 1946 (on Melnica, Volhynia); M. Weisberg, "Life and Extinction of Ghetto Dubno," (Yiddish), *Fun letstn Hurbn,* no. 2 (Munich, September 1946), 14; Mendl Man, "The Uprising in the Tuczyn Ghetto" (Yiddish), *ibid.,* no. 9 (Munich, 1948), 61; *Zamoshz bigona uvshivra* (Zamość in Despair and Destruction) (Tel Aviv, 1953), pp. 168–70 (on Olyka, Volhynia); I. Metzker, in *Forverts,* New York, July 22, 1946 (on Bóbrka, Eastern Galicia); *Pinkes kolomey* (Memorial Book of Kołomyja) (New York, 1957), pp. 325, 329; *Sefer butshatsh* (Memorial Book of Buczacz) (Tel Aviv, 1956), p. 251; a letter in the *Forverts,* October 18, 1946 (on Kopyczyńce, Eastern Galicia); Tania Fuchs, *A vanderung iber okupirte gebitn* (Wandering through Occupied Territories) (Buenos Aires, 1947), pp. 194–95 (on Horodenka); Mordkhe Gerstel, *Hurbn yaritshov bay lemberg* (The Destruction of Jaryczów near Lwów) (New York, 1948), pp. 30–36; Avrom Weisbrod, *Es shtarbt a shtetl* (A Village is Dying) (Munich, 1949), p. 19 (on Skałat, Eastern Galicia); *Der fertsik-yeriker yorbukh fun pliskover gmilus-khasidim-fareyn* (The Fortieth Anniversary Annual of the Pliskov Gmilut-Hasidim Association) (Pittsburgh, 1948), p. 18; Mayer, pp. 9–13; Noe Grüss and Maria Hochberg-Mariańska, eds., *Dzieci oskarżają* (Children Accuse) (Lodz, 1947), pp. 33, 134–35 (on Horodenka and Sambor); Reitlinger, *The Final Solution,* pp. 199, 232, 298 (on the pogroms in Radomyśl, Uman, and in Bucovina); *Sefer hapartizanim hayehudim* (Book of the Jewish Partisans) (Merhavia, 1958), I, 658 (on Ostróg and Międzyrzec in Volhynia).

30. In Buczacz the pogrom was directed by the local Ukrainian intelligentsia (*Sefer butshatsh,* p. 272); also *Yizkor-bukh ratne,* p. 484. The pogrom in Delatyn, Eastern Galicia, was largely the work of the music teacher Sławko Waszczuk; and that in Stanislav, of Professor Łysiak, of the local teachers' seminary (Dov Sadan and M. Gelerter, eds., *Stanislav: arim ve-imahot be-yisrael* [Stanisławów: Cities and Mothers in Israel], V, Jerusalem, 1952, 401) A Jewish teacher in Dubno relates that the pogrom in Dubno was carried out under the direction of several members of the new Ukrainian municipal administration—his former colleagues, whom he enumerates by name (Weisberg, p. 20). A Ukrainian pharmacist, a teacher, and several others participated with the Germans in planning the pogrom in Tarnopol ("Tarnopol," *Entsiklopedia shel galuyot,* III, Jerusalem, 1955, 413). Among the leading figures in the massacre of the Jews in Kosów Huculski was a former Ukrainian school inspector (Fuchs, pp. 221–24). The daughter of a local Ukrainian attorney was the foremost agitator against the Jews in Złoczów (Mayer, pp. 9–13). In some places even Ukrainian priests took part in the anti-Jewish agitation. In Skałat, the Ukrainian priest and a Ukrainian judge were members of a delegation that presented an anti-Jewish petition to the Germans (Weisbrod, pp. 20–21). In Jabłonica, Eastern Galicia, the Ukrainian priest incited the Hutsuls (Eastern Carpathian mountaineers) against the Jews. Thereupon several Jews were

dragged at night from their beds and drowned in the Czeremosz River (Fuchs, p. 215). The massacre in Jabłonica is also recorded by Isaac Huzen, *Kitever yizkor-bukh* (Memorial Book of Kuty) (New York, 1958), pp. 110–11. The Ukrainian priest Hawryluk incited his parishioners against the Jews in Glinany (Halpern, pp. 232–33).

31. In Zbaraż, Ukrainian secondary-school students marched singing through the streets, and on to the Jewish cemetery, where they destroyed the tombstones. See Jakob Littner, *Aufzeichnungen aus einem Erdloch* (Munich, 1948), pp. 80–81. Prior to the massacre of the Jews, the municipality of Kosów Huculski summoned Ukrainian youths to help dig mass graves for the Jews (Fuchs, pp. 221–24).

32. In the village of Shubkov, near Rovno, the Ukrainians established a kind of concentration camp for the local Jews (numbering about a hundred), and tortured them there. When the Germans learned of this camp they ordered its abolition (Man, pp. 61–62).

33. *Yalkut volin, osef zikhronot u-t'evdot (1946–1952)* Files of Volhynia, Collection of Memoirs and Documents, 1946–1952), II, no. 10, pp. 22–23 (on Klesów); Layzer Fishman, "When Jewish Blood was Cheap" (Yiddish), *Dos naye lebn*, Lodz, July 13, 1947 (on Novograd Volynski); Shmuel Druk, *Yidenshtot yavorov* (The Jewish City of Jaworów) (New York, 1950), pp. 34, 45; Diadia Misha (M. Gildenman), *Hurbn korets* (The Destruction of Korzec) (Chicago, 1949), p. 76; "The First to Rebel, Lachva" (Hebrew), *Entsiklopedia shel galuyot* (Jerusalem, 1957), 60, 73–74. The reports of the German Einsatzgruppen state that the cooperation of the Ukrainian population facilitated location and identification of Jews. In some cities, such as Lwów, the Ukrainians themselves seized Jews and turned them over to the German authorities. See report no. 9 of the Einsatzgruppen, Berlin, July 30, 1941, cited in Monneray, *Est*, pp. 290–91. Many Jews who escaped from Tuczyn and Rokitno, in Volhynia, were caught by Ukrainian peasants and were surrendered to the Germans (*Sefer hapartizanim*, I, 617, 683–84; II, 222, 249).

34. This reward varied. As a rule, it was no more than some quarts of vodka, several pounds of sugar or salt, cigarettes, or, occasionally, small sums of money. See *Sefer butshatsh*, pp. 313, 335; also my book, *Their Brothers' Keepers* (New York, 1957), pp. 17, 184.

35. Ereignismeldung, no. 23, July 15, 1941. The German text reads: "With our gratitude [for the liberation] we connect the solemn vow of faithful vassalage in the reconstruction of a Europe freed of Jewish Bolshevist blood rule and plutocrat oppression."

36. *Yizkor-bukh ratne*, p. 529.

37. *Sefer hosht*, p. 16; Weisbrod, p. 28; *Yizkor kehilot luninez-kozhenhorodok* (Memorial for the Communities of Luniniec-Korzen-Horodec) (Tel Aviv, 1952), p. 181; Meir Teich, "The Jewish Self-Administration in the Ghetto Shargorod (Transnistria)," *YVS*, II (Jerusalem, 1958), 228–29.

38. "Tarnopol," *Entsiklopedia shel galuyot*, III, *passim*.

39. Fuchs, p. 220; Halpern, pp. 237–38; Huzen, p. 138.

40. Diadia Misha, p. 33.

41. Gerszon Taffet, *Zagłada Żydów Żółkiewskich* (The Destruction of the Jews in Żółkiew) (Lodz, 1946), p. 16; Mayer, p. 23.

42. *Dokumenty i Materjały*, II, *"Akcje" i wysiedlenia* ("Actions" and Deportations), ed. by Josef Kermisz (Lodz, 1946), p. 392.

43. Halpern, pp. 237–38; Druk, p. 10; *Pinkes kolomey*, p. 329. After a group of young men of the Jewish underground organization in Buczacz killed a Ukrainian informer, the number of Jews delivered to the Germans markedly declined (*Sefer butshatsh*, p. 283).

44. Pankiwsky, in *Listy do priyateliw*, 5, No. 8 (August 1957), 10–12.

45. In many cities Operation Petlura centered chiefly upon the extermination of Jewish intellectuals. Following a prepared list, the Ukrainian militia systematically visited the houses of Jewish physicians, lawyers, teachers, and communal leaders and took them to police headquarters, allegedly for questioning. None of the arrested ever returned. See below, essay 10, "The Destruction of the Jews of Lwów, 1941–1944"; T. Brustin-Bernstein, "The Process of Annihilation of Jewish Communities in the Territory of the So-Called 'District Galicia' " (Yiddish) *BFG*, 6, No. 3 (1953); Metzker, in *Forverts*, August 3, 1946 (on the basis of the deposition of Arthur Rothenstreich); Halpern, pp. 243–44; Eisenstein-Keshev, pp. 43, 54; Holcman, I, 319. There are many depositions on the participation of the Ukrainian police in the extermination of the Jews.

46. Stanislav, p. 396; Diadia Misha, pp. 48, 62; *Sefer butshatsh*, pp. 252, 256, 258, 278, 284, 292; Mark Frumer, "Destruction of Złoczów," in *Bleter fun payn un umkum* (Melbourne, 1949), p. 103; Fuchs, pp. 214–18; *Sefer hazikaron likdoshe bolehov*, pp. 307, 312, 320, 328, 349; *Rovno, sefer zikaron* (Równe Memorial Book), pp. 518–19, 526, 557, 567; *Pinkes kovel* (Memorial Book of Kowel) (Buenos Aires, 1951), p. 83; Weisberg, pp. 15–17; N. M. Gelber, *Toldot yehude brodi, arim ve-imahot be-yisrael* (Documents of Jews from Brody, in his ed. of *Cities and Mothers of Israel*), VI (Jerusalem, 1956), 402, 406; Taffet, p. 18; Holcman, II, 142, 154 ff.; Teich, pp. 229–30; *Schupo- und Gestapokriegsverbrecher von Stanislau vor dem Wiener Volksgericht*, compiled by T. Friedman (Haifa, 1957), pp. 2, 9, 35, 66, 68, 70–71, 75–76; *Schupokriegsverbrecher von Stryj vor dem Wiener Volksgericht*, compiled by T. Friedman (Haifa, 1957), pp. ix, 13, 33–35, 39, 43, 53; *Schupo-kriegsverbrecher in Kolomea vor dem Wiener Volksgericht*, compiled by T. Friedman (Haifa, 1957); Affidavit of Hermann Friedrich Graebe, Doc. PS–2992, *IMT*, XXXI, 441–50; report of General Georg Thomas of December 2, 1941, on the situation in Reichskommissariat Ukraine, Doc. PS–3257, *IMT*, XXXII, 72–75.

Similar reports are available for Bucovina and Moldavia. In the Ereignismeldung of the Einsatz-kommando 106, July 10, 1941, we read: "In Hotin 10b has carried out assignments. Intellectuals, leading personalities of Soviet party and state, Jewish agitators, teachers, lawyers, rabbis were caught in several raids with the help of Ukrainian informants and dealt with accordingly." Cited after the Nuremberg Documents in *Gutachten des Institutes für Zeitgeschichte* (Munich, 1958), p. 143.

In an interview with a first lieutenant of the German police, *Lwiwski Wisti* of August 26, 1941, stated that the number of Ukrainian militiamen in Galicia was about 6,000. Volhynia had a similar number. The figures for the other areas are unknown (Ilnytzkyj, II, 181). A frightful account by an eyewitness, the German officer Erwing Binger, of the Ukrainian militia's killing of 213 Jews in municipal park in Vinnitsa, in September 1941, is found in *YVS*, II (Jerusalem, 1959), 310–11.

47. Jonas Turkow, *In kamf far lebn* (Fighting for Life) (Buenos Aires,

1949), p. 72; below, essay 10, "The Destruction of the Jews of Lwów, 1941–1944"; Shiloni, p. 11; *Bleter fun payn un umkum,* p. 105; *Sefer hazikaron likdoshe bolehov,* p. 328; *Pinkas kremenez* (Memorial Book of Krzemieniec) (Tel Aviv, 1954), p. 511; *Yizkor-bukh khelm* (Memorial Book of Chełm) (Johannesburg, 1954), p. 596 (on Sobibor); Apenszlak, *The Black Book,* pp. 131, 143, 149; Nachman Blumental, ed., *Obozy* (The Camps), *Dokumenty i Materialy,* I (Lodz, 1946), pp. 180–81, 189, 206, 255. According to the testimony of eyewitnesses, there were some 400 Ukrainian policemen in Sobibór. See Yankel Wiernik, *A Year in Treblinka* (New York, 1945), pp. 9, 13, 25, 30 ff.; Zdzisław Łukaszkiewicz, *Obóz Straceńców w Treblince* (Extermination Camp in Treblinka) (Warsaw, 1946), p. 18. Łukaszkiewicz, a Polish judge, appointed by the central state commission for the investigation of German crimes in Poland to study the materials on Treblinka, notes that, according to the testimony of eyewitnesses, Treblinka had 40–50 German SS men and 300 Ukrainian policemen; he is of the opinion that this number was exaggerated, however. See also Kermisz, pp. 312, 318, 320; Władysław Szpilman, *Śmierć miasta* (The Death of a City) (Warsaw, 1946), pp. 98–99; J. Rajgrodzki, "Treblinka" (Polish), *Biuletyn,* no. 25 (Warsaw, 1958), 112. The late Jewish historian A. Lewin wrote in his "Diary from the Warsaw Ghetto" (Polish), *Biuletyn,* no. 25 (1958), 124, entry of January 4, 1943, that about 600 Ukrainian militiamen were scheduled to arrive in Warsaw in preparation for a new German "operation" against the Jews. J. Hirshhaut, *Finstere nekht in paviak* (Dark Nights in Pawiak) (Buenos Aires, 1948), p. 70, states that the prisoners in "Pawiak" were guarded by six Germans and twelve Ukrainians. Several of the Ukrainians, along with a group of Jewish and Polish prisoners, planned to mutiny and escape (p. 149).

48. General Mykola Kapustyanski, "First Ukrainian Division of the Ukrainian National Army," *Istoria ukrainskoho wiska,* pp. 605–8; Reitlinger, *The SS, Alibi of a Nation,* pp. 200, 202–4; Dmytryszyn, pp. 1–10; Kamenetsky, p. 75; Rosenblatt, p. 214, describes a battle between the SS Haliczina division and the partisans of General Sydor Kovpak. See also above, note 20.

49. Shandruk, *Rozbudowa Derzhavi,* see note 22.

50. Shandruk, *ibid.,* Kamenetsky, *Hitler's Occupation of the Ukraine, 1941–1944,* p. 62.

51. Kazimierz Leszczyński, "The Extermination of the Population in the Polish Territories in the Years of 1939–1945, Districts: Bialystok, Gdańsk, and Kielce" (Polish), *BKG,* 8 (1956), 115–204; *idem,* "Extermination . . .Districts: Cracow and Lublin," *ibid.,* 9 (1957), 113–255. Judge Leszczyński utilized for these two studies the materials of the official inquiry conducted by the central state commission for the investigation of German crimes in Poland in 1945 with the aid of Polish courts, local investigation commissions, mayors, justices of the peace, and the Polish Red Cross. In 1939–1945 there were executions of Jews, Poles, Soviet prisoners of war, Jewish and Polish prisoners of war, Soviet partisans, Gypsies, White Russians, and Ukrainians. Most executions were carried out by the Germans (SS, SD, military police, Gestapo, police, *Wehrmacht,* German civilians, *Lagerschutz*). Some were carried out by the Germans' assistants—the Polish police, the Ukrainian police, the followers of Bulba-Borovets, the Ukrainian SS, other Ukrainian units (mostly of the HiWi), the followers of General Vlasov, Cossacks, Kalmuks, Mongolians, and Lithu-

anian and White Russian detachments. A total of 2,687 executions (of individuals and groups numbering in the tens of thousands) were registered in the five districts. Executions of Jews constituted a large part of this total. The aforementioned Ukrainian detachments participated in thirty-seven executions of Jews. On the execution of Jews by the HiWi in Transnistria, see Teich, p. 249.

52. See *BGK,* 8, 175, Kielce district, item 298; 9, 168, Cracow district, item 674; 9, 238, 247, Lublin district, items 908, 1004.

53. The enthusiastic reception of the invading Nazis by the Ukrainians was described by war correspondents in German, Italian, Spanish, and Scandinavian newspapers; some of these accounts are quoted in part in Ilnytzkyj, II, 165–69.

54. A Jewish teacher and journalist who lived on "Aryan" papers in Polish and Ukrainian villages in Eastern Galicia tells of the excellent underground organization of the Ukrainian partisans and of the hostility toward Jews that informed these groups (Shilony, pp. 54, 100–14). Eisenstein-Keshev (p. 62) states that in the forests of Kapyczów and Arianów the Bandera followers killed about a hundred Jews. Attacks on Jews by followers of Bandera or Bulba-Borovets are reported in various testimonies in *Dzieci oskarzają,* pp. 38, 139, 141, 143, 144, 150, 154. Similar instances are reported in *Sefer hazikaron likdoshe bolehov,* pp. 337, 339; *Yizkor-bukh ratne,* pp. 560–61; *Dos bukh fun lublin* (Paris, 1952), pp. 458–59, 552; Weisbrod, p. 145; Rosenblat, pp. 16, 128, 225. A Jew who escaped from the concentration camp in Janów, near Lwów, reported that a Bandera group had surrounded a forest where about eighty Jews had been hiding, and killed them (testimony no. 1247 of the Central Jewish Historical Commission [now Jewish Historical Institute] in Poland). On atrocities against the Jews committed by Bandera's followers and, especially, by the followers of Bulba-Borovets, see Bakalchuk, pp. 126–36, 189–92, and *Sefer hapartizanim,* I, 626, 629, 680–81; II, 244, 246, 250.

55. According to a communication by Lew Shankowsky, a former member of the UPA and a prominent Ukrainian historian, immediately upon assuming the position of commander, General Chuprynka issued an order to his officers to refrain from anti-Jewish activities. No written document to that effect is available, however.

56. Neither the resolutions of the third general congress of the OUN (published clandestinely in 1943) nor the publication *Idea i Chin* (The Idea and Action) has been available to me. I quote from Shankowsky, *Pokhidni,* pp. 21, 22, 24, 117, 128. In any case, these resolutions and instructions came much too late to benefit the Jews of the Ukraine. The work of annihilation had by then been largely completed.

57. "Tarnopol," *Entsiklopedia shel galuyot,* III, p. 400; Eisenstein-Keshev, p. 61. The questionable source on the medical training course mentioned here is the "memoir," allegedly by a Jewish woman named Stella Kreuzbach, in *Nasha Meta,* Toronto, November 27 and December 4, 1954; *Ukrainske Slovo* (Buenos Aires?), October 10, 1954; and *Kalendar Almanakh na 1957 Rik* (Calendar Almanac for 1957) (Buenos Aires), pp. 92–97. *Kalendar* also features an article by Dmitry Andreyewsky (pp. 88–91), in which he states that Stella Kreuzbach went to Palestine after the war, where she was later employed as a secretary in the foreign ministry, and that several

weeks after the publication of her memoirs in the *Washington Post* (which the Ukrainian publication credited for first releasing the memoirs) she was mysteriously shot and killed. I checked the *Washington Post* of that period and did not find the memoirs. At my request, Dr. N. M. Gelber of Jerusalem made inquiry in the foreign ministry there; the reply was that the ministry had never had an employee by that name and that such a case of homicide was entirely unknown. Moreover, a careful analysis of the text of the "memoirs" has led me to the conclusion that the entire story is a hoax. Similarly, the Ukrainian writer B. Kordiuk labels the story "a mystification"; he states that "none of the members of the UPA" known to him "ever met or heard of her" (B. Kordiuk, "About Self-Sacrificing People" (Ukrainian), *Suchasna Ukraina,* Munich, July 20, 1958, p. 7).

58. Petro Mirchuk, *Ukrainska Powstanska Armija* (Munich, 1953), pp. 69–72; Vasyl Mudry, "On Clear Waters" (Ukrainian), *Swoboda,* May 3, 1955, pp. 2–3; *Ukrainian Resistance,* p. 84. Mykola Lebed, head of the OUN in the period 1941–1943, wrote: "The majority of physicians in the UPA were Jews, whom the UPA had rescued. . . . The Jewish physicians were treated as citizens of the Ukraine and officers of the Ukrainian army. It should be duly stressed at this point that all of them discharged their exacting duties faithfully. They rendered service not only to the soldiers but to the entire population. They traveled throughout the area, and organized field hospitals and local medical stations. They did not desert the fighting ranks in trying situations, even then when they had an opportunity to go over to the Reds. Many of them died a hero's death." (Lebed, pp. 35–36.)

59. Lew Shankowsky, "Ten Years of the UPA Struggle (1942–1952)," *Ukrainian Insurgent Army,* p. 27, enumerates several Jewish physicians in the UPA: Dr. Margosh (pseudonym, Havrish), chief of the medical services of the Western Division of the UPA; Dr. Maximovitch, engaged in a training school for UPA officers in the Carpathians; and Dr. Kum (pseudonym), chief of an underground UPA hospital in Trukhanow, near Skole in the Carpathians. (Dr. Kum was killed in a battle against the Soviet army.) Immediately after the war, I met a Jewish physician who, together with his wife, was with the Bandera group; I am under obligation not to divulge his name. Another Jewish physician who served in the Bandera group and was thus saved, together with his brother, lives now in a village near Tel Aviv.

Eisenstein-Keshev, p. 63, states that the Bandera group liquidated the Jewish physicians upon the approach of the Red army; no detailed data on this point are available in her book, however.

60. In a letter to me dated March 7, 1958, Shankowsky wrote that there were fourteen Jews in his unit of the UPA; practically all of them survived. There were undoubtedly some Jews in the underground organization of the OUN as well. A report of an Einsatzgruppe (Doc. NO–4134 in the Ohlendorf trial) states that Jews were active on behalf of the Bandera movement, and that these Jews were provided with false identification papers by the movement (Ilnytskyj, II, 217; also Shankowsky, p. 705). One Jewish woman, Shprintse Feierstein of Lublin, declared that she and another Jewish woman worked as seamstresses for a Bulba-Borovets group and thus survived (*Dos bukh fun lublin,* pp. 458–59). A similar case, of a Jew in Rokitno admitted to a Bandera group, is recorded in *Sefer hapartizanim,* I, 705–6.

61. According to Eisenstein-Keshev, pp. 62–64, seventeen Jews from Camp Kudrynki miraculously survived. Her report is not sufficiently documented, and is subject to question. In the middle of June 1943 the UPA was compelled to disband this camp not because of the advance of the Soviet army, as Eisenstein-Keshev erroneously states, but because of an attack by a German motorized battalion, under General Hüntzler. Conceivably, some of the Jewish inmates were left behind, fell into the hands of the Germans, and were exterminated.

62. Brustin-Bernstein, *BFG*, VI, no. 3, pp. 96–98; deposition of Samuel Weiler in *Ruch podziemny w ghettach i obozach* (Underground Movement in the Ghettos and Camps), ed. by B. Ajzensztoyn (Lodz, 1946), pp. 154–65; report of the SS and police chief in District Galicia, General Fritz Katzmann, Doc. L–18, *IMT*, XXXVII, 391–431.

63. *Sefer hazikaron likdoshe bolehov*, pp. 336–38.

64. Rosenblatt, pp. 21–23, 98, 114.

65. Shankowsky, *Istoria*, p. 662; *Ukrainian Resistance* (p. 86) cites the following official communiqué of the UPA leadership: "Between March 15 and October 4, 1943, all police detachments in Volhynia and Polesie, composed of Ukrainians, upon orders of the High Command of the UPA, went over with their weapons to the Ukrainian Insurgent Army." M. Bakalchuk (pp. 86–88) tells of a group of sixty Ukrainian auxiliary policemen who, upon orders of the Gestapo, attempted to infiltrate a Communist partisan unit in Volhynia, and were discovered and killed. Other cases of infiltration into Soviet partisan units are recorded in *Sefer hapartizanim*, I, 623–24, 626.

66. *Yizkor-bukh ratne*, p. 560; Yekhiel Granatstein, *Ikh hob gevolt lebn* (I Wanted to Live) (Paris, 1950), pp. 100–12. Granatstein tells of a group of Ukrainians who escaped to the Soviet partisans in Polesie. While in his cups, one of the Ukrainians related that he was a policeman and had been trained in Germany, in a special school for Ukrainians, where they had been given such instructions as "could not be divulged." Later on, he confessed that he had killed a number of Jews during the anti-Jewish operations in the Ukraine. For further details on anti-Semitism among the Soviet partisans, see Kaganovitch, I, 316–64. In *Yizkor-bukh ratne*, p. 563, there is a report that a group of Red partisans came to the forest near that town, drove the Jews from their hiding places and killed them. Similarly, Bakalchuk (pp. 167–69) tells of anti-Semitic sentiments and incidents among the Communist partisans.

67. Such a band, led by a notorious criminal, operated in the vicinity of Buczacz (*Sefer butshatsh*, p. 293). Another band operated in the vicinity of Kamień Koszyrski, Volhynia (Kaganovitch, pp. 343–44). A group pretending to be followers of Bulba-Borovets was led by Ataman Fiodor, a common adventurer. A Jewish youth named Berish Arbuz belonged to that group, and was later killed by Fiodor. (Motl Sternblitz, "Jewish Partisans in the Area of Lublin-Bychowa" (Yiddish), *Dos bukh fun lublin*, p. 552.) That various armed groups disguised themselves as UPA partisans is also mentioned by Lebed, *UPA, Ukrainska powstanska armija*, p. 49; and Shankowsky, *Istoria*, p. 674.

68. Lew Shankowsky communicated these figures to me in his letter of March 7, 1958. The same figures are given in Lebed, p. 65. On the other hand, Shankowsky, *Istoria*, p. 698, mentioned a much higher figure, undoubtedly a mistake. The proclamations of the SS and police chief of the Galicia District

(in German, Ukrainian, and Polish) were posted everywhere to warn the population against anti-German activities. A collection of such posters is found in the archives of the Prologue Society in New York; photostatic copies of the posters were made for the archives of the YIVO Institute for Jewish Research and the Centre de Documentation Contemporaine in Paris.

In connection with the notices of executions in Galicia, I should mention that I have found a confidential report, sent by the SS and police chief of the Government General to the higher authorities in Berlin on October 7, 1943, stating that there was a marked increase in the numbers of trials of Christians, especially peasants, for concealing Jews. The writer of the report opined that the concealments had a twofold motivation: pity, and friendship because of former business associations. He was, moreover, of the opinion that such crimes should not be tried, but should be dealt with summarily: death "on the spot, without losing time," especially since it had been the practice for any Christian guilty of such a crime (hiding a Jew) to be executed without trial. The original of this report is in the archives of the Instytut Zachodni (Polish Western Institute) in Poznań. An authorized copy is in my possession.

69. See the article by Vasyl Mudry cited above, note 58. That article is based mainly on testimony (of Jews saved by such Ukrainians) gathered by Joseph Schwarz of Brooklyn. The survivors live in New York, Vineland (N.J.), and Israel.

70. Petro Pik-Pasetski, "How the Ukrainian Foresters Were Saving Jews" (Ukrainian), *Swoboda,* April 9, 1955.

71. On the rescue activities and aid to Jews by Ukrainians, particularly Ukrainian women who had been maids in Jewish homes, see Ada Eber-Friedman, "From the Gallery of My Life-Givers" (Polish), *Nasza Trybuna* (New York, 1949–1950), nos. 109–118; Winfried, *Tagebuch für Ruth* (Vienna, 1946), special issue of the *Wiener Revue,* no. 2, p. 14; S. Szende, *The Promise Hitler Kept* (New York, 1945), p. 194; *Dzieci oskarżają,* p. 139; Rachel Korn, *Tog,* September 23, 1949; M. Borwicz, *Arishe papirn* (Aryan Papers) II, 40–43; *Sefer hosht,* p. 118; *Yalkut volin,* I and II (on Ukrainian peasants who rescued Jews in Hoszcza, Melnica, Klesów, Lutsk, Ozierany); *Yizkor-bukh ratne,* p. 561; *Pinkes biten* (Memorial Book Byteń) (Buenos Aires, 1954), pp. 503–10; Fuchs, pp. 224–25; Ilya Ehrenburg, *Merder fun felker* (Murderers of Peoples) (Moscow, 1944–1945), I, 10–18; II, 100–4, 119–23; Donia Rozen, *Yedide hayaar* (Friends in the Forest) (Jerusalem, 1954); G. Kenig, *Undzere bafrayer* (Our Liberators) (Paris, 1952); Eliezer Ungar, *Zakhor! me-yemei kronot ha-mavet* (Remember! From the Days of the Death Wagons) (Tel Aviv, 1945); N. M. Gelber, *Brodi,* p. 404, notes the names of ten Ukrainians and Poles, intellectuals and workers, who aided the Jews. *Rovno, sefer zikaron* tells of a Ukrainian lawyer friendly to the Jews. The Ukrainian library of the Szewczenko Society in Lwów employed and protected, in a given period, four Jews; see Wolodomir Doroshenko, *Ohnishtche ukrainskoi nauki* (The Center of Ukrainian Studies) (Philadelphia, 1957), pp. 92–93. *Sefer butshatsh,* pp. 275–76, records the very friendly attitude of the local Ukrainian mayor, Iwan Bubik, who rendered many favors to the Jews, and rescued many individuals from danger. Bubik also prevented the establishment of a ghetto in Buczacz.

72. Pinkhes Hirshprung, *Fun natsishn yomertol* (From the Nazi Valley of Lament) (Montreal, 1944), pp. 115–16; Schwarz, p. 314. M. Teich,

head of the Jewish community in Suczawa, Bucovina, who was taken by the Nazis to Shargorod, Transnistria, narrates the following episode: In mid-November 1941, a group of almost 900 women, children, and a few aged people arrived from the Dorohoi District in Shargorod. Their journey northward, in the dead of winter, would mean certain death. Teich intervened with the Rumanian praetor to let the group remain a few days, but in vain. The praetor ordered the immediate departure of the group the next day. When the deportees set out on the march, many of the Ukrainian peasant women who had come to the market that day crowded around them and gave them food for the journey. The women then went to the praetor's office, sat down, and blocked the way. When the praetor arrived, the peasant women cried and screamed, raised their fists and shouted: "You Burjui! How can you be so hard against human beings?" The transport was returned, and eventually the entire group settled in Shargorod (*YVS,* II, 231–32).

73. Ilnytzkyj, II, 176.

74. A photostatic copy of a Hebrew letter sent by Sheptitsky, in 1903, to the Jewish community of Jaworów, Eastern Galicia, was published by me in "The Destruction of the Jews of Lwów" (Hebrew) *Entsiklopedia shel galuyot,* IV (Jerusalem, 1956), 670.

75. Rabbi David Kahane (*Undzer veg,* Paris, September 17, 1948) relates that he visited the metropolitan in August 1942, and Sheptitsky told him of the letter to Himmler and of the rude reply from the German police and SS chief. The story of this letter is told by Sheptitsky's biographers; see T. B[utchko], *Weliki tchernets i narodoliubets* (A Great Monk and Humanitarian) (Prudentopol, Brazil, 1949?), pp. 130–31; Stepan Baran, *Mitropolit Andrei Sheptitski* (Munich, 1947), pp. 114–15. According to Baran, Sheptitsky forbade his priests to minister to Ukrainians who participated in anti-Jewish operations, even under German pressure. Pankiwsky is of the opinion that Sheptitsky's letter provoked the Germans' repressive measures against the Ukrainian national council in Lwów. Other Ukrainian writers, such as Ilnytzkyj, maintain that the days of the Ukrainian national council were then numbered anyway. See Pankiwsky in *Listi do priateliw,* V, no. 3, pp. 11–12; Ilnytzkyj, II, 186–87, 208, 227, 231, 244–46, 250.

76. *Lwiwski Arkhieparkhialni Widomosti* (Lwów Archdiocesan Bulletin), LV, no. 11 (November 1942), pp. 177–83. A photostatic copy of this document came to me through the courtesy of Vincent Shandor, executive secretary of the Ukrainian Congress of America in New York.

77. The wording of the conversation between Sheptitsky and Frederic was in all likelihood doctored by Frederic. His report, dated Berlin, September 19, 1943, is now in the archive of the CDJC in Paris (CXLVa–60).

78. Kahane was a teacher in the secondary schools in Lwów prior to World War II, and after the war was chief chaplain in the Polish army and later chaplain in the Israeli army.

79. Kahane's memoirs, published in *Undzer Veg* (Paris, September 17, 1948). Among the hidden were also the sons of the rabbi of Lwów, Ezekiel Lewin. One of the sons, Izhak (Kurt) Lewin, later published his memoirs, *Aliti mi-spezia,* in which he described his meetings with the metropolitan and the years spent with the Studites (pp. 174–75). Later he added to this description several details, in an article published in the English supplement to the

Ukrainian publication *Swoboda* (January 28, 1954), under the title "Jewish Call for Friendship with Ukrainians."

Marko Stek, a Ukrainian priest in charge of the rescue activities on behalf of Jewish children, left Eastern Galicia for Poland in 1954; later, with the help of Izhak Lewin and Kahane, he went to Germany, and then to America. Another twelve Studite monks managed to leave and settled on a farm in Canada.

In the late 1950s, a movement was started for the beatification of Sheptitsky. An authorized biography of the metropolitan, submitted to the Holy See by the Reverend Michael Hrynchyshyn, mentions Sheptitsky's rescue of Jews (*Romana seu Leopolien. Beatificationis et canonizationis servi Dei Andreae Szyptyckyj Archiepiscopi Leopoliensis Ukrainorum Metropolitae Haliciensis, Articuli pro causae instructione*) (Rome, 1958), p. 30.

80. Hirschprung, pp. 68, 81–82, 112, tells of the Ukrainian priest Tirpovitz in Dukla, Galicia, who saved the Jews there from a pogrom. A similar story of a Ukrainian priest in Wysock, Volhynia, is told by Deborah Neshkes in *Pinkes biten,* p. 500. Natalia Dresdner, a Jewish woman of Lwów, hid in the home of the Ukrainian priest Korduba in Mosty, Eastern Galicia, for eight months (Borwicz, I, 65–66). Sonia Rubinstein, of Poryck, Volhynia, was hidden by the family of a Ukrainian Greek Orthodox priest, named Piereviezov. The priest's daughter, Nina, a member of the Bandera movement, was friendly to Sonia and guarded her. Then trouble came. In the neighboring village of Lachow, about ten miles from the Piereviezov residence, another priest concealed a Jewish physician from Poryck; Bandera followers found this out, surrounded the house of the priest, and killed both the physician and the family of the priest. Piereviezov then arranged for Sonia's admission into a convent in Włodzimierz Wołyński. After the war, she had to remain in the convent until her departure for Palestine, in order not to bring down the wrath of the nationalist partisans on the Piereviezov family. The memoirs of Sonia Rubinstein appeared in *Fun letstn hurbn,* no. 8, pp. 65–75.

81. Mark Khinoy, *Forverts,* October 9, 1945.

82. On aid given by the Ukrainian Baptists, see *Yalkut volin,* I, no. 7, p. 30; Eisenstein-Keshev, pp. 72–73; on aid by the Seventh-Day Adventists, see *Sefer butshatsh,* p. 288; and the testimonies of Elsa Silver (on her experiences in the vicinity of Podhajce, Eastern Galicia) and Simon Schechter (of Korolówka, Eastern Galicia) in the YIVO archives. Shiloni, p. 68, tells how his Ukrainian landlord, a Jehovah's Witness, rescued him and deplored and lamented the conduct of their Ukrainian neighbors who persecuted the Jews.

83. "The Revised Myth of Ukrainian Anti-Semitism," *Ukrainian Quarterly,* V, no. 1, 167–74.

84. Volodimir P. Stakhiw, in *Suchasna Ukraina,* no. 11 (May 31, 1959).

# PART TWO

*1941–1945  Extermination*

# 9

# THE EXTERMINATION OF THE POLISH JEWS DURING THE GERMAN OCCUPATION, 1939–1945

The number of Jews within the boundaries of Poland before September 1, 1939, can be only approximately established. The last official census before the war was on December 9, 1931, and recorded 3,113,900 civilians of Jewish denomination; in addition, 18,681 Jews were serving in the armed forces. In view of an average natural increase of 0.9 percent (about 28,000 persons) per year, we would estimate that the Jewish population increased by 224,000 during the eight years to the end of 1939, and totaled about 3.347 million by September 1, 1939. Investigations carried out by Stefan Szulc, director of the central statistical office in Poland, have shown that the number of births in the Jewish population during that period was at least 50 percent higher than the figure given in the official tabulations.[1] Considering this correction, we can estimate a total of 3.454 million Jews in Poland in 1939, but we must subtract from this figure about 116,000 Jews who emigrated between December 1931 and September 1939; it can then be assumed that the total number of Jews in Poland at the start of the war was about 3.338 million—or, in round figures, 3.34 million. This population was distributed roughly as shown in the following table. The figures in the table approximate the population distribution of these territories just before the war. Actually, by September 1939 changes had

*Estimated Territorial Distribution of the Jewish Population in Poland (prewar figures)*

| *Areas Subsequently Occupied by Germany* | *Population* | *Areas Subsequently Annexed by the USSR* | *Population* |
|---|---|---|---|
| Government General Provinces of Cracow, Warsaw, Lublin, Kielce, Warsaw city, and a part of the Lwów province up to the River San | 1,560,000 | Provinces of Lwów (eastern part), Tarnopol, and Stanisławów Volhynia | 555,000 225,000 |
| Territories incorporated into the Reich Provinces of Poznań, Pomerania, Silesia, Lodz, Bialystok, and a part of the Warsaw province | 665,000 | Western Byelorussia and Lithuania, the provinces of Polesie, Nowogródek, and Vilna | 335,000 |
| TOTAL | 2,225,000 | | 1,115,000 |

already begun to occur in this conjectural distribution. The sudden attack by German tanks and by aircraft and the lightning advance of the invader caused vast movements of population all over Poland. Large masses of civilians fled eastward and southward to escape the horrors of the war. For example, about 10,000 persons (including 5,000–6,000 Jews) fled Cracow alone during the first days of September.[2] Hence, already at the outset of the Second World War, strictly speaking after the end of the Polish campaign in September 1939, great changes occurred in the territorial distribution of the Jewish population.

Demographic changes were caused not only by large-scale migratory movements, but also by civilian and military deaths resulting from the war. In the fighting against the German invader, 32,216 Jewish soldiers and officers were killed, and 61,000 were taken prisoner.[3] Most of the Jewish prisoners-of-war taken by the Germans must also be considered casualties. Only a small group of them survived; the rest were murdered by the Germans. (From September 13, 1939, to September 30, 1940, 449 Jewish prisoners-of-war were released by the Germans, and returned to Cracow;[4] this case, small as it was, was almost unique.) Many thousands of Jews also perished in air raids when the Germans bombed civilian populations in the cities and refugees on the roads.[5]

Immediately before and after the outbreak of hostilities, about 20,000–25,000 Jews succeeded in escaping to neutral countries: Hungary, Rumania, and the Baltic states.[6] After the cessation of military operations and the establishment of a frontier between Germany and the Soviet Union, the exodus of the Jewish population continued. They fled from the Germans— who had begun their rule with a series of violent acts against Jews and

Poles—to the territories annexed by the USSR, where they found safer living conditions and possibilities for work. As a result of these migrations to the east, which reached their peak in the fall of 1939 (the German-Soviet border was closed in November), at least 300,000 Jews from the territories under the German occupation settled in the Soviet area.

The question arises: How many Jews remained in the German-occupied areas during the period of relatively stable Russo-German political relations (September 1939 to January 1940)? If we assume that the total Jewish population decline (caused by emigration to neutral countries and by war casualties in the military and civilian sectors) was distributed proportionally in the German (66.6 percent of the Jewish total) and Soviet (33.4 percent) areas of occupation, then the Jewish population in the German-occupied territory would have declined by about 120,000, not including the 300,000 emigrants to the USSR. Thus the Jewish population in German-occupied Poland fell to about 1.8 million.

Important dislocations of Jews also occurred within the German zone. In the first year of German rule, considerable transfers to the east took place; in September 1939 about 60,000 Jews fled from the western part of Poland to central Poland (the so-called Government General), and were unable to return to their homes in the west, because total expulsion of Jews from that part of the country was being enacted. As a result of this expulsion, the Germans transferred (between September 1939 and July 1940) 330,000 Jews from the territories incorporated into the Reich to the territory of the GG.[7] The Jewish population of the incorporated territories was thereby reduced to about 240,000 (if we also count the losses due to emigration and the war casualties), while the Jewish population in the GG rose to about 1.5 million. Moreover, a huge number of Jews from Western Europe (mainly from Germany, Austria, and Czechoslovakia, with smaller numbers from Holland, Belgium, and other countries) were resettled in the GG by the Germans. By the end of 1942, about 200,000 to 300,000 Jews had been so transferred. But this influx did not make up for the Jewish population losses due to starvation, persecution, executions, and "special actions" (*Sonderaktionen*), which affected the deportees from the West as much as the Polish Jews. It can be assumed that the number of Jews in the GG probably did not exceed 1.5 million, notwithstanding the influx from the West. In the summer of 1941, after the Germans had overrun the territories evacuated by the Soviet Army, about 1.0 million Jews were added to the total in German-occupied Poland, and they remained in those areas taken by the German military.

Polish Jewry was concentrated in cities and towns. The census of 1931 showed that 77 percent of Polish Jewry lived in cities, and only 23 percent in the country. According to Peter-Heinz Seraphim, 88 percent of the Jewish population in the GG in mid–1940 lived in the cities. The concentration of Jews in certain defined centers was intensified by the Germans, for it facilitated their policy of repression and constituted an important step in the implementation of their anti-Jewish program. At the outbreak of the war, the Jewish population in Poland was distributed in about 1,000 urban and rural localities in Poland. By the end of 1942, when the massive exterminations were already in progress, the Germans had concentrated all of Polish Jewry in no more than fifty-four urban centers; Jews had been completely eliminated from all the rural settlements.

This tendency to clump the Jews in large urban centers (*Zusammenballung*) is clearly illustrated by the growth of some of the larger Jewish communities in German-occupied Poland. The most striking case is Warsaw, where the Germans organized a "monster-ghetto." At the end of October 1939, Warsaw was inhabited by 359,827 Jews;[8] by the middle of 1942, notwithstanding the high mortality rate and the deportations for forced labor, the number had risen to 540,000, according to some authors. About 150,000 Jews from other localities were resettled in Warsaw by the Germans during this period; 72,000 Jews had been transferred from the Warsaw suburbs on the left bank of the Vistula River in the spring of 1941.[9] Smaller concentrations of Jews were effected in other cities. In Cracow, which had a Jewish population of 56,000 in 1931 and about 60,500 in 1939 (estimated from the conjectured birth rate), the number of Jews rose to 70,000 by the spring of 1940, because of the "military events and relocations."[10] The number of officially registered Jews in summer 1940 was 68,482.[11] According to official statistics of the Jewish community in Cracow, on July 1, 1940 (the first incomplete census of the Jewish population), there were 54,517 prewar residents and about 11,000 newcomers.[12] In Lublin, which had a Jewish population of 38,000 in 1931, and 37,034 in 1939 (according to the official register of the Jewish community, October 25, 1940), the number of Jews rose to between 47,500 and 50,000 in 1940.[13] In Częstochowa, the Jewish population increased from about 25,000 in 1931 to over 30,000[14] in 1940 (mainly because of resettlement); according to municipal records for the year 1940, in January 1940 there were 28,714 Jews and in December of that year, 33,365.[15] Of the 13,800 Jews in Piotrków, 3,625 had been resettled there by the Germans.[16] At the end of 1941, 23,025 Jews were deported to Lodz, among them about 20,000 from Germany, Vienna, Prague, and Luxembourg, and 3,082 from Włocławek and its vicinity. In the first half of 1942, 7,649 Jews were expelled from the so-called Warthegau (districts of Lodz and Poznań, and part of the district of Warsaw) and deported to Lodz.[17] The number of Jews in Kielce rose from 18,000 in 1931 to about 25,400 in 1940.[18]

Bialystok, with a Jewish population of 39,165 in 1931, contained about 56,000 Jews in the years 1942–1943.[19] These few examples suffice to show the changes German policy wrought in the distribution of the Jewish population.

Under normal conditions a demographic study would not be complete without a detailed report on population movements. But the Jewish "migrations" had a peculiar character: they were compulsory, and were accompanied by loss of property, health, and often life. Neither can we speak here of natural increase or decrease in the Jewish population. The number of deaths rose catastrophically, and the birth rate fell sharply until finally there were no births at all.

## The Nazi "Solution of the Jewish Question"

The political program of Nazi Germany included not only the conquest of Poland and other countries on the eastern border but also the partial extermination of the native population, so that Germans might colonize the depopulated areas. According to testimony at the Nuremberg trials, Hitler considered the liquidation of 30 million Slavs. The plan for the physical destruction of the Jews had already been envisaged at the outbreak of the war in 1939, as shown by the testimony at Nuremberg,[20] as well as by official German documents,[21] the speeches by Hitler and Streicher, and articles by Goebbels.[22] The Nazis began to carry out their program in the first days of the war, although the precise steps leading to its implementation were still to be formulated and there apparently were also differences of opinion among the leaders of the Third Reich regarding this problem. In some circles, in the years 1939 and 1940 and even in the beginning of 1941,[23] plans for a less cruel solution of the Jewish question were put forward.[24] While these plans were being debated, however, the gradual extermination of Jews by all possible means was already taking place.

Jews were put outside the law. While Poles in the territories annexed to the Reich were considered second-class citizens (*Schutzangehörige des Reiches*), Jews and Gypsies were excluded even from this category and were thereby deprived of the protection of the state.[25] A series of oppressive regulations was enacted against the Jews. By an order of November 23, 1939, special marking of Jews was introduced; by an order of January 26, 1940, Jews were deprived of the right to travel or to change their place of residence. Orders for the confiscation of Jewish property were issued for German-occupied Poland on September 22, 1939, and January 24, 1940, and for the incorporated territories on September 17, 1940. Contributions were imposed on the Jewish communities—that is, fines to be paid in money, gold, silver, furs, and other valuable objects. The food rations allocated to Jews were far inferior in quantity and quality to those of other inhabitants. Starting in 1940, Jewish ghettos were established in various Polish cities. The worst parts of town were chosen for this purpose. The living quarters assigned to Jews were insufficient to accommodate the masses of people, and there was constant overcrowding, filth, and disease. Thus massed in one place, the Jewish population was an easy target for persecution of any kind, and for actions aiming at their annihilation. Accordingly, the ghettos became the main instrument toward the Nazi extermination of the Jewish people.

Another major instrument of annihilation was introduced by the Nazis in this period: the forced labor camps (*Zwangsarbeitslager*), sometimes ironically referred to as "training camps" (*Erziehungslager*). On October 26, 1939, at the very beginning of the occupation of Poland, the Germans issued an order introducing compulsory labor for Jews between the ages of fourteen and sixty. The first camps were set up by the end of 1939, where Jewish inmates, regardless of their age, education, ability, or professional training, were compelled to perform all kinds of onerous physical labor, under Draconian discipline and all sorts of chicanery, abuse, and frequent corporal punishment at the hands of their guards. The "labor" camps were, of course, merely another device for destroying the Jewish population. Many of the Jewish workers perished in the camps because of the conditions prevailing there, while those who returned home were, in most cases, physically broken and unfit for work.

During this initial period from the beginning of the German occupation, the Jewish population was kept under constant terror. It was subjected to severe punishments, fines, forced contributions, and to group executions. Attempting to leave the ghetto was punished with death. Hundreds of death sentences were issued for this offense by the German special courts (*Sondergericht*) and all of them were carried out. The death penalty was also imposed for not wearing the Jewish badge, for buying food illegally, for using means of transportation forbidden to Jews, for absenteeism from work, for sabotage, and other transgressions. Moreover, Jews received no protection under the law, and could be abused by anyone with complete impunity. No German official (military, civil, or police) was ever held responsible for killing, wounding, or robbing a Jew.

Though these repressive measures inflicted terrible casualties on the Jewish population, they were not sufficient to accomplish the goal of complete extermination. A plan to achieve this goal had already been hatched in the minds of the leaders of the Third Reich, however, during the period preceding the war with Soviet Russia.

## "Small Terror" and "Cold Pogroms"

It can be said that there were two stages in the destruction of the Jews under the German occupation. In the first, the Germans used various methods to concentrate and weaken the Jewish population. From the perspective of the mass exterminations that followed later, this stage was called the period of "small terror" (*Kleinterror*), because the massacres and executions generally did not affect more than tens or hundreds of victims in each instance (there were some exceptions, however, such as Bydgoszcz). In the second stage, the Germans proceeded to a swifter, mass annihilation of the entire Jewish population in the ghettos and camps.

At the very beginning of the war, as soon as the Germans invaded Poland, Jews unable to escape from the onrushing Nazi armies were horribly persecuted. The soldiers overtaking would-be fugitives tormented them, often beat them, seized their possessions, and, in many cases, shot them. Sometimes the invaders would drive together a large group of Jewish fugitives, several thousand of them, allegedly to put them in quarantine. After being incarcerated without food or drink, exposed to mockery and torments of various kinds, the victims would finally be released, barefoot and half-naked. When the Jews returned home, new troubles awaited them. Most of their homes and shops had been looted, and they were reduced to abject poverty. In some localities, the Germans arrested Jewish refugees for attempting to escape and subsequently treated them as enemies of the "New Order."[26]

Although the goal of exterminating the Jewish population had already been adopted by the Nazis, the Germans persisted in their strategy of deception. They tried to lull the Jews into a false sense of security, by making reassuring promises which they had no intention of keeping. Thus the German officials negotiating the terms for the capitulation of Warsaw pledged that the Jewish population would not be harmed. This assurance was repeated over the radio, in good faith, by the mayor of Warsaw, Stefan Starzyński. In his radio speech on September 4, 1939, Field-Marshal Walter von Brauchitsch, commander-in-chief of the German army, reassured the Polish Jews about their fate; and General Blaskowitz, commander of the German troops occupying Warsaw, issued a proclamation on September 30, 1939 (which was posted on the streets of Warsaw), repeating the same assertion and ordering Jews to return without fear to their occupation. No such promise was ever kept by the Germans, even temporarily. From the very beginning of the German invasion, cruel anti-Jewish acts were committed, involving all the elements of the future extermination policy—save only, perhaps, the gas chambers and crematoria. There were robberies, "inspections," fines and forced contributions, confiscations, the taking of hostages, beatings and tortures, mockery and derision, humiliation, forced participation in crude and insulting spectacles before movie cameras, Jew-hunting, hard labor, the rape of Jewish women, the desecration of religious objects, the burning of synagogues and Jewish libraries, expulsions, executions, and murders, both individual and collective.

In a number of localities, for instance, Warsaw, Lublin, and smaller towns like Bełżyce and Gorlice, immediately following the German invasion Jews were ordered to reopen their stores, to facilitate looting by the invaders. Shopkeepers who disobeyed this order were severely punished. In other places, for instance, Włocławek, Radziejów, Częstochowa, and Przemyśl,[27] all Jewish stores were sealed and put at the disposal of the German authorities. In Rzeszów, on the other hand, the German commander ordered on September 18, 1939, that all Jewish shops be seized and be put in the charge of the non-Jewish pensioners of the city—another example of the Nazi strategy of "divide and rule." In all cities, larger establishments were directly appropriated by the German authorities. Major factories and industrial plants were immediately taken over by the state. The German army confiscated stocks of textiles, leather, and ironware owned by Jews. Huge military lorries drove up to Jewish-owned warehouses in Warsaw, Lodz, and other manufacturing cities, and carried away all the goods; owners and employees were often ordered to act as porters.

Individual looting of Jewish property was carried out by German soldiers and police, often abetted by the local rabble and the *Volksdeutsche* (ethnic Germans). Vandalism and looting of Jewish homes, under the pretext of searching for incriminating evidence or without any reason at all, were everyday occurrences in almost all localities. Gold rings and earrings were taken by force from their wearers; often fingers were twisted or broken, ears were injured or torn.[28] The individual plunder of Jewish property, especially in larger cities, was passed off under the guise of an "inheritance," sometimes of a Jewish apartment with all its possessions. In actuality, a German or a *Volksdeutsch* would rush into an apartment owned by Jews, look at his watch, and order the owner to get out within five to twenty minutes, leaving everything behind. Sometimes the residents would be permitted to pack a small valise, but generally even this was prohibited. In rare instances, the time allowed for leaving the apartment was extended to several hours or more.

Contributions were exacted from Jewish communities under every possible pretext, and sometimes with no pretext at all. The amount and conditions of payment, and the penalties for nonpayment, were enormous. Each local authority levied them according to individual whim. In some places contributions were imposed repeatedly. Sometimes they were as high as tens of millions of zlotys for a community. Besides money, the Germans extorted gold, silver, jewelry, and other articles of value, by means of terror, beatings, and torture. Hostages were taken, and were rarely released after the contribution was paid. If the sum imposed was not raised by the given time, punitive sanctions were used: hostages, members of the Jewish militia, or employees and members of the Jewish Council might be deported to the camps or executed outright. There was no hope of appeal to a higher authority against these local actions, since the Jews were considered outside the law.

Moreover, during the first weeks of the occupation, the Germans organized pogroms in all Polish towns and villages. In front of the local populace, forcibly assembled in the marketplace, the Germans would arrange public spectacles in which Jews were humiliated, derided, beaten, tortured, and then killed.[29] In some places Jews were forced to dance and sing, scream, and recite absurd self-deprecations.[30] Street raids were organized allegedly for taking Jews to work. Large numbers of Jews were ordered to assemble at a given hour, and were driven straight to another town or camp that was hastily set up.

Religious Jews were particularly exposed to derision. Their beards were cut or pulled off (often together with pieces of skin), or were set on fire (which the victims were kept from extinguishing).[31] Rabbis and Orthodox Jews were forced to dance and sing before crowds or were dragged along the streets garbed in prayer shawls.[32] In Cisna the Germans ordered Jews themselves to set fire, in the marketplace, to Jewish liturgical vestments and religious books, and dance around the pile, singing in chorus: "We are so glad that the 'dirt' is burning" (*Wir freuen uns, wie das Dreck brennt*). Jews were ordered to sweep streets, wash floors, and clean latrines with their prayer shawls. In Kalisz, Jews were forced to jump over a fire in which religious books and ritual vestments were burning. Germans set synagogues on fire, or forced Jews to do it themselves. During that period several hundred synagogues in Poland were destroyed by fire or blown up. In the first fortnight after the invasion, the Germans burnt down all the synagogues in Bielsko. In Bydgoszcz the first building destroyed by the Germans was the local synagogue. Between September 5 and 10, the Germans burnt completely all synagogues in Piotrków and Aleksandrów. In Zgierz, after destroying the synagogue, they forced the rabbi to sign a statement that the Jews themselves had done it. On the Day of Atonement (September 24, 1939), the Germans burnt down the synagogue in Włocławek. The fire was filmed, and then twenty-five Jews were arrested, and were forced to sign a statement that they themselves had set the fire. Consequently, a fine of 100,000 zlotys was imposed on the Jewish population. On the same day, the synagogues in Grudziąc, Toruń, Zamość, Mielec, Częstochowa, Tarnów, and Katowice were burnt down. In Grójec, Jews were forced to set fire to their synagogue, and afterward a number of the "incendiaries" were executed. At Radziejów, the Germans set fire to the synagogue, and later arrested several Jews as the culprits, because a box of matches was found in the pocket of one of them. Between November 11 and 15, 1939, about ten Jewish houses of prayer were burnt down in Lodz. In Sosnowiec, the Germans destroyed three synagogues and arrested 250 Jews. In Siedliszcze, the Germans placed a bomb in the synagogue. In Poznań, they burnt down several synagogues and desecrated the central synagogue by converting it into a swimming pool during festivities honoring the Hitler Youth and the Nazi party. In Cracow and Będzin, the destruction and burning of Jewish synagogues and study houses was assigned to special brigades, called *Brennkommandos*. For their acts of desecration, for example, in Włocławek, Płońsk, Bełżyce, and Mielec, the Germans deliberately chose solemn Jewish holidays. From place to place, they turned synagogues into stables (Gniewoszów and Maków), into factories (Przemyśl), into ballrooms (Nowy Tomyśl), into health centers (Góra Kalwarja), into a jail (Kalisz), and even into a public latrine (Ciechanów).[33]

Germans assigned to Jews the hardest and most humiliating and loathsome tasks: the clearing of rubble from the streets, the removal of corpses, the carrying of heavy loads, the digging of ditches, and the cleaning of latrines. The work imposed on an individual usually exceeded his strength (Jews, instead of horses, were harnessed to carts and were ordered to pull heavy loads), but if he was unable to complete his assignment, he was beaten unmercifully. Jews were forced to clean out latrines with their bare hands; to gather horse-droppings in the marketplace and put them in their pockets or caps (in Cisna); to smear their faces with excrement (in Kalisz).[34]

Jewish women as well as men were the victims of torment, persecution, and acts of violence at the hands of the Germans. In spite of the Nuremberg racial laws, Jewish women and girls were raped by Germans.[35]

As soon as the Germans arrived, they began to expel Jews from the area which they intended to incorporate into the Reich—mainly the provinces of Poznań, Pomerania, and Silesia, and the cities and towns on the borders of Eastern Prussia (such as Bielsko, Wysokie Mazowieckie, Kalisz, Toruń, Bydgoszcz, and Suwałki).[36] Expulsions also took place on the German-Soviet border, the Germans trying to drive the Jewish inhabitants across to the Soviet side. Jews were driven from Chełm and from Hrubieszów to Sokal, for example, near the Soviet border; during their march of several days, many of them were shot.[37] From Jarosław, Łańcut, Przemyśl, Tarnobrzeg, and other border towns, Jews were pushed into the

Soviet territory by the Germans. A week after their invasion of Jarosław, the Germans ordered the Jews to evacuate within half an hour.[38] An eye-witness report from Łańcut describes how the Jews were pushed by the Germans across the River San:

We arrived at the banks of the River San on the third day of the move. Gestapo men were waiting there. They started to push people into a boat, or rather onto a raft of two unbalanced wooden planks, from which women and children were falling into the river. Everywhere we saw floating corpses, dead victims from days before; women were standing in the water closer to the banks of the river, holding their children above the heads, crying for help, to which the Gestapo men reacted by shooting them. Blood, dead bodies, masses of floating corpses. It is impossible to imagine the despair, or to describe the weeping and the crying and the utter helplessness of people in a situation like that.[39]

The Germans afterward boasted in their newspapers that these towns were now completely "free of Jews" (*judenrein*).[40]

According to a report by the English journalist Baker-Beall, the Bydgoszcz area was dejudaized by a more direct method, by exterminating all the Jewish inhabitants. Several thousand Jews—men, women, and children—were driven into a Bydgoszcz stable that had been converted into a latrine, and were shot.[41] Also pertinent to the liquidation of the Bydgoszcz Jews is this terse report of November 14, 1939, from SD-Einsatzkommando Bromberg to the headquarters of the Security Police and Security Service in Berlin: "The Jewish problem no longer exists in Bydgoszcz, for this city is completely free of Jews. During the clean-up operation, all Jews who did not know enough to disappear on their own before, have been removed."[42]

During these first weeks, there was hardly a town or village in occupied Poland where the Germans did not shoot or torture Jews to death. In the township of Wieruszów, immediately after their arrival, the Germans killed twenty Jews in the marketplace.[43] In Częstochowa, on September 3 and 4, 1939, they killed between 100 and 200 Jews. Entering Aleksandrów on September 7, the Germans shot sixty Jews; and on September 14, 1939, they tortured and then shot forty-five more of them. In Ostrów Mazowiecki, they slaughtered 500 Jewish men, women, and children.[44] In Trzebinia, 150 Jews were killed. In Łaskarzew, almost all the Jewish men were murdered. In Warta and Sosnowiec, a number of Jews were arrested and slaughtered.[45] In Przemyśl, several hundred Jews were shot. In Lodz, a pogrom took place on October 8, 1939, during a visit by Goebbels. Many Jews were murdered on this occasion; and Jewish children were thrown out of windows by the SS. In Włocławek, the Germans organized a pogrom on Yom Kippur, and the wounded were buried alive with the dead, at no. 69 Długa Street. In Zgierz, seven Jews were killed; one of them, named

Zysman, was burnt alive, allegedly for resisting.[46] This was not a unique case, however. There are reports by witnesses stating that in Lipsko (near Kielce in the Iłża district) a whole group of Jews were burnt alive in a synagogue.[47] In Mielec, on the eve of the Jewish New Year (September 13, 1939), the Germans drove thirty-five naked Jews from the bathhouse into a slaughterhouse nearby, where they locked them up, and then set fire to the building. This was reported by eyewitnesses, Poles and Jews.[48]

Similar incidents, only on a larger scale and with even greater brutality, occurred in Bialystok after the Germans occupied the city. On June 27, 1941, they burnt alive about a thousand Jewish men and boys in a synagogue.[49] According to eyewitnesses, pogroms on such a scale also took place in Chmielnik, Końskie, Kutno, Łask, Łowicz, Łuków, and Sieradz.[50] In several cities (such as Cracow, Lodz, Warsaw, Tarnów, and Kielce), the Germans arrested and/or murdered outstanding Jewish leaders and intellectuals. In the areas formerly within the Soviet zone occupied by the Germans in 1941, immediately after the outbreak of the war with the USSR, anti-Jewish actions and pogroms, exceeding in scale and intensity the "blitz" pogroms of 1939, were organized everywhere.

## "Liquidation Actions" in Ghettos and Camps

During the first two years of the occupation, the anti-Jewish actions of the German authorities did not yet point to the *total* annihilation of the Jewish population. All the above-mentioned pogroms and individual acts of murder accounted for the death of about 100,000 Jews. Losses resulting from "cold pogroms" were much higher: disfranchisement, exclusion from all sources of livelihood, seclusion in the ghettos, starvation, and disease were decimating the Jewish population. Especially in the larger cities, mortality among Jews soared, while the birth rate dropped to almost nothing. Forced labor and intolerable working conditions also killed many thousands of Jews. All of these tactics would lead ultimately to the gradual extermination of the Jews. But the pace, in the opinion of the German masters, was too slow. They realized that the old-fashioned pogroms alone, no matter how merciless, could not "solve the Jewish problem" quickly enough. Dr. Stahlecker, chief of Einsatzgruppe A, wrote openly on this subject in a report (dated October 15, 1941) to his superiors: "It was easy to foresee from the beginning that the Jewish problem in the East could not be solved by pogroms only. In accordance with the basic directives, the object of the 'clean-up operations' by the police is the complete extermination of the Jews."[51]

Rather than sporadic pogroms, the Germans favored a policy of pauperization and starvation of the Jews. Their expectations were expressed quite clearly in August 1942, by Governor-General Hans Frank. Speaking of the reduction, by half, of the food rations for Poles, Frank stated: "It must be done in cold blood and with no pity." He then added: "The fact that in this way we condemn 1.2 million Jews to death by starvation is only a secondary matter. But, should the Jews not die out from hunger, I sincerely hope that this will serve to accelerate anti-Jewish regulations. Therefore, if hunger and pogroms are not sufficient to solve the Jewish question, one should strive for more effective measures."[52]

The idea of totally annihilating the Jews most probably crystalized in the spring of 1941, before the outbreak of the war with Soviet Russia. The Nazis decided to destroy, first of all, the Jewish population of the territories to be conquered from the USSR, because those were considered to be "contaminated with Communism" and, therefore, particularly dangerous. According to witnesses at the Nuremberg trials, that decision was taken within the circle of Hitler's closest collaborators. At a staff meeting held before the Soviet campaign, Hitler informed the top commanding officers of the plan. To carry out the program in agreement with the high command of the German army, four "operational groups for special tasks," the so-called Einsatzgruppen, were organized from the ranks of the German Security Police and the SD and put into action on the Eastern front. These mobile units (i.e., massacre squads) moved directly behind the advancing combat troops and performed their "special tasks" in the army rear areas. They received definite instructions and operational directions from the chief of the security police and SD, as is shown in the report of Stahlecker, chief of Einsatzgruppe A.[53] The four groups, designated A, B, C, and D, were entrusted with different areas of operation. Groups B and C were assigned to the central sector of the Eastern front, and the territory behind it, which included Poland. Group A was charged with the annihilation of Jews in Baltic countries, Group D was operating in an area extending from Cernauti to the Caucasus.

The entire propaganda apparatus of the Third Reich was set in motion to work out an ideological justification for this crime. In his speech of January 30, 1941, Hitler repeated the gloomy forecast of annihilating the Jews which he had explicitly proclaimed in his speech in the German Reichstag on January 30, 1939:

And I should not refrain from the warning I have already given before in this regard, . . . on September 1, 1939, in the German Reichstag—namely that, if the rest of the world is plunged into a universal war by Jewry, then Jewry as a whole will have thereby played out its role in Europe! They may still laugh at that today, just as they have laughed at my prophecies. The coming months and years will prove that here, too, my predictions were also correct. Already we see how our racial theory [*Rassenerkenntniss*] stirs up one nation after another—I hope that even those nations which at present are hostile to us will yet one day recognize their mightier, internal enemy and will then join us in a broad common front of an Aryan world community against the international Jewish exploitation and corruption of mankind.[54]

Hitler's speech on June 22, 1941, the day of the invasion of the USSR, set the tone for further anti-Jewish propaganda:

Germany has never tried to bring its National-Socialist ideology to Russia, but the Jew-Bolshevist leaders in Moscow have firmly resolved to impose their rule upon us and on the other European nations. . . .[55]

The war with the Soviets was proclaimed as the "Jewish war," a war against the "Jew-Bolshevist" rulers of the Kremlin. The same opinion was repeated by Hitler in his speeches of October 2 and November 8, 1941. Josef Goebbels, the minister of propaganda, in an article in *Das Reich* of July 20, 1941, predicted "a merciless and irrevocable judgment for the Jews." His hateful article of August 16, 1941, entitled "Die Juden sind schuld" (The Jews Are Guilty), explicitly proclaimed the goal of exterminating the Jews. Articles in journals published for the German police, who were carrying out the annihilation program, emphasized the axiom that the Soviet Jews were a "virus that can be destroyed only through extirpation,"[56] and stressed that the aim of the war was a "Europe free of Jews."[57]

Whereas in summer 1941 the official pronouncements of the Nazi leaders focused specifically on the destruction of the Soviet Jews, by the end of 1941 a systematic extermination operation would be initiated deep in the rear of the Eastern front and would extend to the Government General and later to the areas incorporated in the Reich (the so-called Warthegau).

At the end of 1941, Governor-General Frank informed his closest associates that in January 1942 an important conference would be held in Berlin—under the chairmanship of Reinhard Heydrich, chief of the Reich Security Main Office—at which significant decisions concerning the Jewish question would be taken. Speculating about the results of the conference, Frank laid his cards before the gathering of his associates:

What are we to do with the Jews? Do you think we will resettle them in the villages in the Ostland [Baltic Countries]? This is what they [will] tell us in Berlin: "Why all this prattle? We will have nothing to do with them either in Ostland or in the Reichskommissariat [Ukraine]. . . . In short, liquidate them by your own means. . . ." In any case we must take steps that will lead to their extirpation. . . . The Government General, like the Reich, must be free of Jews.[58]

Hans Frank, one of Hitler's closest advisers, proved himself no false prophet. The Berlin (Wannsee) Conference lead to policies quite in accordance with his prediction. It was there that the program for the total extermination of Jews was officially formulated. In April 1942, Hitler issued an order for the "Final Solution of the Jewish Question" (*Endlösung der Judenfrage*). Only Jews fit to work were to be spared, and were to be concentrated in camps. This order thus was extended to all countries under German occupation, and Goebbels expressed his hope that the annihilation (*Ausrottung*) would spread not only over the whole of Europe but even to the countries outside.[59] The specific task for preparation and organization of the Final Solution was given to SS-Obersturmbannführer Adolf Eichmann, head of Section IV–B–4 (Jewish affairs) of the RSHA.

With their typical efficiency, the Germans began to carry out their plan of destruction. In the summer and autumn of 1941, the first blow was struck on the Jews living in territories newly conquered from Soviet Russia. The second blow, in the winter of 1941, fell upon Jews remaining in the areas incorporated into the Reich (Warthegau and East Prussia); and the third in the early months of 1942, upon those living in the GG. The advance of the German army into the territory of the USSR was accompanied by a series of bloody actions against the Jewish inhabitants. The actions differed from the unplanned, chaotic pogroms of 1939. Now, in 1941, the actions were systematically organized. In the larger cities, the victims numbered in the thousands, rather than in the hundreds, as had been the case earlier; in the smaller towns, the Jewish population was immediately liquidated.

The worst terror reigned in the districts of Vilna and Bialystok. The city of Vilna had the heaviest toll. The action against the Jewish population of 65,000 lasted without interruption, from June 22 to September 5, 1941, when the ghetto was established. The bloodshed was renewed in mid-October, and went on until Christmas Eve. Throughout the Vilna action, which lasted half a year, Jewish men were taken, allegedly for work, and were transported to a small wayside halt, called Ponary (about 10 kilometers from Vilna, on the Vilna-Landwarowo railway line), where they were shot and buried in trenches that were dug by the Soviet army against air raids. From October 1941 on, during the "cleaning-out" actions in the ghetto, women and children were also brought to Ponary to be killed. During the first stage of the Vilna action, before the establishment of the ghetto, about 30,000 Jews died; in the second stage, there were more than 15,000 victims.[60] Other towns in the Vilna district that suffered extremely heavy losses in the period of September–October 1941 were Nowowilejka (5,500 Jewish victims), Mołodeczno (4,000 victims), and Troki (1,000).[61]

The Jewish inhabitants of Bialystok (56,000) also paid a very high toll. Immediately after the Germans marched into the city, they set fire to the central synagogue and immolated a thousand Jews. On July 2, 1941, they killed about three hundred Jewish intellectuals and professionals. On July 11, about 4,000 Jews were driven outside the city and were shot to death on the outskirts of Bialystok, in the so-called Pietrasza.[62] In several regions of the Bialystok district (Szczuczyń, Grajewo, Tykocin, and Wasilków), groups of Jews were massacred by the Germans in the summer of 1941. In some localities, the actions amounted to a total liquidation. In Czyżewo Szlacheckie, for instance, several thousand Jews were slaughtered on August 28, 1941. Final liquidation actions were carried out in the smaller towns of Byelorussia. At Slutsk, for example, the commander of the eleventh battalion of the Security Police liquidated the Jewish population in two days (October 1941). Jews were shot on the spot in their homes and in the streets, and their bodies were left where they fell. The commander of the execution battalion refused the request of the Gebietskommissar (district commissioner) to delay these operations for even one day, explaining that he had orders to carry out liquidation actions in all the towns of the region and was therefore in a great hurry. About 9,000 Jews were cruelly murdered at Słonim. Ruthless actions were carried out in other towns in the district of Nowogródek (fall 1941): in Lachowice (several thousand victims), Mir, (2,000), Nowogródek (2,500), Wołczyn (1,800), Ejszyszki (2,200), Kleck (1,800), and Siniawa (2,200).[63]

In Lwów (Jewish population, about 160,000), in the first three months after the German invasion, three pogroms were staged: from June 30 to July 3, 1941, from July 25 to 27, and again at the very end of that month. During each action, thousands of Jews were murdered.[64] In other towns of the Galicia District, similar mass actions took place. For instance, in Kołomyja, where 3,400 Jews were shot in the Szyparowski forest; in Drohobycz and Borysław; in Kamionka Strumiłowa, Złoczów, and Stanisławów. In Stanisławów, where Hungarian troops were stationed in the beginning of the war, the Jews were not persecuted. Only after the Hungarians were replaced by the German army, did the first action take place (October 12, 1941).[65]

In Volhynia, the most terrible massacre was carried out in Równe, where 15,000–17,000 of the original 25,000 Jews were killed in two days (November 5 and 6, 1941).[66] In the murderous actions in Łuck and in Włodzimierz Wołyński (October 1941), about 10,000 Jews in each city lost their lives.[67] During the fall of 1941 in the Polesie region, the heaviest losses were suffered by the Jewish population of Brześćnad Bugiem (6,000 victims), Pińsk (8,000), Kobryń (5,000), Motol (5,000), and Chomsk (3,000).

Soon after, in the winter of 1941–1942, a new wave of liquidation actions began in the areas incorporated into the Reich. By early 1940, the number of Jews in this territory had fallen from 680,000 to 240,000 as a result of ruthless expulsions, often carried out with extreme brutality (as in Kalisz and Będzin in Silesia and at Włocławek),[68] and sometimes turning into outright massacres (as in Bydgoszcz and Kalisz, among others).[69] The second phase, the so-called *judenrein* actions, began in this area in the winter of 1941–1942. In contrast to their conduct in the East, the Germans refrained here from mass shootings, and carried out their liquidation actions in a more discreet manner. First on their list was the remaining Jewish population in the Lodz area. A special extermination camp for Jews was established at Chełmno (Kulmhof), near Koło.[70] It was put into operation on December 8, 1941, when the first transport of Jews arrived from Dębie, Sompolno, and Koło. Other transports followed, from Turek, Poddębice, Włodawa, Bełchatów, Pabianice, and elsewhere. The Lodz ghetto, too, soon paid its share of blood (on January 15 and April 29, 1942). The Germans killed their victims by gassing them in vans specially constructed for the purpose. The extermination camp of Chełmno was not the first place on Polish soil where this method of mass murder was used, however. Somewhat earlier, around September 15, 1941, the first experiment in wholesale murder by gas had been carried out with "positive result" in the concentration camp of Oświęcim (Auschwitz) in Silesia, the first victims being a group of Soviet prisoners-of-war and Polish political prisoners. It is not known when the first transports of Jews were sent to the gas chambers at Auschwitz.

March 1942 marked the beginning of the first series of larger liquidation actions in the GG. In comparison, the sporadic earlier actions—as in Rejowiec (Lublin area) during the Easter period in 1941,[71] in Dąbrowa near Tarnów in July 1941,[72] and in Węgrów on Yom Kippur—can be regarded as experimental maneuvers. In September (according to another source, November) 1941, a major action (3,800 victims) was carried out in Zagorów (Hinterberg, in the Poznań province), where almost all the Jews from the Konin area had been herded together before the start of the action.[73] Several "small" actions took place in Radom in October 1941,[74] and again on December 3; there were also some "small" actions in Lwów.[75]

The action in Mielec was particularly tragic.[76] Preparations had already begun in January 1942. After several delays, the action was carried out, with marked brutality and cruelty, from March 7 to 9. Large numbers of Jews were shot on the streets of the town, and in the airfield nearby. The remaining Jews (about 4,500) were deported to different localities in the Lublin district.[77]

March and April 1942 were filled with actions and deportations: in Rzeszów,[78] Brzesko,[79] Zamość,[80] Kraśnik,[81] Sanniki,[82] Kielce, [83] and Włocławek;[84] Lwów, Lublin, Ostrowiec, Lodz, Nowy Sącz, and elsewhere. It is significant that, in the same period, actions against leaders and members of the left-wing Jewish organizations were staged in such localities as Warsaw, Nowy Sącz,[85] Ostrowiec,[86] and Rzeszów.[87]

The most brutal and extensive anti-Jewish actions were focused around Passover 1942. The massacre of 15,000 Jews in Lwów ended just before that holiday.[88] One of the bloodiest and most cruel operations, in Lublin, began on the night of March 16–17, 1942, and lasted till April 21. That action virtually liquidated the Lublin ghetto. About 2,500 to 3,000 Jews were killed, and about 35,000 were taken to the camps at Bełżec and Trawniki, while some were sent to the Poltava region and to Krivoj Rog (USSR). The remainder, about 3,000 in number, were taken to Majdan Tatarski, where they were "housed" in provisional, primitive shacks. Shortly thereafter they, too, were executed.[89]

The urgent need to dispose of the masses of Jews seized in the actions prompted the Nazis to establish special extermination centers to serve eastern Poland, just as Chełmno and the Auschwitz camps, situated on the left bank of the Vistula River, served western Poland. For the quick disposal of the Jews from the eastern territories of the GG, new extermination camps were created in that area. Consequently, the labor camp at Bełżec and the concentration camp for prisoners-of-war at Majdanek near Lublin were "elevated" to the rank of extermination camps. Larger transports of Jews, such as those from Lublin and Lwów, were directed to Bełżec; smaller ones (like that from the village of Bełżyce in May 1942) were, for the time being, taken to Majdanek.[90] In April or May of 1942, an extermination camp with gas chambers was put into operation at Sobibór. The first transports of Jews sent there for gassing were from Siedliszcze.[91]

Steadily, the extermination activities were gaining momentum. "Liquidation" actions, innocently referred to by the Germans as "deportations," were methodically carried out in every Jewish community.

On May 12, 1942, a confidential circular was transmitted by the authorities of the Lublin District to the regional offices (*Starosta powiatowy*) requesting that preparations be made for deportation of the Jews.[92] Similar circulars were undoubtedly issued by the governors' offices of other districts. The liquidation of Jews was entering its final stage. In the summer of 1942, a whole series of deportations to the extermination camps took place in Silesia (Jaworzno, Sosnowiec, Dąbrowa Górnicza, and Bielsko); in the GG (Bełżyce, Żółkiewka, Siedliszcze, Rabka, Cracow, Tarnów,

Radom, Rzeszów, Mielec, Dębica); in the Galicia District (Lwów, Prze-myśl, Tarnopol); in Byelorussia (Słonim); and in Volhynia (Równe). In some localities (Równe and Słonim), the Jews resisted, and the Germans responded by burning down their houses.[93] The numerous actions in the summer of 1942 were even more brutal and savage than those in the spring of this year. One of the major actions, in Przemyśl, resulted in the death of about 12,000 Jews.[94]

During August, September, and October 1942, the actions reached their climax in scope and in intensity. The tragic fate of the Warsaw ghetto overshadows in monstrosity all the other calamities of this most cruel period of the Holocaust. Beginning on the eve of Tishah be-Av (July 22, 1942), the horrors continued, unabated, for two and a half months, until October 3. According to the official report of SS-Brigadeführer Jürgen Stroop, 310,322 Jews were "deported" during that time; very likely the actual number of victims was even greater. During the same period, catastrophe also befell the Jewish population of Lwów: during the action that lasted from August 10, 1942, until the end of that month, about 40,000 to 50,000 Lwów Jews perished.[95] A third major action was carried out, in mid-August in the towns and villages of the coal-mining region of Zagłębie Dąbrowskie, where about 60,000 Jews lost their lives.

In Radom, about 20,000 Jews, including the members of the Jewish Council, perished during the action on August 16; in Międzyrzec, about 10,000, on August 28; in Piotrków, about 15,000; in Ostrowiec, about 9,000 (October 10, 1942); in Kołomyja, the whole Jewish population of the city and the surrounding area. A series of actions was also carried out in the vicinity of Warsaw (in Otwock, Falenica, and Rembertów); in Cracow, Łańcut, Rabka, Rymanów, Rzeszów, Drohobycz, Borysław, and Kielce; in Częstochowa (the first action on September 22, 1942); in Siedlce, Biała Podlaska, Łuków, and the entire area of Podlasie; in Bełżyce, Szydłowiec, Nowy Sącz, Wieliczka, Wolbrom, Lodz, Stanisławów, Buczacz, Brzeżany, Brody, Sokal, Borszczów, Kopyczyńce, Skole, Zbaraż, and Dolina, to name but a few of the many.

The existing extermination camps were inadequate. On July 23, 1942, at the beginning of the action in Warsaw, a new extermination camp was opened, Treblinka "B," near the railway station of Małkinia. It is im-possible to assess precisely the number of Jews who lost their lives in the monstrous actions during the fall of 1942. In the Galicia District, according to the report of SS-Brigadeführer Katzmann, 254,989 Jews were deported up to November 10, 1942—that is, about 50 percent of the entire popula-tion in this area.[96] Undoubtedly, the number of victims in other regions of the GG was even larger, probably involving 70 to 80 percent of the Jewish population.[97] Similar results were obtained in the area incorporated into the Reich, where (aside from some small communities) only two large ghettos, in Lodz and Bialystok, were left.

In the winter of 1942–1943, the intensity of the operations diminished. The largest action, in Pińsk, lasted four days, from October 28 to November 1, 1942, and took about 16,200 victims.[98] At the same time, the whole region of Bialystok was cleared of Jews, except for the two ghettos of Bialystok and Jasinówka. About 130,000 Jews lost their lives. Two actions (on November 18–20, 1942, and January 5–7, 1943) reduced the population of the Lwów ghetto by more than 20,000.[99] On December 5–6 and 25, 1942, 7,000 to 8,000 Jews were deported from Chełmno to their death in Sobibór. In Warsaw, on January 18, 1943, the Germans "combed out" still another 6,500 Jewish victims. On February 5, 1943, in Bialystok, 11,000 people were murdered on the spot, and 12,000 were "deported," to the death camp at Treblinka.

As a result of continuing small actions, the Jewish population of Galicia was rapidly diminished. The death camp at Bełżec was no longer adequate to cope with the masses of people sent for liquidation. The Janowska camp in Lwów opened its gates for the multitudes of deportees from other ghettos of the Galicia District. The city of Warsaw had only about 60,000 Jews left; Lwów, about 20,000; and the Galicia District about 45,000.[100] There were still Jewish remnants in some other towns of the GG: in Częstochowa (working in the Hasag labor camp of the Hugo Schneider Aktiengesellschaft, a German firm engaged in heavy industry), and other such camps in Skarżysko, Radom, and Cracow. The number of Jews left in the GG at that time was probably about 150,000.

There were still over 100,000 Jews left in the Incorporated Territories. About 70,000 of them were in Lodz; the rest in Bialystok, and the towns of the Warthegau.

During 1943 and 1944 the Germans were engaged in the liquidation of the remaining Jews in Poland. In 1943, the heroic battle of the Warsaw ghetto took place. It started on April 19 and ended on May 16, when the Germans blew up the central synagogue in Tłómackie Street.[101] About 56,000 to 62,000 Jews had been killed. The liquidation of the Bialystok ghetto started on August 16, 1943. A Jewish uprising broke out during the action. After the unequal battle, the ghetto fell a few days later.[102] The liquidation of the Sosnowiec ghetto took place between June 1–6, 1943. Ten thousand Jews were deported to Auschwitz. During the liquidation of the Lwów ghetto (early June 1943), about 20,000 Jews were killed.[103] On January 25, 1944, Governor-General Hans Frank stated with satisfaction that in the whole of the GG there were perhaps 100,000 Jews left.[104] By that time, there was only one ghetto left in Poland, the Lodz ghetto with its 70,000 inhabitants. The Germans were liquidating Lodz in stages, by repeatedly dispatching groups of workers, mostly to Auschwitz. In August 1944, when the front line was approaching Lodz, more than 60,000 Jews were transported to Auschwitz in one mass deportation (August 2–30). This was the largest contingent of Jews ever sent from a single ghetto. There remained in Lodz only the so-called *Aufräumungskommando* (clean-up brigade), consisting of 870 persons.

And yet the "final solution of the Jewish question" as directed by Himmler had not yet been accomplished. There were still small remnants of Polish Jews in various camps, since (in compliance with Himmler's own orders) men and women capable of work had been temporarily exempted from extermination. During each major liquidation action, selections had been made, and those fit to work had been sent off to camps. Their death sentence was not revoked, only postponed.

In the labor and concentration camps, Jews were exploited to the utmost limits of their endurance; they were subjected to ruthless discipline, to hunger, and to the worst possible living conditions. Among the concentration camps, Auschwitz and Janowski (in Lwów) were almost prototypical for their inhuman exploitation of Jewish inmates; for their variety of sadistic tortures, both physical and mental; for their inconceivable working conditions. Work requirements in the munition factories in Skarżysko-Kamienna (belonging to the Hasag Company) endangered the lives of the inmates who, with no protection whatsoever, were exposed to highly poisonous chemicals. The mortality in these camps was terrifying. Not content with the high "natural" death rate in the labor camps, the Germans periodically arranged actions, roll calls, and selections, in which hundreds of thousands of inmates were murdered. In addition, there were more than 300 forced-labor camps for Jews, the first of which was established by 1939. Usually they were shortlived, very often being closed down after two or three years of operation, having served their purpose in the restructuring of rivers, the construction of fortifications, roads, and so forth. In these camps the majority of Jewish workers lost either their health or lives. In only a few camps of this type did Jewish inmates survive till the liberation.[105]

With the stepping-up of anti-Jewish operations, some of the labor camps (for example the Janowski camp, in Lwów; the Płaszów camp, near Cracow; Poniatów and Trawniki, in the Lublin District; Szebnie near Jasło) were transformed into concentration camps. The Jews working in these camps were not treated as workers but as working prisoners.[106] Hundreds of thousands of Polish Jews passed through this kind of camp in their march to death. The relatively low number of inmates in the individual camps at any given time can be explained by the enormous turnover. For instance, the number of inmates in the Janowski camp at Lwów rarely exceeded 20,000 and sometimes fell as low as 8,000 (for example, on March 1, 1943, the camp had about 15,000 Jews, on June 26 only about 8,000). Yet a total of some 200,000 persons perished in this camp. Indeed, a much larger number of Jews than even this passed through the camp, including many murdered in the woods of Lesienice, near Lwów, and those deported for extermination to Bełżec. For them, the Janowski camp served as a so-called *Dulag (Durchgangslager)*, or "transit camp."[107] On June 27, 1943, after the final liquidation of all the ghettos in the Galicia District, there were still twenty camps in this district, with a total of 21,156 Jews, as reported by SS-Brigadeführer Katzmann to the chief of the SS and Security Police in the GG, Friedrich Wilhelm Krüger. But this number, Katzmann reassured Krüger, was "continually diminishing."[108] In addition to the Janowski camp, the camps at Kurowice, Jaktorów, Łackie, Kozaki, Drohobycz, and Borysław were widely known.

There were also a number of labor concentration camps in the Cracow district. The most notorious were in Płaszów near Cracow, and Szebnie, near Jasło; in both camps about 20,000 Jews, mainly from Cracow, perished. In the Jewish labor camp in Wieliczka (liquidated in September 1944) the average number of working inmates was about 6,000. In each of the camps set up in the territories of Małopolska, in Pustków near Dębica, in Rozwadów and in Stalowa Wola, several thousand Jews perished.

In Central Poland, the largest number of such camps was in the Lublin district. According to an inquiry conducted by the Central Commission for the Investigation of German Crimes in Poland, twenty-eight Jewish labor camps of a considerable size were set up within the Lublin District (Województwo Lubelskie) during the German occupation. The average number of inmates in those camps was over one hundred.[109] Best known were the camps in Trawniki, near Lublin, and Poniatów, near Puławy. In each of them more than 15,000 Jews perished. The five labor camps in Częstochowa, under the control of the Hasag Company, employed a total of about 14,000 Jews; the four camps in Kielce, about 8,000; Skarżysko-Kamienna, 8,000; Starachowice, 8,000; Piotrków, 4,700; Biała Podlaska, 3,000.[110] Far to the north was the concentration camp at Stuthof, near Gdańsk. Of the 110,000 persons who passed through it, 40,000 were Jews—from the various countries of Europe, mainly Poland and·Lithuania. It should be recorded here that, on the day before the evacuation of the Stutthof camp, the Germans drove the Jewish inmates, men and women, toward the sea. Several thousand of them were pushed into the sea, where they drowned or were finished off by machine-gun fire.[111]

There were numerous forced-labor camps for Jews in the territories incorporated into the Reich, especially in Silesia and the Poznań district. In the city of Poznań proper, there were twelve such camps, with a total population of 13,500 in the year 1942. According to the inquiry by the Central Commission for the Investigation of German Crimes in Poland, there were twenty-five sizable Jewish labor camps in the Poznań district, with an average of one hundred inmates in each. In the county of Poznań alone, there were nine labor camps with a total of about 11,500 Jewish workers.[112]

All these figures seem insignificant, however, in comparison with the frightful number of victims consumed by the extermination camps, which were organized by the Germans on Polish territory, expressly to accomplish their diabolical task. Some of the larger concentration camps, such as Auschwitz and Majdanek, which had been set up in 1940, were now put to use for the liquidation of Jews. In addition, new specific camps were set up. In 1942 and 1943, the camp in Auschwitz was expanded and specifically adapted for the purpose of genocide, with the construction of huge gas chambers and crematoria. The numerous transports of Jews arriving there were immediately directed, almost in their entirety, to the gas chambers. Only small groups of Jews were saved, for work in the camp. In September 1944, the Jewish Sonderkommando, a special unit servicing crematorium IV at Auschwitz II (Birkenau) revolted. The insurgents, numbering about 300, killed several SS men and injured a number of others. They cut the barbed wire that surrounded the area, terrorized the guards, and escaped from the camp; but they were pursued by the Germans, who caught up with them and killed nearly all of them. Before their escape, the insurgents succeeded in blowing up the crematorium. After putting down the revolt, the Gestapo started an investigation to determine who had supplied the insurgents with arms (guns, grenades, ammunition, and bombs). They subsequently arrested four Jewish girls who worked in the munition factory Union. These heroic girls, though tortured by the cruel inquisitors, did not disclose the names of the resistance organization. The girls were publicly executed in the camp by hanging. Only 5,000 Jewish inmates at Auschwitz survived to the end of the war—a small fraction compared to the millions of Jews who lost their lives there. Besides Polish Jews, hundreds of thousands of Jews from Hungary, Czechoslovakia, Austria, Germany, Greece, Belgium, France, and other countries perished at Auschwitz.[113]

Majdanek, near Lublin, was the second largest concentration camp that also served as an extermination camp. Several hundred thousand Jews were killed there. In both Auschwitz and Majdanek, the majority of Jews confined there were exterminated in gas chambers with hydrogen cyanide or "Zyklon B," a gas which killed its victims in three to five minutes. In the concentration camp at Gross Rosen in Silesia, where tens of thousands of persons perished, the number of Jews was relatively small.

The extermination camps designated almost exclusively for Jews were Treblinka (Treblinks "B"), Chełmno, Bełżec, and Sobibór. At Treblinka (county of Sokołów Podlaski, in the Warsaw district), between July 22, 1942, and the early fall of 1943, about 730,000 to 1 million persons were killed, almost exclusively Jews. On August 2, 1943, an uprising broke out in the camp. It was organized by the inmates under extremely difficult conditions. The insurgents managed to destroy some of the camp's installations, and killed several of the crew servicing the camp. A sizable number of insurgents escaped from the camp, but most of them were caught and killed. Only a small group (about twenty or thirty) got away. Soon after the revolt, the camp was liquidated by the Germans (November 1943).

The camp at Chełmno (a village in the Lodz district about fourteen kilometers from Koło, on the Lodz-Poznań railway line) was in operation until January 1945. About 350,000 Jews were murdered there, in specially constructed gas vans. On the night of January 17–18, 1945, when the German Sonderkommando began to liquidate the camp, a small group of about forty-seven Jewish survivors resisted, killing two German guards. The Sonderkommando set fire to the building where the Jewish group had concentrated its defense. Only two of the insurgents survived, miraculously.

The camp at Bełżec, near Rawa Ruska, was established at the beginning of 1940 as a labor camp, and was transformed into an extermination camp in 1942. Between the spring of 1942 and the end of 1943, several hundred thousand Jews were murdered there—mainly from Galicia and the Lublin and Cracow districts, but also from the districts of Warsaw and Radom.

The extermination camp of Sobibór (near Chełm, in the Lublin district) was established in the spring of 1942. Hundreds of thousands of Jews perished there, mostly in the gas chambers. In addition to Polish Jews, numerous Jews from France, Holland, the USSR, and Czechoslovakia died there. On October 14, 1943, a revolt broke out at Sobibór. After killing a number of SS men, a group of several hundred inmates escaped; the majority lost their lives under fire from the camp guards or on the minefields surrounding the camp.[114]

Soon after entering the city of Lwów, the Germans established, in September–October 1941, a concentration camp on Janowska Street. About 200,000 Jews, mostly from Lwów and the Galicia District, perished in the Janowski camp. In November 1943, a revolt broke out, in which a small group of inmates managed to escape after killing several of the guards, but the revolt only accelerated the liquidation of the camp, which took place on November 20, 1943. That same day, an uprising broke out in the "Death Brigade" in Lesienice (outside Lwów). A small group of bold and desperate inmates killed several SS men, attacked the startled guards at the gates, forced their way out of the camp, and escaped to freedom.[115]

It must be stressed that the above-mentioned concentration and death camps were not the only places of extermination for the Polish Jews. In the vicinity of nearly every large center of Jewish life in Poland, temporary places of execution were to be found, where tens of thousands of victims perished daily—as in Ponary, near Vilna; in Lesienice, near Lwów; Pietrasza, near Bialystok; Radogoszez, near Lodz; in the Rakowice forest, near Cracow. Besides the widely known camps mentioned above, there were lesser-known places of mass murder by gas. One was in the Kazimierz forest, near Kazimierz Biskupi (40 kilometers from Chełmno), where the Germans used gas vans as early as September 1940. Executions also took place in the so-called "Gęsiówka," the Jewish prison on Zamenhofa Street in Warsaw.

## Estimate of the Total Jewish Losses in Poland

The "final solution of the Jewish problem" in Poland was accomplished almost in its entirety. The number of Jews in Poland before September 1, 1939, amounted to about 3.34 million. How many of them survived?

The Central Committee of Polish Jews, organized at Lublin in August 1944, ordered a registration of the surviving Jews. This registration, carried out by local Jewish committees in the individual towns, gave the following results: Up to June 15, 1945 (computation date for the total figures received), 55,509 Jews were registered in Poland. To this number must be added 5,446 Polish Jews registered in the camps on German territories, and 13,000 Jews in active service in the Polish army. The resultant total of 73,995 persons does not accurately represent the actual number of Polish Jews saved from destruction under the German occupation, however.

First, the figure of 55,509 must be reduced, as there were numerous inaccuracies in registration. As a consequence of much internal migration in the first months after the liberation, many Jews were registered twice or even several times in the different towns through which they passed. (Multiple registrations are impossible to check out, even after careful study of the registered material.) Moreover, included in the total registration figure of 55,509 were a certain number of Jews repatriated from Soviet Russia.

Likewise, the figure of 13,000 (Jewish soldiers and officers in the Polish army) must be reduced, as it does not refer to Jews who survived in the German-occupied territories, but mainly involves Jews who were in the USSR during the war and who enlisted in the Polish army which was organized there. On the other hand, the figure of 5,446 Jews registered in the camps in the German territory is probably too small, since few of the Jews in these camps registered with the Central Committee of Polish Jews or any of the local committees. In addition, the total figure of Jewish survivors should include those who were still using Aryan papers and did not register with the Jewish committees; but there is no accurate basis on which to assess their number (perhaps several thousand). Still, many Jewish survivors who continued to use an Aryan identity after the liberation nevertheless registered with the Jewish committees and gave their true Jewish family name—perhaps so that they might get in touch with friends and relatives abroad in the hope of arranging for future emigration from Poland. There were probably no more than 1,000 to 2,000 registered Jewish "Aryans."

Neither does our estimate include the number of Jews repatriated, after June 15, 1945, from western White Russia and Lithuania. They will be considered in a different context below.

To summarize, the total number of Polish Jews who survived the war in German-occupied Poland probably did not exceed 50,000. Included in this figure are about 5,000 children.[116] There remained some 40,000 to 50,000 Jews who were saved by hiding among the Poles, or by living in disguise; some survived in woods as partisans and even in some camps. This is a maximum number, which includes Jews returned from the western Ukraine, western White Russia, and the Lithuanian Soviet Republic, before June 15, 1945. (Migratory movements that took place after June 15, 1945, and affect the later distribution of Polish Jews in Poland and in Germany are of course not pertinent to the question under discussion.) We must remember, however, that a number of Polish Jews escaped the Holocaust by fleeing abroad or to the territories of the USSR in 1939; in 1941, after the outbreak of German-Soviet hostilities, some of the Polish Jews in the USSR saved themselves by fleeing into the interior of Soviet Russia. Altogether, about 250,000 of these Polish Jewish émigrés survived in various European countries (USSR, England, Sweden, Switzerland, Rumania, Hungary), as well as in Palestine and in the United States. In addition, a number of Polish Jews survived in the camps in Germany, Austria, and the Protectorate, and in the territories of western Ukraine, western Byelorussia, and in Lithuania, but did not return to Poland until after June 15, 1945, and were, therefore, not registered; lacking any exact data, we can only roughly estimate that these Jews numbered about 40,000 to 50,000.

Of the 3.34 million Jews in the territory of Poland before the onset of World War II, only 3 percent remained at the end of the war: that is, about 50,000 within the new Polish boundaries and almost the same number in the territory of the former German Reich and in the western part of Soviet Russia.

Five stages can be discerned in the Nazi extermination of Polish Jewry. The Jewish losses in each stage can be estimated as follows:

1. During the first months of the German occupation of Poland (that is, September 1, 1939, to the end of that year): 32,000 Jewish soldiers killed in the September campaign; 100,000 prisoners-of-war taken during the September campaign and murdered by the Germans; civilians killed during the military operations; and victims of early persecution and pogroms.

2. During 1940 and the first half of 1941 (until the outbreak of Soviet-German hostilities): 300,000 Jewish victims of individual and mass murders, compulsory resettlements, forced labor, disease, and hunger. Total Jewish losses from September 1, 1939, to June 22, 1941—about 450,000 persons.

3. From June 22, 1941 (when the German army occupied the Polish territories previously occupied by the USSR) to the end of December 1942: 2,250,000 Jewish victims of extermination actions, disease, and hunger (out of about 2.65 million Jews under the German rule in Poland).

4. During 1943: 250,000 Jews (including the remnants of the Jewish communities in Warsaw, Lwów, and Bialystok; concentration camp inmates; individuals who had escaped to the woods; Jewish partisan groups; and Jews living in hiding on the Aryan side).

5. During 1944: 100,000 Jews (including inhabitants of the last large ghetto, Lodz, now liquidated, numerous individuals on the Aryan side, caught especially during and after the Polish uprising in Warsaw; and workers from the concentration camps still in operation).

Besides Polish Jews, a considerable number of Jews from abroad were murdered on Polish territory by the Germans. According to the information published by the Institute of Jewish Affairs in New York, out of a total prewar population of 9,612,000 Jews in Europe, 5,787,000 perished during the Nazi era. Of this number, more than half (over 3 million) were Polish Jews. Of the other half, about 1 million European Jews perished in Poland; and the remainder in the territory of the Soviet Union, in Rumania, Bulgaria, Hungary, Yugoslavia, Greece, and elsewhere.

The million foreign Jews killed by the Germans in Poland included 300,000–400,000 from Hungary; 200,000 from Czechoslovakia and Slovakia; over 100,000 from Germany; tens of thousands each from Austria, France, Holland, Belgium, and Greece; and numbers varying from a few hundred to several thousand each from Yugoslavia, Italy, Norway, Luxembourg, and Denmark.

Jews from abroad were sent to Poland by the Germans as early as the end of 1939 (from Czechoslovakia and Austria), allegedly for settlement, or for work on fortifications. Further transports, during 1940–1941, were directed mainly to the small towns of the Lublin district and to the ghettos of Warsaw and Lodz. Because of unspeakable living conditions, inadequate food, great poverty, and hard labor, these Jews died in large numbers. In 1942, the deportation of Jews from Western and Central Europe to Poland was accelerated, but then the deportees were not resettled there for work, but were directed straight to the extermination camps to be killed.

Jews from Greece and Hungary were the last to be deported to Poland for extermination. The mass deportation of Hungarian Jews started as late as the summer of 1944. But the brutality with which these Jews were treated exceeded all that the Nazis had previously been guilty of.

The murder of several million Jews in Poland constitutes a crime that differs in its uniqueness and its magnitude from the many crimes committed by the Germans during World War II. It is a crime to which all Jews, or more accurately speaking, all Europeans whom the Nazis considered "non-Aryan" would have fallen victim. Jews were the first obstacle to be removed, and, as stated before, the experiment certainly succeeded.

In the extermination of Jews in Poland, the German authorities proceeded according to a precisely conceived plan, in which not only the Gestapo, the SS, the police, and the members of the Nazi party all took an active part, but also German military authorities, German railway personnel, and German industry. The vast majority of Germans who were in Poland during the war knew perfectly well that millions of Jews were being tortured and murdered, as did the many Germans in the Reich who shared in the plunder from the Jewish victims.

The destruction of the Jews in Poland was for the Nazis only the first experiment in a particularly radical solution to obstacles confronting German imperialism, however. Jews were the first obstacle to be removed, and this experiment was very successful. As the fate of Soviet prisoners-of-war and of hundreds of thousands of Russian and Polish civilians murdered by the German authorities shows, the Poles and the Russians, as ethnic elements posing a threat to German expansion in the east, were the next candidates for mass extinction. Setting aside all moral and ethical principles, taking advantage of the indifference and apathy of the German people, and applying terror in the occupied countries, the Nazis—had military events taken a different turn—would have murdered millions more in Poland and Russia.

⁌ The earliest version of this essay first appeared in *Biuletyn Komisji Głownej dla Badania Zbrodni Niemieckich w Polsce* (Bulletin of the Central Commission for the Investigation of German Crimes in Poland), I (Warsaw, 1946), 163–208, and simultaneously in English in *German Crimes in Poland,* published by the Central Commission for the Investigation of German Crimes in Poland, vol. I (Warsaw, 1946), pp. 125–67.

In 1947 an enlarged and corrected version of this study—from which the present essay was translated—was published by the Federation of Polish Jews in Munich, under the title *Zagłada Żydów Polskich w okresie okupacji niemieckiej 1939–1945* (The Extermination of the Polish Jews in the Years 1939–1945). This version includes information from documents and scholarly publications that appeared subsequent to the volume published by the Central Commission (for instance, acts and documents of the Instytut Pamięci Narodowej in Warsaw, and documents made public during the Nuremberg trials, and in other court inquiries and pretrial investigations).

## Notes

1. Stefan Szulc, "The Accuracy of the Registration of Births and Deaths" (Polish), *Statystyka Polski,* series C, no. 41, p. 150.
2. Bericht über die Tätigkeit der jüdischen Gemeinde in Krakau (Cracow, 1940), p. 69 (mimeographed copy in the archives of the CJHC in Poland).
3. Communiqué of the Polish general staff of October 9, 1939; quoted by Israel Cohen, *The Jews in the War* (London, 1943), p. 67.
4. Bericht der jüdischen Gemeinde in Krakau, p. 13.
5. Apenszlak, *Black Book,* p. 200; *Hitler's Ten-Year War on the Jews* (New York, 1943), p. 148. In both books the number of civilian victims is given as 60,000, but is not documented. Therefore, we cannot use this figure in our statistical material.
6. Apenszlak, *Black Book,* p. 169; *Hitler's Ten-Year War,* p. 155.
7. Peter-Heinz Seraphim, "Die Judenfrage im G.G. als brennendes Problem," *Die Burg,* I (Cracow, October 1940), 61.
8. Apenszlak, *Black Book,* p. 32.
9. Maximilian du Prel, ed., *Das General Gouvernement,* 2nd ed. (Würzburg, 1942), pp. 348–49; *idem, Zwei Jahre Aufarbeit in Distrikt Warschau* (Warsaw, 1941), pp. 72–73.
10. *Krakauer Zeitung,* December 14, 1941.
11. Bericht der jüdischen Gemeinde in Krakau, p. 87.
12. *Ibid.,* p. 99.
13. Seraphim, p. 61; Maximilian du Prel, ed., *Das deutsche Generalgouvernement Polen,* 1st ed. (Cracow, 1940), p. 169.
14. *Ibid.,* p. 100.
15. *Rocznik Statystyczny Rady Starszych w Częstochowie* (Statistical Annual of the Town Council of Częstochowa), II, 134. Archives of the municipality of Częstochowa, sect. III, no. Ks. B III/5044/689.
16. *Gazeta Żydowska,* Warsaw, June 30, 1940.
17. *Statistisches Jahrbuch der Juden in Litzmannstadt.* Unedited proof sheets. Also other statistical material from the archives of the CJHC in Lodz.
18. Du Prel, *Das deutsche Generalgouvernement Polen,* p. 100.
19. Szymon Datner, *Walka i Zagłada Getta Białystockiego* (The Battle and the Destruction of the Bialystok Ghetto) (Lodz, 1946).
20. Lahousen's testimony (on January 21, 1946) on the guidelines de-

termined by Ribbentrop and Keitel during the conference held on September 13, 1939, in Hitler's railway train in Poland. *IMT,* Document PS–3047. See also essay 3 above, "The Jewish Ghettos of the Nazi Era."

21. In particular, the express letter sent by Reinhard Heydrich, chief of the Security Police, on September 21, 1939, to chiefs of the Einsatzgruppen, concerning the Jewish question in the occupied territories. See essay 3 above, "The Jewish Ghettos of the Nazi Era."

22. Hitler's speeches of January 30 and December 31, 1939, January 30, 1941, January 30, 1942; Streicher's speech of October 31 (Nuremberg Doc. PS–2583); articles by Goebbels in *Das Reich,* July 20, 1941, and June 14, 1942.

23. Speech by Alfred Rosenberg on March 28, 1941, at the opening of the Institut zur Erforschung der Judenfrage at Frankfurt.

24. See essay 2 above, "The Lublin Reservation and the Madagascar Plan."

25. Decree of March 3, 1941, *RGBL,* I, 118, §7; decree of January 31, 1942, *ibid.,* I, 51; see also essay 3 above, "The Jewish Ghettos of the Nazi Era."

26. Apenszlak, *Black Book,* p. 6 (on Kalisz).

27. *CJHCA,* Eyewitness records nos. 376, 30, 32, 676.

28. *Ibid.,* nos. 43 (on Oksza) and 84 (on Bełchatów).

29. *Ibid.,* Eyewitness records nos. 38, 458, 372 (Siedliszcze, Minsk Mazowiecki, Radziejów).

30. Such spectacles were staged at Bełżyce, Bełchatów, Węgrów, Oksza, Zgierz, and other places.

31. For instance, at Warsaw, in the Sejmowy Park, at Oksza, Zgierz, Węgrów, and Piotrków.

32. Apenszlak, *Black Book,* p. 11 ff.

33. *Krakauer Zeitung,* June 16, 1942; L. Brenner, "Chronicle of Częstochowa" (Yiddish), manuscript in CJHC; Apenszlak, *Black Book,* pp. 226, 227; *The Jews in Europe* (London, 1945), p. 26; *Jewish Survivors' Report,* no. 1 (London, 1945); *The German New Order in Poland* (London, 1941), p. 246; *CJHCA,* Eyewitness records nos. 280, 458, 826, 818, 372, 133.

34. Apenszlak, *Black Book,* p. 6.

35. Apenszlak, *Black Book,* p. 8; on Bełżyce, Diary of H. Ferstman in *CJHCA.*

36. *CJHCA,* Eyewitness record no. 969.

37. *The Jews in Europe,* p. 26; *The New Order,* p. 220; *CJHCA,* Eyewitness record no. 640, affidavit of S. Turteltaub.

38. *CJHCA,* Eyewitness record no. 837.

39. *Dokumenty Zbrodni i Męczeństwa* (Documents of Crime and Martyrdom) (Cracow, 1945), p. 143.

40. *Krakauer Zeitung,* November 16, 1939, and July 17, 1940; *CJHCA,* Eyewitness records nos. 694, 840.

41. Baker-Beall, *The German Invasion of Poland,* quoted in Apenszlak, *Black Book,* p. 6; *German New Order,* p. 137.

42. Quoted from the Polish newspaper *Ilustrowany Kurjer Polski,* Bydgoszcz, December 25, 1945.

43. Apenszlak, *Black Book,* p. 5.

44. *Jews in the War,* p. 36; *German New Order,* p. 220.

45. *Jews in the War,* pp. 35–37.
46. Apenszlak, *Black Book,* p. 10; *Jews in the War,* p. 36.
47. *CJHCA,* Eyewitness record no. 82.
48. *Ibid.,* no. 217; Apenszlak, *Black Book,* p. 12.
49. *CJHCA,* Eyewitness record no. 546; Datner, p. 12.
50. *Jews in the War,* p. 35; *Jews in Europe,* p. 26.
51. *NMT,* Doc. L–180.
52. Hans Frank's Diary (entry of August 24, 1942), *IMT,* Doc. PS–2233.
53. See above, note 51; see also statements of SS-Brigadeführer Otto Ohlendorf, Chief of RSHA Office III and chief of Einsatzgruppe D at the Nuremberg trials on January 3, 1946.
54. Translated from *Der Grossdeutsche Freiheitskampf. Reden Adolf Hitlers,* II, 222.
The date of the speech in which Hitler threatened the Jews with their total annihilation was January 30, 1939, not September 1, 1939. In that speech he said: ". . . In my life I have often been a prophet, and most of the time I have been laughed at. During the period of my struggle for power, it was in the first instance the Jewish people that received with laughter my prophecies that I would some day take over the leadership of the state and thereby of the whole people, and that I would, among other things, solve the Jewish problem. I believe that . . . the hyenic laughter of the Jews of Germany has been smothered in their throats. Today I want to be a prophet once more: If international-finance Jewry inside and outside of Europe succeed once more in plunging nations into another world war, the consequence will not be the Bolshevization of the earth and thereby the victory of Jewry, but the annihilation of the Jewish race in Europe." (Translated from Max Domarus, *Hitler: Reden und Proklamationen, 1932–1945,* II [Munich, 1965], 1058.)
55. Translated from Domarus, II, 1727.
56. *Hitler's Ten-Year War,* p. 189. Quotations from an article in the official German publication *Die Deutsche Polizei.*
57. *Mitteilungsblätter für die Weltanschaulige Schule der Ordnungspolizei.* Published by the Chief of Order Police. Group: "Ideological Instruction" (*Weltanschaulige Erziehung*), December 1, 1941, class A, series 27. Only for the internal use of the Order Police.
58. Hans Frank's Diary (October–December 1941), *IMT,* Doc. PS–2233.
59. *Das Reich,* June 14, 1942.
60. G. Jaszuński in *Dos naye lebn* (Lodz), no. 6; B. Balberyski, *ibid.,* in no. 9; S. Kaczerginski, "Ponary," *CJHCA,* records from Vilna.
61. Documents of the Instutut Pamięci Narodowej in Warsaw.
62. Datner, p. 14.
63. Documents of the Instytut Pamięci Narodowej.
64. See essay 10 below, "The Destruction of the Jews of Lwów, 1941–1944."
65. *CJHCA,* Eyewitness records nos. 45, 515, 679, 1068, 1162, 801.
66. *Ibid.,* no. 1190; Apenszlak, *Black Book,* pp. 113 ff.
67. Documents of the Instytut Pamięci Narodowej.
68. *CJHCA,* Eyewitness record no. 375.

69. *Ibid.,* no. 559.

70. "The Extermination Camp at Chełmno," *German Crimes in Poland,* I (Warsaw, 1946), 109–21.

71. *CJHCA,* Eyewitness record no. 89.

72. *Ibid.,* p. 1209.

73. *Ibid.,* no. 38.

74. *Ibid.,* no. 28.

75. See essay 10 below, "The Destruction of the Jews of Lwów, 1941–1944."

76. *CJHCA,* Files on Mielec. See also German documents, *ibid.*

77. *Ibid.,* Files on Mielec; eyewitness record no. 217.

78. *Ibid.,* Eyewitness record no. 768.

79. *Ibid.,* no. 611.

80. Records of JUS.

81. *CJHCA,* Eyewitness record no. 275.

82. *Ibid.,* Eyewitness record, on Sanniki.

83. *Ibid.,* nos. 65, 64a, 67.

84. *Ibid.,* no. 375.

85. *Ibid.,* no. 1203.

86. *Ibid.,* nos. 270, 146.

87. *Ibid.,* no. 678.

88. See essay 10 below, "The Destruction of the Jews of Lwów, 1941–1944."

89. *CJHCA,* Eyewitness record no. 6 (memoirs of Ida Glückstein); no. 640 (Turtletaub affidavit); Apenszlak, *Black Book,* pp. 95–96 (on Lublin).

90. *CJHCA,* Eyewitness record no. 228.

91. *Ibid.,* no. 458.

92. *Ibid.,* Lublin documents.

93. *Ibid.,* nos. 1190, 141.

94. *Ibid.,* nos. 676, 691.

95. See essay 10 below, "The Destruction of the Jews of Lwów, 1941–1944."

96. *Ibid.*

97. In October 1942, the Chief of the SS and Security Police in the GG, Friedrich Wilhelm Krüger, ordered the establishment of fifty-four ghettos in the GG. The order was never carried out, as most of the Jews were already exterminated. See essay 3 above, "The Jewish Ghettos of the Nazi Era."

98. Staff reports of the fifteenth police regiment on the operation in Pińsk. An official German document published in Yiddish by Ilya Ehrenburg in *Merder fun felker* (Murder of Peoples), I (Moscow, 1944), 7–10, contains materials concerning the atrocities committed by the Germans in the occupied parts of the USSR.

99. See essay 10 below, "The Destruction of the Jews of Lwów, 1941–1944."

100. According to official statistics for the period of the German occupation (Akta Instytutu Ekonomiki Ukraińskiej Akademii Nauk we Lwowie [Acts of the Institute of Economics of the Ukrainian Academy of Science in Lwów]), the Jewish population in the District Galicia amounted to 42,162 on March 1, 1943, distributed as follows: in the region of Drohobycz, 7,078;

Złoczów, 10,202; Kamionka Strumiłowa, 5,723; city of Lwów, 259; Stryj, 153; Tarnopol, 9,854; Czortków, 8,893. All other districts were already *judenrein*. Judging from the figures above, showing the number of Jews in the city of Lwów as only 259, we can assume that Jews confined to the concentration camps were not included in the statistics. Figures including the Janowski concentration camp would have totaled at least several thousand Jews.

101. According to the report by Jürgen Stroop, SS and Police Leader, Warsaw (Nuremberg Doc. PS–1061), who had directed the operation, the blowing up of the central synagogue marked the end of the action. Actually, the "clean-up" operation in the ghetto to dispose of still active centers of resistance continued for several weeks.

102. Datner, as in note 19.

103. Report of SS Gruppenführer Katzmann, SS and Police Leader in Galicia, to SS Obergruppenführer Krüger, Higher SS and Police Leader in the GG. *IMT*, Doc. L–18; see also essay 10 below, "The Destruction of the Jews of Lwów, 1941–1944."

104. Hans Frank's Diary (January 1–February 29, 1944), *IMT*, Doc. PS–2233.

105. Such as the Hasag labor camp in Częstochowa, the *Aufräumungskommando* ("clean-up commando") camp in Lodz, and the Płaszów camp, near Cracow.

106. Katzmann report to Krüger (as in note 103).

107. See essay 10 below, "The Destruction of the Jews of Lwów, 1941–1944."

108. Katzmann to Krüger, see note 103.

109. *BKG*, I (1946), 22.

110. *Ibid.*, pp. 27, 35–39, 42–45.

111. *CJHCA*, Eyewitness record no. 381 (Log of Aldo Coradello, and memoirs of Leon Szeftel, former inmate of Stuthof).

112. *BKG*, I, 22, 47–51.

113. See my *To jest Oświęcim* (This Is Auschwitz), 1st ed., Warsaw, 1945; 2nd ed., Warsaw, 1946; *This Was Oświęcim* (London, 1946); *Oshventsim* (Yiddish), new and enlarged edition (Buenos Aires, 1950); *Auschwitz* (Spanish) (Buenos Aires, 1952).

114. The judicial inquiry into the German crimes committed in the extermination camps of Bełżec and Sobibór found that very few persons escaped from these camps. But it is difficult to estimate the number of victims there, as the Germans did their best to wipe out all vestiges of their crimes.

115. See essay 10 below, "The Destruction of the Jews of Lwów, 1941–1944."

116. *Biuletyn ŻAP'u* (Bulletin of the Jewish Press Agency), November 12, 1945. Figures given by S. Herszenhorn, Director, Section for the Assistance of Children, the Central Committee of Jews in Poland.

# 10

# THE DESTRUCTION OF THE JEWS OF LWÓW, 1941–1944

In the early morning hours of June 22, 1941, before daybreak, the inhabitants of Lwów were awakened from sleep by the thunder of bombs which German planes rained down upon the tranquil and unsuspecting city. A few hours later, the Soviet Union's minister of foreign affairs announced that a state of war now existed between Russia and Germany because of the Germans' sudden attack.

At that time the Jewish population of Lwów totaled about 150,000–160,000. It is difficult to establish the exact figure. The last official census had been recorded on December 9, 1931, when 99,595 Jews were counted. Their numbers increased by at least 10,000 prior to 1939. At the outbreak of Polish-German hostilities in September 1939, many Jews residing in Poland's western districts fled from the Nazi troops and settled in Lwów. With the German military victory (at the end of September 1939) a new migratory movement commenced, from the Nazi-controlled western area of Poland to the eastern area, then under Soviet administration. Some Jews sneaked across the border to escape Nazi persecution. Some were expelled from their homes by the Nazis and were forced to cross the border. In any case, the number of Jews who crossed the border during the autumn and winter months of 1940 was very large. The majority of refugees who settled in Lwów came from the Cracow, Lodz, Warsaw, and Kielce districts. At the beginning of 1940, the total population of Lwów was about the same as before the war. (In addition to Jews, many Polish refugees had fled to Lwów.) The city's total population at that time was about 700,000 people, including about 180,000 Jews.

With the German invasion in 1941, the Jews of Lwów were stricken with mortal fear. The Soviet authorities began to evacuate Russian citizens from Lwów but managed to move out only a small number of officials and military recruits. Due to the suddenness of the attack, the task of evacuation was beset with many difficulties. The modes of transportation and conveyance were totally ill-suited for a large-scale transfer operation, and the German air attacks caused great disruption. Consequently, the Russian authorities did not abet the impulse to escape that gripped the Jews; indeed, they placed obstacles before the many Jews who attempted to flee eastward on their own initiative. In Tarnopol, Podwołoczyska, and other cities on the old border between Galicia and Russia, refugees were arrested and were ordered to return to their former places of residence. Hence, an insignificant number of Lwów Jews managed to escape the Nazis. Only a few thousand young Jews (most of them associated with leftist movements and the Communist political machine), officials, experts, and a few thousand mobilized into the Russian army fled to the Soviet Union. According to the estimate of General Katzmann, SS and Police Leader in District Galicia, there were about 160,000 Jews in Lwów during July–August 1941. According to the estimate by the Lwów Jewish Council, the figure at the end of August was about 150,000.

## "Pogrom Blitz"

The last detachments of the Russian army left Lwów on the night of June 28, 1941; on that day, the first detachments of the German army entered the city. The Germans were received with cheers by the Ukrainian masses, who hoped, with German assistance, to detach eastern Ukraine from the Soviet Union and unite the two parts of the Ukraine into one independent country. No sooner had the leader of the Ukrainian Nationalist Party, Stefan Bandera, arrived in Lwów than proclamations appeared bearing his signature, calling for war against the Bolsheviks, and containing venomous incitements against the Jews. Simultaneously, the Ukrainian militia was organized, which immediately began attacking the Jews. In contrast, Metropolitan Andreas Sheptitsky, head of the Uniate Church, issued a manifesto warning his Ukrainian adherents against bloodshed and wanton acts.

But the Germans did not wait for the Ukrainians to start pogroms against the Jews, whose destruction had been planned several months prior to the outbreak of Soviet-German hostilities. The plan for "the liquidation of the Jews in Eastern Europe" (see above, essay 9) had been drawn up during meetings between Hitler and his closest collaborators, in consultation with representatives of the SS, Gestapo, and the supreme military staff. During these sessions, it was decided to establish four "Liquidation Groups" (Einsatzgruppen), whose task would be to exterminate the Jews in all the areas of Soviet Russia to be conquered. Group "C," headed by SS-Brigadeführer Otto Rasch, was assigned to Galicia.

One of Group C's ranking officers, Erwin Schulz, Chief of Einsatzkommando 5, provided the following details in sworn testimony before the Nuremberg Military Tribunal concerning the liquidation activities in Lwów:

On or about June 23, 1941, Einsatzgruppe C, which comprised Sonderkommando 4A and 5B and Einsatzgruppen 5 and 6, proceeded to Gleiwitz, on the way to Lwów. At the beginning of July, we reached Lwów and were informed that a number of Lwów's inhabitants had been killed before the retreat of the Russian armies from the city. A short time after we arrived in Lwów, the commander of Einsatzgruppe C, Dr. Rasch, informed us that Jewish officials and Jewish inhabitants of Lwów had participated in the killing. The military command had already organized a local Ukrainian militia in the city. Dr. Rasch, who worked in close cooperation with the militia, ordered the Sonderkommando to support it. Those who had participated in the killing mentioned above, and those suspected, were arrested that very day and on the morrow. Additionally, the special detachment of Schöngarth was transported from Cracow [to Lwów] for this purpose.

The true meaning of this euphemistically worded testimony is clear. The Germans had dispatched Einsatzgruppe C to Lwów to incite the non-Jewish inhabitants against the Jews. They spread rumors that it was the Jews who had killed prisoners whose corpses were found in the Lwów prisons after the departure of the Russians. In this manner, the Nazis wished to influence the non-Jewish residents of Lwów to take vengeance upon the Jews, while the directing hand of the German leadership should remain concealed. For this reason, the Germans attempted during the first days to utilize the Ukrainian militia as the principal agent of their criminal policy. By inciteful proclamations, pamphlets, and oral propaganda, the Germans stirred up mass hatred of the Jews. Persecution and pogroms began immediately after the entry of the German army. From June 30 to July 3, German soldiers spread through the streets of the city in the company of Ukrainian nationalists and an unruly mob of the local population. They fell upon Jews in the streets, beat them murderously, and dragged them away for "work" —especially for cleansing of prisons filled with corpses and blood. Thousands of Jews were seized and conveyed to the prisons on Zamarstynowska, Jachowicza, and Łąckiego Streets; to the Brygidki prison on Kazimierzowska Street; and to the Gestapo headquarters, at 59 Pełczyńska. A deadly fear gripped the Jews. They hid in cellars and ceased to show themselves on the streets of the city. Then the destroyers, chiefly the newly organized Ukrainian militia, began to roam through Jewish houses, to remove men—and frequently, women also—ostensibly for "purification of prisons." Most of the Jews thus taken to the prison courtyards never emerged again. They died after grievous agonies and tortures, or were shot outright. Eyewitnesses who escaped from the hoodlums during these terrible days, relate that the courtyard walls of the Brygidki prison were spattered with fresh blood up to the second floor, and with human brains. One eyewitness saved from the Brygidki slaughter estimates that 2,000 Jews were tortured to death there, while only 80 persons were saved and set free.[1] Among the martyrs put to death in the courtyard of Brygidki was Yechezkel Lewin, rabbi of the Reform Synagogue in Lwów and editor-in-chief of the Jewish Polish weekly *Opinja*. He died a hero's death. When the acts of brutality began and the first Jewish victims fell, Rabbi Lewin approached Metropolitan Sheptitsky to beseech him to stay the hands of the Ukrainian masses from the Jews:

I have come, Your Excellency, in the name of the community of Lwów, in the name of about half a million Jewish people living in the area of western Ukraine. You told me once: "I am a friend of Israel." You have always emphasized your friendship to us, and we ask you now, at this time of terrible danger, to give proof of your friendship and to use your influence over the wild crowds rioting against us. I am begging for the salvation of hundreds of thousands of Jews, for which the Almighty and Omniscient will reward you.[2]

Apparently, the metropolitan promised to fulfill Lewin's request, for he did issue a proclamation to the Ukrainians—which did not have much influence upon them, however. He even suggested that Rabbi Lewin remain in the palace until the violence had subsided. But Lewin responded: "My mission is completed. I have come to make a request for the community, and I shall return to the congregation, where my place is. May God be with me." When Lewin crossed from Plac Św. Jura, the location of the metropolitan's palace, to his apartment on Kołłątaja Street, near Brydigki, a few Christians approached him and urged him to go back, because Ukrainian patrols in the vicinity of his house were dragging Jews off to prison. Lewin did not listen to them. When he reached the threshold of his house, the Ukrainian militiamen seized him and took him to the Brygidki prison yard. Lewin's son Isaac, who was there, describes the final moments of his father's life thus:

At ten I saw my father. Two Germans pushed him and beat him with their rifle butts. He was pale as a corpse in his official robes. He marched toward death. . . . When he came among a group of Jews, he made his confession and in a loud voice cried: "Hear O Israel." At that moment the Germans opened fire on that corner. All those who were working on the removal of corpses heard the prayer. . . . They joined, and the roar of the gunfire could not be heard over the force of the cry "Hear O Israel." The threats and the beatings did not stop our prayers, which inspired us with superhuman strength.[3]

Among the other martyrs in the July slaughter were the renowned Rabbi Aaron Lewin, brother of Yechezkel Lewin, and head of the rabbinical court of Rzeszów, as well as leader of the Agudat Israel, and a deputy of the Sejm; Henry Hescheles, editor-in-chief of the Polish daily *Chwila*; and the editor, Dr. Igiel.

It is difficult to estimate how many Jews were killed in the prisons and streets during these riots. According to one eyewitness, the number totaled upwards of 4,000.[4] The Germans estimated the figure much higher. In an official "top secret" report prepared by the Reich Security Main Office, and dated July 16, 1941, the action was summarized as follows:

During the first hours after the departure of the Bolsheviks, the Ukrainian population took praiseworthy action against the Jews. In their assault upon the Jews inhabiting Lwów, they seized about 1,000 of them and brought them to a prison that had previously belonged to the GPU and was now in the hands of the German army. About 7,000 Jews were seized and shot by the police in retribution for inhuman acts of cruelty [allegedly perpetrated by the Jews before the departure of the Russians]; 73 persons [Jews] regarded as officials and spies of the NKVD were also shot. Forty persons were liquidated on the basis of substantive information from the inhabitants [in Lwów]. The age of most of the Jews seized was 20–40. To the extent feasible, the artisans and experts among them were set free.

The report goes on to detail similar "acts of retribution" and "praiseworthy" acts of killing in other places—such as Dobromil, Jaworów, Tarnopol, Złoczów, and Sambor in Eastern Galicia.

## Other "Actions" in Summer 1941

The Germans did not relent after the "spontaneous pogroms" of July 1941. Their tactic was to maintain the constant threat of death so that the Jews would have no respite in which to catch their breath or take heart. If the Jews were kept in a state of perpetual danger, they would have no time to engage in whispering campaigns against the Germans or to traffic in the black market, which damaged the German economy. This was the official explanation provided daily by Berlin's own propaganda ministry to camouflage the liquidation plan that had been drawn up in Berlin.

The goal of total annihilation could not be realized through sporadic pogroms or other schemes like those utilized in former times by the czarist authorities. In lieu of the pogrom, the Germans instituted a new strategy— the *Aktion*—a military type of operation methodically planned and directed. Throughout July 1941, the action continued, with searches and arrests of leftist Jewish activists, particularly of Jews denounced as members of the Komsomol (Communist Union of Youth). All suspects caught were executed in the forest of Lesienice (in the vicinity of Lwów) without due process. At the same time, a second action took place, the "Petlura action," which was carried out with terrible zeal during the three-day period of July 25–27. Thousands of Jewish men and women were seized by Ukrainian militiamen, ostensibly for "work." The unfortunates were for the most part brought to the prison in Łąckiego Street; intermittently, Ukrainian mobs would burst in, howling "revenge for Petlura," and would beat many Jews to death. Some of the Jews seized disappeared without a trace. Only a few managed to save themselves. Rumors spread through the city that the Germans had given the Ukrainian nationalists "three days" to do with the Jews as they saw fit to avenge the death of Semyon Petlura, killed in Paris on May 26, 1926, by the Jew Shalom Schwarzbard. According to the most cautious estimate at the time, the Jewish fatalities resulting from the Petlura action totaled at least 2,000 Jews.

A series of smaller-scale actions continued throughout the summer of 1941. One atrocity particularly shocked the Jews of Lwów: German soldiers apparently complained that a shot had been fired into a German military hospital, located in the Św. Anny School, from one of the houses opposite the hospital. Without any investigation, German troops attacked the Jewish houses (nos. 1, 3, 5, 7) on Św. Anny Street and on Jachowicza Street (nos. 11 and 18). Ignoring the Christian occupants, the Germans removed all the Jewish males, and shot almost all of them (nearly 80 persons).

## *"Economic War"*

Concomitant with the murder actions, an "economic war" was waged against the Jews which consisted primarily of plunder and theft, both official and private. The private acts of theft would occur quite simply: a German would enter a Jewish house and take whatever he desired. Frequently, the despoiled Jew had to pack up his belongings and deliver them to the German's house. The Jew was quite fortunate, indeed, if he managed to return home safely at the end of his "errand."

The official German plunder began with the imposition of a fine ("contribution") on the Jews in the sum of 20 million rubles (according to some witnesses, 22 million rubles). The announcement regarding the contribution, signed by Infantry General von Roch, was promulgated at the beginning of August 1941 and gave the following explanation for the imposition of the fine: Whereas the city had sustained much damage from acts of war (that is, from the bombing and bullets which the Germans rained down upon it during their attacks), it was only just and proper that the Jews, who were responsible for this war, should "contribute" with their own money to the "reconstruction" (the other inhabitants, of course, were not called upon to participate). The indemnity decree was received by the Jews with a feeling of relief. They viewed it as betokening the end of the invasion period, with its frenzied pogroms, and the beginning of a new period of civil administration, which would content itself with extorting money from the Jews. Henceforth, the Jews hoped, it would be possible to barter lives for cash. "A contribution will save your life," was the watchword in those days. Citizens' committees were established by independent initiative in all quarters of the city to collect the requisite sum. Jews hurried to make their contributions. During the first days, long lines queued up before the committees' offices—with persons bringing large sums as well as those making a token contribution of 18 rubles (for *chai,* "life"). The committees accepted gold and silver objects, watches, jewelry, candelabra, and wedding rings from contributors who had no cash. Some Polish gentiles also brought contributions, mostly anonymously. Despite the general readiness to pay, the Germans took hostages from among the Jews. Before the promulgation of the order, small groups of German and Ukrainian policemen entered the houses of Jewish notables and seized them, on the pretext that the hostages were needed. The action involved principally the Jewish professional class—intellectuals, doctors, lawyers, engineers, etc.—as well as prominent merchants, factory owners, bankers, and civic leaders. In this manner, over 1,000 people were arrested (according to one estimate, almost 2,000 people). This event accelerated payment of the fine, since the Jews believed that if they paid on time and in the full amount, the hostages would be freed. Many Jews therefore sold the balance of their property to make up the ransom, and they scrupulously guarded the receipts given them for their money. The fine was paid on time, the first installment being transferred to the Germans as early as August 8, 1941. Aside from cash, the Jews had brought many jewels, gold, and a substantial amount of silver (about 1,400 kilos). But the hostages weren't freed. They disappeared without a trace. This cynical deception was the first encounter the Jews of Lwów had with the "new ethics" of Nazi Germany. The Germans utilized the same stratagem of taking hostages in other cities as well, and everywhere the results were duplicated. Thus many civic and cultural leaders were lost. This policy of liquidating the leadership of the conquered people was employed by the Germans vis-à-vis other groups—the Poles, the Czechs, etc.—but never with such thoroughness and cruelty as against the Jews.

In the period during which the contribution was being exacted, another action was instituted. The Germans began to set fire, systematically, to synagogues, first the venerable synagogue of the Turei Zahav (also known as the synagogue of "the Golden Rose"), together with the other synagogues on Sobieski, Boimów, and Blacharska Streets; then the synagogue on Szajnocha Street, as well as the Reform temple on Żótkiewska Street (its ruins and burnt walls were finally demolished in the summer of 1942). SS-Officer Wallenburg (or Wallenburger) headed the 1941 arson activity. The remaining Lwów synagogues were destroyed later, particularly during the liquidation of the ghetto in 1943.

The Germans also engaged in "economic exploitation" of Jewish cemeteries. They removed headstones from the cemeteries and used them to pave roads, paths, sidewalks (they used some of the headstones for building the floors of the concentration camp on Janowska Street). I do not have exact figures on the total scope of this "economic action," but the report of General Katzmann states that from one cemetery alone on the outskirts of Lwów, the Germans removed 2,000 square meters of stone for the paving of roads. Jewish workers seized by the Germans were compelled to perform the backbreaking work of uprooting the monuments, shattering them, and transporting them.

## The Judenrat (Jewish Council)

The Judenrat was established at the time of the "contribution action"; its first official activity was the collection of the contributions and the payment of the fine to the Germans. In Eastern Galicia, the Jewish community councils had been abolished under Soviet rule. It was the Germans' policy to organize a Jewish Council in every area of Jewish settlement and transform it into an apparatus for implementing their orders. At the beginning of July 1941, the German command met with various Jewish functionaries to negotiate on the creation of a Jewish Council. The Germans proposed that Moses (Maurycy) Allerhand—famous scholar of law and professor at Lwów University, who had been a government-appointed director for the Lwów Jewish community prior to the war—be chairman of the Judenrat. Allerhand declined, pleading old age and illness. A few others (among them Judah Ehrlich) refused to be council members. Finally,

seeing that there were no volunteers from among the important function-
aries and city notables, the Germans gave up "negotiating" and simply ap-
pointed council members from their list of candidates. At first, five members were appointed, but later additions were made (until July 20, 1941).
The composition of the Judenrat in the autumn of 1941 was as follows:
Józef Parnas, chairman; Adolph Rotfeld, vice chairman; council members:
Henryk Landesberg, Oswald Kimmelman, Edmund Scherzer, Naftali
Landau, physician Izydor Günsberg, Jacob Chigier, Seidenfrau, Josef Hoch,
Szymon Ulam, Marceli Buber, Chaim Zarwincer, and others. Changes soon
ensued. Józef Parnas, a lawyer, who was then about seventy years old and a
representative of the assimilationist Jews, could not adapt to the modus
operandi of the Germans. He was an attorney, a scion of wealthy estate
holders. In his younger years he had been a cavalry major in the Austrian
army. Being of strong character, he was not submissive to the German
authorities and even dared to refuse a few of their demands. In October or
November 1941, Parnas was arrested by the Germans, because (according
to the rumors that spread through the city) he had refused to provide the
quota of workers demanded by the Germans for forced labor. Parnas was
brought to the prison in Łąckiego Street, where he was shot to death in the
courtyard. Adolph Rotfeld, a lawyer and member of the Zionist Executive
Committee in Eastern Galicia, took Parnas' place, but died from a severe
illness in February 1942. Henryk Landesberg—prominent lawyer, former
community leader, and active member of B'nai B'rith before the war—then
became chairman. Landesberg did not serve long either: he was murdered
by the Germans in September 1942. The fourth chairman, Ebersohn, a
decent man but lacking in power and effectiveness, filled the post until the
Germans executed him, together with the other members of the committee,
in February 1943.

The prerogatives of the Jewish Council were very broad, and surprised even the optimists in the Jewish community. Ostensibly, the Germans assigned an extremely wide sphere of activity to the Jewish "self-
rule," to be administered according to German instructions. After the
establishment of the ghetto, this task of administration turned into full territorial self-rule. The Judenrat organized a finance division and a taxation
division, with various autonomous sources of income. It opened social-
assistance establishments, including infirmaries, hospitals, orphanages, old-
age homes, soup kitchens, and inexpensive restaurants. It supervised economic matters, industrial and trade plants, food stores. It organized Jewish
labor through a labor office, supervised nutrition, and distributed ration
cards to the Jewish population. It purchased raw foodstuffs, established
bakeries, and managed stores, the sole places where Jews could receive the
rations allotted to them. It distributed and assigned living quarters, through

the housing division; distributed Jewish mail; and ultimately provided the Jewish community with a judicial authority, through its legal division and the formation of a Jewish militia.

These wide-ranging activities necessitated a huge apparatus. At first the community employed a thousand officials, but the number rose to 4,000 in 1942 (according to Farber and Maltiel, there were as many as 5,000 functionaries and manual laborers, in addition to the artisans and skilled workers in shops and plants under the aegis of the community). These were the branches of the apparatus: (1) the personnel division, which hired and supervised officials and workers, was headed by Joseph Hoch, an energetic and influential member of the Jewish Council (in a satirical poem on the Lwów Judenrat, the entire apparatus of the Jewish Council was dubbed the "Organization Hoch," in allusion to the "Organization Todt," German labor organization); (2) the supply division, headed by Egid and his adjutant, Beno Teichholtz; (3) the housing division, headed first by Dr. Schutzman of Przemyśl, then by Ludwik Jaffe of Bielsko, Silesia (one of the directors in the housing division was Samuel Pacanowski of Lodz, head of the Noar Hatzioni movement, who was murdered by the Germans in August 1942); (4) the economic division, headed by Zarwincer, Stanisław Rotfeld, Bardach, and others; (5) the labor division; (6) the taxation division; (7) the health division, first headed by Dr. Günsberg and afterward by Dr. Alexander Blaustein; (8) the social welfare division, headed by Józef Kohn, an experienced communal leader; (9) the legal division, headed by Dr. Hirschprung and others; (10) the statistical division, headed by Fryderyk Katz; (11) the building division; (12) the burial society; (13) the educational division, headed by Abraham Roth, former director of the Jewish Commercial Gymnasium, and Cecilia Klaften, a very active leader in the sphere of professional education in the prewar period (but since the Germans banned the opening of Jewish schools, the educational division could not develop this activity); (14) the cultural division, whose basic activity was the administration of religious affairs (by the Orthodox Rabbis Yisrael Wolfsberg, Moshe Elchanan Alter, and Natan Leiter, and the Progressive Rabbi Kalman Chameides, formerly of Katowice, and David Kahane, together with six rabbinical judges). The activity of this religious council was severely limited because the Germans banned public worship. Almost all the Lwów synagogues had been burned, and the houses of study had been transformed into shelters for Jewish refugees expelled from their homes by the Germans. There was even a ban on the prayer of private *minyanim* (Jewish religious quorums). Not infrequently, the Germans, at the start of the occupation, would burst into such prayer groups and arrest all the worshipers, who would vanish without a trace. Secular cultural activity among the Jews was totally banned in Lwów.

An old house in the vicinity of the flea market, near the old synagogue at 2 Starotandetna Street, was assigned to the Jewish Council. But the structure was too cramped to house all the divisions. Later, the old Jewish community building at 12 Bernstein Street was returned to the council, and the statistical and cultural divisions were transferred there. On the main floor was the Jewish Social Self-Help office, which was not directly dependent upon the Judenrat apparatus. As a branch of the Jewish Social Self-Help organization for the Government General, it was the sole independent institution outside the aegis of the Jewish Council. The center of the Jewish Social Self-Help Organization was in Cracow; Michael Weichert, a Jewish author and theatrical expert, headed the organization. The head of the branch in the Galicia district headquarters in Lwów was the prominent attorney Leib Landau, while the Lwów section was headed by Max Schaff. The Jewish Council also had a social welfare division, which somewhat paralleled the work of this organization; it was housed in the synagogue on Jagielońska Street that was salvaged from the Germans. In the synagogue at 2 Rappaporta Street, the tax division was housed, while the burial society division was on nearby Szleichera Street. The housing division was at first located in the large synagogue on Bóżnicza Street and was later transferred to the Abraham Kohn School on Stanisława Street. The office for distributing ration cards, under the aegis of the economic division, which employed many officials and maintained a huge file, was located on Żółkiewska Street. The Jewish militia (or police), officially named the Jüdischer Ordnungsdienst Lemberg (Jewish order-service of Lwów), occupied a special position in the framework of "self-rule." The militia was organized during August-September 1941 (as one of the chroniclers of that period details).[5] The head of the Jewish police in the Warsaw ghetto was brought to Lwów to train and organize the police there. The number of persons in the Lwów police force rose from 100, at the time of its establishment, to 500 and subsequently to 750 persons. The militia was divided into four districts: the first, which included the supreme command and the criminal division, was located in the Yad Charutzim headquarters at 11 Bernstein Street; the second, at 112 Zamarstynowska; the third, in the Kleparów suburb; the fourth in the Zniesienie suburb. The criminal section (Kripo) and the special service (Sonderdienst) constituted a special division within the Jewish police, and maintained close cooperation with the Gestapo. The chiefs of this division (Max Goliger, Szapiro, and his adjutant Krumholc) were anathema to the Jewish community for their wanton acts.

There was a continual deterioration in the activity and position of the Jewish police vis-à-vis the Jewish community. The militia, which was created as an aid to the Jewish Council to ensure order and sanitation in

Jewish neighborhoods, gradually began to collaborate with the Germans, who compelled it to carry out shameful acts and turned it into a German tool, thus nullifying its affinity to the Jewish Council. The composition of the ghetto police also changed in the course of time. At the outset, young men from the Jewish intelligentsia enlisted in its ranks. Once its role as a German tool for persecuting Jews became apparent, individuals possessed of civic responsibility departed: some left of their own volition, some fled to the Aryan neighborhoods, and others were removed by the Germans. In their stead came a motley crew of thugs and fortune hunters, who sought to feather their nests during this terrible turmoil and were prepared to implement the commands of their German bosses.

The activities of the Judenrat, too, developed in a direction more harmful than beneficial. The strategy of the Germans was to create in the Judenrat a body which would deceive the Jews into cooperating in the Nazi scheme for their destruction. The Germans succeeded in concealing this strategy from the Jews, or at least from the great majority of them, until a much later period of the Nazi conquest. The council served the Germans as a means by which to extort money and valuables and obtain a labor force. One of the important departments of the council was the supply division; but we would be mistaken to assume that its task was to supply the Jews with their needs. The work and duty of this division was to supply the Germans with whatever their hearts desired, and the list of demands and requests swelled from day to day. One day they might ask for a hundred Oriental rugs; and the next day for a dozen sets of fine china, silverware, kitchen tools, luxurious furniture, crystal, gems and diamonds, fine clothing, works of art, kegs of the best coffee, caviar, and other delicacies that had long disappeared from the market. Although, officially, the supply division had only to fill the requests of German officers or their representatives, woe to the individual who tarried in filling the requests of other Germans, many of them officials in the SS or the Gestapo. Egid, the head of the supply office, once refused to fill some private "orders" for a German police official. The next day, he was invited to the Gestapo office for a "meeting," and was shot there. The Germans justified their demands upon the Jews with the declaration that all Jewish property in the conquered lands had been expropriated by the German state and remained in Jewish possession only on a temporary basis: Jews were permitted the use of that property only when it was not required by the Germans.[6] The scope of this law was expanded to encompass the area of Eastern Galicia by virtue of a decree dated August 7, 1941.

The supply office employed many officials whose entire activity lay in making the rounds of Jewish houses to seize articles required by the Germans. In addition to filling the regular "orders," the office deemed it necessary to prepare special gifts for the German representatives, "to soften their hearts" so that they would "waive" some of their "excessive" demands. Other communal officials became expert in negotiating with the Germans and bribing them in a "refined" manner. Accordingly, they could at times intercede on behalf of the community or certain individuals. In some cases established ties were created and a stratum of traffickers and go-betweens developed, proficient in "fixing" matters, who earned huge sums of money through their intercession. Corruption prospered, to the disgust of the Jewish community. The scope of this "official" German piracy was vast. According to the estimate of a Judenrat functionary, the value of the articles claimed in this way in August-December 1941 exceeded by 30 percent the fine (contribution) paid to the Germans in early August of that year.[7]

Aside from implementing the supply, taxation, and work schemes (which supplied the Germans with free labor), the Judenrat was used by the Germans to divide the Jews, to create a deep abyss between the officials of the community and the rest of the population. This was part of the Nazi strategy of "divide and rule," also applied to relations between Jews and Poles, Jews and Ukrainians, and Poles and Ukrainians. Members of the Jewish ghetto police and, to a large extent, officials of the Jewish Council (members of the Judenrat, officials of the supply division, and other functionaries) were granted extra privileges. For example, they enjoyed immunity (such as protection from searches and evictions); freedom of movement in the streets, without threat of being seized for forced labor; extra rations; and so on. On the other hand, officials of the police and the community did not receive a fixed salary for their work, and the cost of living rose daily. As a result, some of them exploited their official position. Indeed, hierarchies of privilege and "class divisions" developed. Judenrat members and division heads constituted the upper stratum. Middle strata comprised officials with "hard" work permits (identification tickets on firm paper, or bound documents), whereas the temporary workers had "soft" work authorizations (typewritten or handwritten notes on plain paper). Other privileged groups were professionals, experts, technicians, engineers, physicians, and medics—who worked primarily in offices and German plants. Less important were the former storekeepers, merchants, agents, ordinary workers, and professionals: teachers, lawyers, rabbis, cantors. Last of all was the large mass of unemployed persons; these poor people were not protected either by work permits or through intercession. They were ripe for plucking by the Germans. Members of this lowest stratum were exterminated and liquidated pitilessly from the very first moment.

The class stratification within the Jewish community under Nazi occupation differed totally from the prewar professional and social structure.

It turned things topsy-turvy. The new class distinctions were far more bitter, for they jeopardized not just a person's income but his life as well. A person bereft of means, official protection, or a trade useful to the Germans was surely condemned to death—either a "natural" death (by disease or hunger) or a quicker, violent death through "forced labor," extermination in a concentration camp, or as the victim of an "action."

Finally it became clear to all that the "miniature Jewish state" established under the German authorities was a terrible delusion—a malicious caricature of independent rule, designed entirely to serve the Germans.

## Legal Limitations, Anti-Semitic Incitement

As early as their first few months of rule, the Germans began to implement their racial policies in the sphere of housing. They intended to set up boundaries between the various nationalities resident in the city, particularly to divide the Jews from the Slavic peoples (Poles and Ukrainians) and the Germans (including the Volksdeutsche). The loveliest part of the city, with palaces and luxurious houses—where heretofore Poles and many Jews had dwelled—was chosen for the Germans. The Jews living on streets in the vicinity of Listopada, Potocki, Lisa Kuli, Wólecka, and Kadecka, and the streets adjacent to the Stryjski Park (Dwernickiego, Św. Zofji, Żyżyńska, and Snopkowska) received an order to vacate their homes without delay. In the majority of cases, they were granted only a few hours to get out, and they departed with what they could carry by hand. Occasionally, they were ordered to leave without taking anything. This action, accompanied by terrorist tactics, felled many Jewish victims (according to estimates, more than 200 people were killed). Fear seized the Jews dwelling in streets in the "Aryan" parts of the city. Not wishing to wait until the decree reached them, they sought housing in the Jewish neighborhoods. Large numbers of them queued up daily before the housing office of the Judenrat. But the evacuation action was soon terminated, and new blows came in its stead.

The law annexing Eastern Galicia to the GG as the Galicia District was issued on August 1, 1941. The law sorely disappointed the Ukrainians, who had trusted Nazi propaganda promising that the Germans would abet them in establishing a "united, indivisible, free, and sovereign" Ukrainian state. Now the Germans seized Ukrainian nationalist leaders and imprisoned them. Among those imprisoned was Stefan Bandera, leader of the extremist Ukrainian Nationalists, who was sent to a concentration camp and was freed only after Germany's downfall. Members of his party (dubbed

"Banderovtsi") went underground, and established partisan brigades to fight the Germans. Eastern Galicia was full of them. But while they were fighting the Germans, they exterminated the Jews as well. A large number of the Ukrainian masses, especially the peasants, followed Bandera. Among the bourgeoisie, some collaborated with the groups, others abstained from any political activity. Even the democratic groups did not assist the Jews or attempt to restrain the Ukrainian masses, however. The Metropolitan Sheptitsky was an exception. He gave refuge to a large number of Jews, especially children, saving about 150 of them.[8] But no imitators arose from the ranks of Sheptitsky's adherents.

After the annexation of the Galicia District to the GG, all anti-Jewish laws promulgated in the GG during the past two years were applied to the Jews of Galicia, Lwów included. One of the decrees published earlier (July 15, 1940), was that every Jew (and every person of Jewish extraction, up to the third generation) over ten years of age had to wear on the left arm a white armband bearing a blue Star of David. This distinguishing mark served as an invitation to attack.

While the armband was intended to divide Jews from non-Jews, other limitations were intended, in the main, to limit movement from place to place in order to seek support or foodstuffs. The curfew, applied to non-German gentiles (not to Germans) from nine in the evening onward, was advanced to eight in the evening for the Jews. Individuals found in the street even a few minutes after the curfew hour were shot or sent to labor camps. On the trams, a special compartment "for Jews only" was set aside; later, even this dubious privilege was withdrawn and they had to walk to work, sometimes a distance of several kilometers—a long trip, which would exhaust them and expose them to danger and persecution in the streets. Train travel was forbidden, and the right to leave the city was withdrawn. Jews were permitted to purchase foodstuffs in the markets only between two and four o'clock in the afternoon. Employment in many professions was forbidden. Instead, the Jews were compelled to do forced labor. Their property, both in movables and real estate, was confiscated. All sums of money over 2,000 zlotys were to be confiscated, but the Germans did not succeed in implementing this law.

The first governor of the Galicia District was Karl Lasch, former governor of the Radom District. On January 24, 1942, Lasch was arrested on multiple charges: unlimited embezzlement of state funds; falsification of accounts; theft of rugs, furs, and objects of art; and bribing the wife of Governor-General Hans Frank. He was also alleged to have desecrated his race and betrayed the fatherland by having sexual relations with a non-Aryan. SS-Brigadeführer Karl Otto Wächter, former governor for the Cracow District, was appointed in his place. SS-Brigadeführer Fritz Katzmann was appointed SS and police chief for the Galicia District, and Robert

Ulrich of Gratz (Austria) was nominated chief of the German police (Schutzpolizei) in Lwów. In the first few days after the German conquest, the Ukrainian scholar and geographer Professor Jurij Polański served as mayor of the city, but after Galicia was annexed to the GG, the Germans abolished this last vestige of Ukrainian autonomy. The office of mayor was eliminated and a German official, Kujath, was appointed Stadthauptmann. Kujath was succeeded by another German, Dr. Höller.

By means of civil restrictions, physical assaults, insults, and abductions, the Germans sought to inspire terror in the Lwów residents, especially the Jews. By establishing a discriminatory pecking order of privileges and persecutions, they sought to prevent the development of a spirit of solidarity among the city's inhabitants. The Ukrainian felt himself superior to the Polish "slave," who was more persecuted and therefore beneath him. And both the Ukrainians and the Poles viewed themselves as "Aryan" aristocrats vis-à-vis the Jews. The Germans incited the non-Jews' contempt for Jews through vicious and vulgar anti-Semitic propaganda, via frequent radio broadcasts, various publications, posters, "exhibitions," popular songs, and slanderous press. The Lwów press, comprising two non-German dailies (Polish and Ukrainian) and an official German daily, poured out torrents of mendacious accusations and libels fabricated by the German propaganda machine against Jews and converts alike. An article entitled "They Have Forgotten Their Origin," in the Polish *Gazeta Lwowska* on October 22, 1941, expressed the opinion that converts should wear the white armband with the Star of David, as should any Christian man or woman tied to a Jew by marriage. It appears that during the first period of the German invasion, many assimilationists naïvely believed that conversion would save them from the anti-Jewish decrees and actions (conversion also occurred on a large scale in Slovakia and Hungary). According to an item in the *Gazeta Lwowska* on November 8, 1941, the number of Lwów Jews willing to convert to Christianity in November 1941 was about 4,000. Although we should not place too much credence in this newspaper devoted to attacking Jews and Jewish converts, we may assume that the number of candidates for conversion was quite large. The office of the Catholic bishop of Lwów arranged a series of special lectures and established a trial period of six months for such candidates. Particularly active in the conversion of Jews was a priest in the Church of St. Vincent de Paul; and the *Gazeta Lwowska* launched a bitter attack upon him (November 9–11, 1941). Converts and candidates for conversion soon learned that their apostasy would not save them, however. German laws, which precisely defined their use of the term "Jew," were based upon racial rather than religious objectives, and converts were clearly included under the decrees. Only a small portion of those who had gentile friends or relatives were hidden, or obtained forged Aryan documents, and were thus saved.

## *"Labor" Decrees and "Labor" Camps*

Among the earlier laws of the GG was the "forced-labor" law which required every Jew, male and female, aged fourteen to sixty to work for the Germans. The Germans established a labor office in the city with a special division for Jewish labor (*Judeneinsatz*), which was housed at first in the school in Zamknięta Street (in an alleyway adjoining Gródecka Street) and was later transferred to the Mikołaja Reja School in Misjonarski Square. Heinz Weber—a cruel, crude, and uneducated German— headed the office. The officials were Jews, some of whom became notorious within the Jewish community for their fawning attitude toward the Germans and their mistreatment of their own brothers. The new office conducted a census of all the Jews aged fourteen to sixty. Anyone who could not present a work authorization from an institution beneficial to the Germans was compelled to work at a place assigned to him—often at brutal physical labor, to which Jews were generally not accustomed. Many evaded registering in the German labor office (*Arbeitsamt*); the Germans therefore instituted a new procedure. The office employed Jewish "snatchers" (*khapers*) to hunt down Jews without work authorizations; Jews seized were held captive in the office until a new "transport" went out to the place of labor.

The activities of the German labor office paralleled those of the Judenrat's labor office. There were two reasons: First, the Germans didn't trust the Jews. Second, they sought to introduce confusion into the labor market—because the essential goal was not Jewish labor, but the persecutions and oppression that accompanied it. The Judenrat's labor office attempted, in vain, to work with the Germans to introduce order into the method of labor conscriptions and to establish a precise quota of Jewish workers. One agreement was reached, after much toil, but the Germans failed to respect it. They fired workers displaced by the community, and again let loose the "snatchers," whose prey were sent to places from which they would never return.

"Work" served as a pretext for any German to brutalize the Jews. In addition to the two labor offices, military transports and SS vans would cruise the city streets and seize Jews for work. Individual Germans in uniform or in plain clothes frequently seized Jews and forced them to work without pay. In many cases, the task was a futile one, whose entire purpose was simply to mock the Jew. In general, the jobs were backbreaking beyond human endurance. Old men, for example, were ordered to carry bags of cement weighing 100 kilograms, and then to return them back to the place from which they had originally been picked up. Young people were compelled to transport railroad ties weighing 200 kilograms and more. Occasionally, Jews were compelled to carry a burden while running. Those who tarried or fell were assaulted, shot, even killed.

In most army-related work, the Jews received a salary, albeit a trivial one (2 to 4 zlotys a day), and were occasionally given food supplies, depending upon the generosity of the foreman. Jews working in plants organized by the German office also received payment in cash or in food stamps. During the period of Soviet rule (1939–1941), the nationalization of factories and private businesses owned by Jews or gentiles was implemented. Although the Germans at first announced that they would return such establishments to the former owners, all the industrial plants and consumer cooperatives were instead transferred to the ownership of the German trust offices (*Treuhandstelle*). Jews who had been factory owners or businessmen were fortunate if they could be employed as workers in the establishments they had owned. Nor were buildings confiscated by the Russians returned to their owners; thus a former landlord might be reduced to working as a doorman in his own building.

Most of the Jewish workers in German institutions worked not for the insignificant salary but to obtain a work certificate, believing it would protect them from greater evils, particularly from conscription for the labor camps. The labor camps for the Jews were deceptively dubbed "educational institutions" (*Erziehungslager*) by the Germans. The SS and police leader for the Galicia District, General Katzmann, explained the need for such camps:

It is our [the German police's] duty first of all to positively combat the extensive activities of the Jews—especially the lazy, the unemployed, and the idlers—in the black market throughout the entire Galicia District. The most effective method was the establishment of forced-labor camps by the chief of the police and SS. The most perfect opportunity was provided us when there was a need to repair road D. G. 4—of vital importance to the entire southern front—which was in a very poor condition. . . . On October 15, 1941, we began to set up camps along road D. G. 4 and, despite the many obstacles, we established seven new camps in the course of a few weeks, and we could announce in our report the existence of fifteen such camps, where 20,000 Jews worked.[9]

Katzmann's report indicates that, in their transfer of Jews to the camps, the Germans were not motivated solely by "educational" purposes. Nor were these the first camps established in Lwów and its vicinity. Other camps were established prior to October 15, 1941. A small labor camp (30–60 workers) was established as early as July 1941 on Herbutów Street. A larger camp located in swampy marshland in the suburb of Sokolniki, near Lwów, was organized in mid-July 1941, and employed 200–400 Jewish workers at a time. The Ukrainian Czubak and his adjutant

Jaworski headed a Ukrainian police contingent that supervised the work. Jewish workers were compelled to wade into the swamps—the water reaching above their knees—to uproot weeds and water plants and transfer them to dry land. During the winter months, when the cold grew more intense, the workday still lasted more than twelve hours. There was severe illness and high mortality. From 70 to 80 percent of the workers were felled by illness, cold, lack of food, and inhuman housing conditions. Many died from wounds or from the blows that the Ukrainians inflicted on the "lazy." Some were shot by overseers. The Judenrat's labor office was compelled to supply replacements for the deceased and the ill; approximately 100 persons were sent every two weeks. The camp's police prevented any contact between the prisoners and their families or the outside Jewish community. The camp was sealed: only additional workers entered, none but corpses left. Complete secrecy surrounded the Sokolniki camp during its entire existence. It is not known how many Jewish victims this camp consumed or when it was liquidated. Some writers say that it was liquidated in December 1941; others claim that it continued during 1942.

Lwów Jews were sent to other camps outside the city: Łacki Murowane, Hermanów (west of Lwów), Winniki (Weinbergen), and Ostrów, Kurowice (between Lwów and Podhajce), Kozaki (near Złoczów), Jaktorów (in the Złoczów area), Medyka, Unterbergen, and others. Actually these "labor camps" were death camps. Few Jews emerged alive from these labor camps, and the percentage of wounded and permanently disabled among them was very high.

The police and the SS also set up two camps within the city: the SS labor camp on Czwartaków Street, in the vicinity of the SS residential quarter (between Listopada and Potockiego streets); and the Janowska Street camp (more on this will follow). The Czwartaków camp became notorious for the ferociousness of the SS men and their cruel brutalization of Jews. The camp was liquidated in the spring of 1943, after most of the Jewish workers there had been murdered by the SS.

## The Ghetto Decree and New Actions

In October 1941, the Germans announced the establishment of a ghetto in Lwów for Jewish residents. The ordinance was signed by the governor for the Galicia District. The poorest and most dilapidated sections, Zamarstynów and Kleparów in the northwest portion of the city, were set aside for the ghetto. These were areas, without municipal sewage or water facilities, and with almost no electricity. There were few large houses, and the living quarters were mainly in shacks and low, decrepit clay huts. Among the poor that lived there were a motley crew of libertines, prostitutes, thieves, and armed robbers. Elevated railroad tracks separated these suburbs from the city proper. Only four streets—Kleparowska, Żródlana, Pełtewna, and Zamarstynowska—connected these neighborhoods to the city through underpasses. The topographical situation was well suited to the creation of a ghetto, for it readily isolated the areas from the rest of the city and enabled the Germans to closely supervise the connecting links. A communiqué in the official German paper, *Lemberger Zeitung,* on November 15, 1941, stated that all Jews had to transfer their residence from other parts of the city to the new ghetto within the month, from November 16 to December 15 of that year. Of the four streets leading to the ghetto, the Jews were permitted to use only one, Pełtewna Street. Under the railroad bridge was stationed a detachment of Ukrainian police and SS men to inspect the possessions of the Jews. The inspection station was in an old bathhouse which became a barracks for the German Ukrainian "garrison." The guards fastidiously inspected the never-ending stream of Jews carrying the pitiable remnants of their property. From dawn to dusk Jewish caravans streamed down Pełtewna Street under the railroad bridge, everyone bearing bags and bundles or transporting their movables in wagons or wheelbarrows. But under the bridge, dubbed by the Jews the "bridge of death," patrols of German and Ukrainian Jew-haters waited. Whoever could not show a certificate of work, or seemed hungry, sick, or elderly, was immediately dragged over the fence to the old barracks. There they were slapped and beaten, often fatally, by the supervisors and gate-keepers. (Among the overseers were a few Jewish outcasts, specially trained, who served the Germans; particularly notorious was a tall Jewish woman named Malkele.) Anyone who did not please the inspectors was arrested and was later transferred to the prison on Łąckiego Street. The course from there was well known. Victims were thrown onto trucks which would take them to the forest for execution. The lives of thousands of Jews, many of them women, were lost in this "bridge of death" action. This was the first major "action" in Lwów against Jewish women.

The initial purpose of the ghetto appears to have been the reduction of the Jewish population in Lwów and the creation of confusion and panic by the forced relocation. For a time, the Germans were content with this, and in the period after the established date for the closing of the ghetto, December 15, 1941, nothing happened. Most of the Lwów Jews, who had not yet managed to find a place in the ghetto, had no choice but to remain in their homes in the city and await, in fear, their punishment. The Germans now seemed to ignore but did not explicitly revoke their ghetto decree. The Judenrat therefore conducted lengthy negotiations with them. Though we do not have documents and proofs, the representatives of the community apparently sought to soften the Germans through bribery and suitable gifts. It is clear that the Germans did not enforce the order concerning the establishment of the ghetto, and the uncertain situation of the panicky residents in forbidden neighborhoods stretched on for another year, until September 1942.

The total Jewish population of Lwów decreased from month to month, as a result not only of the repeated actions and the conscription for the labor camps but also of a voluntary exodus of Jews from the city. Many Lwów Jews were refugees who had arrived from western Poland at the time of the Soviet conquest, and rumors now began to spread that Jews in the western districts of the GG led more tranquil, orderly lives despite persecutions and limitations, than Jews in the areas which the Germans conquered from the Russians. Indeed the reports were true to some degree, because in that period the Germans planned to exterminate mainly Jews "infected with Communist progaganda," who had resided in the former Soviet area of occupation. Refugees who had relatives in the western districts began to flee Lwów to return to their former places of residence. Also many indigenous Lwów residents sought to leave their native city of birth, and settle in smaller, quieter towns. Thus many thousands left Lwów, despite the German ban on travel. It is impossible to establish their exact number, because their exodus was illegal and clandestine.

From January to February 1942 there was a brief respite, during which there were no mass murder actions. Mini-actions continued, however; among them, the expulsion of Jews from Żółkiewska Street and its vicinity from December 1941 to January 1942. The Jews residing in that area were compelled to transfer immediately to the Zniesienie suburb—a barely inhabited place, a semirural neighborhood which was a perennial refuge for thieves and thugs. Bereft of conveniences and personal security, the Jews suffered great privations in their new neighborhood. This is how one Lwów Jew described his new apartment:

A new apartment. Two rooms, the size of rat holes. Little windows facing the ground, and in this shack, nine people live. The stench is nauseating. The lack of ventilation for many years is dizzying. But it does have one thing that the rich take pride in—a toilet near the table, from which the stench rises up. There is no cellar, but there is a pit for potatoes. The well supplying drinking water is tens of meters away. During our sojourn in Zniesienie, thieves broke in at least thirty times. For two to three days we were "honored" by visitations from guests of the neighborhoods. They would drag away anything that came to hand—foodstuffs, firewood, coal, furniture parts, fence pickets—everything was worthy of theft.[10]

In December–January 1942, the fur action was carried out. The Germans demanded that the Jews turn over all fur and rawhide garments, fur coats, fur collars, woolen cloth, and woolen clothing, needed for the soldiers "fighting for the Third Reich" in the cold areas of Russia. Jews alone were drafted to contribute to this patriotic enterprise. Any Jew who violated the law faced the death penalty. Not all of the horde of furs and woven goods were sent to the fighting army. The administration and German police kept a large supply of furs, particularly luxury furs, for their own use, and they even embezzled some to sell in the black market. (As noted, even the governor, Lasch of Galicia, was caught helping himself to the booty.) The extent of the thievery is indicated by the fact that from the entire Galicia District only thirty-five railway cars loaded with furs were sent to the army. The official report of General Katzmann provides no breakdown as to what portion of the spoils was confiscated from Jews of Lwów and what portion from Jews in outlying cities. A few Jews caught concealing their furs were killed.

Nevertheless, the fur action was one of the quietest, causing mainly economic damage and few fatalities. Many more victims fell in other small actions (winter 1941, spring 1942). One time the Germans moved to rid the city of Jewish beggars; another time, they seized orphan children; yet another time, they spent several days hunting down elderly men and women. The victims of these actions were taken to an unknown place, and were never seen again. All the while, the actions of snatching people for the camps never ceased. Fifty to one hundred Jews disappeared daily without a trace. After the slaughter and carnage of the previous months, the Jews of Lwów grew accustomed to these losses and even began to regard them with equanimity, as a propitiation of the Moloch.

## Living Conditions

The German rule brought in its wake a total revolution in the economic lives of the Jews. This was the second economic revolution in their lives since the outbreak of World War II. The first had occurred at the time of the Soviet occupation when all property (both movables and real estate of landlords, industrialists, and businessmen) was socialized. Other groups, such as officials, lawyers, and religious instructors, were deprived of their means of livelihood by the changes in the social order. In contrast, many Jews found employment in the collectivized trades and industries as workers, officials, and instructors. Capitalists, bankers, industrialists, and prominent merchants, officials, and former army officers, as well as all unemployed persons (including many refugees) were suspect in the eyes of the Russian authorities, and in 1940–1941 many were transferred from Lwów to the outlying areas of Eastern Galicia or to Russia proper. Thus the economic conditions of the Jewish community during the Soviet period were highly unstable.

In the Nazi period, new onslaughts disrupted the life of the community, whose economic norms had already been sorely disturbed. All collective economic institutions passed automatically to the ownership of the Ukrainians and the Germans, who fired the Jewish workers. In one blow almost all officials, workers, artisans, and professionals were deprived of their source of income. In general, only heavy physical labor remained open to the Jews—in most cases forced labor, with no pay. When wages were paid, they were insignificant and could not support even a meager existence. The expulsions and frequent forced moves caused severe economic losses in most households, the remnants of whose capital were diminished by the payment of the "contribution" and other extortions. Moreover, many families lost their source of support when the young men, the sons and the fathers, were seized for forced labor in the camps. No healthy economic base was left to the Jews, almost all of whom were forced to eke out a hand-to-mouth existence from the sale of objects and movables still in their possession. They sold furniture, clothes, bricks of gold, and silver objects which they had succeeded in hiding from their persecutors. When their merchandise ran out, they became beggars, dependent upon public or private charity. Others tried, at the risk of their lives, to support themselves by trafficking in the black market, or through temporary clandestine work.

But the Jews' troubles in the economic sphere did not end there. The Germans instituted food rationing among the population of Lwów. Each individual would receive his portion on the basis of the ration card issued to him. But the rations were not allotted equally to each nationality. The Jews received only 10 percent of the supplies that were given to the Germans (*Volksdeutsche*), 50 percent of the food ration for the Poles and Ukrainians.

At first the Jewish ration comprised 1,400 grams of bread per week (later cut to 1,050 grams, then to 700 grams, and finally to 500 grams); 250 grams (later 100 grams) of sugar per month; half a kilogram block of salt (formerly used for consumption by animals) once every two or three months; every two months, 200–400 grams of moldy flour (black flour, dubbed by the Germans *Judenmehl,* "Jewish flour"), and some groats; half a liter of vinegar from time to time; on occasion 200 grams of beet-sugar jelly, a box of matches, a small amount of mustard, and very rarely a few other supplies of no nutritional value. In the winter of 1941, each Jew received 25 kilograms of potatoes. The Jews were allotted no kindling wood or coal at all. They had to purchase their rations in food stores set up especially for them by the Judenrat. It was permissable to purchase vegetables in the city markets without restriction, but the Jews were permitted to come to the market only between the hours of two and four in the afternoon, when most of the produce was gone.

Since the ration supply was insufficient to live on, Jews who could afford to bought groceries on the black market. Prices on the black market skyrocketed. By 1941 the price of bread had risen to 30–40 zlotys per loaf (1,400 grams); butter, to 200 zlotys per kilo; a box of matches to 150 zlotys. Aside from the high prices, purchases in the black market involved mortal danger. Poles caught holding merchandise or making purchases in the black market were sent to prison or to concentration camps. Jews caught in these acts were killed. One woman, surnamed Barbasch (a Latin teacher in the Jewish high school, she was the wife of a noted scholar of Polish literature), was caught attempting to buy a few kilos of potatoes from a gentile caretaker. The Gestapo police immediately took her to prison, from which she never returned. Similar cases concerning other Jews are known.

However, the Jews' money soon ran out, and they had to make do with the official ration. Hunger, poor housing, cold, inadequate clothing, the disruptions, and the physical and moral torments—all combined to exhaust the endurance of the Jews. Mortal illnesses spread—especially among the children, particularly those whose parents had perished during the actions; their homes and possessions confiscated, these children roamed through the city streets naked, and attempted to support themselves by begging, through small trade, and even thievery. Men dropped dead in the streets. One member of the Judenrat speculated that, at the existing rate of mortality from hunger, disease, and suicide, combined with the low birth rate, in five years there would not be a single Jew in Lwów, even without the actions.[11] But even this pessimistic estimate fell short of the mark, for natural increase had totally ceased during the years 1942–1943. According to an estimate made by the Jewish doctors of Lwów, more than 50 percent (others estimated the figure at 90 percent) of the women stopped menstruating. In those years, 60–80 percent of the ghetto residents were bloated with hunger, stricken with typhus, tuberculosis, and scurvy. No organized social service could ease this mass tragedy. The Lwów branch of the Jewish Social Self-Help and the Judenrat's department for social assistance had severely limited funds at their disposal. The officials of the social service agencies were at their wits' end and could do nothing, despite their devotion, to prevent the general disaster; the Germans impeded them at every turn. Disease could not be successfully combated under such conditions. The former Jewish hospital, the Lazarus on Rappaporta Street, was expropriated by the Germans immediately upon their arrival, and all the furnishings and medical equipment confiscated. Through great efforts Jews succeeded in establishing three small hospitals. One, in the Tadeusza

Czackiego school building on Alembeków Street; a second, in the school on Kuszewicza Street; a hospital for contagious diseases, at 112 Zamarstynowska Street; and an outpatient clinic on Misjonarski Square. Daily the wounded and maimed were brought from the "labor" and work camps, mortally ill and dying from hunger.

## Despite Everything: The First Resettlement from Lwów

With all their suffering, the Jews of Lwów maintained hope of a better future, "despite everything." They assumed that the Germans had already employed the maximum number of Jews in hard physical labor, and that the industry and transport systems in Lwów, of great value to the army's fighting front, depended upon the work of Jewish laborers and professionals. Therefore, they thought, the Germans would not wish to exterminate the Jews and bring about the collapse of these important economic bases. Although they realized that they would yet suffer more oppression and barbaric persecutions, they were confident that Germany's downfall would ultimately come, and with it an end to their sufferings.

But these thoughts, based on normal human logic, did not coincide with the inhuman policies of the central German authorities. We know from documents and papers at our disposal today what the Jews under Nazi rule did not know; namely, that the goal of the total extermination of European Jewry had already been decided on in Berlin at the end of the year 1941, and that early in 1942 the Germans commenced large-scale liquidation actions in the areas of Poland annexed to Germany (the provinces of Poznań, Silesia, and Lodz). On January 20, 1942, the momentous conference of the major officials of the German government and the Nazi party on the "Final Solution of the Jewish Question" took place in Berlin, and the extermination plan was authorized. In the beginning of March 1942 the liquidation actions were started in the GG: first, the great expulsion of Jews from Western Galicia took place, and the long-delayed deportation of Jews from Mielec (in the Cracow District), followed by the resettlement of Jews from other cities in Poland (Rzeszów, Brzesko, Nowy Sącz, Kielce, Kraśnik, Zamość, Ostrowiec, and Sanniki). The massive action in Lublin took place from March 17 to April 20, with 35,000 Jewish victims.

In March the Nazis also began their action in Lwów. They utilized there the same tactics of deceit that they employed elsewhere. They informed the Judenrat that it was necessary to resettle the Jews of Lwów because the city was filled to capacity and the situation was having devastating effects. Indeed, the Nazis claimed, in order to lighten the excessively heavy burden of social assistance on the Judenrat, they would transfer the "nonproductive elements"—criminals registered in the police files, prostitutes, door-to-door beggars, and persons existing on social-assistance funds. In order to strengthen the impression that the evacuation was merely a transfer of residence, they promulgated a very detailed order on the articles that each of the "emigrants" was permitted to take with him: 200 zlotys in cash, food for the road, clothing and bedding, up to twenty-five kilos in weight. The Germans also wanted to entice the Judenrat into implementing the resettlement. To give the action a humane appearance, they ordered the Judenrat to prepare the lists of those to be resettled and to organize groups of Judenrat officials and Jewish police to make the rounds, remove the designated persons from their houses, and bring them to the collection points. To foster the impression that the entire population would be handled in a just and humane manner, the Nazis established a screening committee in the central transfer point (*Durchgangslager*) in the Sobieski school on Zamarstynowska Street. The committee was made up of representatives of the police (Robert Ulrich, the chief of the German Police [SCHUPO] in Lwów); the German labor office (the head of the *Arbeitsamt*, Weber, participating); of representatives of the economic department of the Lwów municipality; the SS and Gestapo; and finally of the Judenrat. Alternately participating in the committee were: Ludwik Jaffe, Chigier, Seidenfrau, Natan Buksbaum, Samuel Pacanowski, and others. The position of the Jewish appointees on the committee was not easy. Only the German representatives, of course, could make decisions. They treated the Jewish appointees—who attempted to save at least a few souls—with contempt.

Even before the beginning of the resettlement, differences of opinion emerged within the Jewish community regarding cooperation in the action. Various associations and parties apparently were against the community's cooperating in any form, and notified the Judenrat of their negative stand. We do not have exact knowledge regarding the discussions and meetings that took place, however, save for a single intervention, seemingly one of many. Rabbi David Kahane (who, after the liberation of Poland, became the chief rabbi of the Polish army) has related that before the expulsions began, a delegation composed of Rabbis Yisrael Leib Wolfsberg, Moshe Elchanan Alter, Kalman Chameides, and David Kahane came to the head of the Judenrat, Dr. Landesberg, and warned him against assigning community officials to assist in the action. According to Rabbi Kahane, Landesberg did not make any clear reply, but complained that the Judenrat could not act freely, since it was dependent in all its activities on the German authorities. Yet the Judenrat probably may have hoped that Jewish officials and the Jewish militia might manage to save some individuals from deportation. But after a few days the Judenrat realized that the Germans merely wanted to trick the Jews into implementing the action. Not limiting themselves to the removal of the original "nonproductive elements," the Germans were also seizing unemployed persons, old people, sick children, the handicapped, as well as go-betweens and speculators. Occasionally, even work permits were of no avail. As one of the high German officials told a Jewish acquaintance, "a good hiding place is the best document" (*Ausweis*).

The men of the Jewish militia, who were appointed to assist in the resettlement action, performed their task halfheartedly. The Jewish patrols brought in so few people during the first few days that the Germans soon dispensed with Jewish help and took over the entire operation. The action lasted for three weeks. The Germans occasionally blockaded specific neighborhoods to conduct a thorough search. On April 1, 1942, the action was finished. At the start of the Passover festival, on the evening of the first *seder,* the last of the victims was taken.

Lwów Jewry had suffered catastrophic losses. Over 15,000 people had been taken. At first, rumors were rife that they had been settled in outlying cities. Only after several months did it become known that they had been sent to the extermination camp of Bełżec near Rawa Ruska, where they had been murdered, according to the first reports that arrived, by electrocution or in gas chambers. Lwów Jewry was immersed in grief and the stillness of death. Not a single Jewish family failed to mourn a loved one who had fallen prey to the Germans. Even children ceased their laughter and games and fled in mortal panic at the sight of a German or Ukrainian policeman. People began to search for new stratagems to escape the threat of extermination hovering over them.

## "Work Will Save You from Death"

Immediately after the conclusion of the resettlement action, the Germans conducted a new registration of Jewish workers. New identity cards were issued, and the workers received special permits and armbands, different from those worn by the unemployed. Each Jew received a red registration card (*Meldekarte*) with his picture and a precise personal description. The registration card also included a typical warning (whose purpose was to "protect" the Jews): "It is illegal to seize the owner of this card on the street." The large white armbands of the workers bore the letter "A," for *Arbeiter* (worker), and a serial number was sewn on the cloth. Each worker was also entitled to receive a special registration card for one woman (his wife, mother, or sister) to run his household. These women, too, who were given the letter "H," for *Haushalt* (household help), were ostensibly under the protection of the labor office. About 50,000 men and 25,000 women received the registration cards and the new armbands.

After the census a new spirit swept over the Jews. Again they focused on the slim hope which the Germans deceptively held out to them. Again the Nazis succeeded in splitting the Jewish community—between those "armed" with registration cards and armbands and those who lacked such protection and were therefore condemned to death. The Jews believed that every person with an "A" armband and a work card was protected. Unemployed Jews attempted to seek work through all sorts of means, since the Germans continued to distribute cards and armbands to every Jew accepted for work in a German plant authorized by the labor office. Jews stormed the new work places; the watchword was, "Work will save you from death."

Thus a new complex for large working establishments was created and a great fictive "prosperity" was generated. In those days a gigantic plant, the municipal workshops (*Städtische Werkstätten*), was established. Its existence was to be brief and dramatic.

As early as January 1942, a *Volksdeutscher* named Dorman came to Lwów with plans to establish a plant, employing Jewish workers in tailoring and weaving for the *Luftwaffe*. By employing Jewish workers, whose salaries were very low, German contractors and industrialists made huge sums. To this end, Dorman entered into negotiations with the German authorities, but did not obtain an agreement till the conclusion of the action at the end of March 1942. D. Greiwer (Grajower), a Jewish merchant from Cracow who had already established workshops in the city of Bochnia in Western Galicia and had made a great success there, also arrived in Lwów. Greiwer employed a few hundred Jewish workers in the Bochnia plants and boasted that he had saved them from deportation. Upon his arrival in Lwów, he apparently worked in tandem with Dorman and some of the communal leaders in Lwów who were seeking a way to save thousands of unemployed Jews. They entered into negotiations on this matter with the Stadthauptmann, Höller, and with his assistant for economic affairs, Reisp, on one hand, and with Greiwer and Dorman on the other. The officials were Tremski, an industrialist; Izydor Reisler (Leib Landau's son-in-law), the lawyer who became prominent after the war as Jerzy Sawicki, a prosecutor of the Supreme Polish Court in the Nazi war criminals trials in Majdanek, Lublin, and Nuremberg; and the attorney Dawid Schächter. These were appointed directors of the municipal workshops organized in April 1942; the chief director was Greiwer. The new institution was supported actively by the president of the Jewish Self-Help, Leib Landau, and by Mehrer, a noted leader of the Jewish artisans union of Lwów. The founders of these plants hoped to save through industrial employment a few thousand Jews, not only from the ranks of skilled workers and artisans but also from among the Jewish intelligentsia. The municipal workshops were projected to engage in all sorts of light industry, manufacturing of fancy goods, luxury items, baskets, brushes, bookbindings, linens, women's millinery, paper boxes, small leather goods. Most of the crafts were easy to learn, and it was possible to take on former lawyers, editors, rabbis, teachers, and merchants who might learn the trade in a short time. They were also accepted for other jobs in the plants, jobs that did not require any special skills. Among the doorkeepers and night watchmen were the famous pianist Leopold Münzer, the attorney Julius Menkes, the journalist Adolph Friedman, and others.

Reisp was appointed on behalf of the German municipal authorities. He was a Viennese lawyer and a devotee of the theater—an amiable man to deal with, serious, but lacking economic experience. He promised one of the Jewish directors that in times of deportation or other dangers the municipal workshops would be "an island of peace and tranquility" to the workers employed there. Jews began streaming to this place for work and protection, and in a short time over 3,000 Jews found employment there. The directors of the workshop required that workers bring their own sewing machines and tools; the Germans would supply only the work space, at Nos. 17 and 20–22 Kazimierzowska Street and 9 Furmańska Street. The workers brought not only the few sewing machines and other tools still in their possession but whatever money they had, and even the furniture required for the establishment. But despite the zeal and energy which the directors invested in organizing the plant, the workshops did not become the secure refuge that was hoped for.

The basic error lay in the fact that the plants were established through an agreement with the civilian municipal authorities, Höller and Reisp, rather than with the army and the SS. According to the agreement, the workshops were to supply the German civilian population with tailored and luxury goods. Representatives of the army and especially of the SS (Wagner, director of the economic division; Seiss-Inquart; General Katzmann) claimed that the plants were of no importance to the war effort. In 1942, competition between Germany's civil administration and industry and the SS had sharpened. The disputes between Albert Speer, the German minister for armament and war production, and the SS are well known; likewise, the dispute of Ernst Zörner, governor of the Lublin District with the SS and police leader Odilo Globocnik. Similar conflicts arose in Lwów as well, not merely between the municipal authority and the SS. There was a perennial conflict, too, between Greiwer and the Judenrat and between Greiwer and Heinz Weber, head of the German labor office. Weber felt that Greiwer's activity caused Weber's loss of supervision over thousands of Jews. The Judenrat had more fundamental misgivings about Greiwer, a very energetic but coarse and megalomaniacal individual who could not accept criticism from even his most intimate codirectors. The Judenrat intimated that Weber desired to amass a fortune in a short time, was unscrupulous about the means, and would even resort to partnership with Dorman. As the Judenrat had no influence over the management of the municipal plant they feared that the plant would gradually turn into a private venture. They therefore planned to create new workshops under their own aegis and supervision.

The economic basis of the municipal workshops was unsound. Most of the machinery brought there was unsuitable for large-scale production, and the proliferation of unskilled workers further slowed up the work. But the greatest obstacle was the shortage of raw materials, which prevented large-scale production. The workshops had to limit themselves to the production of small-scale luxury items, shoe repairs, tailoring, and fur work, while the management prepared attractive statistics and presented exhibitions in an effort to pacify the Germans.

Private German firms, interested in the cheap market of Jewish labor in Lwów, began to establish branches there; the largest was set up by a Berlin industrialist, Schwarz, in a block of houses on Marcina Street (nos. 3, 5, 7, 9, 11). About 3,000 Jews worked in this establishment, in three shifts. One of the chief functions of the plant was the repair and alteration of the clothing, sent there from all over Eastern Galicia by the SS, of Jews killed in the murder actions carried out by the Germans. The clothing was reconditioned, sanitized, and repaired, and then sent to Germany for German charitable institutions, particularly the Winter Help Fund. Another German firm utilizing Jewish labor was Victor Kremin's plant for seizure of raw material (*Rohstofferfassung*). The working conditions there were revolting. Some of the workers would collect sundry rags and waste materials in the streets and the garbage dumps; other workers would sanitize and repair what was collected. In addition, lice-ridden, bloody, pus-stained, torn, and patched uniforms from the front were sent there for sanitization and repair. Most terrible of all was the work on the clothing of Jews killed in actions. The private firms made a good profit. The Jewish workers were paid little or nothing and in many cases even had to pay an "admission fee" (sometimes thousands of zlotys) for the privilege of working. Finally, there were intermediaries, both Jews and non-Jews, who extorted substantial fees for their services as "employment agents."

But the Jews speedily became convinced that work in the German plants would not save them and that the sword of destruction hovered over them all.

## Disaster Is Imminent

In the midst of the illusory work "prosperity," the Germans initiated a blitz action against the Jews of Lwów. In late June 1942, a mobile SS brigade assigned to murder actions burst into Lwów and began a sudden and cruel action. The action, which lasted about twelve hours, from two in the afternoon to two at night, was conducted by two SS officers in Lwów: Engels (Katzmann's assistant and one of the Gestapo heads in Lwów) and his adjutant Wepke. Soldiers made the rounds of the Jewish houses, removed the "unemployed" (that is, old people and children), and took the victims (6,000–8,000 souls according to some estimates) to the transit camp—the *Durchgangslager,* or "Dulag"—near the Janowski camp, and there tortured them to death. Rumor had it that among the other terrible murders repeated during this slaughter, the Germans utilized trained dogs to attack the victims and tear them to pieces.

During the early summer there were other small actions. One night all Jewish veterinarians were removed from their houses and brought to the Janowski camp, where nearly all of them perished within a short time. Another time the Germans seized all the Jews who had worked for insurance companies before the war, and took them to an unknown place. At the end of April 1942, a roll call of the Jewish police was taken, and approximately 200–250 individuals were transferred by the SS and the Gestapo to the Janowski camp allegedly to serve as camp policemen. Their fate was the fate of all the inmates of the camp—execution.

In July 1942 the Jews were again ordered to make a contribution. This was the third such payment. The second contribution had been made in the spring of 1942, and the Germans complained that it did not bring them enough money. Now it was even more difficult to extort the requisite sum. Tens of thousands of Jews had been killed; the remainder were poverty stricken. A few optimists among the Jews still believed that the new contribution was a favorable omen, signalling a German change of heart—that the fine would be in lieu of blood. But they were again mistaken.

After the goal of total extermination of the Jews had been decided upon at the Conference on the "Final Solution of the Jewish Question" in Berlin in January 1942, basic changes ensued in administration. Previously, in all matters, the Jews had been subject to two authorities: on one hand, the civil (governor, mayor, and others) and military authorities; on the other hand, the SS and the Gestapo, which constituted part of the SS. During the summer of 1942, the entire handling of Jewish affairs passed to the SS. This was a victory for the fanatical Nazis over the more "moderate" group, who wanted to postpone the extermination of Jews. Their opposition to immediate extermination did not emanate from humanitarian motives, but from economic considerations. High officials of the civil administration (for example, Wilhelm Kube, the Kommissar-General of White Russia, and Peter-Heinz Seraphim, expert for economic and population matters in Poland and the Ukraine) and German generals sent protest letters to the central German authority, warning of the dangers involved in a "premature" liquidation of the Jews. The German civil authority in Lwów also raised its voice on this matter, in an official report dated August 29, 1942 (the document is now in the archives of YIVO in New York):

The labor force in the [Galicia] District is stretched to its limit. On top of this comes the removal of Jewish manpower from the labor market, which is being carried out in a most radical manner. The administration of the [Galicia] District has had only one year to prepare for the liquidation of Jewish labor. The Aryan population of Galicia is less proficient in handiwork and industry than the population of other districts. Hence the war economy will suffer far more grievously there than in other parts of the Government General.

It appears that the basic problem regarding the liquidation of the Jews— priority to political considerations or to the necessities of war—was settled by the high command in favor of the political motive, in full realization of the fact that economic production will decrease markedly in these areas. I must especially emphasize that the implementation of this policy will cause very severe consequences in Galicia.[12]

In contrast, General Katzmann submitted this triumphant report to his superior, the higher SS and police leader for the GG, Krüger, in Cracow:

The [civil] administration lacked authority and was too weak to contend with the disorder that prevailed in this field [forced labor of the Jews]. Therefore, the head of the SS and police assumed the entire management of Jewish labor. All Jewish labor offices in the Galicia District, where hundreds of Jews worked, were dissolved. All work authorizations provided Jews by various firms or offices were invalidated. Work certificates provided to Jews by the labor offices were nullified if they were not authorized by a new signature of the SS. During this period of inspection, thousands of Jews who had forged identity cards or had obtained their work authorizations fraudulently or by various stratagems were seized. They were all turned over for "special treatment" [*Sonderbehandlung;* i.e., for execution].[13]

Katzmann's report accurately conveys what transpired in Lwów and the entire Galicia District. The Jewish labor office in Lwów was liquidated at the start of August 1942, and all Jewish labor was thereafter supervised by the SS. In a farewell speech by Heinz Weber to his Jewish employees, who had been dismissed, he advised them how to manage in the future: "It is better for you to be ragpickers than bookkeepers and office clerks." Weber also noted, in a private conversation with a Judenrat representative: "From now on matters concerning the Jews will be arranged not from the viewpoint of economic needs but from the political viewpoint."

The new masters, the SS men, immediately launched a scrutiny of all Jewish workers. In each shop, a "tour" was conducted, and the number of Jewish workers was cut. Those fired were not merely sent to their homes, but were arrested by the SS. Women and infirm men were sent to so-called *Schmeltz* (*Schmeltz* literally means "discarded scrap metal" and was used to refer to execution). Stronger persons were transferred to the Janowski camp. On the work certificates of persons spared during the inspection, a new signature was affixed by the SS. It was recognized that even this constituted only a temporary reprieve, that there was no security in the new working certificate or the "A" armbands. It is said that Katzmann was wont to express his contempt for the presumed "protection" in these cynical words: "The armband isn't something to be ashamed of. The armband is a death sentence."

Katzmann's assistants in the division for "Jewish employment" were the SS officers Hildebrand, for the District Galicia, and Linhart, for the city of Lwów.

An inspection of workers similar to the ones in other industrial plants was staged in the municipal workshops. But here all those "worthy of being saved" were given a red SS seal in lieu of the black seal given in other plants. No one paid attention to this petty detail at the time, for it appeared to be a mistake of minor importance. Only during the massive action of August 1942 did it become clear that this "mistake" foreshadowed disaster.

As for the employees of the Judenrat, whose number had reached 5,000, their situation was special. The SS refused to stamp their work certificates at all, which was a most gloomy portent.

## The Massive Action of 1942

On August 10, 1942 (a Monday), at dawn, a massive action began, carried out by the Germans in Lwów. It was apparent that military and political experts had planned the action in advance in a very systematic manner. The special extermination brigade of the SS (*Vernichtungskommando*) took part, as did the Gestapo, the German police (SCHUPO), and the Ukrainian militia. The direction of the action was entrusted to Katzmann. Officers of the German army relate that Katzmann had postponed initiation of the action several times because he received from the Jews a bribe of one-half million zlotys for each postponement. At the start of the action, Katzmann let slip the following remark to a German army officer: "Katyń! What's Katyń in comparison to this action of ours, in Lwów? Katyń is just the work of a single day for us."[14] The Germans and Ukrainians carried out the action punctiliously, with equanimity and satisfaction. They would blockade the houses, streets, and sections one after the other, and would conduct searches and systematic patrols. After they had removed all inhabitants from the houses, they would conduct a second search, and after that a final inspection which was called "fine-combing" (*auskämmen*). With this exacting method of search they would remove and transfer to the Janowski camp a few thousand victims a day.

The Jews were unprepared for the sudden action. There were few instances of resistance. Many Jews tried to hide—in cellars, tunnels, sewers—but with little success. Places of concealment found at the last minute and in great haste were easy to discover, especially through the assistance of police dogs. In many cases, gentile children betrayed the fugitives to the police. There were many cases of suicide. Others attempted flight from the transports, or direct physical resistance. Hundreds of such "criminals" were immediately shot by the police.

Generally, the Germans spared persons with work permits stamped with the SS seal during the previous inspection, but they displayed extreme cruelty toward workers from the municipal workshops, the old bone of contention between the civil administration and the SS. On August 13, 1942, the SS burst in with barbaric shouts upon the workshops and conducted a scrutiny. Now the base deception perpetrated during the inspection came to light. All these had received red seals; now the Germans claimed that only black seals were valid. About 3,500 Jews were employed in the municipal workshops at the time, and because the place was supposed to be (according to Reisp) "an island of tranquility," the workers had also brought their families (about 2,000 additional persons) with them for protection. The Germans transported 4,000 persons to the Janowski camp, and spared only 1,000 persons from the workshops.

Most terrible and cruel was the action in hospitals and orphanages. The Germans seized not only the sick but the physicians and staff members as well. Infirm persons who could not move from their beds were shot on the spot. Children were thrown into wagons, where they were heaped like sacks, one on top of the other.

All the victims were brought to the Janowski camp, where the Germans compelled them to stand for hours in a large field, to await an additional inspection. In the interim, the policemen beat them murderously and searched them for money, gold, jewelry, etc. A very small number were freed after the additional inspection. The rest were sent off to the death camp in Bełżec.

The massive action, concluded on August 23, 1942, resulted in the death of more than 50,000 persons. During the first days, the Germans had tried to cloak the action in a "cultural" guise. Such a posture could not be long maintained, however, in the midst of mass murder. Lwów quickly turned into a city of nightmare and blood. Matters reached such a pass that even the German civil administration, which in principle agreed with the SS regarding the "final solution" of the Jewish question, opposed the means for attaining this end. In a report dated October 26, 1942, a representative of the civil administration wrote:

The action of resettling the Jews often assumes forms unworthy of the cultured nation as it fosters the notion that there is a similarity between the methods of the Gestapo and the GPU. They say that the transport trains are in such bad condition that it is impossible to prevent Jews from escaping. As a result, shots break out and there are regular manhunts at the stations and transit points. . . . Although the German population and the entire non-Jewish population is convinced of the need to liquidate all the Jews, it would still be worthwhile to implement these acts of extermination in a manner which would create less sensation and less disgust.[15]

## Establishment of the Ghetto in Lwów

After the massive action of August 1942, the order to establish the ghetto was issued, not by the civil administration but by General Katzmann, the SS and police leader for the Galicia District. The final date for establishing the ghetto was set for September 7, 1942. Any Jew found outside the ghetto after this date faced a mandatory death penalty, as did any gentile providing concealment for a Jew.

The erection of the ghetto was an additional victory for General Katzmann in his struggle with the German civil administration over the Jews. In a report to his superior, the Higher SS and Police Leader in the GG, Katzmann accused the civil administration of having neither the requisite talent nor the courage "to solve the Jewish question," and he set forth the reasons that persuaded him to erect a ghetto. Even in a report intended for the internal use of the SS, Katzmann resorted to libels and deceptions to sustain his motivations and grounds for creating the ghetto:

In the course of time it becomes ever clearer that the [civil] administration does not have the power to solve the Jewish problem in even a partially satisfactory manner. For example, the civil administration attempted several times to restrict the Jews in a closed Jewish area, but failed. The problem has therefore been solved by the head of the SS and Police Leader for the District Galicia [i.e., Katzmann himself] and his adjutants, without any hesitation. The order was an urgent matter that could not suffer any delays, since, in the winter of 1941, cases of typhus were registered in various sections of the city. This constituted a grave danger, not only to the local population, but, additionally, to the army— both the Lwów garrison and the soldiers passing through Lwów to the front. At the time of the Jews' transfer from the city to the ghetto, a few barriers were created whose purpose was to carefully sift out the antisocial Jewish mob repelled by work. All elements of this type were seized and transferred for "special treatment" (*Sonderbehandlung*).

Katzmann's words clearly show that the SS planned a "purge" of the Jews during the move from the city to the ghetto. Many Jews were murdered during this new "inspection."

Many other victims fell in various barbaric actions—the cruelest occurring very early in September (about September 1) in the area of the new ghetto. After the ghetto ordinance was promulgated, the offices of the Judenrat were transferred from Starotandetna (outside the boundaries of the ghetto) to the corner house at 15 Jakóba Hermana Street and 2 Łokietka Street. In addition to the central office of the Judenrat, the housing office was also relocated there. Crowds of panic-stricken Jews mobbed the housing office, begging for any sort of living space in the ghetto. Suddenly, tens of SS and Gestapo officers emerged from their cars, rushed into the masses, and staged a massacre. According to rumors that spread through the city, this action was in retaliation for an event that had occurred the previous day: a Jew attempting to defend himself from a German official had injured or killed him. The German officer who directed the massacre (various eyewitnesses divulged different names: some said it was Engels, others said it was Wepke or Gustaw Wilhaus) sent a special car to bring the head of the Judenrat, Landesberg, to the place of the massacre. (Landesberg had been incarcerated a few days previously in the Łąckiego Street prison. It was said that Landesberg was accused of conducting secret negotiations with the Polish underground and of giving them financial support.) When Landesberg arrived, the Germans had already managed to snatch and shoot tens of men and women from the crowd, which was fleeing in panic. The dead were piled up in front of the Judenrat headquarters. The Germans next selected twelve Jewish officials and policemen to be hung publicly from the roof of the house and from the lamps in the street. Lacking sufficient rope, they ordered new and stronger ropes from the city and submitted the bill to the Judenrat, with the demand that the community pay it (the original receipt was preserved by Jaffe, head of the housing office). Some of the ropes broke, and the unfortunate victims fell from the roof to the pavement. Bloody, mutilated, they were forced by German beatings again to mount the steps to the roof, where they were hanged a second time. Among the dead were the Jewish Polish author Ludwig Rath, the high-school teacher Leon Taube, and the physicians Teofil Taffet and Tunis (head of the Judenrat's assistance division for the Jewish camp inmates). Tunis, a former Austrian officer, was granted a "reprieve" from this shameful death by hanging—his sentence was commuted to an "honorable" death by shooting. The other victims were hung from the balconies of the first floor and from the lampposts on the street. For Landesberg the Germans staged a special show to mock and shame him. Since he was the head of the Judenrat, the Germans decided to hang him above his officials—that is, from the second floor—as a mark of recognition. Landesberg was first hung with very thin ropes which quickly split. He fell to the ground, and was brought back to the second floor to be hung again. This scene was repeated three times. Semi-conscious, wounded, bleeding, Landesberg begged for a reprieve from the hangmen, relying on the legal principle that the death sentence of the condemned must be commuted if his life is not terminated during the execution. The Germans ignored his supplication and carried out the hanging to death.

They then ordered that the dangling bodies of the hanged should be left on public view for a full day (according to some other testimony, two days) in order that the entire population might witness this display as a reminder of German "justice." One survivor of the Lwów ghetto has described the atrocious sight:

I went with my mother to the office of the Jewish community regarding an apartment, and there in a light breeze dangled the corpses of the hanged, their faces blue, their heads tilted backward, their tongues blackened and stretched out. Luxury cars raced in from the center of the city, German civilians with their wives and children came to see the sensational spectacle and, as was their custom, the visitors enthusiastically photographed the scene. Afterward the Ukrainians and Poles arrived by tram, with greater modesty.

## The Ghetto Regime and Internal Life

The area of the ghetto established at the command of Katzmann was greatly constricted from that planned by the municipal authorities a year earlier as the Jewish population had dwindled by more than 70,000. The ghetto comprised part of the Kleparów and Zamarstynów outskirts (without Zniesienie). On the south side, the ghetto had a natural boundary, the railway embankment. The western boundary was Zamarstynowska Street, from the bridge under the railway track to the house at no. 105. To the north the Pełtew River was the boundary; in the east, Tetmajera and Warszawska Streets. But for the remaining Jewish population of Lwów (about one third of the total before the actions and the deportations), the ghetto area, a place of small clay and wooden shacks, did not suffice. A large house was rare in these neighborhoods and in most cases the newcomers had to find dwellings, in the horribly overcrowded conditions, in less than two weeks from the promulgation of the order until the closing of the ghetto. The Judenrat was still in a condition of confusion and bewilderment from the recent actions. Its apparatus, especially the housing office, was now sorely overburdened with the task of relocation.

Communal and family life were shattered; not one family remained intact. The uprooting to the ghetto, with all the persecutions, searches, and oppressions that occurred along the way, was a new destructive action. Jewish families who failed to find a roof over their heads camped out in the streets, in the courtyards behind buildings, in hallways, in barns and shanties. The season was autumn, with chill weather and heavy rains, which impaired the health of the people and caused great damage to their few belongings and foodstuffs. The sole plaza in the ghetto, Kleparowski Place, was filled with such "dead of the desert," dwelling in tents and shanties or lying naked under the sky. The Germans, to further vex and embitter the Jews' wretched existence, had not arranged for the Aryan families to leave the ghetto prior to the entry of the Jews. Only after the Jews had arrived did the Aryan residents begin to leave, either changing their abject dwellings for spacious Jewish apartments in the city (the Jews still had to pay a substantial "fee" for such exchanges) or simply evacuating the Jewish area, out of fear that they would be lumped with the Jews. After a few months most of the Aryan families had left the ghetto, somewhat relieving the overcrowding. Congestion was also reduced by the death of many Jews—some through disease, others as victims of the unrelenting actions. But there was still not sufficient space. Officially, each Jew was entitled to apartment space of three square meters, but such "luxury" apartments were only on the books. In practice, in each small room with a single small window, at least ten persons were crammed; that is, two, three, or even four families. Since there was not adequate sleeping space for everyone at one time, they devised various strategies. Some households arranged to sleep in two shifts, one during the day and one at night (day workers might alternate with persons on night shifts). Some split up sleeping time into three shifts. Others built two-tiered bunks in the room which were set up only when they were to be slept in and had to be disassembled during the day so that the inhabitants would be able to move about the room and perform household chores. The housing is described by a ghetto resident:

Dwellings in the normal sense were few and far between. In the main they were ruins, collapsing shacks, marked for condemnation before the war. Common people of all sorts had previously lived in these rooms. Such a room must be described: Tiny windows, most without window panes, patched and stuffed with rags, paper, splinters of wood and filthy pillows, or "luxuriously" covered with boards. The color of the outer walls was a grayish brown layered with grime and mud stains—splattered by wagons which wended their way slowly through stinking puddles, stagnating through summer and winter. The walls were covered with mold and slime . . .; the northern walls damp and rotten to the roof; the roof was covered with shingles, and the gutters were rotting and disintegrating. The hallway to the house, covered with wooden boards, constituted an abyss of mines and traps for the feet of the unknowing. An apartment with "conveniences" had a broken toilet and a smelly sink difficult to envisage as a drinking-water faucet. The rooms were not plastered or maintained, the walls and floors were in disrepair, and in each room and far corner there was an iron stove and a rusty, sooty pipe for exhaust.[16]

The ghetto in Lwów was surrounded by a wooden fence. The job of erecting the fence, entrusted to the engineer Naftali Landau of the Judenrat, took a long time. Landau deliberately delayed the work and blamed the slow progress on the lack of lumber. But in the end the fence was completed, and the Jews could enter or leave only through the ghetto gate, inside which the Jewish police stood guard, while detachments of the German and Ukrainian police were stationed on the other side. At first all workers were permitted to leave; but later on they had to go out group by group for inspection and present their work cards. The guards carefully inspected all those passing through, lest they take anything out or smuggle food or other things into the ghetto. The supply situation of the Jewish population severely worsened from the time the ghetto was established.

In general, contact and trading with gentiles on the black market was severed. Jewish and gentile traffickers who smuggled merchandise into the ghetto at the risk of death demanded prices that exceeded black-market prices on the Aryan side by 300 to 400 percent. The amount of food allocated to the Jews was insignificant, the quality was execrable. The main meal of the ghetto resident (either lunch or dinner, in accordance with the work hours of the members of the family) consisted of a soup made of beans, potatoes, or coarse groats; and bread. Instead of coffee, ghetto inmates would drink the extract of roasted beets, with saccharin instead of sugar. They prepared vegetable dishes from mustard greens or from peels and scraps of potatoes. The basic staple was bread, of extremely poor quality.

This bread resembled real bread externally, but internally it seemed to be a dough concocted from a secret recipe. It contained a certain portion of flour, but by its brownish blackish greyish color it resembled street mire. This sticky, damp, and soggy something that didn't completely dry was the food that we craved, despite its disgusting appearance and nauseating taste. And let no one suppose that this so-called bread was brought to the ghetto in the regular manner. On the contrary, for this smuggled commodity we paid a Midas' treasure [30 zlotys for one kilo of bread].

Various diseases spread throughout the ghetto. Combating illness was very difficult, since there were no hospitals (all the infirmaries and Jewish hospitals had been liquidated in the big action of August 1942). There was one tiny provisional infirmary, but not a single pharmacy. All medications had to be smuggled in from the Aryan side at exorbitant prices.

The typhoid epidemic spread and intensified, and there was no way to check it. One of my friends, a doctor who shared my room, told me that he would daily count up to twenty-five new cases. Tens of doctors still lived in the ghetto, and they were all swamped with work. Ghetto dwellers protected themselves as best they could. They sterilized clothing and tried to wash themselves thoroughly despite the lack of privacy. The ghetto did not have a bathhouse, and the one outside the ghetto was set aside for the militia and had room for only 100 bathers per day.[17]

There was an additional hardship: a person found ill in the ghetto immediately fell victim to the Germans, who sent him for "special treatment." The sick would therefore walk around in the winter chill, sometimes with fevers of 39° to 40° centigrade, and would pretend that they were healthy, stay on their feet in the workshops, and do their jobs as usual. The desire to live and overcome all obstacles was so strong that some among the dangerously ill managed to recover and return to full strength, at least ostensibly.

## New Actions in the Ghetto

On November 18, 1942, the Germans conducted a new registration in the ghetto. This time, every worker in military installations received a metal plate inscribed with the letter "W" (for *Wehrmacht,* army) or "R" (for *Rüstungsindustrie,* munitions industry). About 12,000 men and women received the new insignia during the registration, which also provided the Germans with an opportunity for "purging" about 5,000 "nonessential" persons, who were sent directly to their death.

The survivors were divided into two categories: (1) Holders of the metal tags with the letters "W" or "R" were billeted in the ghetto's "better" houses which were converted into barracks; on each barracks was designated the specific detachment residing there, and the plant in which its occupants worked. (2) Those without metal tags were, from that time on, considered superfluous, and were persecuted. The shanties and clay huts were assigned as their dwelling quarters, and their very existence was tantamount to illegal. Many of them were killed each time the Germans conducted searches in the ghetto. The largest such action was on January 5, 6, and 7, 1943, when about 15,000 persons were murdered, among them many officials of the Judenrat. Prior to the action, all officials of the Jewish Council were ordered to gather together in the Judenrat building. When they had assembled, the Germans burst in, removed the officials, and sent them off to Bełżec or to the Janowski camp. A short time later (apparently February 4), the Germans ordered the members of the Judenrat (there were still about twelve) to report for a meeting. Several of those who appeared were murdered, among them Eberson (the head of the Judenrat) and his associates Marceli Buber, Oswald Kimmelman, and Jacob Chigier. Others were sent to the Janowski camp, among them Szymon Ulam, who was later transferred to Dachau, where he perished. Most of those who managed to go into hiding were subsequently caught and killed by the Germans. Two members of the Council who hid out in Aryan neighbor-hoods, Dr. Schertzer and Leib Landau, were apparently betrayed by their Aryan neighbors. They were found in their places of hiding by the Germans, who brought them to the Jewish jail in the ghetto and from there led them to execution. One Council member, the physician Ginsberg, escaped from the Germans, and for some time went about disguised as a gentile, on forged Aryan papers. Later he hid in the cellars and ruins of the ghetto, after it was emptied of Jewish residents as a result of the un-ceasing actions.

Hundreds of men and women went into hiding in the ghetto ruins—persons whose extermination had been ordered by the Germans: the un-employed, the elderly, children, orphans. They were in perpetual danger, as the ruins were abandoned and exposed. Nevertheless, they were treated to periodic visits by the Ukrainian police and common thugs and extortion-ists, who searched out Jews in hiding for any valuables that might remain with them, and for information about the vast treasures allegedly buried (according to popular rumor) by other Jews before their death. When the searchers found "rats"—that is, Jews hidding in the ruins—they threatened to expose them, and extorted hush money and the remnants of their property. On many occasions, the fugitives were betrayed to the Gestapo even after the bribery. Ginsberg, in desperation, took his own life, and we can assume that there were many other cases of suicide among these hunted individuals.

In the actions implemented in the ghetto in the winter of 1942–1943, the Germans adopted new military tactics. In order to prevent the Jews from fleeing the transports en route to the death camps—a regular occur-rence in previous actions—they now stripped all prisoners (men, women, and children) of their clothing and transported them naked to the place of execution. Occasionally, the wagons and box cars were open, though it was in the depth of winter. A picked guard, consisting of German and Ukrain-ian police with rifles and machine guns and aided by bloodhounds, was placed over the transports. The closed cars were double-locked; the open cars were surrounded and packed with barbed wire. Jews were not per-mitted to get out at the stations, even to perform their bodily functions.

But despite all the security measures, many persons escaped. Some broke windows, others cut holes in the floor, and jumped from the moving transport. Many were killed in their fall, or were shot on the spot, or fell victim to attacking dogs. Many died of cold and starvation after they roamed naked through the fields and forests. Many of the escapees fell into the hands of the Gestapo agents. Few managed to obtain food and clothing from merciful peasants, who were rare. The "leapers" (*shpringers*), as they were called, achieved notoriety in the Jewish community. Some had been through the experience three or four times, and were singled out as "extraordinary" persons. Generally, the *shpringers* could no longer be considered members of the community. Not many were able to return to Lwów. They had no work permits, no place to live, no clothes, no private property whatsoever. They would generally camp out in the Judenrat building or in the streets until a new search or action, when they were again sent to the death transports. The police would pack into the ghetto prison those destined for the transports, until the quota for a shipment was filled. The prison was first located at 25 Wierzbickiego Street in the Kleparów suburb, but after that suburb had been partially liquidated the prison was transferred to 15 Weyssenhofa Street. It was customary to "clear out" the prison once a week and transfer the prisoners either to the liquidation site located in the "Sands" (*na Piaski*) near the Janowska Street cemetery or to the Lesienice forest. The expression "He was sent to the Sands" was used to signify an execution.

## The Ghetto Is Transformed into a Julag

At the start of 1943, far-reaching changes in the management of the ghetto took place, on the basis of a decree of Heinrich Himmler, Reichsführer-SS and chief of the German police. The Germans wanted to transform all remaining ghettos into work camps; the pertinent "order" was given to the German command in Warsaw in the spring of 1943, to Lodz (Litzmannstadt) in September 1943, and so on. In Lwów, the change ensued subsequent to the action of January 1943. Instead of a "ghetto," the Jewish quarter was henceforth designated as a "Jewish camp"—a *Judenlager,* or Julag. Norms of life in the Julag were different from those in the ghetto. The Germans instituted strict military discipline. A large portion of the old ghetto was liquidated, and all Jews working there were transferred to barracks. Some parts, including Żródlana Street and the Kleparów suburb, were removed completely from the area of the ghetto. The Judenrat was totally liquidated (the last head of the council, Feil, was left without any influence in Jewish communal life), and no other central communal institution took its place. The Germans would appoint "Jewish elders" over each labor detachment—but of course the post had no prerogatives. Jewish workers were forbidden individual exit from the ghetto, and could go out only in groups during fixed hours, to their place of work. The nonworkers —including parents, wives, and children of the workers—were considered superfluous. The Germans conducted frequent searches to apprehend these "illegal" Jews—and succeeded in reducing the number of Julag inhabitants to 12,000 "legal" workers. Just a few thousand "illegals" remained alive after all the actions, until the liquidation of the ghetto.

An SS-appointed commandant was placed in charge of the Julag: first, SS officer Mansfeld (his assistant was Siller); afterward, SS-Hauptsturmführer Josef Grzymek (his adjutant was Hainisch). Grzymek, who assumed office in February 1943, was the cruelest of all. Even prior to his arrival in Lwów he had "excelled" as the commandant of the Jaktorów concentration camp for Jews (in Eastern Galicia). He liquidated the camp after he had exterminated all the Jewish inmates. After that he organized the ghetto in Rawa Ruska—in his words, a "model" ghetto because of the iron discipline and brutal regime there—which was also liquidated by him. Grzymek tormented and tortured the Jews of the Lwów Julag, and made excessive demands in the realms of discipline and cleanliness—all of which bordered on insanity.

"Grzymek set about to purify the ghetto"—related one of the Julag residents. The ghetto streets were litter-strewn. The houses were, even before Jews moved in, decrepit and grimy. There were piles of trash in every courtyard and cranny, and the houses themselves were in ruins. However, Grzymek would not suppress his obsession. He put up twenty-four semicircular signs with the slogan "There must be order" (*Ordnung must sein*), as well as plaques with this injunction: "If your house is clean, you will be a healthy person."

He especially persecuted the "sanitation workers"—Jewish women charged with responsibility for cleanliness in the ghetto. He began to inspect their activity daily. He cruelly beat them for any slight disorder, and he ordered that his plaques be hung in all barracks and all houses. With white gloves he would inspect the dust in every nook and cranny, and he would torture to death janitors who could not fix a broken piece of plumbing or a stuffed-up sewer. When he would catch a negligent janitor, would give him twenty-five lashes with a whip which he always carried.[18]

Every morning Grzymek would pass in a horse-drawn carriage through the entire ghetto, for a first inspection. The carriage would move very fast, and a group of Jewish police would run behind it, in accordance with his command. He would cast a critical eye on the streets and houses, and if he saw a trace of filth on one of the window sills, he would immediately smash the window to bits. He would enter the houses for inspection, and if something did not please him, he would make a mess of the place, shattering all the furniture and crockery, and tossing out food. If he caught "illegals" roaming through the house or Jewish workers absent from work for one reason or another (whether sickness or a day off) he ordered the police to imprison them. In this way, he caused the death of hundreds of Jews. Additionally, Grzymek carried out large actions as well. In one such action, on March 17, 1943, 1,500 people were killed. In another action, 800 people were sent to Auschwitz.

Grzymek organized a Jewish orchestra, which was ordered to play daily by the gate of the Julag when the work detachments went into the city. By German command, the orchestra played dance music, marches such as the well-known Radetzky march, and works by Mozart and Beethoven (a German soldier, Alfred Greiner, relates that he heard this orchestra play Beethoven's Third Symphony in the ghetto courtyard).

Grzymek was the commandant of the Lwów Julag until its liquidation. Afterward, he was sent to command the Szebnie camp near Jasło in Western Galicia. He was infamous there, too, for his cruelty and sadism. After the war, he was captured and placed on public trial in Warsaw, in April 1949; the court found him guilty and executed him.

## Statistics on the Casualties

The changes in the total Jewish population of Lwów serve as a horrifying indicator of the pace of the Germans' extermination program. The numbers cited here were provided to me immediately upon the liberation of Lwów by Dr. Weiser (head of the food ration card office in the Lwów Judenrat), from notes that remained in his possession. These figures only approximate reality, for a variety of reasons. On one hand, the total population may have been less than that listed in the office file, as many families, in order to have additional ration cards, did not notify the authorities of deaths among them. There were also many families who believed that members who had been taken for "work" or to a camp would still return, and therefore did not remove them from the records. On the other hand, a large number of "illegal" Jews were not recorded. "Criminal refugees," political activists, and other ordinary Jews preferred to waive their paltry food allotment rather than have their names listed in a file open to the Germans. Those who prepared to go into hiding or disguise themselves as gentiles with forged Aryan papers likewise were not recorded. Indeed it is hard to know what number should be added to the total on file and what number should be deducted. Probably the differences balanced themselves out, so that the numbers listed do approximate the truth. These are the numbers as they were provided:

In June 1941, 150,000 to 160,000 Jews were in Lwów, according to the estimates of the community and of General Katzmann (see above). In subsequent months, the number registered in the ration card office were as follows:

| Date | Number of Jews (in thousands) | Date | Number of Jews (in thousands) |
|------|-------------------------------|------|-------------------------------|
| *1941* | | *1942* | |
| October | 119 | May | 84 |
| November | 109 | June | 82 |
| December | 106 | July | 82 |
| *1942* | | August | 76 |
| January | 103 | September | 36 |
| February | 97 | October | 33 |
| March | 96 | November | 29 |
| April | 86 | December | 24 |

There are no official data beyond December 1942. The Judenrat was liquidated the following month.

## Cultural Life in the Ghetto

It is impossible to draw a complete picture of the cultural life in the Lwów ghetto, because cultural activities were conducted secretly, in closed circles, for fear of punishment and imprisonment by the Germans. As noted above, even participation in the private prayer quorum was, in the eyes of the Germans, a grave transgression, subject to the death penalty.

In the cities of Vilna and Lodz, and to some extent Częstochowa, Będzin, Cracow, and Sosnowiec, Jewish cultural life was allowed to develop; there were Jewish schools, synagogues, and houses of study. It was also possible to hold lectures and concerts, establish a theater and sports organizations for youth, and even publish periodicals (such as the *Vilner Geto Yediyes* [Vilna Ghetto News]; *Litsmanshtetishe Geto-Tsaytung* [Lodz]; *Gazeta Żydowska* [Cracow]). All forms of public cultural activity were denied the Jews of Lwów, however. Immediately upon the arrival of the Germans, the Jewish communal activists called for a meeting of representatives of all parties and factions to consult with them regarding the establishment of a school. The meeting took place in the summer of 1941. The participants, about twenty persons, weighed the questions of education and culture, and a department of educational affairs was established in the

Judenrat. Because of the strict prohibition by the Germans, however, not a single school was opened. All efforts to obtain a permit for any sort of cultural activity—lectures, courses, theatrical performances—were futile. No other major Jewish community met with such a restrictive attitude on the part of the Germans. The division for education and culture of the Judenrat ceased its activity after a few months of deliberation and futile intercession. Indeed, not a single organized, public, cultural, or religious activity took place. Only in secret would worshipers gather; children were taught in private houses; a few authors convened for meetings; and representatives of parties and youth groups met to hold discussions.

A number of literary gatherings, not at all public in character, took place in the offices of the Judenrat, at the initiative of Henryk Graf, a lawyer who worked in one of the council's offices. To avoid arousing suspicion, the gatherings were conducted each time at a different locale (this was during the first months of the German conquest, when the offices of the community were spread throughout the city). Generally, Abraham Brat, a member of the editorial board of *Chwila* (a Polish-Jewish daily) before the war, opened the meeting with a topical speech. Afterward, the actress Hoffman would read a few chapters from the Bible. Occasionally, the poet Maurycy (Moshe) Szymel recited some of his sorrowful lyric poems. After the literary portion, a sort of "live newspaper" was offered, with satire about the Judenrat and the like (usually written by J. Berman and the young refugee authors from Cracow, Elisha Weintraub, Kornreich, and Maximilian Boruchowicz). After a while a short notice on the literary gatherings was published in the journal *Gazeta Żydowska* in Cracow. Fearing persecution, the persons conducting the gatherings canceled them (apparently, their fears were unfounded, because the Germans paid no attention to the matter).

Only in one realm, music, did the Germans permit—or to be exact, compel—the Jews to conduct a public cultural activity. Lwów was rich in Jewish performers and singers, some quite famous in their art. The Germans and the anti-Semitic Poles utilized this for their propaganda. In the daily *Gazeta Lwowska* a satirical song appeared about the Jewish musicians in Lwów and the names of over forty artists were noted. The Germans organized two orchestras from among the Jewish musicians—one in the Julag and the other in the Janowski camp. The musicians were forced to perform against their will at very tragic moments, during the terrible roll-calls and the "selections" at the ghetto gate and in the camp.

To summarize what is known to us about the cultural life of the ghetto confirms that it did not emerge from a normal development but from a bitter struggle and from the destruction of Jewish culture and its creators. We have succeeded in gathering some information on the fate of the cultural leaders during the Holocaust, their actions and death, and we will hereby provide this information, albeit abridged, for posterity.

There were many Jewish writers in Lwów, writing in Yiddish, Hebrew, or Polish during the Russian occupation. These Jews constituted a specific Jewish division of the general writers' guild of Lwów. The Yiddish writer David Königsberg headed the division (he had translated the poem "Pan Tadeusz" by Adam Mickiewicz, into Yiddish). The secretary was the young Yiddish poet Yaakov (Yankel) Szudrich. A small number of the Yiddish writers managed to escape from Lwów and reached Russia prior to the arrival of the Germans. Those remaining in Lwów were almost totally exterminated by the Nazis. David Königsberg was sent to the Janowski camp, where he died. The Yiddish writer Yerachmiel (Miltche) Grin, the author of *Di verter fun Kolomei* (Notes from Kołomyja), who labored as a porter in one of the divisions (nutrition or transport) of the Judenrat, also was sent to the Janowski camp, and continued his literary work there. He wrote a novel on the life of the camp, portions of which he read to his friends when the opportunity presented itself. The work was lost when he died. His wife, the poet Helena Grin, was also killed in the Janowski camp. She was the author of the doleful prisoner's song (in Yiddish) that opens with the words: "We sit at the foot of the Sandhill and drink *l'chaim* with Death," which quickly became a sort of hymn for the camp's inmates. Yankel Szudrich wrote songs about the Baal Shem Tov and the Ukrainian bandit Dobosz (according to popular legend, there was a friendship between the sainted founder of Hasidism and Dobosz) and apparently other songs. In one letter that survives, Szudrich described his feelings and his work (the year was 1942):

I am leaving these poems unpolished, in a raw state, without improvement or any embellishment. I see that the extermination of my people is an accomplished fact. So let these songs remain at least as a testimony that I lived and I created even at a time when the sword was hanging over my neck. . . . All the time I dreamed of at least fighting shoulder to shoulder with the partisans somewhere in the forests—even though there was never a rifle stock in my hand. I would have wished to learn this skill. I would have done the most dangerous things. Unfortunately, I have not been lucky.

In 1943, Szudrich finally saw the partial fulfillment of his dream. He was one of a group of youths who organized an attempt to break out of the ghetto and link up with the partisans. They entered into negotiation with some gentiles, who promised to bring them to the forest in a wagon. Apparently this was a trap planned by the Gestapo, and the youths fell into it. The vehicle was surrounded by armed police, and all its passengers were killed.

Other writers disappeared, and their deaths are concealed from us: Maurycy Szymel, Sanie Friedman (who was in the Janowski camp), Debora Vogel-Barenblüt (who wrote Polish songs and philosophical essays), Berl Schnapper, Daniel Ihr, Esther Schuldenrein (a young graduate student of YIVO), and others. It is said that Yisrael Weinlös was caught during the action directed against old people (at the end of 1941), and was led to his death.

Not everyone who escaped before the entry of the Germans, saved his life thereby. The talented poet and publicist Shmuel Yaakov Imber was forced to leave Lwów during the days of the Russians, because his poetry was denounced as "controversial" from a Marxist-Leninist viewpoint. He settled in the little town of Jezierna with his in-laws, and from there moved to the city of Złoczów, to the home of his brother-in-law Hertznik (director of the Jewish hospital), where he continued his literary work. He was returning from reading his poems to a group of infirmary workers and patients, when he was caught, during the action of November 3, 1942, and sent to Bełżec. His wife and friends preserved his literary legacy until they too were killed. The last writings of Imber were lost with them.[19]

The famous Yiddish writer Alter Kacizne, who came to Lwów as a refugee in 1940 and settled there, died a tragic, tortured death. During the Soviet period he was a spokesman for the Jewish writers, and was appointed literary director of Radio Lwów's Yiddish-language broadcast. An opera which he composed, *Die Judens-Opera,* was accepted for performance by the State Theater of Kiev. At the outbreak of Soviet-German hostilities, Kacizne fled from Lwów, but when he reached the vicinity of Tarnopol, Ukrainians fell upon him, tortured him gruesomely, and killed him.[20]

Many of the Hebrew writers also perished. Among them were Moshe Feld, a writer and teacher (in the Jewish Gymnasium at 17 Zygmuntowska Street); and Moshe Waldman Goliger, researcher in Semitics, lecturer at the Institute of Jewish Studies in Warsaw. Goliger, who later was active in the office of the Jewish Self-Help, and aided Jewish authors and scholars, disappeared at the end of 1942. Apparently he was captured in the action of 1942. Israel Ostersetzer, lecturer on the Talmud at the Institute of Jewish Studies in Warsaw, and a famous scholar, was taken during the first days of the German entry, in July 1941, and never returned.

There was a large group of Jewish authors writing in Polish in Lwów. Incarcerated in the Janowski camp were the poet and literary critic Karol Drezdner, the poet Alexander Dan, and the satirist Zygmunt Schorr. Schorr continued his literary work, writing notes on camp life, but Dan and Drezdner were overcome by depression. The following writers vanished without a trace: Halina Górska; Rafael Lan (his real name was Lichtenstein; he was the son of the Bundist activist Israel Lichtenstein of Lodz), who became famous as a writer of radical-socialist novels; the critics Mojzesz Kanfer and Chaim Lew, both from Cracow; and Ludwik Roth, who was, as stated earlier, murdered by the Germans on September 1, 1942.

Many Jewish scholars and scientists were also among the Jewish victims in Lwów—in particular, Jakób Schall, the Jewish Polish historian and teacher in the Jewish Gymnasium, who was arrested in the action of August 1942. Until the last moment, Schall gathered historical data on the catastrophe of Lwów Jewry. His notes, hidden away by him, were all lost at his death. During the occupation, Schall was also preparing a historical survey on the origins of the Karaites in Poland at the request of Leib Landau (head of the Jewish Self-Help), who was ordered to provide the German authorities with historical material regarding the Karaites and their racial origins. (See above, essay 7.) In this group were also the before-mentioned Israel Ostersetzer and Mojżesz Goliger, lecturers at the Institute of Jewish Studies in Warsaw; and Falik Hafner, a young historian who was a student of Meir Bałaban. Hafner was in charge of a food distribution store for the Jewish community and used his office, with the consent of the economic section of the Judenrat, to organize secret assistance for Jewish writers and scholars, and was truly devoted to his work. During the action of August 1942, he hid in a bunker that was discovered by the Germans; while attempting to flee from the ranks of the arrested, who were being led to their doom, he was shot and killed by the Germans. S. Czortkower, a noted Jewish anthropologist, was killed in the action in the end of August 1942. Jakób Willer, a linguist and researcher in the Yiddish language, died of starvation in the Zniesienie outskirts. Isachar Madfes, author of a history of Zionism in Polish and Yiddish, was seized in the streets one night, shortly after the eight o'clock curfew (in 1942). The following notables vanished without a trace: the literary critic and Hebrew philologist Ozjasz Tilleman, teacher in the Jewish Gymnasium; the Jewish librarian Jehuda Kohn; the art collector Maksymilian Goldstein; and the Orientalist Leon Gutman.

Aside from the Jewish educators and teachers enumerated among the authors and scholars, one should mention as well Isachar Reiss, founder of the Hashomer Hatzair movement in Vienna and pre-World War I Galicia, and director of the Hebrew high school Tarbuth in Równe, who died at the end of 1942 (or at the beginning of 1943) during an outbreak of typhus in the ghetto; Barlas, director of a Hebrew school in Zbaraż and later a Hebrew teacher in the Lodz high school, who also died of typhus; Abraham Roth, director of the Jewish commercial high school in Lwów, later head of the education section of the ghetto, who perished in one of the actions during 1943; and Cecylja Klaften, noted pedagogue, founder, and director of a professional school for girls, who was seized during one of the actions and sent to the death camp at Bełżec (at the end of 1942 or the start of

1943). Nothing is known about the fate of Siwek, the teacher of Hebrew and author of textbooks; or about Szlomo Igiel, a psychologist, director of the Jewish Gymnasium; or about Zgymund Sens-Taubes, a teacher of religious studies. They all disappeared.

The number of Jewish journalists among the victims of the Nazis is large: Henryk Hescheles, editor of *Chwila,* was one of the first victims in the Brygidki massacres. Disappearing without trace were the editors Abraham Brat (*Chwila*), Zygmunt Reich, Szulim Rettig, and Joel Spiegel, director of the ITA Bureau in Lwów; Naftali Hauser, administrative director of *Opinja;* Adolf Kruman and Morus Sobel, active members of the Poalei Zion party, died in Lwów in the massacre of St. Anne's Street. Benzion Ginsberg and David Frenkel were in the Janowski camp. Both were active in the organization of Jewish inmates there—Ginsberg, in secret literary activities; and Frenkel, in the underground and resistance movement. The fate of the following has likewise remained unknown: Henryka Fromowicz-Stiller, Stanisław Saltzmann, Henryk Passierman, Itzchak Dam, Emil Igiel, Dreikurs, Jakób Istener, Maximilian Schönfeld, Moshe Rabinowicz, the Yiddish writer Fischel Witkower, Roller, Józef Markus, Jakob Bodek, and Dawid Schreiber (both Bodek and Schreiber had been members of the Polish Senate).

Among the scholars killed were the noted legal authority Maurycy Allerhand; the mathematicians Szymon Auerbach and the lecturer Sternbach, of the University of Lwów; the lecturers in physics Fuchs and Griffel (killed in the Janowski camp); the psychologist Leopold Blaustein; the philosopher Stefan Rudniański; the classical scholars Marian Auerbach, Jakób Handel, and Miss Schulbaum; the Romance linguist Helena Schlusser; the Germanists Izydor Berman, Arnold Spät, and Herman Sternbach, all of whom wrote on Jewish affairs and German culture and literature; the scholar of Polish Wilhelm Barbasz; Henryk Balk, lecturer at the University of Lwów, who was researching the origins of Polish literature (he committed suicide upon the entry of the Germans into Lwów).

Little is known to us of the fate of the rabbis and religious officials who were martyred in Lwów. Among those who perished were Aaron Lewin, the noted rabbi and leader of Agudath Israel in Poland, and deputy to the Polish Sejm; his brother, Yechezkel Lewin; Rabbis Yisrael Leib Wolfsberg, Moses Elchanan Alter, Natan Leiter, Szmulka Rapaport, and Kalman Chameides, the Hasidic leader, and Avraham Yaakov Friedman of Bojanów, a Turkish citizen, who was arrested by the Gestapo during one of the actions.[21]

Losses were heavy among Jews in the field of art and music. Among the musicians who fell were the conductors Alfred Stadler, Marceli Horowitz, and Jakób Mund (killed in the Janowski camp); the composers Leonid Striks (Janowski camp), Maks Striks, Józef Frenkel, Skolka, and

Wilhelm Kristal; the cellist Leon Eber; and Leon Zak, Schatz (Janowski camp), Józef Herman (Janowski camp), Edward Steinberg (Janowski camp), Hildebrand, Breyer, Aron Dobszyc, Priwes (committed suicide); the professors of the Lwów conservatory of music, Lepold Münzer, the famous pianist Mark Bauer, and Artur Hermelin; the piano prodigy Pollak; the Lwów Opera singers Feller, Fiszer, Szrage, and Buxbaum. From the ranks of Jewish artists perished Arno Erb, Marcin Kicz, Henryk Langerman, Julia Acker, Gabriela Frenkel, Aleksander Rimmer (died in Paris), the caricaturist Fryc Kleinman (killed in the Janowski camp), and the graphic artist Menkes.

During the Soviet occupation a state Jewish theater existed, directed by Ida Kaminska. Most of the actors and directors of the theater managed to escape from Lwów before the Germans arrived. Those who remained in the city perished: the director Mark Katz, the actor Rot and his wife Sonia Altman, and others. Among the Nazi victims were Jewish actors from the Polish theater in Lwów: Roman Grodniewski, Helena Flusner, and the administrative director, Maurycy Axer.

It is my duty as well to mention those Jewish physicians and lawyers who became well known in their profession through their public activity. Prior to the arrival of the Germans, there were a few hundred Jewish physicians in Lwów. According to the statistics prepared by an anti-Semitic Polish paper,[22] there were about 662 Jewish physicians in Lwów before the war—in addition to dentists, who numbered at least 200. In 1939–1940, refugees from Germany, Austria, and western Poland increased the total to at least 1,000 Jewish doctors in Lwów. Only a few tens of them were saved—the ones who fled as military physicians with the Russian armies, those who managed to hide, the few who emerged alive from the camps. Space is insufficient to record the names of all but the most prominent of them: the gynecologist Adolf Beck; the dentist Henryk Allerhand; the veterinarian Adolf Gizelt; the surgeon Stanisław Ruf (slain with a group of other professors of Lwów University); Marek Gimpel, Maximilian Jurim and his wife Blanka (a pediatrician)—all three committed suicide; the internist Schnitzer, the ophthalmologists Wiktor Reiss, Oswald Zion, Oksner (according to rumors, he committed suicide); Eugeniusz Wolner, M. Bickeles, Adolf Rosmarin, and Mendel Brill.

In 1934, there were 265 Jewish lawyers in Lwów, in addition to a large number of "applicants" (those who had graduated from the university's law school and were waiting for licenses to open law offices). Only a few of them remained alive after the Holocaust. Among those who perished were Leib Landau, E. Schertzer, Henryk Landesberg, M. Achser (the Jewish activist), Max Schaff, Anzelm Lutwak, Leon Chotiner, Henryk Graf, and Lauterstein.

## *Attempts at Resistance and Revolt*

After the actions carried out in Lwów in 1942 and the reports arriving from other cities, especially Warsaw, it became clear to everyone that the Germans were planning to exterminate all the Jews of Poland. The first attempts to organize a resistance movement among the Jews arose then. But the difficulties were very great. Many of the Jewish party and youth leaders were gone. Some had fled to Soviet Russia; some had been killed by the Germans. The Polish underground in Lwów was particularly weak, because the city had a mixed population of Poles and Ukrainians. A tremendous migration from the villages and outlying towns during the Soviet occupation had increased the Ukrainian population. The Ukrainians remembered full well the persecutions and oppressions under Polish rule prior to 1939, and the German strategy of divide and rule had succeeded in intensifying their hatred of the Poles. Also, the parties of the right, which had decisively rejected any cooperation with the Jews, maintained a decisive majority in the Lwów underground. Hence the Jews could negotiate with Polish underground groups only from the democratic or leftist camps, whose strength in Eastern Galicia was very small. The Ukrainian underground organized partisan groups in Eastern Galicia, but most of them were followers of Stefan Bandera and fought against Germans, Poles, and Jews simultaneously. During the years 1942–1943, the extreme nationalists of the Bandera camp (Banderovtsi) liquidated the other partisan Ukrainians who were liberal or more democratic (for example, the Bulba group in Volhynia). From that time on, the forests of Volhynia and Galicia were under their control.

These unfavorable circumstances did not allow either the formation of a centralized Jewish resistance movement or a mass exodus to the forest. There were only isolated attempts at underground activity in small groups and in the main Jewish youth organizations. At the close of 1942, a group of young officials of the Judenrat (most of them members of the Zionist youth organizations) organized clandestine military training courses in one of the cellars under the Judenrat's offices, but these courses did not result in the creation of a military detachment. There were also attempts to flee to the forest, but the young people who fled could not find partisan groups to link up with. In many cases, Ukrainian peasants turned them over to the Germans. Bandera's partisans killed any Jews who crossed their path. One survivor of the Janowski camp tells about such a meeting:

I fled from the Janowski camp to the forest. There I met a group of thirty-four refugees, who had also escaped from the camp. The Banderovtsi pursued us. We heard that there had been about eighty Jews in one forest. The Banderovtsi surrounded the woods, blockaded the Jews, and slaughtered all of them. After that they cut up their bodies, hung the limbs of flesh on the trees, and attached notes to them: "This is Jewish meat."[23]

Sometimes, escaping Jews were caught and killed even before they could get out of the city. This occurred with a group which included the poet Jankiel Szudrich. In his report of June 30, 1943, to Krüger, General Katzmann mentions other attempts that also ended in failure.

Most of the Jewish youth who attempted to flee to the forest were armed. Generally they purchased arms—pistols and rifles (the average price for a pistol was 2,000 zlotys)—from Italian or Hungarian soldiers, who were their principal accomplices in organizing escape. Katzmann records that a group of twenty to thirty armed Jewish youth who escaped from the Janowski camp attempted to reach the vicinity of the city of Brody in order to link up with a group of Jewish partisans active in the forest. They approached two German drivers and offered them 20,000 zlotys for a ride from Lwów to Brody. The drivers agreed but then betrayed them to the German police. All the Jews were murdered (May 15, 1943). On May 21, 1943, Katzmann relates, the Germans again liquidated a Jewish group armed with Italian weapons. Katzmann points out that "in proportion to the decrease in the number of Jews in the district [Galicia], the spirit of revolt within them grew." The Jews used all sorts of arms. Despite the bitter end to many attempts, Jewish youths, as individuals or in organized groups, succeeded several times in escaping to the forests, and remained there until the downfall of Germany. A small group (led by the physician Boris Pliskin) even managed to penetrate the Carpathian Mountains. According to one testimony, a group of youths organized by Goldberg, an officer of the Jewish police in Lwów, linked up with one of the partisan bands in the city's vicinity. After the ghetto in Lwów was decreed a Julag, Goldberg was dispatched by the partisan command to organize the resistance movement there, but was caught and killed by the Germans.

The Jewish underground in Lwów put out a typewritten, illegal newspaper in a very limited number of copies. Six issues were published in all. Abraham Wahrman ("Bronek"), a leader of Hashomer Haṭzair, who was the technical manager of the paper, smuggled a typewriter into the ghetto at the risk of his life. He managed to camouflage the machine, hoodwink the police at the ghetto gates, and bring it by horse-drawn cart to the residence of the "editorial board" (the editor was M. H. [Michał Hofman]). The paper provided political and military details secretly culled from radio broadcasts or copied from the press of the Polish underground, as well as local coverage of Lwów ghetto life and proclamations and editorials to

Lwów Jewry calling for courage, resistance, and rebellion. The realization that the Jewish community would pay in blood for any attempt at resistance was a major detriment to any preparations for revolt. The Germans adopted the practice of cruel collective punishment for each private act of resistance by Jews. We have already noted the massacre of September 1, 1942. A similar action occurred on March 16, 1943, in the SS camp at 56 Czwartaków Street. One of the Jewish workers (according to reports, it was construction engineer Kotnowski) killed an SS policeman (Keil, according to testimony) noted for his extreme cruelty. The next day, the Germans burst into the ghetto and hung eleven or twelve Jews from the balconies on Łokietka Street, including militia officers (the attorneys Mahler and Mandel), but were not satisfied with this. That same day, the commandant of the Julag, Grzymek, ordered a roll call, from which one thousand Jews were selected and sent to their deaths at the "Sands." According to one eyewitness:

> The orchestra played at the gate as usual. The detachments were marching out [for work into the city]. At the gate . . . the doctors were giving vaccines against typhus. Behind the gate stood Engels, Pugaszewski, and Wepke [Gestapo officers] and presided over the action. They haphazardly selected people from the detachments—some because they were blondes, or wearing glasses, or with another special characteristic—loaded them onto the van and brought them to the "Sands." Those marching to the gate did not notice anything. Here they played, there they inoculated, and a few steps away death seized them by the neck. Eleven hundred people were dragged away to their execution.[24]

At the same time, the SS men conducted a "retaliatory action" in the Janowski camp. Nearly two hundred persons were killed.

## Liquidation of the Ghetto

The bloody action of May 23, 1943, was a prelude to the liquidation of the Lwów ghetto. In order to understand the nature of that action, one has to describe the organization of Jewish labor. The Germans had divided all the surviving Jewish workers into two large labor centers: the Julag and the Janowski camp. The Jews in the camp were incarcerated; only a few "lucky" ones belonged to *Aussenbrigaden* (outside detachments), and went to work outside the camp each morning. Most of the workers in the Julag lived in barracks, and were organized into work detachments that departed to work outside the Julag in the morning and returned at night. The Germans now moved to transfer the outside detachments of the Julag to the camp. They first staged a terrible massacre in the Janowski camp to make place for the new detachments. Then an order was given for the Julag outside detachments to go straight to the Janowski camp after work and not to return to the Julag as usual. The detachments were incarcerated in the camp, and for a few days no one entered or left. The outside detachments from the camp proper were not dispatched to their work in the city either. During that time, the Germans conducted a systematic slaughter among the horde gathered in the Janowski camp, and thousands of lives were lost.

Then all those still remaining in the Julag—children, women, youth, workers from the inside detachments—grasped the fearsome intentions of the Nazis, and awaited in terror what lay in store for them. They camouflaged and secured hiding places; some Jews even obtained arms. In the words of General Katzmann (in his report of June 30, 1943, to his superior, Krüger):

The Jews tried every means to evade evacuation. They not only attempted to escape from the ghetto, but hid in every imaginable corner, in pipes, in chimneys, in sewers, and canals. They built tunnels under the hallways, underground; they widened cellars and turned them into passageways; they dug trenches underground, and cunningly created hiding places in lofts, woodsheds, attics, and inside furniture, etc.

In various parts of the ghetto, the Jews received the Germans with shots and grenades, and hurled Molotov cocktails at them. The Germans did not dare enter Jewish houses anymore on their patrol, but poured benzine on the houses and set them ablaze, thus forcing the Jews out. Men and women who resisted or attempted to flee were killed on the spot. The Germans murdered the children, often in the most cruel manner: they threw them alive into the fires or dashed the heads of babies against the walls and street lights. The Nazi youth (*Hitler-Jugend*) participated in this action, and they held shooting practice, using Jewish children as live targets. A large number of the men who were caught (nearly 7,000) were sent to the Janowski camp, where an additional selection was carried out. The weak were sent to the "Sands," the strong were assigned to the work detachments. But these detachments were exterminated not long after.

The liquidation of the Lwów ghetto was carried out with a cruelty that exceeded all precedents. Even Katzmann's report confirms this:

Extraordinary measures were needed at the time of liquidating the Lwów ghetto. Special bunkers and dugouts had been built. . . . We were compelled therefore to act brutally from the beginning in order to avoid sustaining greater casualties among our men. We had to blast and burn many houses. Upon this occasion an amazing thing came to light. Instead of the 12,000 legally registered Jews, we succeeded in capturing 20,000. We had to remove about 3,000 Jewish corpses from various hiding places. These were people who had committed suicide by poison.[25]

The last two actions were conducted by Katzmann, who had returned to Lwów (which he had left at the start of 1943), apparently from activities in the rural towns of Eastern Galicia, where he also headed extermination actions. While General Stroop was "busy" in Warsaw from April 17, 1943, on, Katzmann returned to Lwów in order to conclude the matters there. After the conclusion of his mission, Katzmann prepared the "final" report on the solution of the Jewish question in Galicia and presented it to the "Highest SS and Police Leader in the General Government, General Krüger or his adjutant in Cracow."[26] Regarding Katzmann himself, he disappeared after the war ended. There were rumors concerning his whereabouts but they were difficult to verify. Actually, he lived until 1957, and died in Darmstadt, Germany.[27]

## *Jews on the Aryan Side*

After the liquidation action, the ghetto area became a wasteland, its ruins inhabited only by bands of thieves, beggars, and other suspect persons. There remained an insignificant number of Jews in the city, who were legally quartered in small, isolated camps and in barracks of the military factories. A strict guard was placed over them. In addition, the Janowski camp still contained thousands of Jewish prisoners.

A few thousand Jews had managed to escape and had gone into hiding. Some were hidden in various "bunkers" and hiding places among gentile families, some lived in the Aryan neighborhoods on forged documents, under the guise of Poles, Ukrainians, Karaites, Moslems, and even Gypsies. A small number, among them many converts and assimilationists, had set themselves up as Aryans immediately upon the arrival of the Germans. But in 1942, a mass escape to the Aryan neighborhoods began. An entire enterprise for the forging of Aryan documents and Aryan identity cards, marriage certificates, birth certificates, registration cards, and work permits developed. There were originally genuine documents (of Aryans who had died in the war or had been seized by the Germans), and there were totally forged documents (dubbed *Lipa* in the lingo of the dealers). Persons passed to the Aryan side with extreme caution. As best they could, they tried to conceal their escape plan from all their acquaintances until the very last moment.

The slow infiltration to the Aryan neighborhoods was intensified during the spring months of 1942, and reached its peak after the action of August 1942. The number of Jews who went into hiding on the Aryan side or used forged Aryan documents, with the assistance of non-Jewish acquaintances, reached thousands during the years 1942–1943. The German secret police, which ceaselessly patroled the residences and the streets, discovered many of these Jews in the course of time, often as a result of betrayals. Gentiles who aided concealed Jews were condemned to death, and the special courts (*Sondergericht*) in the Lwów docket were filled with such cases. In the report from Cracow of October 7, 1943, the head of the SS and police in the GG wrote to the Reich Security Main Office Department VII in Berlin:

According to reports reaching us from the Galicia District, the number of cases immediately pending before the special court in Lwów, regarding people providing refuge for Jews, has in the last period increased greatly in number and in scope. The death penalty is the sole punishment under the law for this crime. In the present situation, the special courts, have had on occasion to carry out successive death penalties. Judicial circles more or less oppose this. The nature of their criticism is that the death penalty should be implemented by the secret police. Nevertheless, everyone agrees that the death penalty is entirely necessary, since under present conditions, the Jews in hiding have the legal status of pirates.[28]

It appears from this that many death sentences were carried out against gentiles who concealed Jews. In fact, at the time of the report, SS and Gestapo personnel did not always wait for a trial, but sometimes murdered both the "guilty" gentiles and the Jews they were hiding. Court-ordered executions, however, which took place amid great publicity, served the Germans to impose upon the gentiles a dread of offering Jews any assistance. Particularly infamous was the death sentence carried out against Józefek, who had concealed a few Jews in his house in the Kleparów suburb. This execution instilled fear in the gentiles, and greatly disheartened the Jews who still remained in hiding.

In such an atmosphere, concealment in the Aryan neighborhood was not a safe undertaking at all. Few gentiles concealed Jews for purely idealistic reasons—out of friendship, loyalty to former party members or coworkers, or simple humanitarianism or opposition to the Nazi regime. In most cases, gentiles hid Jews for material gain. Some Jews turned over all their remaining property—silver, gold, precious stones, clothing, paintings. Others were asked to make a monthly payment for the privilege of concealment; this was the prevailing custom. Generally, the Jews paid a substantial sum, at least 2,000 zlotys, as an entry fee. In addition, they had to pay a monthly "rent" of anywhere from 2,000 to 10,000 zlotys, depending on the place and the time. Not infrequently, the gentiles would throw the Jew out when his money ran out. There were even cases in which extortionists who found out about concealed Jews demanded huge sums or monthly payments as hush money.

Whereas Jews whose features betrayed their origin had no choice but to hide out among the gentiles, many Jews of "good appearance" (those who did not resemble Jews) tried to pass themselves off as gentiles on purchased Aryan papers, took up residence in Aryan neighborhoods, and found work as gentiles. Of course, to accomplish this—to find living quarters, register with the police, and obtain ration cards and other necessities—they required the assistance of non-Jewish acquaintances who shared their secret. The lives of these Jewish "Aryans" were filled with fear and perpetual danger. SS men, as well as civilian agents and spies, extortionists, even gentile children, roamed the streets in search of persons disguised as "Aryans." The hunters became so proficient that they could detect at a glance a Jew posing as an Aryan, if his actions or behavior departed slightly from the "norm." Any male suspect would be taken to a neighborhood courtyard and would be ordered to remove his pants to show whether he was circumcised. Jewish women, who could more easily evade detection on physical grounds, would be especially subjected to "ideological" examination on the fundamentals of Christianity, its customs and prayers. If these examinations proved of no avail, the suspects were brought to the Gestapo office, which resorted to other "more expeditious" methods of examination.

Tens of Jews in hiding or posing as Aryans were caught daily. Those who were not murdered immediately upon being discovered were brought to the Janowski camp, to a "death cell," and from there were taken to be executed.

Many of those with Aryan papers thought that they would be safer in another city, where the risk of being betrayed by acquaintances would be diminished. Many moved to Warsaw or Cracow. Many others were apprehended on the way during the numerous inspections conducted by the secret police in railway stations and on trains. Among those who reached Warsaw, some were subsequently caught, and some were killed during the Polish uprising of 1944. Only a few survived.

## Establishment of the Janowski Camp

There were three principal extermination areas for Lwów: First, the citadel in the center of the city, between Kopernika and St. Lazar streets; thousands of Russian prisoners of war were murdered there. Second, the forest of Lesienice, a village outside Lwów, on the road to Tarnopol, east of the Łyczaków outskirts; there 140,000 to 200,000 persons were murdered, including Jews. Third, the "Valley of Death" or the "Sands"—a vale between the hills northwest of Lwów, at the foot of Kortumowa Mountain and about half a kilometer from both the Janowski camp and the Catholic and Jewish cemeteries; according to an official Soviet report,[29] over 200,000 Soviet citizens, almost all of them Jews, were killed in the valley of death near the Janowski camp.

One of the principal roads leading northwest from Lwów was Janowska Street (the Germans changed the name to Weststrasse), so named because it led to the city of Janów. At 132–134 Janowska Street was a factory for manufacturing grinding machines, owned by a Jewish firm, Steinhaus and Company (Towarzystwo Budowy Maszyn [T.B.M.]). During the Soviet regime, the factory had been nationalized and annexed to the construction division of the Ministry of Transport and Communication (as construction plant no. 56). At the time of the German occupation, the factory first passed under control of the municipal government, and then, a few weeks later, to supervision of the SS in Lwów. SS-Oberscharführer Wolfgang von Mohrwinkel was appointed factory manager, but was soon succeeded by SS-Hauptscharführer Fritz Gebauer, a young man of about thirty from Berlin, who had been an employee in the industrial firm Siemens and Schuckert of Berlin—Gebauer was pleasant in appearance and could pass for a genial and cultivated person both in speech and manners. The factory on Janowska Street began supplying the needs of the SS and the German army.

The Jews considered a work card for the Janowska factory very valuable—who would dare to seize or brutalize a Jew carrying a work certificate from the SS itself? Hence many sought to find employment in the Janowska plant. In addition to Jewish workers sent there by the labor office, Polish "criminals" were sent there; in September 1941, there were 580 Jews and 320 Poles. At the close of September 1941, the entire factory area was surrounded by barbed wire, and bunks were erected, but the workers were still permitted to return home after work. A basic turnabout took place in October 1941, when Gebauer assembled all the Jewish workers and informed them: "As of today you'll remain here." From that day on, the factory was turned into a forced labor camp, called by the people the Janowski camp. Along the barbed-wire fence a few watchtowers were set up, manned by SS personnel armed with automatic rifles. The SS officers Schlippe, Stellwerk, and Soernitz headed this guard. Soernitz was habitually accompanied by his dog, Aza, who was trained to attack and tear men apart at his command.

From that time on, all contact between the Jewish workers with the outside world was cut off. The camp was divided into two parts. In the principal area were the barracks of the workers, the offices, the SS apartments, and also the "transit camp" (*Durchgangslager,* Dulag) for those to be sent to Bełżec. A new supervisor was appointed for this area, SS-Untersturmführer Gustav Willhaus, a young man, printer by trade, born in Saarbrücken. According to one witness, Willhaus assumed his post on March 2, 1942. A short while later (apparently on April 1, 1942), SS-Untersturmführer Richard Rokita, forty years old, who had been a violinist before the war and leader of a jazz band in a city in western Poland (apparently Katowice), was assigned as Willhaus's first assistant. Willhaus's second assistant was SS-Scharführer Adolf Kolanko, about thirty years old, a plasterer, born in Raciborz in Silesia. In the second part of the camp were the factories and workshops, now considerably extended and developed. They remained under the supervision of Fritz Gebauer, and were called the *Deutsche Ausrüstungswerke,* or D.A.W. (German workshops for armament equipment). Workers from the principal part of the camp were employed here, but competition and hatred between the two commandants prevented any cooperation and coordination between the two areas. Irena Szajowicz, a Jew employed in the office of the camp, wrote in her diary: "There were always arguments between Willhaus and Gebauer. Willhaus would issue an order, and Gebauer—to infuriate him—would cancel it." Only harm derived from these disputes and quarrels between the two "iron men." In the end, after a big brawl, matters approached a severance of relations between the two rulers. Willhaus even set up a separate office, independent from the D.A.W., for the area under his authority.[30]

## Hangmen of the Janowski Camp

In one respect, Willhaus and Gebauer were in total accord—their sadistic attitude toward their Jewish prisoners. Their wanton cruelty and brutality toward the Jews served as an example for other German officers in the camp. Much has been written of these atrocities by Janowski camp survivors. Rokita, Willhaus's adjutant, excelled in a more "refined" and deliberate cruelty. He was a "gourmet" who took delight in inventing "delectable" tortures for his victims—tortures both physical and mental. One camp survivor recalls that Rokita would kill tens of prisoners during roll call or during a visit to the bathhouse. Yet he loved to converse with the prisoners, and even, on occasion, distributed slices of bread among them. He would say that he was by nature a "good person" and he couldn't bear the fact that people trembled before him. If he discerned any movement whatever among the rows of people standing before him at roll call, however, he would kill a few people on the spot; afterward, he would light a cigarette and say, with a slight smile: "I am so good to you, and you are getting me angry. Look what you are making me do."[31]

Rokita appointed as camp overseer (*Lager-Ältester*) a Jew named Kampf, who had played in the same orchestra with him in the coffee houses before the war. But Kampf's "career" quickly came to an end. According to a rumor circulating in the camp, Kampf had disclosed that Rokita was sending home accordions from the camp and that the instruments were crammed with gold and precious stones. When the rumor reached Rokita, he killed Kampf, Kampf's wife, and their small daughter.

Lower-level SS officers were no less cruel than their superiors. SS-Scharführer Kolanko, head of the investigation division; the young sadist Heine, or Heinen (about twenty years old), presumably a former member of the *Leibstandarte Hitler*; the Hungarian SS officer Peter Blum, then seventeen years old, previously a shoemaker's apprentice; Hainisch, who prior to his arrival in the Janowski camp was Grzymek's adjutant in the Julag; the SS men Bitner, Grishaber, and the *Volksdeutscher* Bencke—all excelled in their cruelty.[32]

In the summer of 1943, changes took place in the camp personnel. Rokita was appointed head of the Jewish labor camp in Tarnopol. A short time later (on July 1, 1943), Willhaus was also transferred, and was succeeded by Franz Warzog. Many officers and SS men were transferred from service in the camp to active service in the SS brigades on the Eastern front (Waffen-SS). The internal policy of the hangmen in the Janowski camp oscillated, as in other camps, between two contradictory goals: on one hand, they had been trained to act "with devotion" to "liquidate" the enemies of Germany; on the other hand, with each marked decrease in the camp population, surplus SS men would be dispatched to the front. Indeed, as the situation on the Eastern front worsened, the Germans transferred more and more SS men from the camps, where they were replaced by policemen of non-German origin—SS detachments of Hungarians and *Volksdeutsche,* Ukrainian police, and Russians from the brigades of General Vlasov. They were called "Askaris" by the inmates (the sobriquet for the auxiliary police formed of residents born in the German colonies in Africa prior to 1914). Ukrainian and Russian police were also called "blacks," because of the color of their uniform. The non-German camp policemen served as regular soldiers, whereas the officers and commandants were still members of the German SS.

## Inmates of the Janowski Camp

The Janowski camp was primarily a forced-labor camp for Jews and for non-Jewish criminals. Secondly, it was an extermination camp for the Jews of Lwów and Eastern Galicia. Thirdly, it served as a transit camp, through which tens of thousands of Jews passed on their way to their doom. An examination and selection point was established there to determine who would die immediately and who would work, and who would go "to the transport" to Bełżec. The first transports from the provincial towns began arriving in the Janowski camp in the spring of 1942; in early April, a large transport arrived from Gródek Jagieloński, near Lwów; in May and June 1942, from Przemyśl; in July 1942, from Drohobycz, etc. At the same time, transports began arriving from the southeast of Galicia: Kołomyja, Kosów, Stanisławów, Dolina, and Delatyn. Small groups were also brought from abroad to the Janowski camp—from Czechoslovakia, Hungary, Yugoslavia, Holland, Belgium, Germany, and so on. For them, the camp was not a transit point, but the last stop.

It is estimated that between 300,000 and 400,000 Jews passed through the Janowski camp. At least 200,000 of them were murdered at the execution points in the "Sands" and in the forest of Lesienice. The number of inmates who stayed in the camp was small in comparison. All the official statistical material from the camp was lost or destroyed by the Germans before their flight. Only a single figure (included in the statistical survey of Lwów by the Stadthauptmann [head of the civil administration]) has been retrieved: according to a provisional census which the Germans conducted in Lwów on March 1, 1943, the number of Jews in the city proper was "0"!—and the number of Jews in the Janowski camp was 15,000.[33] It appears that this figure was an exaggeration, however. According to Jewish witnesses, the number of Jewish residents in the camp never exceeded 10,000, and was usually less, though it is possible that on the day of the census a few thousand Jews in the Janowska transit camp (Dulag) were added to the number of regular prisoners.

At first the Janowski camp was intended for males only, but after the massive actions of 1942, many women were brought there, and a section was established for them. Ultimately, a special women's camp, separate from the male camp, was created. The women's camp bordered on the "field of death" (where executions were carried out). The camp's female population at first was seventy women, brought there after the liquidation of the Żółkiew ghetto. The women worked at the camp's knitting machines (in the D.A.W.). As more women were brought into the camp, the Germans began to employ them in other tasks—in the kitchen and sanitation work, packing, and tailoring. The commandant of the women's camp was the SS officer Brumbauer.

The social structure of the camp prisoners was markedly stratified. On the highest level were those who worked as clerks in the camp offices. Next came the skilled workers, foremen, supervisors, engineers, artisans, technicians, and machinists, who were employed either in the choice outside detachments or those inside the camp, and constituted the aristocracy of the camp's workers. Lowest in the camp hierarchy were the unskilled workers, most of whom were professionals and intellectuals—lawyers, former government officials, teachers, writers, and rabbis. Only a few professionals managed to find posts as clerks in the camp offices or as factory workers. Most of them worked at back-breaking labor. They were often murderously beaten by the guards, and occasionally their more skilled comrades would treat them with derision. They were given the worst bunks in the camp barracks; they were last on line when rations were distributed. The horrible living conditions felled many of them. Rabbi David Kahane relates that almost all of the rabbis who were brought with him to the camp died within a short time from hunger, overwork, disease, and physical brutality.

## Living Conditions in the Janowski Camp

During the years 1942–1943, the Janowski camp expanded several times, and its area eventually totaled 2–3 square kilometers. The first expansion took place in March 1942, during the first major action in Lwów. From that time on, construction took place at a rapid pace during the entire summer, until the August action. The lecturer Griffel, of the Lwów Poly-technical Institute, a brilliant engineer, later killed by the Nazis, super-vised the construction.

The barracks were all built of wood in a long rectangle. Within the barracks were four levels of dirty, grimy bunks, one on top of the other. There were no heaters—though a terrible cold reigned during the winter—and no toilets in the barracks. One outhouse, with twelve seats (later forty), and one bathhouse served the entire camp. As these two facilities could be used only during the recess hours in the morning and the evening, the crowding was terrible. The barracks, where the prisoners slept, were locked from ten in the evening until five in the morning, and exit from them was completely forbidden even to go to the toilet. Some barracks lacked even a broom or a chamber pot or pail—though such a utensil would have soon filled up anyway, creating an unbearable stench and contaminant. A shower over two open troughs leading to a water pipe was in every barrack.

The food was far worse than the housing. The principal staple was bread, with the official per capita ration set at one-eighth of a loaf per day; that is, 150–160 grams per day. But those who supervised the distribution of bread knew how to decrease even this meager ration. The doughy bread, made of inferior ingredients, would disintegrate into crumbs when it was sliced. As a result, each inmate usually received at most 100 grams of bread per day. In the morning, the prisoners were given some sort of coffee substitute; in the afternoon, a plate of "soup" (water on which floated a few cabbage leaves), some groats, and, rarely, a bone or a piece of meat of very poor quality. Occasionally, the "soup" was so bad that prisoners, however hungry, could not eat it. In the winter of 1942, the soup was prepared from frozen potatoes that had lain in a heap where the German police often urinated. The soup made from these potatoes, which were neither cleaned nor peeled, raised such a stench that most of the prisoners refused to eat it. Another time, a soup was made from the carcass of a horse; most of the prisoners who ate it took sick, and some of them died.

The wives, mothers, and daughters of the prisoners kept trying to smuggle food to them. They would stand for hours before the gate of the camp or near the barbed-wire fence and wait for an opportunity to pass something to their relatives via an acquaintance or a bribed policeman. Waiting around the camp was very dangerous, because the police would beat the loiterers, even shoot them on occasion. In 1943, when any Jews caught outside the ghetto were condemned to death for this activity, the women stopped coming.

Earlier the Judenrat had attempted to arrange for a legal dispatch of extra rations to the prisoners. In return for very valuable gifts to Gebauer and his wife, a permit to send rations to the prisoners twice a week was granted. But this also proved useless, because the rations were not given directly to the prisoners but had to be distributed through the camp office. The SS personnel supervising the distribution of the shipments would confiscate the best portions, ostensibly as punishment for some offense. Occasionally, they even threw the rations to the dogs, before the eyes of the hungry inmates.

A black market for foodstuffs developed at the camp. The "merchandise" was provided by the policemen and workers who were in charge of the camp kitchen, bread distribution, the warehouse, and food parcels from family members. A substantial quantity of food was brought in by the workers—both Jews and Gentiles—in the outside detachments. The camp always had a number of Polish and Ukrainian inmates, who were distinguished from the Jews (the Poles wore a red patch on their clothes; the Ukrainians, a blue one; the Jews a yellow patch), and were not life-term prisoners (after a stated period of incarceration they were set free); during their sojourn in the camp they had more freedom than the Jews, could go to work outside the camps, and were permitted to visit with their families. These non-Jewish prisoners became go-betweens in the black market. Many Jewish workers in the outside detachments also engaged in this activity. The Jews who were taken to the city to work—on the railroad tracks, in the railway stations (Ostbahn and Betriebswerke-West), in the city sanitation bureau (Reinigungskommando), in the factories and military establishments—bartered with the gentiles in the city, trading in silver, gold, precious stones, or cash, for groceries and medications to bring back to the camp. The prices in the black market were exorbitant. The principal site for black-market activities was in the latrines because here the supervision of the police was not as rigid as in other places.

The black market constituted an attempt on the part of the camp inmates to thwart the scheme of the SS to starve the Jews to death, but it could not make a dent in the prevalent hunger. Moreover, this new economic order became the basis for a new social order in the camp. Everything was turned topsy-turvy. A "nouveau bourgeoisie" arose among the black-market traffickers, the "strong men," the skilled workers in the outside brigades, and a number of prewar "tycoons" who had managed to preserve a remnant of their former fortunes. At the same time, a new proletariat was created, which included the vast majority of inmates. Whereas the new bourgeoisie knew how to derive all the benefits from the unusual situation, the camp proletariat—made up mostly of inmates who worked at forced labor, many of whom had been professionals or government officials before the war—was quickly decimated by starvation.

The unsanitary conditions of the camp caused many illnesses. Not only were the bunks filthy and lice-ridden, but every aspect of camp life was intended to destroy the health of the inmates. At first, there was no bathhouse at all. When one was finally built, Gebauer forbade its use for a long time, ostensibly as a punishment because it was not completed on schedule. The use of soap (obtainable only on the black market) was totally forbidden. Nevertheless, Gebauer demanded that inmates be strict about their bodily hygiene, for which he conducted periodic inspections. One day in the middle of winter, when the temperature was −20 degrees centigrade, the inmates were forced to stand naked in the camp field during such an inspection. In the end, Gebauer chose five inmates to be punished for their lack of cleanliness. The unfortunates were immersed in barrels filled with water, and froze to death.

Occasionally, the camp inmates were sent to the bathhouse on Balonowa Street, which had an installation for delousing. But that bathhouse, with a capacity of 100–150 men at a time, was too small. It was later arranged that the prisoners would go by detachment to the bathhouses on Żródlana and Szpitalna streets. This activity provided the police with a new opportunity to brutalize the prisoners—to beat them on any trivial pretext. Usually each trip to the bathhouse left victims who had had their limbs broken or had been beaten or shot to death.

Many diseases spread as a result of these terrible conditions. One severe typhus epidemic, in September–November 1942, felled fifty persons per day (according to the testimony of Dr. Edgard Zwilling).[34] The best treatment that the Germans provided for seriously ill people was to shoot them to death. Far worse, they would remove the critically ill to the no man's land outside the camp, and would abandon them there till they died. Sick people therefore attempted with all their strength to conceal their illness, and to work even when disease was consuming them. Occasionally sick persons, with the aid of friends, succeeded in concealing their illness from the eyes of the police, and managed to recover despite everything. In the fall of 1941, the Jewish Council and the newly organized committee for assisting camp inmates obtained, through relentless effort and extensive bribery, permission from the camp authorities to transfer the chronically ill to the hospital in the ghetto. The chief physician, Dr. Maximillian Kurzrock, set up a special division in the hospital for these prisoners, and treated them with great devotion. This situation did not continue for long, however. After the massive actions at the end of 1942, the Jewish hospital was liquidated. The Germans then organized a "hospital" in the Janowski camp. An unheated wooden shack was set aside as a "hospital," devoid of medical instruments or sanitary care. Twice a month, the SS men Brumbauer and Birmann would burst in to conduct a "roll call." The sickest inmates would be taken out to be executed. The ill tried, to every extent possible, to avoid going to the "hospital." Medical supervision in the camp was entrusted to Dr. Kurzrock, and subsequently to Dr. Zygmunt Rapaport.

To ferret out the ill and the infirm, the SS men would conduct a form of "track meet" once a week. The inmates were ordered to race through the entire camp, from one gate to another, in perfect order, column by column. Whoever stumbled or fell behind was condemned to death. A more "sophisticated" version of this death race was called the "Vitamin Race"— apparently Willhaus's innovation. The "vitamins" were three types of heavy loads: beams (in Polish, *belki*) were "vitamin B"; bricks (in Polish, *cegły*) were "vitamin C"; boards (in Polish, *deski*) were "vitamin D." At the end of a ten- to twelve-hour workday, the inmates were commanded to transport—on their backs and at a run—the beams, bricks, and boards from the Kleparów railway station to the camp. The memory of this terrible "race" has left a deep mark on the survivors, several of whom have given terrifying descriptions of the ordeal in their memoirs:

The SS-policemen, the Askaris, and the Jewish camp police formed lines along two sides of the road leading from the camp gate to the railway station. The road was brightly lit. Row after row of prisoners would run between the two lines. A row of five, followed by a row of five, column after column, hundred after hundred, thousand after thousand. . . .

All this after a day of back-breaking labor. Legs were already as heavy as lead, but we had to march sprightly, for the pace was determined by the whips and pistols of the SS-officers and the rifle butts of the Askaris. When the order "run" was given, it was not sufficient just to run. We had to be careful not to step out of line during the race. . . . Behind the railway station, we had to go downhill, some tens of meters, in order to reach the railway bridge. Here we had to speedily gather up our load and return quickly with the burden. Above stood the SS officers, their rifles ready to fire, their whips unfurled in the air, and they would goad us on with wild shouts, kicks, beatings, shots in the air, and shots into the mass of inmates, increasing the confusion through these acts. They piled on the burdens without mercy. In particular, they would load upon the sick and infirm persons a load that would have to be carried by five people under normal conditions. Most of those who fell while transporting a load did not rise again from the ground. Those who could no longer carry on were removed from the column and were taken "outside the barbed wire," where they remained all night. In the morning, their half-frozen bodies were piled into lorries and removed to the "Sands" for liquidation. One time, after a Vitamin Race, which lasted from six in the evening until midnight, 130 persons were taken to the "Sands."[35]

The entire order of life in the camp was intended to speed up the extermination process and to suppress any thought or attempt at resistance or revolt. To impose a deathly fear upon the inmates, the Germans carried out punishments and executions in public. These acts excelled in sadism and barbarism. The regular place for executions was the death field, where the SS police would also carry out all cruel and unusual punishment. One common form of execution was to hang a male "criminal" upside down, with his hands and feet bound. Such a hanging caused a prolonged death agony amidst assorted horrible tortures. Women were hung by their hair. Another form of torture was to strip the "criminal" of all his clothing, tie his body up with barbed wire, and leave him outside for a few days. For any petty "offense," the Nazis might give 50–200 lashes, and occasionally would whip a person to death. Such punishments awaited anyone who attempted to escape. A fugitive who was caught was put to death through excruciating torture. In addition, the members of the fugitive's brigade were punished. When one Jew escaped from his work brigade, the police immediately seized twenty persons from his detachment and shot them.

Among the hangmen at the camp were "experts" who excelled in special forms of punishment. Gebauer took particular delight in strangling his victims with all his might until they were dead. Another form of torture practiced by him was "the bath in the water barrel," mentioned above. In another gruesome instance, Gebauer ordered that a person who had been caught stealing a few potatoes be tossed alive into a boiling kettle so that he could enjoy his potatoes straight from the pot.[36] The young SS officer Heinen was said to have had two pet methods of torturing inmates:

he would stab them with a sharp rod, and he would remove the fingernails of women.

The practice of murder developed into a habitual pleasure for the SS men, and they began to kill people without any pretext whatsoever, simply for the "sport" of it. Unusual "exercises" were particularly common among Gustav Willhaus and his family. Willhaus regularly enjoyed himself by firing at live targets: without any prior warning, he would fire into a crowd of inmates camped near the kitchen or the bathhouse and would kill or maim many of them. Willhaus's wife, Otilia, also had a pistol. When guests came to visit the Willhaus family, and sat on the spacious porch of their luxurious house, Otilia would show off her marksmanship by shooting down camp inmates, to the delight of her guests. The little daughter of the family, Heike, would vigorously applaud the sight. Various authors also tell about another young Nazi child, the son of one of the SS officers, who would stand for long periods at the camp gate to throw rocks at the heads of the prisoners going out to work, and would hit them until they bled.

The SS police also tormented the inmates with various forms of humiliation. Two old men, a rabbi and a *shohet* (presumably from Jaworów) wearing beards and side curls, were forced to get up daily on a high platform and dance, holding umbrellas.

According to accounts by Itzhak Lewin, Itzhak Farber, and Gerszon Taffet, the SS also held competitions in killing Jewish children without the use of weapons—by tearing them in two, or dashing their brains out. Every unusual event served as a pretext for new acts of cruelty on the part of the SS men. On Hitler's birthday, April 20, 1943, Willhaus selected fifty-four Jewish prisoners to be shot in honor of the Führer. On July 25, 1943, the day of Mussolini's abdication as ruler of Italy, a particularly horrible incident took place. One of the Gestapo men accused a young Jew who had crossed his path, of mocking him. The youth claimed that he had greeted the Gestapo man politely, according to protocol and discipline of the camp. The German insisted that he detected in the Jew's greeting a veiled mockery (*Schadenfreude*) and a rejoicing over Mussolini's downfall. A merciless execution was arranged and carried out by the SS men Brumbauer and Birman.[37] They hung the youth upside down, cut off his male organ and placed it in his mouth, and kicked him ceaselessly in the stomach to make the blood flow to his head. The youth died in terrible agony.

An orchestra was organized in the camp at the initiative of SS-Untersturmführer Rokita. It was composed of the musicians Józef Mund, Józef Herman, Edward Steinberger, Schatz, and others, with Leonid Striks as its conductor. Rokita, a connoisseur of music, would listen to the music with his gifted ear, and if he detected a false note, would storm the orchestra and shoot the performer who dared to impair the harmony. At Rokita's order a special tune, "Tango of Death," was composed (reportedly by Schatz). The macabre "Tango of Death" would be played on frequent occasions, especially when work brigades were leaving the camp or when groups selected for execution were being taken to the "Sands."

Aside from the frequent "selections" and other small-scale methods of execution already reported, many mass slaughters took place in the Janowski camp. One of the last big actions occurred in mid-May 1943, when several thousand inmates were killed (eyewitnesses' estimates vary, from 2,000 to 6,000).

## Resistance and Underground Activities in the Camp

All the severe tortures of body and soul inflicted on the inmates were intended to dehumanize and degrade them to the level of animals for slaughter. But instead, the atrocities turned the perpetrators themselves into beasts—beasts of prey. As for the inmates, there were those who preserved the spark of humanity within them; the many manifestations of solidarity, friendship, and fraternity reported in the memoirs of the survivors attest to this, as do the cultural activities and the preparations for armed resistance that were carried on in the camp.

Underground activities in the camp were difficult and disjointed. At each effort, many of the leaders died or were killed. Therefore a full description of the resistance movement has not come down to us, only some segments preserved by the few resisters who managed to escape the "valley of death." It is known that during the year 1942, a self-help organization arose, headed by Jakubowicz and Richard Axer (the son of a well-known lawyer), a young man of character and sensitivity. In the part of the camp belonging to the D.A.W., another group was active, led by the journalist David Frenkel (one of the leaders of the Hashomer Hatzair), Abraham Wahrman ("Bronek"), and others. The self-help group laid the groundwork for armed resistance, and in the meantime abetted the escape of individuals by providing clothing, hiding places in the city, and forged documents. Another important area of activity was assistance to the ill and the hungry in the camp. Particularly active in this sphere were the physicians Boris Pliskin and Lust, S. Kohn, M. Hausman, and L. Birnbaum.

Literary activities were also carried on by the camp underground. For example, a secret poetry session was organized by the popular song-writer Schlechter, on New Year's eve, 1941. Apparently, this was the first such gathering in the camp. A series of literary gatherings was organized in the camp during the years 1942–1943 by members of the outside brigade working in the city sanitation department: M. Borwicz (Boruchowicz), Leon Birnbaum, and M. Hausman, with the participation of M. Bernstein, Benzion Ginsberg, and Boris Pliskin. Works recited at these gatherings were copied by Jewish clerks in the camp offices who were members of the underground, and the copies were disseminated among the prisoners. Some authors continued writing in the camp. Whereas the work of Yerachmiel Grin, Zygmunt Schorr, and others has been lost, the popular poem of Halina Grin and some "folk" songs have survived. Many of the camp inmates kept notebooks and diaries, most of which have been lost, unfortunately. Among those that were preserved and published after the war, one should note the two volumes, in Polish, by Michał Borwicz (Boruchowicz), about the Janowski camp: *Uniwersytet Zbirów* (University of Villains) and *Literatura w obozie* (Literature in the Camp). Borwicz wrote poetry as well, some of which was published during the war (in 1944) by the Jewish underground in Warsaw in a booklet entitled *Z Otchłani* (From the Abyss) and was later included in a collection entitled *Ze śmiercią na ty* (Intimate with Death). Janina Hescheles, daughter of the editor Henryk Hescheles, wrote a book of memoirs, *Oczyma 12-letniej dziewczynki* (In the Eyes of a Twelve-Year-Old Girl); and Leon Weliczker wrote *Brygada Śmierci: Sonderkommando 1005* (The Death Brigade: Sonderkommando 1005).

Various cases of individual resistance occurred in the camp. We can assume that in addition to events recorded in the memoirs of survivors, there were acts of resistance that went unrecorded and are lost to memory forever. Space will not suffice to relate all the resistance efforts described in the reminiscences (see the memoirs of Borwicz, Szajewicz, Farber, Lewin, Maltiel, and Weliczker, and others). Many incidents were also described in the affidavits of eyewitnesses, preserved in the archives. Of these, I cite three characteristic episodes:

One day, in the bathhouse, the SS man Bitner attacked without provocation an elderly Jew from a rural village, and was beating him violently and cold-bloodedly. The Jew fell to the ground, did not ask for pity from his attacker, who continued to beat him, but raised his head from time to time with the cry: "Nonetheless, Hitler will not win"; and with these words on his lips, he died.

One day, Rokita stood watching a group of Jews carrying bricks. From time to time, he would aim his whip and strike. His attention and whipping were particularly directed at a Jewish peasant who, while no longer a young man, was nevertheless solid and well built. Several times Rokita aimed his revolver at him, and eventually began to whip him. The Jew ceased his work and began throwing bricks at the SS officer, shouting: "Here are the bricks, let us see how you carry them." Rokita was so astonished by the sudden reaction that he turned around and began to run away. But he immediately regained his composure, returned to the Jew, and shot him dead.

Another time, Willhaus tormented a young Jew, Szajewicz, until he could bear it no longer. Szajewicz uttered courageous words against the SS and finally fell upon Willhaus and slapped his face. The unexpected slap drove Willhaus berserk, he jumped up and shot the Jew. Soon regretting that he had given him such an easy death, he began to brutalize the corpse.

In addition to such incidents of individual resistance, there were attempts in the camp to organized armed resistance. At various opportunities, the inmates purchased and smuggled arms into the camp, particularly knives and revolvers. The camp kitchen served, in the summer of 1943, as a meeting place for the underground. With the assistance of sympathetic kitchen personnel the underground made contact with people from the city who provided foodstuffs to the camp to get their assistance and much needed help for the escapees. Kitchen meetings between the author Sanie Friedman (a member of the Jewish police in the camp) and a group of Jewish youths organizing the resistance effort were carefully arranged; but these meetings did not result in any action.

There were instances in which groups of prisoners resisted the policemen who were taking them to the "Sands." Rumors also spread through the city of an armed revolt by the inmates being transported in a lorry in the vicinity of Place Strzelecki. A few groups of camp inmates attempted to flee to the forests surrounding the city, and some of them succeeded, with the help of the Askaris. Once a lorry left the camp filled with Jewish prisoners under the guard of an Askari armed with an automatic rifle. Apparently there was a secret agreement between the Askari and the Jews, for the lorry disappeared with all its passengers. Occasionally, small groups who fled to the forest, to try to form partisan units or join partisans active in the forest, disappeared completely. In most cases, the escapees died in the forest or fell into the hands of the police or Ukrainian partisans, who killed them. Despite this, the attempts were repeated. One of those who fled to the forest was the Jew Czermak, who returned several times to the camp and each time smuggled out a few persons, until he was informed upon to the Nazi police. Czermak was executed, together with his accomplice, Dr. Zimet. Nevertheless, underground activities did not cease. Two Askaris who began to investigate the secret organization were killed by underground members. Attempts at escape and revolt were also made by other groups (see the memoirs of David Kahane and M. Borwicz). Apparently there were underground groups at work in various places in the camp at different times, but there was no centralized, unified organization.

Many of the resistance efforts were nipped in the bud. One of the biggest was a plan for a revolt in November 1943. Preparations for this revolt are mentioned in the works of various authors, but the data are contradictory and we have no full, reliable account. From the various versions, we can infer that the Germans discovered the plan, decided to anticipate the rebels by liquidating the Janowski camp, and set the liquidation date for November 20, 1943. Although the underground was not really ready for this sudden action, an armed confrontation occurred on November 20, and a small number of prisoners managed to flee to the forest. According to another version, a group of Jewish inmates made a pact with a group of rebellious Askaris, killed some German policemen (guards) a few days before the liquidation of the camp, and fled to the forest.

At the same time, a revolt of the Jewish brigade that worked in the Lesienice camp broke out. This brigade, termed the "death brigade," had been established by the Germans in mid-June 1943 from inmates of the Janowski camp. At that time the Germans began to concern themselves with destroying the traces of the terrible atrocities they had perpetrated. A special German brigade, Sonderkommando 1005, was created, whose task it was to exhume corpses from all the places of slaughter near the ghettos and camps and incinerate them. The officers of the Sonderkommando 1005 organized the "death brigade," employing about 150 persons from the camp. The Jewish members of the brigade plotted a revolt, and on November 20, 1943, attacked the German guards. Though a few guards were killed and the inmates began forcing their way out of the camp, which was surrounded by barbed wire, the revolt was only a partial success. In some places SS guards fired shots, and hurled grenades at the rebels. Of the tens of prisoners who managed to escape and hide in the forests and in the city, most were caught and killed within a short time. Fewer than ten persons survived.

After all the Jewish inmates of the Janowski camp had been slaughtered, the camp served as a place for forced labor and internment for non-Jewish prisoners. There were a few hundred Polish, Ukrainian, and *Volksdeutsche* inmates. In 1944, the Germans again brought in a small group of Jewish workers and artisans, mostly Jews caught on the Aryan side. The Germans chose not to execute these Jews because they were in need of tailors, shoemakers, tanners, electricians, gardeners, and launderers. During the Soviet air raids on Lwów in April 1944, there was great confusion in the camp and fifteen of the Jewish inmates managed to escape. In May there were still sixty-eight Jewish inmates in the Janowski camp. In June, the Germans transferred the remainder to a more secure place in the west; during the evacuation, some Jews escaped and took refuge in the areas surrounding Dobromil and Grzybów in Western Galicia.

The Germans continued to burn corpses in the Lesienice forest after the liquidation of both the Janowski camp and the "death brigade." In January 1944, their work was completed.

## The Jewish Remnant of Lwów

Between July 26 and 29, 1944, the Russian army liberated Lwów from the Germans. Immediately after the liberation, a Jewish committee was spontaneously created which resided in a small hall on Jabłonowska Street and began to record the Jews who remained. Not all the surviving Jews had the courage to admit their identity publicly, for some of the gentile population did not regard them benevolently. There were cases in which Jews were murdered by members of the Polish, Ukrainian, or nationalist underground. For example, Dr. Bartfeld, a religious teacher, was killed after he emerged from hiding.

One can divide the surviving Jews into three categories: First, there were Jews who had disguised themselves as gentiles and owned forged documents. Many of them did not reveal their true identity after liberation. This group includes Jewish children protected by gentile families during the Nazi period—most of whom did not return to the Jewish community and religion, either because the gentile families had become attached to them and did not want to be separated from them or because the children found that their parents and families had been exterminated. Second, there were the "forest people," who had either been in hiding in the forests or had roamed with the partisan bands. They returned to Lwów, in rags, without any belongings. Third, there were the "rats," the Jews who had hidden in pipes, sewers, and bunkers. They emerged weak and exhausted from lack of exercise, air, and light. Their legs were wobbly, their eyes dim, their faces pale, and their bodies bloated.

In addition to the Jews of Lwów, Jewish survivors from the provincial towns preferred to take up residence in Lwów, rather than return to their former dwelling places—either because everything in their home towns reminded them of the Holocaust or because their personal security was greater in the larger community. Indeed, Lwów remained the single "large" community in Eastern Galicia. Whereas the Jewish remnants in other cities totaled a few hundred souls at most (such as Borysław, Drohobycz, Stanisławów, Tłuste), the postwar Jewish population in Lwów totaled a few thousand persons.

The total Jewish population in Lwów after the war does not provide an accurate picture of the number of Jewish survivors from Lwów itself. Among the survivors listed by the Lwów committee and those who settled in Lwów after the liberation, the Jews from the provincial towns constituted a decisive majority. The Jewish committee on Jabłonowska Street had neither the technical means nor the personnel to conduct an accurate census. Approximately 3,400 Jews were listed as of September 21, 1944. This list (which I received from the members of the Jewish committee of Lwów at the end of September 1944) constitutes the single source of information available; the breakdown according to age and sex is as follows:

| | |
|---|---:|
| Women, aged 20–60 | 2,080 |
| Men, aged 18–55 | 1,215 |
| Elderly (over 55 years) | 20 |
| Children and youths (to 18 years) | 85 |
| Total | 3,400 |

Sixty percent of the survivors indicated that they had been artisans, merchants, or functionaries before the war; 15 percent were of the learned professions, teachers, or artists. (Among these were: 32 doctors, 8 dentists, 42 lawyers, 27 engineers, 16 teachers, and 9 artists.)

The Jewish committee began to organize help for the survivors. Both the support provided by the municipal authorities and the other financial resources at the disposal of the committee (mainly contributions from wealthy Jews) were very meager. The assistance provided up until September 21, 1944, comprised 1,300 lunches, 8,000 loaves of bread, 20,000 rubles in cash, and some light clothing.

Later a new local Jewish committee was created in which experienced community leaders functioned (for a few months, Dr. David Sobol served as head of this committee). The new committee received from the municipal authorities the single synagogue that survived the Nazis—the synagogue on Węglana Street, which the Germans had transformed into a storehouse and a stable. Although it was not suitable as an office, the offices of the provisional Jewish committee were transferred there, and prayers were conducted during the holidays. The committee prepared new statistics in November 1944: at that time, only 2,571 Jews were counted, including 134 children aged three to sixteen. Apparently many who were listed in Lwów during the first days after the liberation stayed in the city only temporarily on their way to Poland. This committee also conducted a more accurate investigation, which showed that of the Jews either born in Lwów or resident there at the time of the German conquest, only 823 survived.[38]

The Jewish committee was not given legal authorization by the Russian authorities, who did not want to approve a religious community. The authorities tolerated the activity of the committee only for a few months, after which the committee had to resign. The exodus of the Jews from Lwów continued. According to the agreement between the Soviet Union and the Polish Republic, Lwów was annexed to the Soviet Ukraine, and Lwów's residents could opt for Soviet-Ukrainian or Polish citizenship. Generally, the Jews preferred Polish citizenship, and left Lwów. The repatriation to Poland lasted from October 1944 to the end of 1945, and almost emptied Lwów of its Jewish inhabitants. Lwów survivors migrated to various cities of Poland (such as Warsaw, Lodz, Cracow); from there to the Displaced Persons camps in Germany, Austria, and Italy; and finally to Israel and the United States.

❑ This study was published in Hebrew under the title "Hurban yehudei Lvov" (The Destruction of the Jews of Lwów), *Entsiklopedia shel galu-yot,* IV, *Lwów Volume* (Jerusalem, 1956), 599–746. It is a later version of a booklet in Polish, *Zagłada Żydów Lwowskich w okresie okupacji niemieckiej* (The Destruction of the Jews of Lwów) (Lodz, CJKH, 1945); a second, enlarged edition (also in Polish) was published in 1947, in Munich. Facsimiles of maps, documents, and pictures, which appear throughout the text in the *Entsiklopedia,* as well as the Supplements (pp. 735–46), are not included in the present version.

## Bibliographical Note

I lived in Lwów through the Nazi occupation (June 29, 1941–July 27, 1944) and after the liberation, until November 1944. In addition to direct observation, and daily conversations with many persons during the occupation and after the German retreat, I used the following sources for this essay: *Lemberger Zeitung* (a German daily), 1941–1944; *Gazeta Lwowska* (a Polish daily), 1941–1944; *Lwiwski Wisti* (a Ukrainian daily), 1941–1944; *Ukrainski Shtsho-denni Wisti* (a Ukrainian daily), 1941; *Verordnungsblatt für das General-gouvernement; Amtsblatt des Gouverneurs für den Distrikt Galizien* (published by the German government); "The Population of the District Galicia on 1 March 1943," statistical report (in German and Ukrainian), manuscript, Ukrainian Academy of Science, Department of Economics, Lwów; "Die Land-wirtschaft des Districts Galizien in Polen, 1 Juli 1943," statistical report (German), manuscript, Ukrainian Academy of Science, Department of Economics, Lwów; "German Crimes in the Lwów District: Reports of the Special Commission of Investigation of the USSR," *Pravda,* December 23, 1944 (also in *Izvestia,* December 23, 1944); twenty-five written statements, testimonies of witnesses, and memoirs of Jewish survivors, collected by members of the CJHC and its branches in Lodz, Warsaw, Cracow, and Przemyśl (archives of CJHC in Poland); handwritten statements by twenty-one witnesses, collected by the CHC in Munich (the documents have been transferred to Israel); twenty-four eyewitness reports from the Holocaust era in Lwów, in the archives of YIVO in New York; *IMT.*

In addition to the above sources, the following published materials provide much information on the events in Lwów during the Nazi period: Vladimir Belayev, in *Czerwony Sztandar,* Lwów, October 20, 1944 (Polish), in *Vilna Ukraina,* Lwów, September 28, 1944 (Ukrainian), and in *Ogoniok,* nos. 14–17, Moscow, 1945 (Russian); N. Blumental, ed. *Obozy (Dokumenty i Materiały,* I) (Lodz, 1946); Michał Borwicz, *Uniwersytet Zbirów* (Cracow, 1946); idem, *Literatura w obozie* (Literature in the Camp) (Cracow, 1946); idem, *Ze śmiercią na ty* (Intimate with Death) (Warsaw, 1946); Michał Borwicz, Nella Rost, Józef Wulf, *Dokumenty Zbrodni i Męczeństwa* (Documents of Crime and Martyrdom) (Cracow, 1946), pp. 122–31, 171–73; Jerzy Broszniewicz, *Oczekiwanie* (Expectation) (Warsaw, 1948); "Escape of the Remnants through the Ukrainian Front," *Reshimot,* n.s., 2 (1947), 48–59; Itzhak Farber, "Diary of a Jew from Lwów: Sufferings of a Jewish Community in the Days of the Nazi Occupation" (Hebrew), *Reshimot,* n.s., 1 (1946), 5–33; Shlomo Feier, *Der Untergang fun Zlotshev* (The Destruction of Złoczów) (Munich, 1947); Ada Eber-Friedman, "From the Gallery of My Life-Givers" (Polish), *Nasza Trybuna,* Nos. 109–18 (New York, 1949/1950); Philip Friedman, "Megillat Lwów" (Hebrew), *Annual of Davar,* 5605 (1945), 220–33; idem, *Zagłada Żydów Lwowskich* (The Extermination of the Jews in Lwów), first edition (Lodz, 1945); second enlarged edition (Munich, 1947); Tania Fuchs, *A Vanderung iber okupirte gebitn* (A Voyage through the Occupied Territories) (Buenos Aires, 1947); Noe Grüss, ed., *Kindermartyrologie* (Child Martyrs) (Buenos Aires, 1947), pp. 101–2, 141–45, 186–94, 220–21; Israel Gutwirt, articles in *Yiddishe Tsaytung,* Landsberg, May 16, 1947, in *Ibergang,* Munich, March 30, 1947; Janka Hescheles, *Oczyma 12–letniej dziewczynki* (Through the Eyes of a Twelve-Year-Old Girl) (Cracow, 1946); Itzhak Lewin, *Aliti mi-spezia* (Notes from the Lwów ghetto translated from the Polish manuscript, by Dov Stock [Sadan]) (Tel Aviv, 1946); "Lwów—Śniatyn—Sandomierz," in A. Silberschein, ed., "L'Éxtermination des Juifs en Pologne: Dépositions des témoins oculaires," 5th series (Geneva, 1945), mimeographed; Yaakov Maltiel, *Be'ein nikum* (Tel Aviv, 1947); Shmuel Niger, ed., *Kiddush ha-Shem* (In Sanctification of His Name) (New York, 1948); Rudolf Reder, *Bełżec* (Cracow, 1946); Manfred Reifer, *Massa ha-mavet* (The Death March) (Tel Aviv, 1946), pp. 92–105; Fela Schnek, "How the Jews of Lwów Were Destroyed" (Hebrew), *Davar,* Tel Aviv, November 5, 1946; Wacław Śledziński, *Swastyka nad Warszawą* (Swastika over Warsaw) (Edinburgh, 1944), p. 104; Zygmunt Sobieski, "Reminiscences from Lwów," *Journal of Central European Affairs,* 6 (1947), 351–74; Stefan Szende, *Den Stila Juden from Polen* (The Last Jew from Poland) (Stockholm, 1944); *Der letzte Jude aus Polen* (Zurich, 1945); *The Promise Hitler Kept* (New York, 1945); Gerszon Taffet, *Zagłada Żydów Żółkiewskich* (Extermination of the Jews in Żółkiew) (Lodz, 1946); Israel Unger, *Zkhor! Me-yemei kronot ha-mavet* (Remember! From the Days of the Death Wagons) (Tel Aviv, 1945); Józef Weinberg, *Tam gdzie smierć była ulgą* (Where Death Was a Relief) (Katowice, 1946); Abraham Weisbrod, "While the World Looks on with Red Eyes" (Yiddish), in *Oyf di vandrungn* (On the Move) (Munich, 1947), pp. 51–59; Leon Weliczker, *Brygada śmierci (Sonderkommando 1005)* (The Death Brigade) (Lodz, 1946); Yudka, "Before the Calamity Spread" (Hebrew), *Mebifnim,* June 1947, pp. 457–69; Tadeusz Zaderecki, articles in Yiddish in *Dos naye lebn,* Lodz,

1949, nos. 289, 338; *idem,* articles in Polish in *Opinja,* Lodz-Warsaw, 1946/1947, nos. 11, 12 and in *Nasze Słowo,* Lodz-Warsaw, 1947, nos. 11, 12, 13; *Zvirstva Nimtziv na Lvovshchini* (German Crimes in the Lwów Area), a collection of articles and documents, Lwów, 1945 (in Ukrainian).

## Notes

1. Itzhak (Kurt) Lewin, *Aliti mi-spezia* (I Left Spezzia) (Tel Aviv, 1946). Cf. above, essay 8, "Ukrainian-Jewish Relations During the Nazi Occupation."

2. Quoted from the book of Itzhak Lewin, son of Rabbi Yehezkiel Lewin, who translated his father's address from Polish into Ukrainian.

3. *Ibid.*

4. Itzhak Farber, "Diary of a Jew from Lwów" (Hebrew), *Reshimot,* n.s., 1 (1946), 7.

5. Yaakov Maltiel, *Be'ein nikum* (Without Vengeance) (Tel Aviv, 1947), p. 9.

6. *RGBL,* I (1940), 1270.

7. Maltiel, p. 29.

8. In his *Aliti mi-spezia,* Lewin tells the story of his own rescue and that of other Jews, by Sheptitsky; cf. above, essay 8.

9. Report of June 30, 1943, by General Katzmann, SS-and Police Chief for the District Galicia, to his superior Krüger, Higher SS-and Police Chief for the Government-General, *IMT,* L–18.

10. Maltiel, pp. 63–64.

11. *Ibid.,* p. 143.

12. *Entsiklopedia shel galuyot, Lwów Volume,* Part I, pp. 746, appendix VII.

13. Katzmann to Krüger, *IMT,* L–18.

14. Testimony by a former German soldier, Alfred Greiner, Munich, in *Entsiklopedia, Lwów Volume,* pp. 739–43, appendix VI.

15. *Ibid.,* pp. 746, appendix VIII; YIVO archives.

16. Maltiel, pp. 201–2.

17. *Ibid.,* pp. 210–11.

18. *Ibid.,* p. 245.

19. Shlomo Meier, *Der untergang fun zlotshev* (The Destruction of Złoczów) (Munich, 1947), pp. 21–22.

20. J. Blitz, a Jewish writer, who escaped from Tarnopol and survived, recounts in details his ghastly experiences in an article published in *Dos naye lebn,* Lodz, 1945.

21. Israel Unger, *Zkhor! Me-yemei kronot ha-mavet* (Remember! From the Days of the Death Wagons) (Tel Aviv, 1945), pp. 190–91.

22. *Warszawski Dziennik Narodowy* (1937), p. 36.

23. Eyewitness report of Moshe Erlich, archives of the JHI, no. 1247.

24. Maltiel, pp. 246–47.

25. Katzmann to Krüger, *IMT,* L–18.

26. The report contains over sixty typewritten pages and many photos, and was signed by Katzmann on June 30, 1943. After the defeat of Germany,

the report was attached as Doc. L–18 to the documents of the International Military Tribunal at Nuremberg in 1946–1947. For a facsimile of the front page of the report, see *Entsiklopedia, Lwów Volume,* p. 746, Appendix VII.

27. Raul Hilberg, *The Destruction of the European Jews* (New York, 1961), p. 708.

28. From the archives of Instytut Zachodni w Poznaniu (Western Institute in Poznań), files of the documentary section. See also, *Entsiklopedia, Lwów Volume,* pp. 737, 740, Appendix V.

29. "German Crimes in the Lwów District. Report of the Soviet Extraordinary State Commission for Investigating Crimes Committed by the German-Fascist Invaders and their Accomplices," *Pravda* (Moscow), no. 307, December 23, 1944.

30. Memoirs of Erna (Irena) Szajewicz, in *Dokumenty i Materjały* (Documents and Materials): Vol. I, *Obozy* (The Camps), ed. by N. Blumental (Lodz, 1946), pp. 40–44; *idem,* "The Janowski Camp" (Polish), typescript in the archives of CJHC.

31. Michał Borwicz, *Uniwersytet Zbirów* (University of Villains) (Cracow, 1946), p. 38.

32. Rumors spread that among the hangmen of the Janowski camp were experts from the Dirlewanger Brigade, whose task was to train the camp policemen in murder operations. The Dirlewanger Brigade was composed mostly of convicted criminals, freed from jails and concentration camps to serve in this brigade. The task of the brigade was to "liquidate" the population in areas showing signs of resistance or revolt. The members of this commando group, who were expert in massacring civilians, women, and children, were dispatched to Warsaw during the Polish uprising of August–October 1944. However, until today, there is no definitive proof of the presence of Dirlewanger men in the Janowski camp. Cf. Włodzimierz Bielayew (Belayev), "It Happened in Lwów" (Polish), *Czerwony Sztandar,* no. 57, October 25, 1944; testimony of General Erich von dem Bach-Zelewski, chief of antipartisan warfare, *IMT,* IV, 481–82.

33. The document is in the archives of the Ukrainian Academy of Science, Lwów branch, economic department.

34. Affidavit no. 858 in the archives of JHI in Warsaw.

35. This description is from Borwicz, pp. 34–35; other accounts can be found in Lewin, pp. 139–40; Farber, p. 24.

36. These activities are described in the memoirs of three survivors of the Janowski camp: Farber, p. 24; Borwicz, p. 58; Szajewicz, in *Dokumenty i Materjały,* I: *Obozy,* p. 44.

37. This terrible episode was related to me by survivors of the Janowski camp who witnessed it.

38. This datum was provided me by Dr. David Sobol, head of the Jewish committee.

# CRIMES IN THE NAME OF "SCIENCE"

Block 28 in Auschwitz: Thirty healthy young Jewish boys are in room 13, which is tightly sealed. They may not go out, even to the lavatory. The room is shrouded in the mystery of a great "scientific" secret. Dr. Geza Mansfeld, professor of pharmacology and experimental pathology at the University of Pecs in Hungary, who was a prisoner in Auschwitz, has recalled:

I was terribly interested in the investigations carried on in room 13, and I tried hard to get inside. Dr. Laszlo Schwartz, a physician who had been my pupil, worked there, and one evening he took me inside. I saw a group of young people being given subcutaneous injections of benzine and naphtha. I asked: "Why are you doing this? Such experiments can be performed on animals. Besides, the effect of benzine and naphtha on the [human] organism has long been known and investigated in medical science." My companion replied that the experiments were being conducted by Haupsturmführer Dr. Klein, the German camp doctor, on the order of an army doctor, to test the effect of benzine and naphtha injections on Jews. Many German soldiers, it seemed, had given themselves benzine and naphtha injections to get sick and avoid being sent to the front. We therefore had to test the symptoms of such injections.[1]

The injections were deep; 2–3 cc. of the above-mentioned liquids were generally injected into both of the prisoners' legs. After eight days, large abcesses developed, into which incisions were made, and the extracted pus was put into sealed containers and sent to the Institute for Histology in Breslau. The end result of these "scientific experiments" was death: Dr. Klein's patients fell ill, their wounds healed badly, and at the next "selection" they were sent to the gas chamber.

Various other experiments were performed upon the prisoners in Block 28. Different kinds of salts, pastes, and powders, as well as an 80 percent solution of acid mixed with alum, were applied to the skin to produce rashes and irritations. Strips of skin and deeper tissues were then cut out and sent to Breslau for histological study. These details have been provided by Samuel Stern of Budapest, who worked as a medical orderly at Auschwitz. Other groups of inmates were given fifteen to twenty tablets of acridine daily to give them jaundice, or were injected with the blood of malarial patients. Dr. Klein's assistant in all these experiments was SS-Oberscharführer Emil Kaszub.

The Nazi scientists were also anxious to find out whether East European and West European Jews react in the same way to typhus injections. They infused nine West European Jews, selected at random, with the blood of persons suffering from typhus. Though the East European Jews apparently had somewhat more resistance than the West European Jews, within ten days, all the Jews subjected to the experiment died.

The SS-Untersturmführer Dr. König, who was investigating the effect of electric shock on the human system, conducted other "interesting experiments" on Jewish inmates of Monowice (Auschwitz III). Placing two electrodes against the patient's temples, he would release an electric current through the brain. Many young persons died during this experiment.

Young German doctors came to Auschwitz to gain surgical experience. They performed operations on inmates without any medical justification. The young Dr. König, for instance, amputated hands and legs in cases of simple tissue inflammation, where simple medical therapy would have effected a cure within a few days or weeks. To gain practice in amputation, the SS doctor would amputate a finger for an ordinary inflammation curable by a simple incision; he would amputate a leg for an abscess. After the operations, the patients were sent to the gas chambers.

Two other doctors, Thiele and Fischer, selected large groups of inmates and, without their consent or any medical reason, performed appendectomies, hernia, and gynecological operations on them. If anyone complained of slight stomach trouble to the chief medical officer of Auschwitz, SS-Hauptsturmführer Endress, his practice was to perform an operation known as gastroenterostomy (forming a passage between the stomach and the small intestines), or to "diagnose" it as a stomach cancer and perform an operation called Billroth 1 or Billroth 2. These are major operations, and most of the patients died during the surgery. Those who survived were sent by Dr. Endress to the gas chambers in the next selection.

Various experiments, the nature of which is not precisely known, were also made in Block 11. The men who were injected there, with an unspecified fluid, died within a few hours.

German pharmaceutical firms sent products to the camp to be tried out on the inmates—for instance, preparation B.1034 of the sulfanilamide group, projected as a new treatment for erysipelas. New sleeping tablets and powders were tried out on four prisoners, who were given coffee treated with the drugs. The initial experiment was "unsatisfactory" (i.e., the prisoners survived) and had to be repeated. This time the inmates were first given alcohol to drink and then coffee in which larger doses of the drug were dissolved. Now the experiment was "successful": two inmates died immediately, the other two the next day.

A medical commission of SS doctors experimented on Jewish prisoners in yet another way. They injected a substance into their muscles and, at the same time, gave them an unspecified ingredient by mouth. After fifteen minutes, the doctors tested to see if the experiment had produced signs of complete indifference to life. A revolver was put to the patient's head, and he was asked whether he wanted to live or die, whether he was afraid, and what he thought about his personal enemies. The commission wanted to induce (1) a willingness to make straightforward statements, and (2) a complete mental indifference. The experiment was inconclusive (March 1944).

Auschwitz inmates tell of another form of criminal action, whose purpose has not yet been determined—the macabre ambulances of human flesh. The Nazi executioners would shoot attractive young people, men and women, cut off their arms and legs while the bodies were still warm, and transport the limbs in Red Cross (!) ambulances, to unknown destinations. According to rumor in the camp, the limbs were intended for grafts for wounded German soldiers, but there is no evidence of this.

Merciless, criminal experiments were often carried out on victims selected for the gas chambers. In the name of science, the Germans installed at Auschwitz, in April 1944, a huge laboratory near crematorium no. 3. There the most terrible experiments were performed on persons selected from among those designated for the gas chambers. One woman was given an overdose of anesthetic, and the length of time it took for her to die was measured. In another case, a vein of a victim was opened to demonstrate that the whole five liters of blood which it is calculated the body contains would actually flow out of the organism (this "experiment" was reportedly conducted by Dr. Golze).

Before continuing with this horrifying subject, I should like to note that there was yet another aspect of Nazi interest in "medical science," rather innocent and harmless in comparison with the above. One example is the "institute of hygiene" at Rajsko, about three or four kilometers from Auschwitz. One hundred and ten inmates worked there—fifty of them trained doctors and scientists—under the direction of several SS doctors. The institute was nothing but a German propaganda front to make the world believe that the Germans were concerned about the health of the "native" population and the inmates. Actually, no practical use was made of the investigations or research conducted at the institute, except that the Germans passed off as their own the discoveries of several famous scientists and professors sent to the camp as prisoners and employed at the institute. Professor Geza Mansfeld, for instance, was instructed to collect material about typhus. Some time later Mansfeld found out that del Monte, deputy director of the institute, a *Volksdeutsch* from Liège, had passed off this material as his own in a dissertation presented to a Belgian university, which awarded him a doctorate for the work.

Such reports sound innocuous compared to descriptions of the "scientific research" conducted by the SS-Obersturmbannführer Dr. Josef Mengele, assistant at the Institut für Erbbiologie und Rassenhygiene (Institute for Hereditary Biology and Race Research) at the University of Frankfurt. Dr. Mengele caused terror among the Auschwitz inmates. His brutality manifested itself in the selections for the gas chambers and in the reception at the railway station of new transports to Auschwitz. Mengele would mercilessly send huge masses of the new arrivals directly to the gas chambers—everyone except twin children. Mengele was engaged in research on the inheritance of physical and mental traits—particularly in twins, persons with birth defects, and malformed persons. Mengele's work, of special importance to racial studies, was known to the members of the Sonderkommando, and whenever a transport arrived at Auschwitz they would somehow pass on the information to the unfortunate people that they might save some of the children (unfit to work, children were doomed to die) if they could present them as twins. Pairs of children of about the same age and of some physical likeness would be hurriedly selected and taught to memorize new personal data invented for them. Then the children, self-assured in their new role, would boastfully introduce themselves to the executioners: *Wir sind Zwillinge!* ("We are twins"). Thanks to this special scientific interest of Mengele, about two hundred children lived to see the liberation. It is difficult to say how many of them really were twins—probably very few. The subjects of Mengele's research—twins, dwarfs, and various individuals with birth defects—were placed, on his orders, in Birkenau, in Block 15, along with syphilitics.

Mengele repeatedly measured his patients, drew blood from them, performed blood transfusions upon them, and so on. From one pair of twins (tattoo no. 5107A), for instance, he extracted blood nine times. Mengele experimented with "his twins" as if they were rabbits. One day he found two Jewish women from Czechoslovakia who were twins, and though both were married, he chose for them new husbands, also twins. Fortunately, before he could carry out his genetic experiment, the evacuation of the camp was ordered.

The eyewitness reports of inmates regarding castration experiments lead us deeper into the horrifying aspects of the Auschwitz death-factory. These experiments had far-reaching geopolitical aims: they were closely connected with the criminal Nazi plans to create a *Lebensraum* ("living space") for the Aryan race in Europe through slaughter and sterilization of the "native" populations. Both methods were studied, researched, and "improved" in Auschwitz. There are many reports describing those experiments. The most detailed report is that of Dr. Shmuel Steinberg, who was employed in Block 21, hall no. 1, where the patients were confined after castration.[2] The usual procedure was to select a group of 100–200 healthy young men (eighteen to thirty-five years old) and take them to Birkenau, where there was a special sterilization unit. After examination by the camp doctors, the men were exposed to Roentgen radiation for five to six minutes. Because the attendants were usually unskilled, many victims were badly burned. They were sent directly to the gas chamber. The rest were, after a time (about one month later), taken to Block 21 at Auschwitz I, where they were first subjected to cruel, brutal "tests"— carried out in sadistic, perverted ways by the attendants—and were later surgically castrated. The castrated organs were sent to the histological institute in Breslau. In some cases, the castration was carried out in two or even four separate stages over a period of time, a different part being amputated at each operation. In the "busy season," twenty or thirty castrations were performed daily. After the operations, the patients were in excruciating pain. Most of them did not suffer too long, but were sent to the gas chambers.

A few castrated inmates, by some miracle, survived to tell of their experience:

*David Sures, of Salonika:*
I was sent to Birkenau in July 1943 with ten other Greeks, and was sterilized by Roentgen rays. We were all castrated a month later.

*N. Waligora:*
When I was brought to Birkenau at the beginning of December 1942, all the young men in our transport between eighteen and thirty years were picked out

and subjected to a Roentgen sterilization. Two hundred men were sterilized the same day that I was. The castration was performed eleven months later, in November 1943.

*Aaron Wald, from Poland:*
In April 1943 the SS doctor Schumann arrived in our block, no. 27, in Birkenau, and took all the men between 20 and 24 years old to Auschwitz, Block 21. First they shaved us, bathed us, gave us an enema (2 liters), and two intramuscular injections. At first, I resisted, I wanted to run away. Professor Schumann said: "We need it for an experiment." After the operation I was in terrible pain for forty-eight hours. Ninety percent of the patients died. After eight days, I had to go back to work.[3]

The castration operations were performed by German camp doctors of the SS and one doctor who was an inmate—Władysław Dehring, a *Volksdeutsch* from Warsaw, who was released from the camp early in 1944. There were cases in which patients who knew what the operation would be ran to the electrified fences enclosing the camp and committed suicide. Men who survived the castration began to lose all sexual characteristics: the hair on their faces disappeared, their bodies took on female characteristics, their voices changed, and their sexual impulses completely disappeared. According to the report of the surgical department at the camp hospital, the following operations were performed during October, November, and December 1943: eighty-nine castrations, five sterilizations, and five ovariectomies.

Apparently, this did not suffice for Hitler's doctors. At that time, Himmler was very interested in the experiments of SS-Hauptsturmführer Rascher, a doctor in the *Luftwaffe,* who was performing freezing operations on groups of concentration camp inmates. Rascher forced naked inmates to spend nine to fourteen hours in an open field in sub-zero weather. Later he would take them back indoors and put them in a hot bath, to "revive" them. These experiments were considered by Himmler of such importance that he personally suggested to the head of the *Luftwaffe,* General Milch, that Milch release Rascher from the air force so that Rascher might conduct his experiments under Himmler's own immediate authority.[4] From this time on, Himmler's protégé apparently devoted all his effort to this research. On February 17, 1943, he wrote a letter to Himmler, shameless in its cynicism and obsequiousness:

Highly esteemed Herr Reichsführer:
It would be the best solution if I went to Auschwitz myself to clear up the problem there of reviving frozen persons, at a quicker pace and on a larger scale, by mass experiments. Auschwitz is, under any circumstances, much more suitable than Dachau for large-scale experimentation. First of all, it is colder there; secondly, the camp is very spacious, as a result of which [the experiments] will not be that obvious, despite the fact that the experimental subjects make a noisy

commotion [!] when they are more intensely cold. Highly esteemed Herr Reichsführer, if it concurs with your wish to speed up these experiments, which are so important for our infantry, I humbly beg you to issue the proper orders, so that we can take advantage of the last months of winter cold.

With my most reverential greetings and sincerest gratitude, I remain always devoted to you,

Heil Hitler,

S. Rascher.

It was in Block 10 at Auschwitz that the Nazis performed their principal gynecological "experiments." To this center of the "scientific department" were brought 400–500 healthy Jewish girls and young women, between the ages of sixteen and thirty. Not only eyewitness statements but documents found in the camp after the war testify to the atrocities committed there in the name of science.

In a telegram (No. 2678) dated April 28, 1943, SS-Obersturmführer Sommer instructed the camp commandants to place 120 women on the list of "prisoners for various experimental purposes." The "Statistical Report on the Number and Distribution of Women Prisoners in Various Categories," bearing the signature of the deputy camp commandant Sell, contains a special column for "women prisoners intended for various experiments," under which we find the following items: April 15, 1944, 400 women; June 5, 1944, 413 women; June 19, 1944, 348 women; July 30, 1944, 349 women. Rumors in the camp—that these women had been "bought" from the camp commandant by the German chemical and pharmaceutical firm I. G. Farbenindustrie, for use as experimental subjects— were confirmed by a former German prisoner, Dr. Erwin Valentin, in his statement to the Soviet Extraordinary Commission for the Investigation of German Crimes. Dr. Valentin stated that representatives of the German chemical industry, Professor Clauberg of the University of Königsberg and the chemist Dr. Goebel, "bought" 150 women from the camp commandant for experimental purposes. The experiments were carried out by two leaders in German medicine: SS-Obersturmbannführer of the *Luftwaffe,* Obermedizinalrat Prof. Dr. Horst Schumann of Berlin, and Dr. Karl Clauberg, professor of gynecology at Königsberg (East Prussia) and author of many scientific books and articles. Clauberg was said to be a good businessman. For every successful experiment on women, he allegedly received a large sum of money from I. G. Farben. Working with Clauberg and Schumann were Dr. Wirths and Dr. Bruno Weber. Scientific supervision was in the hands of Clauberg and Goebel, his assistant. The department chief was Mayor Schmidt of Breslau. Two doctors co-opted from among the camp inmates—the above-mentioned Dehring and Samuel (a Jew from

Cologne, or perhaps from Berlin)—also participated in the work. The Nazis gave Samuel a laboratory in Block 10, where he was allowed to perform his own scientific research; they also supplied him with better food than the other Jewish inmates. In addition, he was allowed to write letters to his daughter in Switzerland, though all the letters were later intercepted and destroyed by the SS man Draser, on the orders of higher authorities. One day a German professor arrived from Berlin and confiscated all of Samuel's scientific writings; a few days later, Samuel disappeared. He knew too much and had seen too much.

Dr. E. Wind, who gave a special deposition on the Nazis' gynecological experiments, stated that, in addition to the above-mentioned physicians, Clauberg had two other collaborators: Maks Ippe and Sylvia Friedmann. Ippe, an electromechanical engineer from Prague, worked with Dr. Samuel to construct a device for intravaginal photography; he repeatedly carried out long, painful experiments to test this apparatus. Ippe was of Jewish descent, about thirty years old. Sylvia Friedmann, twenty-one years old, of Slovakia, was a close coworker of Clauberg, and his trusted confidante.

The young girls on whom the experiments were carried out soon became old and decrepit in appearance, probably because of the damage done to their sex glands by the experiments. The victims' wounds healed badly, too, causing prolonged suffering and, very often, death. The experiments were veiled in secrecy. Block 10 and its residents were isolated from the rest of the camp. The windows were shuttered, so that the women could see only through cracks in the shutters what was going on directly opposite their own block. There they saw the "Death Square," the execution ground for Block 11, where mass murders of inmates were constantly taking place. The daily sight of these executions only intensified the women's fears. When they heard that professor Clauberg was coming on one of his regular visits, they would hide in corners and become hysterical, crying out in despair: "The obese butcher is coming! The revolting rooster is here!"

The first experiments were carried out by Schumann on a number of young Jewish girls (between the ages of fifteen and eighteen) from Greece. First, they were sterilized by Roentgen rays; after that their ovaries were removed. Or, three months after the sterilization, parts of their reproductive organs would be removed and sent to the Research Institute in Breslau. Schumann performed such experiments two to three times weekly. Each time he would "use up" about thirty women. Wirths and Dehring performed the operations in Block 21. Hundreds of women were mutilated by them and then sent to Birkenau to the gas chamber.

One group of 170 women was subjected to the following experiment:

A fluid similar to iodine was injected into the uterus and ovaries, and a Roentgen photograph was taken; with internal instruments the experiment was repeated four or five times on the same women. The purpose of the experiment was to test, for German pharmaceutical firms, new substances to replace Lipiodol for the radiography of internal organs. These experiments were carried out by Clauberg himself or by his unskilled aides, who inflicted terrible pain on the women. In general, the experiments were performed with horrible brutality. The German doctors took no measures to spare the patients pain. In some cases, they even carried out their "experiments" simultaneously on mothers and daughters. For example, Hedi Schlesinger, a sixteen-year-old girl from Berlin, and her mother were operated upon at the same time.

A third group of women was subjected to the following experiments by Wirths and Samuel: Cancer tissue was inserted in the uterus, parts of which were later excised, and sent to Breslau for research on the early detection of cancer.

Other experiments involved artificial insemination. Attempts were also made to influence the sex of the fetus through injections of various substances. Dr. Benesh relates the following incident:

One day, at the time when I was working as a *Schreiber* [scribe] in the *Schonungsblock,* I was ordered to assemble all young men between the ages of twenty and thirty years. There were about 180 young men in this age group in my block. They all dispersed when the news got around, and it took me two hours to collect them. The block commandant took them over to the camp doctor, and they were told by him that their sperm would be used for artificial insemination of Jewish women. Rumors began to spread in the camp that Jewish men would be forced to sleep with the sterilized women for experimental purposes. It is impossible to prove if those stories had any sound basis.

The pregnancies that were artificially induced were also artificially terminated. Zofia Flachs of Cracow has stated:

During the examination, the SS doctor Koenig found that I was pregnant. He had me put in Barrack B-3 in Birkenau. There I found sixty-five other women in the same plight. On three consecutive days, I was given intramuscular injections to induce premature birth. On the fifth day, I gave birth to a child. I was seven months pregnant. The child was taken away. During the time I was there, I witnessed fourteen such cases. The children were always taken away.

The German scientists chose not to perform abortions during the first and second months of pregnancy, when the procedure is relatively safe and simple. They preferred to abort women who were six to seven months pregnant, when abortion is very difficult and very "interesting" (!). Many late abortions were carried out by a gynecologist named Thiele.

It is quite possible that many other experiments were performed on those wretched women, but we have no further concrete evidence. The small number of women who have survived can speak only of their own nightmare experiences; they cannot report on the ghoulish acts perpetrated on those who perished. Mutilated for life, sterile, internally burned by X-rays, with faces frozen into an expression of terror, the survivors may yet be carrying the germs of some undetected malignant disease—a last stigma of the black arts of Hitler's "men of science."

Finally, it is important to emphasize that the primary objective of these "scientific" experiments was to create the illusion that important and earnest work was being done for the Reich, so that these men might retain as long as possible their secure positions and avoid being sent to the front lines. At the same time, these scientists saw themselves as true patriots and German heroes, who were torturing the "dangerous enemies" of the Third Reich, the young Jewish experimental subjects.

❦ This essay is a translation from Yiddish, with some revisions, of two chapters in Philip Friedman's *Oshventsim* (Auschwitz), Buenos Aires, Union Central Israelita Polaca en la Argentina, 1950, pp. 113–29. Those chapters, in turn, were an enlarged treatment of the author's earlier work on the topic: *To jest Oświęcim* (This Is Auschwitz), 1st ed., Warsaw, Państwowe Wydawnictwo Literatury Politycznej, 1945, pp. 53–63; 2nd ed., Warsaw, "Książka," 1946, pp. 67–76; *This Was Oswiecim: The Story of a Murder Camp* (translated from a Yiddish manuscript by Joseph Leftwich), London, United Jewish Relief Appeal, 1946, pp. 43–49; *Auschwitz* (translated into Spanish by Elias Singer), Buenos Aires, Sociedad Hebraica Argentina, 1952, pp. 89–102; "Crimes in the Name of Science" (Spanish), *Davar*, Revista Literaria, Sociedad Hebraica Argentina, Buenos Aires, 1950, pp. 65–79.

The materials presented in this essay were gathered by the author while he was a member of the Polish State Commission for Investigating the German Crimes in Poland and attended the meetings of the Commission, which heard evidence about what had been done in Oświęcim (Cracow, March/April 1945). In addition to hearing eyewitness testimony before the Commission, he also interviewed witnesses privately, and received a great deal of additional material, including personal memories, diaries, statistics, and so on. Still other material was obtained through the Central Jewish Commission in Poland of which he was the director.

## Notes

1. Testimony before the Polish State Commission for Investigating the German Crimes in Poland (April 1945).
2. Testimonies of Dr. Benesh, Andrei Kobiletzky (tattoo no. 139,021); by F. Schechter, R. Goldman, and many others; by Dr. Golze in his book in Hebrew, *Parashat Hashoa* (Story of the Holocaust).

3. *Documents pour 'servir à L'Histoire de la Guerre* (Paris, Office Français d'Edition). Vol. IV. *Camps de Concentration. Camps d'Extermination. Auschwitz et Birkenau* (1945).

4. *IMT,* Doc. PS–1617. Letter of Himmler to Milch of November 13, 1942.

# 12

# PSEUDO-SAVIORS IN THE POLISH GHETTOS: MORDECHAI CHAIM RUMKOWSKI OF LODZ

The appearance of false messiahs in ancient Israel was almost always bound up with spiritual revolutions. The inmost urgings of the people, their hopes and their dreams, found expression in the messages of the false messiahs. Thus the term "false messiah" does not really suit those Jews who arose in the ghettos of Nazi-occupied Poland and took upon themselves the task of saving Israel. They were false saviors, not false messiahs. While these ghetto "dictators" occasionally used concepts and expressions seemingly drawn from the messianic tradition, those references were more than fundamental. The pseudo-saviors who emerged in the Polish ghettos derived not from the messianic tradition of Israel, but from foreign and profane sources.[1]

By twisted and strange paths, "messianic" notions had become central to fascism, especially Nazism. In distorted fashion, the false messiahs of the fascist states promised salvation to their masses, spoke about their mission and their election, announced that their regime would endure for a thousand years, and sacrificed to their nation's glowing future, tens of thousands human lives. The pseudo-saviors of the ghettos were, consciously or unconsciously, influenced by the great "messianic" craze of the fascists, and aspired to be saviors of their people in ways that were devoid of Jewish spirit. They were ruthless men who ruled, like their Nazi masters, by coercion. They believed that they would manage to save at least a portion of their people by autocratic deeds in the spirit of the German Führer. It is clear that they had little support in the Jewish community, which regarded them with fear and hatred (or, occasionally, with indifference), though it sometimes fixed its hopes upon them. Messianic feelings were profound among ghetto inhabitants, especially among pious Jews. The popular song "Ani Ma'amin" (I Believe)—affirming the Jewish faith in the coming of the Messiah, as enunciated by Maimonides—bears witness to a deep religious sentiment.[2] But that sentiment did not generate a messianic movement. There is no connection whatsoever between the people's messianic beliefs and the activities of the ruthless pseudo-saviors.

As is well known, the Germans ostensibly broadened the authority of the Jewish communities, giving them economic, administrative, and judicial self-rule, to make the Jews partners in their own destruction. The political model was based on the Nazi *Führerprinzip*. At the head of the community was appointed a leader (variously called *Präses, Leiter,* chairman, elder, *Judenältester*) in whose hands all power was concentrated. In several of the Jewish communities—especially Warsaw, Lodz, Vilna, and Sosnowiec—the historical role imposed upon the appointed leaders was unparalleled in the history of their people. Their egos were inflated with the power, honor, and prestige that the Nazis thrust upon them. In the final reckoning, not one of these ruthless men who entered the "paradise" of power went unscathed. One of them "peeked out and perished" (Adam Czerniakow of Warsaw, who committed suicide in the summer of 1942 when he understood the Nazis' scheme); three of his colleagues who entered the same "paradise"—Jacob Gens of Vilna, Mordechai Chaim Rumkowski of Lodz, and Moses Merin of Sosnowiec—"apostatized."[3]

Despite their historical shortsightedness and their incomprehension of the spirit of Israel's destiny, these were not simple brutes or tyrants, nor were they traitors in the ordinary sense of the word. Their struggles were a dramatic new phenomenon in the history of the Jewish people. There is, in the tragedy of these pseudo-saviors, a terrible historical lesson, entirely different from the case of Josephus or the Spanish Marranos. A profound complex of internal and external contradictions is bound up in the personalities of the Polish pseudo-saviors. Much more time and study will be needed for us to arrive at a full, objective appraisal of their roles. It is my intention in this and the following two essays merely to tell their story.

The largest of the Polish ghettos, after Warsaw, and the last to be destroyed, was Lodz. Though the Jewish community of Lodz was of relatively recent origin (the Jewish settlement there began to expand only in the early nineteenth century), population had risen quickly and reached nearly 250,000 by 1939. Famed for its wealth, philanthropy, erudition and culture, the Lodz community was an important center of Jewish life in Poland before the outbreak of the war. When the Germans took the city in early September 1939, they immediately set out to "solve the Jewish question." As elsewhere, they began by establishing in the Jewish community a form of "self-rule" which they could manipulate toward their own ends. The head of the prewar community, Leon Minzberg, had left Lodz before the arrival of the Germans. The Nazis chose, as head of the community, Mordechai Chaim Rumkowski, who had remained in Lodz. Rumkowski was then a personable old man of about seventy. Before the war, he had been director of the Jewish orphanage in Helenówek, near Lodz. He was known as an impetuous, energetic man of autocratic character. His enemies accused him of being excessively familiar with female students and teachers.[4] Rumkowski was exceedingly hot-tempered, and found it difficult to bow to authority. Many years before the war, he had entered the council of the Jewish community as a representative of the Zionist party. When the council became dominated by the Orthodox Agudath Israel and ignored the views of the Zionist minority, leading to the Zionist withdrawal from the body, Rumkowski defied his party and remained in the council. Afterward, during the Nazi period, Rumkowski would boast of his nonpartisanship: "I have put aside my party card for the duration of the war."

Rumkowski was clearly not a coward. To a German soldier who came to him with demands and began to beat him, he once replied: "What can you do to me? I am seventy years old and have already had my share of life."[5] He did not take lightly his role as chairman of the Lodz Judenrat. The journalist Tania Fuchs, widow of the editor-in-chief of the *Lodzer Folksblat,* has related in her memoirs that when the Germans came she could not decide whether to stay in Lodz or to flee, by a perilous route, into the Soviet zone of occupation. When she asked Rumkowski's advice, he told her: "You can leave? Go! There is no reason to remain here and wait. Hurry, hurry and escape. The situation here is very bad."[6] If that was the case, why did Rumkowski assume responsibility? Did the Nazis force him? On the contrary, it was he who sought the appointment, by all sorts of stratagems,[7] though the position was fraught with danger. In the first days of his administration, Rumkowski had a taste of things to come. The secretary of the Jewish community had been seized by the Nazis for work. When Rumkowski went to the Nazis to plead with them to set the man free, they seized Rumkowski and threw him into a tub of water, then threw him out with kicks and blows.[8]

Why did Rumkowski seek so dangerous an office? An important

motive was a desire for power and honor. But as we study his deeds and words, we see that he was also impelled by a profound feeling of historical mission, which only a chosen few merit and which he was obliged to fulfill. The madness of the Nazi policy regarding the Jews was still not clear to him, nor to the rest of the Jews. Rumkowski naïvely believed that he would be the redeemer of his fellow Jews, not only in Lodz but elsewhere as well. He did not understand that, by accepting the Nazi system's methods of autocratic government, he himself became an instrument of that system with regard to his brothers. He exemplified the maxim, "One sin induces another."[9]

The first period of Rumkowski's chairmanship ended grimly. The Germans had ordered Rumkowski to choose a council (*Beirat*) to assist him. In Nazi style, there were no free elections; Rumkowski simply informed thirty-one men by a circular letter (on October 16, 1939) that they had been appointed to the Judenrat and that it was obligatory to accept the appointment.[10] The members of the council, though inexperienced in public affairs, often disagreed with Rumkowski's policies.[11] Less than a month after the formation of the council, the members were invited to the Gestapo offices, where they were brutally tortured. Only two or three of them survived. On February 5, 1940, Rumkowski informed the German authorities that he had chosen a new council of twenty-one members.[12] What was Rumkowski's part in the fate of the original council? Had he complained to the Germans about the intransigence of the council members? If so, did he know what was in store for them? These are grave questions, which we cannot answer on the basis of the evidence at our disposal.

The second council was one after Rumkowski's own heart. The members had not yet served in any but third-rank positions. Rumkowski chose for his assistants and officials men without any standing in the Jewish community, even assimilationists and converts, whom the Nazi racial laws returned to the Jewish fold against their will.[13] These men, who were far removed from Jewish life and without any support in Jewish society, were completely dependent upon Rumkowski's will (a similar phenomenon occurred in other ghettos, such as Warsaw). After Rumkowski had removed his first obstacle, opposition within the Judenrat, he began to rule arbitrarily. However, as long as the Jews lived scattered about the city, his sovereignty was not complete. The reins of his government were strengthened when all the Jews of Lodz were enclosed within the ghetto (by a German order of February 8, 1940). But the number of people under his sole control decreased sharply. Of the 250,000 Jews in Lodz at the outbreak of the war, only 160,000 entered the ghetto. A large number of Jews had fled before the arrival of the Germans, and many were expelled or escaped in the first months after the ghetto decree was published. The Lodz ghetto was the first large ghetto in Poland (several earlier experiments had been made in certain small cities like Piotrków, but they were of little significance, and its establishment of course spread terror among the Jews). But the Germans soon increased the number of Rumkowski's "charges." About 40,000 Jewish deportees who had been expelled from various cities in western Poland, from the vicinity of Kalisz, Lutzl-bach, Poznań, and other cities, were brought into the crowded Lodz ghetto. In addition, about 20,000 Jews deported from cities in Germany, Austria, and Czechoslovakia were likewise sent to Lodz. To add insult to injury, the Germans increased Rumkowski's empire by adding a colony which was the only one of its kind: in the fall of 1941 he was ordered to vacate several buildings in the narrow northern corner of the ghetto, into which 5,000 Gypsies were moved. The Judenrat was obliged to take care of these Gypsies, especially with regard to food, health care, and postal service. The Gypsy quarter was liquidated by the Germans in the spring of 1942.[14]

The estimate of the historian Artur Eisenbach, that nearly 300,000 persons passed through the Lodz ghetto, is convincing.[15] With the establishment of the ghetto, Rumkowski began to rule by force. His official title was "elder of the Jews" (*Ältester der Juden in Litzmannstadtghetto*).[16] The Jews officially called him *Präses* (chairman); unofficially they called him King Chaim, Emperor Mordechai Chaim, *Der Alter* (Old Man). Emanuel Ringelblum recalls that Rumkowski was also called Chaim the Terrible (*Chaim der shreklekher*).[17] Rumkowski organized an entire state apparatus: supply section (the principal section), health section, welfare (social assistance), education (of children), culture, press, bureau for labor, housing and relocation, finance, tax offices, purchasing, transport and communication, mail, police, judicial matters, and prisons. The Jewish police (*Jüdischer Ordnungsdienst*) had about 1,200 officers. It had a "special squad" (*Sonderabteilung*) for "confidential matters" (greatly feared by the ghetto), and a "search unit" (*Überfallskommando*). There was also a German police in the ghetto, the *Kriminal-Polizei* (*Kripo*)— some of whose officers knew Yiddish and Hebrew—as well as agents recruited from the Jewish rabble. In addition, Rumkowski had a kind of a special guard, a private police—the "white brigade"—for special assignments. (Members of the "white brigade" had to work in the transport section when they were not on special assignments.) Rumkowski's right-hand man for police matters was Shalom Hertzberg, chief of the Czarneckiego Street prison. A coarse-spirited boor, Hertzberg was Rumkowski's devoted *shames* (assistant).[18] As chief justice of the ghetto, Rumkowski authorized the verdicts of the ghetto court (whose presiding officer was Stanisław Jakubson), and decided appeals of court decisions. He also sought to institute capital punishment. The Germans supported him, but four members of the court opposed the idea that Jews should pass death sentences upon their brothers during the Nazi regime. This one time Rumkowski acceded to the majority opinion. He did impose other forms of corporal punishment, however, such as whipping.[19] Like Robespierre in his time, Rumkowski sought to endow his office with a sacred and priestly character by performing religious functions. He schemed to monopolize the function of arranging and performing marriages, a function open to any Jew. Glorying in this role, he would deliver a sermon at the wedding and present the bride and groom with a special gift of food. The many photographs of these ceremonies show that Rumkowski took pains to publicize these acts, rather like a high priest. On the day of the Jewish New Year, 1939, Rumkowski appeared in the synagogue wearing a splendid costume—an embroidered blue and white hat and a long robe with a silver-studded collar[20]—which gave him the aspect of the founder of a strange new sect. This "high priest," who was a widower, married a beautiful young woman. The women of his entourage were always young and beautiful. In one of the women's garment factories, only pretty young women were employed (about seventy of them); it was called "Rumkowski's harem." Despite all the rumors that circulated about Rumkowski's attitude toward women, however, no sexual offenses or licentious acts like those identified with Jacob Frank, the eighteenth-century mystic, and his sect are known to have occurred in Rumkowski's circle.

The Lodz ghetto's administration was a model of its kind. Rumkowski was very strict about order, punctiliousness, cleanliness. He chose as his chief secretary a young woman from Hanover, Dora Fuchs.[21] Rumkowski solved the problem of discipline within his considerable "empire" in an exemplary fashion. Large sums of money were required for the communal institutions with their officers, the factories and production centers with their tens of thousands of employees, the agricultural settlements, schools, orphanages, and hospitals, and for the bribes that had to be paid to the German officials. Rumkowski expropriated all the houses and commercial facilities in the ghetto; he demanded that the ghetto residents surrender all their gold, silver, precious stones and valuables, coins and foreign securities—most of which he was obliged to turn over to the Germans. The special brigades of the police organized searches in the ghettos and confiscated whatever they found. The ghetto was full of spies and informers, who would tell the police about caches of valuables. Rumkowski oversaw whatever came into the ghetto from outside, whether from other Polish towns or from foreign countries via the ghetto postal system.

The ghetto postal system received within the first year of its existence

135,000 packages from Polish sources and 14,300 from foreign sources, 10,000 telegrams, more than a million letters and cards and, in addition, more than 64,000 checks, whose value was 1.7 million marks (the official exchange rate was 5 reichsmarks for 1 dollar). In the succeeding years, the income from checks rose: in 1941, to 4 million marks; in 1942, to more than 5 million. Aside from this, German, Austrian, and Czech deportees brought into the communal treasury currencies equal to more than 4 million reichsmarks.[22] The postal boxes in the ghetto were decorated with pictures of "King Rumkowski" as an impressive-looking old man (the Germans called him "the man with a chrysanthemum head"). He always had a good-natured smile, and would be pictured with various community groups, such as the ghetto economic council, a group of admiring children, or a group of ghetto poor stretching out their hands to him in supplication and gratitude. The Jewish postal revenues became a substantial part of the communal budget.[23]

How did Rumkowski manage to extract such large sums from the Jewish population? He introduced a "revolutionary fiscal reform"—a coin decorated with the menorah and the Star of David, signed in his own hand, and decreed to be Jewish currency in the ghetto. Polish and German money were prohibited in the ghetto. Since all the necessities of life (food, shelter, heat, clothing, etc.) and all social services were administered by the Judenrat, and all ghetto dwellers were obliged to use the new Jewish currency, they had no choice but to exchange at least some of their hidden money. The ghetto bank for issuing Jewish currency (*Ghettoemissionsbank*) opened on June 26, 1942; two days later no other currency, not even the German reichsmark, would be accepted in any institution or store in the ghetto.[24] The coins of the Lodz ghetto were called *Chaimki* by the Jews and Poles, after Rumkowski. An important source of revenue was the trade with the Germans—the export of goods produced in the ghetto, and the resale of imported (raw) materials for the ghetto. Rumkowski's opponents claimed that the Judenrat charged for such materials two, three, or more times the price it paid the Germans. The Jewish community also received occasional revenues. In August 1940, for example, when Moses Merin, the Jewish dictator of Upper Eastern Silesia, visited Lodz, he assured the community that the American Jewish Joint Distribution Committee would send $100,000 to the Lodz ghetto by way of Lisbon. Hans Biebow, German chief of the ghetto administration, wrote in disbelief to the Reichsbank in Berlin for confirmation. The Reichsbank forwarded the sum to the ghetto, in reichsmarks, of course.[25]

Rumkowski, an educator by profession, tried to save all that could be saved of the system of Jewish schools, in which Lodz excelled. The school division, headed by Eliyahu Tabaksblat and Moshe Karo, organized elementary schools which, by the spring of 1940, taught 7,400 boys and girls, and high schools with 730 students. These numbers doubled by 1941. The elderly Zionist businessman Shmuel Lev, the well-known scholar A. S. Kaminski, and the authorized representative of religious Jews, the teacher Y. L. Gersht, were subsequently attached to the school division. It was difficult to find teachers for the schools, because most of the Hebrew and Yiddish teachers had left Lodz before the arrival of the Germans. Many teachers from assimilationist circles, who had taught in the Polish schools and scarcely knew the shape of a Hebrew letter, were hired. The language of instruction in the ghetto was Yiddish. The curriculum developed according to Rumkowski's orders gave ample place to Jewish studies: religion, Yiddish language and literature, and Hebrew. These schools continued until 1943. Afterward education was pursued in secret. Even in 1945 classes were still held clandestinely for children who worked in the various production facilities in the ghetto.[26]

There were also hospitals in the ghetto. Of the 450–500 Jewish doctors who had been in Lodz before the war, no more than 150–170 (according to Ringelblum, only 30) remained. One objective of Rumkowski's visit to Warsaw in September 1940 was to try to bring back about 200 doctors.[27]

The "crowning gem" in Rumkowski's government was the organization of propaganda in support of the chairman. Several official and semi-official publications like the *Chronicle of the Lodz Ghetto* (in Yiddish, Polish, and German) were issued, as well as mimeographed newspapers and calendars. The official organ of public information was the Yiddish *Geto-Tsaytung,* which appeared from March to September 1941 (a total of eighteen issues).[28] Not a single issue of the *Geto-Tsaytung* appeared without an essay or poem dedicated to Rumkowski, the *Präses.* The "court poet" was L. Berman, who had been a teacher of stenography and penmanship before the war. He used to sign his "topical" poems in the *Lodzer Tagblat* with the pen name Graf Cali (Caligraph). During the ghetto period, Berman, apparently anxious to be counted among the *Präses's* supporters, abandoned his pen name for his real name. In the first issue of the *Geto-Tsaytung,* Berman opened with a poem in praise of the mighty chairman, entitled "The President's Strong Arm":

Our President, Mr. Rumkowski,
Is blessed by the Lord Almighty
Not only with wisdom and charm
But with a strong and powerful arm.
At number twenty, Dworska Street,[29]
People are working with great speed,
And all the lazy elements

Feel the power of the President.
The unruly persons, once and for all,
Have been put against the wall.
In the ghetto now reigns order and calm
Thanks to the President's mighty arm.

In another flattering poem, Berman wrote:

The President is passing through.
Men and women, old and young,
Gather here; they come in throngs.
Crowds are pushing, pressing, shouting:
"Look, our *Präses* is passing, our *Präses* is passing through."
Their hearts and minds are turned to him,
And their eyes beseeching him.
Hands are stretching out
With supplications and implorations.
    But the *Präses* is absorbed in thought.
    He does not deign to see them.
    Yet then he spots a child of seven
    And, smiling, stops to meet him.

Hundreds of similarly fawning poems, letters, and solicitations were sent to Rumkowski, together with the works of painters, designers, and sculptors. Adulation of the chairman became obligatory in the schools. For Rumkowski's birthday in 1941, the Lodz ghetto schools presented him with an elaborately decorated album filled with adulatory notes and addressed to "Our Master, the leader" (*Adonenu Ha-Nasi*): "Thou art the leader, provide for us!" He was also referred to as the "father of orphans" in the album, which contained the signatures of 14,587 children and 715 teachers.[30] Similar albums, some of them works of art requiring months of craftsmanship, were presented to Rumkowski by almost all the production groups in the ghetto. The surfeit of power and glory turned the president's head, and he began to preach his "social doctrine" and his plans to save his people. At one meeting, before the outbreak of Soviet-German hostilities, he explained: "I am both a Communist and a Fascist at once. I don't accept [the principle of] private property. Everything belongs to the state. I am also a Fascist in the sense that I require everyone to do what I command him. No man has the right to tell me what I must do, and I have the power."[31]

    Rumkowski expressed his thoughts more precisely to his secretary:

A few years ago I wrote a book that resembles Hitler's *Mein Kampf*. Hitler will win [this war], and then we shall be faced with the problem of solving the Jewish Question. Hitler will set aside for us some stretch of land where the

Jews of Europe will be able to settle. I have taken care to establish good relations with Greiser,[32] and they even know my name in Berlin. They will give
us authority over the Jews; I shall create there [on the territory to be obtained
from the Nazis] a model state.[33]

Did the recorder of these words, Grinberg, one of Rumkowski's opponents,
give us an accurate account? All that we have heard from Lodz survivors
who worked with Rumkowski confirm that Grinberg did not exaggerate.
Several shreds of information from other sources confirm his testimony.
Rumkowski's messianic dreams were known to Jews outside the Lodz
ghetto and a faithful witness to that is the well-known historian Emanuel
Ringelblum, who wrote in his diary on September 6, 1940:

Today Rumkowski, who is nicknamed King Chaim, arrived in Warsaw from
Lodz. An old man about seventy years old, a man of extraordinary ambitions
and somewhat eccentric, he told marvels about the [Lodz] ghetto: it is a Jewish
kingdom, which has 400 policemen and three jails. He has a ministry for
foreign affairs and all the other ministries. The question is, if the situation is
so good, why is it so bad? Why is there such a high mortality rate? He didn't
answer. He believes himself to be God's Messiah.[34]

As early as 1940, Rumkowski had moments when he thought that
he was the only one who could save "his ghetto" from destruction. Ringelblum testified in his diary on September 19, 1940: "When he was in
Warsaw, Rumkowski boasted: 'You will see, within a year or two my
ghetto will be the only one left in Poland.' "[35] One chronicler of the ghetto
believes that the object of Rumkowski's visit to Warsaw was to obtain
authority over all the Jews of Poland, but there is no proof of this hypothesis.[36] Rumkowski did not long enjoy his glory, however. When it became
obvious to everyone that "the emperor had no clothes," that the "Redeemer" lacked the power to redeem and was merely an instrument in the
hands of the Nazis, Rumkowski's opponents grew in number daily. The
political parties opposed him in principle. An association of Zionist organizations (the General Zionists, Right Poalei Zion, Hitachdut, Mizrachi,
and the Jewish State party) decided, in a joint meeting in April 1940, to
express opposition to Rumkowski. A similar resolution was also approved
in a joint meeting of the leftist parties (the Bund, the Communists, and
the Left and Right Poalei Zion) in October 1940.[37]

Within the ghetto, Rumkowski, friend of the children, sought to win
the hearts of the youth. Agricultural enclaves (kibbutz-like farms) were
established on the ghetto outskirts, in the Marysin suburb, for the youth
groups (Gordonia, Zionist Youth, Revisionists, Left and Right Poalei Zion,
the Bund, Mizrachi, and Hashomer Hatzair), which settled more than a
thousand members there and used the enclaves as centers for educational

and cultural activities. This development did not please the dictator Rumkowski, for he could not accept the idea that there were other independent powers in the ghetto. He may also have feared that the matter might become known to the Germans. At any rate, after a short time, Rumkowski took back what he had given the youth groups, and expelled them from the "paradise" of Marysin. The farms and gardens became places of recuperation for children, the sick, community officials, and especially for Rumkowski's friends and supporters.[38]

In 1942, opposition to Rumkowski spread throughout the ghetto, and found expression in graffiti all over the ghetto.[39] In a secret report (February 24, 1942) to the Polish underground in Warsaw, a Polish businessman, Wacław, described the spirit of the ghetto: "Rumkowski is the object of bold criticism and attacks. They accuse him of ruling by coercion and in a despotic manner—and, it goes without saying, of showing too much submission to the Germans."[40] The ghetto theater, and even more, the ghetto street singers, came out against Rumkowski with sharp satirical barbs. One Yiddish song, sung to the tune of "Du vest zayn a gvir, mayn Dzhamele," was very popular: "You will be emperor, Mr. Chaim, / You will show us an exodus from Egypt. . . ." Another, to the tune of "Hot a Yid a vaybele, hot a vayb a yidele," went: "The German has a little Jewboy, / And the Jew has a little Caesar." Still another verse went: "Two Chaims met and agreed / To divide the government between them."[41] And, "He gave us / Into the Germans' hands."[42]

The truth is that Rumkowski lacked the power to fulfill even his minimum program of protecting the Jews of Lodz from starvation and persecution. Either Rumkowski did not realize that the fate of the Jews was sealed or he wished to pretend to himself that there was yet some avenue of salvation open to them. Rumkowski was a firm believer in the "rescue through work" theory: "The ghetto must work with the precision of a clock." The most important events in the ghetto, such as the establishment of a new production facility or group, were noted in the ghetto calendar, as was Rumkowski's birthday, which fell on Purim. The chairman hoped to convince the Germans that the Jewish workers were industrious, that the Reich derived great benefit from them, and that they should therefore be spared. His was an empty hope, however. Hans Biebow, head of the German administration for the ghetto, wrote: "Everything which the Jews produce in the ghetto is, from the point of view of essential military supply, superfluous. They do not render any profit at all, but cause shortages [because they] waste raw material in an irresponsible way."[43]

In return for the finished goods produced in the ghetto, Rumkowski received foodstuffs from the Germans. During a conference (October 24, 1940) in the food and economic office, dealing with the food supply for the ghetto, the chairman, Moser, deputy of the *Regierungspräsident,* complained: "The Jews, most of whom are living indolent, useless lives at the expense of the German people, must be fed. . . . If that is the case, one must give the ghetto only the most inferior stuff." Matters reached the point where even the hangman Hans Biebow remarked, in a letter of March 4, 1942, to Gestapo Kommissar Fuchs: "For over a year now, the food supply to the ghetto has been so deficient that the per capita ration of food has fallen below the amount allocated to prisoners. To the ghetto they always give spoiled foodstuffs [vegetables, flour, fat, and the rest]." On April 19, 1942, Biebow wrote to Oberbürgermeister Ventzki: "The Jewish workers are collapsing [from hunger] at their jobs."[44]

The situation had been precarious even in the first year of the Nazi occupation. In December 1940, it was necessary to allocate to the public kitchens the potato peelings that had been set aside for the horses. Afterwards, ration cards were issued for this "luxury item," and ghetto residents used all sorts of influence to obtain those cards. In January 1941 all the factories had to be closed because the workers were starving and demonstrations were feared. The wormy flour given to the Jews was called *Judenmehl* ("Jewish flour") by the Nazis. Between December 15, 1941, and May 12, 1942, during the massive deportation action, the food supply given to the Jews often consisted of ten-year-old borsht that was rancid and wormy. Hepner, chief of the population division in the *Statthalterei* Wartheland in Poznań, noted in a "humanitarian" letter (July 16, 1941) to Adolf Eichmann:[45] "It would be better to eliminate the Jews by any quick method, it would be more convenient than to let them die from misery and starvation."[46]

In June 1940, the first hunger riots broke out in the ghetto. They were repeated in August and September 1940. Workers' demonstrations in the factories forced Rumkowski to make changes in his "economic policy." At the end of September, he issued a proclamation to the ghetto residents, promising various liberalizations, with financial assistance to children, the elderly, and the unemployed. This announcement endeared him to the masses. He was accustomed in those days to go out in the streets of the ghetto in a carriage drawn by a white horse, without any protection. He made speeches and was received by the people with cries of "Hurrah!" But his popularity quickly declined again. The winter of 1940–1941 was very difficult. Every wooden building and every fence in the ghetto disappeared for firewood. Unknown hands stuck these words on the walls of the houses: "Don't feed us paper promises any longer! We demand wood and coal for the winter! Now sell us the food we need at the price the community pays the Germans! We demand public kitchens for all the people of the ghetto, we demand communalization of the bakeries and welfare money for the sick! It is better to die in battle than from hunger!"[47] In 1941, strikes were called in several factories and in hospitals. In February 1942, a children's demonstration was staged in front of Rumkowski's house. The children carried a placard on which was written: "Rumkowski, you are our tragedy." One of the children made a speech, and the march continued to Bałucki Rynek, where it dispersed. In 1943, a strike of child laborers that lasted two weeks was organized in the women's garment factory in Łagiewnicka Street.[48]

Rumkowski fought with ferocity against these signs of disobedience. At the end of 1940, he took away the factory workers' representation in the Judenrat. In March 1941, he jailed the official representatives of the workers, and then released them during Passover. In 1941, he also imprisoned thirty-five striking physicians and hospital workers. Among those who most opposed him were the transport workers, especially the teamsters. Rumkowski got rid of them in a deportation from Lodz in May 1941. At the end of 1941, Rumkowski closed the public kitchens, because he saw them as a center for his opponents. On one occasion, he called for help from the German police, who fired upon the demonstrators and shot several of them.[49] Rumkowski also struck at his opponents, the poets, writers, and the artists. In complete contrast to Jacob Gens (dictator of the Vilna ghetto), who knew how to appear to enjoy a good joke at his own expense, Rumkowski had no sense of humor. He was badly hurt by the barbs of the Lodz satirists.[50]

It was not the internal dissensions that felled Rumkowski, but the terrible pressure from outside. The awful massacre of the Jews of Poland really began after the outbreak of the war between Germany and the Soviet Union. Until then, the Germans had contented themselves with sporadic attacks and "minor" deportations and with sending a number of victims to labor camps (generally to the Poznań area), where most, if not all, of them died of starvation, disease, and overwork, or were murdered. The first large "resettlement" (i.e., deportation) was in the fall of 1941; it affected mostly "foreigners," deportees from Central Europe who had reached Lodz about six months earlier. Of the 20,000 deportees, only about half remained after the fall action. At the end of 1941, the massive deportation action began, which continued for several months. The Germans demanded that Rumkowski and his officers implement the deportation. This time Rumkowski hesitated and sought the advice of the rabbinical council, pointing out: "I would perform this operation mercifully, while the Germans would do it with the desire to destroy." The rabbinical council agreed with Rumkowski.[51]

According to accounts in the ghetto, Rumkowski again put this moral question to the rabbis before the deportation of the children and the elderly in September 1942. When the rabbis were in doubt about whether the Torah permitted him to participate in the action, Rumkowski argued: "If the boat is sinking and may only be saved by lightening the load, we are obliged to throw the excess burden overboard."[52] Moses Merin, dictator of the ghettos of Silesia, had used exactly the same argument to defend his actions. The debate over whether some Jews might be surrendered to an enemy in order to save others, was conducted in other Polish communities under Nazi rule. Rumkowski was not softhearted; the opposition to, and criticism of, his acts provoked in him a spirit of defiance. After the great deportation of December 1941–May 1942 had started, he delivered a long speech at a mass meeting dealing with the factories (January 17, 1942), and in it he said: "To tell the truth, it was within my power to mitigate the ruthless order. But why and for what purpose? Can't you see that it is better for us to be rid of those sinners?" As if those sentenced to death by the German murderers were sent to die only because they were lawbreakers, vandals, thieves, and shirkers (*asoziale Elementen*)![53]

Rumkowski's relations with the religious Jews were complicated and contradictory. The religious Jewish masses were not organized into a political party; their opposition to Rumkowski was passive—but obstinate. In general, they were careful not to eat meat, even though several rabbis sanctioned the eating of nonkosher meat (the Nazis had forbidden ritual slaughtering, under penalty of death). They also refused to eat in the communal kitchens and in the canteens of the factories, not only meat but any food prepared on the Sabbath. The rabbis did not approve Rumkowski's moral principle of sacrificing some Jews to save others. Rumkowski, in turn, did not protect all rabbis. Rumors circulated in the ghetto that he agreed, without much hesitation, to the Germans' demand that rabbis be sent to die in one of the transports.[54] Very few managed to escape. On the other hand, Rumkowski did defend individual rabbis—for example, Mendele Rosenmunter, a Lubavitcher adherent.[55]

Rumkowski's dream of saving a portion of the people by rendering the sacrifices demanded by the Nazis collapsed with the deportation of the children and the elderly from the ghetto in September 1942. In early August 1942, Rumkowski called a meeting of parents in the Great Square (Lutomierska Street) and asked them to make a good will offering of their children to the German Moloch. He referred to Jewish history to justify the act. If the children weren't handed over, all the Jews would perish, and the destiny of Israel would be cut short. But if the adults could be saved, they could have other children when times improved. "Fathers and mothers! Give us your children!" he cried. Rumkowski's love of children was genuine, and his terrifying speech to the parents was heartbreaking, even for that stubborn old man. The square was filled with sighs and crying. The parents did not respond to Rumkowski's call, however, and would not give their children to the murderers. Rumkowski sent his police to implement the action, but even they, after two terrible days, withdrew. In the end, the Germans took over and finished the action with their own hands. During all the days of that massacre, Rumkowski did not leave his house.[56]

After the September action, a revolt against Rumkowski broke out, not a popular uprising but a "palace coup," which had been prepared for some time (since the beginning of 1942) by David Gertler, Rumkowski's deputy and head of the Sonderkommando of the police. Gertler served as a spy for the Germans, reporting on all that happened in the ghetto, and he also took part in some shady affairs. In 1940–1941, he helped (for a fee) wealthy Jews escape from Lodz to Warsaw, where he had connections with two Jewish Gestapo agents, Kon and Heller, and in 1942, when the deportations from Warsaw began, he helped people escape from Warsaw to Lodz. After the great "resettlement" from Warsaw in the summer of 1942, Gertler began to look for other sources of income. Thus he started to lay plans to take the power from Rumkowski, and the Germans supported him, apparently with the thought of "divide and rule." On the order of Hans Biebow, the allocation of food was removed from Rumkowski's control and was assigned to Gertler, who was given permission to establish special defense, police, and purchasing. Even the labor section (supervision of the factories) was turned over to Gertler's men, Aron Jakóbowicz and Mordechai Kluger. At first the people of the ghetto hoped that these men would be a change for the better. The new rulers began by distributing larger rations of foodstuffs and introducing slight improvements in the labor division. But the ghetto dwellers quickly discovered that the new rulers were no better than the first. To the earlier afflictions, new ones were added, in a war between the two camps of the "Old Man" and the "Youngsters." In the end the "Old Man" won. Gertler was arrested by the Gestapo and disappeared in July 1943. The crown had returned to its former possessor.[57]

But the roar of the now-wounded lion did not evoke the fear it used to. Rumkowski's prestige had declined in the eyes of the Germans, too. After the September 1942 action, Rumkowski did not remove the names of all the deportees from the list of ration cards; he left 3,000 "angels" (individuals who had died but were still listed as requiring food). The surplus food for these 3,000 "angels" was divided between Rumkowski and Biebow, the German representative. A German official informed the Gestapo about the arrangement, and Rumkowski was arrested. Apparently he said too much about his dealings with Biebow. Biebow, enraged, began to hunt for Rumkowski, who had been freed by the Gestapo in the interim. Several people came to Rumkowski, in his office, to warn him about Biebow, but Rumkowski paid no attention to them. Biebow arrived and beat Rumkowski savagely. He had to spend several weeks in the hospital.

This affair made a bad impression in the ghetto, though Biebow afterwards apologized to Rumkowski.

In mid-June 1944, there were still 73,267 Jews in the Lodz ghetto. The Germans, whose troops were retreating along the Eastern Front, decided to liquidate the Jews of Lodz as quickly as possible. They demanded that Rumkowski arrange for the "transport of Jewish workers to German cities in order to clear them of ruins left by British bombing." They first required 500 men a day, then quickly raised the daily allotment to 3,000. Nobody in the ghetto believed the Germans' promises any longer. Rumkowski invited the party heads to a meeting. He suggested, as a tactic of delay, that the Germans be given between 400 and 800 men a day, so that the execution of the action by the Germans would be impeded. In this tragic dilemma, the parties could not come to an agreement. The Left Poalei Zion supported Rumkowski's suggestion; the Bund opposed it, recommending a revolt against the Germans; the Communists wanted to consult their comrades; and the Zionists were divided in opinion. In the end Rumkowski took it upon himself to satisfy the Germans' demands.[58] By July 15, 7,196 persons were deported. On that day, the deportations were halted, and Rumkowski rode about the ghetto streets in his carriage to announce in person the good news to the masses, who heard it joyfully.

But the interruption of the deportations was only temporary. In August, announcements were posted in the ghetto, under the heading "Transshipment of the Ghetto" (*Verlagerung des Ghettos*). Rumkowski arranged a mass meeting (August 7), and Biebow took upon himself the charge of principal speaker; he addressed them as "my Jews," and promised them on his "word of honor as a German officer" that this resettlement was to save lives, not to destroy them. The Jews would be moved, together with all their tools and all the industrial machines, to safer places, within Germany, far from the front.[59] Several times, Biebow and Rumkowski appeared together as speakers. The Jews listened and did not believe. The number of Jews who went voluntarily to the reception areas for transport was very small. In the end Rumkowski said no more. The last announcement that he signed was dated August 7.[60] The remaining announcements after that were signed by the German administration. On August 30 the last transport left the Lodz ghetto, and the Germans summoned the dictator's brother, Joseph Rumkowski, to enter the train. Chaim Rumkowski, furious, told the German official that he did not want to be separated from his brother. The German then curtly invited Rumkowski and his family to join the transport, and he complied. They perished in the gas chambers, together with the rest of the Jews of Lodz.[61]

❧ This essay was first published in Hebrew, in *Metsuda,* VII (London, 1954), 602–18.

# Notes

1. See also essays 13 and 14 below, and my essay, "Two 'Saviors' Who Failed: Moses Merin of Sosnowiec and Jacob Gens of Vilna," *Commentary* 26 (1958), 279–91.

2. "I believe, I believe with complete faith, in the coming of the Messiah do I believe, . . . and even if he should be delayed, still do I believe." It was sung, primarily in the Warsaw ghetto, by religious Jews. See the anthology of ghetto songs compiled by S. Kaczerginski and edited by H. Leivik, *Lider fun getos un lagern* (Songs from the Ghettos and Concentration Camps) (New York, 1948), p. 314. The song "Ani Ma'amin" (words and music) is printed together with Yosele Ostrovtser's story of the Warsaw ghetto in a special collection edited by Fishel Schneeurson (Tel Aviv, n.d.), p. 16. See also *YK,* 28 (May 2, 1946), 8–12.

3. A paraphrase of Yer. Haggigah ii.1, fol. 9a: "Four sages entered paradise: Ben Azzai, Ben Zoma, Aher, and Akiva. Ben Azzai peeked out and died; Ben Zoma went mad; Aher destroyed the plants [i.e., apostatized]; and Akiva alone came out unhurt."

4. He was publicly accused of that in a book written by a physician, which I read in the late 1930s. It was published in Yiddish in Lodz or Warsaw. The author was, to the best of my recollection, a Dr. Pecker, or Preger. I do not recall if Rumkowski took legal action against the author.

5. Tania Fuchs, *A vanderung iber okupirte gebitn* (Wandering through the Occupied Territories) (Buenos Aires, 1947), pp. 36–37. A slightly different account of this event appeared in the Lodz underground newsletter *Min ha-Metsar* on July 8, 1941, and was published in *Dapim le-heker ha-sho'ah ve-ha-mered* (Pages for the Study of the Catastrophe and Revolt), I (Tel Aviv, 1951), 122.

6. Fuchs, pp. 36–37.

7. Of this the Jewish community in Lodz was well aware, as many survivors testify. See Israel Tabaksblat, *Hurban Lodz* (The Destruction of Lodz) (Buenos Aires, 1946), p. 32; Jacob Nirnberg, "The History of the Lodz Ghetto" (Yiddish) in *In di yorn fun yidishn hurbn* (In the Years of the Jewish Catastrophe) (New York, 1948), p. 236; Y. Okrutny, "Chaim the First" (Yiddish), *Folkstsaytung* (Lodz-Warsaw), May 14, 1947; and W. Herszkopf, "The Lodz Ghetto under the Rule of Rumkowski" (Yiddish), *Der Ibergang* (Munich), September 7, 1947.

8. Fuchs, p. 37.

9. *Avot* 4.2.

10. Tabaksblat, p. 33; *Dokumenty i Materiały,* III, *Getto Łódzkie* (The Lodz Ghetto), ed. by Artur Eisenbach (Lodz, 1946), pp. 13–31, esp. p. 20 reproducing the circular letter signed by Rumkowski, with a list of the thirty-one members (not including Rumkowski) of the Judenrat.

11. Y. L. Gersht, *Min ha-Metsar* (Out of Affliction) (Jerusalem, 1949), p. 87.

12. Tabaksblat, p. 33. Eisenbach, pp. 18, 21. The names of the new council members were mentioned in the underground newsletter, *Min ha-Metsar,* July 8, 1941 (see *Dapim,* I, 121–22).

13. Tabaksblat, p. 35, calls the members of the second council *di drite garnitur,* "the third-hand outfit."

14. With regard to the destruction of the Gypsies in general, especially their fate in the Lodz ghetto, see my "A Bizarre, Fatal Partnership" (Yiddish), *Kiyoum* (August-September 1950), pp. 1661–67; also essay 15 in this volume.

15. Eisenbach, pp. 13, 243; also "Statistik der Jüdischen Bevölkerung in Lodz. Lodz 1942. Statistisches Amt bei dem Judenältesten in Lodz," which was prepared for publication but was never issued, for unknown reasons. The proofs of the entire work are in the archives of the Jewish Historical Institute in Warsaw. A large part, but not the complete work, is in the YIVO archives in New York. Also see Abraham Melezin, *Przyczynek do znajomości stosunków demograficznych wśrów ludności żydowskiej w Łodzi, Krakowie i Lublinie podczas okupacji niemieckiej* (A Demographic Study of the Jews of Lodz, Cracow, and Lublin During the German Occupation) (CJHC: Lodz, 1946).

16. The Germans called Lodz Litzmannstadt in honor of the German general Litzmann, who in World War I won a battle in the vicinity.

17. Emanuel Ringelblum, "Notes from the Ghetto" (Polish), *Biuletyn*, no. 2 (1951), p. 174. Ringelblum's notes covering the years 1940–1942 were found with the second lot of Warsaw ghetto archives discovered in the ruins of the ghetto toward the end of 1950. The notes published in the *Biuletyn*, no. 2, (1951), pp. 81–207, are from the year 1940 only. One should not confuse these notes with Ringelblum's "Notitsn fun varshever geto" (Notes from the Warsaw Ghetto), which were found with the first lot of ghetto archives, discovered in the fall of 1946, and were published in the *BFG*, 1 (1948), 5–54.

18. Bendet Herszkowicz, "Litzmannstadt Ghetto" (Yiddish), *YB*, 30 (1950), 25; Nirnberg, p. 254.

19. Nirnberg, pp. 233–34; Herszkowicz, pp. 42–43.

20. I. Rosenbaum and M. I. Fajgenbaum, "Fragments from the Lodz Ghetto" (Yiddish), *Fun letstn hurbn*, no. 3 (Munich, 1946), 68–71.

21. Herszkowicz, p. 27.

22. Tabaksblat, pp. 48–51, with photographs of the Lodz ghetto currency; and Solomon F. Bloom, "Dictator of the Lodz Ghetto," *Commentary*, 7 (1949), 111–22.

23. There are photographs of the Lodz ghetto postal stamps in Tabaksblat, p. 46; see also A. Slabaugh, "Obsolete Notes of World War II: Money Issued in the Jewish Concentration Camp (?) Litzmannstadt," *The Numismatist*, 40 (1947), 579.

24. This episode is scrupulously recorded in the "Chronicle of the Lodz Ghetto," circulated in the ghetto in typewritten copies, in Polish, Yiddish, and German. Large parts of the "chronicle" are in the archives of the Jewish Historical Institute in Warsaw and in the YIVO archives in New York. [Since this writing the Chronicle was published under the title *Kronika Getta Łódzkiego* (Chronicle of the Lodz Ghetto), ed. by Danuta Dąbrowska and Łucjan Dobroszycki, 2 vols. (Lodz, 1965).—*Ed.*]

25. Eisenbach, pp. 118–19.

26. Gersht, pp. 105–13; also his "Teachers' Course for Yiddish in the Lodz Ghetto" (Yiddish), *YB*, 30 (1947), 152–55.

27. Ringelblum in *Biuletyn*, 2 (1951), 145. According to Tabaksblat (p. 13), there were about 170 physicians in the Lodz ghetto at that time, not

thirty as Rumkowski stated in Warsaw. Apparently, Rumkowski deliberately misrepresented the number in order to induce Jewish physicians in Warsaw to settle in Lodz. In the end he succeeded in bringing only five or six doctors from Warsaw.

28. The complete set of the *Geto Tsaytung* can be found in the Jewish Historical Institute, Warsaw. Individual numbers and photocopies are in the YIVO archives in New York, in the Historical Institute of Beit Lohamei ha-Geta'ot in Israel, and in the collection of the CJHC (now in Israel).

29. The address of the central office of the Jewish community was Ulica Dworska 20.

30. This album is in the YIVO archives in New York. Many similar albums can be found there, as well as in the collection of the Jewish Historical Institute in Warsaw.

31. Nirnberg, pp. 232–33.

32. Artur Greiser, the Nazi administrator (Gauleiter und Reichsstatt-halter) for the Wartheland, the strip of western Poland integrated into the Reich. Lodz was within that territory.

33. Quoted from Nirnberg, pp. 235–36.

34. Ringelblum, in *Biuletyn,* pp. 138–39.

35. *Ibid.,* p. 144.

36. Nirnberg, p. 326.

37. Tabaksblat, p. 99.

38. *Ibid.,* pp. 88–98. On the youth movements and their activities, see Betti Eisenstein, *Ruch podziemny w getach i obozach* . . . (The Underground Movement in Ghettos and Camps: Materials and Documents) (Lodz: CJHC, 1946), pp. 72–81. See also Rywa Kwiatkowska, "Youth Organizations in the Lodz Ghetto" (Polish), *Nasze Słowo* Warsaw, April 19, 1948.

39. See also: the collection *Zagłada Żydowstwa Polskiego* . . . (The Extermination of Polish Jewry: Album of Pictures) (Lodz: CJHC, 1946), pp. 11, 27, 33, 36, 40.

40. Documents of the Polish underground are to be found in the archives of the Instytut Historii Najnowszej (Institute for Modern History) in Warsaw and in the private archives of Philip Friedman.

41. The satirical objective was to contrast Rumkowski's absurd and presumptuous fantasy with the Zionist program of Chaim Weizmann.

42. From the song "Lodzher geto" by Yehonatan Karp, which was published in the periodical *Fun letstn hurbn,* no. 7 (Munich, 1946), 73–75. Songs of the ghetto were assembled in "A Special Section for the Collection of Folksongs from within the Ghetto" (Hebrew), in the first issue of *Min ha-Metsar* (July 8, 1941), later published in the book by S. Kaczerginski, pp. 41, 42–43, 60–61, 66, 67, 68, 86, 92, 93, 150, 171.

43. Eisenbach, p. 108; Bloom, pp. 114–15.

44. Eisenbach, pp. 245–47.

45. Head of the section in Reich Security Main Office (RSHA) dealing with the Jewish question, Eichmann was subsequently in charge of the program to exterminate the Jews of Europe. (Doc. 1410 Police file Eichmann Trial.)

46. Nirnberg, pp. 252–54; Eisenbach, p. 182. *Proces Artura Greisera przed Najwyższym Trybunałem Narodowym* (The Trial of Artur Greiser Before

the Highest National Tribunal) (Warsaw, Central Commission for Investigation of German Crimes in Poland, 1948), pp. 125–29.

47. Tabaksblat, p. 55; Nirnberg, pp. 246–47; A. Wolf-Jasny, "Demonstrations and Strikes in the Lodz Ghetto" (Yiddish), L. Fogel et al., eds., *Unzer Lodz,* I (Buenos Aires, 1950), 23–25. A collection of photostats of the protests against Rumkowski has been published (from the archives of the Warsaw Institute of Jewish History) in *BFG,* I (1948), 214–21.

48. Nirnberg, p. 230.

49. A. Wolf-Jasny, *Di oysrotung fun lodzher yidn* (The Extermination of the Jews of Lodz) (Tel Aviv, 1950), pp. 44–46; Nirnberg, pp. 228, 230, 246–49.

50. Tzvi Shner, "Toward a History of the Cultural Life in the Lodz Ghetto" (Hebrew), *Dapim,* I, 98; Isaac Goldkorn, "The Liquidation of the Jewish Writers in Lodz" (Yiddish), *Yidishe bilder,* Munich, no. 2 (February 1947); Moshe Pulaver, "Jewish Theater in Lodz" (Yiddish), *Morgn Journal,* April 20, 1952, followed by a series of articles on several Sundays; Yerahmiel Briks, "Folksingers in the Lodz Ghetto" (Yiddish), *Forverts,* June 11, 1950; Aaron Eisenbach, "The Jewish Literary-Artistic Circle in the Lodz Ghetto," *Yidishe Shriftn,* no. 2 (1947), 171–73.

51. Nirnberg, p. 258.

52. Herszkopf, in *Der Ibergang* (Munich), September 7, 1947.

53. Nirnberg, p. 257; Bloom, note 22.

54. Nirnberg, p. 258.

55. Gersht, p. 122; Mordecai Zar-Kavod (Ehrenkrantz), "The Journal of Menasseh Oppenheim from the Lodz Ghetto" (Hebrew), *Sinai,* 14 (1951), 241–78.

56. *Dokumenty i Materiały,* II, *"Akcje" i wysiedlenia* ("Actions" and Deportations), ed. by Josef Kermisz (Lodz, 1946), 243–51; Bloom, p. 120.

57. Tabaksblat, pp. 159–71; Nirnberg, pp. 272–78; A. Wolf-Jasny, "David Gertler, the Gestapo Agent in the Lodz Ghetto" (Yiddish), *Dos naye lebn* (Lodz), November 18, 1949; H. Gnieslaw, "The Establishment and the Liquidation of the Lodz Ghetto" (Yiddish), *Dos Fraye Vort,* no. 47, Feldafing (D.P. camp, U.S. Zone, Germany), September 6, 1946.

58. In the meantime, the matter became known in the ghetto and panic seized the inhabitants. Dr. Oscar Singer and Dr. Karol Bondy, representatives of the deported intellectuals of Central Europe, came to Rumkowski and asked him to protect them. Rumkowski ordered that a list be drawn up of seventy intellectuals and marked it "chosen to remain." A second delegation, of Yiddish writers (Josef Zelkowicz, Isaiah Spiegel, and Samuel Rosenstein), appeared before the lawyer Naftalin, a high and influential official in the Judenrat, and asked him to protect them. One of Rumkowski's broad objectives was to save Jewish intellectuals from the Holocaust. A. Wolf-Jasny, "The Final Liquidation of the Lodz Ghetto" (Yiddish), *BFG,* I, (1948), 94.

59. *Dokumenty i Materiały,* III, *Getto Łodzkie* (The Lodz Ghetto), ed. by Artur (Aaron) Eisenbach, pp. 267–68; Bloom, pp. 121–22.

60. *Ibid.,* pp. 271–74.

61. A. Wolf-Jasny (see above, note 49); Rywa Kwiatkowska, "The Last Path" (Polish), *Nasze Słowo,* August 3, 1947; Bloom, p. 122.

# 13

# THE MESSIANIC COMPLEX OF A NAZI COLLABORATOR IN A GHETTO: MOSES MERIN OF SOSNOWIEC

The question of the Judenräte—the Jewish community councils under Nazi occupation—has not yet been adequately discussed. Some writers judge them harshly, while others try to defend them. The entire Judenrat question deserves special treatment and careful analysis. Among the communal leaders who headed the Judenräte several personalities have become the subject of particular controversy. Men like Jacob Gens in the Vilna ghetto, Mordechai Chaim Rumkowski in Lodz, Moses Merin in Sosnowiec-Będzin, and Joseph Diamond in Radom, have evoked hatred and harsh criticism in Jewish circles. Many ghetto writers and chroniclers have regarded them as Nazi "collaborators," enemies of their own people. This reaction is understandable, especially among victims of the Holocaust. Historically and sociologically, however, so simplistic and superficial an interpretation will not suffice. These ghetto leaders were not simple "villains." Their downfall was the result of complex internal conflicts, coupled with tremendous pressure from the German enemy. At the root of their spiritual struggles lay the conviction that through political tactics they would manage to save a portion of the Jewish population from destruction. Moreover, some of these leaders believed that they were chosen by God to play a special role in the deliverance of their people. Such was the conviction of Moses Merin, head of the Silesian ghettos. An analysis of the psychological and sociological phenomena in the career of this false deliverer should lead us to a deeper understanding of the spiritual and moral processes which the Jews underwent during the Nazi occupation and destruction.[1]

## Merin's Rise

In 1939, the population of the twin cities of Sosnowiec and Będzin (in the mining district of Silesia, on the Polish-German border) was about 180,000, including 55,000 to 60,000 Jews. On September 4, 1939, the Germans entered Sosnowiec, and immediately began to persecute the Jews. A number of Jews were dragged by the Germans to the bathhouse and beaten: their hair, beards, and earlocks were cut off; many were injured, and some were killed. While this horror was going on, the German commander in charge of the pogrom demanded that the head of the Jewish community appear before him. The communal leader, Lazarowicz, who was among the tortured Jews, was afraid to respond to this demand, and did not budge. The commander repeated his demand several times, but no one responded. The situation was tense and perilous. Finally, a slight young man, Moses Merin, emerged from among the injured. He was immediately honored by the Germans with blows and kicks. Afterward he was found fit to be in charge of the Jewish community, and to act as the intermediary between the Nazis and the Jews. Thus began Moses Merin's rise to glory.

What sort of man was Moses Merin? Though in his late thirties, he looked no more than twenty-five, because of his slight build (he weighed no more than 90 pounds); his expression was sharp and energetic, his eyes keen and deep. His family was well known in the town. During the German occupation in World War I, Merin's father was appointed by the Germans to head the Jewish community. In spite of this, Merin did not master the German language. Before World War II, Merin was a commercial broker. He was separated from his wife, and led a bachelor's life. He spent most of his days and nights in coffeehouses, playing cards and billiards, at which he lost considerable sums of money. Merin's favorite pastime was politics, but his political reputation was not above reproach. Emanuel Ringelblum wrote in his diary (April 26–27, 1940):

I have heard an interesting characterization of "King Merin." Before the war, Merin was bankrupt. He used to switch from party to party. First he was a member of the rightist Zionist workers, then a General Zionist. For a while he was among Rabbi Hamer's followers; he was always politically active.

Before the outbreak of the war, Merin allegedly belonged to the Revisionist party, and served as a member of the Jewish community board. During the first few weeks of the German occupation, Merin's function was not officially defined. At the end of October 1939, the city of Sosnowiec was annexed to the Reich, and the German municipal administration was re-organized. Then Merin's career began. In Sosnowiec, a Jewish community council was established, on the model of the Jewish communal organization in Germany, and Moses Merin was appointed its head. Within a few weeks, the Germans organized the Central Committee of Jewish Councils of Elders for East Upper Silesia (Zentrale der jüdischen Ältestenräte in Ost-Oberschlesien), comparable to the Centralverein in Germany. It was called, for short, "Centrala," and Moses Merin was designated as its head, and thus became the leader of the thirty-seven Jewish communities in Silesia, with a total of 100,000 Jews.

Merin was the embodiment of administrative vigor. Of course, there was no hint of democracy in Merin's appointment. He ruled the entire district with an iron hand. He appointed and fired community heads and committee members. At the head of each community stood a minor despot, appointed by Merin and answerable solely to him. Merin levied heavy taxes upon the Jews, exacted special "contributions," confiscated furniture and household goods for the Germans, as they demanded various items, and enlisted, through the labor department, many Jews to work for the Germans. Since many Jews had begun by then to understand what "work" for the Germans meant, Merin used labor conscription as a threat or pun-ishment for persons who disobeyed him. Those who refused to pay contributions were immediately threatened with "work" or the camps. Naturally, a Jewish militia was not absent from Merin's dominion. On the other hand, there were also schools for children. But the schools had to be closed a few months later, by German orders.

Merin's Centrala worked even more efficiently than the individual communities. Twelve hundred employees worked at the Centrala. In addi-tion, Merin had a "brain trust" of high Centrala officials, heads of depart-ments, and elders of the larger communities. Merin's chief secretary was Mrs. Fanka Czarna, who had been secretary of the Jewish gymnasium in Sosnowiec before the war. She accompanied Merin to all important meet-ings and served as his interpreter on his extensive travels.

Merin's aspirations were still higher. He developed direct contacts with the German authorities. At the same time, he managed to keep in touch with the large Jewish organizations abroad. It is impossible to ascertain from the extant documents or memoirs how Merin was able to accomplish this under the terror of the Nazi regime. In any case, he was among the few selected Jews who were permitted to travel freely in Nazi

Germany and to negotiate with both the central German authorities and with the various Jewish communities. He went to Prague, Mährisch Ostrau (Moravska Ostrava), and Berlin. It is reported that he negotiated with Adolf Eichmann in Berlin concerning the emigration of Jews. In Poland, Merin visited Warsaw, Cracow, Lodz, and perhaps some other cities. In August 1940 he surprised the Jews of Lodz by promising to arrange a payment of $100,000 from the American Joint Distribution Committee. It is probable that Merin received considerable support from the Joint Distribution Committee for the Silesian communities under his authority.

Paweł Wiederman, chronicler of the Sosnowiec ghetto and Merin's biographer, recalls that Merin revealed to his secretary Fanka Czarna in 1942:

No man before me ever had as much power over the Jews as I have in my district. I wanted to extend my rule over most of European Jewry, but small-minded people blocked my way because of their personal pride, and thus condemned their communities to destruction. The blame belongs to Dr. Hirsch from Berlin, Biberstein from Cracow, Rumkowski in Lodz, Czerniakow in Warsaw.

It is difficult to say whether Wiederman may have recorded Merin's words verbatim, but the gist of the statement is consistent with what is known from other sources. Besides Merin's visits to the above-mentioned communities, a meeting (mentioned in various memoirs) took place, in September 1940, in which three ghetto "dictators" participated: Merin, Mordechai Chaim Rumkowski, and Adam Czerniakow. The conference was called by ghetto humorists the "three emperors' conference." In all likelihood, this conference resulted in nothing significant. None of the "emperors" was willing to give up his own "rescue plan" or his own main role in that plan. Evidently, Merin was no more successful in his other visits. In the spring of 1942, he reported to his closest advisors:

You have probably heard, gentlemen, that I have visited, in the company of Mrs. Czarna, practically every Jewish center, and I am thoroughly familiar with what is happening there. We were in Berlin and Prague, and what did we see? Depression, and the absence of a strong hand that could control the situation. The German and Czech Jewish leaders were helpless. . . . I reminded them that a year and a half ago I visited them and suggested the creation of a central organization of all the Jewish communities under German rule, but these men refused to listen. They did not want to relinquish their own power, and secretly bore ill will toward the Polish Jews. . . . They objected primarily out of fear that Sosnowiec would become the capital of the central organization and that power would fall into my hands.

Did Merin believe that such a daring scheme might be realized? Did he not understand that the Germans would never consent to the creation of a central Jewish organization? Reports and information recorded by Ringelblum in his diary clearly show that Merin's plans reached beyond the Polish border; Merin probably thereby increased his prestige in the eyes of Jews outside Poland. According to Ringelblum's diary (April 26–27, 1940):

Merin was welcomed in Moravska Ostrava and in Prague. He succeeded in freeing the Jews who were sent from Moravska Ostrava to the camp in Nisko [in Western Galicia]. . . . In general, he was lucky on many occasions. I think that he is willing to do anything in order to obtain emigration permits for Jews. Recently he tried to obtain authorization from the Jewish community leaders in Warsaw. He probably needed to do so because of the [German] Jews who ask, Who is he? Recently he disgraced himself because his promises to obtain 20,000 [emigration] certificates did not materialize. This hurt his position. But he succeeded in postponing the Jewish deportation from Silesia. . . . Merin "the King" intends to move to Cracow now to rule over the Jews of the "Reich" and the Protectorate in general.

Merin apparently visited Warsaw several times. In addition to the visit of 1940 (see below), some interesting details are known about his visit in April 1941. Merin was Abraham Gancwajch's brother-in-law, and some say that he recommended Merin to the Gestapo. Gancwajch was appointed by the German police in Warsaw to head an office to combat "speculation" in the ghetto. He was permitted to create his own private investigative service, and in a short time he was considered the "ghetto king" in Warsaw. When Merin arrived in Warsaw in the spring of 1941, Gancwajch had his office employees and his policemen give Merin a royal welcome, culminating in an elaborate public party in his honor at the Warsaw ghetto theater.

Like Rumkowski, the despotic leader of the Lodz ghetto, Merin sincerely believed that he had been entrusted with a historic mission, extending beyond the narrow confines of the Silesian Centrala. Merin, too, invented a "philosophy of rescue":

The Jews were always a stubborn people, just as Moses characterized them. They never wanted to obey their leaders or follow orders. Throughout our history there has never been a leader who could command obedience. . . . I am the only one who has been able to force my flock to total obedience. An inner voice tells me: "You, Moshe, were chosen to deliver your people from Hitler's yoke, as Moses delivered his people from Egypt's bondage." I deeply believe in this voice.

In times of disorder and oppression, even more than in periods of tranquillity, despots do not lack flatterers, sycophants, or simpletons to nurture their megalomania. Before the great deportation of June 1942, when Merin was to address a large youth assembly to persuade the young people to obey his commands during the deportation (he claimed that it had to be done, for the public good), a Sosnowiec rabbi introduced Merin with the biblical verse: "But they hearkened not unto Moses from impatience of spirit and for crude bondage," and added: "Moses Merin today is comparable to Moshe Rabbenu in his time. . . . He indicates the path we must take." According to another version of the incident, the allusion to the biblical Moses was even more flattering to Merin. Rabbi Grossman of the Mizrachi reportedly said: "From Moses to Moses there is none like Moses." To which the audience responded: "What an outrage! That a rabbi should utter such thoughts!"

Merin persisted in his delusion of delivering the Jews. If we can believe his biographer, Wiederman, there was no limit to his egotism.

I would not refrain [admitted Merin in conversation with Fanka Czarna] from sacrificing 50,000 of our people in order to save 50,000. Then my reputation will spread to the entire Jewish world. In the land of Israel, our new homeland, they will welcome me as a victor. Only then shall I appear in all my glory. My talents as leader and administrator will find their proper arena. I shall create a great army, equipped with modern weapons, which will support our influence on world politics.

There was a limit to the degree of arrogance and conceit that his coreligionists would tolerate, however. Merin's messianic pretensions now became the object of ridicule and criticism of his actions became widespread. Before the great deportation of 1942, a discussion of fundamental principles was held in the ghetto. Merin called for a meeting of his "brain trust," and suggested that the Centrala oversee the deportation, rather than have the Germans do it themselves. A long discussion ensued, in which several committee members opposed Merin's suggestion. They supported their objections with the quote from Maimonides' *Mishneh Torah*: "If a heathen said to you: Give us one of yours and we shall kill him, and if you don't we shall kill you, all shall die, but you shall not turn over one soul of Israel to them." The discussion on Maimonides lasted for a long time, and the committee members could not arrive at a consensus. Finally, it was decided that this important legal and moral question should be referred before the council of the rabbis and religious scholars of Sosnowiec. According to one of the Sosnowiec ghetto chroniclers:

Merin called together all the rabbis and religious scholars of Sosnowiec-Będzin. Rabbi Levin [Rabbi Hirsch Heinrich Levin's son and Rabbi Magor's brother-in-law] and Rabbi Grossman from Mizrachi participated, and [Merin] posed the following important question to them: "The Germans demand 10,000 Jews for deportation. The Gestapo reduced the number to 5,000 and perhaps I can reduce it still further. Should I carry out what I am ordered?"

Rabbi Levin answered in the negative: "Although Israel sinned, they are still Israel." Rabbi Grossman, too, claimed that Merin's demand went counter to the Jewish religion.

Merin had announced in advance that he would accept the decision of the rabbis on this question, and went out to wait for it. After a long discussion, the rabbis and judges announced that there was no alternative but to choose the lesser evil. They expressed their wish that he might be the rescuer of the *remaining part* [emphasis mine]. Rabbi Grossman was the spokesman for the assembly.[2]

The decision of the rabbinical assembly did not alter the negative attitude of the parties and youth organizations toward Merin. When Merin sent 2,500 notices of deportation to residents, advising them to appear of their own free will in the Judenrat's office, the parties called on the people to passively resist. When eleven instead of 2,500 persons appeared voluntarily, Merin was outraged. This time he personally oversaw the deportation roundup. The Jewish police surrounded homes and lined the deportees up in rows, and Merin himself turned them over to the Germans. Sosnowiec's Rabbi Englard strode majestically at the head of the tragic procession; behind him followed the well-known Mizrachi worker, Chaim Kupferminc. Eyewitnesses report that the following conversation took place: "We are going for the sanctification of the Holy Name, Rabbi," said Kupferminc, "and we must accept it magnanimously, if this is God's will." To which the rabbi responded: "Blessed be He for this, too. Let us not despair, we must set an example for the others."

When it was necessary to prepare a second transport, Merin forced the communal officials to take part in the police work. This operation lasted until July 1942, involving not only Sosnowiec but the other Silesian communities as well. Nearly 15,000 persons were deported to an unknown destination, and never returned. Opposition to Merin now appeared even among his friends and coworkers at the Centrala and in the communal administration. High officials and the heads of several Judenräte rebelled against him. Apparently the greatest changes occurred in the Będzin community. Jacob Ehrlich, a member of Poalei Zion and head of the Będzin Jewish community, objected to being manipulated by Merin, and resigned his position. A member of the Centrala, Władek Boehm, who was appointed head of the Sosnowiec and Będzin communities was transferred from this position by Merin for publicly criticizing him. For a while, Benjamin Graubart, the late rabbi's son, was head of the Będzin community. Then he, too, was transferred and Merin's brother Chaim replaced him. Apparently Merin realized that he was being criticized for his nepotism, and Chaim Merin was replaced by Chaim Mołczadski.

Moses Merin also employed his brother Chaim as a special messenger to the district's communities. The head of the Chrzanów community (10,000 Jews) was a decent and respectable man, Josef Umlauf, who was not among Merin's supporters. A dispute broke out between Umlauf and a member of the Judenrat, Zyg Weber, who had some influence with the Gestapo. Weber was known as a "Jewish Quisling" because of his close relations with the Gestapo. In December 1939, Merin sent his brother Chaim to Chrzanów. Chaim Merin reorganized the Judenrat, naming Bezalel Zucker, an honorable man, as its chairman. Apparently Zucker did not submit to Merin, and was critical of him. In any case, he was suddenly arrested by the Gestapo, and vanished. It was rumored that Merin was involved, though this has not been confirmed.

Meir Bajeski, the Centrala labor department's director, was among Merin's first assistants. Merin conducted a propaganda campaign among the youths, persuading them to volunteer for work in Germany, promising them that they would thereby save themselves and the rest of the Sosnowiec community from death. Meir Bajeski saw the "work in Germany" in a different light and finally relinquished his position (at the start of 1941), as a gesture of protest against Merin's policies. Handel Altmann, a member of the Zionist Council and an old friend of Merin's, criticized Merin harshly, and in punishment was sent first to a transit camp and then to a labor camp. When Altmann became ill, his friends persuaded Merin to free him. Merin agreed, on condition that Altmann write a letter of apology. Altmann refused, and died in the camp.

Bitter conflict arose between Merin and the still well-organized youth movements of the towns of the Zagłębie region. As a Zionist worker, Merin was aware of the importance of the youth, and was especially desirous of gaining the confidence of the Zionist youth. He was cognizant of what went on among the youth and did not suppress their criticism, using instead persuasion and propaganda to win them over. Once, during a youth meeting in an orphanage, the Judenrat was harshly censured. After this, Merin attended a meeting of the Zionist youth and announced that he was willing to help in their organization, particularly in arranging courses in Hebrew instruction. The youth representatives refused this offer, but Merin did not give up. He called on the youth representatives again, also in vain. Finally, after several unsuccessful attempts, Merin founded the "youth counseling bureau," composed of representatives from the various Zionist pioneering organizations: Gordonia, Hashomer Hatzair, the Zionist Youth, and the Kibbutzim. Dr. Lieberman was named the Judenrat representative in the Youth Bureau. After several meetings, Lieberman resigned, as did the second and third representatives appointed by the Judenrat. The fourth appointee was Josef Kożuch, one of the youth movement's directors and a high official at the Centrala. When he was ordered to assist in the deportation of the Jews of Kłobuck, Kożuch resigned his job at the Judenrat.

In the meantime, the youth organizations continued with their legal work as well as with their wide range of activities in the underground, activities aimed not only against Merin and the Judenrat but also primarily against the Germans. They published pamphlets and organized propaganda among the Jewish population. They encouraged Jewish workers to sabotage German industry, they distributed anti-Nazi pamphlets among German soldiers, prepared for an uprising in the ghetto, collected weapons and taught their members how to use them, forged documents for their members, organized escapes, smuggled news out of the ghetto (especially across the Hungarian and Czech borders), and sent messengers abroad and to other Polish towns.

Some representatives of the central leadership of the several youth organizations in Zagłębie went to Sosnowiec. Eliezer Geller, from the central leadership of Gordonia, went twice to Sosnowiec. The first time, in 1941, he spent several months there to organize leadership for the whole Zagłębie region. It is not known whether he met with Merin. When he was there a second time, in September 1942, he did meet with Merin, and was treated respectfully. Geller offered Merin a scheme whereby they could rescue several young men by sending them to work in Germany and Italy with forged Aryan certificates. Merin agreed at first, but then changed his mind and forbade Geller to proceed with this plan in his district. In the summer of 1942, Mordechai Anielewicz, a leader of Hashomer Hatzair (who was to be one of the chief fighters of the Warsaw ghetto uprising), went to Sosnowiec and spent about two weeks in organizational resistance work in the Zagłębie district.

Eventually, the relationship between Merin and the youth organizations deteriorated totally. Merin could not reconcile himself to the existence of an independent group in the ghetto. He demanded obedience from the youth leaders, and insisted that they work under the supervision of his youth bureau. Furthermore, he insisted that letters arriving from the communication bureau in Geneva be addressed to him. The youth leaders would not agree to any of these demands. Merin threatened to suppress youth activities, and appointed a special commissioner for youth organizations, Chaim Mołczadski, who had absolutely no influence. Finally, Merin even tried to found his own youth organization. Not only did he fail in this, but he further antagonized the youth. Ghetto humorists mockingly called the new organization the Merin Jugend (in obvious allusion to the Hitler Jugend), and thus ridiculed the whole idea. The youth organizations finally decided to make an attempt on Merin's life. Zvi Dunski, leader of Hashomer Hatzair in Sosnowiec, volunteered for the task. The attempt (in the fall of 1942) was unsuccessful; Merin was, as usual, surrounded by a strong detachment of Jewish policemen.

In the meantime, Merin organized, on German orders, a "mass inspection" in August 1942. All the Jewish inhabitants of Sosnowiec, Będzin, and Dąbrowa were called to three gathering points, where selections took place. About 50,000 persons were gathered by the SS for this inspection; fewer than half of them survived, the rest were sent to the slaughter. It is difficult to describe the horror and the sorrow. But even this terrible calamity did not break Merin's spirit or rid him of his delusions. He continued to philosophize and dwell on his thoughts of "saving the Jewish remnant." "I feel," he said, "like a captain whose ship is sinking; only by throwing overboard part of the precious cargo will it be possible to save the rest and reach a safe shore."

The "safe shore" that Merin reached with his flock were two wretched, crowded slums, where the survivors were incarcerated. Merin continued his work with great diligence. He was full of energy and ambition—to organize, to build, to create! For what purpose? Apparently Merin could not, or did not wish to, confront himself with this fatal question. He began a complete reorganization of the Jewish police, and thereby achieved two objectives simultaneously. First, he won over the Jewish masses by getting rid of the most hated policemen, those who had been guilty of excessive cruelty during the deportation (though they had participated by order of Merin himself). Second, bitterness about the deportation was deflected from Merin to the Jewish police. Merin tried to renew the people's confidence in him by addressing them publicly. Now he did not try to attract the youths, but censured them harshly. The speech which Merin delivered (early in 1943) in the Judenrat courtyard in the new Środula ghetto (a suburb of Sosnowiec) was typical in its "confession" and public soul-searching:

I am aware of the schemes and plots of some young men and women . . . also the foreign "certificates" which have come from Switzerland. . . . I warn you . . . I am in a cage, confronted by a raging, hungry lion. I stuff flesh down his throat, human flesh, my brothers' and sisters' flesh. . . . Why? Because I am trying to keep the lion in his cage, so that he doesn't get out and trample and devour every one of us at once. . . . No one will dissuade me from this course! I shall not follow what Czerniakow did in Warsaw. . . . I shall not commit suicide! I tell you that I shall continue to gorge the lion with my brothers' and sisters' flesh! May the day come . . . when you can judge me! If I live to see the day when a Jew from Tripoli leads me to the gallows, I shall cry out with the noose around my neck, *Shehecheyanu vekiyemanu vehigiyanu lazeman hazeh*. . . . I shall fight all those men who would disrupt my work. . . . I shall not let the youth distract me from my bloodstained labor. . . . No! . . . I shall fight them with all the means at my disposal, and let history judge me!

Extreme fanaticism and a belief in his "historic mission"—whose extraordinary cruelty has never been equaled in human history—permeates

Merin's words. However, Merin's hopes of saying *Shehecheyanu* on the gallows were disappointed. When Merin's "empire" had been squeezed into one narrow ghetto, the Germans did not need him any longer. They rewarded him as they rewarded all their collaborators. In mid-June 1943 Merin received an invitation to a meeting with the head of the SS. He was accompanied by high officials of the Centrala (Fanny Czarna, Chaim Merin, Lewensztajn, and Borensztajn). None of them returned. According to reports that reached Sosnowiec, they were sent to Auschwitz and died there. The Germans never officially explained what happened to Merin and his colleagues. The Gestapo commissioner, Dreier, simply handed Merin's deputy Śmietana, without elaboration, a short postcard (presumably from Merin) whose date was deleted, which read: "All is well. Keep up the work, as usual."

Merin's end threw the ghetto into a panic. Many, especially the simple folk, believed in him despite all, and hoped that he would find some way of rescuing them. After his death they felt like a flock without a shepherd. Some saw him as their "guardian angel." But many of his opponents were relieved when this despotic tyrant disappeared. One thing was clear to all: Merin's end signaled the total annihilation of the ghetto. The last big roundup began on August 1, 1943, and completely destroyed the remnant of the Jewish community of Silesia.

❧   This essay was first published in Hebrew in *Bitzaron,* XXVIII, no. 5 (1953), 29–40 (in the series "Collaborators and False Messiahs in the Ghettos During the Nazi Holocaust"). A more concise presentation of the subject, incorporating material in essay 14, was published by the author, under the title "Two 'Saviors' Who Failed," in *Commentary,* 26 (1958), 479–91.

## Notes

1. This study is based on the following sources: Paweł Wiederman, *Płowa Bestia* (The Blond Beast) (Munich, 1948); Natan E. Szternfinkel, *Zagłada Żydów Sosnowca* (The Extermination of the Jews in Sosnowiec) (Lodz, 1946); Emanuel Ringelblum, "Notes from the Ghetto" (Polish), *Biuletyn,* no. 2 (Warsaw, 1951), pp. 81–207; David Lior, *Ir Hamatayim* (City of the Dead) (Tel Aviv, 1946); Abner Feldman, "In the Ghetto and in the Camps," *YB,* 30 (1947), 223–48; C. A. Rosenberg, "The 'Thirteen' " (Yiddish), *BFG,* 5 (1952), 203; *Hurbn Chrzanów* (The Destruction of Chrzanów) (Regensburg-Munich, 1949); Ka-Tzetnik, 135638 (pseud. for Yehiel Diniur), *Salamandrah* (The Salamander) (Tel Aviv, 1946).

2. Similar discussions on the moral issue, as the one referred to by Wiederman in his book (p. 98), were held in other communities. For instance, in Lodz at the end of 1941, Mordechai Chaim Rumkowski had consulted the

rabbis as to whether Jewish law required him to yield to the demand of the Germans to deliver some Jews (and thus save the rest), or to refuse. See Jacob Nirenberg, "The Story of the Lodz Ghetto" (Yiddish), in *In di yorn fun yidishn hurbn* (In the Years of the Jewish Catastrophe) (New York, 1948), p. 259. A similar case occurred in Vilna, where the rabbis came to Jacob Gens, Gestapo-appointed head of the Vilna ghetto, and told him that he had no right to deliver even one single Jew to be killed by the enemy, that they were supported by the above-mentioned text from the *Mishneh Torah*; M. Dworzecki, *Yerushelayim delite in kamf un umkum* (The Jerusalem of Lithuania in Struggle and in Destruction) (Paris, 1948), p. 294.

The same argument arose in the community of Turek (between Lodz and Kalisz)—according to the account of S. Glube, "The Rabbinical Judgment" (Yiddish), *Fun letstn hurbn,* no. 6 (August 1947), pp. 44–47—and in other communities in the vicinity of Lodz. In the "collective ghetto" (*Sammelghetto*) of Heidemülle (Poznań province), the German authorities demanded that the Judenrat submit a list of all Jews, from which persons would be chosen for deportation. If the Judenrat did not comply, the Germans threatened to carry out the operation on their own. The head of the Jewish council consulted the rabbis on what course to follow. After a long deliberation, the rabbis authorized him to draw up the list, because, according to the words of the Germans, the deportation was to be to forced labor, not to execution. In the town of Oszmiany in Lithuania, a similar question was put to the local rabbi, who decided that a certain number of elderly people should be delivered to the Germans in order to save the younger Jews; Zelig Kalmanovitch, "A Diary of the Ghetto in Vilna" (Yiddish), *YB,* 35 (1951), 41. From the volume of responsa of Rabbi Ephraim Oshri, *Divre Ephraim* (The Sayings of Ephraim) (New York, 1949), we learn that this moral question was also deliberated in the Kovno ghetto. In the pamphlet *Me-emek habkha* (From the Vale of Tears), the supplement to *Divre Ephraim,* pp. 95–103, Rabbi Oshri discusses whether one is permitted to save oneself by the death of a fellow human being, and answers in the negative, citing the passage in the *Mishneh Torah* of Rambam; Rabbi Oshri notes that Maimonides proved his contention with a statement from the Jerusalem Talmud—namely, that it is forbidden to give up one single life in Israel. This tragic moral conflict must have engaged many communities, though we have salvaged evidence from only a few places. From the material available to us, it is clear that opinions were divided on this matter.

There is a vast literature on the youth movement and underground activities in Zagłębie. We mention here only the most important books and articles: Renya (Kukiełko), *Binedudim uvemahteret* (Wanderings and Underground) (Jerusalem, 1945); Aron Brandes, *Ketz ha-yehudim be'maarav Polin* (The Destruction of the Jews in Western Poland) (Merhavia, 1945); on two sisters who belonged to the Hehalutz in Poland and fell in the battle in the Warsaw ghetto, Gilead (Zerubavel), ed., *Chantche v'Frumke* (Hayka and Frumka [Płotnicki]) (Tel Aviv, 1945); Israel Klausner, ed., *Hazit yehudit b'Erope* (Jewish Front in Europe) (Jerusalem, n.d.), pp. 86–95; "The Battle and the Destruction of the Jewish Będzin" (Polish), *Nasze Słowo,* no. 7 (April 19, 1947); Fela Kac, "In Upper Silesia" (Polish), *Mosty,* no. 4 (1947); "From the History of the Hanoar Hatzioni in Sosnowiec" (Polish), *Opinja,* no. 16 (April 17, 1947).

# 14

# JACOB GENS: "COMMANDANT" OF THE VILNA GHETTO

Before the outbreak of German-Soviet hostilities there were approximately 60,000 Jews in Vilna (some estimates put the number at 65,000–70,000). In spite of the many restrictions imposed during the Russian occupation (1940–1941), Jewish life in the "Jerusalem of Lithuania" flourished. The political parties and youth organizations pursued their work, covertly or overtly, and cultural and social life continued as before the war. On June 22 war broke out, and on June 24 the German army invaded the city. Terror and the destruction of Jews began immediately. In the brief period between the beginning of the occupation and the establishment of the ghetto (September 6, 1941), 21,000 Jews were killed in Vilna; by December 21, 1941, 48,000 had been killed. The ones who survived were assembled in two ghettos: the "large ghetto" and the "small ghetto." The latter was liquidated soon after. The Germans established a Judenrat and a Jewish militia (September 1941), and placed a young man, Jacob Gens, at the head of the Jewish police.[1]

Gens was a new face in the Vilna ghetto. Born in Kovno, he was a member of the Revisionist party. At the end of World War I, he had taken part as a volunteer in the Lithuanian war for independence and served as an officer. He married a Lithuanian gentile, and was friendly with influential Lithuanian nationalists. Probably these friends recommended to the Germans that Gens be appointed head of the Jewish police.

Why Gens accepted the position remains something of a mystery. When he came to Vilna, his wife and daughter managed to stay in the Aryan part of the city. Gens could have hidden with one of his many Lithuanian acquaintances. Apparently he felt, however, that his historic moment had arrived. Mark Dworzecki, a Zionist communal worker and member of the underground movement in Vilna, has discussed Gens's decision in his book *Yerushelayim delite* (The Jerusalem of Lithuania). He quotes a conversation Gens had with a remarkable Lithuanian woman, Ona Simaite, who saved many Jews. Simaite, who knew Gens's family, stated that, in his first letter to his wife from the ghetto, Gens wrote: "This is the first time in my life that I have to engage in such duties. My heart is broken. But I shall always do what is necessary for the sake of the Jews in the ghetto."

The duties Gens had to perform as head of the Jewish police were hard indeed. The Germans carried out one mass murder action after another. The Jewish police had to aid the Germans by bringing the victims forth, often by physical force, and guarding them so that they wouldn't escape. One terrible massacre occurred on the night of November 24, 1941, the "night of the yellow certificates." Yellow certificates, later called "life certificates," had been issued by the Germans to 16,000 Jews who were "economically useful" to Germany. These Jews and their families would be permitted to live. The rest had to be turned over to the Germans by the Jewish police. To snare these unfortunate people, Gens summoned the entire ghetto to a roll call. Though the people did not know what the order meant, they sensed that their lives were in danger. Row after row of people filed past Gens, while he, surrounded by Jewish police and SS officers counted, "One, two, three," dividing the crowd in three groups with a motion of his cane. Persons with a yellow certificate were sent to the yard next to the Judenrat offices, while the rest were doomed to die. Gens's cane divided families, parents wept, and the crowd whispered: "Gens is a Jewish murderer. Gens is a traitor." One family of five marched up. Gens waved the man, the wife, and two of their children into the yard, but the third child, a boy, to the other side. The parents uttered heart-breaking cries. Another family of three came toward him, and Gens counted: "One, the father; two, the mother; three, the child!" Suddenly he pounced on the father, shouting, "You scoundrel, where have you left your second child?" The father mumbled in confusion: "I have no other child." Gens beat him mercilessly, while terror and confusion swept through the crowd. In the midst of the confusion, Gens lowered his cane on the neck of the twelve-year-old belonging to the other family, and pushed him toward the man, crying: "Here, scoundrel. Here is your second son. Next time don't abandon him, you fool!" With a haughty motion of his cane, Gens indicated that they go to the yard, and live. The crowd stirred and whispered: "Gens saved the boy's life. Gens is a Jew after all. Two souls struggle within him. Gens is a riddle." After the night of the yellow certificates, L. Rosenthal composed a song called "One, Two, Three," which quickly became one of the most popular songs in the ghetto.

After the many actions of the fall of 1941, a period of relative quiet occurred in the Vilna ghetto. Eighty percent of the Jews of Vilna had already been murdered. The rest reassured themselves with the thought that perhaps the Germans had filled their "blood quota." After all, only the young and the strong remained, who were "economically useful." German industry required workers, and Jewish workers excelled. "Work will save the ghetto," Gens himself declared.

We must show [the Germans] that we are very useful. . . . Work, especially work for the military, is the order of the day. . . . There are now 14,000 workers in the ghetto, and we must do all we can to increase our production. . . . Jewish workers must give up easy, convenient jobs and take on more difficult work, in order to increase their usefulness. . . . This is essential for the collective interest of the ghetto.

Though there was a Judenrat in the Vilna ghetto, communal authority resided in the head of the police, Gens. The Jews of Vilna called him "Commandant." This title remained with him when the Germans dismantled the Judenrat (in July 1942), because it was "too democratic," and turned over all authority to Gens. Gens issued a proclamation, in virtual military style, at this time, reemphasizing the question of work: "The foundations of the ghetto's existence are work, discipline, and order. Every ghetto inhabitant who is capable of working is a pillar on which our lives depend." Gens was not content with issuing this "manifesto." On the day of his "coronation," he and his friends decided to celebrate the event with all the trappings of royalty. They invited the Jewish police to serve as an honor guard that evening. Gens invited the elite of the ghetto, police officers, section heads of the Judenrat, and heads of the labor brigades to a gala banquet. For the first time, the Germans permitted Jews to buy flowers in the Aryan section of the city, and that evening ghetto notables could be seen dragging themselves, dressed in tatters, to the "king's feast," carrying baskets filled with flowers.

The witty Jews of Vilna, however, could not be presented with a dictatorship as humorlessly as had been done in Lodz or Sosnowiec. Gens understood that the seriousness of his appointments had to be cloaked in self-mockery. He ordered that a cage be placed in the garden of the

Judenrat, and that a live goose be placed in it as an emblem of the Gens dynasty that now ruled the ghetto (*gens* in Yiddish means "geese"). The inhabitants of Vilna understood the subtle joke, and came in droves to see the only fatted goose in the ghetto. Poets and humorists made frequent references to the "king's goose."

In the first period of Gens's rule, literature, art, and science flourished in the ghetto. A Yiddish theater, an experimental Hebrew theater, a workers' house in which lectures, parties, and meetings were held, children's and youth clubs, a music school, an orchestra, a choir, *yeshivoth* and *cheders,* elementary and vocational schools, athletic and health clubs, a weekly publication, science clubs, and associations for writers, teachers, engineers, physicians, pharmacists, and other professionals were founded. The most popular activity in the schools and cultural groups was studying Hebrew. The well-known Bund activist Herman Kruk complained in his memoirs about the "hebraization" of the ghetto. Parties and celebrations were often dedicated to such great Jewish literary figures as Sholom Aleichem, Mendele, Peretz, Yehoash, Bialik, Opatoshu, and Leivick. In addition to this cultural revival, however, there were other "revivalist" phenomena. Speculators and brokers of all sorts appeared in police circles, and a lust for all kinds of pleasures spread. People were consumed with a lust for the life of the moment and the pleasures of the body. Drinking parties, especially, elicited disgust and resentment among many of the ghetto inhabitants.

"Jacob the First," as Gens was dubbed by ghetto humorists, supported the arts and sciences, inviting Jewish writers to literary gatherings in the Judenrat hall. At Gens's initiative, the "Vilna Ghetto Publishing House" was established. Although it didn't publish a single book, Gens paid the authors for every page of manuscript that he was given, and thereby supported the writers of the ghetto. In 1942, Gens consulted the authors' representative in order to create a literary prize in the Vilna ghetto. He was also responsible for the collection and preservation of important documents and manuscripts relating to the history of the ghetto. In July 1942, Gens invited several writers to discuss with him the erection of a "monument to the ghetto." He intended to create a museum and archives for the ghetto. Gens also supported the ghetto's Jewish theater, which had a substantial repertoire; in 1942 alone, it produced 120 shows and entertained 38,000 persons.

Gens also showed great interest in schools, visiting classes, examining curricula, attending the children's ceremonies. During Passover 1943, he was invited to the schools' festivities. The children acted out the ghetto's Haggadah, in which Gens was depicted as one of the main heroes. Gens delighted in all the theatrical events. In the closing ceremonies for the

1942–1943 school year, Gens said to the children: "Little brothers, be good comrades, respect your parents, love your people, work for the ghetto, and be proud and brave Jewish children!" In addition, Gens also gave a summer practice field to the athletic club (which numbered 400 youths), and spoke at the field's inauguration. Shortly thereafter the field became the center for underground activities. Was Gens perhaps aware of this?

New manufacturing plants were established in the ghetto. The "Commandant" also undertook to ameliorate the food situation. Since there was a constant fuel shortage in the ghetto, Gens obtained permission from the Germans to cut down trees in the forest near Vilna for firewood. Groups of workers would leave the ghetto to work in Gens's Forest, as it was mockingly called (in allusion to Herzl's Forest in Palestine). Forest work soon became the favorite occupation of the ghetto inhabitants. Not only was the work healthier and freer, it also provided the opportunity to establish contacts with peasants, exchange various commodities for food, and prepare future hiding places. Above all, it was possible, with great caution, to communicate with partisan couriers in the forest. Might Gens have known about this, too?

Gens's authority and reputation grew from day to day. Several months after his appointment as head of the Vilna ghetto, he was designated head of all ghetto and civilian work camps in Lithuania and part of White Russia. The Vilna ghetto became the "capital" of the region, and Gens dispatched functionaries and policemen to all the new "colonies," the smaller ghettos in the area. Ghetto courts under his authority could pass sentences and had the power to execute them—including the death penalty. In June 1942, six persons, five of whom were Vilna residents, were executed for murder. The sixth, a resident of the ghetto of Lida, was executed for an incident of informing which had resulted in the slaughter of many Lida Jews. Gens praised the Jewish police, who carried out the sentence, for performing a great service in freeing the ghetto of criminals and murderers.

Gens was a strong-minded man who showed no signs of submitting to the Germans. They called him "the proud Jew" (*der Stolzer Jude*). Once, after a Russian air raid on Vilna, a group of Germans rushed into the ghetto calling for vengeance on the Jews. Gens thereupon ordered his policemen to apprehend the Germans and deliver them to the SS. Gens was feared and respected by the Lithuanian police, which guarded the ghetto gates. Until the massive deportations of the summer of 1943, the Jewish masses trusted Gens. They felt that their situation could be gauged by Gens's moods. "He is smiling," they would say, "therefore all is well!" Or, "Gens is depressed. A bad sign. Danger awaits the ghetto." The masses wanted to believe that, in spite of everything, they had an advocate and protector in Jacob Gens.

While Gens did his best to win the trust of all the Jews, he did not manage to win over, even during the more peaceful days of his reign, the more politically conscious and responsible elements. Anonymous persons organized protest meetings during the period of the terrible roll calls in the fall of 1941. Rallies were organized against police brutality, and the youth clubs organized debates around issues and personalities in Jewish history. A mock trial of Josephus Flavius and King Herod was staged, and it was no secret that these figures represented Gens although his name was never mentioned. Gens perceived himself somewhat differently. He compared himself not to Josephus or Herod but (according to the memoirs of Nusia Dlugi of the Vilna underground) to Moses. He would say again and again: "You Jews will see, I will lead you out of the ghetto."

Opposition to Gens was expressed in various ways. When, at his initiative, the theater opened in the ghetto, his opponents distributed leaflets framed in black that read: "The cemetery is no place for a theater!" After the "action of the yellow certificates," a delegation of Vilna rabbis advised Gens that, according to Jewish Law, he lacked the authority to undertake "selections" and to decide who should live and who should die. The rabbis based their opinion on the famous quotation from Maimonides, also used against Moses Merin in Sosnowiec (see above, essay 13).

In the first months of the ghetto's existence, an "assistance committee," composed of twenty members representing all the political parties, was formed. Since it had great influence in the ghetto, Gens always had to consider its attitudes. In general, Gens never enjoyed the same monopoly of power as was exercised by Rumkowski or Merin.

Faith in Gens and his promises slowly began to erode in the ghetto. The inhabitants began to formulate new rescue plans, and built a second city, an underground city—the "secret city" (*Geheimstadt*) as it was aptly described by the Vilna Yiddish poet Abraham Sutzkever in his famous poem of the same name. "Hotels" and "bunkers" were constructed in cellars and attics. In one of the "hotels," there was a hall for a school for eighty children. Gens's Judenrat was commonly called the *Judenverrat* ("Treason to the Jews").

Gens tried to influence public opinion in his speeches, providing detailed explanations for his various actions. This speech delivered in the coffeehouse at the presentation of a literary prize was typical:

Many of you think of me as a traitor, and wonder what I am doing here among you at ghetto literary gatherings. I, Gens, order you to uncover your hiding places; I, Gens, struggle to obtain work certificates, jobs, and benefits for the ghetto. *I take count of Jewish blood, not of Jewish honor.* When the Germans ask me for a thousand persons, I hand them over, for if we Jews will not give them on our own, the Germans will come and take them by force. Then they will take not one thousand but thousands, and the whole ghetto will be at their mercy. With hundreds, I save a thousand; with the thousands that I hand over, I save ten thousands. You are refined, learned people, you do not come in contact with the ghetto scum. You will come out with your hands clean. If you survive, you will be able to say, Our conscience is clear. But, I, Jacob Gens, if I survive, I shall come out of here unclean, my hands dripping with blood. Nevertheless, I shall willingly declare before a Jewish court: I did my best to rescue as many Jews as I could to bring them to the gate of redemption. I was forced to lead some to their death in order that a small remnant may survive; in order to have others emerge with a clear conscience, I had to befoul myself and act without conscience.

This was probably the most powerful speech Gens ever delivered. Gens appeared sensitive and sincere, but did his audience believe him? To what extent was Gens concerned with the public welfare, and to what extent might his actions be attributed to false pride, lust for fame and honor, intoxication of power, narcissism, and moral confusion? Can any human being withstand such trials and temptations and not be affected by them?

Harsher tribulations soon began. The Germans ordered Gens to conduct a "census" of the Jewish population in the town of Oszmiany, and to "transfer" (deport) a certain number of Jews. The Gestapo fixed the number at 1,400 (some sources say 1,000), but Gens managed to have the number reduced to 400 and obtained the concession that the Jewish police be in charge of the "resettlement." Gens and the police went to Oszmiany. Upon his return to Vilna, Gens appeared before a gathering of police officers, Judenrat members, the rabbinical council, and town notables, and declared:

In the towns of Kimieliszki and Bystrzyca, the Germans themselves carried out the deportation, without the aid of the Jewish police, and the entire Jewish population was destroyed. In contrast, in Oszmiany only 400 Jews out of a population of 4,000 were destroyed. In this manner, we saved as many people as possible, even though it has wrenched my heart.

Gens's words, and the additional reports by the police about the Oszmiany "action," shocked the audience. But not everybody judged Gens harshly. Zelig Kalmanovitch wrote in his diary on October 25, 1942: "This evening at the commandant's, the young policemen recounted the events in Oszmiany. They turned over 400 souls to the murderers instead of 1,000. They therefore saved 600 people. The old rabbi of Oszmiany decided that they should give up the old people." The turn of other towns soon followed. When preparations were being made to go to Święciany, Gens insisted that not just the police but the ordinary Jews of Vilna ghetto also participate in the action. Kalmanovitch comments (in his diary on November 1) on this matter in a heartbreaking manner:

Gens demanded that we all become his accomplices in the Święciany action. Truthfully, we are not innocent—we bought our lives at the price of the destruction of tens of thousands [of Jews]. If we have determined that we would go on living . . . then we must follow this inexorable path. . . . The old rabbi of Oszmiany may serve as an example.

After these actions, Kalmanovitch reports, Gens declared: "It is true, our hands are stained with the blood of our brothers, but we have had no choice but to accept this terrible task. We are innocent in the eyes of history. We shall take care of the survivors."

As time passed, Gens became increasingly involved in the horrible chain of killings. At one point, Gens was cruelly deceived by the Germans. During the period of deportations from the small towns, the Germans spared some of the deportees and sent them to the crowded Vilna ghetto, instead of to the extermination camps. It was understood that this was only a temporary reprieve. When the Germans demanded 5,000 workers for Kovno, the news was received cheerfully (ghetto Jews always thought that other ghettos were faring better than their own). Gens collected 5,000 persons, among them refugees who volunteered for this "work," and Gens himself accompanied the transport to Kovno to make sure of their safe arrival. After the transport left Vilna, however, the destination of the transport was changed, and the Germans brought the Jews to the notorious execution grounds of Ponary. The Germans detained Gens, and released him only after the massacre. Gens returned to Vilna, remaining secluded in his home, refusing to communicate with anyone.

The myth of Gens's power as "Commandant" to save and liberate began to lose its credibility. Gens's own faith began to falter. Until that point, he had believed the promises of the Gestapo commander, Martin Weiss. Gens would invite Weiss to his home for lunch, and the honored guest would promise Gens that the Vilna ghetto was not going to be destroyed because it was an important labor camp for German production. Gens had repeated these promises, from a "reliable source," to the ghetto population. Now, however, he was bitterly disappointed, and realized that his tactic of "buying time" from the Germans was bankrupt, that a better strategy had to be devised. But Gens was too late. He had missed the opportunity.

At the end of 1941, the *Fareynikte partizaner organizatsye* (FPO) (United Partisans Organization) was founded in the Vilna ghetto. On January 1, 1942, the FPO issued its first manifesto to the ghetto residents: "We do not want to go like sheep to the slaughter, we want to fight." The

Zionist parties, the Zionist Revisionists, the Bund, Hashomer Hatzair, and the Communists participated in the FPO. Gens's attitude toward the organization was vague and inconsistent from the outset. While he was a moody man, full of contradictions, he was attuned to the people and events around him. Vilna ghetto chroniclers and historians are divided about Gens's position on the FPO. Some claim that he helped the FPO and knew that groups from the ghetto were infiltrating partisan units in the forests. In some instances, he apparently ordered the guards at the ghetto gates to keep the gates unlocked at night in order to make escape easier. According to some chroniclers, Gens cautiously began to prepare his men to join forces with the FPO at the proper moment. Other scholars, however, assert that Gens opposed the FPO from the outset, and wanted to break it up. One group of ghetto fighters felt that Gens was a total traitor to their cause. Perhaps the comments of Szmerke Kaczerginski, author and Vilna partisan, come closest to the truth: "Gens wanted to befriend the FPO, but he was entangled in such a thick net of intrigues and corruption that his good intentions were of no avail." The relationship between Gens and the FPO finally became clear in two dramatic confrontations, which greatly affected the fate of the Vilna ghetto and the resistance movement. In these bitter struggles, the FPO's foundations and underground work, carefully organized over a period of many months, would collapse.

The first of these crucial struggles was between Gens and Joseph Glazman. Before the war, Joseph Glazman was a commander of the Revisionist Betar and an editor of the Revisionist newspaper *Hamedinah*. After the German occupation, he was appointed deputy chief of the Jewish police in the Vilna ghetto. Prior to accepting the position, he consulted his party, which advised that the appointment could benefit the Revisionist party, affording them wider freedom of action in the underground, as well as other administrative advantages. At the same time, Glazman was a member of the central committee of the FPO. According to some authors, the founding meeting of the FPO took place at his home. The FPO had a special intelligence section devoted to uncovering Gestapo agents and others who infiltrated the underground and to surveillance of the FPO itself for cowardice and treachery among its members. To observe the Jewish police force, the espionage section planted some of its members there. Glazman was the head of the section.

Glazman was an energetic and ambitious man with a great deal of administrative talent. His reputation grew daily in the ghetto, and Gens became jealous. Suddenly, Glazman resigned his position as deputy police chief, and was made head of the ghetto housing section. The reasons for the transfer have never been adequately clarified. Some claim that Gens did it at Glazman's request, because Glazman could not tolerate his dual role. The matter did not end here, however. When preparations began for the Święciany action, Gens ordered Glazman to go there to clear up the "housing situation" of the ghetto. Glazman understood, however, that "housing problem" was in this case a euphemism for deportation. When Glazman refused, Gens lost his temper, railed against the "intelligentsia, which criticizes the hard work of the police," and had Glazman arrested. On the way to prison, armed members of the FPO (apparently members of the Revisionist party) attacked the police and freed Glazman, after a skirmish. It was the first time two armed Jewish groups had confronted each other in the ghetto. The threat of civil war was in the air, and both sides retreated in the face of this possibility and attempted to find a compromise. Negotiations between Gens and the FPO were not easy. The FPO was unwilling to disclose its leaders, and sent its Communist members as representatives to meet with Gens. This occurred at the end of June 1943, when rumors were rife in the ghetto about an impending Russian invasion of Vilna. Under these circumstances the FPO assumed that Gens would not dare harm the Communist delegation and would be more amenable to compromise. Apparently, Gens was able to gain the confidence of the FPO, for all its leaders participated in subsequent meetings. Gens explained that Glazman's actions were disrupting discipline in the ghetto, and that without discipline he, Gens, could not manage ghetto affairs. They finally reached a compromise: Glazman received the token punishment of being sent, without police escort, to the labor camp in the marshes near Vilna. A few days later he was released from the camp, and returned to Vilna.

Gens had won a victory. Glazman could do nothing after his return, since he was now too well known to pursue his underground activities in the ghetto. He thus decided to leave the ghetto. In July 1943 he organized a band of fighters and departed for the forests. The forests around Vilna were filled with German and Lithuanian police. After several heated battles in which many of his friends were killed, Glazman managed to break through the circle of German police and reach the partisans. He became the commander of a partisan group known as "Revenge," and increased the number of members by several hundred. He was killed in a forest battle with either the Germans or the Lithuanians.

Before the ghetto could recover from the Gens-Glazman dispute, a second, more dramatic conflict erupted. On July 9, 1943, the German secret service captured two Polish Communists in Vilna. During the interrogation, one of the men broke under the torture and revealed some information, including the fact that he had communicated with a Vilna ghetto Communist, Yizhak Wittenberg. The Gestapo demanded that Gens turn over Wittenberg, apparently without knowing that Wittenberg was commander-in-chief of the FPO. Gens, who knew what the Gestapo did not know, decided to use guile. Since the days of the Gens-Glazman conflict, Gens had met regularly with the FPO on matters of mutual interest. He arranged an urgent meeting at his home at midnight of July 16, 1943. During the meeting, Lithuanian policemen and Salek Desler, deputy chief of the Jewish militia, broke in and handcuffed Wittenberg to turn him over to the Germans. Here Gens had miscalculated, however. Apparently he did not know that whenever the FPO met with him they took the precaution of stationing guards outside. When the FPO guards saw what was happening, they sounded their alarm, "Liza is calling,"[2] all over the ghetto. A half-hour after Wittenberg was arrested, he was freed by armed members of the FPO.

Gens realized that if he did not act immediately he would lose his influence in the ghetto forever. His reaction was quiet and determined. At 2 A.M., Gens summoned his policemen and the ghetto inhabitants. Frightened inhabitants poured into the courtyard near the Judenrat not knowing what had happened. Gens announced, in a voice filled with rage, that the Gestapo demanded that a certain Communist Jew, who had contacts with non-Jewish Communists, be turned over to them. If the order was not obeyed, the entire ghetto would be destroyed. Should the entire ghetto be destroyed for the sake of one man? Gens asked. The crowd answered with a cry of terror: "No! Turn over Wittenberg! We shall save the ghetto from destruction!"

The masses were clearly on Gens's side. They wanted to live. Once again there were rumors that the Russian army was drawing near, and that the Vilna ghetto would soon be liberated. Now, just before the moment of impending liberation, the entire ghetto's safety was jeopardized because one man had communicated with Poles and Lithuanians, people who had never lifted a finger to help the Jews. Moreover, they reasoned, how could a Jew put the affairs of his party above the general welfare of the people at such a time? The middle class and the moderates among the intellectuals also followed this line of reasoning, opposing the idea of resistance and the FPO. Their stand strengthened Gens's position. Kalmanovitch's diary entry for July 16, 1943, is typical of their attitude: "The movement [i.e., the FPO] might bring disaster upon the whole Jewish population. . . . Jews attacked Jews. Weapons which were meant to protect Jewish lives took Jewish lives. . . . Some were injured. . . . Self-defense is a false hope. It is not realistic."

Vilna residents did not really know Wittenberg. As head of the FPO, he had necessarily avoided publicity and public appearances. Even many of the members of the underground who knew him personally did not know that he was commander-in-chief of the FPO. Wittenberg had the qualities of a born leader: quiet and self-controlled, energetic, strong-willed, and consistent, he inspired his friends with his serene and confident nature. Courage and composure did not leave him, even in his most difficult moments.

Wittenberg was staying in a house where the FPO had brought him after freeing him; he was protected by guards ready to defend him against any attack. In the meantime, Gens mobilized the thugs and mobsters of the ghetto, who marched at the head of an angry crowd, surrounding the house where Wittenberg was being kept, and threatening to destroy it if Wittenberg were not handed over by the FPO. In addition, Gens and Desler went from house to house making inflammatory speeches in every yard. Gens declaimed: "The Gestapo has set the deadline for six in the morning. If by then we do not deliver Wittenberg, they will come with tanks and planes to destroy us. Who will defend us then? The small fry with their toy guns?"

At that very moment, the "small fry," FPO youth, were standing ready for battle, arms in hand. In their hearts, however, an inner struggle was taking place. The Jews look on us as their murderers, they thought. We collected guns together and dreamed of a war with the hated Germans, and instead, against whom do we intend to fight? Against our brothers, sons of Israel? Gens understood the FPO's dilemma, and was prepared to take immediate advantage. He sent emissaries to the headquarters of the FPO. At first, the FPO refused to negotiate, but finally agreed to talk. Gens explained:

You fell into this trap because of your carelessness. You yourselves are to blame for what has happened. Resistance to the Germans is impossible in this moment. If we start a battle now, you will be defeated. It is better than you lose one man than that you lose all. You must wait for the proper moment, gain time, and at the right moment you can organize a breakthrough from the ghetto into the forests.

Wittenberg sat quietly listening to the heated debate between the members of the FPO, but took no part in it. The high command of the FPO could not reach a decision. The mob's cries of "We want to live! We want to live!" penetrated through the window. Finally, Wittenberg spoke up: "Listen, please! I would like to turn the decision over to my party." They all agreed to this, and the Communist members of the FPO went into another room to consult. The decision they reached was that Wittenberg turn himself over to the Germans of his own free will. Several party members, including Sonya Madejsker (later caught by the Germans and executed), were selected to tell Wittenberg of the decision. When Wittenberg heard their plan, he could not believe his ears, and asked: "Sonya, was this your decision? Are you serious, Sonya?" His friends repeated their decision and explained that it was the only way out. Finally, Wittenberg understood and accepted their decision. One account relates that he abruptly replied: "If this is what you want, I shall go then." According to another version, he said: "It has never happened that an organization would surrender its leader. Any party which acts this way is bankrupt."

Wittenberg surrendered to the Germans, and was accompanied by the Jews to the ghetto gates. He was imprisoned and tortured for several days. Some accounts relate that the Germans then threw his dying body into the city streets. According to one rumor, Wittenberg took poison, and was thus spared further torture. Several poems were composed concerning his death, one of which (by Shmerke Kaczerginski) became a very popular Yiddish folksong.

Did the Germans know what had happened in the ghetto during the "Wittenberg days"? There is no doubt that they had a number of spies and informers who provided them with detailed reports. And it is likely that reports about the FPO's preparations for an uprising hastened the liquidation of the ghetto. A few days after the Wittenberg affair, new, accelerated actions began: July 27, August 1, 6, and 19–24, 1943. Between August 19 and 24, the small Lithuanian ghettos were also emptied of their Jews. From September 1 to 5, the great deportation to Estonia took place. It was rumored that this deportation really meant a transfer to labor camps, not extermination camps. Genuine letters, in contrast to the customary forged ones, arrived from the Vayvari camp, which was soon dubbed "Camp Veh-Veh" (lit., "Woe, Woe"). Once again Gens delivered confident, optimistic speeches: "We must all go. We shall work there and we shall live."

But the ghetto no longer believed in Gens's promises. No one would board the transports voluntarily to go on the train to Estonia, and Gens was enraged. He got drunk, ran back and forth with his stick, beating and prodding Jews who refused to enter the transport cars. When a Jew hesitated, Gens, infuriated, would pull out his revolver and kill him. The Jewish police also lost all restraint, brutally shooting deportees with guns provided by the Germans. The action ended "successfully": 5,000 Jews from Vilna were sent to the camps in Estonia.

Gens appeared before the survivors, and declared: "This time there shall be peace." But the eternal peace which descended on the ghetto was not the one which he had hoped for. The German informers in the Jewish police spied on Gens, especially on his communications with the partisans. On the basis of their information, the Gestapo ordered Gens to appear at headquarters on September 14. One of Gens's friends in the Gestapo (apparently Martin Weiss) warned him to flee, but Gens replied: "If I—

the head of the ghetto—run away, thousands of Jews will pay for it with their lives." He summoned the Jewish police for inspection, informed them of his imminent visit to Gestapo headquarters, and appointed a deputy. The following day, Gens went to the Gestapo, and did not return. Kittel (of the Vilna SD) summoned the Jewish police and informed them that Gens had been shot for disobeying German orders. It was rumored in the ghetto that the Gestapo had accused Gens of maintaining ties with the FPO and aiding the partisans. That evening the Jewish police held a memorial service for Gens, at which a rabbi began with these words: "We have lost our father." Gens's brother said the *Kaddish,* and memorial services were held in Vilna synagogues for the "holy Rabbi Jacob Gens." Two girls slipped out of the ghetto to place flowers on Gens's grave on Russa Hill.

It is difficult to judge whether the melodramatic account of Gens's demise is reflective of the true feelings of the Vilna Jews. In any case, on September 23, 1943, only nine days after Gens's death, the Vilna ghetto was liquidated. The Generalkommissar of Lithuania reported succinctly: "Because of a great shortage of labor in the oil-producing region of Estonia and because of special difficulties which arise in the Vilna ghetto, the Vilna ghetto was totally evacuated."

## Epilogue

My purpose in relating all this has been to involve the reader in the inner conflicts and spiritual struggles of the inhabitants of the ghettos. If these contemptible people who cooperated with the Nazis suffered from inner struggles and spiritual turmoil, Jews who were faithful to their people must have suffered even more. It is simplistic and superficial to speak of helplessness, apathy, defective moral feelings, and passivity as characterizing the ghetto experience. One of the most important moral problems in the history of the Jewish ghettos of the Nazi era is the position and function of the Judenrat. Since it is impossible to explore the problem in its full scope and depth in one short essay, I have selected one controversial personality who possessed an arrogant faith in his special mission. I have tried to analyze this "misguided soul" to shed light on the reasons for his rise and fall.

There was no room for normal moral perceptions under the conditions of Nazi terror. No one could assume a moderate position. In the ghetto, a powerful man would emerge either as an angel of deliverance or an angel of death. In normal times, the ghetto despots whom I have described here and elsewhere probably would have led ordinary lives. The circumstances of the Nazi occupation elevated them to functions beyond their wisdom and capacity. Although they had engaged in communal activities previously, their scope was limited. When they rose to exalted positions in the ghetto, they lacked the inner resources to cope with their new responsibilities.

Why did they succumb so easily to the destructive forces within and without? Why did they not remove themselves from the stage before it was too late? The historical, sociological, psychological, and moral questions that arise are legion; the answers to them must await further research.

But I did not intend to judge, only to describe. The final assessment, if one is possible, must be made in the future—as Jacob Gens and Moses Merin had hoped—by history.

❮ This essay was first published in Hebrew in *Bitzaron,* XXIX, no. 8 (1953/54), 151–58; XXIX (1954), 232–39 (in the series "Collaborators and False Messiahs in the Ghettos During the Nazi Holocaust"). A more concise presentation of this subject, incorporating material in essay 13, was published by the author, under the title "Two 'Saviors' Who Failed," in *Commentary,* 26 (1958), 479–91.

## Notes

1. This essay is based on the following sources: M. Dworzecki, *Yerushelayim delite in kamf un umkum* (The Jerusalem of Lithuania in Struggle and in Destruction) (Paris, 1948); Shmerke Kaczerginski, *Hurban Vilne* (The Destruction of Vilna) (New York, 1947); Hayim Lazar, *Hurban va-mered* (Destruction and Rebellion) (Tel Aviv, 1950); Abba Kovner, "Flames in the Ash" (Hebrew), in *Yediot ha-tenuah la-ahdut ha-avoda* (Tel Aviv, 1946); Reizl Korczak, *Lehavot be-efer* (Flames in the Ash) (Merhavia, 1946); Z. Kalmanovitch, "A Diary of the Ghetto in Vilna" (Yiddish), *YB,* 35 (1951), pp. 16–91; in English in *YA,* 8 (1953), 9–81; Abraham Sutzkever, *Vilner geto* (Paris, 1946); *Bleter vegn Vilne: Zamlbukh* (Pages about Vilna: A Collection) (Lodz, 1947); M. Feigenberg and Moshe Weisenberg, *Vilne untern natsi-yokh* (Vilna under the Nazi Yoke) (Landsberg am Lech, 1946); Abraham Eisen, *Dos geystike ponim fun geto* (The Spiritual Face of the Ghetto) (Mexico City, 1950); Josef Musnik, "The Life and the Liquidation of the Vilna Ghetto" (Yiddish), in *In di yorn fun yidishn hurbn* (In the Years of the Jewish Holocaust) (New York, 1948); Niusia Długi, Brayne As, Zenia Berkon, Shimon Palewski, M. Dworzecki, "The Wittenberg-Day in the Vilna Ghetto" (Yiddish), *YB,* 30 (1947), pp. 188–213; S. Kaczerginski, "The Death of Itzik Wittenberg" (Yiddish), *Epokhe,* no. 6 (1948); S. Kaczerginski, comp., *Dos gezang fun vilner geto* (Songs from the Vilna Ghetto); music arranged by Ada Eber-Friedman and Dov Botwinik (Paris, 1947); *idem, Lider fun getos un lagern* (Songs of the Ghettos and Camps) (New York, 1948); M. Balberyszki, "The Tragedy of Wittenberg" (Yiddish), *Kiyoum,* nos. 11–12 (Paris, 1949); Abba Kovner, "Stains on the Wall" (Yiddish), *Yidishe Kultur,* no. 9 (1947); Itzhak Rudashevsky, "Diary from the Vilna Ghetto" (Yiddish), *Di goldene keyt,* no. 15 (1953);

*Vilner geto yidiyes* (News from the Vilna Ghetto) (YIVO archives, New York); Herman Kruk, *Togbukh fun vilner geto* (Diary of the Vilna Ghetto) (New York, [YIVO], 1961), of which a condensation, entitled "The Diary of Dr. Herman Kruk," was published in *YA,* 13 (1965), 9–78.

For a more detailed bibliography on the Vilna ghetto, see Philip Friedman's "Bibliography of the Literature of the Jewish Catastrophe in Lithuania" (Yiddish), in *Pinkes Lite* (Memorial Volume, Lithuania) (New York, 1951).

2. Liza Magun was a young FPO courier who was caught and tortured by the Germans without revealing any secrets. After her death under interrogation, the FPO, as an honor to her memory, selected the phrase "Liza is calling [for revenge]" as an alarm.

# 15

# THE EXTERMINATION OF THE GYPSIES: NAZI GENOCIDE OF AN ARYAN PEOPLE

The original home of the Gypsies was in northern India, the cradle of the so-called Indo-Germanic, or Aryan, race. Many scientists believe that the Gypsies are the most direct present-day descendants of this prehistoric race. For reasons unknown to us, the Gypsies left their ancient home about two thousand years ago and became nomads. This form of life evidently suited their tastes, for they displayed no inclination either to return to their native land or to become a sedentary people in the lands of their wandering.

The Gypsy migration to the west proceeded slowly. In the third century of the Christian era they were in Persia. By the year 1000 they reached Europe via the Balkan peninsula. By the beginning of the fifteenth century, they had made their appearance in Germany, Austria, Italy, and other Central European countries. At this stage, they no longer constituted a homogeneous people but broke up into tribes, each of which had its own king, dialect, and beliefs. Some adopted the Christian religion. Others were converted to Islam.

The people of medieval Europe were suspicious of the Gypsies, who consequently, were accused of all sorts of crimes: idolatry, witchcraft, and kidnaping. In reality, they led a life of poverty, and depended for sustenance on handouts, fortune-telling, music, primitive handicrafts, and the repair of old utensils. Under these circumstances, they might, from time to time, resort to stealing animals or even kidnaping. Consequently, they were always shunned. Some countries forbade their entry or limited their residence to specific localities. Others prohibited their participation in specified trades. On many occasions they were subjected to bloody pogroms and expulsion. As a general rule, the Gypsies were deprived of all rights; only in the Balkan lands did they enjoy a measure of tolerance.

As time passed, the anti-Gypsy laws were abrogated. Toward the end of the eighteenth century, they were freed from nearly all restrictions throughout most of Europe. Germany and Austria were the exceptions to this rule. These two countries, always marked by intolerance and rigid bureaucracy, retained on their books numerous detailed and vicious regulations against the Gypsies.

The Gypsies were not in a position to take full advantage of the rights conferred upon them during the nineteenth century. By and large they remained nomadic, and not until after World War I did they begin to adapt themselves to modern forms of life. Gypsy cultural centers—with schools, theaters, orchestras, and a class of intellectuals—arose in Czechoslovakia, Yugoslavia, and elsewhere. But despite this transformation, the bulk of the people still retained their nomadic ways, to such an extent that it was impossible to determine their exact number on the eve of World War II. Some Gypsy authors made exaggerated claims that their people numbered over 5 million in Europe alone. Other students of Gypsy life gave more reliable estimates. Rabbi Moses Gaster of London estimated their number in Europe at 885,000, with perhaps another 350,000 on other continents. The Swedish scholar Arthur Thesleff, an authority on Gypsy problems, estimated the total number of Gypsies at the beginning of the twentieth century as 1.4 million.

The Nazi treatment of the Gypsies was an indication of the lack of sincerity with which the Nazis regarded their own racial theories. By consensus, the Gypsies are the purest of Aryans, but Hitler was ashamed of these poor relations. To get rid of them was a simple matter. He commanded his "scientists" to declare the Gypsies "non-Aryans," and the Nazi professors obediently attempted to comply.

It was not an easy assignment. The accumulated data on ethnography and anthropology had to be turned upside down to prove the point. Some Nazi scholars failed, and were promptly punished for their failure. It remained for the high priest of Nazi "racial science" to deliver the goods, and he did not fail. In his book *Rassenkunde Europas,* the bible of Nazi anthropology, Professor Hans F. K. Günther wrote: "The Gypsies have indeed retained some elements from their Nordic home, but they are descended from the lowest classes of the population in that region. In the course of their migrations, they have absorbed the blood of the surrounding peoples, and have thus become an Oriental, western-Asiatic racial mixture, with an addition of Indian, mid-Asiatic, and European strains. Their nomadic mode of living is a result of this mixture. The Gypsies will generally affect Europe as aliens."

Thus were the Gypsies expelled from the Aryan family. Nor was this a purely academic formulation. To be declared an alien in the Nazi empire meant condemnation to death. Having received the opinion of their expert advisor, the Nazi leaders energetically applied themselves to the "final solution of the Gypsy problem."

There has been little study of the tragedy of the Gypsies under Nazi rule. The *Journal of the Gypsy Lore Society of London* contains some materials. A valuable article on this subject by Dora E. Yates has appeared in *Commentary* (November 1949). Compared with the extensive literature on the extermination of the Jews and on the tribulations of other peoples under the Nazi yoke, the literature on the Gypsies is meager and full of gaps. It has not even been clearly established when the Nazi extermination of the Gypsies actually began.

Some light is shed on this last question by a memorandum from Portschy, Nazi Gauleiter of Steiermark, to Reichsminister Heinz Lammers. The memorandum is dated January 9, 1938, but refers to previous communications to Lammers on the same subject. In it Portschy stated, among other things, that the Gypsies constituted a threat to public health (how well European Jews understood the meaning of this statement!), were "parasites on the body of our people," a danger to the "racial purity of our peasants," and in general "confirmed criminals." Portschy suggested a characteristic Nazi solution to the problem: sterilization of the Gypsies and their mobilization for slave labor. These suggestions were made in peacetime.

After World War II broke out, the Nazis became more severe in their policies toward "alien elements." At a conference held in Berlin on January 30, 1940, the decision was taken to expel 30,000 Gypsies from Germany into the Government General in Poland. Many Jews and Poles were also included in this decree. At that time Josef Goebbels issued a directive to his propaganda offices that Jews, Poles, and Gypsies be treated as equals in the "educational work." Some of the occupied countries promulgated laws placing Gypsies in the same category as Jews. On May 30, 1941, the German military commander in Serbia ordered the confiscation of all property of Jews and Gypsies. Attempts were made in Poland to confine Gypsies to Jewish ghettos, and when the mass extermination of the Polish Jews commenced, German propaganda included attacks on the Gypsies as well. Toward the end of 1942, the *Lemberger Zeitung* and the *Krakauer*

*Zeitung* published a spate of articles declaring that it was intolerable to permit an entire nation of "parasites" to go on eating while the "New Europe" went hungry as a result of the Allied blockade.

As a final step in their campaign, the Nazis resorted to a charge of cannibalism against the Gypsies. A major trial of an entire Gypsy tribe accused of cannibalism was staged in Slovakia. The entire Nazi press seized on the hateful accusation and demanded that the "cannibals" be severely punished. The fate of the Gypsies was sealed.

Late in 1941, Mordechai Chaim Rumkowski, "Eldest of the Jews in the ghetto of Lodz," was ordered by the Germans to clear the area on Brzezinska Street, extending from numbers 70 to 100. Jews living there had to vacate the premises at once, and the area was blocked off with a triple fence of barbed wire and a wide moat.

The establishment of this special area was preceded by an extensive correspondence among the Germans. In the fall of 1941, Hans Biebow, the notorious hangman of the Jews of Lodz, received an order to prepare the Lodz ghetto for the admission of another 20,000 Jews and 5,000 Gypsies. He objected to the order, on the ground that it would tend to disrupt the production of war materials in the ghetto. He particularly objected to the introduction of Gypsies into his domain. But his protests were disregarded. Between October 16 and November 4, 1941, twenty transports of Jews from Germany and a number of transports of Gypsies arrived. The Jews were distributed throughout the ghetto. The Gypsies were quartered in the area blocked off for them. The ghetto thus acquired a "colony" for whose support it was responsible, although it had no say in the colony's administration.

As soon as the Gypsies were installed in their special area within the ghetto, terrible screams and cries were heard from there. Every evening, Jews of the ghetto saw cars crammed with drunken Germans going into the Gypsy camp. All windows had been smashed there—in the dead of winter. Two weeks after the Gypsies were brought to Lodz, a typhus epidemic broke out among them. The Germans gave no medical assistance. But after the German chief of the criminal police died of typhus, the Jews were ordered to provide doctors. Two doctors volunteered; one of them, Dr. Glasser, died in this service. Each day vans loaded with the dead left the Gypsy compound. Alongside those who had died of typhus lay the mutilated bodies of those who had been murdered by the Germans.

The number of Gypsies in the Lodz ghetto rapidly declined. In March and April of 1942, the Germans moved the few survivors to the extermination camp at Chełmno. A leather goods shop and a factory for straw shoes were set up in the vacated quarters.

Except for the two volunteer doctors, the Jews of Lodz did not know who the inmates of the compound had been. For some time rumors circulated in the ghetto that the place was occupied by Jews from Hungary. Other rumors maintained that they were Yugoslav partisans. The Polish underground movement believed that they were Yugoslav partisans. Only after the war ended was the true identity of the inmates established. It is possible that the Germans intentionally planted false rumors.

A similar strategy of obfuscation was used by the Germans in other ghettos. Thus, the Polish underground announced on June 23, 1942, shortly before the great extermination of the Jews commenced, that there were more than 100,000 Gypsies in the Warsaw ghetto. A Jewish survivor from Siedlce testified that of the three blocks of houses in the ghetto of his native city, one was occupied by Gypsies.

Fortunately for the Gypsies, the Germans did not apply their extermination policy to them with the same single-minded consistency that they employed toward the Jews. The directives issued concerning them were of the same severity as those applying to the Jews, but were not always carried out with the same ruthlessness. The Einsatzgruppen established on the eve of the war against the Soviet Union were ordered to destroy Jews, Gypsies, Communists, "undesirable elements," partisans and the mentally ill. But in 1942, when the work of extermination was intensified, Minister of Justice Thierack wrote to Martin Bormann that the job of liquidating the above-mentioned groups was not under the jurisdiction of the ministry of justice. The fate of the doomed groups thus remained in the hands of the local administrators, the police, and the SS, who had the power to postpone the execution of the decree, at least for a while.

Within Germany itself, Himmler forbade the free movement of Gypsies and ordered their incarceration in concentration camps, but his order was not always carried out. The French Vichy government also tried to end the roaming of the Gypsies, and sent some of them to camps where they perished. In Eastern Europe there was great confusion in the treatment of the Gypsies. In some localities, such as Latvia, the Germans even tried to draft them into the army. Curiously enough, in the midst of the extermination, the Gypsy scholar Vanya Kochanowski was asked to write a paper to prove the Aryan origin of his people. At the very time when the Gypsies of central Poland were being herded into extermination camps, those of Eastern Galicia were treated liberally. As late as 1944, the Gypsies in Lwów were allowed to go about freely and engage in their traditional trades. I know of one Jewish boy who tried to save his life by pretending to be a Gypsy, and for some time traveled freely throughout Galicia.

But despite such exceptions, few Gypsies survived the Nazi regime. Of the more than 16,275 Gypsies in Germany, only 12 percent survived.

The vast majority of those in Latvia perished. The 3,000 Gypsies of White Russia and the Crimea perished together with the Jews. In Croatia only 1 percent survived. Similar low percentages of survival were recorded in other countries. It is impossible to obtain exact figures, because the statistics concerning the prewar Gypsy population are unreliable. Gypsy spokesmen estimate the number who perished at 500,000, fully one-third of all the Gypsies in the world.

The surviving Gypsies who returned to Germany in 1945 were quartered in the same barracks at Lierenfeld where their suffering had begun. Isolated from the "Aryan" Germans, they waited for justice and grew ever more skeptical of finding it. Justice in Germany is not known for its swiftness, and the Gypsies were no exception to this rule when they sought compensation for their losses (though it may well be asked whether one can speak of compensation for losses of the kind they suffered). The attitude of German officialdom toward the Gypsy claims was clearly stated in a circular letter published by the Würtemberg ministry of the interior in 1950. This letter stated that in all cases of Gypsy claims for restitution, it should be remembered that the Gypsies had been persecuted by the Nazis not for any racial reasons but because of their "asocial and criminal record." This official statement evoked the protest of some democratic German papers. One such newspaper in Düsseldorf wrote: "Hitler has fallen; racial hatred has remained. Those who do not believe this are invited to be seen in the company of a Gypsy. They will have to run the gauntlet of insults and contempt. . . ." And the trustee of the Gypsies, Herr Sippel, summed up the situation in the following words: "In Western Germany there are again in force unwritten laws like those of the Third Reich."

❰ This essay was first published under the title "Nazi Extermination of the Gypsies, A Nazi Genocide Operation against the 'Aryan People'," *Jewish Frontier,* 18 (1951), 11–14. It also appeared in a slightly different form under the title "The Fate of 500,000 Gypsies" in *The Star Weekly,* Toronto, March 24, 1951. A Yiddish version, "A Strange Common Destiny—The Extermination of Gypsies," appeared in *Kiyoum,* nos. 8–9 (1950), 1661–67. For further bibliography on the Nazi period, see above, essay 3, note 18.

# 16

# JEWISH RESISTANCE TO NAZISM

During World War II over 8.3 million Jews came under the rule of the Nazis, or of Nazi-controlled or -dominated countries. Most of this Jewish population was concentrated in Eastern Europe (5.65 million), while over 1 million Jews lived in the Balkan countries, almost 1 million in Central Europe, and 0.6 million in Western Europe and the Scandinavian countries. Prior to the war, at least some of these Jews, particularly in Western and Central Europe, were so fully integrated into the life of their countries of origin that one cannot logically deal with the phenomena of Jewish experience in the prewar period apart from the historical fate of non-Jews. This argument can by no means be applied to the Nazi period, however. No matter how much the Jews had become integrated into the life of a country, the Nazis marked them as a separate racial unit (designated as including converts and half-Jews), isolated and segregated from the rest of the community, and subjected to discriminatory legislation and, ultimately, annihilation. Just as the Jewish predicament was something distinct and apart, so was the Jewish reaction to Nazi persecution. Though Jewish resistance to Nazism shared some similarities with non-Jewish resistance efforts, it was, in many more respects, fundamentally different.

## Strategic Base

One of the essential conditions for a successful resistance movement is a favorable strategic base from which operations can be safely conducted. In Europe, for example, such a base might be provided by the inaccessible mountain regions of France, Yugoslavia, or Greece, and by the marshes and tick-infested forests of Poland, Lithuania, Byelorussia, and western Ukraine, Volhynia, and Galicia. At the outset, the Jews in Eastern and parts of Central Europe were denied such a base, when they were herded by the Nazis into hermetically sealed ghettos, where their every move could be observed and checked, and from which escape was banned, on penalty of death. Liaison between scattered Jewish underground groups could be maintained only by daring couriers at the risk of their lives. Weapons and explosives had to be smuggled into the ghettos, through heavily guarded gates, or brought in through sewers or by other ingenious means. In a later period of the resistance movement, when the Jewish underground tried to get its fighting groups from the ghettos to the woods and mountains, many were caught and executed. Such was the fate of the group headed by the Yiddish poet Yankel Szudrich in Lwów.[1] Thus, the Jewish underground was unable to prepare the necessary strategic base outside the ghettos for future activities. It could not establish arsenals or arms caches, food depots, hospitals, dugouts, or the other military installations essential to a successful resistance effort.

Nazi surveillance was not the only obstacle. In the ghettos of Warsaw, Bialystok, and others, the Jewish underground became involved in a strategic and moral debate: Should they stay in the ghetto or flee to the woods, where they might establish a base of operations? Could they justify leaving the ghetto population to face the enemy alone, or were they morally obliged to stay on and take the lead in the fight when the crucial moment of the extermination actions arrived? After heated debates, the opinion that prevailed was to stay on in the ghetto as long as possible, despite the strategic disadvantages of this position, and to leave only at the last moment, when they could no longer fight to protect the people in the ghetto. The minutes of the dramatic debates that took place on this issue in the Bialystok underground have survived and have been published in several languages.[2]

An effective strategic base required the friendly cooperation of at least a part of the nonfighting population, in order to secure vital information, supplies, and shelter for the sick and wounded, and in time of retreat to hide the partisans and their weapons. Jewish partisans often lacked this support. In many Nazi-occupied countries, the general population did not identify with the Jewish resistance movement and had an equivocal, even hostile, attitude toward it. Few peasants were willing to suffer for a cause they did not consider their own. On one hand, they were urged by the Jewish partisans to supply food, fuel, and transportation; on the other, they were savagely punished by the Germans for doing so. Several villages were burned and their inhabitants executed for helping or hiding partisans. In addition, the Jewish partisans in Eastern Europe sometimes maintained "family camps" in the woods for the children, elderly people, and women threatened by Nazi annihilation. The peasants were particularly unwilling to supply the family camps. One of the biggest camps, attached to Tovie Bielski's fighting group in the forests of Byelorussia, and called New Jerusalem, harbored about 1,200 inmates.[3] Bielski would tour the peasant country, delivering speeches to the villagers, petitioning aid for the camp. The sad experience of the Jewish resistance demonstrated the truth of the Chinese proverb: Partisans in the country are like fish in the river. The river can live without the fish. But the fish . . . ?

## Arms and Leadership

A steady supply of arms is a sine qua non of successful resistance operations. Most of the non-Jewish underground movements had the backing of their national organizations abroad and received vast supplies of arms and other materiel from their governments-in-exile. In addition they received assistance from the Allied governments. Between 1942 and 1945, 43,000 tons[4] of materiel were flown into various European countries for distribution to the underground, through the Special Operations Executive (SOE), the London center of European resistance movements. (The amount of aid given to the guerrillas in Eastern Europe by the Soviet government has not been disclosed.) Yugoslavia alone received 16,000 tons of arms and other supplies;[5] beyond this, after Italy's capitulation, seven departing Italian divisions left their entire equipment to the Yugoslav partisans. But in no country was the Jewish underground treated on an equal footing with the national underground organizations. Whatever the Jewish underground was to receive had to go through the national channels, and the supplies allotted were often too late or too little. Sometimes, Jewish requests for weapons were refused outright, as, for example, in Bialystok and Vilna. In Warsaw, after long negotiations, the Jewish underground received, in February 1943, a small supply of arms: 50 revolvers, 50 hand grenades, and 4 kilograms of explosives.[6] Thus, the Jews had to resort to other sources of supply—to buy arms at black-market prices from peasants, illegal arms dealers, and deserters, or to produce their own weapons in small, clandestine factories and repair shops. Eventually, they managed to scrape together some meager, obsolete equipment, no match for the powerful German arms. Marek Edelman, a leader of the Warsaw ghetto fighters, one of the best-organized and -equipped ghetto groups, estimated that for each fighter there was, on the average, one gun, with 10 to 15 bullets, or 4 to 5 hand grenades, and 4 or 5 incendiary bottles. Each fighting unit, consisting of 5 to 10 persons, possessed, in addition, 2 or 3 rifles. There was one automatic pistol in the ghetto.[7]

Another great disadvantage of the Jewish underground was the dearth of competent leaders. The seasoned leaders of the prewar period were gone. Many of them had escaped before Germany invaded Poland in 1939, or were deported during the period of Soviet and German wartime occupation. Those who remained were eliminated by the Nazis, in a particularly ruthless and systematic campaign. Jewish intellectuals; professional, political, and trade-union leaders; and former Jewish soldiers and officers were arrested and exterminated under various pretexts. Other able-bodied men were drafted to forced labor-camps, where many perished; the few who returned were usually invalids.

Fortunately, in the first months of the war, the Nazis did not pay too much attention to the Jewish youth. Both the leadership and the rank and file of the Jewish youth organizations survived that period to become the cradle and cadres of the Jewish underground. But they had to learn everything about underground warfare. While the non-Jewish underground movements also had a shortage of leadership (the Polish, Czech, and Russian partisans had lost many leaders at the hands of the Nazis, though fewer than the Jews), they had more opportunities to replace the losses. In the years 1942–1945, the number of persons of eighteen European nationalities who were clandestinely transported by boat and aircraft to work in various parts of the European underground was 6,700.[8] Yugoslavia alone received 2,500 volunteers, and 19,000 partisans were flown out, most of them wounded, for medical treatment.[9] When the Soviet army retreated, the authorities left specially trained leaders for underground warfare, and later flew in a constant supply of new instructors and officers. Partisans who excelled in guerrilla warfare were flown into Russia for supplementary training in special schools and were brought back, after completion of their studies, to work with their guerrilla units.

From these efforts to bolster the guerrilla leadership, the Jews benefited only in a very small degree. Many young Jews in Palestine volunteered for the parachute units, to be dropped by the British into Nazi-occupied areas; they hoped in this way to make contact with the Jewish underground. The British reluctantly drafted and trained 240 of them and, after much delay, agreed to send to Europe, in the spring of 1944, only 32, all of whom reached their destination. A few were caught and executed by the Germans before they could accomplish their assigned tasks. The others established useful contacts with the Jewish underground.[10]

## Timing and Objectives

Jewish underground groups were formed in almost every Nazi-occupied country. The groups were of various political persuasions, and initially had little or no contact between them. In general, the resistance movement of the European nations was a grassroots phenomenon, not organized from above by a central body, except perhaps in the Soviet territories. Time was necessary for a long educational campaign, for training in underground tactics and in the use of weapons, and for welding the small, scattered groups into a centralized, efficient fighting body. For instance, a central resistance council, Conseil National de la Résistance (CNR), was created in France only one year, and in the Netherlands the "Superior Consultation Committee of the Underground" only ten months, before the liberation. But the Jews had much less time than the non-Jews for such preparations. The Nazi campaign of genocide started in the winter of 1941–1942. By the fall of 1943 the ghettos of Europe were almost depopulated. The Jews could not wait. While the non-Jewish resistance groups could time their operations to coincide with the Allied strategy, the Jews who survived the Nazi massacres had to act immediately. They could not expect much help from the non-Jewish underground. In 1942 and 1943, for example, the Polish underground told Jewish partisans that it was too early for the Poles to launch a revolt, because it might jeopardize the attainment of their ultimate goal.[11] Polish political parties opposed the action as suicidal and futile. But for the Jews in the ghettos, this was the last moment. A similar situation prevailed in the concentration camps. The Jews at Auschwitz knew that they were being taken to the gas chambers and furnaces. The non-Jews were not being taken; they were therefore in no hurry to stage a suicidal uprising. It was only with great difficulty that the Jews of the Sonderkommando (those working at the removal of bodies in the crematoriums) who belonged to the resistance organization in the camp, and in the fall of 1944 were facing death, secured from the Polish underground leadership in Auschwitz permission for a revolt, in which the general underground movement did not take part.[12]

Clearly, the Jewish and non-Jewish underground movements had vastly different objectives. The non-Jewish groups were fighting to regain political freedom; the Jews were engaged in a hopeless struggle against total annihilation. Hope is an important psychological factor in any struggle. If a definite goal and a terminal point of the struggle can be identified, it bolsters the movement and the morale of the fighters. But there was no hope, no attainable objective for the Jewish underground movement. The only objective was to die with honor instead of in infamy—a desperate suicidal struggle. Only a few Jewish partisan groups in the woods and swamps of Eastern Europe could cherish a dim hope of survival and significant retribution.

## Traditions and Moral Values

The patterns and forms of reaction to the Nazi occupation and persecution developed differently in each nation. Underground activities and propaganda were influenced by the national historical experience, traditions, and moral values developed through centuries. France, for example, had its tradition of revolution since the end of the eighteenth century, as well as the more recent historical experiences of the German occupation in 1870, and World War I. The Belgian underground was in many ways conditioned by bitter memories of the German occupation during World War I. The Poles, with their history of repeated uprisings (1794, 1812, 1831, 1863, and 1905), had a well-developed insurrectionist tradition, in which cadres of leaders had been reared. The elaborate Polish underground organization during the Nazi occupation resembled, in many ways, the underground system the Poles had created in 1863. Members of the Ukrainian underground, who thrived on the traditions of the Cossack rebellions and the Haidamak revolt, frequently reverted to them to kindle the imagination of their countrymen. Yugoslav partisans were, in a way, a direct continuation of their forebears who had fought against the Turks. There were traditions of passive resistance as well. The Czechs, facing complete political isolation after the crushing defeat of the Hussite rebellion, had developed, during the centuries of Hapsburg domination, tactics of passive resistance, which in their case may have been the more effective course. This course, so graphically represented in the immortal character of Jaroslav Hašek's novel *The Good Soldier Schweik,* they also adopted against the Nazis.

Different and peculiar in their own way were the Jewish traditions. They were themselves diverse, because the Jews were greatly differentiated both culturally and socially. The intelligentsia, the acculturated members of the middle class, and the working class adopted the traditions and values of their host nations. Among the youth movements, both of Zionist and of socialist persuasions, a new feeling of physical prowess began to develop in the late nineteenth and early twentieth centuries, and led eventually to some spectacular, even heroic, acts of courage (such as the Jewish self-defense groups in Russia, the revolutionary groups of the Socialist Bund, and the Shomrim organization in Palestine). But the mass of Orthodox Jews, particularly in Eastern and Southeastern Europe, had a quite different tradition. Whereas most nations have legacies of heroism involving physical and military prowess, in Orthodox Jewish tradition the concept of heroism is inextricably identified with the idea of spiritual courage. Among Orthodox Jews, the bearers of the ancient tradition of the Jewish people, this is not an empty ideal, but one requiring sacrifice for the sake of religion. The ideal of "bravery with holiness," known in Hebrew as *Kiddush ha-Shem* (lit., "sanctification of God's name") characterized the resistance carried out by Orthodox Jews during the Nazi domination. Their resistance, stemming from religious inspiration, can be epitomized by the saying: "not by force but by strength of the spirit," an attitude maintained during many centuries of religious persecutions and reinforced by various philosophical and mystical movements (the Kabbalah, messianism, Hasidism, and so on). The guiding principle is that the evil of the world should not be fought, and cannot be defeated, by mortals through physical force; that the struggle between good and evil will be decided elsewhere, by Divine Providence. In accordance with this view, the true weapons of resistance are conscience, prayer, religious meditation, and devotion—not military arms. Orthodox Jews did not believe that it was possible or even desirable to resist the Nazis in any other way. They believed that the reciting of a chapter of the Psalms would do more to affect the course of events than would the killing of a German—not necessarily immediately but at some point in the infinite course of relations between the Creator and His creatures. There are, no doubt, similar attitudes among other nations. It would perhaps be rewarding to seek, for instance, similarities, between the "nonresistance" of Orthodox Jews and the passive resistance or "noncooperation" of Gandhi and his followers in India. Although different in their backgrounds, both attitudes are based on a definite philosophy. There is no question here of tactics or strategy. It is a normative philosophy of life. Religious sects in various periods of human history have acted in this manner.

## Passive Resistance

Resistance to Nazism was carried on in various forms. In the postwar literature, controversy developed over the subtle distinctions to be made between them, particularly in defining the forms of spiritual or moral resistance, sometimes called symbolic resistance. Several writers refused altogether to recognize any form of spiritual or moral opposition to Nazism as a manifestation of resistance. They argued that moral or spiritual resistance did not constitute an active fight against Nazism or contribute anything to its defeat, and that moral resistance involved no particular danger to those who engaged in it. Such passive forms of opposition, they concluded, could not be considered true manifestations of resistance. Their derogatory attitude toward passive resistance is largely unjustified, however. Many forms of spiritual and moral resistance involved risk of life. Numerous groups and individuals, for reasons of moral or religious principle, could not and would not engage in armed resistance, and preferred to suffer, or even to die, rather than violate these principles or comply with the demands of the enemy. One example is the sect of Jehovah's Witnesses (called Ernste Bibelforscher, in Germany), many of whose members were killed because they refused to serve in the German army. There were individuals among them who were executed only because they refused to say *Heil Hitler* (they believed that the word "hail" was to be used only in connection with God).

On the forms of spiritual resistance engaged in by religious Jews, there is much documentation in the memorial volumes of destroyed Jewish communities, in the commemorative literature, and in other sources. There are records of prayer groups that congregated in ghettos and concentration camps, under threat of heavy penalties, including death; there are accounts of fatal attempts to rescue Torah scrolls from burning synagogues; there are stories of Hasidim who assembled and prayed and danced in religious ecstasy until the last minute of their life. One memorial book, for example, describes how a group of Hasidim congregated and prayed in devotion to God one day before the extermination action in Częstochowa.[13] There are many accounts of religious self-sacrifice performed by groups and individuals, by rabbis and laymen. But spiritual resistance was not motivated solely by religious inspiration. There were various instances of moral resistance by nonreligious people. The action of the famous educator and writer Janusz Korczak, of the Warsaw ghetto—who voluntarily went to his death with the children of his orphanage, although he could have been exempted—was secular in character. It is unjust to assert that such an act lacks heroism. Yet several writers in postwar Poland seriously criticized Korczak because they saw his deed as one of passive surrender rather than active resistance.[14] Korczak, these writers contended, was not a hero, because he did not fight against those who came to take his life. Korczak is only one example. Many other educators acted as he did, accompanying their wards on their last journey.

Various other forms of passive resistance may be noted. One Jewish group, led by Hayim Widawski, in Lodz, listened to Allied broadcasts and spread the news, until they were caught and deported or executed.[15] Elsewhere, artists in ghetto theaters poked fun at the Nazis and their collaborators and engaged in veiled satire. Children were clandestinely educated. Another form of "passive resistance," economic in character, was the slowdown or sabotage carried out individually or collectively by Jewish workers in German factories, particularly in armament plants. Further affecting the German economy was the controversial activity of smuggling. Was not smuggling, with its dislocation of the economy, also a form of resistance? Some writers have argued that the smugglers were rather shadowy characters, recruited from the dregs of society, who wanted only to profit from the general disaster. Whatever their motives, however, smugglers did create confusion in the German production and supply apparatus, and thus caused trouble for the Nazis. Every currency smuggler, every contraband carrier, every peasant who delivered his goods not to the Germans but to the black market, produced chaos in the German economy and forced the Nazis to deploy police and military personnel against this form of sabotage.[16] (See essay 3 above, "The Jewish Ghettos of the Nazi Era.") Many of the ghetto and non-Jewish city dwellers alike would have died of starvation without the steady supplies provided by the smugglers. In the records of that period are many moving stories of children who sneaked through holes in the ghetto walls to bring provisions to their starving families. Many of them were caught by German guards and executed on the spot.

Escape from the ghetto and concealment (either in the woods or in specially prepared hideouts or in Christian homes, or through forged "Aryan papers") was another form of passive resistance. Before the German extermination operation in several of the ghettos of Eastern Europe, the Jews set the ghetto afire and attempted to escape in the ensuing confusion, through the line of the German police and SS detachments. Such desperate actions have been recorded in accounts by the survivors of Kleck, Głębokie, Nieśwież, Łachwa, Krzemieniec, Tuczyń, and other towns.[17] In still other ghettos and camps, the Jews managed to build, during long weeks of secret labor, underground tunnels of escape—always uncertain of what awaited them on the other side. The Jews who attempted to tunnel their way to freedom from the dreaded "Ninth Fortress" (the prison in Kaunas, Lithuania) and from the camp of Nowogródek, for instance, later encountered German patrols, and almost all were killed.[18]

Sometimes groups of Jews rounded up for deportation resisted by refusing to board the train and thus provoked the Germans to open fire on them. In the town of Marcinkonis near Grodno this organized form of passive resistance involved the entire Jewish population. In the ensuing confusion some of the Jews managed to escape to the woods and join the partisans.[19] In Slovakia all the young men of a small town lay down on the railway tracks when the deportation train arrived.[20]

A widespread form of passive resistance was the building of various, often ingenious, dugouts, or bunkers. There were bunkers in almost every town, and the Germans sometimes had great difficulty in discovering and seizing them. In Warsaw alone, General Jürgen Stroop's troops had to blast, during and after the Warsaw ghetto uprising, 631 bunkers.[21] General Fritz Katzmann, chief of the SS and police in Galicia, describes in a report a network of veritable underground fortresses in Rohatyn, and tells of his difficulties in liquidating the numerous bunkers in Lwów.[22] Jews succeeded in building elaborate underground networks in Baranowicze, Warsaw, and Vilna as well.

## Unarmed Active Resistance

Unarmed active resistance was in many cases the first phase of underground work, and later developed into armed resistance. However, unarmed underground work often became a goal in itself. One example is the work of La Sixième in France.[23] This group of Jewish youths of Les Éclaireurs Israélites de France (the French Scout Movement), and perhaps of some other youth movements as well, organized a network for the preparation of forged Aryan documents, which were then supplied to Jews. In Western Europe, among a generally sympathetic and supportive Christian population, Aryan papers were often enough for evading the Germans. La Sixième also founded a network of bases for the rescue of children and, indeed, saved many of them. The same was done by the devoted educator David Rapoport, with a group of faithful coworkers, in the Oeuvre des Secours aux Enfants (Committee for Rescuing Children) at 36 rue Amélot in Paris, which later became an important center of the French-Jewish underground. Rapoport was eventually arrested and killed by the Germans, but many children owed him their lives.[24] Mention should also be made of the illegal frontier crossings frequently made in France, Belgium, and Holland. In Holland, a group of Halutzim (a Jewish pioneer youth organization preparing for agricultural settlement in Palestine), headed by "Shushu" (pseudonym of Yehoyahim Simon) and his Christian coworker Joop Westerweel, a Dutch teacher, smuggled a number of Jewish youths through the Pyrenees to Spain. In Belgium a large Christian youth group cooperated with the Jewish underground in the work of hiding and smuggling Jewish children out of the country. This work required extraordinary courage; it meant traversing Belgium and France and escorting groups of children and youths over the Pyrenees to neutral Spain and Portugal. Several leaders of this underground work, including "Shushu" and Westerweel, were eventually caught by the Germans and killed.[25] Children and youths were also smuggled across the frontier into Switzerland. There were hundreds of such cases, impossible to list here. Among them were the well-known attempts by the French priest Father Marie Bénoit, who cooperated with the Jewish underground in Nice and Marseilles, especially with Joseph Bass and the so-called Group André.[26] Many illegal frontier crossings also went on in Poland, especially from the ghettos of Sosnowiec and Będzin (Bendzin) and their vicinity to Slovakia, as has been described in several books. The smuggling of Jews also went on in Galicia. An "underground railroad" from southern Poland through Slovakia, Hungary, and Rumania was aided by the Jewish underground organizations in those countries.[27] There were also escape routes from Hungary and Rumania through Bulgaria and the Black Sea to Turkey and Palestine, and from Greece to Turkey and Palestine.[28]

Intermediate between passive and active resistance were acts of sabotage. In general, slowdown and sabotage in factories were effected by individuals or groups without preliminary planning or organization. Some acts of sabotage were the result of careful preparation, however, and were supervised by an underground center. One such case was the arson strategy against the German armament factories in 1942 by the underground in Warsaw. In addition, the Germans accused the Jews of starting gigantic fires in Daugavpils (Dvinsk) and other centers of Latvia, in Kaunas, Kiev, Ushomir, and Zhitomir.[29] It is possible, however, that the Germans exaggerated or even fabricated these charges to use them as pretexts for mass slaughter of Jews.[30] The records of these years reveal curious and complex entanglements. Jews using forged Aryan papers did manage to penetrate into crucial positions in German industry and even into the ranks of the SS, and used their position to help their Jewish brothers to sabotage German plans. Thus it was revealed, at an area trial in Kaunas, that the guilty director of a sabotaged factory, allegedly a German, was a full-blooded Jew. In the Byelorussian town of Mir, a member of a Jewish youth movement managed to become employed in the local SS commando as an interpreter, under the Aryan guise of Oswald Rufajzen. Before long, he became the right hand of the SS commander, and in this capacity he advised the leaders of the Jewish youth movement about the Nazi extermination schemes. Eventually, his dangerous double role was discovered. "Rufajzen" was arrested but managed to escape, and survived. Another Jew on Aryan documents became the director of a great German plant in Volhynia, and in this capacity favored and protected the Jewish workers. He, too, was discovered by the Germans and was killed.[31]

## Armed Resistance

Spontaneous acts of individual or collective armed resistance have been recorded in numerous memoirs and eyewitness accounts by Jews and non-Jews, as well as in some official German reports. In addition, preparations for armed resistance were carried on in various ghettos by the Jewish underground.[32] Jewish underground organizations existed in Warsaw, Vilna, Bialystok, Cracow, Częstochowa, Będzin, and many other Polish towns. We also know of organized Jewish underground activities in other cities, such as Kaunas, Riga, and Minsk, and in Slovakia, Holland, Belgium, and France. Some of these groups were discovered and destroyed by the Germans before they could carry out their plans. However, apart from the Warsaw ghetto uprising in April 1943, there was organized armed resistance in Bialystok, Lachwa, Minsk Mazowiecki, Słonim, Nieswież, Kleck, Brasław, and Głębokie, among others. Jewish underground groups also organized uprisings in the concentration camps of Treblinka, Auschwitz, Sobibór, Kołdyczewo, and in the Janowski camp in Lwów.[33] In Paris, Jewish underground groups managed to ambush and kill several high German officials; in Cracow they succeeded in blowing up a café, where several German officials were killed.

As time went on, many Jews who escaped to the woods and mountains began to band together into guerrilla units. Prior to the Soviet-German hostilities, partisan warfare was still in its infancy. Thus, the small Jewish groups were still able to play a considerable role, particularly, in Poland and France, where the right-wing elements, the pro-Vichyists, the isolationists, the "attentists," and the people who kept aloof from political engagement were a strong obstacle to the development of guerrilla warfare during the period of the Hitler–Soviet pact. In that period, the extreme left, the Communists, also abstained from anti-German activities.[34] Among the Jews in France and Poland the situation was quite different, however. One group of Jews in France was particularly ripe for resistance and underground work. They were the uprooted, stateless refugees who had been in France since 1933 or earlier (some, since 1918–1920—from Eastern Europe) and whose plight was so graphically depicted by Erich Maria Remarque in his novel *Flotsam*. Uprooted intellectuals and members of the middle class, they had no economic stability and were gradually sliding down the social ladder and turning to radicalism. Moreover, they became the first objects of German persecution. It is clear that this group was not willing to wait: there was no hope in waiting. Before long, these foreign-born Jews would be threatened with deportation and death, whereas no such danger yet faced the others. A similar situation prevailed in Poland. For non-Jews the question of escaping to the woods and forming guerrilla units there was still a remote possibility; but for these Jews time was running out.

In France, the Jews joined the *maquis* (underground), whenever possible, or formed their own small, separate guerrilla groups, which were neither coordinated nor unified until much later. In Poland, the Jewish guerrilla groups were too weak for military operations, except in self-defense, and they lacked the cooperation of the native population and the

Polish underground. As in most underground organizations, the central authority of the Polish underground was weak in the field, and the local groups often behaved as they liked. In addition, various "wild" groups developed, sometimes only loosely connected with the legitimate underground home army. Sometimes, even groups of brigands assumed the guise of fighters for independence. The Jews in the woods, individuals as well as guerrilla bands, were often persecuted and sometimes annihilated by these Polish "boys of the woods." The Polish democratic and socialist underground was in general too small to be of any real help to the Jews. Without aid, many of the Jewish underground groups in Poland disappeared before long.

These conditions gradually changed, particularly in Byelorussia and the western Ukraine after the outbreak of Soviet-German hostilities. Soviet prisoners escaped to the woods and formed fighting bands and guerrilla units. Later on, a steady flow of Soviet supplies and officers welded these groups into a well-organized guerrilla army. In the initial stage of World War II, the Communists were almost entirely passive. But after Russia went to war against Germany, they became very active. Furthermore, despite their small numbers in 1941–1942, they had a considerable impact, especially in Eastern Europe, where they were operating at a distance of only a few hundred kilometers from the Russian army, which was attacking the Germans and advancing daily. Russian partisans and parachutists soon virtually took over the command of most of the guerrillas who had not already joined the Polish or Ukrainian nationalist guerrilla forces. Jews in the underground movements of the Western countries were able to draw support in one form or another from the largely sympathetic populations there, but in Eastern Europe they had to depend primarily on the Communist underground. There have been published many memoirs of Zionist or Orthodox Jewish guerrilla fighters who deplored the fact that they had no other choice than to join Communist-led or -influenced partisan units, if they wished to survive and to fight the Nazis.

## Jewish Resistance: Elite or Mass Movement?

The non-Jewish underground movements in some countries (such as Poland, Belgium, France, Holland, Denmark, and Yugoslavia) were, in the second phase of the war, mass movements with many well-organized members and a large number of sympathizers. In other countries (Czechoslovakia, for example), the underground was a secret group, with limited membership and tenuous contacts with the masses; emphasis was laid there on the development of a tightly knit revolutionary elite. Neither situation corresponds to that of the Jewish underground, however.[35] In some respects, the Jewish underground developed as a secret, elite group. The Jewish Orthodox masses, for reasons already mentioned, could not be won over to the idea of armed resistance. Moreover, among many Jews the German terror generated an attitude of complete apathy. The number of persons who wanted only to adapt somehow and survive was very great. Many opportunists were ready to do anything they could to jeopardize the resistance activities. Thus, the underground groups in the ghettos were rather further isolated from the Jewish masses. On the other hand, the Jewish guerrilla movement was not an elite movement, because many of the most qualified people and underground leaders were annihilated before they could leave the ghettos for the woods. But neither was it a mass movement, because mass escape from the ghettos was impossible. It was rather an accidental gathering of diverse individuals, many of them persons of enterprise and courage, who had managed to find their way to the woods. In only a few cases, mainly in Western rather than Eastern Europe, was the formation of a Jewish partisan unit a carefully planned undertaking, stimulated by purely ideological pursuits.

## Composition of the Jewish Underground

While the partisan units in the woods sometimes were haphazard gatherings of fugitives from the ghetto, without clear political objectives or leadership, the underground groups in the ghetto were, from the beginning, closely knit ideological groups formed along party lines. On the basis of the literature available to date, it appears that underground movements were sponsored by the Socialist-Zionists, Socialist Bund, Hashomer Hatzair, General Zionists, Revisionists, and Mizrachi. In several countries, there were also other sponsoring groups, less clearly defined politically, such as the Jewish Scout Movement of France. After the outbreak of Soviet–German hostilities, there was a Communist underground as well.

## Jewish Guerrillas in Action

Henri Michel, an authority on the history of European resistance under the Nazis, stated in one of his studies that the European resistance would have disappeared or remained powerless without outside help. The statement is only partly true of the Jewish resistance. Though the Jewish resistance, too, was in need of outside help, it received almost none; yet it managed to survive and function.

Although in Western Europe (with the exception of France) the Jews had virtually no guerrillas of their own, in Eastern Europe there were Jewish guerrilla units in Poland, Byelorussia, and the Ukraine. Almost every Jewish underground group in the East European ghettos attempted, with variable success, to send partisans into the woods. In the Government General the fugitives of the ghettos of Cracow, Warsaw, Częstochowa, Pilica, Żelechów, Minsk Mazowiecki, and other towns formed guerrilla units in the woods.[36] Particularly numerous were the Jewish partisans in the district of Lublin. Some of the better-known units were those headed by Samuel Jeger in the neighborhood of Puławy, and by Hil Grynszpan in the southeastern part of the district; the Bar Kochba group in the woods of Parczew; and two groups operating in the neighborhood of Łuków and Hrubieszów. In Upper Silesia, the Jewish underground of Będzin and Sosnowiec tried to establish guerrillas in the woods. In Eastern Galicia, the undergrounds of Lwów, Drohobycz, Stryj, Brody, and other towns sent guerrillas to the woods and mountains. The Jewish guerrillas of Brody and the neighboring towns suffered heavy losses in an armed encounter with the German forces.[37] Other Jewish partisan units such as Di Yidishe Bande (The Jewish Gang) operated in the neighborhood of Borszczów;[38] in the "Dark Forest" near Przemyślany; in the woods near Stryj, Dolina, and Tlumacz; and in the Carpathian Mountains. During the march of the Soviet partisan division of General Sidor Kovpak through Polesie, Volhynia, and Galicia to the Carpathians and back, many Jews, individuals as well as groups, joined Kovpak's army, and eventually formed a special Jewish detachment.[39]

The largest Jewish guerrilla movement developed in the formerly Polish provinces of western Byelorussia, Polesie, and Volhynia, which were Soviet controlled after September 1939. Particularly well known were the guerrilla units of the Bielski brothers and of Dr. Atlas in Byelorussia, and of "Dyadya Misha" (Moshe Gildenman) in Volhynia. It has been estimated that at least 10,000 escapees (some estimates run as high as 20,000) of the ghettos of Eastern Europe formed their own guerrilla bands or joined the general partisan units in those areas. The numbers do not really matter, however. The efficacy of the guerrilla units cannot be measured by numbers alone, since a small but resolute guerrilla group engaging in harassment and sabotage can often be more effective than a very large but inactive regular army. Nor can these figures be meaningfully compared with those for the various national resistance movements. The Soviets, for example, boasted of 1.5 million partisans in Eastern Europe; but a large part of these alleged guerrillas were virtually organized, equipped, and commanded, on a strictly military basis, from the Moscow army headquarters.[40] The Belgian historian Le Jeune estimated at 50,000 the number of Belgian resisters in June 1944; but more than 136,000 have been recognized in Belgium to date (such a posteriori inflation of figures has not been limited to Belgium). Finally, it must be noted that guerrilla warfare was in some cases the least effective way of fighting the enemy; the Czechs, for example, had no more than 5,000 guerrillas in 1944.

In the west, a certain number of Jewish guerrillas operated in southern France, and created various directing bodies, such as the Jewish Franc-Tireurs (French Sharpshooters), with headquarters in Lyons (founded in 1942); the United Jewish Committee of Defense of the Communist, Bundist, and Zionist Socialist groups in Grenoble (1943); and the United Jewish Fighting Organization in southern France. Several armed Jewish groups engaged in field operations. (For example, a group of the Jewish Scout Movement attacked, in 1944, a German garrison in Castres, near Toulouse, and forced the Germans to withdraw.) In all, about 140,000 guerrillas were fighting in France in 1944, but it is impossible to establish how many Jews were among them.[41]

Guerrilla warfare was impossible in the lowlands of northern France, Holland, and Denmark (on the other hand, the underground activities in the urban areas there were very strong). In the mountainous regions of Slovakia, Jewish guerrillas joined Slovak rebels in the battle of Banska Bystrica and were, with the other insurgents, annihilated by the overwhelming, superbly armed German forces.[42] In Yugoslavia, many young Jews joined the 250,000 guerrillas under Tito; some of them eventually formed separate Jewish battalions that went into action in several engagements with the Germans.

## Jewish Participation in National Resistance Movements

In some countries there were no special Jewish underground organizations, but a considerable number of Jews were active in the national underground. This was true of Italy, as well as Bulgaria and Greece. In other countries, such as France, many Jews were active both in the national resistance effort and in Jewish underground units. Jewish and non-Jewish groups sometimes cooperated in special joint enterprises, such as the rescuing of children in France, Belgium, and Holland. In Belgium the Jewish and non-Jewish undergrounds joined forces to attack a deportation train from the camp at Malines (Mecheln), and rescued several hundred Jewish deportees.[43] Sometimes, cooperation between Jewish and non-Jewish groups arose spontaneously to meet the challenge of an emergency. The anti-Nazi riots and strike in Amsterdam in February 1941 are a case in point.[44] In Brody, Eastern Galicia, a Jewish resistance group maintained close relations with the leftist Ukrainian underground in Lwów, which helped by providing arms and instructors. Even in the Ukrainian nationalist resistance groups under Stefan Bandera, a number of Jewish physicians and other medical personnel, as well as craftsmen, participated.[45]

Jews took part in the Polish democratic and socialist resistance movements, too. In the principal Polish resistance force, the Home Army, however, there were few Jews. The rank and file of the Home Army units were, in most cases, unfriendly to Jews and did not admit them. In fact, Jewish units and individual Jews hiding out in the woods were sometimes attacked. The same also happened in areas controlled by Ukrainian nationalist partisans.

In Eastern Europe, generally speaking, Jews succeeded in joining nationalist resistance groups only when they were able to pass themselves off as non-Jews. Though there were a number of such cases, they are often difficult to discover because of the concealed identity involved. Several Polish authors mention the activities of some of these camouflaged Jews, but fail to mention their Jewish descent, out of either ignorance, ill will, or indifference. For instance, though the peasants in the neighborhood of Lublin greatly honored the memory of one "Szymek," a valiant partisan who was in a command of a Polish guerrilla unit, everyone thought that he was a Pole; he was buried in a Christian graveyard, and every year a ceremony has been held at his grave and flowers have been laid on it. After the war it was revealed by Dr. Michael Temchin, a former guerrilla medical officer and Szymek's friend, that Szymek was a Jew.[46] But there were many Jews for whom no trace of their real identity has been left. It is likely that in some cases only the leaders of the guerrilla units knew the true identity of their Jewish members and took the secret with them to the grave. A similar situation also developed in a few Ukrainian nationalist guerrilla groups.[47]

## The Psychological Factors

The German mechanism of terror kept Jews and non-Jews alike under extreme stress, so that the large mass of the population cooperated out of fear and shunned any anti-German activities. But the Nazi terror hit Jews much harder than non-Jews. The rigors of forced labor, of camps, prisons, and various penalties were applied with much more vigor and ruthlessness against Jews, whose physical and moral isolation generated among them a feeling of hopelessness and lethargy. The methods of discrimination employed against Jews—the compulsory resettlements and deportations and the systematic starvation—produced a feeling of degradation and humiliation, which broke the spirit of many. Moreover, for a long while the German tactics of deception succeeded in obscuring the real meaning of "work assignments" to the camps and the plants; the sending of children to "children's homes" or "colonies"; "resettlement"; and so on. In a tragic kind of self-deception, people clung to the last straw of hope and would not jeopardize the "German truce" by any imprudent act of resistance. In many places, public opinion opposed the underground movement. The Nazis knew how to utilize these psychological factors by applying the primitive principle of collective responsibility in the most ruthless way. When twenty German soldiers were killed in a partisan raid near Kragujevac in Yugoslavia in 1941, for example, 2,000 Serbs, most of them entirely unconnected with the resistance, were executed in retaliation. For the killing of a German policeman in Warsaw in December 1939, 170 Poles were executed. Several acts of sabotage in Kiev in September 1941 provoked the execution of 800 Ukrainian citizens and of many thousand Jews (at Babi Yar). Similarly, when a particularly brutal German SS guard in Lwów was assassinated by a Jewish worker, the SS retaliated by killing 1,000 Jews taken at random from the ghetto. (See above, essay 10.) These examples could be multiplied indefinitely. Massacres of civilians, as reprisal in Oradour (in France) and Lidice (Czechoslovakia), belong to the same category. The sense of family and communal responsibility, particularly strong among the Jewish population, thus became a deterrent to underground activities. Several authors who have written about Budapest and Theresienstadt have pointed out that Jewish self-restraint, rather than prowess, saved the lives of the inhabitants of these two ghettos. If a resistance movement had arisen in Theresienstadt, they contend, it would not have been possible to save its last 17,000 Jews, and if the underground movement in Budapest had attempted a revolt like that in the Warsaw ghetto, the 100,000 Budapest Jews would have suffered the same fate as the last Jews of Warsaw.[48] The Jewish leadership in Budapest and Theresienstadt managed to save their Jews by different means, these authors contend. It is highly disputable whether the self-restraint on the part of the Jews was the main factor responsible for saving these two communities, however. It is rather more reasonable to assume that they were saved by various circumstances connected with the general political and military situation. Jewish self-restraint might delay the deadline for annihilation by the Nazis but could not prevent it.

## Conclusions

While Jewish resistance shared some characteristics with the resistance efforts of other nations under the Nazi occupation, there were other forms of religious and moral resistance innate in (and more suited to) the mentality and philosophy of the large Orthodox Jewish masses of Eastern Europe. As we have seen, various factors handicapped the development of the Jewish resistance movement: the lack of a strategic base, the absence of the operational and tactical media for an underground warfare, the lack of outside support and of an attainable objective, the inevitably poor timing of actions. Nevertheless, there were Jewish underground groups in almost all the Nazi-occupied countries, and various individual and collective acts of armed resistance were performed.

It is not easy to discover Jewish participation in the general resistance movement because of the rules of anonymity and conspiracy applied by the underground. Nor is it easy to estimate how much the Jewish (or any other) resistance movement contributed to the war effort in general. The military effectiveness of guerrilla warfare is still a controversial issue. Thus a historian of the Greek resistance movement, C. M. Woodhouse, believes that the guerrilla warfare in Greece was more damaging to the civilian population than to the enemy.[49] I take exception to this view and believe that the partisan effort in places like the Russian hinterland and in France considerably harassed the German armies. On the other hand, the underground could never be the decisive and final weapon, only a complementary one— and this only if it had powerful outside support. Where this was lacking, the underground was doomed to defeat, as the fate of the uprisings in Banska Bystrica (Slovakia) and Warsaw in 1943 and 1944 demonstrated. In fact, history knows more examples of heroic defeat than of victory for the isolated resistance movements.

However, the psychological effect of a resistance movement can be long lasting, regardless of how little is accomplished in actual warfare. The Polish sociologist Felix Gross makes the excellent remark that both the Serbians and the Poles celebrate national defeats as days of victory (the Kossovo battle of the Serbians; and the Polish uprisings of 1831, 1863, and 1944). Thermopylae is perhaps the most striking and celebrated example. In the Jewish community it has become almost a religious observance to celebrate the anniversary of the Warsaw ghetto uprising, as a symbol of Jewish resistance to the Nazi tyranny. It is a celebration of resistance without victory. Heroism cannot be measured solely by its ultimate achievement. The decision of a handful of men and women to take up an unequal and hopeless struggle against the most powerful and ruthless force of their times—a decision requiring suicidal sacrifice and great moral strength— must always be celebrated and revered.

❆ This essay is based on a paper read at the First International Conference on the History of the Resistance Movements held at Liège–Bruxelles–Breendonk September 14–17, 1958 and published in *European Resistance Movements 1939–1945* (Oxford–London–New York–Paris,

1960), pp. 195–214. The author treated the same subject, from a different perspective, in "Preliminary and Methodological Problems of the Research on the Jewish Catastrophe in the Nazi Period, Part Two: Jewish Resistance," *Yad Vashem Studies on the European Catastrophe and Resistance,* 2 (1958), 113–31; that essay contains bibliographical footnotes relevant to the material here. Philip Friedman also published a series of articles on the Jewish resistance to the Nazi regime in *Yidisher Kemfer* (April 3 and May 8, 15, and 22, 1953). Shortly before his death, he revised and expanded his original paper to the present study, which is here published for the first time.

## Notes

1. See essay 10 in this volume.

2. An English translation by Milton Himmelfarb from the Yiddish text in S. Kaczerginski, *Hurbn Vilna,* appeared in *Commentary,* 8 (August 1949), 105–9, under the title "On the Agenda: Death. A Document of the Jewish Resistance." See also Philip Friedman, ed., *Martyrs and Fighters: The Epic of the Warsaw Ghetto* (New York, 1954), pp. 193 f.

3. Joseph Tenenbaum, *Underground: The Story of a People* (New York, 1952), p. 408.

4. Louis de Jong, "Between Collaboration and Resistance," in *Das Dritte Reich und Europa* (Munich, 1957), p. 149.

5. *Ibid.,* p. 146.

6. Friedman, *Martyrs and Fighters,* pp. 208–14; Melech Neustadt, ed., *Hurbn un oyfshtand fun di Yidn in Varshe* (The Destruction and the Uprising of the Jews in Warsaw) (Tel Aviv, 1948); "Wladka" (Feigele Peltel-Międzyrzecki), *Fun bayde zaytn geto moyer* (From Both Sides of the Ghetto Wall) (New York, 1948).

7. Marek Edelman, *The Ghetto Fights* (New York, 1946), pp. 32–33.

8. De Jong, in *Das Dritte Reich und Europa,* p. 149.

9. *Ibid.,* p. 146.

10. Marie Syrkin, *Blessed Is the Match: The Story of Jewish Resistance* (Philadelphia, 1947), p. 21.

11. See Abraham Berman, "Jews on the Aryan Side," in *Entsiklopedia shel galuyot,* Warsaw, vol. I (Jerusalem–Tel Aviv, 1953), 685–732.

12. On the Auschwitz camp see my book *Oshwiencim* (Buenos Aires, 1950); also see above, essay 9, "The Extermination of the Polish Jews During the German Occupation."

13. Benjamin Orenstein, *Hurbn Czentochov* (Bamberg, 1948), p. 101.

14. This debate was carried on especially in Poland in 1946–1947. It was not until later that a favorable evaluation of Korczak was heard in Poland. See, for example, Barbara Eysymont "Defense of a Sensitive Heart" (Polish), *Kierunki* (Warsaw), no. 26, November 11, 1956.

15. Hayim Nathan Widawski and a group of his coworkers regularly heard the foreign radio broadcasts in Ghetto Lodz and circulated the news among the Jewish population. In 1941 they were caught by the Gestapo.

Widawski committed suicide. The twelve other Jews were deported and never came back. Israel Tabaksblat, *Hurban Lodz* (The Destruction of Lodz) (Buenos Aires, 1946), pp. 104–7. See also S. D. Bunin, *The House no. 29* (Hebrew) (Tel Aviv, 1955), pp. 68–71.

16. See above, essay 3, "The Jewish Ghettos of the Nazi Era."

17. *Ruch Podziemny w Ghettach i Obozach: Materjały i Dokumenty* (The Underground Movement in the Ghettos and Camps: Materials and Documents), ed. by Betti Ajzensztajn (Warsaw, 1946), pp. 91–108.

18. *Ibid.,* pp. 182–85.

19. Leib Koniuchowski, "The Liquidation of the Jews of Marcinkonis," *YA,* 8 (1953), 205–23.

20. This is reported in Oscar J. Neumann, *Im Schatten des Todes* (Tel Aviv, 1956).

21. Nuremberg document, PS–1061.

22. See above, essay 10.

23. The activity of the "Six Department" was described in detail by David Knout, *Contribution à l'histoire de la résistance juive en France, 1940– 1941* (Paris, 1947).

24. See Knout, *passim,* and also J. Jakubovitch, *Rue Amélot, hilf un vidershtand* (Rue Amélot, Help and Resistance) (Paris, 1948).

25. See my *Their Brothers' Keepers,* pp. 65–67, 194; also essay 17, " 'Righteous Gentiles' in the Nazi Era."

26. See my *Their Brothers' Keepers,* pp. 55–59, 192; James Rorty, "Father Bénoit; Ambassador of the Jews," *Commentary,* 2 (December 1946), 507–13; Leon Poliakov and Jacques Sabille, *Jews under Italian Occupation* (Paris, 1955); see also essay 17.

27. P. E. Singer, *They Did Not Fear* (New York, 1952); Oskar J. Neumann, *Im Schatten des Todes* (Tel Aviv, 1956).

28. Jon and David Kimche, *The Secret Roads* (London 1954).

29. See my Yiddish essays on "Jewish Resistance to the Nazi Regime," in *YK,* April 3, 8, and 15; and May 22, 1953.

30. Jews who fought against the Germans as partisans, rebels, or saboteurs are mentioned in various German sources such as the report by Franz Stahlecker, chief of the Einsatzgruppe A, which operated in the Baltic countries (Nuremberg document, L–180). See also American Jewish Committee, *Nazi Germany's War Against the Jews,* prepared and compiled by Seymour Krieger (New York, 1947), Part III, p. 56–74; Max Weinreich, *Hitler's Professors* (New York, 1946). For further German sources, see my "The Destruction of the Jews of Vitebsk" (Hebrew), in *Sefer Vitebsk* (Tel Aviv, 1957), pp. 439–52.

31. Ajzensztajn, *Ruch podziemny,* pp. 109–19.

32. See essays 9 and 10.

33. *Ibid.*

34. Franz Birkenau, *European Communism* (New York, 1953).

35. Moshe Kaganovitch, *Di milkhome fun di yidishe partizaner in mizrakh-Eyrope* (The Struggle of the Jewish Partisans in Eastern Europe, 2 vols.) (Buenos Aires, 1956).

36. Kermisz, *Dokumentry i Materjały,* II, *passim.*

37. Ajzensztajn, *Ruch podziemny,* pp. 154–65.

38. *Ibid.,* p. 34.

39. Affidavit by Fruma Gelfand in YIVO Archives.

40. Edgar M. Howell, *The Soviet Partisan Movement* (Washington, D.C., 1956); D. Karov, *Partizanskoe dvizenie v SSR v 1941–1945 gg.* (The Partisan Movement in the USSR, 1941–1945) (Munich, 1954); John Armstrong and Kurt DeWitt, *Organization and Control of the Partisan Movement* (Maxwell Air Force Base, Ala., December 1954).

41. Massimo Adolfo Vitale, "The Destruction and Resistance of Jews in Italy" (Yiddish), *YB,* 37 (1953), 198–204; Isaac Kabeli, "The Jews in the Greek Resistance," *YA,* 8 (1953), 281–88; also in Yiddish, *YB,* 37 (1953), 205–12; Leon Poliakov, "Jewish Resistance in France," *YA,* 8 (1953), 252–63; also in Yiddish, *YB,* 37 (1953), 185–97. For more bibliographical information on France, see my *Their Brothers' Keepers,* pp. 48–49, 191.

42. Neumann, *Im Schatten des Todes,* p. 264.

43. *Their Brothers' Keepers,* pp. 69–70, 194–95.

44. B. A. Sijes, *De Februari Staking 25–26 Februari 1941* (The Hague, 1954). Also see essay 17.

45. See essay 8, "Ukrainian–Jewish Relations During the Nazi Occupation."

46. See my *Their Brothers' Keepers,* pp. 128, 211; Jonas Turkow, *In kamf far lebn* (Fighting for Life) (Buenos Aires, 1949).

47. See essays 8 and 9.

48. On Theresienstadt see: Zdenek Lederer, *Ghetto Theresienstadt;* H. G. Adler, *Theresienstadt, 1941–1945, Das Antlitz einer Zwangsgemeinschaft.* On Budapest, see my *Their Brothers' Keepers,* pp. 80–91; *ibid.,* pp. 197–200 indicate the extensive bibliography on the subject.

49. C. M. Woodhouse "On the History of the Resistance in Greece," *Vierteljahrshefte für Zeitgeschichte,* 6 (1958), 150.

# 17

# "RIGHTEOUS GENTILES" IN THE NAZI ERA

Relations between nations and between ethnic, religious, and racial groups are a complicated matter. Jewish historians must be especially aware of this, since international and intergroup relations have always had a greater impact on our history than on that of other peoples. Our dispersion among many nations, our often involuntary coexistence with other groups— especially in areas with large, mixed populations with strained relationships—has brought us into all sorts of confrontations, antagonisms, conflicts, and dangers, and has involved us, at various times, in problems of adjustment, acculturation and assimilation, dissimulation, discrimination, and so on. Under such circumstances, "enemies of the people of Israel" and "friends of the people of Israel" have always been important factors, even in normal times. These factors have been still more decisive, often affecting our very existence, in crucial periods of historical change—for instance, the epoch of the Crusades; the chaotic period of the "Deluge" in Eastern Europe (1648–1654); the era after World War I; and of course, the period of World War II.

During World War II, intergroup relations became much more tense in many European countries because of the Nazis' deliberate tactic of instigation (*Hetz-Politik*) in their strategy of "divide and rule." The

German propaganda machine tried with great intensity to aggravate the conflicts between Jews and other groups and to inflame, as far as possible, existing anti-Semitic sentiments. The Nazis thereby sought to gain support for (or at least avert opposition to) their merciless *Judenpolitik* and, whenever possible, to involve other groups in the process of pillaging and destroying the Jews.

The European countries reacted differently toward the Nazi *Judenpolitik*. The peoples of Western, Northern, and much of Southern Europe were almost totally against it, and many individuals aided the Jews in their struggle for survival. In Eastern and some parts of Central Europe, reactions varied. Nazi collaborators and sympathizers were in the majority; they were particularly numerous among East European peoples—Ukrainians, Poles, Lithuanians, Latvians, Rumanians, and Slovaks. There were also large numbers of indifferent people in Eastern and Central Europe—with the exception of Czechoslovakia and Hungary. Far less numerous were the persons who had compassion for the Jews; fewer yet were those who actively helped the Jews. There were some "passive humanitarians" in all the countries under Nazi occupation or Nazi influence. Active helpers, or "righteous gentiles," though a small minority in Eastern and Central Europe, were far more numerous in Western and Southern Europe (France, Belgium, the Netherlands, Italy, Finland, Denmark, Bulgaria, and Greece), where a vast majority of the people were in sympathy with the Jews. Even among the collaborators and traitors in those countries the anti-Semitic program was not as popular as other parts of the Nazi plan.

For accuracy, we must emphasize that in some countries, especially Sweden and Switzerland, strong sentiments of compassion for the Jews were evident, and a number of persons in those countries participated, directly or indirectly, in rescue operations. It is sufficient to mention here such well-known examples as Raoul Wallenberg (plenipotentiary of the king of Sweden) and Charles Lutz (the Swiss consul), who rescued, through their intervention and persistent efforts, several tens of thousands of Hungarian Jews from imminent death; and Jean-Marie Mussy, former president of the Swiss Confederation, who managed, through his skillful negotiations with the Germans, to snatch several thousand doomed Jews from Theresienstadt and Bergen-Belsen almost in the final hour.

I do not include the German people in this study. My main concern here is intergroup relations in the occupied countries and in the countries that were allied with the Germans (for instance, Finland, Bulgaria, Italy). The issue of "righteous gentiles" in Germany cannot be considered apart from the broader question of German (not only Nazi) responsibility for the crimes committed—a problem that deserves special and thorough investigation.

It is impossible to determine, even roughly, the number of "righteous gentiles" during the Nazi era. Many of them worked clandestinely and remained unknown. Others considered the work a "sacred duty," for which they would accept no acknowledgment or publicity after the liberation. Still others feared reprisals after the war by anti-Semitic neighbors or anti-Semitic organizations. I could quote many such cases from my collection of documents—clear evidence of the danger and the oppressive moral climate in which the righteous people worked while saving Jewish lives.

It is also impossible to determine accurately the number of Jews who owe their lives to the noble saviors. At the beginning of World War II, about 8.3 million Jews were living in the territory later occupied by the Nazis and their satellites. About 6 million were exterminated. Of the 2.3 million survivors, some were saved by special political conditions, as in Rumania and Hungary; some had escaped to the central regions of Soviet Russia or to Siberia or had managed to emigrate abroad. The rest, about a million Jews, survived on the then-occupied territory of Europe—some in camps, some as partisans in the forests, some in disguise as Aryans, some in hiding. Most of these Jews would not have remained alive without help rendered, in varying degrees, by non-Jews. Surely, these "righteous gentiles" must have numbered in the thousands.

Our bibliography of the Holocaust and collections of eyewitness reports contain a great quantity of material pertaining to Jewish individuals or groups rescued by gentiles. Each record is a thrilling account of miraculous personal experiences. Volumes would be needed to describe them all. Yet this vast documentation available to us today still leaves many pages unwritten in the amazing chronicle of "righteous gentiles."

## Motives

I do not include here the considerable number of gentiles who saved wealthy Jews and accepted payment for their help. Though even in such cases the risk of death, the constant fear, the strain and tension, were of far greater magnitude than the amount of money received, I consider the "righteous gentiles" to be only those who performed their noble deed without remuneration. What motivated them to risk their lives for Jews? Friendship or love was very often the motive. Especially among the intelligentsia and the working class, friends rescued colleagues, comrades, and acquaintances. Aryans married to Jews saved their Jewish relatives and loved ones. Another motive was party affiliation. Individuals and underground organizations helped Jewish party members. Underground organizations and intellectuals also saved Jews who had distinguished themselves in science, literature, art, and social services—among them many converts, who were equally threatened by the Nazi policy of annihilation. Some of these were the famous art historian Bernard Berenson, the French novelist Colette, the world-renowned Polish bacteriologist Ludwik Hirszfeld, the Warsaw theater director Arnold Szyfman, the prominent scholar and historian of Polish literature Juliusz Kleiner, the piano virtuoso Władysław Szpilman.

Many gentiles who helped Jews did not belong to any of the above-mentioned categories, however. Their motives were purely humanitarian, and they extended their help indiscriminately to all Jews in danger. Humanitarian concerns were clearly manifested in the attempts to save the Jewish child—a rescue operation considered of top priority and carried out with great zeal by both individuals and by organizations, with no regard to party affiliation or political orientation. While some adult Jews managed to save their own lives largely through their initiative, courage, and ingenuity, the majority of rescued Jewish children owed their lives primarily to the help rendered by noble gentiles, individually or in groups (church or secular, charitable, educational, or political). In several countries, there have been attempts to give statistics on the rescued children. Though the figures which follow are conjectural and incomplete, they give some idea of the magnitude of the phenomenon:

*Belgium.* The number of rescued Jewish children was estimated as between 3,000 and 4,000. A substantial number of Belgians took part in the rescue activities. The children were kept in many Christian homes, in convents, and in scattered villages. Post-office employees helped by intercepting letters from informers to the Gestapo, and by warning the threatened families. Physicians took care of sick Jewish children in hiding. The Belgian underground organization Oeuvre National de l'Enfance (ONE) has estimated that it aided 3,000 Jewish children (unfortunately, not all the children lived until the liberation). Several individuals distinguished themselves in the rescue work: Jeanne de Mulienaere, the young editor of a Flemish newspaper; Jeanne Damman, a young teacher; the Catholic nuns from Louvain; and the director of a sanitarium for boys near Brussels.

*Holland.* About 4,000 Jewish children were saved.

*France.* An extensive rescue operation was organized in France. According to some reports, perhaps somewhat exaggerated, about 12,000 Jewish children were rescued in Paris alone. Particular praise is due two Catholic priests, Father Chaillet and Father Devaux, and the Protestant clergyman Paul Vergara. A number of Jewish children were rescued in Lyons by Abbé Glasberg, a converted Jew. Jewish and non-Jewish organizations worked together smuggling numerous Jewish children out of France to Switzerland and also, in smaller numbers, to Spain. In addition, individual Frenchmen hid children.

*Czechoslovakia.* The Catholic Caritas society placed orphaned Jewish children in their orphanages and children's homes.

*Poland.* The number of rescued children was small in proportion to the once large Jewish population. In prewar Poland, there were 921,000 Jewish children up to fourteen years of age. In 1946, the Central Committee of Polish Jews estimated the number of Jewish children as about 20,000. Of these, 15,000 had returned from Soviet Russia, and only 5,000 from the camps, the forests, or from hiding among gentiles. There was no large-scale action in Poland to save Jewish children, except as part of the activities of the Rada Pomocy Żydom (Council for Aid to Jews), to which we shall return later. In Poland and other East European countries, Jewish children were rescued mostly through the efforts of individuals and, in some cases, of church organizations. In many instances, former maidservants, wet nurses, and governesses hid "their children" out of compassion, frequently under extremely difficult conditions. One peasant woman saved a small Jewish child in her baking oven; another hid a child in a dung box. A Polish woman at Mordy, a village near Siedlce, snatched a Jewish child from a death convoy, nearly before the eyes of the police escort. Given these circumstances, she could not keep the child, who was sent at once to Warsaw and placed in an orphanage. In Czerniakow (a suburb of Warsaw), in an orphanage under the guidance of the Rada Głowna Opiekuńcza (Central Relief Council), there were eight Jewish children and, among the orphanage's six employees, two tutors of Jewish descent.

According to a news item in *Lachayal* (The Soldier), a journal of the Jewish Brigade, there were, at the beginning of 1944, thousands of Jewish children and adults in scattered Italian villages and convents, where they might be converted. Indeed, the rescue of Jewish children was often motivated by missionary zeal, especially among clergymen and persons strongly influenced by the Church. The Jewish children saved from death were not necessarily saved for the Jewish people or for their Jewish families. Numerous children did remain in convents. Also, a number of gentile families became so attached to their Jewish foster children, and vice versa, that they refused to be separated after the war. In Holland, for example, out of the 4,000 Jewish children rescued, only about 1,750 were returned to Jewish families; the others remained in gentile homes. The government of the Netherlands even went so far as to form a Christian-Jewish commission to deal with that sensitive problem, which evoked a passionate debate in the press. In all the other European countries, tragic conflicts developed over adopted or converted Jewish children, and court cases were initiated by relatives or by Jewish organizations to force the return of the children. It is sufficient to recall the case of the Finaly brothers in France.

On the whole, women played an important role in the rescue of Jewish children. Many women were involved in the rescue activities. More easily moved by their emotions than men, women very often acted on their first impulse, and thought less of the consequences. How much gentile women were influenced by emotional motives can also be seen in cases of mixed marriage. Many non-Jewish women saved the lives of husbands, and in-laws, or shared the tragic fate of their husbands, following them to the ghetto and later to death. Many gentile women also remained equally loyal to their employers and were hiding them, risking their own lives. In the underground organizations, more women than men were engaged in the section dealing with aid to Jews. A number of gentile girls and women were also of great help as contacts or couriers for Jewish underground organizations.

The scope of this essay prevents me from reviewing even a fraction of the many episodes concerning courageous and compassionate women in all the nations of Europe. I shall here mention only a few of the better-known names. For example, Anna Simaite, the Lithuanian Socialist-revolutionary, a librarian at the University of Vilna, who saved many Jews, especially children, is known to Jewish readers through her articles in the Jewish press about the sufferings during the Nazi era. Because of her activities, she was sent by the Nazis to a concentration camp. After the war, in 1952, she went to Israel to visit her adopted daughter, a Jewish girl rescued by her. Another example is the mother superior of a Benedictine convent in Vilna, a graduate of the University of Cracow, who sheltered a number of Jews in the convent—among them, the writers Abba Kovner and Abraham Sutzkever. Later, when they returned to the ghetto and established the Jewish Fighters' Organization, she provided them with their first hand grenades and implored them to let her join their ranks. There was the merciful "Mother Maria," the former Elizabeth Skobtzoff, from Paris, an inmate of the Ravensbrück concentration camp, who sacrificed her own life to save that of a Jewish woman. Let me also mention here Janina Bucholz, a psychologist, director of the secret bureau for helping Jews, in Warsaw; and Irena Solska, famous actress of the Polish stage; the young and beautiful Lena Zelwerowicz, also an actress; the writers and teachers Wanda Żółkiewska and Roma Dalborowa—all of them noble rescuers.

Christian organizations and clergy performed an important role in the rescue operations. With respect to the Catholic Church, we must distinguish between official Vatican policy and the purely humane, Christian-ethical motives of individual clergymen, monasteries, convents, and other Catholic institutions. In the official attitude of the Vatican and the higher clergy, there was a certain sanctimony. Though Pope Pius XI had, before the war, officially condemned racism and anti-Semitism (in his famous encyclical *Mit brennender Sorge,* in 1937), his successor, Pius XII, was very cautious and restrained in public utterances with regard to the Jews. The Vatican was more concerned with the political interests of the Church in the occupied territories and Italy than with the tragic situation of the Jews. Pius XII issued no official protest against Nazi persecution of the Jews, not even against the deportation of Jews from Rome (October 1943); neither did he dare to rebuff the Vichy government when Marshal Pétain of France tried, through Léon Berard, his ambassador to the Vatican, to sound out the attitude of the Vatican toward anti-Jewish legislation planned by Vichy.

As far as is known, in only three countries did papal representatives make efforts to intervene on behalf of the Jews. As the defeat of the Nazis grew closer, interventionist moves became stronger. At the end of 1941, Monsignor Andrea Cassulo, the papal nuncio in Rumania, approached the deputy chairman of the Rumanian governmental council about extending help to the Jews in camps in Transnistria and about stopping further deportations from Bucharest. The deportations ceased temporarily in 1942. By the end of 1942, the papal nuncio in Slovakia warned the Slovakian government that the Jews deported to Poland were being killed there. This information moved the Slovakian clergy to redouble their protests against the deportations, which were stopped for a period of time as a result of the protests. Toward the end of June 1944, Monsignor Angelo Rotta, the papal nuncio in Hungary, sent a strong protest to Regent Horthy against the deportation of Jews. This was the beginning of broader, international pressure—by representatives of Switzerland, Sweden, and the Vatican, by the International Red Cross, and by the U.S.A. (through the radio messages of Secretary of State Cordell Hull). During the bloody terror of Szálasi's Arrow-Cross regime in Hungary, the papal nuncio supposedly distributed about 13,000 safe-conduct letters to Hungarian Jews, letters which saved their lives.

Apart from the officially promulgated policy of the Vatican, the pope (who was of course the highest representative of a religion preaching love and charity for those in need) unofficially extended help to victims of Nazi anti-Semitism. At his invitation, a number of prominent individuals survived the war peacefully, behind the safe walls of the Vatican, in the papal summer residence, or in other hiding places. Among these individuals were the famous art historian Bernard Berenson (a convert) and Dr. Israel (Eugene) Zolli, former chief rabbi of the Jewish community in Rome (a puzzling epilogue was the conversion of Dr. Zolli). The pope also helped the Jewish community in Rome (in September 1943) with a large sum of money toward the huge contribution imposed by the Nazis, which the community could not raise in full on its own.

A similar discrepancy between official policy and individual principles can be noticed among other high Church dignitaries. Many of the higher-ranking clergy (such as the archbishops of Toulon, Montauban, and Lyons) sent out formal letters of protest and strongly objected in their sermons and pastoral letters to the criminal actions of the Nazis, but limited themselves to these pronouncements. Cardinal Sapieha of Cracow, not a very good friend of Jews, who had many times interceded with Governor General Hans Frank on behalf of the Polish population, only once voiced his protest, and this only in passing, over the fact that young Polish men were being used as helpers in the extermination actions against the Jews. Some individuals went further, however; Cardinal van Roey in Belgium and the bishops in Slovakia and in Hungary intervened before their governments on behalf of Jews. Metropolitan Andreas Sheptitsky, archbishop of Lwów, lodged a protest with Heinrich Himmler and was severely reprimanded for it. Sheptitsky did not limit himself to formal protests or to pastoral letters to his Ukrainian coreligionists. He personally helped to save the lives of about 150 Jews, who were hidden, at his request, in the monasteries of the Studite Order in Eastern Galicia. Alois Stepinac, archbishop of Croatia, also rescued hundreds of Jews, by transporting them to Italy or across the Rumanian and Turkish borders to Palestine.

How important the individual feelings were for the rescue operations of Jews can be proven by the different attitudes of two bishops in Lithuania in 1941. When a delegation of Jews from Kovno approached Bishop Brizgys to ask for help, he answered: "I can only cry and pray myself; the Church cannot help you." On the other hand, Bishop Rainis of Vilna preached to the monasteries that help be given to Jews. He also refused to bestow his blessing on a Ukrainian auxiliary battalion attached to the German army, because the battalion participated in actions against the Jews.

The lower ranks of the clergy were freer to follow their own humanitarian impulses. On the whole, the attitude of the lower clergy paralleled that of the various ethnic groups. Where the local population was full of sympathy for the persecuted Jews, almost all the priests participated in rescue activities; this was the case in Italy, Belgium, France, Czechoslovakia, and parts of Hungary as in the Protestant countries and in Greek Orthodox Bulgaria and Greece. Where the majority of the population was anti-Semitic, there were also anti-Semitic clergymen whose attitudes encouraged the enemies of the Jewish people.

How much more should we appreciate, then, that amidst those East European peoples devoured by anti-Semitism, some clergymen had the courage to oppose the anti-Jewish wave, sometimes paying for it with their own lives. In January 1941, according to Emanuel Ringelblum, in all churches in Warsaw, priests preached to their parishioners to forget all misunderstandings with the Jews and resist the instigations of the enemy, who desired only to sow discord among the people. Ringelblum also mentions a certain priest in Kampinos (a village near Łowicz), who frequently asked in his sermons for help for the Jewish labor camp inmates. Father Lipnianus, a priest in Vilna, had to pay with his life for similar sermons. In Vilna, two elderly clergymen from the Uniate Monastery were arrested by the Gestapo for helping Jews and were heard from no more. Their monastery was sealed up. A priest from Vidukle was shot, not far from his convent, for trying to shield Jewish children. Pastor Krupovitchius, who protested the murderous actions against the Jews, was deported to a forced-labor camp near Tilsit.

One group of clergy formed a secret circle to help Jews. Heading the group was the above-mentioned "Mother Maria," a distinguished Russian poet. The group sheltered many Jews and provided them with "Aryan" papers. In February 1943, the group was discovered, and all members were deported to camps. The greatest triumph for the Nazis was the arrest of Dimitri Klepinis, a Russian priest, caught forging documents. He was dragged to three different camps (Compiègne, Buchenwald, and Dora), was compelled to wear a special armband marked "friend of Jews" (*Judenfreund*), and was eventually condemned to death. Another well-known group of clergymen, the French Amitié Chrétienne (Christian Friendship), not only worked to rescue Jews but published a series of pamphlets entitled *Cahiers du Témoignage Chrétien,* in which they attacked the Nazi racial theories and called for resistance against the crimes perpetrated on the Jewish people. The editor of this series, Father Chaillet, was also engaged in the rescue of Jewish children in Paris, as mentioned above. Also connected with that group was Abbé Glasberg, secretary to Archbishop Gerlier, who himself exerted a great influence on Marshal Pétain and courageously protested the Nazi crimes against Jews.

A particularly interesting personality was Father Marie Bénoit, a Capuchin monk, who began his rescue activities on behalf of the Jews in Marseilles. In a short time, he got into close contact with Jewish underground organizations and with the Italian general Lospinoso (Mussolini's special commissioner for Jewish affairs in Nice), who was favorably disposed toward the Jews. Father Bénoit worked out an elaborate system for smuggling Jews across the border to Spain and Switzerland. He quickly realized that if southern France fell into German hands, Jews there, just like the Jews in northern France, would be threatened with destruction. Father Bénoit, together with the Jewish organizations, General Lospinoso, and Lospinoso's Jewish adviser Angelo Donati, worked out a plan to extricate 30,000 Jews from southern France, to North Africa. Father Bénoit went to Rome, was granted an audience with the pope, received the pope's consent, and also obtained the permission of the Italian government. At the beginning of September 1943, four Italian boats stood by, ready to transport the Jewish refugees to North Africa. But the capitulation of Italy and the quick German military actions against the Badoglio regime ruined the whole ingeniously prepared rescue plan. Only a small number of Jews managed to save themselves in Italy. Father Bénoit had to move his headquarters to Rome, where it was cleverly disguised in the Capuchin convent on the Via Siciliano. There, under the name of Father Benedetti, he again saved large numbers of Jews, by providing them with forged false identification papers. In this work he was aided by the staffs of the Swiss, Hungarian, Rumanian, and French embassies and also by a number of Italians—among them the "marshal of Rome," Mario di Marco, a high official of the police, who was later tortured by the Gestapo but did not disclose what he knew. (In 1952 and again in 1954 Mario di Marco visited New York, where he was enthusiastically welcomed by Jews.) Father Benedetti was also aided by Dr. De Fiore, chief of the Italian bureau for refugees; by Charrier, chief of the bureau for food allotment for foreigners in Italy; by the Protestant priest Monsignor Dionysius; and others.

Important rescue work was carried on in all the European countries by the underground organizations, especially by the liberal, democratic, and Communist groups. The Polish underground established a special "Council for Aid to Jews," which provided thousands of Jews with forged documents, hiding places, apartments, and also money (received by the council from Jewish organizations abroad). In several instances, non-Jews became leaders of Jewish underground organizations or partisan groups. For instance, in Holland, when "Shushu" Simon, the young Jewish leader of the Halutz movement (a widespread youth organization that smuggled Jewish children from Holland across Belgium and France to Spain), was caught by the Gestapo and shot, his place was taken by Joop Westerweel a Dutch teacher, who later met the same fate as "Shushu." Joop's wife and collaborator, Wilhelmina Westerweel, was sent to a concentration camp, but survived (after the war she visited her Jewish friends in Israel). Another example was Rudolf Masaryk—twenty-eight-year-old veterinarian, captain in the Czechoslovak army, and relative of President Tomás Masaryk—who refused to part with his Jewish wife and voluntarily went with her to Treblinka. He became one of the chief organizers of the famed revolt there, and fell in the battle of August 1943, together with his comrades.

Innumerable Jewish lives were saved through compassionate efforts of noble gentiles acting on their own initiative, not on orders from any party, group, or organization. It is impossible to categorize these noble people. Among them were workers, aristocrats, intellectuals, peasants, servants, government officials and, not infrequently, members of the police, beggars, and criminals. There were among them even some anti-Semites who became *bal-shem-tovniks* (saintly saviors), such as the well-known Polish former anti-Semite Jan Mosdorf, who perished in Auschwitz for allegedly helping Jews, among other "crimes."

The limits of this essay do not allow me to treat at length all the large-scale rescue operations and collective expressions of sympathy for the persecuted Jews in the European countries. These manifestations deserve to be specially treated in a separate volume. Let me mention here only a few of the outstanding episodes in which the entire population stood loyally behind the Jews and tried to save them. Such a shining episode was the "Exodus from Denmark" in October 1943. As soon as the Danish population learned of the German plan to deport the Danish Jews, several rescue committees were spontaneously set up. Risking their own lives, they transported, without delay, the whole Jewish population (6,000 to 7,000 persons) across the sea from Denmark to Sweden. One leader of this rescue action, Aage Bertelsen, was the director of a high school. Bertelsen visited the U.S.A. in the fall of 1954, and on that occasion the Jewish press wrote extensively about him. He also published a book in English about his rescue operation. A similarly miraculous sea crossing was carried out by the Greeks, who transported several hundred Jews from the Greek islands to Turkey. On the Greek mainland, several thousand Jews were sheltered in the mountains and other hiding places, thanks to the friendly attitude shared almost unanimously by the Greek population (except in Salonika, where the prevailing conditions were unfavorable and much more complicated). In Holland, the first attempt by the Nazis to carry out a mass deportation of Jews provoked a general strike by the workers in Amsterdam, in February 1941. In Finland and Bulgaria, the pressure of public opinion averted the deportation of Jews ordered by the Germans.

## Conclusion

For the first time in the history of humanity, mass murder, with millions of victims, was carried out, by the Nazis, in a methodical, efficient, cold-blooded manner. For the first time in the history of humanity, mass murder was committed as the culmination of a series of quasilegal acts by a bureaucratic governmental apparatus, with the aid of the military, with specially trained murder brigades, scientific "experts," and death chambers built with funds provided by the Nazi state. Anyone who opposed the murderers and sought to rescue the victims was treated as a dangerous criminal, deserving the death penalty. All previous ideas of law, justice, and morality were abolished. It is understandable that this policy had to be opposed by all organizations, especially the Church, whose basic *Weltanschauung* was threatened by that legal and moral revolution. The Church had to oppose the Nazi ideology, not so much for their "love of Mordecai" as for "their hatred of Haman." Likewise, the liberal, democratic, Socialist, and Communist movements also opposed the destruction of Jews. But the parties were shattered at the beginning of World War II. They lost their leadership, their funds, their prewar apparatus, and could work only underground, under constant police terror and impending arrests. This inevitably hampered their efforts to rescue Jews. The Church had much greater opportunities, because its organization, its apparatus, funds, and leadership remained intact. But inspired leaders were lacking; moreover, missionary motives became involved in some cases. The third major force engaged in helping Jews was made up of individual righteous gentiles. This was a completely unorganized force, which worked haphazardly, independently, and without the proper connections and without the necessary means. Still one may ask: If there were so many righteous gentiles, why were so few Jews saved? The same question could be asked with regard to the resistance movement, Jewish as well as non-Jewish, and with regard to the military defeat of the Allies in the first years of the war. The Nazis had the advantage of the first offensive (*Blitzkrieg*), the new method of attack. In addition, cynical, deceptive tactics; the fifth column; Quislings, collaborators, and informers had never before been used in so systematic a manner or with such calculated, merciless, scientific efficiency. Finally, systematic mass murder, starvation of entire populations, mass deportations and population transfers, the slave labor of millions, the seizing of children and young women, mass sterilization, were methods for which no one was prepared. To combat such methods, new strategies of counterattack and of defense had to be developed. Resistance movements and rescue workers using old, conservative tactics suffered defeat in their initial fight against the enormous terrorist and destructive machinery of the Nazis. Before the new methods of military and partisan resistance were worked out, millions of Jews had perished.

In conclusion, we must carefully examine the Nazi example of genocide—unprecedented in the history of the world—to develop a defense against any recurrence in the future. Intergroup relations and experiences during World War II have put before us a series of fundamental questions: How far-reaching and penetrating are the teachings of humanity and merciful compassion? Why did not thousands of years of ethical education and concern ward off the horrible massacres or prevent the participation in them of so many "civilized" and "educated" peoples? At what point does the conscience of "normal human beings" compel them to resist evil at the risk of their own lives? In such critical moments how valid and how effective are the feelings of humanity and solidarity among distressed groups.

Perhaps an analysis of these questions will someday bring a reevaluation of the entire educational system and a reform in other areas of human life, especially in the realm of intergroup relations. We must try to place relations between different groups on such a plane that the humanitarianism of less oppressed, more secure groups will prevent the destruction of threatened minorities. This is the lesson to be learned from the history of the Nazi madness and its tragic consequences.

❧ This essay first appeared under the title "Khasidey umoys ho'oylom in the Nazi Period" (Yiddish), in *Yidisher Kemfer,* vol. 36 (1955), 54–58. Two years later, Philip Friedman published *Their Brothers' Keepers: The Christian Heroes and Heroines Who Helped the Oppressed Escape the Nazi Terror* (New York, 1957; reprinted in New York, 1978). This volume includes almost forty pages of references and sources, which cover all the materials mentioned in this essay.

# WAS THERE AN "OTHER GERMANY" DURING THE NAZI PERIOD?

The period of Nazi barbarism has, as it were, relegated to the dim, distant past the years in which Gotthold Lessing wrote *Nathan der Weise* and *Die Juden,* the epoch in which German scholars, poets, and diplomats found inspiration in the Jewish salons of Berlin and Vienna and in correspondence with prominent Jewish men and women. The twenty-odd years in which Hitlerism cast its shadow over world history have been subjected to intensive research. Nonetheless, there are some aspects of this dreadful period which remain relatively neglected. Moreover, the approach to the subject is at times burdened by subjectivity and partisan motivations.

Among the most neglected questions is that of the attitude of the German people—its cultural and religious leaders as well as the masses—toward Jewish persecution. Were their sympathies with the Nazis or with their victims? If the latter, was their opposition to Nazi barbarism limited to moral sentiments, or did it extend to open protest and a readiness to aid the victims? What were the attempted or actual achievements of anti-Nazi Germans on behalf of the Jews?

Despite the paucity of research on this question, much has been written bearing directly or indirectly on the subject, particularly in German.

This material ranges from expressions of regret and repentance to attempts at a whitewash. The literature of the former type contains forthright, unequivocal statements by individuals and organizations, particularly Protestant groups. The resolution adopted by the Protestant Synod in Berlin in April 1950, and the comments made by Pastor Martin Niemöller, one of the synod's leaders, in proposing the resolution, are striking expressions of contrition. The text of the resolution reads as follows:

We openly declare that through indifference and silence we became before the God of Mercy accomplices to the vile deeds committed by the people of our nation against the Jews.

"I regard myself as guilty as any SS man," Niemöller added. "We let God wait ten years. Yet we must confess our guilt, not only before Him but also before the people."[1] Other church leaders,[2] writers, and scholars, such as Rudolf Pechel[3] and Karl Jaspers,[4] have spoken in the same vein.

Some of the problems touched upon in this repentance literature are symptomatic of certain postwar spiritual trends in Germany and are not quite pertinent to my present inquiry. The literature contains ample material on the Nazi period, however. These books, pamphlets, and articles, as well as the literature on the resistance, constitute an important source for the study of the attitudes and behavior of organized and unorganized anti-Nazis with respect to Jews and the Nazi persecution of Jews. The phrase "the other Germany" is not a precise phrase. To some writers it denotes organized anti-Nazi resistance; to others, all manifestations of anti-Nazi sentiment or behavior on the part of the people at large. In the present study, I have used the term in the second, more inclusive sense.[5] I have also included materials on anti-Nazism in Austria after the *Anschluss* in 1938.[6]

Finally, I would like to note that research in this difficult, complex area is subject to the intense pressures of various ideological and emotional factors. It is the responsibility of the historian to assemble all relevant materials, to present them as objectively as possible, and thus to aid the reader in finding a solution to the perplexing questions of our generation on the basis of the soundest evidence available.[7]

## The Clash Between Christianity and Nazism

The conflict between the Christian churches and the Nazis was both political and ideological. The political factor was predominant in Nazi-Catholic relations, whereas the conflict with the Protestant Church and with smaller sects was primarily ideological. Ideological friction was manifested as early as the beginning of the 1920s. It did not become pronounced until 1933, after the Nazis had come into power. The struggle was waged orally, from the pulpit, and in writing. There is a rich potential literature on the subject: books, pamphlets, periodicals, pastoral letters, documents, miscellanies, sermons, memoranda, and the like.[8]

The Nazis accused the Church—particularly the Catholic Church—of having political ambitions, of being universalistic and cosmopolitan, and of opening its ranks to Jews and other alien elements, thereby corrupting the ideal of the racial purity of the German nation. Alfred Rosenberg (in his *Myth of the Twentieth Century* [1930] and elsewhere) went further, accusing the Catholic Church of betraying Germany. Subsequently, Hitler made it quite clear that the Nazi attack was directed not against this or that one of "the hundred and one different kinds of Christianity" but against Christianity in general.[9] In conversation with his associates, Hitler allegedly said:

[Italian] Fascism, if it likes, may come to terms with the Church. So shall I. Why not? That will not prevent me from tearing up Christianity root and branch, and annihilating it in Germany. . . . Whether it's the Old Testament or the New . . . it's all the same old Jewish swindle. . . . A German Church, a German Christianity, is distortion. One is either a German or a Christian. You cannot be both.[10]

The Nazi war against the Church was conducted on several fronts. Most important was the fight over the education of the young. Shortly after their assumption of power, the Nazis—through the state and the party—monopolized the entire educational system, taking over both schools and youth organizations from the Church. Nazi education was strongly anti-Christian and anti-Jewish. Children were taught songs mocking Christianity.[11] A secret guide for leaders in Nazi youth camps in Austria, issued Easter 1938, reads:[12]

Point 2. Christianity is Communism. They are one and the same. . . .
Point 4. The New Testament is a Jewish invention. . . .
Point 20. Christianity derives from Judaism, and was brought into being by Jews. . . .
Point 26. Jesus is a Jew.

Not long after Hitler's rise to power, arrests and persecutions of clerics began. Many were sent to concentration camps, there to undergo torture and ridicule of their clerical garb as well as of their faith.[13]

How did the Christian churches meet the Nazi attacks? There is a sizable literature, both Catholic and Protestant, which attempts to show the intensity with which the churches fought the Nazis. On the other hand, there are those who admit that the struggle might well have been greater than it was, particularly with respect to opposition to the persecution of Jews. An official Protestant publication grants: "The conduct of Christians, including members of the Confessional Church, with respect to the National Socialist persecution of Jews, presents a picture of great weakness and uncertainty."[14] How can we account for this weak, equivocal attitude?

It must be remembered that the German masses, Catholic and Protestant alike, looked on in passive apathy as the Nazi terror engulfed Germany in 1933, and subsequently allowed themselves to be harnessed to the Nazi chariot of victory. Evidently the Christian churches felt too weak to oppose the Nazi wave. At first, the churches strongly desired to reach a compromise and avoid a break with the new regime. We shall consider later the substantial differences, in this respect, between the Protestant and Catholic churches. On the whole, it seems, some of the clergy, the lower ranks in particular, were sympathetic to the Nazis at first; some of them even joined the party.[15] From the very beginning, however, there was a minority, including many of the leading figures of both churches, which opposed Nazism. Their protests against the Nazis grew ever louder. These were the only voices of protest which were not always silenced by the totalitarian terror of Nazi Germany. It was only rarely that the Nazis dared arrest high church dignitaries, though the number of lower clergy arrested reached into the thousands.[16] They had no desire to increase the popularity of leading church figures by granting them martyrdom.[17]

During the first phase of the Nazi-Christian conflict, the Jewish question was raised only within the theoretical realm of theological discussion. After 1933, however, more concrete issues came to the fore. On April 7, 1933, the Nazi government issued a decree removing all "non-Aryans" from government positions.[18] This move was followed by pressure to introduce the "Aryan paragraph" into the churches, pressure to which the Protestant denominations quickly yielded. Overriding the energetic opposition of a bold minority, the synods of the various Protestant churches decided to exclude non-Aryans and spouses of non-Aryans from appointment to the clergy or church offices. Non-Aryans occupying church positions were to be dismissed.[19] The Catholic Church, thanks to its different legal and organizational status, was able to avoid a total capitulation to the "Aryan paragraph."

On the heels of their first important triumph, the Nazis began to demand that Jewish converts be isolated into special "Jewish-Christian congregations." This demand ceased to be actual with the introduction of the Nuremberg Laws in 1935. Converts and baptized children of mixed marriages were thenceforth considered Jews, subject to all anti-Jewish decrees—such as those regarding compulsory membership in the Jewish community, residential limitations, the required wearing of distinguishing marks, deportations, and similar measures.

The number of Christians of Jewish descent affected by the Nuremberg Laws was great. The noted statistician, Friedrich Burgdörfer, estimated the figure at 340,000 in Germany in 1933: 50,000 converts; 210,000 "half-Jews" (children of mixed marriages); and 80,000 "quarter-Jews" (those with one Jewish grandparent). To this total should be added many tens of thousands of converts and *Mischlinge* (half- or quarter-Jews) in Austria.[20]

With the progressive deterioration of the legal and economic position of "non-Aryan" Christians, the churches began to organize special relief activities for their benefit. The first organization set up in this field was the Reichsbund Christlicher Deutscher Staatsbürger nicht-arischer oder nicht-rein-arischer Abstammung, in 1933, which became the Protestant Paulsbund Vereinigter nicht-arischer Christen in 1937. It was followed by the formation of other Protestant groups with the same purpose (see below). A parallel Catholic organization was the St. Raphael Verein (headed by Bishop Berning of Osnabrück), which was instrumental in the escape from Germany of many non-Aryans. In Berlin, Catholic relief was centered in the diocesan office and was headed by a highly courageous woman, Dr. Sommer. The German Quakers engaged in relief activities for the benefit of non-Aryan Christians belonging not to the Catholic or Protestant churches but to various sects, and also aided some Jews. By and large, cooperation among the various relief organizations was quite common. At critical moments, requiring emergency relief and instant decisions, a rigid division of rescue work along confessional lines was impossible. Most Christian organizations also cooperated with Jewish groups and, under certain circumstances, aided Jews directly, particularly Jewish children.[21] Jewish organizations likewise assisted non-Aryan Christians, at the request of Christian relief administrators.

The problem of persons in mixed marriages was closely related to that of non-Aryan Christians. Though most often the Jewish partner converted to Christianity, it was not uncommon to find Jewish members of mixed marriages who had not relinquished their religion. The Aryan partners were subjected to various legal restrictions and administrative discrimination.[22] The Nazis, intent upon breaking up mixed marriages, met with strong opposition from the Christian churches on this issue, and were forced to retreat. Until the very end of the regime, the Nazis respected these marriages, and treated the Jewish partners much more leniently than they did other Jews. As a result, many Jews married to Christians managed to survive.

The firm stand of the churches on this issue is attributable to a number of factors. For Catholics, the Church's dogmatic, fundamental opposition to divorce was crucial. Equally unequivocal was the stand of the Protestant Confessional Church. On its behalf, Bishop Wurm addressed the Nazi government, on July 16, 1943, as follows:

In particular, we raise vigorous objections against those measures which threaten the marital union in legally inviolable families and the children resulting from such families.[23]

A second significant factor was the fact that the churches sensed the moral support of the German people on this issue. As noted above, the number of children of mixed marriages in Germany and Austria was very large. There is evidence that in many cases the German partner in mixed marriages stood up to the Nazi terror and remained loyal to the Jewish spouse. Reporting the results of a survey conducted on this question in 1945, an American anthropologist writes:

We were very much struck by the large number of German men who refused to divorce their Jewish wives and did all they could to protect them under the Nazis. In one case we know of, a husband whose Jewish wife was gassed in a concentration camp committed suicide. In another instance, the Jewish wife of a former naval captain was hidden by her husband in their home for eight years. . . . We encountered a number of German women who had been forbidden to marry Jews or half-Jews under the Nazis; all of them remained single, waiting for a change in the government which would permit them to marry their lovers.[24] One physician's wife had waited 13 years to marry him. . . . Another woman . . . waited 12 years. . . . In all our contacts we came across only one case of betrayal . . . but we heard many stories of loyalty involving great sacrifice.[25]

One hears, too, of German women married to Jews imprisoned in the *Judenhaus* in Munich who visited their husbands in disregard of the SS commandant's wrath.[26] Similar cases of the loyalty of Germans to their Jewish spouses are described elsewhere in the literature.[27] The story is told of a German doctor who voluntarily followed his deported Jewish wife to the Warsaw ghetto and perished in the ghetto revolt of 1943.[28] So strong were the sympathies of the population with couples who had intermarried, that the Nazi regime was compelled to take this factor into account, even in cases where its own prestige was at stake. On February 27, 1943, the Nazis conducted mass arrests of Jews in Berlin (the so-called factory-action).

On the same day Jews who had non-Jewish wives were arrested and placed in the administrative building of the Jewish community. The wives of the arrested persons gathered in front of the building every morning to demand the release of their husbands. Despite the police who harassed them they persisted in their demonstrations until the men were released.[29]

There were no demonstrations protesting the deportation of other Jews from Berlin, however.

During 1943, Christian circles became increasingly fearful that "about 400,000 'half-Aryans' would follow the Jews to their death."[30] The

Protestant Church began to protest sharply against the Nazi policy of extermination and proposed to the Catholic Church that it take similar steps.

During the first years of the Hitler regime, the churches had spoken out on the Jewish question only insofar as their own ideological fundamentals or the interests of converts were invoived. Not until the last years of the regime were direct protests against the persecution of Jews voiced by the central church organizations, though protests by individuals had been heard earlier. During the pogroms of November 1938, in particular, a number of Christians assisted Jews in hiding from the murderous SS bands. There were clergymen who spoke, from the pulpit, of the persecution of Jews, albeit in veiled language. A number of them were arrested. Generally, the Nazi regime, especially the Gestapo, portrayed the Church as "the agent of Jewish world politics," and accused certain clergymen of "defending the Old Testament" and of "recommending more and more that children be given at baptism 'Judeo-Christian' (biblical) names."[31]

The various aspects of the conflict between Christians and Nazis over the Jewish question can best be clarified by considering each of the confessions separately.

## The Catholic Church

The Catholic Church was not only an ideological opponent of the Nazis but a political one as well. The Catholic Center party was one of the strongest political parties in Germany. After the Social-Democratic and Communist parties had been crushed, the Center party was one of the most serious obstacles to a Nazi monopoly of political power. The Catholic Church, moreover, had the support of a powerful world political force totally independent of the Nazis—the Vatican—and was therefore constantly attacked as "the politicizing church," the "Romanists" (that is, Vatican subjects), "pacifist traitors," "birds befouling their own nests," and the like. In a speech in March 1933, Göring said that the Weimar Republic's tricolor symbolized the triumvirate of Germany's international enemies: the black for Catholics, the red for Communists, and the yellow for Jews. No sooner had th, Nazis taken power than they proceeded to arrest a number of Catholic priests (June 20–28, 1933). Within a few days, an edict was issued liquidating all the larger Catholic youth organizations.[32]

The world was therefore amazed to learn, on July 8, 1933, of the signing of a concordat between the Vatican and Nazi Germany, which made the Vatican the first political power in the world to formally recognize Hitler's regime. The concordat heightened the regime's prestige outside Germany and solidified its rule within. The concordat met with strong criticism. One scholar later referred to it as the Roman Catholics' Munich. The view was expressed that the concordat precluded any potential Catholic opposition to Hitler.[33] Only after years of bitter disillusionment due to the concordat did the Vatican, in 1945, justify it, on the grounds that it had "at least prevented worse evils."[34] There is no doubt that the concordat weakened the fighting spirit of the Catholic Church. Some politically naïve members of the lower clergy accepted the early Nazi propaganda. One priest, with avowed Nazi sympathies in the period from 1929 to 1938, justified his attitude as follows:

I must admit that I was glad to see the Nazis come into power, because at that time I felt that Hitler as a Catholic was a God-fearing individual who would battle Communism for the Church. . . . The anti-Semitism of the Nazis, as well as their anti-Marxism, appealed to the Church in Germany as a counterpoise to the paganism which had developed after 1920. . . . It was not until after 1938 that I saw that Hitler and the Nazis hated Catholicism as much as they did Communism.[35]

Yet, despite the fact that a number of Catholic clergymen had positive attitudes to Hitler and that leading Catholic dignitaries[36] made several official as well as individual peace overtures, the Nazi party and regime continued to persecute Catholic priests and conduct anti-Catholic propaganda.[37] German Church leaders, as well as the Vatican itself, often protested that the German government was failing to live up to its responsibilities as detailed in the concordat. Finally, Pope Pius XI issued his famous encyclical of March 14, 1937, *Mit brennender Sorge,* in which he openly condemned Nazi racist principles:

Whoever transposes Race or People . . . from the scale of earthy [*sic*] values and makes them the ultimate norm of all things . . . perverts and falsifies the divinely created and appointed order of things. . . . Only blindness and self-will can close men's eyes to the treasure of instruction for salvation hidden in the Old Testament. He who wishes to see Bible history and the wisdom of the Old Testament banished from church and school blasphemes the word of God, blasphemes the Almighty's plan of salvation and sets up narrow and limited human thought as the judge of God's plans.[38]

The encyclical was read aloud from all German Catholic pulpits, despite the efforts of the Gestapo to prevent it. It is noteworthy that certain German Catholic leaders played a part in the issuance of the encyclical, particularly Joseph Wirth, former German Reichskanzler and leader of the Catholic Center party. Wirth was active during the 1930s in fighting anti-Semitism in various European and American lands, and was in contact with various Jewish figures.[39]

At first, the protests of the leading Catholic dignitaries referred only to the persecution of Catholics and the vilification of Catholic dogma and doctrine. The ideological aspect of the conflict inevitably drew the Church into a defense of the Bible and of "biblical Jewry" against the onslaught of Nazi propaganda. This development is manifest in the anti-Nazi struggle waged by the "Lion of Munich," Cardinal Faulhaber. In December 1933, the cardinal delivered a series of three sermons, from the pulpit of Munich's St. Michael's Cathedral, on the value of the Old Testament.[40] Faulhaber's sermons created a stir. He defended boldly and unequivocally the moral, ethical, and religious value of the Bible and of "biblical Jewry" and affirmed the closeness of the (biblical) people of Israel.[41] Though Faulhaber, as far as is known, had nothing more to say about the Jewish question in his official statements—his scholarly competence, he declared, was limited to the period of the Old and New Testaments—he personally assisted a number of converts as well as Jews, as reported by his secretary, Monsignor Joseph Weissthanner,[42] and by several German Jews.[43] In October 1938, Faulhaber dispatched a truck to the chief rabbi of Bavaria to rescue the scrolls of the Law and other religious articles from the Great Synagogue, and had them brought to his palace for safe-keeping. In November, after he delivered another powerful sermon attacking the totalitarian regime, an enraged mob stormed the palace of "Faulhaber, the friend of the Jews."[44] In November 1941, when deportation to Eastern Europe began, Faulhaber again aided a number of Jews and "non-Aryan" Christians.[45]

In western Germany, the bishop of Münster (later cardinal), Count Klemens August von Galen, headed the Catholic opposition. He was thus characterized in a confidential Gestapo report of January 1942: "He has had a Jewish and Jesuit education" and " he continues to correspond, to this very day, with leading Jewish figures. . . . As late as 1939 he consistently voiced the opinion that the Jewish people was God's Chosen People."[46]

Bishop von Galen made a great impression with three strong speeches in 1941 and a declaration the following year. About that time, a pastoral letter adopted at a conference in Fulda on July 20, 1941, was circulated by the German bishops, explicitly declaring: "It is impermissible to destroy human life, except in the event of a just war."[47] Nonetheless, these were all only indirect allusions, whose lack of forthrightness was criticized in a rather interesting Polish pamphlet (presumably put out by an underground organization among Polish forced laborers in Germany). The pamphlet reported the slaughter of 500 Jews in Oszmiany (Vilna district) by the German police shortly after the Germans had occupied the area. Further details are given about massacres of Jews and Poles, and the German Catholics are bitterly criticized for their silence in the face of such crimes. The pamphlet then describes the courageous anti-Nazi struggle of Bishop von Galen, and the persecution of German Catholics, and concludes: "No matter how great our sympathies with the German Catholics . . . we do not believe that they can be absolved of this terrible responsibility [of failing to oppose the Nazi persecution of Jews and Poles]."[48]

On December 13, 1942, Cardinal Conrad Count von Preysing, bishop of Berlin, issued a forthright pastoral letter, which reads, in part:

Every human being has rights of which no earthly power can deprive him . . . the right to live, not to be hurt, to be free, to own property, to have a family life. These rights cannot be infringed upon by the government. . . . No one can be deprived of them because he is not of our blood or does not speak our language. . . . We must understand that taking away these rights or acting cruelly against our fellow men is an injustice, not only to the stranger, but also to our own people.[49]

The sharper the conflict between the Nazis and the Catholic Church became, the more forthright were the latter's protests against the persecution of Jews. In a joint pastoral letter in 1943 the German bishops declared:

The extermination of human beings is per se wrong, even if it is purportedly done in the interests of society; but it is particularly evil if it is carried out against the innocent and defenseless people of alien races or alien descent.[50]

In 1944, a Gestapo report complained: "From various places we hear that priests have recently begun to praise Jewry very highly in their sermons." A second report noted: "The Catholic Church wishes to know nothing of a war against Judaism and Bolshevism. Her 'faithful' embrace both sides of the battlefield, praying not for a German victory, but for peace."[51]

In contrast to the aforementioned Nazi policy of not arresting high church dignitaries, lest they become martyrs, was the frequent arrest of clergy of middle and lower rank. The detention of one such priest, Monsignor Bernhard Lichtenberg of St. Hedwig Cathedral, Berlin, received widespread attention. Lichtenberg, a man of profound piety and moral stature, was head of the bishop's relief program in the German capital for many years. Throughout the worst years of Nazi persecution, he called daily upon the faithful in his church to pray for the "poor persecuted Jews," for those imprisoned, and for "our non-Aryan coreligionists." In a sermon on August 29, 1941, he declared that, unable to bear Nazi vandalism any longer, he would thenceforth include the Jews in his daily prayers, "since the synagogues had been set aflame and Jewish businesses had been closed." An American writer who visited St. Hedwig's (presumably before the war, or, at the latest, in 1940; no date is given), described the strong impression made by Lichtenberg's sermons, the words "that came out of the depth of his heart, beautifully spoken, moving, stirring."[52] Lichtenberg was arrested by the Gestapo on October 23, 1941 and sentenced to jail. After serving his term, he was consigned to a concentration camp for "reeducation." He asked to be sent to the Jewish ghetto in Lodz, but instead was assigned to Dachau. The ailing priest did not live to complete the journey, however. He died on November 3, 1943, on the way to the concentration camp, in the city of Hof.[53]

Jews as well as "non-Aryan" Christians received considerable assistance, particularly during the period of deportations, from the Catholic Caritas society. In the spring of 1943, the Gestapo learned of these activities and arrested the leaders, among them Dr. Gertrud Luckner and Grete Wünsch. After two years in a concentration camp, the former was, at liberation, "in bad physical shape but spiritually unbroken." Dr. Luckner returned to her home in Freiburg, where she founded the journal *Rundbrief*. A member of the Bonn Parliament, she visited England at the invitation of Leo Baeck in 1950, and was warmly received by German Jewish refugees, who knew her relief work well. Dr. Luckner received a similar reception on her visit to Israel in 1951.[54]

## The Protestant Church

It might have been anticipated that the Protestant opposition to Nazism would be greater than the Catholic, for, in 1938, 64 percent (45 million) of the total German population (70 million) were Protestants. Their power, however, was not proportionate to their numbers. Protestants were divided into twenty-nine independent regional organizations and denominations, among which there had been sectarian strife for many years. Moreover, they had no international body upon which they could rely, as the Catholic Church had. A further source of weakness lay in the institutional ideology of Protestantism. According to Lutheran tradition, the relationship between "altar and throne" was one of subordination of the church to secular authority. This disciplined attitude of deference was so deeply rooted that it paralyzed large numbers of Protestants, even under the anti-Christian regime of the Nazis. Finally, many Protestants were ensnared by point 24 in the Nazi program, which spoke of a "positive Christianity."

Possessed of no political ambitions, German Protestants hoped that they would be accorded freedom in religious affairs by the new government. They were therefore initially disposed to be loyal to the Nazi regime. This led the twenty-nine Protestant groups to unite voluntarily in a Deutsche Evangelische Kirche. Friedrich von Bodelschwingh was elected the first German Protestant Reichsbischof. The Nazis were not appeased, however.

Pro-Nazi Protestants who had organized themselves into the Glaubensbewegung Deutscher Christen in March 1932, urged the formation of a "German Church of Christians of the Aryan race." Their activities finally compelled Bodelschwingh to resign. In the church elections of July 1933, the National Socialist candidates received a majority, and the Nazi military chaplain Ludwig Müller was elected Reichsbischof. In short order, the Protestant Synod introduced the "Aryan paragraph" into the church regulations.[55]

The rapid victory of the National Socialist elements, in part a result of government pressure, wrought widespread confusion in Protestant ranks. Several outstanding theologians, such as Karl Thieme, turned to Catholicism in protest.[56] But a substantial number of Protestant pastors opposed to Müller and to the "Aryan paragraph" resolved to fight. Some 2,000 pastors left the official Protestant Church to form the Pfarrer Notbund, which later became the Confessional Church, led by a Vorläufige Kirchenleitung der deutschen Evangelischen Kirche (VKL). The Confessional Church never received official recognition from the Nazi regime. Nazi persecution notwithstanding, the church grew steadily. One of the early public demonstrations of the Pfarrer Notbund in Berlin, on November 27, 1933, attracted 10,000 persons. The number of pastors enrolled in the organization doubled within a short time. By February 1936 the Confessional Church was reported to number 9,000 pastors. According to an estimate made in December 1938, about 40 percent of German Protestants were sympathetic to the Confessional Church, 10 percent supported the official German Protestant Church, and half remained indifferent.[57]

One of the founders and outstanding leaders of the Confessional Church was Martin Niemöller. Captain of a U-boat in World War I, Niemöller had the aura of a military hero, a fact of some import to the Germans. This was not his only qualification for leadership, however. One writer refers to the following aspects of his character: "Courage . . . resolution . . . wisdom . . . dynamism . . . a gift for words . . . kindness . . . and simplicity."[58] He also proved to be nimble and flexible in politics. His talent for political maneuvering was particularly displayed in the years following World War II.[59] Politically, Niemöller was a German nationalist, and his early attitude to Hitler and the Nazis was not entirely negative. In this he agreed with other leaders of the Protestant opposition, such as the leader of the Altona circle of Protestant theologians, Hans Christian Asmussen, and the noted religious philosopher Karl Barth. At first, these men were not opposed to the National Socialist regime, only to the religious innovations of the "German Christians."[60] Niemöller apparently accepted Hitler's declarations and promises about the creation of a "positive Christian church." Not until he was convinced that they were deceptive did he become the driving force in organizing the Protestant opposition. Its struggle was oriented to a defense of the Bible against the attacks of the Nazis and to opposition to the "Aryan paragraph."[61] The Jewish issue, in the early period, was of no concern. Much as various Catholic leaders did, Niemöller defended "biblical Judaism" and the Old Testament, while disregarding the fate of contemporary Jewry in Nazi Germany. (After the war, when he was reproached for having failed to protest the Nazi persecution of Jews, Niemöller is reported to have replied that his struggle had been ideological and theological, and that he had kept out of politics.[62]) In 1933, Niemöller issued a statement opposing the "Aryan paragraph" in principle, but with qualifications:

In the [church] community we must recognize converted Jews . . . as full-fledged members, whether we like it or not. . . . A church edict which excludes non-Aryans or those not wholly Aryan . . . from church offices is contrary to religion [*bekenntniswidrig*]. . . . Such a stand requires great self-sacrifice from us, a people that has suffered severely from the Jewish influence. . . . It is, indeed, unfortunate that, in days such as these, a pastor of non-Aryan descent should occupy a position in church leadership . . . but we cannot permit the introduction of such an edict.[63]

Further developments led Niemöller and his colleagues to adopt bolder steps and formulations in regard to both the general ideological struggle and the Jewish question. Evidently, Hitler had not anticipated such strong Protestant resistance. He regarded with disdain the "insignificant people, submissive as dogs," who "will betray anything for the sake of their little incomes."[64] He was, therefore, surprised at the extent of the Protestant opposition. Opposition to the "Aryan paragraph" was so great that even Reichsbischof Müller's resignation was demanded.[65]

In March 1935, the opposition pastors issued a manifesto stating that Nazi doctrine, based on a "racist and nationalist world outlook," constituted a "deadly danger" for the German people. To prevent the reading of this manifesto from the pulpit, the government subjected some 700 pastors to home arrest for a brief time. The struggle grew more and more intense, and gradually was transformed from a biblical-theological controversy to a conflict over problems of race and over the Jewish question. Speaking to a large audience in March 1935, Niemöller defiantly pointed out: "The Jews are not the only ones who crucified Christ."[66] On May 27, 1936, a memorandum was submitted to Hitler by the leaders of the Confessional Church, dealing, in part, with the Jewish question:

When blood, race, nationality, and honor are regarded as eternal values, the first Commandment obliges the Christian to refuse this valuation. . . . While the Christian is compelled by the Nazi *Weltanschauung* to hate the Jews, he is on the contrary bidden by the Christian commandment to love his neighbor.[67]

Nevertheless, none of these manifestoes or declarations makes explicit reference to the bitter fate of the Jews of Nazi Germany. None other than Niemöller himself confirmed this. In a speech delivered before students at Göttingen on January 17, 1946, he said: "I am guilty . . . I kept silent! I only began to speak up when the Church was affected. I feel that I am guilty!"[68]

On June 23, 1937, the Gestapo arrested most members of the Vorläufige Kirchenleitung, and closed its Berlin offices. Niemöller was arrested on July 1, 1937. When asked after the war to account for his arrest, he replied: "I think the concrete and final motive was provided by the memorandum at the end of 1936."[69] The Nazi regime preferred to avoid a public trial of Niemöller, lest it enhance his popularity. The special court which tried him in closed session ruled that the seven months of internment which he had completed constituted sufficient sentence. On "medical advice," however, he was transferred for "convalescence" to the Sachsenhausen concentration camp.[70]

Until his arrest, Niemöller had been pastor of the Protestant congregation in Dahlem, a surburb of Berlin. This congregation was a stronghold of the Confessional Church and remained so even after its spiritual leader had been arrested. A German painter, Valerie Wolffenstein, a Protestant of Jewish descent, thus describes her visit to the Dahlem church at the beginning of 1943:

As I entered the church, the congregation was reciting the 126th Psalm: "When Jehovah brought back those that returned to Zion, we were like unto them that dream." This was January 30, the tenth anniversary of Hitler's accession to power. At the end of the service, at which point the prescribed prayer for the Führer is recited, Pastor Dehnstedt, Niemöller's successor, said: "O Lord, perform what seems impossible to us mortals, perform a miracle—turn the obdurate heart of our Führer." . . . He then read the names of those pastors who had been sent to prisons or concentration camps. Members of this congregation did much to hide Jews and faced many risks in aiding them.[71]

Once again, we see the same state of affairs as among the Catholics: an open, official declaration against the Nazi persecution of the Jews was avoided but help was extended to persecuted individuals.

Toward the end of the 1930s and the beginning of the 1940s, the Jewish lot grew so critical that the Protestant Church could no longer continue its policy of "staying out of politics." After the pogroms of the Kristallnacht (November 1938), an "atonement service," which filled the church completely, was held in Dahlem. At its conference of December 10–12, 1938, the synod of the Confessional Church circulated a call to its member congregations, with clear reference to the pogroms: "We remind our congregants to care for the physical and spiritual needs of their

Christian brethren and sisters of Jewish descent and to pray to God on their behalf." A second statement issued by the synod referred to Protestant pastors who, "on seeing the treatment meted out to the Jews, ardently preached the Ten Commandments, for which act not a few were persecuted."[72]

The dangers confronting opposition pastors were not limited to official acts—to arrests, confinement in concentration camps, compulsory military service, or being sent to the front.[73] After the November 1938 pogroms, Pastor von Jan of Oberlenningen, Württemberg, said the following prayer, in which the word "Jew" was not even mentioned:

. . . Openly and in secret much evil has been done. . . . Men's lives and livelihoods have been damaged and destroyed. . . . Property has been robbed and the honor of neighbors assailed. Lord God we confess before Thee these our sins and our nation's sins. Forgive us and spare us from Thy punishment. Amen.

The pastor was shortly thereafter dragged out of a Bible class by a band of Nazi hooligans bearing placards with the word "Jew-lackey"; he was beaten brutally, and was thrown into the local jail. At the same time, his vicarage was wrecked. In the town of Ludwigsburg, a mob demonstrated against Deacon Dörrfuss, carrying similar posters. The pastor of Böckingen, near Heilbronn, was fired upon, and the windows of his home were broken.[74]

Despite the double pressure of the government and the mob, Protestant opposition and courage grew steadily. Reference to the Jewish question was made more and more openly. The story of Theophil Wurm, regional bishop of Württemberg, exemplifies the progression from biblical-theological controversy to political opposition. During the early 1930s, Wurm and Hans Lilje, bishop of Hanover, were regarded as leaders of the moderate wing of the Confessional Church, in contrast to Niemöller, who led the radical wing.[75] Wurm was, nonetheless, the first bishop to be arrested by the Nazis—in September 1933, as a consequence of his vigorous protest against Nazi efforts to create a "Nordic-Christian hybrid religion." His arrest was followed by that of the Bavarian bishop, Hans Meiser. His followers staged protest demonstrations in the streets of Munich, and both bishops were freed in October 1933.

On December 3, 1938, Bishop Wurm addressed a plea to the minister of justice to "do all within your power to restore authority, law, and the sense of justice."[76] Though this plea was an explicit reaction to the November pogroms, the word "Jew" was not mentioned. In the various memoranda and declarations he issued up to the end of 1942, Wurm protested only against the persecution of non-Aryan Christians, not against that of Jews.

By the beginning of 1943, a significant departure was made—at least by some members of the Protestant opposition—from the policy of caution with respect to Nazi persecution of Jews. During Easter 1943 Bishop Meiser of Munich received an anonymous memorandum from two members of the Protestant Church. He could not prevail upon them to sign their names. After the war, it was learned that the author was Pastor Diem, chairman of the Württemberg "Theological Society." The anonymous message did not mince words:

As Christians, we can no longer tolerate the silence of the Church in Germany about the persecution of the Jews. In the Protestant Church, all congregants are equally responsible for the failure of the clergy to fulfill its duties. Hence we, too, feel guilty for the fact that we have failed in our duty in this matter. . . . Every non-Aryan in Germany today, be he Jew or Christian, is as one who has fallen among murderers. We must ask ourselves whether we are to meet him as did the priest and the Levite, or as the Samaritan? No talk of a "Jewish question" can absolve us from facing these alternatives. . . . The Church must bear witness against the regime, testifying to the significance of the people of Israel for the idea of redemption, and must oppose with all its might the attempt to "resolve" the Jewish question according to an artificially conceived gospel; that is, the attempt to exterminate Jewry.[77]

Bishop Meiser transmitted the memorandum to Bishop Wurm in Württemberg, who had just then begun his own campaign of protest against the extermination of Jewry. In the spring of 1943, Wurm addressed the German government as follows:

There must be an end to all these measures of putting to death members of other nations and races, without either civil or military trial, solely on the basis of membership in a certain nation or race. One hears more and more about such deeds from [military] personnel on leave, and this weighs heavily on the consciences of all Christian fellow-citizens, for such deeds are a direct controversion of God's commandment. . . . For this, our people will some day be subjected to a terrible retaliation.

An even direr warning was issued by Wurm to the government at the end of December 1943:

From the depths of my religious and moral feelings, and in agreement with the thoughts of all true Christians in Germany, I must declare that we Christians consider the policy of extermination of Jews to be a grave wrong, which will have fatal consequences for the German people. To kill beyond the necessities of war and without a trial . . . is against the commandments of God. . . . Our nation widely regards the suffering wrought by enemy fliers as a just retribution for what has been done to the Jews. The houses and churches aflame, the walls crashing during air raids, the flight from destroyed homes with the remnants of one's belongings, the helpless wandering in search of a refuge—these are agonizing reminders of the sufferings the Jews have undergone.

That the destruction wrought in Germany by enemy planes was an act of God in retribution for the extermination of the Jews was a charge for which the Nazis could not forgive the bishop. In the spring of 1944, they threatened him with arrest, though they did not carry out the threat.

Finally, in the fall of 1943, an official body of the Confessional Church had its say openly on the extermination of Jews. The Confessional Synod of the Old-Prussian Union, the Church's largest group, issued the following declaration:

Such concepts as "extermination," "liquidation," "worthless lives" are unknown to Divine Providence. . . . God has not granted the right to the government to destroy people because they belong to an alien race. . . . The lives of men— including those of the people of Israel—are in the hands of God alone, and sacred to Him.[78]

In addition to the Paulsbund, the Confessional Church set up a second central organization to assist Protestants of Jewish descent, which later included Jews among those it aided. After an earlier attempt in 1934–1936, the Confessional Church, at the fourth synod in February 1936, set up an "Office for Christians of Jewish Descent"—headed by Pastor Martin Albertz of Berlin-Spandau. Among his colleagues were Pastor Hermann Maas and his secretary, Charlotte Friedenthal, herself "non-Aryan." This relief organization really began to expand in September 1938, when a central office was set up in Berlin, headed by Pastor Heinrich Grüber of Berlin-Kaulsdorf. This became known as the Grüber Bureau. It had a permanent council, which included Albertz, Maas, and other important Protestant figures. In addition to the Berlin office, it had branches in Heidelberg, Breslau (headed by the wife of the vicar Staritz), Kassel, and other cities.

One of the Grüber Bureau's leading tasks was to assist converts and Jews in emigrating from Germany. Until 1940, the Gestapo favored a rapid emigration of Jews; hence the bureau's activities were tolerated by Nazi authorities. It also extended aid in various other ways: provision of jobs, material and legal aid, and, for converts, religious support. Since the children of converts and mixed marriages were, after August 1939, not permitted to attend secular public schools, and since the only alternative was the Jewish religious schools, the bureau founded a Christian school for these children in Berlin. Grüber went several times to Switzerland, Holland, and England in efforts to obtain visas. The bureau often worked closely with Catholic and Jewish relief organizations, and among those it assisted in emigrating were a substantial number of Jews, particularly children.

In 1940, however, Nazi policy on Jewish emigration underwent a major change, and Grüber's activities came into disfavor. On December 19,

1940, he was arrested and sent to Sachsenhausen, later to Dachau. The Berlin office of the bureau was closed, though the local offices were permitted to operate for some time thereafter.[79] Grüber has related a moving story about his arrival in the concentration camp:

On my arrival in Sachsenhausen camp shortly before Christmas, I was approached by one of the long-suffering, tortured Jews, who had known me in Berlin. It was in the evening that he stole out of the Jewish barracks and came to me, saying: "Herr Pastor, your having been brought to the camp is the most wonderful holiday gift for us Jews." Throughout the years [of camp imprisonment], this childlike, simple sentence was gospel and mission to me.[80]

The closing of the Grüber Bureau bore heavily on Protestant converts, for they could receive little aid from either the Catholic or the overwhelmed Jewish relief organizations. Grüber's successor, Pastor Werner Sylten, continued the bureau's activities in semiclandestine ways until he too was arrested in 1941 and deported to Dachau, where he died in 1942. His work was carried on to the extent possible by Martin Albertz and his three "non-Aryan" secretaries, aided by a number of Protestant pastors. The rescue activities of this group, too, were uncovered, and Albertz and some twenty-five of his assistants were arrested and sentenced to various prison terms. Several months later, Mrs. Staritz, head of the Breslau office, was also arrested.[81]

The Heidelberg division of the organization was headed by Pastor Hermann Maas. An ardent Zionist (in his own words, "a silent 'Lover of Zion' since the Fifth Zionist Congress . . . since 1903"), Maas had visited Palestine in 1933. His daughter Brigitta lived in Palestine for many years, where she and Ahuva Yellin, daughter of the Hebrew educator David Yellin, founded a weaving school for Jewish youths in Jerusalem. Maas's rescue activities on behalf of Jews and "non-Aryan" Christians began immediately after Hitler's assumption of power. He was particularly active in arranging the emigration of Jewish children, which work took him to England a number of times. When the Nazis learned of his activities, he was deposed from his post as pastor of Heidelberg's largest church, the Church of the Holy Spirit. This was a heavy blow to Maas, who came from a family with a clerical tradition going back to 1625. He continued his illegal work, suffered arrest a number of times, was sent to France for forced labor, and was sentenced to death several days before the end of the war. After the liberation, Maas wrote letters to his Jewish friends, which are marked by a great warmth and affection for the Jews.[82]

Maas was the first German to receive a formal invitation from the Israeli government. The Jewish National Fund honored him on his seventy-fifth birthday by planting a forest in his name.[83] Maas published his impressions of his trips to Israel in 1950 and 1953 in two books.[84] On his return from the first trip, he addressed a meeting of the German Parliamentary Society in Bonn. In this talk, he dwelt on the problem of "our guilt toward Jews"—using "our" rather than "Nazi." He said:

Every man is judged in two courts. He defends himself in the first, in the earthly court, in order to receive a lighter punishment. We—even those who were not directly guilty, but who were, and even today remain, thoughtless, silent, or forgetful—have deserved the death sentence even from an earthly judge. How much greater, then, is our guilt in the sight of the Eternal Court.

Maas also urged his listeners to understand Jews' feelings of disgust, hatred, and mistrust toward Germany. His address made a strong impression on his audience, which included the president of the Bonn Republic, Theodor Heuss, the vice chancellor, many professors, government officials, and members of Parliament.[85]

Another philo-Semite who aided Jews during the Nazi period was Pastor Albrecht Goes, a student and follower of Martin Buber and of his philosophy of Hasidism. Goes has written:

When in 1933–1934 Nazi tyranny was capturing one position after the other before our very eyes, we had one consolation: the certainty that Martin Buber was still at his home on the Bergstrasse in Heppenheim, and that we could still come to him for help and advice, much as the Hasidim would come to the Great Magid or to Reb Shmelke of Nikolsburg.

Soon thereafter, however, Buber left Germany for Palestine, and his followers were left leaderless. Goes has published a tale describing Jewish suffering in Nazi Germany and the action of a simple German woman in helping the persecuted.[86]

Further examples of aid rendered to Jews by Protestants could be cited. Thus, before emigration became impossible in February 1940, Pastor Zwanziger of Munich aided sixty-five people to flee the country.[87] Several members of the Berlin Dahlem congregation saved the lives of a number of converts and Jews by providing them with forged Aryan papers. Dr. Kaufman, himself a convert, headed this work. He was captured by the Gestapo and sentenced to death.[88] Most of the defendants in a large-scale trial of "defenders of the Jews," which took place in Berlin in January 1944, were members of the Confessional Church.[89]

## Other Christian Denominations

That Jews received little aid from the various other Christian denominations in Germany was due to a number of reasons. In the first place, their membership was quite small—only 150,000 out of a total population of 70 million.[90] Secondly, most of these sects were themselves objects of political persecution. Almost all members of the Ernste Bibelforscher (Jehovah's Witnesses), for example, were sent to prison or concentration camps. Thirdly, some of the sects were unfavorably disposed toward Jews.

One group which manifested great sympathy for Jews from the very onset of the Nazi persecution was the Quakers. They set up an organization to help non-Aryan victims of Nazism with food, clothing, and secret shelters. This organization was known to the British consul general in 1938. Various Jewish writers also refer to the assistance rendered by the small Quaker communities in Berlin, Munich, and Isarthal (near Munich).[91]

The Baptists, too, were well-disposed toward the Jews. Emanuel Ringelblum wrote about a German Baptist in a high post in the administration of the Warsaw District who had a friendly attitude toward Jews. In the Lodz area, too, even during the worst of Nazi persecutions, there were German Baptists who maintained a sympathetic attitude. One Pietrick, a German weaver, and his wife were sent to the concentration camp at Dora (near Buchenwald), and their property confiscated, as a result of their aid to Jews and their open anti-Nazi talk.[92]

The story of the Jehovah's Witnesses is a chapter in itself. They were hated by the Nazis for a number of reasons. They were, in the first place, a sect which had originated abroad, with headquarters in New York.[93] The Nazis and their ideological predecessors had conducted an intense propaganda campaign against the sect since the early 1920s, accusing them of being "collaborators and servants of Judaism and of Jewish world imperialism."[94] Jehovah's Witnesses, particularly in America, openly proclaimed their opposition to totalitarianism. Shortly before his death in January 1942, Judge Joseph Franklin Rutherford, leader of the sect, published a pamphlet predicting the downfall of the Axis powers.[95] In consequence of their opposition to military service, the sect underwent much hardship in many countries.[96] Their categorical refusal to use the "Heil Hitler" salutation—a grave offense in Nazi Germany—enraged the Nazis. They were furthermore accused of spreading anti-Nazi propaganda and prophecies about the coming downfall of "anti-Christ" (Hitler) and of the Day of Judgment for his regime.[97] According to Annedore Leber (widow of the murdered Socialist leader Julius Leber), there were 6,034 Witnesses in Germany from 1933 to 1945, of whom 5,911 were arrested.[98] In the concentration camps, the Witnesses were treated far more leniently than the Jews; nevertheless, more than 2,000 were killed, often as a result of their refusal to compromise their beliefs. The literature of concentration camp memoirs contains many instances of individual Witnesses being tortured to death for their fearless behavior. The same sources report the existence of friendly relations among Jews and Witnesses in the camps.[99] Since so few members of the sect retained their freedom, there was little possibility of their rendering aid to the Jews. There are some cases in which Witnesses at liberty—both German and others (for example, the Estonians and Hungarians)—did help the Jews.[100] The suffering of the Jehovah's Witnesses did not end with the war. In Eastern Germany, they were tried in 1950 for "systematic boycott, incitement to war, espionage in the service of American imperialism, and illegal activities." A number of their leaders were imprisoned, and the sect itself was declared illegal.[101]

## The German Resistance Movement and the Jewish Question

The discussion about the historical significance of the German resistance movement is far from over. It has been the subject of innumerable books, pamphlets, and articles, written in a critical, polemical, or reminiscent vein. Among the critics are those who maintain that the chroniclers of the movement have, for various reasons, gone too far in exaggerating insignificant facts and personalities. These critics hold that there were only a few, tiny isolated groups, which either limited themselves to theoretical discussions about opposition or invariably failed when they did formulate concrete plans, such as inciting the German people to revolt against Nazism or to unseat Hitler. It may be that these critics are too extreme and biased. Perhaps the most judicious approach is that of the historian Hans Rothfels, who suggests that the role of the historian today is primarily that of a finder, recorder, and analyst of relevant factual materials, leaving evaluation to a later date.[102] In my opinion, this approach is even more valid with respect to the Jewish aspect of the German anti-Nazi opposition.

The various scattered groups constituting the German opposition drew their members from all social strata of the German people—from the working class, professionals, aristocracy, military, and, to some extent, from the differing religious groups.[103] Between 1933 and 1945, no fewer than 3 million Germans were sent to prison or concentration camps for political crimes. Of these, about 500,000 paid with their lives. Nevertheless, it cannot be inferred that German resistance was a mass movement. Most of the arrests stemmed from the Nazi policy of "prophylaxis"— the attempt to imprison all potential enemies: the functionaries and activists of all other political parties, and all those upon whom any suspicion fell of being actually or potentially disloyal to the Nazi regime. It is estimated that 800,000 of the 3 million arrested were real anti-Nazis, and that the number of Germans who "went underground" because of their anti-Nazism amounted to no more than 150,000 (of whom about 10,000 were Jews).[104]

The backbone of any potential large-scale resistance movement was broken by the mass arrests. The German resistance movement was caught in a moral dilemma, particularly after the outbreak of the war in 1939. Resistance to the Nazis meant, in effect, working for Germany's defeat and seeking aid from its military and political enemies. The Nazis took advantage of the opportunity to label the resistance movement as unpatriotic and traitorous. It took great moral courage to make a declaration such as that of one leader of the Protestant opposition, Pastor Dietrich Bonhöffer. Asked for whom he prayed, Bonhöffer answered: "Truth to tell, I pray for the defeat of my country, for this is the only possibility of atoning for all the suffering which my country has inflicted upon the world."[105]

Prior to the introduction of the Nuremberg Laws in 1935, Jews participated in the resistance movement, particularly in the labor groups. Thereafter, however, their number was constantly decreased. The greater the anti-Jewish terror became, the more Jews became liabilities to a conspiratorial group, for they were subject to special persecution (the yellow badge, limited mobility, deportation, arrest). Jews were placed under close surveillance by the German police and the Gestapo, which added to the dangers facing any illegal group.[106]

Thus, there are few known cases of Jewish participation in the German resistance groups. One exception is Max Fleischmann, professor of international law at the University of Halle. He was in close contact with the opposition leader Fabian von Schlabrendorff and with the bitter enemy of Nazism, State Secretary Herbert von Bismarck. Nevertheless, in 1943, when Fleischmann, like all other Jews, received the order to be prepared for deportation to Poland, his highly placed friends could be of no assistance to him, and he committed suicide.[107] The young Jew Hans Dankner played an important role in the Communist underground movement in Dresden. He was responsible for all border activity in the Sudeten region until 1939 (this involved smuggling people across the Czech border and bringing illegal literature into Germany). In March 1939 he was imprisoned and in 1943 he was deported to Auschwitz, from which he did not return.[108]

The two leading figures of the most influential opposition group, Colonel-General Ludwig Beck, chief of the German general staff, and Dr. Karl Friedrich Gördeler, spoke out clearly on the Jewish question on various occasions. General Beck prepared a manifesto, addressed to the German people, which was to be published after the Hitler regime had been overthrown. The manifesto sharply condemned the "blasphemous racial theory" and "frightful crimes" of the Nazi regime, and declared that the Jews should be compensated for their suffering.[109]

As is well known, the submission of the Western powers to Nazi Germany, and Hitler's unanticipated victory in the Sudetenland in 1938, frustrated the plans of the German opposition for an uprising against him. The leaders of the opposition made various attempts at the time to convince the Western powers that appeasement of Hitler was a mistake. They warned that it would strengthen his prestige in Germany and make a revolution impossible. Among the political figures approached was Chaim Weizmann. In September 1938, shortly before the Munich conference, Gördeler transmitted a document to Weizmann in London, which described the political situation in Germany in detail, and called upon Prime Minister Chamberlain not to be fooled by Hitler. Weizmann immediately turned the document over to a high British official, but Chamberlain did not even take the trouble to read Gördeler's missive.[110]

Gördeler was undoubtedly the leading figure among the civilian members of the resistance movement. In certain opposition circles, he was seen as the country's future president after the defeat of Hitler. He had been mayor of Königsberg since 1920, and mayor of Leipzig since 1930. In 1931, he also took on the responsible position of Reichs commissioner for price control. The Nazis took advantage of Gördeler's absence from Leipzig on vacation to remove the Mendelssohn memorial from the square in front of the "Gewandhaus." On his return, Gördeler vigorously demanded the return of the statue. The Nazis refused, and in March 1937 Gördeler resigned his post as mayor in protest.[111]

Subsequently, Gördeler played a leading role, both in the preparations of the opposition within the country, and in negotiations on behalf of the German opposition with various refugee organizations abroad. He maintained close contact with the Wallenbergs of Stockholm (a gentile banking family), especially with Raoul Wallenberg, who was later (1944–1945) to rescue thousands of Hungarian Jews. Gördeler was arrested after the unsuccessful attempt on Hitler's life on July 20, 1944. Evidently Heinrich Himmler knew of Gördeler's political contacts, for he proposed that Gördeler, through Weizmann, Raoul Wallenberg, and King Gustav of Sweden, try to persuade Prime Minister Winston Churchill to agree to early peace negotiations. The plan fell through when Gördeler specified the condition that he be allowed to go to Sweden to undertake the mission. Shortly thereafter, he was sentenced to death.[112]

A second opposition group sympathetic to the persecuted Jews was the Kreisau Circle. The group was named after the Silesian estate of one of its leaders, Count Helmuth James Moltke, nephew of a famous German general of Bismarck's days. The Kreisau Circle included people from various walks of life—aristocrats, military men, Catholic and Protestant leaders, Social Democrats, diplomats, intellectuals, and the like.[113] The Kreisau Circle was instrumental in helping a number of Jews to flee Germany. Count Moltke was also connected with the noted rescue of

Danish Jews. Through his friends in high government positions, Moltke had learned that the deportation of Danish Jews was scheduled for October 1943. He transmitted this information to his friends in Copenhagen, who in turn informed the Danish government and the Jewish community administration.[114] Moltke and a number of his colleagues were arrested at the beginning of 1944, and were executed shortly thereafter.

The Solf Circle was closely connected with the Kreisau Circle. Wilhelm Solf had been state secretary in the German colonial office before World War I. From 1921 to 1928 he served as German ambassador to Japan. He helped a number of persecuted academicians, among them some Jews, to leave Germany in the first years of the Nazi regime, and obtained posts for them in Japan. After his death in 1936, his wife Hanna and daughter Lagi, Countess Ballestrem-Solf, continued the rescue work for victims of Nazism. Among the members of the group were the former German consul-general in New York, Otto Karl Kiep. On Albert Einstein's arrival in New York, Kiep received an invitation to the banquet arranged in the physicist's honor. Although he was a high-ranking German official (Kiep was also German chargé d'affaires in Washington) at the time, he accepted the invitation. This was a transgression the Nazis could not overlook and he was soon relieved of his post.[115] Countess Ballestrem-Solf has written:

As the persecution of Jews intensified, I made it my special task to aid them. . . . My mother and I did our best to get emigration affidavits for Jews and she visited innumerable embassies and consulates in quest of visas. . . . It became increasingly important to save Jewish families by getting them out of the country illegally or by hiding them. We sheltered some in our house and helped others to find hiding places. . . . One day we learned of a chance to smuggle some of our protégés into Switzerland . . . [through] a small farm close to the border in Baden, from which a few field paths led to Switzerland.[116]

The Gestapo knew about the Solf Circle. In the first months of the war, the countess was called in by the Gestapo and was warned against being a "Jew-lackey." In January 1944, both mother and daughter were arrested. They were sent to Ravensbrück concentration camp, where they managed to survive. They were fortunate, for most of the other members of the Solf Circle, arrested at the same time, were condemned to death. No fewer than 80 percent of the members perished, among them Otto Kiep.[117]

Another opposition group, consisting of high officials in the German foreign office, was known as the "Red Orchestra" (probably because its members favored cooperation with the Soviet Union in the overthrow of the Nazi regime). They aided Jews with food, money, and shelter. In a German diary, we find reference to the activities of a group called "Uncle Emil," presumably the same group as the "Red Orchestra." One of the heroes of this book is called Erich Tüch, easily identified as the noted German diplomat Erich Kordt (a member of Ribbentrop's staff).[118] Another member of the group, Philipp Schaeffer, a distinguished Sinologist, attempted to save a Jewish couple from suicide. In his attempt, which proved futile, Schaeffer fractured his pelvis and thigh, and was caught by the Gestapo. He was sentenced to death.[119]

Another small, isolated group consisted of students and faculty at the University of Munich. It was known as the Scholl Circle, after its leaders, Hans Scholl and his sister Sophia. One of its members, Hans Karl Leipelt, was half-Jewish. He had gone through the early war years in Poland and in France, and had received an Iron Cross, but was discharged because of his "racial impurity." He and the other members of the group were caught by the Gestapo and sentenced to death. Under the name *Die Weisse Rose,* the Scholl Circle distributed anti-Nazi circulars and leaflets. One of the leaflets (issued in the spring of 1942) dwelt at some length on the Jewish question:

As an example, we wish to mention that 300,000 Jews have been bestially murdered in Poland since the German occupation. This is the most horrible of crimes, unparalleled in all human history. . . . Why is the German people so apathetic in the face of such revolting, inhuman crimes? Almost no one takes any note of it. The facts are known, but are set aside as mere documents. And the German people goes on in a stupor, giving these fascist criminals the courage and the opportunity to continue their berserk rampages, which they indeed do. . . . Will the German finally awaken from this stupor, protest as only he can against this clique of criminals, sympathize with the hundreds of thousands of victims, and sense his guilt? . . . For there are none free of guilt. Each [of us] is guilty, guilty, guilty![120]

Another illegal group which hid Jews and provided them with false documents was located in Berlin. A leading part in this group was taken by Kurt Christian Knudsen, who became, after the war, a book publisher and noted Protestant leader and writer.[121]

Annedore Leber's account tells of other anti-Nazis, presumably in Socialist circles. Among others, Lili Glöder and her husband are mentioned. Both were sincere opponents of Nazism, who hid victims of anti-Jewish persecution and Nazi political terror. For this activity, husband, wife, and mother were sentenced to decapitation in November 1944. The nurse Gertud Seele was also sentenced to death for this type of activity.[122] Otto Heinrich Greve, a Social Democratic member of the Bundestag, helped Jews to flee Germany. After the war, Greve visited Israel in 1955 at the invitation of the committee which observed the tenth anniversary of the liberation of Bergen-Belsen.[123]

At the first world congress of the reconstituted Socialist International, held in Frankfurt am Main in July 1951, a question arose concerning the extent to which German Socialists had aided Jews during the Nazi period. Leibman Hersch, speaking for the Jewish Socialist Bund, issued a declaration "On the German Question." Kurt Schumacher, leader of the German Social Democrats, replied in a lengthy address to a mass meeting called in honor of the congress. Schumacher touched on the events and problems of the Nazi period in a general way, devoting himself mainly to a sharp attack on recent signs of "fascism, chauvinism, and anti-Semitism," and calling for a struggle "against the danger of new bestiality."[124]

The Communist underground organizations published a number of illegal pamphlets sharply censuring Nazi anti-Semitism.[125] Their relief activity was centered on the rescue of party comrades, among whom were undoubtedly a number of Jews. Since Communist publications rarely mention "racial," religious, or ethnic origin, it is difficult to obtain a clear picture of the Jewish aspect of their rescue work.[126] In Communist literature occasional reference is made to rescue acts on behalf of Jews as such, irrespective of party membership. One such case is told about the Auschwitz concentration camp.[127]

Assistance rendered to Jews by various unidentified underground organizations is described by Ruth Andreas-Friedrich.[128] The pogroms in November 1938 had a particularly strong impact on opposition circles and led many new people to participate directly in the illegal activity on behalf of Jews, or at least to see that the Nazi crimes were recorded. Andreas-Friedrich writes in the introduction to her book: "The burning of the synagogues on November 10, 1938, moved me to resolve to write [this book.]"[129] Ulrich von Hassel, former German ambassador to Italy and a leading figure of the German opposition, entered the following in his diary on November 25, 1938:

I am writing under crushing emotions evoked by the vile persecution of the Jews after the murder of vom Rath. Not since the World War have we lost so much credit in the world. But my chief concern is not with the effects abroad. . . . I am most deeply troubled about the effect on our national life, which is dominated ever more inexorably by a system capable of such things.[130]

Several German poets expressed their sense of sorrow and shame in poems which circulated illegally in thousands of copies throughout the land.[131]

The November pogroms also led a number of Germans to take more direct action. In the middle of November 1938, a number of British Jews in London formed a rescue committee for German Jews. On its behalf, Sir Michael Bruce, a colorful figure with rich experience in special missions of various sorts, was sent to Berlin.[132] In his memoirs, Bruce writes that, on his arrival in Berlin, he approached, through prearranged contacts, a secret

German organization, whose members were jurists, doctors, and military men. According to Bruce, this group did a wonderful job in assisting Jews. All the relief work was conducted in close contact with leaders of the Berlin Jewish community.[133] Several months prior to this, in March 1938, Bruce had carried out a similar rescue action on behalf of Viennese Jews, with the cooperation of Austrian anti-Nazis:

We . . . built up, with the aid of a group of Austrian anti-Nazis, an escape organization. . . . There were, in fact, a number of these organizations, of which ours was only one. How many people were concerned altogether I have no idea. I believe my own section contained eighty men and women. . . .[134]

It is noteworthy that a number of members of the anti-Nazi opposition were stationed in occupied territories and criticized the anti-Jewish Nazi extermination policy in their letters and even in their memoranda to their superiors. For example, one high-ranking officer bitterly criticized, in a letter from Minsk on November 19, 1941, the deportation of German Jews to Eastern Europe and the introduction of the yellow badge in Germany. He warned that just retribution would be meted out.[135] General Georg Thomas, chief of the war production office in the German ministry of war, was also a staunch opponent of Nazism and may have initiated the memorandum of December 2, 1941, prepared by Peter-Heinz Seraphim, German expert on East European affairs. This memorandum pointed out that the mass execution of Jews in the Ukraine had many undesirable consequences: it weakened the economic potential, particularly for military supply production; second, it had negative repercussions abroad; third, it had a bad effect on German soldiers; and, finally, it brutalized the German police responsible for carrying out the executions. At the same time, the memorandum subtly criticizes the extermination not only of young men but of "old men, women, and children. . . . The great masses executed make this action more gigantic than any similar measure taken so far in the Soviet Union."[136]

In a second such case, an active member of the military opposition, stationed in White Russia, prepared a memorandum on the extermination of Jews. On October 19, 1941, an "extermination platoon" of Einsatz-gruppe A celebrated a "festival of the German police," perpetrating a ghastly slaughter of Jews in Borisov, in which over 7,000 persons were killed.[137] Both this memorandum and the aforementioned one on the Ukraine evidently went unanswered.

There were rare instances in which German officers and civilian officials not only protested but aided Jews outright. One high-ranking German police officer in Warsaw took great interest in a farm operated by Halutzim in Grochów, helping them as much as possible.[138] There is no way of knowing whether this German officer was aware that the farm was a base for a Jewish underground organization. But there are recorded cases of German anti-Nazis who knowingly worked with the Jewish underground. In Bialystok there was an entire group, among whose members were one Schade, director of a textile factory, who was a Social Democrat; the afore-mentioned Jehovah's Witness Busse; a Viennese Communist named Walter; several Sudeten Germans; and a German official whose Jewish wife and daughter had been murdered by the Nazis. This group provided the Jewish underground organization with every possible type of assistance. It saved Jews by providing jobs, forged papers, and shelter. It gave arms to the underground, and informed it of impending German moves. Two of these Germans were discovered by the Gestapo and sentenced to death.[139]

The case of Anton Schmidt in Vilna is perhaps the most interesting of this type. Schmidt had been pro-Zionist since his prewar visit to Palestine, and was a thoroughgoing anti-Nazi. He rendered significant assistance to Jews in Vilna, where he was stationed, but was finally caught by the Nazis and sentenced to death by a courtmartial. His friend, the Jewish poet Herman Adler, relates that Schmidt was buried under a wooden cross in the German army cemetery in Vilna.[140]

❧ This essay was first published in *YIVO Annual of Jewish Social Science,* 10 (1955), 82–128, and in Yiddish in *YIVO Bleter,* 29 (1955), 104–64. The first part of the essay appeared in German as a pamphlet, under the title *Das Andere Deutschland: Die Kirchen* (Berlin, 1960).

## Appendix A
## Two Letters from Pastor Hermann Maas

The first of these letters was addressed to the rabbi of Frankfurt, Dr. L. Neuhaus, on the occasion of the first Passover after liberation. It appeared originally in the German Jewish journal *Jüdische Rundschau* (Marburg/Lahn), 1 (1946), 50. The second letter, written to Dr. Frank Rosenthal, rabbi of Winston-Salem, N.C., appeared in the German Jewish New York weekly *Aufbau,* on February 22, 1946, p. 40.

Highly Esteemed Herr Doctor Neuhaus:
Please forgive me, a stranger, for writing you these few lines, but the first issue of the *Jüdische Rundschau,* the impressive rebirth of the earlier *Jüdische Rundschau,* has prompted me to do it. And, in fact, not only that, but also something entirely different.
Although I have known everything about all the horrors it describes, I [must say that] I am shocked anew at all those facts. And though I can do nothing, absolutely nothing, to wipe out all that has happened, or to redeem it, I must add a few words to you in this respect. I know it takes courage. In the end I may hurt you, and the Almighty knows I do not want to do that and should not do that.

How terrible is the burden of guilt that weighs so heavily on the conscience of the non-Jewish German people—strictly speaking, on every single individual and also on myself. We share in the guilt, even if we have sincerely loved Israel and have fought against those evil forces, as I have tried. The prophet Jeremiah takes the thousand and thousandfold smaller guilt of his people upon himself. How much more should we burden ourselves, we dwarfs as compared with this giant. I cannot expiate this guilt only before God, the guardian of Israel, the Supreme Judge who intercedes for His people. I must also atone to you, the faithful protector and spokesman of the Jewish community in Germany.

We can do so little! We can only cover our heads in shame, and with a broken spirit fall on our knees and lament the murdered people of Israel. I tell you this in a state of deep distress, and I beg for forgiveness.

But should there be forgiveness? Is there—perhaps for the first time in the history of Israel—solely and alone, an atonement and downfall for the perpetrator?

Yes, we have to atone! Suffering and acting, confessing and fighting, against hatred and indifference. I say it where I am given the word—that is, in the parishes. I say it as one of the silent "Lovers of Zion" and as a follower of the Zionist movement since 1903, since the Fifth Zionist Congress—and, most important, as the most afflicted in these days.

I would also like to tell you for Pesach, the first that you and I as liberated men in spirit and in prayer celebrate: May God always give us new ways to intercede for Israel, in reverence and love, in prayers for the murdered and the survivors.

With *Shalom al Israel* and a heartfelt *Birchat Zion,* I salute you.
Yours cordially,
Hermann Maas, priest
Heidelberg
Beethovenstrasse 64


My dear Herr Doctor Rosenthal:
Your charming young friends have shown me your very kind letter, and I was delighted to read it. You write so many good things about me—much too much for a modest man, who never did nor does more than to fulfill in a small way his God's commandments. You see, my dear Herr Doctor! When I am being asked what my part is in that dreadful guilt which the German nation has put on its shoulders during those evil years, I have only one answer to this question: My only guilt is that I am still alive! I should have shouted much louder, I should have protected and saved more people, so that in the end they [the Nazis] would have also murdered me. I know quite well that, in the last months, weeks, and days, I escaped the execution by a hair. But, nevertheless, I did escape. Is this not a guilt in itself?

I can only repay it by loving even more those who were put into my heart by our merciful God, who has chosen Israel as His people to suffer so immensely, but whom he never allows nor will allow to perish. I cannot tell you how deeply I feel for Israel and for every member of its people, with whom I have united my own fate and, how my heart beats, bleeds, and burns for them. There is still much misery and much pain to overcome. And for that reason we are gathering again to help everybody who is still here or who returns—to cheer him up, not let him down, to show him our brotherly love, to let him feel the unity of our souls.

You too were forced to let the wild Satan destroy the lives of your parents and murder them and you could not help. God bless the memory of your beloved ones and of the martyred victims, His faithful followers. I am sure that they too went to their death with a *Shema* on their lips and in their hearts. Now we pray for them, and hope that their intercession on our behalf will reach God's throne.

You also have your own community. Please convey regards from someone who so deeply admires Israel's worship of God. Through this I feel a true kinship with you in prayer and in the words of the Almighty who heals all wounds and who overcomes all divisions.

Hermann Maas<br>Pastor of the Lutheran community in Heidelberg

## Appendix B

Werner Bergengruen, "The Last Epiphany," translated from "Die Letzte Epiphanie," in *Dies Irae* (Zurich, 1945), pp. 29–30.

I have taken this land to my heart
And sent many messengers there.
In many shapes and forms have I come,
But you did not know me in any of them.

I knocked at the door nights,
I, an ashen-faced Jew,
A fugitive, hunted,
In tattered shoes.

You called in the sentry,
Gave the nod to the spy,
And only my ashes
At last you let go.

An orphaned boy on the vast eastern plains,
I threw myself at your feet, begging for bread.
But you did not fear future retribution.
You shrugged your shoulders
And sent me to death.

I came as a captive to slave away the days,
Uprooted and sold, lashed by the whip.
But you turned away from the wretched drudge.
Now I come as the judge.
Do you know me now?

# Notes

1. Taken from the detailed report given in *Rundbrief zur Förderung der Freundschaft zwischen dem Alten und dem Neuen Gottesvolk im Geiste der beiden Testaments,* ser. II, nos. 8–9 (Freiburg, August 1950), p. 18. (Hereafter cited as *Rundbrief.*) The intensity of feeling of some of the repentance literature is also seen in this dramatic declaration, recalling a statement by the chairman of the Protestant Synod: "And, at the joint synod in Berlin-Weissensee, we were deeply moved when Chairman Kreyssig clarified our guilt: 'On every train, carrying Jews to the death camps in the East, at least one Christian should have been aboard, going voluntarily!' We did not do it; we avoided the pain, and Israel had to suffer for us. Therefore, we must be silent before the Jews." Erica Küppers, "Kirche und Israel," in *Bekennende Kirche. Martin Niemöller zum 60. Geburtstag.* Supplement (Munich, 1952), p. 16.

Niemöller had been even more outspoken on other occasions. In an address to leaders of the Confessional Church in Frankfurt am Main on January 6, 1946, he said: "The guilt exists, there is no doubt about it. Even if there were no other guilt than that of the six million clay urns, containing the ashes of burnt Jews from all over Europe. And this guilt weighs heavily on the German people and on the German name and on all Christendom. For these things happened in our world and in our name. . . . Can we say it is not our fault? The persecution of the Jews, the manner in which we treated the invaded countries. . . . We cannot get out of it with the excuse: I might have had to pay with my life had I spoken out." Martin Niemöller, *Of Guilt and Hope* (New York, n.d.), pp. 13–15; the original German edition was *Über deutsche Schuld, Not und Hoffnung* (Zurich, 1946).

2. Heinz Schmidt, *Die Judenfrage und die Christliche Kirche in Deutschland* (Stuttgart, 1947), pp. 57–58: "In particular the Christian church in Germany will have to accept God's judgment with remorse and repentance. It was up to her to warn and to save Germany. We have scarcely opposed the arrogance of our people, the hatred of the Jews. Many Christians even collaborated. . . . This is why we, as Christians in Germany, will have to confess our guilt before Israel. . . . It is necessary, as preachers and members of the community of Jesus Christ, to admit our guilt openly, as the Church Theological Society in Württemberg did on April 9, 1946: 'Cowardly and passive, we turned the other way, when the members of the people of Israel in our presence were being dishonored, robbed, tormented, and murdered.' "

3. Rudolf Pechel, "Judentum, Christentum, Abendland," *Deutsche Saat,* 73 (1950), 65–66: "Over every conversation between Jews and Germans, especially Christian Germans, falls the heavy shadow of an unparalleled guilt . . . because the treatment of the Jewish question by Hitler and his henchmen is the point on which we Germans, as a nation, have lost our dignity. Crimes were committed of a magnitude that transcends all the limits of human comprehension, even the most extravagant fantasy."

4. Speaking at the reopening of Heidelberg University on August 15, 1945, Jaspers said: "We might have sought death in the loss of honor in 1933, after the violation of the constitution, when the totalitarian regime was set up by a sham legality and whoever opposed it was swept away amid the intoxication of the majority of our people. We could have chosen death when the crime

of the regime emerged into the open on June 30, 1934, or in 1938, with the plundering, the deportation and murder of our Jewish friends and fellow-citizens, when the synagogues and [Jewish] places of worship were burning throughout Germany, to our irredeemable shame and disgrace. We did not go into the streets when our Jewish friends were taken away, we did not shout in protest until they would take us, too, and destroy us also. We preferred to stay alive, with the feeble, if accurate, excuse that our death would not have helped anyway. . . . That we remained alive is our guilt. We know, before God, why we despair." Karl Jaspers, *Die Schuldfrage: Ein Beitrag zur deutschen Frage* (Zurich, 1946), p. 49.

5. See Heinrich Fränkel, *The Other Germany* (London, 1942); Ulrich von Hassel, *Vom Anderen Deutschland* (Zurich, 1946).

6. The anti-Nazi struggle in pre-*Anschluss* Austria (such as the movement of Irene Harand) is excluded from this study, however.

7. The present essay is part of a projected larger work on "The 'Other Germany' and the Jews," which consists of the following sections: (1) Religious Opposition; (2) Political Resistance Groups and Movements; (3) Opposition within the Wehrmacht; (4) Anti-Nazi Elements in the Administration; (5) Attitudes of the German Populace; and (6) Literary Opposition. It is based on the first two sections of the larger study. [The larger work on "The Other Germany" was not completed.—*Ed.*]

I wish to express my appreciation to Mrs. Sophie G. Fryde for assistance in assembling the materials upon which this study is based.

8. A bibliography on this subject cannot be presented here. The references cited in this essay are those of immediate relevance. Some notion of the extensive literature on the subject can be obtained by reference to the following bibliographies published in the *WLB*: "The German Churches Under Nazi Rule," 2 (1948), 29; "Good Will Toward Men: A Bibliography on Christian-Jewish Relations," *ibid.*, 28; "The Story of Rosenberg's *Mythos*," *ibid.*, 7 (1953), 33–34; Bernhard Lakebrink, "Catholic Action Against Rosenberg," *ibid.*, p. 34; Anonymous, A Student of German History, "Anti-Christian Literature: The Need for a Bibliography," *ibid.*, 1 (1947), 29.

9. *The Nazi War Against the Catholic Church* (Washington, D.C.: U.S. National Catholic Welfare Conference, n.d.), p. 27.

10. Hermann Rauschning, *The Voice of Destruction* (New York, 1940), p. 49.

11. For examples of such songs, see Dorothy Macardle, *Children of Europe* (Boston, 1951), p. 33; Robert d'Harcourt, "National Socialism and the Catholic Church in Germany," in M. Baumont, J. H. Fried, and E. Vermeil, eds., *The Third Reich* (New York, 1955), pp. 803–4.

12. John M. Österreicher, *Racisme—Antisémitisme—Antichristianisme* (New York, 1943), pp. 140–44.

13. The wealth of concentration camp literature, particularly about Dachau, provides much evidence for this. One typical verse anthology describes the suffering of an Austrian Catholic priest in Dachau, and contains many striking examples of the vilification of Christianity in the camps by SS men. See Hugo Huppert, *Der Heiland von Dachau* (Vienna, 1945). See also the material on the Protestant pastor Paul Schneider's experiences in Buchenwald, in *Der Prediger von Buchenwald: Das Martyrium Paul Schneiders* (Berlin,

1953); and Leonhard Steinwender, *Christus im Konzentrationslager* (Salzburg, 1946).

14. *Die Evangelische Kirche Deutschlands und die Judenfrage: Ausgewählte Dokumente aus den Jahren des Kirchenkampfes 1933 bis 1943,* prepared and published for the Flüchtlingsdienst des Ökumenischen Rates der Kirchen (Geneva, 1945), p. 6. On the Confessional Church, see below.

15. See David Rodnick, *Postwar Germans* (New Haven, 1948), p. 202. Rodnick, an American anthropologist, quotes a speaker at a Social Democrat convention in 1946 as saying that "a large part of the [German] clergy joined the Nazi party" and "helped persecute the Jews and turned their backs to the cruelty inflicted on concentration camp inmates." In 1933, pro-Nazis scored an important victory in the elections to the National Protestant Synod of the church in which they received the support of the majority of pastors (see below, note 16).

16. According to the U.S. Federal Council of the Churches of Christ, about 9,000 Catholic and Protestant clergymen were arrested prior to March 1938. See Adolf Lande, ed., *Chronology of Adolf Hitler's Life* (Washington, D.C., 1944), p. 125. According to a statement by Hans Kerrl, Nazi minister for church affairs, an additional 8,000 Catholic monks and lay brothers were arrested prior to December 1937; *ibid.,* p. 108.

17. This is explicitly acknowledged in Alfred Rosenberg's diaries. On December 13 and 14 of 1941, a gathering of Nazi leaders in Hitler's home discussed the strong anti-Nazi utterances of the Catholic bishop von Galen. Rosenberg reports: "The Führer declared that these gentlemen wish to become 'martyrs,' expecting to be accorded an 'arrest of honor.'" See Robert M. W. Kempner, ed., "Der Kampf gegen die Kirche: Aus unveröffentlichen Tagebüchern Alfred Rosenberg's," *Der Monat,* I, no. 10 (1949), p. 37; Philip Auerbach, "Wesen und Formen des Widerstandes im Dritten Reich," unpublished doctoral dissertation, University of Erlangen, 1949, p. 76 (mimeographed copy in the YIVO Library). Another source reports that Hitler overruled Himmler's proposal to execute Bishop von Galen. See Patrick Smith, trans. and ed., *The Bishop of Münster and the Nazis: The Documents in the Case* (London, 1943), p. 52.

18. *RGBL,* I, 175 f., reprinted in Bruno Blau, *Das Ausnahmerecht für die Juden in den europäischen Ländern, 1933–1945,* Part I, *Deutschland* (New York, 1952), pp. 15–19.

19. *Die Evangelische Kirche,* pp. 35–113, contains the text of the decree, and a review of the subsequent discussions in Protestant circles in Germany.

20. Friedrich Burgdörfer, "Die Juden in Deutschland und in der Welt," *Forschungen zur Judenfrage,* III (Hamburg, 1938), 152. The preliminary results of an Austrian census conducted on May 17, 1939, showed that there were 18,106 "part Jews of Grade I" (having two Jewish grandparents) and 8,479 "part Jews of Grade II" (having one Jewish grandparent). The number of converts is not given. It is to be presumed that they were included among the 94,533 "full Jews." *NCA,* IV, 587, 591, Document PS–1949. The number of Jews reported by the census is only slightly more than half the number of Jews in Austria prior to the *Anschluss*. From this we can deduce that the number of converts and *Mischlinge* was also substantially higher before March 1938 than in May 1939. One authority estimates their number at 100,000 in

1938. See Oskar Karbach, "The Liquidation of the Jewish Community of Vienna," *JSS,* 2 (1940), 259.

21. Further details on these relief organizations are to be found in Auerbach, "Wesen und Formen," p. 77; Siegmund Weltlinger, *Hast Du es schon vergessen? Erlebnisbericht aus der Zeit der Verfolgung* (Frankfurt, 1954), p. 19; Hans Lamm, "Über die innere und äussere Entwicklung des deutschen Judentums im Dritten Reich," unpublished doctoral dissertation, University of Erlangen, 1951, p. 90 (mimeographed copy in the YIVO Library); J. Neuhaüsler, *Kreuz und Hakenkreuz,* vol. II (Munich, 1946), pp. 377 f.

22. A survey of such laws, decrees, and discriminations is to be found in Bruno Blau, "Die Verfolgung von Nichtjuden im Dritten Reich—wegen Juden"; *Rundbrief,* ser. III-IV, no. 16 (April 1952), pp. 34–36.

23. *Die Evangelische Kirche,* p. 190.

24. In 1937, the German Reichsgericht annulled several marriages between Jews and Aryans, thereby setting a precedent which acted to prevent mixed marriages. Evidently there were frequent cases of such marriages until that time. See Blau, *Das Ausnahmerecht,* Part I, p. 133. In the summer of 1935, the *Essener National Zeitung,* Göring's organ, complained that in Berlin alone 667 mixed marriages had occurred. See the collection *The Yellow Badge: The Outlawing of Half a Million Human Beings* (London, 1936), p. 273.

25. Rodnick, *Postwar Germans,* pp. 121–22.

26. Else R. Behrend-Rosenfeld, *Ich stand nicht allein: Erlebnisse einer Jüdin in Deutschland, 1933–1944* (Hamburg, 1945), pp. 188–89.

27. See Lotte Päpke, *Unter einem fremden Stern* (Frankfurt, 1952); Ruth Hoffman, *Meine Freunde aus David's Geschlecht* (Berlin, 1947), pp. 127–33; Anna Holtzman, "Experiences as an 'Aryan' of Jewish Faith" (Yiddish), *Fun letstn hurbn,* Munich, no. 7 (May 1948), 87–88.

28. Leon Poliakov, *Brévaire de la Haine* (Paris, 1951), p. 324.

29. Bruno Blau, "The Last Days of German Jewry in the Third Reich," *YA,* 8 (1953), 202.

30. William W. Schütz, *Pens under the Swastika* (London, 1946), p. 42. Presumably Schütz's figure of 400,000 also includes non-Aryan Christians in the territory then considered part of the Reich: Austria, Bohemia, and Moravia, and parts of occupied Poland and France.

31. John S. Steward, comp., *Sieg des Glaubens: Authentische Gestapoberichte über den kirchlichen Widerstand in Deutschland* (Zurich, 1946), pp. 90, 91, 115–16; these reports, marked "streng vertraulich" are mostly from 1942 to 1943.

32. A brief review of the relations between the Nazis and the Catholic Church until about 1940 is to be found in D'Harcourt (as in note 11), pp. 797–810.

33. N. Micklem, *National Socialism and Christianity* (Pamphlets on World Affairs, no. 18: New York, 1938), pp. 13–14. See also A. E. Kerr's review of Monsignor Ronald Knox's book *Nazi and Nazarene,* in *Dalhousie Review,* 21 (1941), 381; and John B. Jansen and Stefan Weyl, *Silent War: The Underground Movement in Germany* (Philadelphia, 1943), p. 243. Karl Jaspers described his reaction to the concordat as follows: "This was the first important affirmation of the Hitler regime, a tremendous boost for Hitler. At

first, it seemed impossible. But it was a fact. A horror had befallen us." Jaspers, *Die Schuldfrage,* pp. 69–70.

34. Ernst von Weizsäcker, *The Memoirs of E. von Weizsäcker* (London, 1951), p. 269.

35. Rodnick, *Postwar Germans,* p. 189. Similar sentiments were expressed in an official publication of the archbishop of Freiburg, Konrad Grüber: *Handbuch der religiösen Gegenwartsfragen* (1937), p. 149.

36. A number of Catholic peace moves toward the Nazis are described in Lande, *Chronology . . . Hitler's Life,* pp. 95–96; and Clifton J. Child, "Germany—1939–45," in A. and V. Toynbee, eds., *International Affairs Survey of 1939–1946: Hitler's Europe* (New York, 1954), p. 35.

37. The following contain much factual material on the persecution of Catholics: Lande, *Chronology . . . Hitler's Life,* pp. 95–96, 108; Österreicher, pp. 136–37; *The Nazi War Against the Catholic Church, passim;* Koppel S. Pinson, *Modern Germany* (New York, 1954), pp. 512 f.

38. Cited in *The Nazi War Against the Catholic Church,* pp. 34–47; and Steward, *Sieg des Glaubens,* p. 9.

39. Details on Wirth's activities against anti-Semitism are to be found in Morris D. Waldman, *Not by Power* (New York, 1953), pp. 81–88, 91–100.

40. Published in English as *Judaism, Christianity, and Germany* (New York, 1935).

41. Faulhaber's views emerge clearly in the three sermons. See Freidrich Stummer, "Kardinal Michael von Faulhaber und das Judentum," *Rundbrief,* ser. VI, nos. 21–24 (February, 1954), pp. 21–23. The well-known Swiss daily *Nationale Zeitung* (Basle), August 18, 1934, reprinted the text of a courageous uncompromising statement by Faulhaber, and reported that the text had been confiscated in Germany. The paper reported Faulhaber as saying: "History teaches that God has always punished the tormentors of His Chosen People, the Jews. No Roman Catholic approved of the persecution of Jews in Germany. When God made June 30 the judgment day for some tormentors of the Jews, the punishment was well deserved. . . . Racial hatred is a wild, poisonous weed in our life. Root out the terrible inhuman prejudice against the forever suffering people." Quoted in *WLB,* 6 (1952), 19.

42. Josef Weissthanner, "Liebe und Recht," in K. C. Knudsen, ed., *Welt ohne Hass,* 2nd ed. (Berlin, 1950), pp. 154–55.

43. Cf., a number of articles which appeared in Israeli papers after Faulhaber's death: Shalom Ben-Horin, in *Yediot Hadashot* (Jerusalem), June 20, 1952; *Mitteilungsblatt Irgun Oley Merkaz Europa* (Tel Aviv), June 27, 1952.

44. Hugh Martin et al., *Christian Counter-Attack: Europe's Churches Against Nazism* (London, 1943), p. 24; Lande, *Chronology . . . Hitler's Life,* p. 125. The Nazi press occasionally published inflammatory articles about Faulhaber, such as, Karl Seitz's "Nochmals Kardinal Faulhaber und das Alte Testament," *Der Weltkampf* (Munich, May 1934), 138–41.

45. *Rundbrief,* ser. V, nos. 17–18 (August 1952), 36.

46. Steward, *Sieg des Glaubens,* p. 104. Alfred Rosenberg referred to Bishop von Galen with great bitterness. See the *Memoirs of Alfred Rosenberg,* with commentaries by Serge Land and Ernst von Schrenck, trans. from the German by Eric Possett (Chicago, 1949), pp. 97–98.

47. Hans Rothfels, *German Opposition to Hitler* (Hinsdale, Illinois, 1948), p. 44; *The Nazi War Against the Catholic Church,* pp. 117, 120–21; Schütz, *Pens Under the Swastika,* p. 35; Heinrich Portmann, *Dokumente um den Bischof von Münster* (Münster, 1948), pp. 154–55.

48. *Ibid.,* pp. 153–55; *idem, Kardinal von Galen: Ein Gottesman seiner Zeit* (Münster, 1948).

49. The full text of the letter is given in *Rundbrief,* ser. II, nos. 8–9 (August 1950), 14. Preysing's anti-Nazi utterances are reprinted in *Dokumente aus dem Kampf der Katholischen Kirche in Bistum Berlin gegen den Nationalismus* (Berlin, 1946).

50. Quoted in Schütz, *Pens Under the Swastika,* p. 35; Auerbach, "Wesen und Formen" p. 78.

51. Steward, *Sieg des Glaubens,* pp. 74, 81.

52. Max Jordan, *Beyond All Fronts* (Milwaukee, 1944), pp. 132–33.

53. A. Leber, W. Brandt, and K. D. Bracher, eds., *Das Gewissen steht auf: 64 Lebensbilder aus dem deutschen Widerstand, 1933–1945* (Berlin, 1954), p. 180; Alfons Erb, *Bernhard Lichtenberg* (Berlin, 1946); *Rundbrief,* ser, III–IV, nos. 12–15 (December 1951), 5; Blau, *ibid.,* ser. VI, nos. 21–24 (February 1954), 36.

54. *Ibid.,* ser. II, no. 7 (April 1950), 24; ser. III–IV, nos. 12–15 (December 1951), 56; Erich Boehm, ed., *We Survived* (New Haven, 1949), p. 232.

55. These developments are discussed in many works. See, for example, Birger Forell, "National Socialism and the Protestant Church in Germany," *The Third Reich* (see note 11), pp. 812–25; Child, *Germany 1939–1945,* pp. 35–36.

56. See Thieme's letter to Martin Buber, reprinted in *Rundbrief,* ser. II, nos. 5–6 (December 1949), 21.

57. *Die Evangelische Kirche,* pp. 38–39; Lande, pp. 96–97, 125. Cf., Kerr, in *Dalhousie Review,* 21, 381. In Berlin in 1937, about 160 of the 400 Protestant pastors belonged to the Confessional Church; 40, to the German Church; and the rest were "neutral." Rothfels, *German Opposition to Hitler,* p. 42.

58. Niemöller is the subject of many biographical and political accounts. His own writing also contains much biographical and historical material. The present quotations are taken from Ludwig Bartning, "Martin Niemöllers Berufung," in *Bekennende Kirche,* pp. 133–34.

59. After World War II, Niemöller became president of the regional Hessian Protestant Church and head of the foreign office of the Protestant Church. In 1952 he journeyed to Moscow to "negotiate" (as he himself puts it) with the Soviet government for the release of the remaining German prisoners of war in Russian camps. Niemöller was severely criticized by a number of German writers and church leaders for making this trip; he was even accused of political careerism. For example, see Herbert Hein, "Pastor Niemöller und Moskau," *Aktion* (Frankfurt a/M), 12 (1952), 17–20.

60. Jansen and Weyl, p. 243; *Der Kirchenstreit in Deutschland: Bibel und Rasse* (London, [1935?]), p. 21; James A. Roy, "Pastor Niemöller," *Dalhousie Review,* 21 (1941), 88.

61. Basil Miller, *Martin Niemöller: Hero of the Concentration Camp* (Grand Rapids, Mich., 1942), pp. 81, 84; Roy, p. 88.

62. See Z. B. Kamaika's report of a meeting with Niemöller in Chicago in the *Morgn-zhurnal* of January 22, 1947, p. 3. In this connection, the complaints voiced by an American rabbi against Niemöller, in 1938, are of some interest. See Leon Fram, *The Story of the Conflict Between Hitler and the Christian Church* (Detroit, 1938), p. 8.

63. The complete German text of Niemöller's 1933 statement appears in Kurt D. Schmidt, *Die Bekenntnisse des Jahres 1933, 1934, 1935,* vol. I: *1933* (Göttingen, 1934–1936), pp. 96 f.

64. A. S. Duncan-Jones, Dean of Chichester, *The Crooked Cross* (London, 1940), p. 2.

65. Eugen Gerstenmaier, "The Church Conspiratorial," in Boehm, *We Survived,* p. 173. Gerstenmaier, later president of the Bonn Budestag, was one of the most active members of an opposition group (the so-called Kreisau Group), which conducted negotiations with groups abroad and aided a number of Jews.

66. Harry Albus, *Concentration Camp Hero* (Grand Rapids, Mich., 1946), p. 64; Miller, *Martin Niemöller,* p. 85.

67. *Die Evangelische Kirche,* p. 152; Rothfels, *German Opposition to Hitler,* pp. 41–42; Schütz, *Pens Under the Swastika,* p. 65.

68. Wilhelm Niemöller, *Macht geht vor Recht: Der Prozess Niemöllers* (Munich, 1952), p. 110; the author is Martin's brother. Other writers have likewise criticized the absence of reference to Jewish persecution in the declarations of the Confessional Church. See Franz Beyer, *Menschen warten: Aus dem politischen Wirken Martin Niemöllers* (Siegen, 1952), p. 118; Herman Z. Stewart, *The Rebirth of the German Church* (New York, 1946), p. 48. This view is disputed by Wilhelm Jannasch in *Deutsche Kirchendokumente: Die Haltung der Bekennenden Kirche im Dritten Reich* (Zurich, 1946), p. 11: "Should one reproach a church by saying that it was a silent church during the Third Reich—when its individual members, as well as its whole congregations, in private and in public argued and made their opinion known from the very beginning on the Jewish question?"

69. Martin Niemöller, *Of Guilt and Hope,* p. 72.

70. Niemöller's trial and sentence, a complicated issue, are discussed in Hans B. Gisevius, *To the Bitter End* (Boston, 1947), pp. 261–64; Lande, *Chronology . . . Hitler's Life,* pp. 124–125; *Die Evangelische Kirche,* p. 157. See also above, note 68.

71. Valerie Wolffenstein, "Shadow of a Star," in Boehm, *We Survived,* p. 86.

72. Rothfels, *German Opposition to Hitler,* p. 32; *Die Evangelische Kirche,* pp. 163–64; Jannasch, *Deutsche Kirchendokumente,* p. 80.

73. By April 1942, about 7,000 Protestant pastors and other church officials were mobilized, and many of them were sent to the front. Of these, 698 were killed. Rothfels, p. 44.

74. Heinrich Fraenkel, *The German People Versus Hitler* (London, 1940), pp. 131–32.

75. Forell, in *Third Reich* (see note 11), p. 820.

76. Heinrich Hermelink, ed., *Kirche im Kampf: Dokumente des Widerstands und des Aufbaus der Evangelischen Kirche Deutschlands von 1933 bis 1945* (Tübingen, 1950), pp. 648–49.

77. *Die Evangelische Kirche,* pp. 196–97; Hermelink, *Kirche im Kampf,* p. 650.

78. *Die Evangelische Kirche,* pp. 190–96; Hermelink, *Kirche im Kampf,* pp. 650–67; Schütz, *Pens Under the Swastika,* pp. 43–44; *Bekennende Kirche,* p. 175; Auerbach, p. 77.

79. *Die Evangelische Kirche,* pp. 150–51, 180–82; Martin Albertz, "Die Vorläufige Leitung der Evangelischen Kirchen," in *Bekennende Kirche,* pp. 168–71; *Schuld und Verantwortung: Zehn Jahre nach der Kristallnacht, Nov. 8, 1938* (Hannover, 1948), pp. 3–5. After the war Grüber held a high position in the Protestant Church in Berlin. In 1947, he was chairman of the Association of Nazi Victims (VVN) in Berlin. His rescue work is described in the special report *An der Stechbahn: Erlebnisse und Berichte aus dem Büro Grüber in den Jahren der Verfolgung* (Berlin, 1951). Unfortunately, a copy of this work was unavailable to me in New York at the time of writing.

80. Heinrich Grüber (Häftling 27832), "Gottes Liebe schenkt die Bruderschaft, die zum Lobpreis Gottes führt," in *Bekennende Kirche,* p. 186.

81. *Die Evangelische Kirche,* pp. 181–84. Her management of the Breslau office was not the only reason for Frau Staritz's arrest. When the Nazis introduced the requirement of the yellow badge in the fall of 1941, she circulated an open letter protesting the new decree. After her arrest, she was the subject of a sharp attack in the December 8, 1941, issue of the official SS organ, *Das schwarze Korps.*

82. See Appendix A above.

83. Hermann Maas is the subject of a number of articles in the New York *Aufbau*: Emil Belzner, "Der Brückenwächter der Menschlichkeit," May 5, 1950; "Ein Deutscher in Israel," April 21, 1950; "Brief von Pastor H. Mass," February 22, 1946. See Miriam Wolman-Sheratshek, "What the German Pastor Dr. Hermann Maas Has Told Me," *Yidishe Tsaytung* (Buenos Aires), November 10, 1953.

84. Hermann Maas, *Skizzen von einer Fahrt nach Israel* (Karlsruhe, 1950); *—und will Rachels Kinder wieder bringen in das Land: Reiseeinddrücke aus heutigem Israel* (Heilbronn, 1955).

85. The excerpt from Maas's talk is taken from an article by Marian Gid in the Buenos Aires *Yidishe Tsaytung,* March 14, 1952, pp. 5 f. Unfortunately, I have not been able to obtain a copy of the original text.

86. Albrecht Goes, "Martin Buber, der Beistand," in *Jewish Travel Guide,* 1953–1954, pp. 97–104; *idem, Das Brandopfer* (Frankfurt a/M, 1954).

87. Auerbach, *Wesen und Formen,* p. 77.

88. Boehm, *We Survived,* pp. 82–84, 87.

89. Jannasch, *Deutsche Kirchendokumente,* p. 6.

90. Forell, in *Third Reich* (see note 11), pp. 813–14.

91. Great Britain, Foreign Office, *White Book: Germany,* vol. II (London, 1940); Behrend-Rosenfeld (see note 26), p. 84; Weltlinger, p. 19. S. Dorfsohn, writing from London, published an account of 56 Jewish orphans who were brought to England from Germany and Austria by the Quakers. There was no thought of converting these children. Moreover, their hosts were concerned to give them a Jewish religious education, saw to it that they attended synagogue, and provided a strictly kosher kitchen. See his "Refugee Children Who Were Brought over During Wartime" (Yiddish), *Morgn-zhurnal,* December 28, 1949, p. 7.

92. Emanuel Ringelblum, *Notitsn fun varshever geto* (Notes from the Warsaw Ghetto) (Warsaw, 1952), p. 99; an entry dated February 1941 reads: "Legendary tales are told about Dr. Schubert from this district. He is a sponsor of Gancwajch. He puts on an armband and enters the ghetto. He is said to save Jewish property occasionally. He is a Baptist." The story of Pietrick is told in *Belkhatov yizker-bukh* (Bełchatów Memorial Volume) (Buenos Aires, 1951), pp. 421–22.

93. The sect was founded in Pennsylvania in 1872.

94. The following important works convey the character and orientation of this propaganda: Alfred Rosenberg, "Die 'Ernste Bibelforscher,' " in his *Kampf um die Macht* (Munich, 1937); pp. 328–32; Paul Braeunlich, *Die "Ernste Bibelforscher" als Opfer bolschewistischer Religionsspötter* (Leipzig, 1926); Theodor Fritsch, "Ernste Bibelforscher," in *Handbuch der Judenfrage,* 30th completely revised ed. (Leipzig, 1931), pp. 263–68; Hans Jonak von Freyenwald, *Die Zeugen Jehovas, Pioniere für ein jüdisches Weltreich: Die politischen Ziele der internationalen Vereinigung "Ernster Bibelforscher"* (Berlin, 1936).

95. J. F. Rutherford, *End of the Axis Powers: Comfort All That Mourn,* cited in Herbert H. Stroup, *The Jehovah's Witnesses* (New York, 1945), p. 167.

96. Stroup, *Jehovah's Witnesses,* pp. 148–49; American Civil Liberties Union, *Jehovah's Witnesses and the War* (New York, 1943).

97. The question of the anti-Nazi propaganda of ⸱ʰe sect is discussed in detail in a memorandum of July 15, 1943, from Ernst Kaltenbrunner, head of the German Security Police, to Himmler. The text of the memorandum is in my *Oświęcim* (Warsaw, 1946), pp. 179–86. On the Witnesses' opposition to Nazism, see Rudolf Pechel, *Deutscher Widerstand* (Zurich, 1947), pp. 106–7.

98. Leber et al., *Das Gewissen steht auf,* p. 20. These figures are almost identical with those given by Judge Rutherford. In his book *Armageddon* (1937), he writes that about 2,000 Witnesses were arrested in Germany. In a second publication, *Judge Rutherford Uncovers the Fifth Column* (1940), p. 20, he reported that over 6,000 Witnesses had been arrested, and that many of them had been executed; cited in Stroup, *Jehovah's Witnesses,* pp. 147–48.

99. Franz Zürcher, *Kreuzzug gegen das Christentum* (Zurich, 1938); *Oświęcim,* pp. 179–86, 210–28; Olga Wormser and Henri Michel, comps., *Tragédie de la déportation, 1940–1945* (Paris, 1954), pp. 229, 262–64; Boehm, *We Survived,* pp. 27, 137, 208; Rothfels, *German Opposition to Hitler,* p. 40; Elie A. Cohen, *Human Behavior in the Concentration Camp* (New York, 1953), p. 27; Eugen Kogon, *Der SS-Staat: Das System der deutschen Konzentrationslager,* 2nd ed. (Berlin, 1946), pp. 51, 241–43; Margarete Buber, *Under Two Dictators* (New York, n.d.), pp. 186, 188, 204, 219 f., 222–23, 233–35, 236–38, 247 f., 261, 265, 271, 274, 277, 280, 317–18; Ernst Wiechert, *Der Totenwald: Ein Bericht* (Munich, n.d.), pp. 148–55.

100. Khayke Grossman, *Anshe hamahteret* (The Underground People) (Merhavia, 1950), pp. 388–94, gives a description of a German, Busse, who headed an artists' studio in Bialystok. Originally from a wealthy East Prussian family, Busse had become a biblical and talmudic scholar. Although a nominal member of the Nazi party, he was an opponent of Nazism. He had a great liking for Jews, and established contact with the Jewish underground organization, often providing a good deal of important information. He was also of great help to

the Jewish workers employed under him. B. Mark, in *Der oyfshtand in bialis-toker geto* (The Uprising in the Bialystok Ghetto) (Warsaw, 1950), p. 346, cites evidence that Busse was a member of the Jehovah's Witnesses. In the article "The Chosen" (Yiddish), in the *Landsberger lager-tsaytung* (DP. Camp Landsberg, U.S. Zone, Germany), May 3, 1946, Isaac Nementchik writes about a Jehovah's Witness in Estonia who regularly brought food to Jews in the concentration camp of Kuremaa, and otherwise aided them as much as possible. The *Morgn-zhurnal* of January 6, 1940, p. 1, reported that there was a "Jehovah's Witnesses Organization" to aid Jews in Hungary, and that thirty-six of its members were arrested; no more precise details on this matter have been found.

101. M. Kalikstein, "Jehovah's Witnesses Are Going Back to the Prison . . ." (Yiddish), *YK*, November 17, 1950, pp. 8–12; "Jehovah's Witnesses' Persecution: Past and Present," *WLB*, 5 (1951), 8.

102. Rothfels, *German Opposition to Hitler*, pp. 158–59.

103. *Ibid.*, pp. 45, 47–48, 53, 141; Boehm, *We Survived*, p. 193; Pechel, *Deutscher Widerstand*, pp. 71–113.

104. Boehm, *We Survived*, p. viii; "Buchenwald: Reverse Allied Atrocity Propaganda," *The Network* (published by the American Association for a Democratic Germany), 2 (1945), 13; *Inside Germany Report* (New York), November 20, 1944, p. 15.

105. W. A. Visser 't Hooft, "Begegnung mit Dietrich Bonhoeffer," in *Das Zeugnis eines Boten: Zum Gedächtniss von Dietrich Bonhöffer* (Geneva, 1945), p. 7; Rothfels, *German Opposition to Hitler*, pp. 141–42; Friedrich Minssen, "Der Widerstand gegen den Widerstand," *Frankfurter Hefte*, 4 (1949), 884–88.

106. Jansen and Weyl, *Silent War*, p. 250.

107. Pechel, *Deutscher Widerstand*, pp. 74–75.

108. Max Zimmering, *Widerstandsgruppe, "Vereinigte Kletter-Abteilungen" (VKA): Ein Bericht von der Grenzarbeit der Dresdener Arbeitersteiger in der Sächsischen Schweiz und dem östlichen Erzgebirge* (Berlin, 1948), pp. 28–29.

109. Rothfels, *German Opposition to Hitler*, p. 107; Pechel, *Deutscher Widerstand*, p. 213.

110. Chaim Weizmann, *Trial and Error* (London, 1950), p. 505.

111. Friedrich Krause, ed., *Gördelers politisches Testament: Dokumente des Anderen Deutschlands* (New York, 1945), p. 16; Rothfels, *German Opposition to Hitler*, p. 85; Auerbach, "Wesen und Formen," .p. 84; *Hjalmar Schacht: 76 Jahre meines Lebens* (Bad Wörishofen, 1953), p. 548; Eberhard Zeller, *Geist der Freiheit: Das zwanzigste Jahrhundert* (Munich, 1952), p. 31.

112. Gerhard Ritter, *Karl Gördeler und die deutsche Widerstandsbewegung* (Stuttgart, 1954), pp. 427–28.

113. More precise details on the members of the Kreisau Circle are to be found in *A German of the Resistance: The Last Letters of Count Helmuth James Moltke* (London, 1946); Rothfels, *German Opposition to Hitler*, pp. 112–29; Pechel, *Deutscher Widerstand*, pp. 117–18; Auerbach, "Wesen und Formen," p. 88; Zeller, *Geist der Freihei*, pp. 73, 75–80; Boehm, *We Survived*, pp. 182–83, 189; Helen Walker Homan, *Letters to the Martyrs* (New York, 1951), pp. 187–206.

114. *A German of the Resistance,* p. 11; Boehm, *We Survived,* p. 178. The German through whom Moltke transmitted the information to the Danish premier about the plan to deport the Jews was G. F. Duckwitz, a high official in the German administration in Copenhagen. See Aage Bertelsen, *October '43* (New York, 1954), p. 17.

115. The Solf Circle's activities are discussed in Lagi Ballestrem-Solf, "Tea Party," in Boehm, *We Survived,* pp. 132–50; Karl O. Paetel, *Deutsche innere Emigration* (New York, 1946), p. 19; Pechel, *Deutscher Widerstand,* pp. 88–93; Leber et al., *Das Gewissen steht auf,* p. 143; and Rothfels, *German Opposition to Hitler,* p. 32.

116. Ballestrem-Solf, in Boehm, *We Survived,* pp. 134–35.

117. *Ibid.,* pp. 142, 145, 149; Rothfels, *German Opposition to Hitler,* p. 32; Gisevius, *To the Bitter End,* p. 433.

118. Ruth Andreas-Friedrich, *Der Schattenmann: Tagebuch-Aufzeichnungen, 1938–1945* (Berlin, 1947); English edition, *Berlin Underground, 1938–1945* (New York, 1947); Rothfels, *German Opposition to Hitler,* pp. 33, 56; Gisevius, *To the Bitter End,* p. 433; Weizsäcker, *Memoirs,* pp. 145, 220. Erich Kordt himself published two books on his work in the foreign ministry and in the German opposition movement: *Wahn und Wirklichkeit: Die Äussere Politik des Dritten Reiches* (Stuttgart, 1947); and *Nicht aus den Akten. Die Wilhelmstrasse im Frieden und Krieg. Erlebnisse, Begegnungen und Eindrücke, 1928–1945* (Stuttgart, 1950).

119. Günther Weisenborn, "Reich Secret," in Boehm, *We Survived,* p. 205.

120. Karl Vossler, *Gedenkrede für die Opfer an der Universität München* (Munich, 1947); Ricarda Huch, "The Action of the Students of Munich against Hitler" (German), *Neue Auslese,* 4 (1949), 12–18; *Rundbrief,* nos. 19–20 (1953), 8; Inge Scholl, *Die Weisse Rose* (Frankfurt, 1952), pp. 91–93. Inge Scholl, a sister of Sophie and Hans, cites an episode (p. 48) from her murdered brother's diary dating from the period of his service as a German soldier in Poland: "The Army transport stopped for several minutes at a railway station, somewhere in Poland. [Hans] noticed on the railroad embankment young women and girls, bent down, with heavy iron pickaxes in their hands, performing hard men's labor. They wore the yellow star on their breast. Hans climbed out of the window of his car and approached the women. The first in the row was an exhausted young girl, with small hands and a lovely, intelligent face in which an unspeakable grief was mirrored. Didn't he have something on him he could give her? Hans remembered his emergency food ration, a mixture of chocolate and nuts. He put it next to her. The girl picked it up and, swift as lightning, with a harassed but immensely proud gesture, threw it back at his feet. He lifted it up, smiled, looked at her, and said,: 'I wanted so very much to cheer you up a little . . . ' He bent down, picked up a daisy and put it, with the package, at her feet, nodding slightly. But the train was already rolling, and with a few long steps Hans climbed up. From the window, he saw the girl, standing and looking at the moving train, the white daisy in her hair."

121. Boehm, *We Survived,* p. 68; Kurt C. Knudsen, ed., *Welt ohne Hass: Aufsätze und Ansprache zum I. Congress über bessere menschliche Beziehungen in München* (Berlin, 1950).

122. Leber et al., *Das Gewissen steht auf, pp.* 76, 81.

123. *Der Tog* (New York, April 18, 1955); *Allgemeine Wochenschrift der Juden in Deutschland,* Düsseldorf, May 20, 1955.

124. Liebman Hersch, "On the German Question" (Yiddish), *Unzer Tsayt,* September 1951, pp. 12–15; Emanuel Scherer, "The New Socialist International" (Yiddish), *ibid.,* pp. 4–12, esp. p. 7. On several other occasions, too, Schumacher touched on the question of Nazi persecution and anti-Semitism in Germany, but was concerned more with the future of German Jewry than with past events, and did not deal with the question of aid rendered by Social Democrats to Jews during the Nazi period. See Arno Scholz and Walther G. Oschilewski, eds., *Turmwächter der Demokratie: Ein Lebensbild von Kurt Schumacher,* vol. II (Berlin, 1952–1954); *Reden und Schriften* (Berlin-Grunewald), pp. 104, 130, 175.

125. In a bibliography of illegal, anti-Nazi publications distributed in Germany during the Nazi period, which includes most of the Communist organs, are at least four pamphlets devoted primarily to persecution of Jews, particularly, the pogroms of November 1938. These rare pamphlets are to be found in the Alfred Wiener Library in London. See *WLB,* 5 (1951), 21.

126. One Communist publication relates how a Communist resistance group in Dresden smuggled, on party orders, a number of "anti-Fascists who were in danger" across the border into Czechoslovakia. This comment is added: "We didn't know the names of the [rescued] persons, nor did we inquire." Zimmering, *Widerstandsgruppe,* p. 14.

127. A transport of 160 Hungarian Jewish orphans, aged 11 to 17, was sent from the Carpathian region to the Yavishovitz coal-mining camp (a division of Auschwitz). The underground political organization managed to have a Communist camp inmate appointed *Stubenältester* ("block elder") of the block in which the children were quartered. In his memoirs, he writes that 158 of the 160 children were kept alive until the day of liberation. See Erich Hoffman, "Im Bereich der Hölle von Auschwitz," *Dokumente des Widerstandes* (Hamburg, 1947), pp. 88–90.

128. The following are quotes from the German edition of Andreas-Friedrich's diary (see note 118): "The Jews don't get any ration stamps for clothing. . . . [We] have prepared among our circle a number of shelters. For fourteen Uncle Heinrichs. And for twenty two Aunt Johannas . . . [p. 81] The children must be taken care of. Frank has four protégés. Heike two. Five have made reservations with Andrik, and those that Flamm expects can hardly be dealt with single-handed. . . . [p. 100] I have a place for two to sleep, tomorrow. . . . For three the day after. From December 15, [1942], there is a good safe apartment available in Lankwitz [p. 102]."

129. *Ibid.,* p. 7.

130. *The von Hassel Diaries, 1938–1944* (Garden City, N.Y., 1947), p. 14. In September 1944, von Hassel was arrested, condemned to death, and executed almost immediately.

131. See Appendix B above.

132. Prior to his departure for Germany, Bruce conferred with the following British Jews: Lord Rothschild, Lord Samuel, Lionel Rothschild, Neville Laski, and Otto Schiff. See Sir Michael Bruce, *Tramp Royal* (London, 1954), pp. 236–39.

133. Bruce writes that he met with Wilfred Israel, proprietor of the noted Berlin department store, and with the following leaders of the Jewish

community: Epstein, Stahl, and Seigishon (presumably Seligsohn). *Ibid.*, p. 239.

134. *Ibid.*, pp. 230–31.

135. "Ausgewählte Briefe von Generalmajor Hellmuth Sieff" *Viertel-jahrshefte für Zeitgeschichte* (Munich), 2 (1954), 302–3; "There are extensive railroad restrictions . . . ; nevertheless, the railways are still capable of dispatching from Germany every other day a train filled with Jews and leaving them there to their fate. It is exactly like the Jewish star in Berlin—as I saw it there in September—worthy of an alleged people of culture (*Kulturvolk*)! All this must bring retribution on us, one day—and with *right!*" General Sieff, a member of the organized opposition of high-ranking officers, was later condemned to death by the Nazis. See Zeller, *Geist der Freiheit*, pp. 171–72. See also essay 1 above, "The Jewish Badge and the Yellow Star in the Nazi Era."

136. "To the Chief of the Economy-Armament Office in the OKW, Herr General Thomas," *IMT*, XXXVII, 71–75, Doc. PS–3257. In 1944, General Georg Thomas was arrested and sent to the concentration camps of Flossenburg and Dachau. After the war, he published a brief account of his experiences and observations: "Gedanken und Ereignisse," *Schweizer Monatshefte* (December 1945), pp. 537–39.

137. Fabian von Schlabrendorff, *They Almost Killed Hitler* (New York, 1947), pp. 37–38: "This report [on the Borisov massacre] raised such boundless indignation among the officers of our staff that several of them, with tears of rage, assailed Bock, the chief of our Army group, with the demand that he should interfere at once and put a stop to such atrocities. But Bock did not dare to use military force and indict the culprits. He merely ordered me to draft a memorandum to Hitler describing the appalling crime." Cf. Gerald Reitlinger, *The Final Solution* (New York, 1953), pp. 196–97.

138. This interesting story is related by Emanuel Ringelblum in his diary, in an entry for October 20, 1940 (*Notitsn*, p. 63), which reads in part: "The *tsadik* among the gentiles has berated the Polish commandant of Grochów for imprisoning the Halutzim. He held him personally responsible for the safety of every last bit of farm property. He provided a Dutch cow for the farm. He is deeply moved by the fact of Jews [tilling] the soil."

139. Mark, *Der oyfshtand in bialistoker geto*, pp. 347–48; Grossman, *Anshe hamahteret*, pp. 388–400.

140. Mark Dworzecki, *Yerushelayim delite in kamf un umkum*, pp. 332, 336, 340; Mordecai Tennenbaum-Tamaroff, *Dapim min hadleka* (Pages Salvaged from the Fire) (Tel Aviv, 1948), p. 124. Tennenbaum, commander of the Bialystok resistance organization, eulogized Schmidt thus: "May his soul be bound up in the bundle of life—one of the pious among the nations, who endangered his life in saving hundreds of Jews in the Vilna ghetto and was a devoted friend of the movement and of the writer. Killed by the gendarmerie because of his contacts with us."

A very detailed account of Schmidt's contact with the Jewish underground and his aid to Jews is contained in a document preserved in the secret Jewish archives in Warsaw (Ringelblum archives). It was printed in *BFG*, 4 (1951), 96–101, but with many deletions and changes. For this reason, the complete text of the original document was reprinted as a supplement to the Yiddish original of this essay (*YB*, 39).

# PART THREE

*Methodological Problems*

# 19

# POLISH JEWISH HISTORIOGRAPHY
# BETWEEN THE TWO WARS (1918–1939)

The purpose of this essay is to provide a picture of Jewish historical writing in Poland between 1918 and 1939. It is not intended as a comprehensive bibliography, but rather as a survey of the achievements of the various historical schools and of the currents and kinds of problems studied, so that a picture of this rich, but now extinguished, phase of Jewish culture may remain for the future. This modest contribution is also intended as a monument to the creators and leading representatives of this branch of Jewish scholarship, as well as to the younger generation of Jewish historians, all of whom were torn from our midst. I shall be concerned in this study chiefly with Jewish historical studies in Poland, but shall also pay some attention to important work on Polish Jewry done outside of Poland—in order to fill out the picture.

Modern Jewish historiography in Poland really began around the turn of the century (1898–1903) with the work of Meir Bałaban, Yitzhak (Ignacy) Schipper, and Moses Schorr. Schorr soon turned his attention to Assyriology. Bałaban produced a series of standard works on Jewish history and trained a whole generation of young Jewish historians, while Schipper laid the foundations for Jewish social and economic history and for the sociological study of Jewish cultural history.[1]

After 1918, the study of Polish Jewish history developed along two lines. First, there was the critical, analytical tendency toward detailed documentation and the study of the rich materials in state, communal, and private Jewish and non-Jewish archives. This approach, especially favored by Bałaban, also came to stress the importance of local and regional Jewish history. A host of books, pamphlets, and periodical articles resulted from these studies, out of which a large monographic literature was built up. The second tendency aimed at a synthesis of the entire history of the Jews in Poland with the main currents of political, economic, and cultural development. This approach was represented most clearly in the work of Schipper. With the accumulation of monographic studies, synthesis obviously became more necessary.[2]

The centers of Jewish historical activity were Warsaw and Vilna. In Warsaw, the Instytut Nauk Judaistycznych (Institute of Jewish Studies) was an important agency for the training of young Jewish historians. Bałaban lectured there on Jewish history; and Schipper (followed by me), on economic and social history. Teaching was concentrated around Bałaban. In his seminar at the institute and at the University of Warsaw, where he occupied a chair for Jewish history, he trained an entire generation of Jewish historians—among them, M. Kraemer, Perla Kramerówna, Arie Rassin, Ester Tenenbaum, Bela Mandelsberg, Falik Hafner, Josef Kermisz, Aaron Eisenbach, Isaiah Trunk, and David Wurm.[3] A second center in Warsaw was the historians' circle of the Society of Friends of the YIVO, led by Raphael Mahler and Emanuel Ringelblum. Whereas Bałaban and his school represented the ideological view, Schipper was an exponent of the economic interpretation of history. In the preface to his *Jewish Economic History,* he wrote that he accepted historical materialism as a method but not as a *Weltanschauung.* Orthodox Marxist historical method was represented by Mahler, Ringelblum, and others of the Warsaw circle of young historians.[4]

In Vilna, YIVO not only had gathered an imposing collection of materials on Jewish history but became, in a short time, an important center of scientific work and a training school for new scholars. The *Historishe shriftn,* the *Ekonomishe shriftn,* and the *YIVO Bleter* published important historical studies, and YIVO research fellowships provided for the development of young scholars.[5] The YIVO never attempted to impose a unified ideological approach or methodology upon the historians grouped around it. Simon Dubnow was a sort of intellectual godfather to the historical section, but representatives of various historical schools published their work in YIVO publications. It was outspokenly Yiddishist in its direction, and also aimed to bring the Jewish masses into the orbit of Jewish scientific activity. More regional in character were the Jewish S. Ansky-Historical and Ethnographic Society of Vilna and the Society of the Friends of the YIVO in Lodz.

A significant place is occupied by the historical works published in the periodical literature of the time. In Yiddish there was the *YIVO Bleter* (founded in 1931), the *Historishe shriftn*,[6] the *Ekonomishe shriftn*,[7] the *Yunger historiker* (later changed to *Bleter far geshikhte*),[8] and *Fun noenten over* (From the Recent Past), founded by Moyshe Shalit in Vilna and devoted to modern Jewish history.[9] Other Yiddish journals, like *Literarishe bleter* and *Sotsiale meditsin*, also gave some space to historical articles and reviews.

In Polish, the following Jewish periodicals published numerous historical articles: *Nowe Życie* (New Life), edited by M. Bałaban;[10] *Miesięcznik Żydowski* (Jewish Monthly), edited by Z. Ellenberg, which appeared in Warsaw, 1930–1935; *Głos Gminy Żydowskiej* (Voice of the Jewish Community), published in Warsaw 1937–1939; and *Myśl Karaimska* (Karaite Thought), founded in Vilna in 1924. Anti-Semitic Polish circles in Posen started the *Przegląd Judaistyczny* (Judaic Review) in 1922, but only a few numbers were published.

Jewish historical research in Russia flourished for a while between 1918–1931.[11] Several important journals, all of which contained a great deal of material on Polish Jewish history, appeared during this time. Saul Ginsburg edited the Hebrew *Heavar* (Jewish Chronicle) in Petrograd in 1918; several volumes of the *Evreiskaya starina* appeared,[12] as well as four volumes of the *Evreiskaya letopis* (1923–1926) and a volume of *Evreiski Vestnik* (Leningrad, 1928). In Yiddish there was the *Tsaytshrift far yidishe geshikhte, demografie un ekonomik, literatur forshung, shprakhvisenshaft un etnografie,* published in Minsk (5 vols., 1926–1931); and the *Visenshaftlekhe yorbikher,* in Moscow (1 vol., 1929). I. Galant edited two volumes, in Ukrainian, of the annual of the Jewish Historical and Archaeological Commission (Kiev, 1928–1929). Gradually, however, the Jewish scientific commissions, institutes, and scholarly groups in Minsk, Kiev, Moscow, Leningrad, and Kharkov were closed down, and the older generation of Jewish historians in Russia (J. Hessen, I. Sosis, T. B. Heilikman, S. Ginsburg, I. Galant, R. Alexandrov, and others) seems to have had no successors.

Up to the advent of Hitler, there was also a significant center for Polish Jewish history in Berlin, where Simon Dubnow, Jacob Lestschinsky, Mark Wischnitzer, Rachel Wischnitzer-Bernstein, Elias Tcherikower, Josef Meisl, and others worked. Periodicals like the *Zeitschrift für Demographie und Statistik der Juden,* edited by Artur Ruppin and others (16 vols., 1905–1920; 3 vols., 1924–1926); *Bleter far yidishe demografie un statistik,* edited by B. Brutzkus and others (1923–1925); and *Der Jude,* edited by

Martin Buber (10 vols., 1916–1928), published many valuable studies on the history of the Jews in Poland.

Centers for the study of East European (especially Polish) Jewish history gradually developed in Israel and the United States as well. In the years since his arrival in the United States, Jacob Shatzky has published an imposing number of books and articles on Polish Jewish history.[13] He was joined by other immigrant Jewish scholars of established reputation, such as Jacob Lestschinsky, Mark and Rachel Wischnitzer, Raphael Mahler, and younger historians such as Abraham G. Duker and Bernard Weinryb. In Israel, there were several historians in this field, notably N. M. Gelber, I. Halperin, and Israel Klausner.

## General History

Attempts at a synthesis of the history of the Jews in Poland were made before 1918. The first volume of Dubnow's *History of the Jews in Russia and Poland* (3 vols., Philadelphia, 1916–1920) dealt with the history of Polish Jewry up to 1795. Josef Meisl's *Geschichte der Juden in Polen und Russland* (3 vols., Berlin, 1921–1925), though sharply criticized for methodological weakness and inaccuracies, did bring together an enormous mass of material. The best work of this kind, in many ways still unsurpassed, was the collective history of the Jews in Poland, which appeared in Russian as vol. XI of the *Istoria Evreiskago Naroda* (History of the Jewish People) (Moscow, 1914; only vols. I and XI appeared). The story of the Jews in Poland up to 1795 was presented in a series of thorough studies written by M. Bałaban, S. Dubnow, S. Kutrzeba, J. Hessen, P. S. Marek, Y. Schipper, M. Wischnitzer, S. L. Zinberg, S. M. Ginsburg, E. N. Frenk, and others, and edited by Wischnitzer, Hessen, and Ginsburg. Julius Hessen's *History of the Jews in Russia* (Russian, 1914; 2nd and enlarged ed., Leningrad and Moscow, 1923; 3rd ed., Leningrad, 1925) also contains numerous chapters on Polish Jewish history particularly, covering the nineteenth century.

After 1918 several attempts at a general history of the Jews in Poland were made in that country. The first was by Samuel Hirszhorn, a journalist and contributor to the Polish Jewish paper *Nasz Przegląd* (Our Review). In 1921, he published *Historia Żydów w Polsce od Sejmu Czteroletniego do wojny europejskiej, 1788–1914* (History of the Jews in Poland, 1788–1914), which appeared in Yiddish in 1922. Hirszhorn did not use archival material, and his utilization of the previously published literature left much to be desired. Despite this, his work had a great success and remained for a long time the only intelligent, factual summary of the modern history of the Jews in Poland. Jacob Schall's *Historia Żydów w Polsce, Litwie i na Rusi* (History of the Jews in Poland, Lithuania, and Ruthenia) (Lemberg [Lwów], 1934) was a more ambitious work. Schall, a trained historian, was able to draw on much erudition but was only partially successful at systematically integrating it into his work, which is more a confused compilation than a genuine synthesis. There is too much unnecessary detail, too much space is given to local communal history, and the author so loses himself in historical minutiae that no overall picture emerges. Economic and social history receive but scant attention, and demographic and statistical material are altogether lacking.

The need for a ·general synthesis was met in some measure by the cooperative work, *Żydzi w Polsce Odrodzonej* (The Jews in Poland Reborn [2 vols., Warsaw, 1934–1935]). Among the contributors were M. Bałaban, W. Fallek, J. Fränkel, A. Hafftka, I. Lewin, M. Mieses, A. Prowalski, Y. (I.) Schipper, M. Schorr, H. Spidbaum, Aryeh Tartakower, and myself. The first 800 pages were devoted to the period before 1918, and the last 600 to the period of 1918–1933. Over 500 illustrations, many reproduced for the first time, added to the attractiveness of the volumes. Two more volumes, dealing with cultural and social problems, were scheduled to appear but were never published. Although the authors of the articles were the most competent historians in Poland, they were forced to adjust to the general outlook of the publishers, who intended the work not as a strictly academic, scholarly synthesis but rather as a deluxe edition after the manner of the German *Propyläen Weltgeschichte*. The form had to be of a popular character, without documentation, in order to attract the lay reader. Despite many failings, this work remains to this day the best synthesis of Polish Jewish history.[14]

## Bibliographies

The work of synthesis was made difficult by the lack of a systematic, comprehensive bibliography. This need was later met in part by Bałaban's *Bibliografia historii Żydów w Polsce i w krajach ościennych za lata 1900–1939* (Bibliography of the History of the Jews in Poland and in Adjacent Countries, 1900–1939) (Warsaw, 1939), which lists books, pamphlets, periodicals, important newspaper articles, book reviews, printed archival and manuscript catalogues, and even catalogues of book dealers. It is not annotated, however, and unfortunately has remained unfinished. The first part, issued just before the war, includes about 3,000 entries of general bibliography. The plan of the entire work, published in the first part, indicated that specialized sections were to follow, arranged according to subject and geographical distribution. These sections, ready to go to press when the war broke out, were lost during the war.

The third volume of Salo W. Baron's *Social and Religious History of the Jews* (New York, 1937), which may serve as a complement to Bałaban's unfinished bibliography, contains a vast bibliography and critical notes with a great deal which pertains to Polish Jewish history. Baron's *Bibliography of Jewish Social Studies, 1938–39* (New York, 1941), provides a comprehensive bibliography of Polish Jewish history for the last two years before World War II. YIVO published in 1926 the first volume of its *Bibliografishe yorbikher* (Bibliographical Annals), and Edward Poznański published his *Sefer hashana lebibliografia yehudit bepolania* (New Bibliography of the Jews in Poland) (Warsaw, 1936).[15] Bibliographical surveys by Hermann Frank are also found in yearbook nos. 6 (1938) and 7 (1939) of *Poylishe Yidn* (Polish Jews), published in New York. Avram Yarmolinsky published an interesting bibliography on the Khazars (New York, 1939). The bibliography by the Nazi writer M. Gunzenhauser should also be mentioned.[16] Pinkas Kon and Jacob Shatzky published many short bibliographical notes in the *YIVO Bleter* and in the *YIVO Historishe shriftn,* and I published a critical and analytical bibliography of the history of the Jews, in the Lodz *voyevodstvo* (province).[17] Scattered but valuable bibliographical material is also to be found in the various Jewish encyclopedias and in the larger histories mentioned above.

During the last years before the war, an increased number of almanacs and biographical dictionaries were published. Most of these have little or no scientific value and were published for either publicity or commemorative purposes. Some are relatively serious publications, however; the biographies of Jewish personalities and the accounts of Jewish institutions may serve as valuable source materials for a history of extinguished Polish Jewry.[18] The most serious attempt was the *Yidisher geselshaftlekher lexikon* (Jewish Social Lexicon) edited by Ruven Feldschuh (Ben Shem), which was to have covered all of Poland. Only the first volume, with several general articles on Polish Jewry, and a second part, entitled *Varshever yidishe institutsies un perzenlikhkeiten* (Jewish Institutions and Personalities in Warsaw) were published (Warsaw, 1939), letters *aleph* to *zayin.*[19] The mass of material for the other volumes was lost during the war.[20]

## Social and Economic History

A considerable amount of work was done in the field of Jewish economic history. The pioneer in this field in Poland was Y. (I.) Schipper. His *Yidishe geshikhte: Virtshaftsgeshikhte* (4 vols., Warsaw, 1930), which covers the medieval period, is, despite some failings in its method and in distribution of material, the best general work on the subject.[21] The chapters dealing with Poland represent an enlarged edition of his previously published *Studja nad stosunkami gospodarczymi Żydów w Polsce podczas średnio-wiecza* (History of the Economic Situation of the Jews in Poland in the Middle Ages) (Warsaw, 1911; Yiddish translation, Warsaw, 1926).[22] Schipper's work, based on rich source materials, is marked by keen analysis, bold hypothesis, and broad historical perspective. Frequently, however, he was inclined to force the facts into his boldly imaginative but sometimes untenable theories. This brought him into controversy with other historians, above all Bałaban—as, for example, on the question of the Khazars and Schipper's theory of the Khazar origins of Polish Jewry and the influence of the Khazars on Polish political institutions in the early period.[23] A second work by Schipper, *Dzieje handlu żydowskiego na zie-miach polskich* (Warsaw, 1937), dealt with the history of Jewish commerce in Poland from earliest times to the present.[24]

Among other works in the field of economic history, the most ambitious study was Bernard D. Weinryb's *Neueste Wirtschaftsgeschichte der Juden in Russland und Polen* (Breslau, 1934), which goes up to 1881. Weinryb collected a great amount of sources and published materials, which he carefully analyzed. Nevertheless, he is unsuccessful at synthesis, and his interpretation of sources and statistical methods are not always sound.[25] Weinryb's second book, *Toledot hakalkala vehahevra shel yehudei Polin* (The Economic and Social History of the Jews of Poland) (Jerusalem, 1939), also contains some valuable material.

In his *Projekty i próby przewarstwowienia Żydów w epoce stanis-ławowskiej* (Attempts at Occupational Shifts in the Period of Stanislaus) (Warsaw, 1934), Emanuel Ringelblum contributed a basic study of Jewish economic history in the reign of the last Polish king (1764–1795). In "Wirtschaftliche Umschichtungsprozesse und Industrialisierung in der pol-nischen Judenschaft, 1800–1870,"[26] I investigated the structural changes in the economic and social life of Polish Jewry during that transitional period.[27] My *Dzieje Żydów w Łodzi od początku osadnictwa Żydów do r. 1863* (History of the Jews in Lodz) (Lodz, 1935); and "Produktivizi-rung un proletarizirung fun Lodzr yidn, 1860–1914" (Productivization and Proletarianization of the Jews in Lodz, 1860–1914)[28] deal with important aspects of Jewish economic history in Poland. Solid studies of the history of Jewish artisans in Poland were published by M. Wischnitzer, I. Sosis, Israel Halperin, M. Kraemer, Perla Kramerówna, Bela Mandel-berg, Emanuel Ringelblum, and R. Notik.[29] The history of Jewish agricul-ture was treated by Brutzkus[30] and Shatzky.[31] Valuable materials on various problems of the economic history of the Polish Jews are to be found in the

YIVO *Ekonomishe shriftn* and in *Yidishe ekonomik* (Vilna, 1937–1939), both edited by Jacob Lestschinsky, as well as in Lestschinsky's own numerous articles in various periodicals. Worthy of mention too are G. Glicksman's *L'aspect économique de la question juive en Pologne* (Paris, 1929), the large cooperative volume on the Polish Jewish industrialist and financier Leopold Kronenberg,[32] and A. Gomer's *Beiträge zur Kultur—und Sozialgeschichte des litauischen Judentums im 17. und 18. Jahrhundert* (Cologne, 1930). Interesting materials on Polish Jewish social and economic history were published by the Russian Jewish historians Sosis, Yuditzky, and Margulis.[33] On the other hand, T. B. Heilikman's *Geshikhte fun der geselshaftlikher bavegung fun di yidn in Poyln un Rusland,* vol. I (Moscow, 1926), does not fulfill the expectations of the title, and contributes nothing new in material or interpretation.

The history of the Jewish labor movement in Poland was treated in many anniversary volumes, *Zamelbicher, Pinkasim, Festschriften,* and publicity material. The most important scholarly work in this field was done by A. W. Buchbinder,[34] A. Tartakower,[35] and A. Wolf-Jasny.[36] An enormous amount of valuable material is also to be found in the third volume of the YIVO *Historishe Shriftn*[37] and in the series of anthologies on the Jewish labor movement edited by M. Rafes and A. Kirshnitz in the USSR.[38]

The history of Jewish emigration from Poland was treated by Tartakower, M. Linder, and Lestschinsky.[39] The Jewish cooperative movement in Poland was studied by Abraham Prowalski, Meir Pollner, and Hermann Parnas.

A subject that received considerable attention was the history of Jewish autonomy and the constitutional aspects of Polish Jewish life. Dubnow, the pioneer in this field, made an important contribution with his edition of the *Pinkas* of the Lithuanian *vaad* and his magnificent introduction to the volume on Jewish autonomy in Poland.[40] Important work on the history of the Council of the Four Lands, the Lithuanian *vaad,* and the provincial councils was done by Halperin and Schipper.[41] Izhak Lewin published significant contributions to Jewish legal history.[42]

An interesting chapter in Jewish social history is occupied by the *hevra kaddisha* (holy brotherhood) societies. The traditional studies in this field limited themselves to the publication of the minute books of the societies and in some cases, to a description of the institutional organization. In a study of the *hevra kaddisha* of Lodz,[43] I attempted to analyze the institution from a sociological standpoint and investigate its social structure, its relationship to the community, its budget and expenditures, and its internal conflicts. The works on the *hevra kaddisha* in Piotrków and that in Kutno by Feinkind and Zomber[44] are more in the traditional manner.

## Political History

A large number of studies were published on Jewish participation in the Polish liberation movement. The tendency to bring this participation into relief went hand in hand with the struggle of the Polish Jews during 1918–1939 to achieve full equality in the new Poland. Even though many of these studies show the stamp of apologetic or polemical character, they are nonetheless valuable as source material. I shall discuss the more important ones in the chronological order of the subject matter.

The memorial volume dedicated to Berek Joselewicz (the famous organizer of the Jewish regiment that fought with Tadeusz Kościuszko in 1794 against the Russians) was edited by Bałaban[45] and contains a considerable number of essays (the one by Bałaban himself is the most significant) of distinctly idealistic tendency. It also contains a great deal of hitherto unknown source material. A work on the same subject is Ringelblum's *Di poylishe yidn in oyfshtand fun Kościuszko* (Polish Jews in Kościuszko's Insurrection) (Warsaw, 1937), with a supplement by Raphael Mahler.[46] This volume approaches the problem more critically and probes more deeply into the attitude of the Jewish masses toward the Polish uprising. It also includes much new material on the reaction of the Jewish population outside Warsaw to the uprising. The participation of the Jews in the Polish uprising of 1831 was thoroughly treated, on the basis of extensive source materials, by Schipper.[47] Jewish participation in the uprisings of 1831, 1846, and 1863 are treated by Gelber,[48] who supplied much new source material for this subject. In his reviews of the Gelber and Schipper volumes, Shatzky[49] also made significant contributions of his own to the history of the uprisings of 1831 and 1863.

The Jewish legion of the great Polish poet Adam Mickiewicz, created at the time of the Crimean War to fight under the Polish–Turkish general Sadyk-Pasha (Czaykowski) against the Turks, was thoroughly studied by Roman Brandstätter.[50] This project, launched by Mickiewicz and the well-known French Jewish publicist Armand Lévy, was tied up with vague messianic ideas and plans for a Jewish state. The plan was to secure the financial support of the Rothschilds and the political sanction of the anti-Turkish Western coalition, but nothing came of the project because of the sudden death of Mickiewicz, in November 1855, and the beginning of peace negotiations. Brandstätter seeks to show that Mickiewicz was poisoned in Constantinople by Polish reactionaries who wanted to prevent him from carrying out his judeophile undertaking. It was previously assumed by all that Mickiewicz had been stricken during the cholera epidemic in Constantinople. Brandstätter's hypothesis unloosed a violent polemic in Polish circles, and the nationalistic Polish press raged against this "Jewish maligning."[51]

A comprehensive survey of Jewish participation in all the Polish wars and rebellions had been prepared for publication by Mattheus Mieses before World War II broke out. Mieses published only a portion of this work in a series of articles in *Nasz Przęglad* (1938–1939). Another work by Mieses, *Polacy Chrześcijanie pochodzenia żydowskiego* (Christian Poles of Jewish Origin and Descent) (2 vols., Warsaw, 1938), indirectly political in character, aroused great interest and had serious political repercussions. Mieses showed that a whole series of prominent Polish families, noblemen, authors, and political leaders were descended from Jewish apostates, among them many Frankists. According to information given to me by Jacob Apenszlak (former editor of *Nasz Przęglad*), influential Poles were preparing racist anti-Jewish laws at the time of the publication of Mieses's volume. The laws were dropped after the appearance of the book, because several of the Poles involved in drafting them were shown to be descendants of converted Jewish families. Unfortunately, Mieses weakened the force of his arguments by going too far in his zeal to ascribe Jewish ancestry—with only forced, insubstantial evidence—to such leading figures as King Stanislaus August Poniatowski, Frédéric Chopin, and the Polish national hero Chrzanowski.[52]

Significant contributions to the political history of Polish Jewry were made by Meir Bałaban. It would be impossible, however, to list them all; even a selected bibliography of Bałaban's work in this field would take too much space.[53] Aron Eisenstein's *Die Stellung der Juden in Polen im XIII. und XIV. Jahrhundert* (Teschen, 1934) deals with the earliest beginnings of Jewish history in Poland, particularly with the first Polish Jewish statutes; and Max Weinreich, in his *Sturmvind* (Vilna, 1927), devotes several chapters to the period of the Cossack revolt of 1648, the influence of Sabbatianism on Polish Jewry, and ritual murder trials during the early period of the Catholic reaction. The persecution of Jews during the Cossack revolt of 1648 is given a new interpretation by Jacob Shatzky in the introduction to his Yiddish edition of Nathan Hanover's work.[54] Instead of religious and national antagonisms, Shatzky gives primary emphasis to economic and social conflicts. Shatzky dissects the social classes and rival interests in Ukrainian society; analyzes the economic and political interests of the wealthy Cossack class, the propertyless mob (*tschernj*), and the dynastic policies of Chmielnicki; and shows how the extermination of Jews was due to the clash of conflicting class interests. Other and equally decisive economic, political, and religious antagonisms between the Jews, the Polish nobility, the clergy, and the state are given too scant attention, however.[55]

New material on the history of the Jews in the duchy of Warsaw was gathered by Aron Eisenbach,[56] and studies on the history of the Jews in the Russian-occupied provinces were published by Hessen, Galant, and

Ginsburg.[57] The interesting problem of relations between Jews and Armenians received the attention of L. Streit.[58] My *Die galizischen Juden im Kampfe um ihre Gleichberechtigung* (Frankfurt, 1929), paid special attention to the revolutionary years 1848–1849 and the debates in the Galician Diet of 1868. The recent history of the Jews in Poland was treated in a series of scholarly articles in the anniversary volume of the *Haj'nt* (Warsaw, 1938), edited by M. Indelmann, and in a more popular manner in the special issue of the Warsaw *Głos Gminy Żydowskiej* (1939). The period 1918–1938 also received attention in Simon Segal's *The New Poland and the Jews* (New York, 1938).[59]

A rich memoir literature began to develop during and after World War I.[60] Two works deserve special mention: S. Ansky's *Der yidisher hurbn in Poyln, Galitsie, un Bukovine* (The Destruction of Jews in Poland, Galicia, and Bucovina) (Warsaw, 1921),[61] and Ruven Fahn's *Geshikhte fun der yidisher natsional avtonomie inem period fun der marev-ukrainisher republik* (History of the Jewish National Autonomy in the Era of the Western–Ukrainian Republic) (Lwów, 1933).[62] Both are scholarly monographs, as well as accounts of personal experiences.

## Cultural History

Much work was done in the field of Jewish cultural history. Most important is Schipper's *Kulturgeshikhte fun di yidn in Poyln baysn mitelalter* (Warsaw, 1926).[63] Israel Zinberg, in his *Geshikhte fun literatur bay yidn* (10 vols., Vilna, 1935–1936; reprinted New York, 1945), devotes numerous chapters of volumes V, VI, and VII to a synthesis of Yiddish literature in Poland to the end of the eighteenth century. Similar material is found in the other standard histories and lexicons of Yiddish and Hebrew literature.[64]

The extremely valuable archives of Josef Perl in Tarnopol fortunately were studied by several scholars before they were destroyed during the war. Several monographs and collections of source material resulted from these studies. Israel Weinlös published a valuable biography of Perl, together with several hitherto unknown writings of Perl;[65] I published various materials on the history of the Haskalah, the struggle between the Hasidim and the maskilim in Galicia, and an extended study on Perl as a pedagogue and the history of his school at Tarnopol.[66] Other material from the Perl archives was published by S. Katz.[67] A very valuable study of the Galician Haskalah, based chiefly on archival material in Lemberg (Lwów), was published by Mahler;[68] and the origin of the Haskalah in central Poland was treated by Schipper.[69] Articles on Jewish influences on Polish literature and Jewish writers in Polish literature, appeared in various Polish journals—written by Wilhelm Fallek, Chayim Lew, and Karol Dresdner.

The history of the rabbinate, rabbinical literature, and rabbinical personalities received the attention of Chaim Tchernowitz, Simha Assaf, and S. M. Chones.[70] Assaf also supplied a valuable basis for a history of Jewish education in old Poland in his source collection *Mekorot letoledot hahinukh beyisrael* (Sources to the History of Education in Israel) (3 vols., Tel Aviv, 1925–1936). Shatzky published several contributions to the history of Jewish education in Poland,[71] and Aron Sawicki described the first rabbinical seminary in Warsaw in the 1860s.[72] The Jewish schools during the period 1918–1939 were studied by Tartakower, Hecht, Kazhdan, and Eck.[73] Saul Langnas treated the problem of Jewish students in Polish universities during 1921–1931.[74] Haim Ormian's *Hamahshava hahinukhit shel yahudut polanya leor hasifrut hapedagogit vehapsikhologit* (Educational Theory of Polish Jewry in Light of Psychology and Pedagogy) (Tel Aviv, 1939) is a fundamental and solid study.[75] The Hebraist movement in Poland was studied in the comprehensive work of Abraham Levinson, *Hatenua haivrit bagola* (Hebrew Movement in the Diaspora) (Warsaw, 1935). Very interesting and valuable articles, bibliographical items, and source materials on Jewish education and educational psychology are found in the two YIVO publications dedicated to these problems and edited by Leibush Lehrer.[76]

The history of Jewish printing in Poland was treated in Ringelblum's *Zu der geshikhte fun yidishen drukwesen in 18ten yorhundert* (History of Jewish Printing in the 18th Century) (Warsaw, 1932–1934) and in C. D. Friedberg's *Toledot hadefus haivri bepolanya* (History of Jewish Printing in Poland) (Antwerp, 1932).

Jewish arts were also treated in numerous monographs, lexicons, and articles. The history of the Jewish theater was described in the large work by Schipper,[77] the volume of essays edited by Shatzky,[78] and in the lexicon of Silberzweig and Mestel.[79] In the field of the plastic arts, the architecture of Jewish synagogues in Poland was a popular theme.[80] This subject also interested several non-Jewish art historians, such as Adolf Szyszko-Bohusz and Georges Loukomski.[81] More comprehensive works on the general subject of Jewish art were not as numerous. Worthy of mention is Otto Schneid's "Yidishe Kunst in Poyln," in *Yidisher geselshaftlekher lexikon,* 1 (1939), 334–58. Bałaban's *Zabytki historyczne Żydów w Polsce* (Jewish Historical Antiquities in Poland) (Warsaw, 1929) is a fundamental study in this field, with rich historical and bibliographical references, but it is more a historical catalogue than a work of aesthetic analysis.[82] The same might also be said of *Kultura i sztuka ludu żydowskiego na ziemiach polskich* (The Culture and Art of the Jewish People in Polish Lands) by Karol Dresdner and Maximilian Goldstein (Lwów, 1935)[83]—essentially an enlarged analytical catalogue of the art collection of M. Goldstein in

Lwów. Jewish art is interpreted by these authors primarily as folk art and folk objects, which occupied a large part of the Goldstein collection.[84]

The study of Jewish sects and Jewish mysticism, begun before World War I, received increasing attention from Jewish scholars in Poland, as well as from those in Germany, the United States, and Palestine. The Sabbatian and Frankist movements were thoroughly treated by Bałaban in his "Zur Geschichte der frankistischen Bewegung in Polen," in *S. Poznański Memorial Volume* (Warsaw, 1927), pp. 25–75; and above all in his *Letoledot hatenuah hafrankit* (History of the Frankist Movement), 2 vols. (Tel Aviv, 1934–1935). Significant additions were made to the literature of Hasidism. Dubnow, one of the pioneers in the scientific study of this movement, completed the synthesis of many years' work in his two-volume history of Hasidism, published in Hebrew, Yiddish, and German.[85] In contrast to this sober rationalist treatment of Hasidism, S. A. Horotdetzky[86] gave more emphasis to the lyrical and emotional character of the movement; and Martin Buber[87] and Hillel Zeitlin[88] read their own philosophies into Hasidism. The literary significance of Nahman of Bratzlav, too, gained esteem.[89] The subject of Hasidism also received increasing attention in the United States, from scholars such as S. Minkin, L. Newman, and K. Pinson, who made available to the wider American public the results of much of the European work in this field.[90] New and important work on the early history of Hasidism is being done in Israel by Benzion Dinaburg and Gershom Scholem. The former is interested chiefly in the social and messianic elements in Hasidism,[91] while Scholem, continuing his work on the history of Jewish mysticism, has sought to establish new relationships between Hasidism and Sabbatianism.[92] A. Z. Aescoly, who died in Israel, published two small yet interesting studies on Hasidism and on the influence of the Towiański messianic movement on Jews.[93]

The history of the Karaites in Poland not only was a subject of scholarly investigation but also became a matter of serious political significance. Scholarly treatment was accorded to the Karaites by Bałaban,[94] and a rather literary elaboration by Fahn.[95] The problem of Jewish versus Mongolian racial ancestry for the Karaites became the subject of a polemic between Jewish and Karaite scholars. Bałaban, Schall, Gedo Hecht, J. Brutzkus, and others were ranged against Karaite scholars like Ananiasz Zajączkowski, A. Mordkowicz, S. Firkowicz, A. Szyszman, and the *hakham* of the Vilna Karaites, J. Seraj Szapszal.[96]

The polemic took on a tragic political aspect during the Nazi occupation. If the Karaites had been officially declared to be racially Jews, they would have shared with the Rabbanites in the Nazi "Final Solution." Fortunately, as we have seen, the Germans were swayed by the various memoranda written by Jewish and non-Jewish scholars (including Bałaban,

Schipper, Kalmanovitch, and Schall, with my assistance) and treated the Karaites as offshoots of the Turco-Mongolian race.[97] I am personally familiar with the small Karaite community in Halicz, Eastern Galicia. They were not bothered by the Nazis, and they were allowed to carry on their normal way of life. The Karaites, on their part, refrained from social contacts with Jews in order not to arouse the suspicions of the Germans. Liberation in 1944 found the Karaites of Halicz (and, it may be supposed, others too) undisturbed as to their lives and possessions.

Jewish folklore and ethnography did not receive much attention before 1914. Much material was gathered in this field in the period 1918–1938. The most important center for the study of Jewish folklore was YIVO. Their publications, especially the five volumes of *Filologishe Shriftn* (1926, 1928, 1929, 1930, 1938) contain a mine of valuable folk material and numerous worthwhile scholarly studies. The anthology *Bay undz yidn* (Among Us Jews) (Warsaw, 1923), edited by M. Wanwild, also contains important material in this field, as does the Minsk *Tsaytshrift*. The most important contributors to this infant branch of Jewish scholarship were S. Ansky, J. L. Kahan, A. Landau, Shmuel Lehman, Noah Prylucki, Max Weinreich, N. Weinig (Norbert Rose), Ch. Chajes, J. Zelkowitz, I. Rivkind, S. Winter, the folk bard Hershele (Hersh Danielevitz), and S. Z. Pipe.[98] Regina Lilientalowa and Gisa Frenklowa wrote on Jewish folklore in Polish; Emanuel Olsvanger, in German. In Vienna, Max Grünewald carried on the work he had started before World War I. The musical aspects of Jewish folklore were given great impetus by the collections of folk songs compiled by A. S. Bernstein[99] and A. Z. Idelsohn.[100]

## Local and Regional History

Great interest was developed for Jewish local history.[101] The most significant and classic work in this field was done by Bałaban in his large monographs on Cracow, Lwów, and Lublin.[102] The study of Lublin was of a much more popular character than the other two. Bałaban treats Lublin as the seat of the central institutions of Polish Jewry and there is little regarding the history of the Jewish community of Lublin per se. Several smaller contributions to the history of Lublin Jewry were made by a pupil of Bałaban, Bela Mandelsberg. Nothing comparable to the studies of Cracow and Lwów was done with Polish Jewry's greatest center, Warsaw. Ringelblum's treatment of the period up to 1527, in his *Dzieje Żydów w Warszawie do r.* 1527 (History of the Jews in Warsaw to 1527) (Warsaw, 1932), was his first scholarly study, and met with severe criticism.[103] Much better are his studies on the social and cultural history of the Jews of

Warsaw in the eighteenth century.[104] Some aspects of the economic life of the Jews of Warsaw and other Polish cities were dealt with by Isaiah Warshawsky.[105] Only very recently, in the United States, Jacob Shatzky has begun a history of Warsaw on a grand scale.[106]

The economic and social history of the Jews of Lodz was treated in the works by me mentioned above. The large volume of essays on the oldest Jewish cemetery in Lodz, *Stary Cmentarz Żydowski w Łodzi,* ed. by J. Szper (Lodz, 1938), contains studies by Aron Alperin, Gliksman, Szper, myself, and others, and is the best monograph on a Jewish cemetery in Poland. It contains not only excellent studies and illustrations of the tombstones but also articles on related aspects such as mortality rates and burial associations. The *Lodzer Almanakh* (New York, 1945), edited by G. Eisner, is devoted mainly to the history of the Jewish labor movement.

The old and revered Jewish community of Vilna was the subject of numerous historical studies. The most systematic work on Vilna, based on rich source material, is the yet unfinished *Toledot hakehilla haivrit b'Vilna* (History of the Jewish Community of Vilna) (vol. I, Vilna, 1938), by the young scholar Israel Klausner.[107] He is continuing his work now in Israel. Numerous articles and documents on Vilna Jewry were published by Pinkas Kon;[108] and Haykl Lunski, for many years librarian of the Strashun Library, published biographical and folklore materials on Vilna's Jews.[109] Z. Szyk's work on Vilna will be discussed later. Less satisfying a work is Israel Cohen's *Vilna* (Philadelphia, 1943), but it contains an extensive bibliography. The large collection of essays in *Vilna* (New York, 1935), edited by E. Jeshurin, varies in quality. Many are important contributions to the history of Vilna Jewry. Valuable material is also to be found in the *Vilner Almanakh,* edited by A. Grodzensky (Vilna, 1939), and the collections of Szabad, Szalit, and Zalmen Reisen, cited below.

A significant contribution to local Jewish history is the *Pinkes Bialystok* (vol. I, New York, 1949), by A. S. Herschberg. This is a work of good scholarship, based on source materials and oral traditions collected over a long number of years. Ready for publication in 1934–1935, the manuscript came by chance to the author's son in New York, where it was published by the Bialystok Historical Society.

Among other Jewish community studies were those on Żółkiew by Schall; on Czortków by Sonnenschein; on Brody by David Wurm; and on Płock by Trunk and Schipper.[110] Schipper's work was of a popular character. Local history was stimulated by the creation of various local and regional associations of scholars, and by their publication of collections of essays and almanacs. One example was the *Lodzer visnshaftlekhe shriftn* (Lodz, 1939), edited by me, with contributions by Eleasar Feldman, S. Posener, R. Mahler, Joseph Zelkowicz, P. S. Gliksman, N. M. Gelber, M.

Schwalbe, M. Balberyszki, and Moshe Feinkind. Of the almanacs, the best were *Pinkes far der geshikhte fun Vilne in di yorn fun milkhome un okupatsie* (Notes for the History of Vilna in the Years of the War and Occupation), ed. by Zalmen Reisen (Vilna, 1922); *Oyf die khurves fun milkhomes un mehumes* (On the Ruins of War and Turmoil); *Pinkes fun gegn-komitet YEKOPO in Vilne* (Minutes of the Regional Committee of YEKOPO in Vilna), ed. by M. Shalit (Vilna, 1932); and the excellent *Pinkes fun der shtot Pruszane* (Prużany, 1930).[111]

Several guidebooks to Jewish Poland were also published in the last years before World War II. Two such volumes appeared for Cracow: Osias Mahler's *Przewodnik po zabytkach żydowskich Krakowa* (Guide to the Jewish Historical Relics in Cracow) (Cracow, 1935), and the handsomely illustrated *Przewodnik po zabytkach żydowskich Krakowa* (Guide to the Jewish Historical Relics in Cracow), by Bałaban (Cracow, 1936). J. Schall published *Przewodnik po zabytkach żydowskich Lwowa* (Guide to the Jewish Relics of Lwów) (Lwów, 1936), a guide to the Jewish places of interest in Lwów; and Zalmen Szyk wrote *Toysnt yor Vilne* (One Thousand Years of Vilna) (Vilna, 1939), a detailed guide to Jewish Vilna.[112]

## Non-Jewish Historians

This survey would not be complete without some attention to the work of non-Jewish scholars in Poland,[113] most of whom were concerned with the Jewish problem for other than purely scholarly motives. Many of them showed unmistakable anti-Semitic tendencies. The well-known Polish publicist Teodor Jeske Choiński published a superficial, anti-Semitic survey of Jewish history in Poland,[114] as well as equally superficial studies of the Frankist movement and of Jewish conversions to Christianity. A more sober, scholarly work is the short survey by the prominent Polish legal historian Stanisław Kutrzeba.[115] Its conclusions, though presented in scientific terms, are equally anti-Jewish, however. The well-known Polish medievalist Jan Ptaśnik has treated the problem of the urban Jewish element in medieval Poland, in several studies.[116] He espouses the cause of the Christian bourgeoisie, who were the bitter rivals of the Jews and engaged in violently anti-Jewish propaganda. A great deal of interesting material is found in Bartoszewicz's work on anti-Semitism in Polish literature of the fifteenth through eighteenth centuries.[117] A similar but less systematic work is F. Rawita-Gawroński's study of the Jews in the history and folk literature of Ruthenia,[118] dealing mainly with the Cossack and Haidamak revolts of 1648 and 1761. The best statistical study of Polish Jewry is the work of Bohdan Wasiutynski,[119] a descendant of the baptized Jewish family Wasercug. While adhering to the external forms of historical objectivity, the author aims to warn his "fellow nationals" of the dangers of increasing Jewish influence in the Polish cities.

As mentioned above, an anti-Semitic group in Posen founded the journal *Przęglad Judaistyczny* (Judaic Review) in 1920. Of the articles published there, the more significant are A. Wojtkowski's study of the economic history of the Jews in the Prussian-occupied part of Poland at the end of the eighteenth century and W. L. Tatarzanka's essay on the economic and cultural history of the Jews in Russian Poland, 1815–1830.

The Catholic priest and historian M. Morawski published *Stanowisko Kościoła wobec niebezpieczeństwa żydowskiego w dawnej Polsce* (The Attitude of the Church toward the Jewish Danger in Old Poland) (Włocławek, 1938). The title of the book is sufficiently indicative of its approach. Of a similar character is Rudolf Korsch's *Żydowskie ugrupowania wywrotowe w Polsce* (The Jewish Subversive Parties in Poland) (Warsaw, 1925). For Korsch, all Zionist and Socialist parties are subversive. More objective are the works of Henryk Mościcki.[120] Free of anti-Semitic bias and containing very valuable material on Jewish history are the works of P. Kontny, Z. Lutman, S. Hoszowski, and J. S. Bystroń.[121]

## Epilogue

The Holocaust of 1939–1945, which destroyed the great East European reservoir of Jewish creative energy, saw the end of Polish Jewish historiography with the annihilation of almost all of its representatives. Not much is known regarding the last hours of these martyrs, but I shall attempt to set down here, as an everlasting testimonial to their revered memory, what I have been able to piece together from various sources.

Moses Schorr was seized by Russian troops, immediately following the outbreak of the war, as he fled to Volhynia before the invading Nazis. He died in prison in Uzbekistan on July 8, 1941.[122]

Meir Bałaban died, broken by moral and physical suffering, in the Warsaw ghetto at the end of 1942.[123] Rumors that he was murdered or committed suicide are not true. To clear up these contradictory rumors, I searched for reliable materials and witnesses, and succeeded in finding several persons who worked with Bałaban during the last months of his life. Among them was his typist, who saved herself by using forged Aryan papers; she has published, under the name of Krystyna Nowakowska, a record of her experiences in the form of an autobiographical novel, *Chciałam żyć* (I Wanted to Live) (vol. I, Warsaw, 1948). In the archives of the Polish underground at the Warsaw Instytut Pamięci Narodowej, I found a handwritten report entitled "The Story of Professor Bałaban," in Polish, by a Polish underground worker who signs herself "Sabina" (perhaps the Polish Socialist leader Halina Krahelska). The report, which corroborates the more general information I received from ghetto survivors, begins:

Prof. Bałaban was shut up in the Warsaw ghetto together with his entire family. In December 1942 he was visited by a delegation of professors from Cologne who had known him before the war and who respected him greatly. During the course of the visit, the German scholars assured him that they would visit him again after six weeks. Prof. Bałaban expressed doubt as to whether they would still find him alive, since the ghetto would most probably be liquidated by then. The Germans said they could not believe it. Such an end, they declared, might at most be meted out to the "crude masses," but not to men of science. Three weeks after this, Prof. Bałaban died as a result of a heart attack. He left a widow and three children between the ages of 20 and 30; a married daughter and two sons. . . . The older son became an employee of the Jewish Council. In February 1943, the widow and her daughter and son-in-law escaped from the train [most likely the death transport to an extermination camp]. They bribed the Lithuanian guard who was on top of the car, jumped from the train, and returned to Warsaw. The son-in-law took advantage of his familiarity with a sanitarium in which he had formerly been employed [he was a physician] and found refuge with the gate-keeper. . . . The daughter, thanks to her Aryan appearance, was able to find living quarters and move freely in the city. . . .

The report goes on to say that the younger son, Alexander (Olek), lived in the ghetto and, during the uprising in April 1943, managed to escape to the Aryan side. On May 17, 1943, however, he was arrested on the street and brought to Gestapo headquarters. Bałaban's daughter left her home on the Aryan side on May 21, 1943, and never came back. The report does not indicate what happened ultimately to Mrs. Bałaban, her son-in-law, or the second son.

Simon Dubnow was killed by the Nazis in Riga in December 1941.[124] Ignacy (Yitzhak) Schipper was seized during the uprising in the Warsaw ghetto in 1943 and was sent to Majdanek. Despite the solicitous care of the other Jews in the camp, his weakened and ailing body could not endure the severity of concentration-camp life. He breathed his last in June or July of 1943 (according to some of his fellow sufferers, he died on July 2, 1943[125]).

Emanuel Ringelblum organized the famous ghetto archives in Warsaw —an activity concealed under the innocent guise of an *"Oneg Shabbat."* Ringelblum diligently collected documents and materials pertaining to Nazi persecution of Jews. During the great Nazi extermination action from July to September 1942, the archive materials were carefully buried in several iron cases. Ringelblum was sent to the labor and extermination camp of

Trawniki, but escaped and returned to the non-Jewish sector of Warsaw, where he concealed himself and continued to work on his historical studies and memoirs. In March 1944, the Nazis discovered his hideout. They tortured him to extract from him the whereabouts of the archives. Ringelblum died in terrible suffering but refused to betray his secret. The archives were recovered in 1946 and were turned over to the Jewish Historical Institute in Warsaw.[126]

During the ghetto uprising in Warsaw, Tulo Nussenblatt, the biographer of Theodor Herzl, was seized by the Gestapo and sent to an extermination camp. In Warsaw or Treblinka the following also met their end: Lipman Zomber, the young historian and statistician; M. Tauber; S. Szymkiewicz; Jonas Szper; the prominent folklorist Shmuel Lehman; and others. Menahem Linder, contributor to *Yidishe Ekonomik* and the Warsaw ghetto archives and organizer of the "Tkuma" movement in the ghetto, was shot by the Nazis on April 17, 1942.[127] Abraham Lewin, teacher of history, author of a volume on the Jewish cantonists in Russia, and active participant in the Warsaw ghetto archives, was killed during the massive Warsaw "action" of September 6–12, 1942.[128] About the same time, Rabbi Simon Huberband—specialist on the history of the Passover Haggadah and on Jewish cemeteries in Poland, and one of the most active contributors to the ghetto archives[129]—also perished.

Mattheus Mieses, thinker and scholar, was murdered in Przemyśl. In Bialystok, the aged S. A. Herschberg perished during the liquidation action in 1943. Here, too, the young historian and archivist Maximilian Meloch most likely met his end. In Vilna, the following were murdered by the Nazis: Haykl Lunski (probably taken to Treblinka); Pinkas Kon (killed on August 31, 1942, in Ponary, near Vilna); Zalmen Szyk (murdered in Lida in May 1942); Moshe Shalit; A. I. Goldschmidt (director of the Jewish ethnographic museum in Vilna); the statistician Moshe Heller; Zelig Kalmanovitch, scholar and one of the founders of the YIVO; the folklorist and philologist Ch. Chajes; and many others.[130]

In Lodz, the following were liquidated: A. S. Kamenetzky, Hebrew translator of Heinrich Graetz; Joseph Zelkowicz, folklorist, whose numerous descriptions of the Lodz ghetto are found in the archives of the Jewish Historical Institute in Poland and, in part, in the YIVO in New York; the Hebrew author Pinkas Selig Gliksman; and others.

In Lwów and Eastern Galicia: M. Kraemer, mobilized in the Red Army in the summer of 1941 and sent to Bessarabia, where he most likely perished in battle or in a German prison. In December 1941 or January 1942, Israel Weinlös was seized in a street roundup and was never seen again. Jacob Schall was killed in the action of August 1942 in Lwów. During the same action, Falik Hafner was shot "while trying to escape."

Karol Dresdner perished in Lwów in the Janowski camp in 1943. In Lwów, too, perished Isachar Matfes, historian of Zionism; Solomon Czortkower, anthropologist; and Maximilian Goldstein, art collector. Nothing is known concerning the fate of Leon Streit, Reuven Fahn, David Wurm, A. Eisenstein, Osias Mahler, Bela Mandelsberg, Arie Rassin, I. Warshawsky, Leopold Halperin, Rivke Notik, and many other Jewish scholars. It is unlikely that any of them survived. Honored be their memory!

Few were able to escape this bitter fate. I was liberated at Lwów in the summer of 1944, and immediately went to Lublin, and founded the Central Jewish Historical Commission (CJHC), the present-day Jewish Historical Institute (JHI) in Warsaw. The first members of the CJHC were the journalists D. Kupferberg and Shabatai Klugman, the poet and partisan leader Abba Kovner, Reuven Feldschuh (Ben-Shem), and myself. We were later joined by the folklorists Melekh Bakalczuk and Nachman Blumental (later director of the JHI, Warsaw), who had returned from the Soviet Union. Soon came Hersh Wasser, secretary of the Warsaw ghetto archives, who had miraculously escaped liquidation. Joseph Kermisz, pupil of Bałaban and author of several studies on Polish and Jewish history, who had been active in the ghetto and the underground, also joined. In 1946, Aron Eisenbach, Isaiah Trunk, Rafael Gerber, and A. Wolf-Jasny, all repatriated from the USSR, were added to the group.

This small group of Jewish historians, joined by a group of young students and amateurs concentrated around the JHI, attempted to carry on as far as possible the brilliant traditions of Polish Jewish historiography. Consciously harking back to the *Bleter far geshikhte* published before the war by the historians' circle of the YIVO, the JHI began publication of a new series of *Bleter far geshikhte*. Three numbers have appeared since 1948, and bear the stamp of serious scholarship. Nevertheless, it must be said that there is little hope for a rebirth of Jewish historiography in Poland. There are no Jewish masses left in Poland; experienced and distinguished historical scholars are lacking; and interest in Jewish historical study has given way to other tasks and aims, which now dominate the Jewish scene in Poland. Many members of the JHI have left Poland. Yet, this small group of Jewish historians, under the most unfavorable conditions, has managed to create imposing archives and a museum, collect great treasures of Jewish scholarship and art, develop a large publishing house, and contribute serious scholarly work. This must be recorded as an unusually impressive achievement.

❦ This essay first appeared in *Jewish Social Studies,* 11 (1949), 373–408.

## Notes

1. On Jewish historiography in Eastern Europe, see M. Wischnitzer, "Jewish Historians in Poland" (Yiddish), *Zukunft,* 48 (1943), 483–87; E. Tcherikower, "Jewish Historical Studies in Eastern Europe" (Yiddish), *YB,* 1 (1931), 97–113 (this deals only with Russian Jewish historiography; the second part, on Poland, never appeared); *idem,* in *Encyclopaedia Judaica,* VIII, 147–55; *Algemeyne Entsiklopedie,* s.v. "Yidn"; *The Jewish People Past and Present,* I, 223–32. See also M. Bałaban, "Jewish Studies in Reborn Poland and Polish Judaizers Abroad" (Polish), *Głos gminy żydowskiej* (1938), p. 285 f.

2. For further details regarding these two tendencies, see my "Jewish Historiography in Poland in the Last Years. A Critical Survey" (Polish), *Miesięcznik Żydowski,* 5 (1935), 182–94.

3. See the annual bulletins of the institute, which appeared in Hebrew and Polish, beginning in 1929. See also I. Ostersetzer, "The Institute of Jewish Studies in Warsaw" (Polish), *Miesięcznik Żydowski,* 1 (1931), 262–73; M. Bałaban, "Jewish Science and Its Educational Institutions in Poland" (Polish), *Pisma Instytutu Nauk Judaistycznych w Polsce* (Warsaw, 1927), pp. 19–33; I. Lewin, "Higher Talmudic School in Lublin" (Polish), *Miesięcznik Żydowski,* 1 (1931), 455–61; M. Alter, "The Tahkemoni School of Higher Learning in Warsaw" (Polish), *ibid.,* 2 (1931), 262–72.

4. See S. Dubnow, "The Present State of Jewish Historiography" (Yiddish), *YB,* 8 (1935), 289–94.

5. On the YIVO research fellowships, see nos. 54–62 in the *Yivo bibliografie* (New York, 1941). This bibliography is a comprehensive list of all YIVO publications.

6. Three volumes of this appeared, in 1929, 1937, and 1939.

7. There were two volumes, in 1928 and 1932.

8. Two volumes appeared under the first title, in 1926 and 1929, and two volumes under the second title, in 1934 and 1938.

9. Six issues of this magazine appeared between 1937 and 1939.

10. It was started in Warsaw in 1924, and only six issues were published.

11. See M. Wischnitzer, "Jewish Historians and Scholars in Soviet Russia" (Yiddish), *Zukunft,* 32 (1928), 461–63.

12. See Abraham G. Duker, *"Evreiskaya starina,* a Bibliography," *Hebrew Union College Annual,* 8–9 (1931–1932), 525–603.

13. A bibliography of Shatzky's publications was published by the American section of the YIVO (New York, 1939).

14. The popular work by Gershom Bader, *Draysig doyres yidn in Poyln* (Thirty Generations of Jews in Poland) (New York, 1927), is not of scholarly caliber. It was subjected to a searching and critical analysis by Jacob Shatzky in *Di fraye arbeter shtime* of November 25 and December 2, 1927. The most recent attempt at a general synthesis of the history of the Jews in Poland is *Di yidn in Poyln* (The Jews in Poland) (New York, 1946), by A. Menes, R. Mahler, J. Shatzky, and V. Shulman; see my review in *JSS,* 11 (1949), 82–85. Mahler's section on the social and economic history of Polish Jewry up to the beginning of the nineteenth century appeared separately

in Hebrew (Merhavia, 1946). Mention should be made here of the many synthetic articles dealing with Polish Jewry in the Yiddish *Algemeyne Entsiklopedie* (Paris, 1934), s.v. "Yidn."

15. See my review of Poznański's book, in *Ster,* no. 28 (1958). Poznański dealt with certain problems of Jewish bibliography in Poland in *Miesięcznik Żydowski,* vol. 1 (1931).

16. M. Gunzenhauser, *Bibliographie zur Nationalitätenfrage und zur Judenfrage der Republik Polen, 1919–1939* (Stuttgart, 1941).

17. *Lodzer visnshaftlekhe shriftn* (Scientific Studies of Lodz) (Lodz, 1939), pp. 133–48.

18. The more important of these are *Almanach gmin żydowskich w Polsce* (Almanac of the Jewish Communities in Poland) (Warsaw, 1939), which contains short accounts of thirty-four Jewish communities; and *Almanach szkolnictwa żydowskiego w Polsce* (Almanac of the Jewish School System in Poland), vol. I (Warsaw, 1938), both edited by J. Zineman; Gershom Bader, *Medinah vehakhameha* (A Land and its Sages) (New York, 1934), a list of Galician celebrities, of which only vol. I (*aleph* to *lamed*) appeared; the lexicon of the Polish Jewish war veterans, *Księga Pamiątkowa Związku Kombatantów Żydowskich* (A Memorial Volume of the Association of Jewish War Veterans), ed. by Zdzisław Żmigryder-Konopka and others (Warsaw); *Ilustrirter Yorbukh far industri handl un finantsen* (Illustrated Annals for Industry, Commerce, and Finances), ed. by Lazar Kahan (Lodz, 1925); *Almanakh fun der alt-shtot* (Almanac of the Old City), ed. by J. Turko (Lodz, 1932); *Biografyes* (Biographies), ed. by M. Frankental (Lodz, 1936); the *Lwów Lexicon of Jewish Personalities,* ed. by Dr. Brenner (Lwów, 1938); *Bialystoker Lexikon* (Lexicon of Bialystok), ed. by P. Kapłan (Bialystok, 1935). Several Vilna lexicons and almanacs will be discussed later.

19. See my review of this work in *Haj'nt* (1939) and in *Oyfn sheidweg,* no. 2 (1939), 227–29.

20. Most of the lexicons, almanacs, and bibliographical works cited here are, unfortunately, no longer available to me, for they were destroyed during the war. My references are for the most part from memory; hence the gaps in some of my data.

21. See my review of this in *Miesięcznik Żydowski,* 1 (1931), 555–59.

22. Cf., Shatzky's review in *Zukunft,* 32 (1927), 180–83, and Bałaban's review in *Przegląd Historyczny,* 17 (1913), 78 ff.

23. For a more detailed discussion of the origins of Polish Jews, see: M. Bałaban, "When and From Where Did Jews Come to Poland" (Polish), *Miesięcznik Żydowski* 1 (1931), 1–17 and 122 ff.; M. Mieses, "Judaisers in Eastern Europe" (Polish), *ibid.,* 3 (1933), 41–62, 169–85; 4 (1934), 143–59, 241–60, 342–56, 566–76; and my "First Thousand Years of Jewish History in Eastern Europe" (Polish), *Głos gminy żydowskiej,* 3 (1939), nos. 1–2.

24. See my review in *JSS,* 2 (1940), 102–5; the review by I. Halperin in *Kiryat Sefer,* 15 (1938), 206–10; and that by M. Wischnitzer in *Zukunft,* 48 (1943), 485–86. Other interesting works on Jewish trade in Poland are M. Wischnitzer, "Die Stellung der Brodyer Juden in internationalen Handel in der 2-ten Hälfte des XVIII Jhdt." in *Dubnow Festschrift* (Berlin, 1938), pp. 113–23; M. Brilling, "Jüdische Messgäste und Marktbesucher in Breslau im 17. Jahrhundert," *Jüdische Familienforschung,* 6–8 (1930–1932), 6 (1930), 315–

18, 364–72, 413–19, 506–509, 577–30; M. Berger, *Zur Handelsgeschichte der Juden in Polen während des 17. Jahrhundert* (Berlin, 1932).

25. See my detailed reviews in *Miesięcznik Żydowski*, 5 (1935), 185–87, and in *YB*, 8 (1935), 258–63; also Weinryb's reply, *ibid.*, 9 (1936), 152–55; and my rebuttal, *ibid.*, 11 (1937), 387–93.

26. Published in *Jewish Studies in Memory of G. A. Kohut* (New York, 1935), pp. 178–249.

27. Cf. the review by Guido Kisch in *Zeitschrift für die Geschichte der Juden in Deutschland*, 7 (1937), 59–60.

28. In *Lodzer visnshaftlekhe shriftn* (1938), 63–132.

29. M. Wischnitzer, in the *Minsk Tsaytshrift* (1928), nos. 2–3; *idem*, "Die jüdische Zunftverfassung in Polen und Litauen im siebzehnten und achtzehnten Jahrhundert," *Vierteljahrschrift für Sozial- und Wirtschaftsgeschichte*, 20 (1928), 33–51; I. Sosis, in the Minsk *Tsaytshrift* (1926 and 1930); I. Halperin, "Artisans Associations in Poland and in Lithuania" (Hebrew), *Zion*, 2 (1936–37), 70–89; M. Krämer, "The Participation of the Jewish Artisans in the Christian Guilds in Pre-Partition Poland" (Yiddish), *BFG*, o.s. 2 (1938), 3–32; *idem*, "Study of the Craftsmanship and Artisan Guilds Among Jews in Poland" (Hebrew), *Zion*, 1 (1937), 294–325; P. Kramerówna, "Jewish Craft Guilds in Ancient Poland" (Polish), *Miesięcznik Żydowski*, 2 (1932), 259–98; Bela Mandelberg, "Jewish Artisans of Lublin in City Guilds During the First Half of the 17th Century" (Yiddish), *Yunger Historiker*, I (1926); E. Ringelblum, "Protocols of the Tailors' Guild in Płock" (Yiddish), *Ekonomishe shriftn*, II (1922), 20–31; R. Notik, "The History of the Handicrafts Among the Lithuanian Jews" (Yiddish), *YB*, 9 (1936), 107–18.

30. B. Brutzkus, *Di yidishe landvirtshaft in mizrakh eyrope* (Jewish Agriculture in Eastern Europe) (Berlin, 1926).

31. J. Shatzky, "The History of the Jewish Colonization in the Kingdom of Poland" (Yiddish), *YB*, 6 (1934), 209–32.

32. *Leopold Kronenberg: Monografia zbiorowa* (Leopold Kronenberg: A Collection of Monographs), ed. by Simon Aszkenazy (Warsaw, 1922).

33. I. Sosis, *Di geshikhte fun di yidishe gezelshaftlekhe shtremungen in 19–tn yorhundert* (The History of the Jewish Social Trends in the 19th-Century) (Minsk, 1929); A. Yuditzky, *Yidishe burzhvazie un yidisher proletaryat in ershter helft 19–tn yorhundert* (The Yiddish Middle Class and the Yiddish Proletariat in the First Half of the 19th Century) (Kiev, 1931), and my review in *Miesięcznik Żydowski*, 5 (1935), 187; and U. Margulis, *Geshikhte fun yidn in Rusland* (History of the Jews in Russia), vol. I (Moscow, 1932).

34. A. W. Buchbinder, *Geshikhte fun der yidisher arbeter bavegung in Rusland* (History of the Jewish Labor Movement in Russia) (Russian and Yiddish) (Leningrad, 1925).

35. A. Tartakower, "Zur Geschichte des jüdischen Sozialismus," *Der Jude*, 7 (1923), 503–16, 591–618; 8 (1924), 16–38, 148–273, 386–99, 455–72, 638–61—later published in Hebrew under the title *Toledot tenuat haovdim hayehudim* (History of the Jewish Labor Movement) (3 vols., Warsaw, 1929–1932). See the review by Morus Sobel in *Miesięcznik Żydowski*, 2 (1932), 542–47.

36. A. Wolf-Jasny, *Geshikhte fun der yidisher arbeter bavegung in Lodz* (The History of the Jewish Labor Movement in Lodz), (Lodz, 1939).

37. *Historishe Shriftn,* vol. 3. *Di yidishe sotsialistishe bavegung biz tsu der entshehung fun Bund* (The Yiddish Socialist Movement Prior to the Founding of the Bund), ed. by E. Tcherikower, P. Kursky, A. Menes, and A. Rosin (Vilna, 1939). See the review by K. Pinson in *JSS,* 3 (1941), 424–28; and my review in *Literarishe Bleter,* no. 5 (1939).

38. *Der yidisher arbeter* (The Jewish Worker), ed. by A. Kirshnitz and A. Rafes (4 vols., Moscow, 1928); *Revoluzionnoye dvishenye sredy Evreev* (Revolutionary Movements Among the Jews), with a preface by S. Dimantshtein (Moscow, 1920); *Arkady: Zamelbuch zum andenk fun grinder fun "Bund" Arkady Kremer* (Arkady: A Collective Volume in Honor of the Founder of the "Bund" Arkady Kremer) (New York, 1942); *Vladimir Medem tsum tsvantsigstn yorzayt* (To the 20th Anniversary of Vladimir Medem's Death) (New York, 1943); J. S. Hertz, *Di geshikhte fun a yugnt* (The History of a Youth) (New York), 1948); J. Kenner, *Kvershnit* (Cross-Section) (New York, 1947); D. Shub, *Heldn un martirer* (Heroes and Martyrs) (2 vols., Warsaw, 1938). For more detailed information, see Koppel S. Pinson, "Arkady Kremer, Vladimir Medem, and the Ideology of the Jewish 'Bund,'" *JSS,* 7 (1945), 233–64; A. G. Duker, "Notes on Bibliography of the Jewish Labor Movement in Europe," *Jewish Social Service Quarterly,* 11 (1935), 267–69.

39. A. Tartakower, *Yidishe emigratsie un yidishe emigratsie-politik* (The Jewish Emigration and Jewish Emigration Policy) (Vilna, 1939), reviewed by Nathan Reich in *JSS,* 2 (1940), 213–14; A. Tartakower, *Yidishe vanderungen* (Jewish Migrations) (Warsaw, 1939); "Pauperism of the Polish Jews" (Polish), *Miesięcznik Żydowski,* 5 (1935), 97–122; M. Linder, "Emigration of the Polish Jew During the Crisis (1929–1933)" (Polish), *ibid.,* pp. 142–72, and a series of articles in *Yidishe ekonomik.* See also M. Wischnitzer, *To Dwell in Safety* (Philadelphia, 1948). Of the numerous studies on Jewish emigration by Jacob Lestschinsky, the most important are *Die Anfänge der Emigration und Kolonisation der Juden im 19. Jahrhundert* (Berlin, 1929); "Die Umsiedlung und Umschichtung des jüdischen Volkes im letzten Jahrhundert," *Weltwirtschaftliches Archiv,* 30 (1929), 123–56; 32 (1930), 569–99; "Jüdische Wanderungen und Staatsräume im Lichte der Vergangenheit," *Monatsschrift für Geschichte und Wissenschaft des Judenthums,* 75 (1931), 429–43.

40. S. Dubnow, *Pinkas hamedina* (Minutes Book of the Vaad of the Lithuanian Province) (Berlin, 1925). See also his article *s.v.* "Jewish Autonomy" in the *Encyclopedia of Social Sciences* (New York, 1932).

41. I. Halperin, "The Attitude of the Council of the Four Lands Toward the Hebrew Book" (Hebrew), *Kiryat Sefer,* 9 (1932), 367–78; "Accounts of the Councils of the Four Lands in Poland" (Hebrew), *Tarbiz,* 6 (1934–1935), 202–10, 527–34; "Zur Frage der Zusammensetzung der Vierländersynode in Polen," *Monatsschrift für Geschichte und Wissenschaft des Judentums,* 76 (1937), 519–22; "Attitudes of the Central Representation of the Council and the Communities in Poland Toward Eretz-Israel" (Hebrew), *Zion,* 1 (1935–1936), 82–86; "The Beginnings of the Council in the Grand Duchy of Lithuania and Its Relations to the Council of the Four Lands" (Hebrew), *ibid.,* 3 (1937–1938), 51–57; "The Council of the Four Lands and Its Relations with Abroad" (Yiddish), *Historishe shriftn,* 2 (1937), 68–79; *Tossafot umiluim lepinkas medinat lita* (Addenda and Supplements to the Protocols of the Great Duchy of Lithuania) (Jerusalem, 1935); I. Schipper, "Jewish Autonomy in

Poland at the Turn of the 18th and 19th Centuries" (Polish), *Miesięcznik Żydowski,* 1 (1931), 513–29; "Polish Records to the History of the Congress of the Four Lands" (Yiddish), in YIVO, *Historishe shriftn,* 1 (1929), 83–114; "The Composition of the Council of the Four Lands" (Yiddish), *ibid.,* pp. 72–82; "Financial Deterioration of the Central and Local Autonomy of the Jews in Pre-Partition Poland" (Yiddish), in YIVO *Ekonomishe shriftn,* 2 (1932), 1–19; "The Warsaw Commission: A Contribution to the History of the Jewish Autonomy in Poland" (Polish), *Publications of the Institute for Jewish Scholarship,* 3–4 (1931), 147–57. Outside Poland there were the publications by L. Lewin, "Aus ostjüdischer Geschichte," *Monatsschrift für Geschichte und Wissenschaft des Judentums* (1929), 177–84; *Die Landessynode der grosspolnischen Judenschaft* (Frankfurt, 1926); "Nachträge zur Landessynode der polnischen Judenschaft," *Dubnow Festschrift* (Berlin, 1930), pp. 124–35; D. B. Teimanas, *L'Autonomie des communautés juives en Pologne en XVI et XVII siècles* (Paris, 1933).

42. Lewin's more important works are "The Vienna Divorce" (Polish), reprinted from *Przewodnik Historyczno-Prawny,* vol. II (Lwów, 1931), reviewed by M. Alter in *Miesięcznik Żydowski,* 2 (1932), 549–52; *Klątwa żydowska na Litwie w 17 i 18 wieku* (The Jewish Excommunication Ban in Lithuania in the 17th and 18th Centuries) (Lwów, 1932); *Protokoły kahalne w 18 i 19 wieku w Małopolsce Wschodniej* (Protocols of the Jewish Kahals of the 18th and 19th Centuries) (Lwów, 1931).

43. My "The Hevra Kaddisha in Lodz and Its History" (Polish), in *Stary Cmentarz Żydowski w Łodzi* (The Old Jewish Cemetery in Lodz) (Lodz, 1938), pp. 37–110.

44. M. Feinkind, "Di hevra kaddisha in Piotrków" (Yiddish), *Lodzer Visnshaftlekhe Shriftn* (1938), 55–62; L. Zomber, "A Picture of Jewish Life in a Polish Town at the Beginning of the 19th Century" (Yiddish), *Yunger Historiker,* 1 (1926), 58–65.

45. *Księga pamiątkowa ku czci Berka Josełowicza* (Memorial Volume in Honor of Berek Josełowicz), ed. by M. Bałaban (Warsaw, 1934), reviewed by J. Shatzky in *YB,* 9 (1936), 123–26.

46. See the review of Raphael Mahler in *JSS,* 2 (1940), 106–7.

47. I. Schipper, *Żydzi Królestwa Polskiego w dobie powstania listopadowego* (The Jews of the Kingdom of Poland in the November Uprising) (Warsaw, 1932), reviewed by me in *Kiryat Sefer,* 11 (1934–1935), 210–12, and in *Literarishe Bleter,* 11 (1934), 172.

48. N. M. Gelber, "Die Juden und die polnische Revolution, 1846," *Aus Zwei Jahrhunderten. Beiträge zur neueren Geschichte der Juden* (Vienna, 1924); *Die Juden und der polnische Aufstand des Jahres 1863* (Vienna, 1923); and "The Jews in the Polish Uprising of 1831" (Polish), published in a series of installments, beginning November 1931, in the Lwów Polish Jewish daily *Chwila.*

49. See Shatzky's review articles in YIVO *Historishe shriftn,* 2, 355–89; and 1, 423–68. Also *idem,* "American Jews and the Polish Uprising of 1863" (Yiddish), *YB,* 4 (1932), 407–18.

50. R. Brandstätter, *Legion żydowski Adama Mickiewicza* (The Jewish Legion of Adam Mickiewicz) (Warsaw, 1931).

51. See the review by Shatzky in *YB,* 7 (1934), 248–53.

52. The most severe indictment by a Polish scholar of Mieses's book is Leon Białkowski's *Żyd o neofitach polskich* (A Jew on Jewish Converts in Poland) (Warsaw, 1938). The general problem of Jewish apostates in Poland had been treated earlier by A. Kraushar, in 1895, *Frank i Frankisci polscy* (Frank and the Polish Frankists), vol. I, ch. 15; and by the Polish anti-Semite Teodor Jeske Choiński, in 1905. Jewish publications on this topic in the period 1918–1939 include S. L. Zitron, *Meshumodim* (The Converts) (Vilna, 1921); E. N. Frank, *Meshumodim in Poyln in 19ten yorhundert* (Converts in Poland in the 19th Century), 2 vols. (Warsaw, 1923–1924); N. M. Gelber, "Die Taufbewegung unter den polnischen Juden in 18ten Jahrhundert," *Monatsschrift für Geschichte und Wissenschaft des Judentums,* 68 (1924), 225–41; S. M. Ginsburg, *Historishe verk,* IV (New York, 1937). From the Polish side come the following: S. Didier, *Rola neofitów w dziejach Polski* (The Role of Neophytes in Polish History), 3 vols. (Warsaw, 1934); L. Korwin (Piotrowski), *Szlachta polska pochodzenia żydowskiego* (Polish Aristocracy of Jewish Descent) (Cracow, 1933); *Szlachta mojżeszowa* (The Mosaic Aristocracy), vol. 1 (Cracow, 1938); *Szlachta neoficka* (The Neophyte Aristocracy) (Cracow, 1939). Mention should also be made of the work of the Nazi "expert" on Polish Jewish history, J. Sommerfeldt, "Zur Geschichte der Judentaufen in Polen," *Deutsche Forschung im Osten,* 3 (Cracow, 1943), 59–78.

53. See my "Majer Bałaban," *Miesięcznik Żydowski,* 3 (1933), 340–46, and the bibliography of Bałaban's works, *ibid.,* 346–51.

54. N. N. Hanover, *Yveyn metzula* (Deep Mire), trans. into Yiddish by S. W. Latzky-Bertoldi with a supplement by I. Israelsohn and an introduction by J. Shatzky (Vilna, 1938). A revised Hebrew edition of the *Yveyn metzula* appeared in Tel Aviv, 1945, with an introduction by J. Fichman and notes by L. Halperin.

55. See the review by me in *Literarishe bleter,* no. 34 (1939); and that by A. Berger in *JSS,* 4 (1940), 217–18.

56. A. Eisenbach, "Documents to the History of the District Councils and Planned Central-Councils in the Duchy of Warsaw" (Yiddish), and "The Central Representation of the Jews in the Duchy of Warsaw, 1807–1815" (Yiddish), *BFG,* o.s. 2 (1938), 49–127 and 33–88; "Jews in the Duchy of Warsaw" (Yiddish), in *A Yor Aspirantur* (Vilna, 1937), pp. 91–99; "Jews in the Duchy of Warsaw" (Yiddish), *YB* (1936), 91–99.

57. S. M. Ginsburg, *Historishe verk* (Historical Studies), 3 vols. (New York, 1937–1938), reviewed by me in *JSS,* 3 (1941), 95–97.

58. L. Streit, *Ormianie a Żydzi w Stanisławowie w XVII i XVIII wieku* (Armenians and Jews in Stanisławów in the 17th and 18th Centuries) (Stanisławów, 1936).

59. Reviewed by N. Reich, in *JSS,* 4 (1942), 184–85. See also Joel Cang, "The Opposition Parties in Poland and Their Attitude Towards the Jews and the Jewish Problem," *ibid.,* I (1939), 241–56. The subject of anti-Semitism in Poland was dealt with in numerous publicistic books and articles, especially treaties on anti-Semitism. A full bibliography of this literature can be found in the article "Antisemitism" in the *Encyclopaedia Judaica* (German ed.) and in the article "Antisemitism in the Post-War Period" by Koppel S. Pinson in the *Encyclopaedia Britannica.* Special mention should be made here of Oscar Janowsky, *Jews at Bay* (New York, 1939), and the economic interpretation of

Polish anti-Semitism by Raphael Mahler in *Essays in Antisemitism,* ed. by Koppel S. Pinson (2nd ed., New York, 1946), pp. 145–72.

60. See J. Shatzky, "Jewish Memoir-Literature from the Times of the First World War and the Russian Revolution" (Yiddish), *Zukunft,* 31 (1926), 241–43, 428–30, 485–86.

61. Reviewed by Shatzky in *Bikhervelt,* 1 (1922), 170–72.

62. Reviewed by Shatzky in *YB,* 14 (1939), 367–70.

63. Reviewed by Shatzky in *Zukunft,* 36 (1927), 546–49.

64. J. Klausner, *Historia shel hasifrut haivrit hahadashah* (History of the Modern Hebrew Literature), 3 vols. (Jerusalem, 1930–1939); F. Lachover, *Toldot hasifrut haivrit hahadashah* (History of the Modern Hebrew Literature), 4 vols. (Tel Aviv, 1928–1933); M. Waxman, *A History of Jewish Literature,* 4 vols. (New York, 1930–1941); Shalom Spiegel, *Hebrew Reborn* (New York, 1930); M. Weinreich, *Bilder fun der yidisher literatur-geshikhte* (Impressions from the History of Yiddish Literature) (Vilna, 1928); A. A. Roback, *The Story of Yiddish Literature* (New York, 1940); S. L. Zitron, *Geshikhte fun der yidisher prese, 1863–1899* (History of the Yiddish Press, 1863–1899) (Vilna, 1923); Zalman Reisin, *Lexikon fun der yidisher literatur, prese un filologie,* 4 vols. (2nd ed., Vilna, 1926–1930); M. Weissberg, "Die neuhebräische Aufklärungsliteratur in Galizien," *Monatsschrift für Geschichte und Wissenschaft des Judentums,* 77 (1933), 513–26, 735–49; 71 (1927), 54–62, 100–09, 371–87; 72 (1928), 71–88, 184–201.

65. Joseph Perl, *Yidishe ksuvim* (Jewish Writings), with a biographical introduction by Israel Weinlös and a philological analysis by Z. Kalmanovitch (Vilna, 1937). Cf., the review by me in *Literarishe Bleter,* 15 (1937), 362, and in *Tenuhim* (1937), and by R. Mahler in *JSS,* 1 (1939), 487–88.

66. My "The Adepts of Enlightenment in Galicia on the Threshold of the 19th Century" (Yiddish), *Fun noentn over,* 2 (1938), 90–102, and "The First Conflicts Between Enlightenment and Hasidism" (Yiddish), *ibid.,* 1 (1937), 259–74. My "Josef Perl as an Educator and His School in Tarnopol" (Yiddish) was first published in vol. 2 of the YIVO *Pedagogishe Shriftn,* in Vilna in 1940, with the special permission of the new Soviet regime. Authority was granted to print only forty copies of the volume. Two of these copies, fortunately, were salvaged and brought to New York, and from them the Perl study was reprinted in *YB,* 31–32 (1948), 131–91. *Habent sua fata libelli!*

67. S. Katz, "New Materials from the Perl Archives" (Yiddish), *Wachstein Bukh* (Vilna, 1939), pp. 557–77.

68. R. Mahler, *Der kamf tsvishn haskole un khasidus in galitsye* (The Conflict Between the Enlightenment and Hasidism in Galicia) (New York, 1942). A part of this was published in English under the title "The Austrian Government and the Hasidim during the Period of Reaction, 1814–48," in *JSS,* 1 (1939), 195–240.

69. I. Schipper, "The Beginnings of the Enlightenment in Central Poland" (Polish), *Miesięcznik Żydowski,* 2 (1932), 311–27.

70. C. Tchernowitz, *Toledot haposkim* (History of the Codifiers), 2 vols. (New York, 1946); S. Assaf, "History of the Rabbinate in Germany, Poland, and in Lithuania" (Hebrew), *Reshumot,* 2 (1927); S. M. Chones, *Toledot haposkim* (History of the Codifiers) (Warsaw, 1929).

71. Collected in J. Shatzky, *Yidishe bildungs politik in Poyln fun 1806*

*bis 1866* (Jewish Education Policy in Poland from 1806 to 1866) (New York, 1943), reviewed by M. Wischnitzer in *JSS,* 6 (1944), 280–82.

72. A. Sawicki, "The Rabbinical School in Warsaw" (Polish), *Miesięcznik Żydowski,* 3 (1933), 244–74.

73. A. Tartakower, "Jewish Communal Schools in Poland" (Hebrew), *Pisma Instytutu Nauk Judaistycznych* (Warsaw, 1931); idem, "Jewish Culture in Poland Between the Two World-Wars" (Yiddish), *Gedank un Lebn,* 4 (1946), 1–35; G. Hecht, "Twenty Years of School Network of the Jewish Minority in Poland" (Yiddish), *Yidisher gezelshaftlekher lexikon,* 1 (Warsaw, 1939), 247–98, with bibliography; H. Kazhdan, *Di geshikhte fun yidishn shulvesen in umofengikn Poyln* (The History of the Jewish School System in Independent Poland) (Mexico City, 1947); reviewed by Emanuel Pat in *YB,* 31–32 (1948), 364–73; N. Eck, "The Educational Institutions of Polish Jewry," *JSS,* 9 (1947), 3–32.

74. S. Langnas, *Żydzi a studia akademickie w Polsce w latach, 1921–31* (Jews and Academic Studies in Poland in the Years 1921–31) (Lwów, 1933), reviewed by M. Pomeranz in *Miesięcznik Żydowski,* 4 (1934), 471–80.

75. Reviewed by B. D. Weinryb in *JSS,* 3 (1941), 436–37.

76. *Shriftn far psikhologie un pedagogik* (Studies in Psychology and Education), vol. I, ed. by L. Lehrer (Vilna, 1933), and vols. 31–32 (1948) of *YB,* dedicated entirely to these problems. See also note 66, above.

77. I. Schipper, *Geshikhte fun der yidisher teatrkunst* (History of the Jewish Theatrical Arts), 4 vols. (Warsaw, 1923–1928).

78. J. Shatzky, ed., *Arkhiv far der geshikhte fun yidishn teatr un drame* (Archives of the History of the Jewish Theater and Drama), vol. I (New York, 1930).

79. *Lexikon fun yidishn teatr* (Lexicon of the Jewish Theater), ed. by Z. Silberzweig and Jacob Mestel (New York, 1931).

80. Rachel Wischnitzer-Bernstein, "Synagogen in ehemaligen Königreich Polen," *Das Buch der polnischen Juden* (Berlin, 1916); A. Breier, M. Eisler, M. Grunwald, *Holzsynagogen in Polen* (Vienna, 1934); S. Zajczyk, *Architektura barokowych bóżnic murowanych w Polsce* (The Architecture of Baroque Synagogues in Poland) (Warsaw, 1936); M. Bałaban, *O warownych bóżnicach w Polce* (Fortified Synagogues in Poland) (Warsaw, 1929); M. Mieses, "Underground synagogues" (Polish), *Miesięcznik Żydowski,* 1 (1931), 145–52; C. Aronson, "Wooden Synagogues of Poland," *Menorah Journal,* 25 (1937), 326 ff.

81. A. Szyszko-Bohusz, "Materials on the Architecture of Synagogues in Poland" (Polish), Publications of the Commission for the History of Art and the Polish Academy of Sciences (Cracow, 1927); G. Loukomski, "Old Polish Synagogues," *Journal of the Royal Institute of British Architecture* (1935); idem, "Wooden Synagogues in Poland," *Burlington Magazine,* 66 (1935), 14–21. An extensive bibliography of this subject is to be found in Loukomski's *Jewish Art in European Synagogues from the Middle Ages to the 18th Century* (London, 1947), even though some of the items contain errors; a great deal of attention is given to Polish synagogues in this volume.

82. Reviewed by Shatzky in *YB,* 3 (1932), 63–68.

83. Reviewed by J. Schall in *Miesięcznik Żydowski,* 5 (1935), 198–200.

84. The most complete bibliography of all aspects of Jewish art and

art history has been compiled by Rachel Wischnitzer-Bernstein. Comprising about 700 items, it has been turned over to the YIVO. An earlier bibliographical article by the same author is found in *Dubnow Festschrift* (Berlin, 1930), pp. 76–81. A great deal of material regarding the cultural treasures of the Jews in Poland before the Nazi invasion is to be found in the series of publications of the Conference on Jewish Relations, published as Supplements to *JSS*: "Tentative List of Jewish Cultural Treasures in Axis-Occupied Countries," vol. 8 (1946); and "Addenda and Corrigenda," vol. 10 (1948); "Tentative List of Jewish Periodicals . . . ," vol. 9 (1947); "Tentative List of Jewish Publishers . . . ," vol. 10 (1948); and "Tentative List of Jewish Educational Institutions . . . ," vol. 8 (1946).

85. Yiddish ed., 2 vols. (Vilna, 1930–1933); German ed., 2 vols. (Berlin, 1931–1932); Hebrew ed., 3 vols. (Tel Aviv, 1930–1932).

86. S. A. Horodetzky, *Hahasidut vehahasidim* (Hasidism and Hasids), 4 vols. (Tel Aviv, 1923; 2nd ed., Berlin, 1928); *Shivhey habesht* (In the Praise of Baal Shem Tov) (Berlin, 1922); *Torat hamaggid mi-Meseritch* (Teachings of the Maggid from Międzyrzec) (Berlin, 1923); *Torat Reb Nahman Mi-Bratzlav* (Teachings of Reb Nahman from Bratslav) (Berlin, 1923). An abridged edition of the first-mentioned work appeared in English translation as *Leaders of Hasidism* (London, 1928).

87. Buber's German rendition of Hasidic lore has been gathered in one volume, *Die chasidischen Bücher* (Hellerau, 1928). Several volumes have appeared in English translation: *Jewish Mysticism and the Legends of Baal Shem* (London, 1931); *Tales of Hasidim: The Early Masters* (New York, 1947); *Hasidism* (New York, 1948).

88. Hillel Zeitlin, *Hasiduth* (Hasidism) (Warsaw, 1922). Cf. *Sepher Zeitlin,* by Isaiah Wolfsberg and Zvi Harkavy (Jerusalem, 1944). See also M. Bałaban, "The Literature of the Hasidism of the Recent Era" (Hebrew), *Hatekufa,* 18 (1923), 488–502.

89. See especially the Yiddish edition of Nahman's *Massiyot* (Tales) by Yona Spivak, with a magnificent introduction by S. Niger (Vilna, 1932), and the Yiddish and Hebrew edition by S. A. Setzer (New York, 1929).

90. S. Minkin, *The Romance of Hasidism* (New York, 1935); Louis I. Newman, *The Hasidic Anthology* (New York, 1934); Koppel S. Pinson, "Chassidism," in *Encyclopedia of the Social Sciences,* vol. 3, pp. 354–57; and his "The Poetry of Hasidim," in *Menorah Journal,* 29 (1936), 287 ff. A section on the study of Hasidism has been established [at the time of this writing.—*Ed.*] by YIVO under the direction of Abraham J. Heschel.

91. B. Dinaburg, "The Beginning of Hasidism and Its Social and Messianic Elements (Hebrew), *Zion,* 9 (1943–1944), 39–45, 89–108, 186–97.

92. Scholem delivered a series of five lectures on Hasidism at the Jewish Institute of Religion in the spring of 1949. See also his "Contributions to the Knowledge of Sabbatianism from XVIII Century Missionary Literature" (Hebrew), *ibid.,* pp. 27–38, 84–88.

93. A. Z. Aescoly, *Introduction à l'étude des hérésies religieuses parmi les Juifs: La Kabbale, le Hassidisme* (Paris, 1928), and *Tenuat Towianski beyn Hayehudim* (Towianski Movement Among Jews) (Jerusalem, 1933).

94. M. Bałaban, "Karaites in Poland" (Polish), *Nowe Życie,* 1 (1924), 1–23, 166–76, 323–40; 2 (1924), 14–26, 192–206; and in Hebrew in *Hatekufa,* 20 (1920), 293–307, 21 (1921), 226–35, 25 (1925), 451–87.

95. R. Fahn, *Kitvey* (Writings), (n.p., 1929), vol. I (*Sepher ha-Karaim* [Karaites Volumes]).

96. M. Bałaban, "When and From Where Did The Jews Come to Poland" (Polish), *Miesięcznik Żydowski,* 1 (1931), 1–12, 112–21; *idem,* "The Karaites in Poland" (Polish) (see note 94). A sharp reply to Bałaban was published by A. Zajączkowski, *Na marginesie studium Bałabana: Karaici w Polsce* (On the Margin of Bałaban's Study: The Karaites in Poland) (Vilna, 1928). See also J. Brutzkus, "The Origins of the Karaites in Lithuania and in Poland" (Yiddish), *B. Wachstein Memorial Volume,* published by YIVO (Vilna, 1939), pp. 109–124; reprinted from *YB,* 13 (1938); G. Hecht, *Karaimi: "Synowie zakonu"* (The Karaites: "Sons of the Covenant") (Warsaw, 1938); A. Zajączkowski, *Karaimi na Wołyniu* (The Karaites in Volhynia) (Równe, 1933); *idem, Elementy tureckie na ziemiach polskich* (Turkish Elements in Polish Lands) (Zamość, 1935); S. Firkowicz, *O Karaimach w Polsce* (On the Karaites in Poland) (Troki, 1938); A. Mordkowicz, *Ogniska Karaimskie* (Karaite Centers) (Łuck, 1934); *idem, Synowie Zakonu* (Sons of the Covenant) (Łuck, 1930); *Księga Jubileuszowa ku czci chachama H. S. Szapszala* (Jubilee Volume in Honor of Haham H. Seraj Szapszal) (Vilna, 1938); A. Szyszman, *Osadownictwo karaimskie na ziemiach Wielkiego Księstwa Litewskiego* (Karaite Settlements in the Grand Duchy of Lithuania) (Vilna, 1936).

97. The story of Dr. Schipper and Prof. Bałaban is told in the memoirs of Dr. Michael Weichert, director of the Jewish Self-Help in the GG (unpublished manuscript). On Kalmanovitch, see M. Dworzecki, *Yerushelayim delite in kamf un umkum* (The Jerusalem of Lithuania in Struggle and Destruction) (Paris, 1948), p. 332. Dworzecki mentions a debate ordered by the Germans in Vilna between S. Kalmanovitch and the Karaite *hakham,* Shapshal (Szapszal). Kalmanovitch, of course, agreed with the thesis that the Karaites are not descended from Jews. According to Dworzecki, the Karaites in Vilna were not persecuted by the Germans, because they were not regarded as Jews. See also essay 7 above, "The Karaites Under Nazi Rule."

98. A detailed bibliography of these works is found in the YIVO *Filologische Schriftn,* esp. vol. 2, and in YIVO *Bibliografie,* pp. 135–42.

99. M. Bernstein, comp., *Musikalisher pinkes* (Vilna, 1928).

100. A. Z. Idelsohn, comp., *Thesaurus of Hebrew Oriental Melodies,* 10 vols. (Leipzig, 1914–1932).

101. See my "Regionalism" (Yiddish), *Landkentnish,* no. 1 (March 1937), 3–7, and the work cited above, note 2.

102. M. Bałaban, *Żydzi w Krakowie i na Kazimierzu, 1304–1868* (Jews in Cracow and Kazimierz, 1304–1868) (Polish) (vol. I, 1st ed., Cracow, 1913; 2nd ed., enlarged, 2 vols., Cracow, 1931–1937); *idem, Żydzi lwowscy na przełomie XVI i XVII wieku* (The Jews of Lwów at the Turn of the XVI and XVII Centuries) (Lwów, 1906); *idem, Die Judenstadt von Lublin* (Berlin, 1919).

103. See the review by the Polish historian Łucjan Siemieński in *Kwartalnik Historyczny* (1932); and that by E. Feldman in *Miesięcznik Żydowski,* 2 (1932), 251–61.

104. E. Ringelblum, "Jews in Warsaw in the 18th Century" (Yiddish), YIVO *Historishe Shriftn,* 2 (1937), 248–68; "The Internal Life of the Jews of Warsaw in the 18th Century as Seen from the Opposite Side" (Yiddish),

*Fun noentn over,* 1 (1937), 179 ff., 275–80; 2 (1938), 119–30; "Shmuel Zbytkower of Poland in the Period of the Partitions" (Hebrew), *Zion,* 2 (1938), 246–66, 337–55.

105. I. Warshawsky, "Jews in the Kingdom of Poland, 1815–1831" (Yiddish), YIVO *Historishe Shriftn,* 2 (1937), 332–54; "Jews in the Newly Rebuilt Cities in the Kingdom of Poland in 1822–1831" (Yiddish), *YB,* 3 (1932), 28–35; "The Social and Economic Structure of Warsaw Jewry in 1840" (Polish), *Miesięcznik Żydowski,* 1 (1930), 55–67, 2 (1931), 245–62.

106. J. Shatzky, *Geshikhte fun yidn in Varshe* (The History of the Jews in Warsaw), 3 vols. (New York, 1947–1953).

107. Reviewed by Salo W. Baron in *JSS,* 3 (1941), 419–20.

108. See YIVO *Bibliografie* (New York, 1943).

109. H. Lunski, *Geoynim un gedoylim fun noentn over* ("Geonim" and "Gedolim" from the Recent Past) (Vilna, 1931), *Fun Vilner geto* (Vilna, 1930); *Mehageto havilnayi* (From the Vilna Ghetto) (Vilna, 1921); *Legendes vegn Vilner Goen* (Legends about the Gaon of Vilna) (Vilna, 1924).

110. J. Schall, *Dawna Żółkiew i jej Żydzi* (Ancient Żółkiew and Its Jewry) (Lwów, 1939); Ephraim Sonnenschein, *Prakim mitoldot hayehudim b'Czortków* (Chapters from the History of the Jews in Czortków) (Warsaw, 1939), D. Wurm, *Z dziejów żydowstwa brodzkiego do 1772 roku* (History of the Jews in Brody to 1772) (Brody, 1935); J. Trunk, *Plozk (1237–1657)* (Warsaw, 1939); I. Schipper, *700 lat gminy żydowskiej w Płocku* (700 Years of the Jewish Community in Płock) (Lwów, 1938).

111. Among the less successful works in this field were the following: P. S. Gliksman, *Ir Łask vehahameha* (The City of Łask and its Scholars) (Lodz, 1926); M. Feinkind, *Dzieje Żydów w Piotrkowie* (History of the Jews of Piotrków) (Piotrków, 1930); M. Steinberg, *Żydzi w Jarosławiu* (The Jews in Jarosław) (Jarosław, 1933); G. A. Goldberg, *Z dziejów m. Słonimia* (From the History of the Jews of Słonim) (Słonim, 1934). Local studies of a more fragmentary character are E. Feldman, "The Jewish Ghetto in Kalisz in the 15th and 16th Centuries" (Yiddish), *Landkentnish,* no. 1 (1933), 19–25; *idem,* "Two Old Jewish Communities in the Lodz Area (Kalisz and Konin)" (Yiddish), *Lodzer visnshaftlekhe shriftn,* 1 (1938), 3–31; E. Ringelblum, "Names of Warsaw Streets" (Yiddish), *Landkentnish,* no. 1 (April 1935), 3–8; R. Mahler, "The History of the Jews in Kowel" (Yiddish), *ibid.,* no. 1 (1933), 26–46; my "Documents to the History of the Jews in Łęczyca" (Yiddish), *Lodzer visnshaftlekhe shriftn,* 1 (1938), 239–47; I. Trunk, "A Jewish Community in Poland at the End of the 18th Century: Kutno" (Yiddish), *BFG,* o.s. 1 (1934), 87–140; N. Bomse, "Jewish Prayer-Shawl Weavers in Sasów" (Yiddish), *Landkentnish,* no. 1 (1933), 81–90; Piotr Kontny, *Oaza srebrnych kwiatów* (Oasis of Silver Flowers) (Lwów, 1934); I. Streit, *Dzieje synagogi postępowej w Stanisławowie* (History of the Progressive Synagogue in Stanisławów) (Stanisławów, 1939); I. Halperin, "The History of the Jews in Tykocin" (Hebrew), *Hazofeh* (Budapest, 1930), pp. 287–98.

112. See my "Jewish Topography Literature" (Yiddish), *Literarishe Bleter,* 14 (1936), 425–26.

113. The work carried on by Nazi writers is a subject in itself, and will not be treated in this essay.

114. T. J. Choiński, *Historja Żydów w Polsce* (History of the Jews in Poland) (Warsaw, 1919), reviewed by M. Bałaban in *Hatekufa,* 12 (1922), 495–501. See also Choiński's older work, *Neofici polscy* (The Polish Neophytes) (Warsaw, 1905).

115. S. Kutrzeba, *Sprawa żydowska w Polsce* (The Jewish Problem in Poland) (Lwów, 1918).

116. J. Ptaśnik, *Miasta w Polsce* (The Towns in Poland) (Lwów, 1922); *Miasta i mieszczaństwo w dawnej Polsce* (The Towns and the Burghers in Old Poland) (Cracow, 1934); "Jews in Medieval Poland" (Polish), *Przegląd Warszawski,* 2 (1922), 215–37; "The Flood of the Polish Cities by Jews from the 15th to the 18th Centuries" (Polish), *ibid.,* no. 35 (1924). A vigorous critique of these writings is to be found in J. Shatzky's article, "History in the Disguise of Publicistics" (Polish), and "Polish Cities and the Jews" (Polish), in *Nasz Kurier,* May 19 and June 2, 1922.

117. Kazimierz Bartoszewicz, *Antysemityzm w literaturze polskiej XV–XVIII wieku* (Anti-Semitism in the Polish Literature of the 15th–18th Centuries) (Warsaw, 1914).

118. F. Rawita-Gawroński, *Żydzi w historii i literaturze ludowej na Rusi* (Jews in the History and Popular Literature of Ruthenia) (Warsaw, 1925). See also *idem, Historia ruchów hajdamackich* (History of the Haidamak Movements), 2 vols. (Brody, 1913).

119. B. Wasiutynski, *Ludność Żydowska w Polsce XIX i XX w.* (Jewish Population in Poland in the 19th and 20th Centuries) (Warsaw, 1930); see the review by Bałaban in *Nasz Przegląd,* December 16, 1931.

120. H. Mościcki, "Jews in Poland Under Catherine II" (Polish), in his *Pod znakiem Orła i Pogoni* (Warsaw, 1915); See also his *Dzieje porozbiorowe Litwy i Rusi* (History of Lithuania and Ruthenia After the Partitions), vol. 1 (Vilna, 1918); and *Białystok: Zarys Historyczny* (Bialystok: A Historical Outline) (Bialystok, 1933). A. S. Hershberg, in his *Pinkas Białystok* (pp. 3–9) seeks to show that Mościcki is definitely anti-Jewish, but his charges are greatly exaggerated.

121. P. Kontny, *Oaza srebrnych kwiatów* (The Oasis of Silver Flowers) (Lwów, 1936); Z. Lutman, *Handel miasta Brodów, 1773–1880* (The Commerce of Brody, 1773–1880) (Lwów, 1937); S. Hoszowski, *Rozwój gospodarczy Lwowa* (The Economic Development of Lwów) (Lwów, 1938); J. S. Bystroń, *Dzieje obyczajów w dawnej Polsce* (History of Customs and Morals in Old Poland), 2 vols. (Warsaw, 1932).

122. A memorial volume for Schorr, *Kobetz maddai* (Scholarly Miscellany), ed. by Abraham Weiss, was published in New York in 1941. A study of Schorr's scholarly work and a bibliography of his writings were published by I. Ostersetzer in *Miesięcznik Żydowski,* 4 (1934), 460–70. See also the *Bulletin of the Polish Institute of Arts and Sciences in America,* 1 (1943), 670.

123. On Bałaban see M. Wischnitzer in *JSS,* 5 (1943), 410–11; I. Lewin, *Hurbn Eyrope* (The Destruction of Europe) (New York, 1948), pp. 151–55; Jonas Turkow, *Azoy iz es geven* (Thus it Happened) (Buenos Aires, 1948); Hillel Seidman, *Yoman geto Varshe* (A Diary from the Warsaw Ghetto) (Tel Aviv, 1946), pp. 273–80; R. Auerbach, "Jewish Writers in the Warsaw Ghetto" (Yiddish), in *Kidush Hashem,* ed. by S. Niger (New York, 1948), pp. 107–10.

124. See Max Kaufman, *Hurbn Lettland* (The Destruction of Latvia) (Munich, 1948), pp. 259–66; K. I. Honig, "The Last Days of Professor Dubnow" (Yiddish), *Ibergang* (Munich), no. 31 (1947); S. Kor, "Professor S. Dubnow in the Column for Death" (Yiddish), *Undzer Velt* (Munich), no. 2 (1946); Hilel Melamed, "How the Nazis Murdered Professor S. Dubnow" (Yiddish), *Zukunft* (February 1946), 320–31.

125. Hillel Seidman, pp. 299–305; J. Turkow, "The Last Days of Dr. I. Schipper" (Yiddish), *Tsionistishe shtime* (Munich), nos. 3–4 (1946); the eyewitness testimony of an inmate of Majdanek in *Obozy* (Camps), *Dokumenty i materiały*, I, ed. by N. Blumental (Lodz, 1946), pp. 167–70; R. Mahler, "I. Schipper," *YB,* (1945), 19–32; M. Neustadt, *Hurbn un oyfshtand fun di yidn in Varshe* (The Destruction and the Uprising of the Jews in Warsaw) (Tel Aviv, 1948), II, 697–99.

126. Jacob Kenner, *Emanuel Ringelblum* (New York, 1945), reprinted in *idem, Kvershnit* (Cross-Section) (New York, 1947), pp. 228–46; A. Eisenbach, "Scientific Research in the Warsaw Ghetto" (Yiddish), *BFG,* 1 (1948), 55–113, no. 2, pp. 69–84. The latter, an exhaustive study, gives a detailed description of the activities and the collaborators of the ghetto-archives. A second article by "A. Bach" (pseudonym of A. Eisenbach), "Survey of the Materials from the Clandestine Ghetto-Archive" (Yiddish), in *BFG,* 1 (1948), 178–82, surveys the discovered and collected materials. See also R. Mahler in *YB,* 24 (1944), 307–17; N. Eck in *Hadoar,* no. 3 (1946). The report of E. Ringelblum and A. Berman addressed to the YIVO in New York, the Pen Club, and several Jewish personalities in New York, was published in the *YB,* 24 (1944), 3–9. Fragments of Ringelblum's diaries were published in *BFG* (January–March, 1948), 5–54.

127. Neustadt, II, 497–99; J. Turkow, *Azoy iz es geven,* pp. 88–95, 246–55, and *passim.*

128. Neustadt, II, 501–3.

129. *Ibid.,* II, 430.

130. See S. Kaczerginski, *Hurbn Vilne* (The Destruction of Vilna) (New York, 1947), pp. 178–216.

# 20

# EUROPEAN JEWISH RESEARCH
# ON THE HOLOCAUST

When the Nazi Holocaust struck, European Jewry was preparing to celebrate the one hundred and fiftieth anniversary of the French Revolution—a turning point in Jewish history, which had initiated a period of emancipation and civil equality for the Jews, resulting in their ever-increasing participation in the general culture and civilization. After a period of such optimistic prospects, the Holocaust, with its unprecedented suffering and enormous losses, hit us even more acutely. The impact of the tragedy, moreover, was widespread in extent. Unlike earlier catastrophes in Jewish history, which for the most part were confined to one country, the Nazi Holocaust spread over continental Europe.

The international character of the Holocaust is of tremendous import in the scientific study of the events. Our historiography has always been faced with problems much bigger than the history of any nation. Instead of covering just one national territory, we have to cover whole continents and dozens of countries with heterogenous political, economic, and social backgrounds and particular problems. The Jewish historiography of the Holocaust has an even more complex basis. Vast quantities of sources, scattered over dozens of countries in various languages, have been and are being compiled by as many governmental, municipal, communal, international, and private institutions, with diverse ideological and political approaches, with different goals and objectives. An attempt will be made here to present some characteristics of these materials, both as to their quantity and quality and as to the methods of reproducing and utilizing them.

The quantity, as already mentioned, is considerable. The Germans, in their sudden collapse, did not succeed in destroying all their records and documents, and much first-class material was found by the victorious Allied armies. Important parts of this official German material have been presented in the war crime trials all over Europe. To indicate the scope and abundance of these sources, it is sufficient to give a few illustrations.

The First Nuremberg War Crimes Trial Commission and the offices of the four Allied prosecutors presented an amazing amount of documents, evidence, and depositions. Some collections of this tremendous assemblage of sources have been edited. The extensive U.S. edition, with its bulky thirty-six volumes published to date, may be mentioned first,[1] as well as the smaller, preparatory edition in eight volumes with two supplementary volumes.[2] The French government followed with voluminous publications, as did the Soviet government.[3] The greater part of the unpublished sources (chiefly mimeographed materials) concerning Jews has been compiled (in multigraphed copies or, sometimes, in the originals) by several Jewish institutions, such as the World Jewish Congress (Institute of Jewish Affairs, New York), the YIVO (New York), and the Centre de Documentation Juive Contemporaine (CDJC) in Paris. This was the output of only one trial. The subsequent Nuremberg Trials and the scores of other trials in Bergen-Belsen, Dachau, Lüneburg, Warsaw, Cracow, Kharkov, Prague, Paris, and elsewhere brought immense quantities of new materials to light.[4]

Besides the central German archives and the archives of the foreign office, of the Oberkommando der Wehrmacht (German commanding staff), the navy, and the Alfred Rosenberg archives (ministry for the occupied territories in the East), the Allied armies seized and secured a considerable number of local archives, such as those of the Gestapo, SS, police, NSDAP, Hitler-jugend, local German administrations, and concentration camps. Archives of the Axis satellite governments (central and local) and of puppet governments in the occupied areas were also seized. In a few cases, some important materials were immediately secured for Jewish institutions. The Jewish underground forces in France were clever enough to get hold of the whole collection of the Commissariat aux Affaires Juives. These archives, containing about 40,000 items, are now in the CDJC, and have already been catalogued. Similarly, the Central Jewish Historical Commission (CJHC) in Poland was successful in preserving the large collection of the German Ghettoverwaltung in Lodz.

Jewish institutions also tried to gather materials in neutral countries. The Historiska Kommissionen (Historical Commission) in Stockholm, attached to the World Jewish Congress (WJC), is doing a useful job in collecting materials—from Swedish governmental archives, the records of the International Red Cross in Stockholm, and the Scandinavian wartime press—concerning rescue activities and Scandinavian public opinion on the Holocaust.

The archives of the Allied governments, which may contain many firsthand records and other important materials, have not yet been explored, as far as I know.

Underground records and archives are an important source of information. Valuable collections of Polish Jewish underground materials are in Warsaw, Israel, and New York; important French Jewish underground sources are in Paris.[5]

A different kind of source is presented by materials of the German-sponsored, Jewish puppet autonomy—in some countries both central and local, as for example the Union Générale des Israélites de France (UGIF), in other countries only local Jewish authorities—the Judenrat. Very important sources, too, are the minutes and records of other Jewish institutions— for instance, the Jewish Welfare Boards, the Jewish militia, and the Jewish civic courts. Only a small part of these archives have been preserved, however, for instance, the documents of the Judenräte in Lodz and Vilna, of some Jewish organizations in Paris, Cracow, and elsewhere.[6]

From the few above-mentioned examples, one may get an idea of the amount and scope of archival sources available for scholarly research. Nevertheless, in the postwar confusion much has been overlooked by the collecting teams, and is now trickling in through various channels. Much scattered material could still be collected.

Our historiography of the Holocaust is also confronted with another important problem: namely, the utilization of sources other than, or beyond the common definition of, "archival materials." The peculiar feature of this contemporary historiography is that the historians and archivists are instrumental not only in collecting and utilizing sources but also in producing sources. Never before in history could firsthand historical material be obtained and compiled from the historical figures themselves on such a large scale. Each German satellite, or collaborationist defendant, beginning with the top officials of the Axis regime, was bound to deliver detailed information, complete depositions, statements, accounts, and evidence. Well known is the story of a group of outstanding German generals, prisoners of war, assigned by a U.S. historical commission to write their personal record and statements on World War II, while awaiting trial. These are unusually intimate sources of information on previously top-secret, highly confidential topics. No other period in our history has been illuminated by this kind of inside information and background on the mechanisms and motives of anti-Jewish actions. These records, court depositions, evidence, prison diaries and confessions, and minutes of judicial inquiries, now number in the thousands. The minutes of almost all war crimes trials contain considerable material of Jewish concern. Unfortunately, not all these trials are being systematically traced, nor are all the Jewish materials being picked out by Jewish institutions. We do not even have an adequate indexing or cataloguing apparatus for all trials completed or in process.

Nor may we forget that these German sources are biased. They must be balanced and complemented by Jewish records and statements—interviews with Jewish survivors, reports by Jewish groups and individuals, and biographical materials. Moreover, the above-mentioned German sources cover only the political background, the organizational and administrative frame, of Jewish life under Nazi occupation. The inner Jewish history, the sufferings and the spiritual life, are rarely or falsely reflected in the German sources, and must be studied in Jewish sources. Jewish records were collected even during the war, from escaped Jewish victims and witnesses, in the neutral and Allied countries by the Vaad Hatzalah and Jewish Agency in Israel, the World Jewish Congress in New York, the Jewish Relief Committee in Geneva, and other organizations. After the liberation, many such records and interviews were collected by the Jewish historical commissions in Poland (about 3,300 items), in Germany (2,500), Italy (800), Linz, Vienna, and (in smaller numbers) in Hungary and Rumania.

Other important sources are Jewish (and non-Jewish) memoirs, diaries, journals, wills, poetry, fiction, and folklore. The assemblage of this material has just begun. The biggest collection of this kind in Europe is to be found in the CJHC in Warsaw (the present-day Jewish Historical Institute—JHI); a smaller but valuable collection is in the Centre de Documentation in Paris. A clear-cut distinction has to be made between this firsthand material and the rather prolific ex post facto memoiristic literature, a product of a postwar opportunism. The postwar literature will be discussed below.

Photographs—taken by the Germans and their assistants, by Jewish or non-Jewish underground members, or by Allied authorities after the liberation—have been collected by the CJHC; the Central Historical Commission (CHC) in Germany, Linz, Vienna, and Rome; the CDJC in Paris; and the Wiener Library in London. In addition, there are the private collections of a few Jewish photographers (for instance, Hirsch Kadushin-Kadish of Lithuania, now in New York; Nahman Sonnabend of Lodz, now in Stockholm). In general, the photographs are few, and are scattered over many places. The biggest collection in Europe seems to be that of the CJHC (several thousand photos).

Even smaller are the collections of songs of the Jewish ghetto, camps, underground, and partisans. We may suppose that most of these songs were lost with the people who sang them. The largest collections of songs are in the archives of the CHCs in Poland and Germany. The CHC in Germany has about sixty recordings of these songs. Some collections of musical scores and texts have been published.[7]

Collections of ghetto art (paintings, sculpture, etchings, and drawings) are in the CJHC and in the Centre de Documentation in Paris. Museum collections of all kinds of material illustrating Jewish life under Nazi rule, particularly in the camps, are in the Jewish sections of the state museums in Majdanek and Auschwitz in Poland.[8] The Jewish museum in Vilna seems to have a valuable collection which I have not seen.[9] The Jewish museum in Prague, greatly enlarged during the German occupation— thanks to a strange Nazi caprice to keep souvenirs of a "lost people"—is devoted to Jewish life.

Remarkable in abundance, the available materials must nevertheless be evaluated as to quality. I pointed out earlier that the vast official German sources are very valuable. But we must be especially cautious and critical with these sources, because they always tried to conceal the most ignominious anti-Jewish activities. For example, official German sources rarely mentioned anti-Jewish "pogroms" or "extermination," but were inclined to use euphemistic terms such as *Gross-Einsatz, Übersiedlung, Überstellung, Transport, Durchkämmung, Aktion, Himmelfahrt, Himmelkommando, auf Schmelz, Hasenjagd,* for extermination; *Sonderbehandlung,* for asphyxiation; *Bad- und Inhalationsräume,* for gas chambers; *Sonderkommando, Rollbrigade,* for extermination squads; *Bäckerei, Ziegelbrennerei,* for crematoriums; *Wohngebiet der Juden,* for ghetto; *Arbeitslager, Erziehungshaft, Schutzhaft, Durchgangslager (Dulag), Judenlager (Julag),* for concentration camps; *Effektenkammer,* for the storehouse for belongings of executed Jews; and *Sicherstellung, Treuhandstelle,* for diverse forms of confiscation of Jewish property. A special lexicon of this German terminology should be compiled. Some attempts have already been made, however unsatisfactory.[10]

In contradistinction to German sources, which endeavor to hide or diminish the true dimensions of the Jewish tragedy, Jewish sources give us a life-size picture of the catastrophe. But they too are biased; they are, understandably, inclined to exaggerate, to lay stress on macabre and gruesome aspects. They are not merely descriptive, but rather passionate and emotional, frequently incriminating, sometimes apologetic (for instance, if they originate from former members of the Judenräte militia, and other

Jewish officials). Not all witnesses are capable of giving a clear, objective report of what happened. For most Jews under the Nazi occupation, their opportunities to move about and make reliable observations were restricted; and, under the tension of Nazi persecution, rumors were frequently taken for truth. Many eyewitnesses were illiterate or too naïve to understand complicated situations, and hence give us a rather simplified record of events. They are not sophisticated enough to understand what an impartial statement is, and they therefore present—unconsciously and bona fide—personal judgments or wishes as facts. Frequently, the interviewers themselves are not sufficiently trained for their difficult task, and their own emotionalism or biases destroy the objectivity of their reports. In sum, I must admit that the collection of contemporary Jewish materials is not satisfactory; either in quality or in quantity. In order to get more and better material, we must train interviewers in this type of work, which is to utilize sociological (questionnaires, interviews, and so forth) rather than historical methods; sometimes there is only a chance of doing the exacting archival job of collecting or checking documents. Some attempts to work out the techniques and instructions for interviewers have already been made and published.[11] In some places where large groups of survivors are living now, the collection of these materials has been completely neglected. This is especially true for the U.S., and in a smaller degree, for Israel; but it is true also for some European countries—for instance, France, the Low Countries, England. The necessity to gather these data with the utmost speed cannot be emphasized enough, since the living source of information is diminishing from year to year, and the memories of the living fade and grow distorted with the passage of time.

## Research Activities in Europe

The activities of the various Jewish historical commissions may be summarized as follows:

### COLLECTING OF MATERIALS

All the historical commissions are engaged in the collection of sources. In addition, the historical commissions in Poland, Germany, Linz, Vienna, Rome, and the Centre de Documentation in Paris are engaged in the production of sources (through interviews, eyewitness records, questionnaires, statistical and social inquiries).

The following institutions are also collecting literature and bibliographical data on the Holocaust: The Wiener Library in London, the Centre Israélite d'Information and CDJC in Paris, the historical commission in Stockholm (preparing a bibliography of Judaica and anti-Semitica in the Scandinavian literature and press since 1939), CJHC (preparing a bibliography of Judaica and anti-Semitica since 1939 in Poland).

To date, no scientific, reliable, annotated bibliography of the Jewish catastrophe has been worked out.[12] This lack has resulted in duplication of research, contradictions, and controversial assertions. The absence of a serious, permanent instrument of evaluation and criticism fosters irresponsible graphomania and even the forgery of historical facts. Lack of an annotated bibliography also means lack of authoritative guidance and information, particularly necessary for this new field of study, and is a handicap in the popularization and consumption of Holocaust research.

## RESEARCH, EDITING, AND PUBLISHING

*Editing and publishing documents:* In Paris the CDJC has edited about ten volumes of documents,[13] approximately the same quantity as the CJHC.[14] Besides this, the CJHC and the CHC in Germany have published memoirs.[15] As to their historical value, and their scholarly apparatus, the books differ. In general, the later editions are the better in this regard. Documents and memoirs have also been published in Hungary, Rumania, and Bulgaria.[16]

*Periodicals:* The CHC in Germany published irregularly in Yiddish the journal *Fun letztn Hurbn,* devoted primarily to eyewitness accounts.[17] The CDJC in Paris issued the monthly *Le Monde Juif,* devoted to documents of the Holocaust and to current events in Jewish life. After a year's interruption, the monthly began reappearing in the fall of 1949 (until now twenty-four issues). The Wiener Library publishes the *Wiener Library Bulletin (WLB),* devoted mainly to bibliography and criticism. The JHI in Warsaw published in 1948 two issues and in summer 1949 the third of its quarterly *Bleter far Geschikhte (BFG),* devoted to scholarly research.

Monographic studies have been published by the CJHC in Poland (about ten volumes),[18] the CDJC in Paris,[19] and the CHC in Rome.[20]

## TRAINING OF SCHOLARS AND PERSONNEL

There is no possibility for training Jewish scholars in Europe. No qualified Jewish institute to do so exists. If some attempts in this direction have been made, they are rather modest and limited only to the preparation of workers for the practical purposes of interviewing, collecting material, and library research. The work of the historical commissions was carried out chiefly by the small number of Jewish scholars who escaped extermination and by amateurs. The largest staff of historians was concentrated in the

CJHC where it was also possible to instruct and introduce younger applicants to scholarly work. The staff of the CJHC is constantly diminished by emigration, however. The CDJC in Paris has some well-trained scholars but has great difficulties in procuring researchers with good Judaic background for its staff. Some of the best publications of the CDJC have been done by prominent outside investigators. The third institution with a competent scholarly, but small staff is the Wiener Library in London. The work of the other historical commissions has been carried on by amateurs. The CHC in Germany has tried to raise the standards of its work by arranging short training courses for field workers. But the courses failed to produce the desired effects, since it was impossible to fill the gaps in the Judaistic and general education of the students by a simple short seminar.

To meet the need for methodological instruction, some historical commissions, as well as some individual scholars, have published papers about methodology and techniques of the Holocaust research. A remarkable further step toward a better elaborated methodology and better cooperation and coordination was the first conference of the European historical commissions in Paris, in December 1947.[21]

### INDIVIDUAL LITERARY, BIOGRAPHICAL, AND SCHOLARLY WORK ON THE HOLOCAUST

Even the amateurish work of some of the historical commissions is an advance over the work in this field by individuals. The prolific semi-historical, autobiographical output on the recent Jewish tragedy has deep psychological and sociological roots. Even the inferior products of this phenomenon cannot be routinely dismissed as mere graphomania but should be carefully studied as symptomatic of significant sociopsychological developments. This is not the place to discuss this sociopsychological background. But I should note that the outpouring of memoirs and chronicles on the Holocaust is enormous, beyond comparison with the production of memoirs after other important events in Jewish history. It seems that the Holocaust has evoked thousands of Nathan Neta Hannovers. But not only Jewish postwar literature is so productive: the French and Polish entries about German occupation are almost as numerous. In France, for instance, I have found more than a thousand entries (books and pamphlets) on this subject; in Polish and Hungarian, several hundred; in Dutch, Czech, and Rumanian, several dozen publications. The preferred subjects of these non-Jewish books are: the concentration camps, prisons, labor camps and plants, and the underground resistance. The Jewish materials in these publications have not yet been explored.

To show how large the Jewish literature is, I will cite only one example. A tentative bibliography on the Warsaw ghetto, prepared by Z.

Szajkowski, cites 113 entries.[22] This list could easily be increased to about 200 entries (only books and pamphlets). It may well be assumed that many of these publications are of little value.

Generally speaking, there are many good books written by individual scholars and litterateurs. There are also several outstanding books among the memoirs. But the bulk of this numerous output may be divided roughly into two groups: First, there are the works written by inadequately trained amateurs, zealous and ambitious, but using unchecked materials and unreliable sources, credulous, taking all for granted, sometimes striving for sensationalism to bring their work into the market. The approach is journalistic; the efforts to give the books a literary form and to embellish them with a "poetic touch" are, in most cases, failures. Second, and even more dangerous and harmful, is a group of publications which tends to adjust the historical facts to preconceived theories or political biases. For instance, in the history of the famous Warsaw ghetto uprising, almost every political party is concerned with its own interpretation. Sometimes the writers are very selective in the choice of sources and facts. Sometimes the writer is a publicity seeker or attempts to put himself or his friends in a favorable light with deliberate or unconscious misrepresentation. *Nomina sunt odiosa.*

It may be admitted that the vulgarization of literary and scholarly work is a common disease and a threatening phenomenon in the postwar cultural life of the *She'erit Hapletah* (The Saving Remnant, that is, the Jewish survivors of the destruction). There are numerous justifications. The almost complete extinction of the Jewish intelligentsia by the Nazis; the major shift of Jewish population, which displaced acknowledged authorities and centers of learning, art, and scholarship, and mixed different milieus; the new type of unsophisticated and naïve reader, hungry for each kind of literature and accepting everything uncritically—all created a favorable public for inferior literary products. As it happens, this "golden age" for newcomers promoted not only serious and gifted men but the crowd of graphomaniacs who entered the field. Pretense, sensationalism, banalities, falsehoods—and the growing mistrust of the public toward all Holocaust literature—are the results. In this case we cannot act according to the principle *tout comprendre est tout excuser.* Indulgence and tolerance, or even indifference, toward these abuses can greatly damage our discipline. If nothing is done to halt this development, these publications may conceivably be used in the future as reliable sources. Monographs based on these sources of information should therefore be instantly checked and corrected. In conclusion, only a systematic, current, critical bibliography can help us distinguish the chaff from the wheat.

## Jewish Institutes of Research in Europe

I have investigated or taken an active part in Jewish research work in Poland, Germany, France, and England, and have met and discussed problems with representatives of historical research institutions in Austria, Bulgaria, Rumania, Czechoslovakia, Greece, Italy, Hungary, the Low Countries, Yugoslavia, Sweden, and Switzerland. This gave me the chance to draw the following picture of the activities in this field across Europe.

### POLAND

Until 1939 Poland was the biggest center of Jewish cultural life and scholarship in Europe. After 1939, that country was the locale of the cruel slaughter of 3 million Polish Jews and the Golgotha of hundreds of thousands of Western and Central European Jews. No wonder that Holocaust research developed there first and on the largest scale. Just after the Germans entered Warsaw, the first Jewish statistical commission (with Lipowski, Chilinowicz, and Moshe Mark-Prager) was established, but was soon discontinued. A few months later (1940), the famous "Oneg Shabbath" (this name was used to conceal the nature of the activities from the Germans), the underground Warsaw ghetto archives, headed by Emanuel Ringelblum, was created. Many contemporary records, statistics, studies, social inquiries, literary and scholarly papers, newspapers, and underground press clippings were collected and buried in safe iron containers during the massive German extermination action, in August 1942.[23] The excavation of this archival treasure began in the summer of 1946 and a portion of the hidden materials have been rescued and have been incorporated into the archives of the CJHC-JHI in Warsaw as a separate unit.[24] Excavation activities and the search for the remainder of the hidden materials are continuing.

After the liberation, the CJHC was founded by me in Lublin in 1944; it was moved in 1945 to Lodz, and in 1948 to Warsaw. Besides the headquarters in Lodz, branches were established in 1945 in Warsaw, Cracow, Bialystok, Katowice, Wrocław, Lublin, and other localities. The staff numbered about twenty scholars and from sixty to seventy technical and administrative personnel. In 1948, the name was changed to the Jewish Historical Institute (JHI) and the objectives of research were enlarged to the study of the "history of the Polish Jews from the beginnings to the present time." But, as I understand, these ambitious plans have not yet been realized.

The development of the CJHC was for the first two years characterized by an inner struggle. The leadership and the executive officers in Lodz favored a scholarly approach without political biases, and prepared publications of a technical, bibliographical, and monographic character. The opponents inside the CJHC (the Cracow branch) and outside (a left-wing group in the Central Committee of Polish Jews, to whose supervision and financial maintenance the CJHC was subject) advocated a policy of publishing for popular consumption, to serve propaganda purposes and fight against fascism. The split in policy is reflected in the respective publications —the headquarters specializing in editions of documents and monographs; the Cracow branch, in publishing belles-lettres, memoirs, poetry, and so forth. Later, the editorial activities of the branches were canceled, and their work was adjusted to the general standards of the CJHC. I can no longer report from personal experience about the latest developments, since I left Poland in the summer of 1946 and resigned from my post as director of the CJHC at that time. As I understand it, the present situation is that the JHI has to adjust itself to the general cultural and political developments in that country.

The CJHC–JHI has, I believe, the largest and most valuable European collection of sources on the Holocaust. The cataloguing of these archives is progressing rather slowly, however, as is the other reference and indexing work. The CJHC has published to date about forty books and pamphlets in Polish and Yiddish.

The research on the Holocaust in Poland is not confined only to the CJHC. For the time being, the most informative bibliography on the German crimes is to be found in a non-Jewish publication—the quarterly of the Institute for National Remembrance in Warsaw, *Dzieje Najnowsze* (Recent History). Also, the three volumes of *German Crimes in Poland* (published in Polish and in English),[25] edited by the Polish War Crimes Commission, contain a series of valuable contributions on the Holocaust. Besides, some good studies on the concentration camps (Oświęcim, Majdanek, Stutthof, and others), with a very large amount of material of Jewish interest, and some commendable memoirs and diaries by Jewish authors have been brought out by Polish publishers. Also, Jewish publishers outside the CJHC have put out some interesting literary and scholarly publications in Yiddish on the Holocaust.[26]

### FRANCE

The most important Jewish institution in France for Holocaust studies is the CDJC founded in 1943 in Grenoble by its devoted and zealous president, Itzhak Schneersohn. The CDJC specialized at first in compiling sources for Jewish history in France and North Africa (Algiers and Tunis). This compilation has been completed in a very remarkable manner and is better ordered and catalogued than, for instance, the archives of the CJHC. The latest development of the CDJC is the extension of its activities to the sources and history of the Holocaust in other European countries. As was mentioned above, the CDJC organized the first European conference of the Jewish historical commissions in Paris in December 1947. Sixteen European historical commissions and more than fifty Jewish scholars, writers, and students participated in this meeting; reports of activities, and technical and methodological addresses were made; scholarly papers were read and organizational problems were discussed. The conference resulted in the creation of a coordinating committee for the Jewish historical commissions in Europe. But the activities of the new body are handicapped by the lack of both financial means and executive power. Nevertheless, in order to strengthen the ties and continue this very necessary and far-reaching program, the CDJC is planning a second European conference in connection with a European exhibition on the Jewish Catastrophe and reconstruction.[27] The publications of the CDJC (about twenty books and *Le Monde Juif*) represent a valuable contribution to the history of the Holocaust. They are all edited in French. The first publications in Yiddish are now in print and others are in preparation.[28]

A second Centre de Documentation (CD) has been established with the Union des Sociétés Juives en France, also originating from underground activities during the German occupation. The CD has very limited financial means, no trained staff, and is sustained mainly by the devotion of its director. The CD has collected valuable material for the history of the Jewish underground in France (particularly of the Jewish leftist and Communist organizations) and of Jewish social and cultural activities in the concentration camps; has stored manuscripts of Jewish writers; has assembled a museum of Jewish paintings, objects, and memorabilia; and has gathered the Jewish underground press. On the basis of this material only three books have been issued to date.[29]

A third institution, the Centre Israélite d'Information in Paris, has perhaps the biggest collection of books, pamphlets, and other printed or mimeographed materials, especially in French, concerning racial problems and persecution. Unfortunately, this institution has no means to order or catalogue its collection. The *Bulletin d'Information* published by the Centre de Documentation Israélite was discontinued in 1948. In general, this center exists today only as an appendix to the Centre de Documentation Politique. Both have been founded and conducted by an expert bibliographer, M. Vanikoff. According to the information given me by Vanikoff, the Centre de Documentation Politique has about 40,000 items, in which many Jewish entries may be included.[30]

Scattered valuable materials have been collected by such institutions as the Consistoire Central de France, the Conseil Représentatif des Juifs de France—CRIF (Central Representation of the French Jews), and the Alliance Israélite Universelle. The Committee of Sephardic Jews and the *Cahiers Sephardis,* under the able and industrious Sam Lévy, assembled almost full documentation on the tragic fate of the Sephardic communities in France.[31]

The Centre d'Études "to study the thousand-year history of the Polish Jews," attached to the Association of Polish Jews (9, rue Guy Patin) in Paris, may be mentioned here merely for registration. Neither in its collections nor in the qualifications of its directors is there any guarantee of a serious approach to its allegedly scholarly objectives. At any rate, the gigantic aims and tasks which this institution claims constantly to be willing to realize cannot be attained in the slightest degree by its material and spiritual capacities, and one cannot help getting an impression of irresponsibility on the part of the leaders.

The existence of so many Jewish research centers in Paris is rather confusing. For numerous reasons a merger of these institutions in the near future is not conceivable. Even efforts to bring about a closer cooperation have failed until the present day.

### ENGLAND

England was fortunately not a Nazi-occupied country, and should therefore be treated in our survey at a later place, together with the neutral countries. But the Wiener Library must be included in one of the first sections in this survey, for several reasons. This library, which originated in Amsterdam in 1934 as part of the Jewish Central Information Office and moved to London in the beginning of World War II, was the first scholarly institution to fight against Nazi discrimination. Its collection of about 60,000 books, pamphlets, and newspapers, only one-half of which is catalogued, is devoted not only to the Jewish Catastrophe but also to general aspects of World War II, the German problem, Nazism and racism, the Arab question, and Zionism. This is the largest and best-organized Jewish collection of books in Europe for the study of the above-mentioned problems. A cross-reference catalogue is now in preparation. I have already noted that the library has a competent scholarly staff and an expert and devoted director (Alfred Wiener). The library has published some books, both of Jewish and non-Jewish interest. In general, in the Jewish field its publishing activities are rather limited (small issues of photostatic reproductions of documents, and a few mimeographed survivors' reports). Like the other services of the Wiener Library, the bibliographical *Bulletin* is aimed to supply general information.[32]

### GERMANY

The CHC in the U.S.-occupied zone of Germany was established in Munich at the end of 1945 by the Central Committee of Liberated Jews. The CHC, a central organization, included about forty regional and local branches in the U.S. zone. In 1947–1948, the CHC extended its activities to the

British, French, and Russian zones. The CHC specialized in collecting eye-witness reports. These reports are not of uniform value, however. Many of them were drawn up by poorly instructed interviewers in the branches, which could not be efficiently controlled by the central office. These records can be used for scientific purposes only with reservation and much critic-ism. The eyewitness reports chiefly cover the East European areas, being col-lected from Jewish displaced persons (DPs) and infiltrees. As few German Jews made depositions or submitted their personal experiences or notes to the CHC, the record of what happened to the German Jews in the Nazi period is very small. Curiously enough, the indigenous German Jewish residents do not show much interest in their past, and the German Jewish communities could not afford up to now to build an apparatus for historical research. Of course, the traditions of German Jewry in this regard are quite different from those of other European Jews. At any rate, the CHC pro-cured some valuable official German documentation—for instance, Nazi documents concerning the Jews in Munich and Bavaria. The CHC has, moreover, worked out an exhaustive inquiry for all Jewish settlements, camps, and execution sites in Germany, and has succeeded in carrying it out through German officials (by order of the military government) in all zones of occupied Germany. This unique collection, even when one-sided, gives a comprehensive picture, covering every place in Germany. Besides materials for the history of the Holocaust, the CHC also collected con-temporary publications of Jewish interest in Germany—DP and German Jewish newspapers and printed materials, photographs, and the like—and created in this way a basis for the archives of the *She'erit Hapletah* in Germany. Among its valuable acquisitions are the abandoned archives of some Jewish communities in Germany (particularly in Franconia), going back to the seventeenth century.[33]

The main purpose of the CHC journal *Fun letztn Hurbn* was to publish eyewitness accounts collected by the CHC and thereby to stimulate further eyewitness depositions. But the approach of the editor is rather un-scholarly; the accounts are editorially corrected and stylistically changed, a method rather unorthodox in the publication of documents. The editor, Israel Kaplan, explains this policy by claiming that his journal is destined for popular consumption, rather than for scholarly research. A smaller portion of the magazine was devoted to the publication of documents from the CHC archives and to current bibliography (including only articles from Jewish newspapers in Germany); finally, few good monographic studies appeared. Notwithstanding the above-mentioned technical shortcomings, this journal was the best of its kind (publication of eyewitness records) in our literature, and credit must be given both to the editor and to the di-rector of the CHC, M. Feigenbaum, for their fine achievement in publish-ing and for their industry, zeal, integrity, and ingenuity in collecting sources, which made the CHC archives one of the richest collections of its kind in Europe.

The recent mass emigration movement from the DP camps of Germany brought an important turn for the CHC. The Central Committee of Liberated Jews soon decided to transfer the materials of the CHC to Israel, and this decision was carried out at the end of 1948; the CHC later discontinued its activities. Before its liquidation, the CHC and its branches still managed to publish a few books.[34]

Besides the CHC and its branches, two independent Jewish historical commissions operated in the British zone of occupation—the historical commission attached to the Central Committee of Liberated Jews in Bergen-Belsen, and the historical commission in Göttingen, with rather limited activities. The historical commission in Bergen-Belsen issued two books (a collection of ghetto songs and an album of pictures). The historical commission in Göttingen issued two small bulletins and was busy with gathering Jewish documents and museum materials.

Also outside the CHC, some research work has been done by individuals on the recent catastrophe. A collection of eyewitness records gathered by a Lithuanian Jew (Leib Konyuchovsky) in three years of devoted work covering all the Jewish settlements in Lithuania except Kovno is remarkable. These records have been prepared very carefully and are the most valuable I have seen in Germany. Recently there have appeared monographic studies on the life and destruction of the Jews in Kovno (J. Gar); Latvia (M. Kaufman); Częstochowa, Otwock, Karczew, and Falenica (B. Orenstein); Poland (myself); Złoczów (S. Mayer); Sierpiec and Warsaw (H. Fenigstein); Lwów (myself); and Szawle (L. Shalit); some methodological and technical studies in the literary journals of the *She'erit Hapletah* (*Shriftn, Hemshekh*); and two Polish books of memoirs, covering personal experiences in seven concentration camps and ghettos (T. Stabholz) and in Sosnowiec (P. Wiederman). Besides these contributions, much inferior material has been published by amateurs. My impression is that only in Germany has so much irresponsible and sometimes harmful writing been published. It has finally evoked a sharp reaction on the part of the more responsible members of the *She'erit Hapletah* against such "irresponsible and illiterate" work and "uncouth" utterances.[35]

### AUSTRIA

Two Jewish historical commissions—one in Linz, U.S. zone, the second in Vienna—are for the most part occupied in gathering evidence against Nazi criminals in Austria. For this purpose they have collected numerous eyewitness records and depositions, of value both from the judicial and the historical point of view; minutes of trials (processed in Austria) on Nazi crimes, and of inquiries and interrogations. These commissions have not engaged in publication to date.[36]

In Vienna a private publisher started a series of small leaflets on the Jewish tragedy, for popular consumption (of little historical value).

There are some items in the Austro-German literature which deal directly with the Jewish problem or indirectly contain some Jewish details. A bibliographical study has yet to be made.

### ITALY

Neither the Central Committee of the Jewish DPs nor the Italian Jewish community has established a historical commission. The CHC of the PHaH (the Hebrew abbreviation for the joint organization of former Jewish partisan fighters, halutzim, and ex-servicemen) plays an important role in the collection of materials in Italy. Established in Poland in 1945, the CHC of the PHaH moved to Austria, then to Milan, and later to Rome. Its aims have been to collect materials and carry on research on the history of the Jewish resistance against Nazi oppression in Eastern Europe. The PHaH CHC now possesses about 700 biographical reports on Jewish fighters; materials on about twenty-five Jewish partisan detachments; about a hundred firsthand depositions by Jewish fighters; and eyewitness records, diaries, and other materials. A well-documented book on the Jewish role in the partisan movement in Soviet Russia has been published by M. Kaganovitch (chairman of the CHC). But the activities of the CHC of the PHaH had to be discontinued for the same reason as in Germany; the collections of the CHC in Rome are already on their way to Israel, where they are to be incorporated in the Yad Vashem archives.[37]

As in Austria and Germany, the indigenous Jewish population has no share in this research work. Some individual efforts in this field have not gone far to date.

### CZECHOSLOVAKIA

In Prague some materials were gathered in 1945–1946 by the Jewish Agency and were shipped to Israel. A few small publications, especially about Terezin (Theresienstadt), appeared. Zidovske Dokumentacna Akcia (Jewish Historical Commission) in Bratislava has started a more systematic collection of sources for research into the history of the Jews in Slovakia.[38]

### BULGARIA

The Jewish Scientific Institute in Sofia has collected a considerable quantity of official German and Bulgarian material for the history of the Jews in that country during World War II. The archives have been ordered and catalogued. A few books and pamphlets have been published. Also the journal *Novi Dni*—primarily devoted to the analysis of actual Jewish problems, fiction, and poetry—has given some place to historical and statistical monographs on World War II. I have no information as to how much the future development of this institute will be affected by the almost complete emigration of Bulgarian Jews to Israel.[39]

### RUMANIA

Although no historical commission exists in Rumania, some important contributions have been made by individuals. Outstanding is the three-volume publication of documentary and statistical materials prepared by Matatias Carp (in his work *Cartea Neagra*). A series of booklets edited by private publishers or by organizations has been written for popular consumption (most of them published by "Cartea Rossa" or by "Hehalutz"). As I understand it, A. M. Halévy, a well-known Rumanian Jewish scholar, is endeavoring to set up a Jewish historical institute to collect materials and centralize the scattered Jewish research in this field.[40]

### HUNGARY

Some institution for Jewish research in this field seems to exist in Hungary, in Budapest. Three years ago representatives of a Jewish historical commission in Budapest got in touch with me in Lodz, reported their activities, and presented their first publications. Since then, I have tried to get in touch with the historical commission, but without results. No representative from Hungary came to the European conference of the historical commissions held in Paris in December 1947. Only a short written report had been sent.[41] Because of the lack of sufficient reliable information, my report on the historical commission in Hungary must be rather general. I have learned from other sources, however, that dozens of books and pamphlets on the Holocaust have been published in Hungary. The valuable report of Rezsö Kasztner and the well-documented books of Eugene Lévai (one has been published in English) must be mentioned first. Some books about concentration camps (particularly about Auschwitz) have appeared. The quantity of books relating to personal experiences in the labor detachments and labor camps is truly remarkable.[42]

### GREECE

No Jewish historical commission exists. Some useful historical publications have been prepared by individuals in Salonika, Athens, and Corfu.[43]

### YUGOSLAVIA

The extermination of the greatest part of the Yugoslavian Jewish population has not yet been reflected in a scholarly Jewish or non-Jewish publication. Dr. Weiss, president of the Union of Jewish Communities formed in Yugoslavia after the liberation and Yugoslav representative at the International Military Tribunal in Nuremberg, was much concerned in initiating a scholarly research project in this field, and discussed with me in 1946 the problems of organization and research. As far as I know, no action followed. In the meantime, the emigration of Yugoslav Jews changed the situation in that country.

In the voluminous publications of the Yugoslavian War Crimes State Commission only scattered materials of Jewish concern may be found.[44]

### RUSSIA

I am unable to present a comprehensive picture about Russia, as information is very scarce. An enormous number of documents, eyewitness records, and depositions of war crimes trial defendants have been collected by the Russian War Crimes Commission and in the numerous local war crimes trials in various Russian cities. A considerable quantity of material was also stored with the Jewish Anti-Fascist Committee in Moscow, and with the Organization Committee of the Polish Jews in Moscow. But neither of these institutions exists any longer (the Anti-Fascist Committee was dissolved at the end of 1948), and detailed information on what happened to the rich archives of these organizations, which seemed to be well arranged and catalogued, has not been available to me. Ilya Ehrenburg's publications of documents and eyewitness records (published in Russian and Yiddish) seem to be based mainly on these collections. Some parts of the materials stored with the official Soviet archives have been published by the Extraordinary State Committee for Investigation of the Crimes of the German Fascist Occupiers in the series *Dokumenty obvinyayout* (Documents Accuse) (Moscow, 1944). The first two volumes of this series contain much Jewish material.

Besides these publications, smaller contributions of rather journalistic character are scattered in periodicals.[45]

### THE LOW COUNTRIES

In Holland a series of books and pamphlets has been printed describing the Jewish fate and sufferings. Some of these publications are very valuable.[46]

In Belgium the historical output on the Holocaust is very modest. A report submitted by the Belgian government to the war crimes trial court in Nuremberg, and some articles in the *Revue Juive* in Brussels, may be mentioned. Jewish historical commissions devoted to research on the Holocaust do not exist in either country.

### SWEDEN

The Jewish Historical Commission collects materials from the archives of the Swedish government, the International Red Cross, and from Scandinavian newspapers during World War II.[47]

### SWITZERLAND

The Jewish Historical Commission, established in 1947, has devised a big program for collecting and research, but has not yet been able to begin carrying it out.[48] During the war, the Jewish Relief Committee in Geneva collected and published, in mimeographed form, a series of eyewitness records from Poland, edited by Dr. A. Silberschein.

## Conclusions

Jewish scholars and Jewish historical societies should give more attention to this field of research, which is abandoned and mostly in the hands of amateurs. These amateurs, among whom we may find many devoted and gifted men, need instruction, leadership, guidance, and assistance. It is particularly necesary to work out a methodology for this research; to train and instruct interviewers, archivists, and librarians, as well as research students; to carry on systematic bibliographic registration; to begin publishing an annotated bibliography and current, critical evaluations of new publications. It would be advisable to coordinate the activities of all the European commissions, to assist them in such tasks as the uniform cataloguing and indexing of their collections, and finally, by means of world-wide cooperation, to draft a minimum plan for a longer period (several years) for a coordinated research program. The Jewish scholarly institutes and historical societies of the United States and Israel should be the initiators and organizers of these activities. This paper is fully justified if it evokes discussion in this direction.

❦ This essay is based on a paper read at the annual meeting of the American Academy for Jewish Research held on December 26, 1948. It was later published under the title "European Jewish Research on the Recent Jewish Catastrophe in 1939–1945" in the *Proceedings of the Academy,* 18 (1949), 179–211. This study is confined to an analysis of Jewish research activities on the Holocaust as far as they were carried on in Europe at the time of this writing.

## Notes

Many sources partially cited in the following notes may be found in the more comprehensive *Guide to Jewish History under the Nazi Impact,* compiled by Jacob Robinson and Philip Friedman (New York, 1960).

1. *IMT*.

2. *NCA*. For a critical examination from the Jewish point of view, see Joseph Guttman, "The American Publication of the Nuremberg Documents" (Yiddish), *YB*, 30 (1947), 3–20.

3. *IMT*, French edition; and *Le Procès de Nuremberg* (Paris, 1946), 4 vols. The Russian edition was not available to me.

4. Herbert Wechsler, professor of law at Columbia University and member of the U.S. Tribunal at Nuremberg, reported, at the annual meeting of the Conference of Jewish Relations on April 3, 1949, on the twelve subsequent Nuremberg cases conducted by the U.S. prosecutors. Each of these cases contains about 10,000 pages of hearings—apart from the documentation, which amounts to approximately 1 million pages. Some parts of this vast material have been mimeographed and stored with the Law Library of Columbia University. In Dachau, 489 separate cases have been conducted against 672 defendants. Nothing of these materials has been published to date. Almost all of the above-mentioned cases contain valuable Jewish material—especially the trials of the German physicians; SS-Obergruppenführer Oswald Pohl and his assistants (the administrators of the concentration camps); Otto Ohlendorf and accomplices (Einsatzgruppen [extermination squads]); SS-Brigadeführer Ernst von Weizsäcker and the other officials of the German foreign office.

To this output of some of the trials conducted by U.S. authorities in Germany, we must add materials from the numerous trials conducted in Germany by British, French, Russian, and German prosecutors; from the trials conducted in all allied countries (for instance, the trials in Warsaw of the top officials of the German administration of the Government General [GG] and of the officials of the Oświęcim [Auschwitz] concentration camp, trials which yielded hundreds of thousands of pages of hearings, proceedings, and documentation), and we can then imagine how large is the total quantity of unpublished materials.

Besides the above-mentioned publications of the Nuremberg Trials, there are other published versions of these sources. The publications of the United Nations War Crimes Commission, *Law Reports of Trials of War Criminals,* 15 vols. (London, 1947), includes the following trials: Bergen-Belsen (vol. II), Zyklon B (vol. VII), Artur Greiser (vol. XIII), Mauthausen (vol. XIV). In Poland the proceedings of the trials of Amon Goeth (commander of the Płaszów concentration camp) and SS-Obergruppenführer Artur Greiser, Gauleiter and Reichstatthalter of the Wartheland (governor of the Nazi-occupied Polish provinces incorporated into the Reich), and the hearings on Josef Bühler and some German generals by the Central Commission for Investigation of German Crimes in Poland were published in Polish in the volume *Zburzenie Warszawy* (The Destruction of Warsaw) (Warsaw, 1946). In France, the proceedings of the trial of Marshal Pétain; Prime Minister Pierre Laval; and of Xavier Vallat, the head of the Commissariat aux Affaires Juives, have been published. See M. J. Goldbloom, "War Crimes Trials," *American Jewish Year Book,* 50 (1949), 494–500 (deals chiefly with the Nuremberg Trials).

5. French Jewish underground materials are in the Centre de Documentation, Paris. Polish and Polish Jewish materials are in the archives of the CJHC in Warsaw; the Instytut Pamięci Narodowej (Institute of National Remembrance) in Warsaw; the private collection of Dr. I. Schwartzbart, New

York; in the collection of the Jewish Labor Bund in New York—published in New York in part in 1949, in the volume *In di yorn fun yidishn hurbn* (In the Years of the Jewish Destruction); and in Israel in the materials of the Zionist movement and the Hehalutz—partly published in Tel Aviv, in 1946–1948, by Melekh Neustadt in Hebrew and in Yiddish under the title *Hurbn un oyfshtand fun di yidn in varshe* (The Destruction and the Uprising of the Jews in Warsaw).

6. Many materials about the UGIF and the Jewish communities in France under the Nazi occupation are included in the archives of the Consistoire Central de France; see the report of Léon Meiss in *Les Juifs en Europe, 1939–1945* (Paris, 1949), pp. 103–7. The archives of the Jüdische Soziale Hilfe in Cracow, a central welfare agency in the GG, were discovered after the liberation and transferred from Cracow to the CJHC.

7. The best of these publications is *Lider fun di getos un lagern* (Songs of the Ghettos and Camps), comp. by Shmerke Kaczerginski, ed. by H. Leivick, with music arranged by M. Gelbart (New York, 1949).

8. See J. Kermisz, "Le Musée Juif à Auschwitz," in *Les Juifs en Europe,* pp. 164–65; J. Słowacki and S. Zborowski, *Oświęcim* (published by the Committee for the Conservation of Oświęcim, 1947); P. Sobolewski-Zagórska, *Muzeum Państwowe na Majdanku* (The State Museum in Majdanek), n.p., n.d.

9. A description of the Jewish museum in Vilna and its collections may be found in F. Novick, *Eyrope tsvishn milkhomeh un sholem* (Europe Between War and Peace) (New York, 1948), pp. 314–20.

10. A few examples are H. Pacht, *Nazi Deutsch: A Glossary of Contemporary German Usage* (New York, 1944); "Aus dem Wörterbuch des Unmenschen" (by several authors signed mostly by initials). A series of articles in *Die Wandlung* (1946, 1947); N. Blumental, *Słowa niewinne* (Innocent Words) (Lodz, 1946), an unfinished compilation from *A* to *I*.

11. Jacob Lestschinsky, *Di yidishe katastrofe: Di metode fun ir forshung* (The Jewish Catastrophe: The Method for its Research) (New York, 1944). Also Philip Friedman et al., eds., *Metodologishe onvayzungen tsum oysforshn dem hurbn fun poylishn yid tum* (Methodological Instructions for Research on the Destruction of Polish Jewry) (Lodz, 1945); this booklet has been partly reprinted by the CHC in Germany and used for instructional purposes.

12. Only scattered bibliographical fragments on special problems have been published, covering but a fraction of the respective materials. Among the more important are the studies of Z. Szajkowski, "The Jewish Press in Germany, Austria, Italy, and Sweden" (Yiddish), *YB,* 28 (1946), 397–408; "Maps of Concentration Camps and Ghettos" (Yiddish), 30 (1947) 259–79; B. Shochetman, "Bibliography of Literature on the Catastrophe" (Hebrew), in *Reshumoth,* n.s. 4 (Tel Aviv, 1947), 209–32; Shmuel Friedman, "The Jewish Catastrophe in Our Literature" (Hebrew), in the *Annual Book of Davar* (Tel Aviv, 1947), pp. 265–96; L. C. Tihany, "Bibliography of Post-Armistice Hungarian Historiography," in *American Slavic and East-European Review,* 6 (1947), 158–75; Hans Mayer, "Vom 'Braunbuch' zum 'SS-Staat' " in *Jüdische Rundschau* (Marburg/Lahn), nos. 14–15 (1947), pp. 43–44, 50; M. Kaganovitch, "Literature of Jewish Resistance and Fighting Against the Nazis" (Yiddish), *Im Gang* (Rome), no. 8–10 (1947), pp. 54–65; Wanda Kiedrzynska, "Recollections from

German Concentration Camps in Polish Literature" (Polish), *Dzieje Najnowsze* (Warsaw), vol. 1 (1947); my "Hundred Books in Yiddish on the Catastrophe and Heroism" (Yiddish), *JBA* 8 (1949), 122–32; 9 (1950), 80–92; Helen Conover, comp., "The Nazi State, War Crimes, and War Criminals," Washington, D.C.: Library of Congress, August 1945 (mimeographed); Raphael Lemkin, *Axis Rule in Occupied Europe* (Washington, D.C., 1944), bibliography of Nazi legislation, pp. 641–64; Franz Ahrens, *Widerstandsliteratur: Ein Querschnitt durch die Literatur über die Verfolgungen und den Widerstand im Dritten Reiche* (Hamburg, 1948).

13. These books are on the following topics: anti-Jewish legislation in Nazi-occupied and Vichy France; Jews in southeastern France under Italian occupation; the looting of Jewish objects of art and libraries by the Nazis; the Jewish resistance in France; and the persecution of Jews in Western and Eastern Europe (at least two bulky volumes of documents, compiled from the collections of the Nuremberg Military Tribunal).

14. These volumes treat the following subjects and materials: documents and eyewitness records about camps, extermination actions, the ghetto in Lodz, Jewish resistance in Poland, an album of photographs, proceedings of the Amon Goeth Trial, eyewitness records about Bełżec, Klementów, Jewish life in hiding and on "Aryan" papers.

15. The CJHC in Poland has published memoirs of the Janowski camp in Lwów, the slave labor factory in Skarzyska, the Jewish resistance movement in Cracow and environs, and Jewish martyrdom in Warsaw. The CHC in Germany has published memoirs about Jewish sufferings in several small towns in Poland (Skałat, Biała Podlaska, Międzyrzec Podlaski).

16. These publications include the three-volume edition of Matatias Carp, *Cartea Neagra* (The Suffering of the Jews in Rumania, 1940–1944) (Bucharest, 1946–1948), in Rumania; *Dokumenty* (Documents) (Sofia, 1945) by Natan Greenberg and the memoirs of Rabbi Daniel Zion, in Bulgaria; the three books of Jenö (Eugene) Lévai (one of which, *The Black Book on the Martyrdom of Hungarian Jewry,* has been published in English translation in Zurich, 1948); and the report of Rezsö Kasztner on the rescue activities in 1942–1944 in Hungary, and some other studies.

17. The first issue appeared in August 1946; the last (no. 10) in December 1948.

18. These monographs are on the following subjects: the extermination of the Jews in Lwów, Sosnowiec, Żółkiew, and Cracow; the uprisings in Warsaw and Bialystok; Treblinka; a statistical study of the Jewish population in Lodz, Cracow, and Lublin under the Nazis; Jewish poetry in the ghettos and concentration camps; a lexicon of Nazi terms, and other topics.

19. These monographs are on Jewish organizations in France under the Nazis; Jewish resistance; the press and public opinion in France; the concentration camps; Drancy; and the yellow badge.

20. M. Kaganovitch, *Der yidisher ontayl in der partizaner-bavegung fun Soviet-Rusland* (The Participation of Jews in the Partisan Movement of Soviet Russia) (Rome–New York, 1948).

21. At the conference of the Jewish historical commissions in Paris (November 30 to December 9, 1947), some papers on the techniques and methods of research were read by E. M. Lévy, N. Moch, L. Poliakov, H. Mon-

neray, A. M. Halévy, I. Schneersohn, myself, and others. These addresses, as well as the proceedings of the conference and the scholarly papers and reports of activities presented at the conference, have been published by CDJC in *Les Juifs en Europe, 1939–1945* (Paris, 1949).

I have published the following studies devoted to problems of the Holocaust research: "The Research on Our Catastrophe" (Yiddish), *Kiyoum* (Paris), no. 1 (1948), 47–54; the same essay was published in *Shriftn fun shrayberfarband fun der sheyres hapleyte in Daytshland* (Munich, 1948), pp. 28–32; "From Antihistoricism to Superhistoricism" (Yiddish), *Kiyoum,* no. 3 (1948), 28–32; "Elements of the Research on the Holocaust" (Yiddish), *Hemshekh*, no. 1 (Munich, 1948), 4–10; continuation in no. 2 (1949), 26–34; "Les problèmes de recherche scientifique sur notre dernière catastrophe," *Les Juifs en Europe, 1939–1945, pp.* 72–80.

22. Zosa Szajkowski, "A Bibliography of Publications on the Warsaw Ghetto" (Yiddish), *YB,* 30 (1947), 280–88.

23. For a detailed description of the activities related to the Warsaw underground ghetto archives, see A. Eisenbach, "Scientific Research in the Warsaw Ghetto" (Yiddish), *BFG,* 1 (Warsaw, 1948), 55–113, and no. 2, 69–84.

24. A survey of the rescued materials is given by A. Bach [Eisenbach], "Survey of the Materials from the Underground Ghetto Archives (Ringelblum Archive)" (Yiddish), *ibid.,* 1 (1948), 178–82.

25. The English edition of *German Crimes in Poland* is in two volumes: Volume I contains a verbatim translation of vol. I of the Polish edition, the *Biuletyn Głównej Komisji dla Badania Zbrodni Niemieckich w Polsce* (Bulletin of the Central Commission for the Investigation of German Crimes in Poland) (Warsaw, 1946)—with contributions on the extermination of Polish Jewry, on the concentration camps of Oświęcim, Chełmno, and Treblinka, and a general survey of all German concentration camps in Poland. Volume II comprises summaries of the articles published in vol. II and III of the Polish edition. Of Jewish interest are, primarily, the papers on the concentration camps in Bełżec, Sobibór, and Stutthof, and on the liquidation of the Warsaw ghetto.

26. On the activities of the CJHC in Poland, see N. Grüss and Diana Grynbaum, *Rok Pracy Centralnej Żydowskiej Komisji Historycznej* (One Year of Work and the Collections of the Central Jewish Historical Commission in Poland) (Lodz, 1946); J. Kermisz in *Les Juifs en Europe, pp.* 140–44; Jacob Pat, *Ash un fayer* (Ashes and Fire) (New York, 1946), pp. 76–82; in the English edition of Pat's book, *Ashes and Fire* (New York, 1947), pp. 61–65; *BFG,* 1 (1948), 198–200, and i–iii (listing publications of the CJHC).

27. See articles by H. Hertz and I. Schneersohn in *Le Monde Juif,* nos. 13 (1948) and 16 (1949).

28. On the activities and collections of the CDJC, see the report of H. Hertz in *Les Juifs en Europe, pp.* 58–62; another exhaustive report, in *Le Monde Juif,* nos. 9–10, 20–27; I. Schneersohn, "The Jewish Documentation Center in Paris" (Yiddish), *YB,* 30 (1947), 248–58; and a pamphlet in English, *Centre de Documentation Juive Contemporaine—The Jewish Contemporary Documentation Center* (Paris, 1949).

29. *Yizkor-Bukh, tsum ondenk fun 14 umgekumene parizer yidishe shrayber in kamf far frayhayt* (Memorial Book in Honor of the 14 Jewish

Writers of Paris Who Perished in the Fight for Freedom), ed. by I. Spero et al. (Paris, 1946); the French edition, *Combattants de la Liberté* (Paris, 1948); and a small pamphlet containing six letters by Romain Rolland to a Jewish underground fighter in 1940–1941 (in French and in Yiddish translation). The center also organized an exhibition in 1947 and published a catalogue of the exhibition in French and Yiddish.

30. See the report by M. Moch in *Les Juifs en Europe*, pp. 34–36; and that by M. Vanikoff, *ibid.*, pp. 144–48.

31. See the report by Sam Lévy, *ibid.*, pp. 66–71.

32. See the pamphlet *The Wiener Library: Its History and Activities, 1934–1945* (London, 1946); and Alfred Wiener's report in *Les Juifs en Europe*, pp. 125–28.

33. See the report of A. M. Faygenbaum in *Les Juifs en Europe*, pp. 149–51 and an exhaustive report in *Fun leztn Hurbn*, no. 10, pp. 162–70. In 1948 the CHC arranged an impressive exposition in Bad Reichenhall (Bavaria) and published an extensive catalogue of the exhibition in five languages.

34. The CHC in Munich published two books of memoirs: the Stuttgart branch, a book about Nazi persecutions of Jews in Radom; the branch in Landsberg, a pamphlet about Vilna under Nazi rule.

35. See the essay by M. Liebhaber, "Spitefully and with Irresponsibility," in the Yiddish journal *Undzer Veg*, Munich (1948); that by Israel Elenzweig in *Landsberger Zeitung* (1947); and that by M. Kroshnitz in *Hemshekh*, Munich, no. 2 (1949), 51–61.

36. See the reports by Simon Wiesenthal (Linz) and Tobie Frydman (Vienna), in *Les Juifs en Europe*, pp. 37–40, 194–96.

37. On the activities of the CHC of the PHaH in Italy, see the report by M. Kaganovitch in *In Gang*, Rome (journal of the Jewish writers' union in Italy), nos. 13–14 (July–August 1948).

38. Report by Frédéric Steiner in *Les Juifs en Europe*, p. 216.

39. Report by Elie Echkenazy, *ibid.*, pp. 40–43.

40. Matatias Carp, *Cartea Neagra*. With a foreword by Alexander Safran, 3 vols. (Bucharest, 1946–1948). See the report by A. M. Halévy, *Les Juifs en Europe*, pp. 160–64.

41. Report by Ernest Munkácsi, *ibid.*, pp. 196–98.

42. See F. Hevesi, "Recent Jewish Literature in Hungary," *JBA*, 6 (1947–1948), 71–75; and the above-mentioned (note 12) bibliography of L. C. Tihany.

43. See the book about the Jews of Salonika edited by Michael Molho, *In Memoriam. Hommage aux victimes juives des nazis en Grèce* (Salonika, 1948); and that by I. A. Matarasso, *He Katastrophe ton Helleno-Hebraion Tessalonikes* (However, not all had been killed . . . The Catastrophe of the Greek Jews of Salonika during the German Occupation) (Athens, 1948); Henrietta Ali, "Thanks to the Passport. A Report of a Survivor from Salonika on the Way from Bergen-Belsen to Palestine" (Hebrew), *Reshumot*, n.s., II (1945–1946), 41–43; Haim Pardo, "Dráma [Macedonia], Eyewitness Account" (Yiddish), *Fun letztn Hurbn*, no. 7 (May 1948), 88–90; Asher Moissis, "La situation des Communautés juives en Grèce," in *Les Juifs en Europe*, pp. 47–54; and the brochure, *Le Drame des Juifs Hellènes, Documents* (Cairo, Département Helléniques de l'Information, 1943, 1944).

44. Especially in vol. II of this series (Belgrade, 1945).

45. Articles in the Yiddish newspaper *Aynikayt* (Moscow, 1944–1948); in the journals of the Jewish writers' union (such as *Tsum Sig, Haymland,* Moscow, 1944–); the reports by the special Soviet Russian Investigation Commissions in various cities, published, from 1944 on, in the newspapers *Pravda* and *Izviestya;* the books by H. Smoliar about the ghetto and underground in Minsk; by M. Yellin and D. Gelpern about Jewish partisans in Kovno; and by others.

46. See the article by L. de Jong, "The Netherlands State Institute War Documentation," *WLB,* vol. III, no. 1 (1949), p. 5; David Scheinert, "Jewish Culture in Western Europe," *Commentary* (March 1949), 281–83; also T. Gutman's review article "Dutch Jews under German Rule" (Yiddish), *YB,* 30 (1947), 107–16.

47. Report by Nella Rost in ʻLes Juifs en Europe, pp. 57–58.

48. Report by J. Bloch, *ibid.,* pp. 214–15.

# 21

# AMERICAN JEWISH RESEARCH AND LITERATURE ON THE HOLOCAUST

Research on the Jewish catastrophe of 1939–1945 is still in a prescientific stage. It began with pure fact-finding and reporting, with collecting raw material and documentation for quick information and, later, for supporting the legal prosecution of war criminals. Not until after the end of the war could the archival and documentary basis for this research be broadened enough to permit a more scholarly approach. A stupendous amount of material had been found in German archives all over Europe; another tremendous source was added by the innumerable war crimes trials in almost all the European countries. These sources were later supplemented and enlarged by an immense flow of testimonies of Nazi victims, eyewitness records, memoir literature, diaries, letters, chronicles, literary works, underground press, clandestine archives, and the like. A large network of historical commissions and institutes sprang up in various parts of the world for the purpose of collecting these materials. Some of the historical institutes started cataloguing and indexing their collections. Some began to work out a methodology of research on the subject. Methodological conferences were held in Warsaw, Jerusalem, Paris, and New York. Among the problems most frequently discussed at these conferences were the following: (1) Can contemporary history be a subject of strictly scholarly research? (This problem received special attention at the Paris conference.) (2) How can the work of the individual research groups be coordinated to avoid duplication and overlapping, and foster mutual assistance and cooperation? Many technical problems are involved: for example, the development of uniform patterns for cataloguing and indexing, the common planning of all-embracing research projects; the systematization of bibliographical work; etc. (3) What sort of methodology is needed for collecting material through interviews, inquiries, questionnaires, and the like?

At first the foremost center of collection and research activities was, of course, Europe. Here were the indispensable sources and facilities; here were the abandoned German and satellite archives to be immediately seized and used; here were the masses of the living human sources (the survivors and eyewitnesses, the defendants and war criminals); here were all the physical traces and clues to the Nazi crimes (the ghettos, the labor camps, the concentration camps and the killing installations); here were the stocks of the now ownerless and derelict Nazi literature and press, the still fresh memories of the Nazi regime and its atrocities. Gradually, however, the activities of the Jewish historical commissions in Europe diminished. The majority of the Jewish survivors emigrated to Israel or to America. Gradually also tremendous amounts of archival materials and documents were concentrated in the United States and in Israel. Only three sizable and vital centers with adequate scholarly staffs, archives, and libraries remained in Europe to continue the work: the Centre de Documentation Juive Contemporaine in Paris, the A. Wiener Library in London, and the Jewish Historical Institute in Warsaw.[1]

In Israel the collecting and publishing of materials on the Holocaust proceeded actively from the outbreak of World War II. The Representation of the Polish Jews and other *landsmanshaftn* (associations of fellow countrymen), the Zionist organizations and institutions, and the publishing houses Min Hamoked, 'Am Oved, Hakibbutz Hameuhad, and Sifriyat Hapoalim were particularly active. A large number of eyewitness records were issued in mimeographed form by the Vaad Hahatzalah. Hundreds of important articles appeared in magazines and in the daily press. A plan for an institute to commemorate the memory of the martyrs and heroes (*Yad vashem lagola*) was elaborated, and a world conference for organizing the research on the last catastrophe (*Kinus olami l'heker hashoa vehagevura*) was held in Jerusalem in July 1947. The dramatic events of the War of Independence, however, interrupted these research activities. It is more than probable that the young State of Israel will be preoccupied for years to come with organizing its political, economic, and social life, and public opinion and literary and research activities will be devoted mainly to these problems. Several new institutes for the study of the Holocaust have been planned in Israel, but only one, the Historical Institute in the Bet Lohamei Hagetaot (the kibbutz of the ghetto fighters and partisans in Galilee), has reached the first stage of concrete realization, with a modest building containing the archives and the library of the institute. The institute also set up a small research staff, and initiated research and publishing activities. The first issue of its scholarly publication *Dapim l'heker hashoah vehamered* (Pages for the Study of the Catastrophe and the Revolt, January–April 1951), edited by Nachman Blumental, Joseph Kermisz, and Zvi Shner, bodes well for its future scholarly efforts.

## Research Institutions in the United States and in Other American Countries

In the United States two important Jewish institutions took the lead in the research activities in this field. The first body founded primarily for, and devoted particularly to, research into the Holocaust in Europe was the Institute of Jewish Affairs, organized in February 1940 upon the initiative of the American Jewish Congress and the World Jewish Congress. At a conference held in 1942, the director of the institute, Jacob Robinson, outlined its work in the following words:

Our chief concern is Europe, where Nazi policy threatens 8 million Jews with extinction. A study of the long truce between 1919 and 1939 is extremely important in this connection . . . [also] . . . an exhaustive study of the minorities treaties. . . . Since the outbreak of the war, our greatest task has been that of obtaining the authoritative and reliable documentation necessary for an accurate contemporary picture.

Methods of studying contemporary history on a scientific basis had to be worked out. The leaders of the institute were ambitious enough to try to "evolve a new type of Jewish reporting, which could concentrate on actual day-to-day Jewish history." The reports were to be based not on Jewish newspapers but on Nazi publications and, if possible, on confidential material. The confidential material was being continually received from "diplomatic and other sources of information." After the war, new sources were collected and added: Nazi newspapers and documents, materials of the war crimes trials, eyewitness reports, pictures, underground archives, and other materials picked up by representatives of the institute in European countries. Since the end of World War II the activities of the institute have been curtailed in general, and most of the work still carried on is in other fields.[2] The research on the Holocaust initiated so efficiently by the Institute of Jewish Affairs has been continued by the Yidisher Visenshaftlikher Institut—YIVO (Institute for Jewish Research). Founded in

1925 in Vilna, the YIVO moved its headquarters to New York City in 1939, and has become one of the most important Jewish research centers in the world.

## Archives

The most comprehensive and systematically organized archives on the Holocaust are those of the Institute of Jewish Affairs. In addition to the materials on the general history of European Jewry and the various political problems with which the institute was concerned, these archives contain material on the following aspects of the Holocaust: (1) anti-Jewish legislation in the various countries; (2) war crimes, atrocities, persecutions; (3) concentration and death camps; (4) the daily life of European Jewry under the Nazi occupation (anti-Jewish propaganda, looting of Jewish property, Jewish war prisoners, children, and the like); (5) refugees and displaced persons (DPs); (6) liberation of the camps; (7) war crimes trials; and (8) actions by world Jewry for the relief and rescue of European Jewry.

The importance of the archives of the Institute of Jewish Affairs cannot be measured solely by the number of items. These archives were, at least until 1945, the most comprehensive on the Holocaust on the American continent, and they still have the fullest and most complete array of materials, covering all European countries and virtually all problems of any importance. But the institute carried on its collecting activities most intensively during and immediately after the war. More recently, particularly since 1946–1947, archival matter pertaining to the World War II period has not been systematically compiled and supplemented. Therefore, the types of material freely available only since the close of the war—such as official Nazi documentation from confiscated Nazi archives; depositions by Nazi defendants and other war criminals; diaries, eyewitness records, and other documentary evidence—are rather scant in the archives of the institute. Fortunately, this gap has been filled by the YIVO.

Immediately after the outbreak of hostilities in Europe, the YIVO began collecting data and materials on the Holocaust and World War II. However, its most valuable collections have been acquired since the end of the war. Early in 1945 the YIVO took steps toward the establishment of archives relating to the Jewish catastrophe under the Nazis. Of foremost importance is the collection of official German materials containing many confidential reports of German authorities, statistics, statements, correspondence between various offices of the German administration, and the like. Some of these documents were presented as evidence at the Nuremberg Trials. These archives contain several hundred bulky units. As catalogued by the YIVO staff, they are divided into the following main categories: Germany; the occupied territories in general; the occupied territories in the West; the occupied territories in the East; the occupied territories incorporated into Germany; the Government General; Ostland, White Russia and Russian-occupied territories; the Baltic countries; the Ukraine; the Balkan countries; Austria and Hungary; the "Protectorate"; and Slovakia.

Another important group of materials in the YIVO is the collection of Lodz (Litzmannstadt) archives. It contains diversified and original materials, such as the periodicals of the Litzmannstadt ghetto, the collection of posters promulgated by the Jewish ghetto council, and by the German ghetto administration, the "chronicle of the ghetto" (typewritten daily reports, amounting to as much as 40 or 50 pages for a single day), official correspondence, statistical materials, and a host of other official, semi-official, and personal papers and photographs (about 400) covering all facets of ghetto life. This collection embraces 1,493 items, and is catalogued in eighteen categories. A third important collection is that on the Vilna ghetto, containing 710 items similar in character to those in the Lodz collection.

For the history of the Jews in France, three collections in the YIVO are important: (1) the collection of documents concerning the activities of French Jewish organizations and communities during the German occupation, containing 313 large files already catalogued and a host of material still in the process of classification; (2) the collection of newspapers and periodicals, clippings, posters, press releases, and other contemporary materials, mainly French, containing over 60 units; (3) the Jacques Belinky collection (covering the years 1940–1942 in Paris) of diaries comprising over 1,000 written pages, supplemented by newspaper clippings, photographs, official announcements, and the like.

In 1947 the YIVO archives were enriched by two new collections: a highly valuable collection of materials on the Jews in Denmark during the period 1927–1947; and the David Trocki collection on the Jews in Belgium, comprising 3,500 documents relating to the period beginning at the close of World War I and ending in the early years of World War II (1942–1943). In 1950 the YIVO received from the Hebrew Sheltering and Immigrant Aid Society (HIAS) the archives of the HIAS–ICA Emigration Association (HICEM), covering its rescue activities during World War II (278 large units). All these archival collections have been classified and indexed. Still not catalogued are the following: (1) a collection of documents from the Baltic states, particularly Lithuania; (2) a very large collection from Germany and Austria, comprising materials on concentration and labor camps, as well as a comprehensive assemblage of materials pertaining to Jewish life in these two countries immediately after the liberation—particularly noteworthy are the archives on the DP camps, some of which delivered to the YIVO their complete documentation from the moment of their establishment to the very hour of their dissolution; (3) part of the archives of the Amsterdam Judenrat (to 1943); (4) archival materials, photographs, diagrams, and literary works from Rumania and Transnistria (the Rumanian Russian-occupied territories).

In order to obtain firsthand accounts by survivors or witnesses of the Holocaust in Europe, the YIVO took steps to encourage reporting, by means of contests and awards. In 1946 an autobiography contest was arranged for surviving Jewish children in Europe. The contest brought in the life histories of 161 children.

Turning back from these lesser items to the larger ones, we must first take into account the YIVO collection of eyewitness records. This is the largest collection of its kind in the American countries and contains over 1,200 items, including the above-mentioned 161 reports written by children. Most of these records describe events in a particular locale. The most remarkable records are devoted to the following cities (the total number of reports for each is given): Warsaw, 190; Radom, 52; Vilna, 39; Lodz, 32; Paris, 27; Lwów, 24; Tarnopol, 17; Częstochowa, 16; Lublin, 13; and Bialystok, 11. Less numerous are the records on concentration camps: Skarzyska, 36; Auschwitz and Birkenau, 26; Bełżec, 9; Treblinka, 9; Majdanek, 9; and elsewhere.

Another rich and unique group of materials in the possession of the YIVO is the Shanghai collection, which was exhibited at the YIVO; an extensive thirty-two-page catalogue was prepared for this exhibition by Z. Szajkowski and was published in 1948. This valuable collection, covering all phases of Jewish life in Shanghai before and during World War II, contains documents and official and unofficial materials relating to the ghetto in Shanghai; the governmental authorities, and Jewish organizations; photographs; posters, books and pamphlets printed in Shanghai; and a priceless collection of the output of the Jewish press in China, embracing more than thirty diverse periodicals.

In addition to the above archival collections, a number of institutions and individual collectors deserve mention. The American Jewish Joint Distribution Committee in New York has amassed a great amount of material on relief activities during World War II, as well as on the plight of Jewish refugees, the sufferings of the Jews in various Nazi-occupied countries, the situation of the survivors immediately after liberation, and similar subjects. Only a fraction of these materials is organized in the committee's headquarters building in New York City; the bulk of this vast collection is stored in a depository.

A small, but good, collection of wartime reports and surveys is with the American Jewish Committee in New York. Important collections of uncatalogued materials are extant in certain non-Jewish institutions—such as the library of Columbia University in New York, the archives of the international and U.S. war crimes tribunals, and the U.S. State Department in Washington. A small, but good, collection of archival material concerning the French Jews under the Nazi occupation has been acquired by the Jewish Theological Seminary in New York.

Mention must also be made of two valuable private collections in New York. The collection of Ignacy Schwarzbart, formerly a member of the Polish government-in-exile in London, covers the interval from the beginning of 1940 to March 1946. Constituting the official archives of the "Office of the Member of the National Council of the Polish Republic, Dr. I. Schwarzbart," this precious assemblage of documents (mainly in Polish) contains several hundred large items and folders classified into many sections and divisions, for example: the interventions of the National Council of the Polish Republic on behalf of the persecuted Jews in Nazi-occupied Poland; the Jews in the Polish armies; conferences with Polish government members and with representatives of other Allied governments; reports from the Polish and Jewish underground in Poland to Jewish organizations all over the world; the organization of relief for the Polish Jews; press conferences; collections of documents, leaflets, and pamphlets about the situation of the Jews in Poland; minutes of conferences, hearings, broadcasts, and the like.

The second important private collection is that of M. Frankenhuis (formerly in The Hague, Netherlands), which deals with the fate of the Jews in Holland and in the Theresienstadt concentration camp (in Czechoslovakia). Besides documents, diaries, and newspaper clippings, this collection also embraces an assemblage of posters from the Nazi period.

## Libraries

An important asset for research on the Holocaust is the library of the YIVO. A separate section of the library is devoted to the large collection of Nazi literature, which has been systematically catalogued. The file contains about 7,000 cards, 5,000 of them referring to books and periodicals in the YIVO collection, and 2,000 to items not in the YIVO (700 are in other libraries in New York City).This catalogue, prepared by Bruno Blau, with many carefully elaborated cross-references, is organized in 53 categories. The YIVO has also systematically collected literature dealing with the Holocaust in Yiddish, Hebrew, English, and other languages. At the time of this writing, this section of the YIVO library contains several thousand books and pamphlets and more than 200 files of current Jewish periodicals from all over the world, particularly from Poland, Germany, Austria, and Italy. These contain a large number of articles, reports, lengthy diaries, and memoirs dealing with the Holocaust. Publications of the Jewish press of Poland and Germany available in the YIVO collection have been carefully studied, and a classified catalogue has been prepared (by "Władka"—Feigele Peltel-Międzyrzecki), comprising 1,120 bibliographical entries, together with numerous cross-references. These entries have been prepared from 16 Jewish periodicals published in Poland and 26 published in Germany between 1945 and the middle of 1948. Also available here is a full collection of the Nuremberg publications and thousands of pages of Nuremberg mimeographed material.

The library of the Institute of Jewish Affairs is similarly of great value, containing a fair collection of books and pamphlets, leaflets and periodicals of the wartime period, mainly in English, with a good cross-reference catalogue. Periodical articles dealing with the Holocaust have been carefully excerpted and added to the cross-reference catalogue; this is very helpful to readers and scholars.

The Jewish Theological Seminary in New York systematically collects literature on the Jewish catastrophe (particularly in Hebrew and Yiddish) and has already accumulated several hundred books and pamphlets. Good collections of books on the Holocaust are also extant in the library of the American Jewish Committee and in the New York Public Library. The Library of Congress, Washington, D.C., has in its stacks a large collection of Nazi literature on the Jewish question, as well as books and pamphlets by Jewish writers on the great catastrophe. The Jewish materials in these vast collections have not yet been explored or classified, however.

## Research and Publications

During the war, the research and publication activities of the Institute of Jewish Affairs were quite extensive. The research staff included about fifty prominent scholars, research students, and editors, and a staff of twenty-five technical and clerical workers. Preparatory work for scholarly studies was carried on in a vigorous and speedy manner; catalogues of the archives and library were prepared; current publications and unprinted materials were critically evaluated; projects for comprehensive monographic studies were elaborated; and drafts and preliminary surveys were drawn up. Some of the studies were prepared for intramural use only; some were submitted to the governments concerned and to official bodies such as the war crimes tribunals, the United Nations Relief and Rehabilitation Administration (UNRRA), international conferences, the United Nations, and the executive board of the World Jewish Congress. Still others remain unpublished, for technical reasons or lack of funds. Altogether about 130 studies, drafts, projects, analytical reviews, and ready-to-print manuscripts are stored in the research files of the institute. Its research activities, therefore, cannot be measured solely by the number of actual publications. The publishing activities of the institute were at their highest during the years 1941–1944, when seven books and about twenty pamphlets appeared.[3] Since then only a few short pamphlets have been published by the institute on the subject of the Holocaust.

About twenty papers on various problems of the Jewish catastrophe have been delivered at annual conferences of the YIVO convoked since the outbreak of the war. In 1947, the YIVO held an extensive exhibition, "The Jews in Europe, 1939–1946." Several smaller exhibitions—on the Warsaw ghetto uprising, on Jewish children during and after World War II, on Jewish life in Shanghai, and similar topics—followed in subsequent years. In its scholarly publication *YIVO Bleter* appeared an array of studies on World War II and its effects by S. Mendelsohn, L. Hersch, J. Guttmann, M. Kligsberg, E. Papanek, L. Lehrer, Z. Szajkowski, and others. Volume 30 (1947) was devoted entirely to the study of the catastrophe and contains bibliographies, articles, testimonies of victims and survivors, documents, and reviews. Among other YIVO publications in this field is Max Weinreich's *Hitler's Professors,* a study of the role of German scholarship in planning the annihilation of the Jews (English ed., New York, 1946; Yiddish ed., New York, 1947).

Scholarly research into the Holocaust has also been carried on by other American Jewish institutions and by individuals. *Jewish Social Studies,* sponsored by the Conference on Jewish Relations (renamed Conference on Jewish Social Studies), has published a number of important research studies on Jewish life in Europe under the German occupation. In 1949, the Conference on Jewish Relations also arranged, in cooperation with the YIVO, the first scientific conference devoted exclusively to the problems of the Jewish catastrophe. Papers were presented by Joshua Starr, Hannah Arendt, Solomon Bloom, Samuel Gringauz, James Wechsler, and myself, and almost all of the papers were published in the January 1950 issue of *JSS.* Particularly relevant also are the four extensive lists of Jewish cultural treasures in Europe destroyed or looted by the Nazis, lists compiled after painstaking study by a staff of the Conference on Jewish Relations under the direction of Hannah Arendt, Joshua Starr, and Adolf Kober. These are the *Tentative List of Jewish Cultural Treasures in Axis-Occupied Countries; Tentative List of Jewish Educational Institutions;*

*Tentative List of Jewish Periodicals;* and *Tentative List of Jewish Publishers.*[4]

Since 1940, the American Jewish Committee has published in its *American Jewish Year Book* studies and surveys of Jewish life in Europe during the Nazi period. The *Contemporary Jewish Record,* a bimonthly published by the same institution and edited by A. G. Duker, devoted a considerable proportion of its issues (1940–1945) to research and information on the Holocaust in Europe. The volume *With Firmness in the Right,* edited by Cyrus Adler and Aaron M. Margalith (New York, 1946), has a section containing official material concerning the policy of the United States government during World War II with respect to the anti-Jewish persecutions and the Jewish refugees. A more recent important achievement of the American Jewish Committee is the publication of the five volumes of *Studies in Prejudice.* Of special interest for our research is Paul Massing's *Rehearsal for Destruction* (New York, 1949), which deals with the background of Nazi anti-Semitism.

The short-lived American Jewish Conference succeeded in publishing only one book: *Nazi Germany's War Against the Jews* (New York, 1947), prepared and compiled by Seymour Krieger, containing selected Jewish materials from the vast files of the Nuremberg International Military Tribunal.

Another attempt at a comprehensive assemblage of monographic studies and articles treating of the Holocaust in Europe is *The Black Book: The Nazi Crime Against the Jewish People* (New York, 1946), published jointly by the American Committee of Jewish Writers, Artists, and Scientists and the World Jewish Congress. Although this volume contains some interesting contributions, it fails, on the whole, to attain desired scholarly standards.

Important contributions in Yiddish have been made by several Jewish publishers in the United States. The Central Yiddish Culture Organization (CYCO) published the huge anthology *Kidush Hashem* (Sanctification of His Name) (New York, 1948), edited by S. Niger, which will long remain a helpful manual; the handsome anthology of the songs of the ghettos and concentration camps, *Lider fun di getos un lagern* (Songs from the Ghettos and Camps) (New York, 1948), compiled by S. Kaczerginski and prefaced by H. Leivick, which is the best work of its kind; and *Hurbn Vilna* (The Destruction of Vilna), by S. Kaczerginski (New York, 1947).

The publications of the Jewish Labor Committee, the American Representation of the Jewish Labor Bund, and the Undzer Tsayt publishing house also contain valuable collections of firsthand records and diaries, among them memoirs of several ghetto fighters. The more important of these are *Fun beyde zaytn geto moyer* (From Both Sides of the Ghetto

Wall), by ("Władka") Feigele Peltel-Międzyrzecki (New York, 1948); *Finf yor in varshever geto* (Five Years in the Warsaw Ghetto), by Bernard Goldstein (New York, 1947; trans. into English under the title *The Stars Bear Witness,* New York, 1949). Marek Edelman's memoirs appeared in *In di yorn fun yidishn hurbn* (In the Years of the Jewish Catastrophe) (New York, 1948), a collection of valuable materials on the underground activities of the Bund in Poland during the Nazi period. Valuable shorter contributions are found in the American Jewish press in the Yiddish and Hebrew journals *Hadoar, Harofe ha-ivri, Kultur und Dertsiyung, Undzer Tsayt, Yidisher Kemfer, Yidishe Kultur, Zukunft, Bialystoker Shtime,* and others; in the Yiddish dailies and weeklies; in Jewish periodicals in English and German (*Jewish Frontier, Commentary, Forum, Aufbau,* and so forth); as well as in American scholarly journals.

Interesting and sometimes important contributions have been published by the Jewish *landsmanshaftn.* The earliest of these publications were *The Black Book of Polish Jewry,* edited by Jacob Apenszlak, and the *Lodzer Pinkes,* both of which appeared in 1943. Since the close of the war from thirty to forty publications have appeared which are concerned with the fate of the Jewish population during World War II in many European countries and cities, particularly in Eastern Europe. Among the more valuable of these are *Tchenstochover Yidn* (The Częstochowa Jews) (New York, 1947); the *Volkovisker Yizkor Bukh* (Wołkowysk Memorial Volume) (New York, 1949); the *Grayever Yizkor Bukh* (Grajewo Memorial Volume) (New York, 1950); publications on Horodec, Briansk, Warsaw, Vilna, Kovno, Łomża, Brzeziny, Zelechów; *Hurbn Chrzanów* (Destruction of Chrzanów) (Regensburg, 1949); *Hurbn Koretz* (Destruction of Korzec) (Paris, 1949); and *Hurbn Dynów* (Destruction of Dynów) (New York, 1950). Of more recent date are the *Pinkes Mława* (Mława Memorial Volume) (New York, 1950), edited by Jacob Shatzky, *Pinkes Belchatów* (Bełchatów Memorial Volume), and a voluminous collective work on Lithuanian Jewry, the *Pinkes Lite* (M. Sudarski, editor), published in 1951.

There still remain to be mentioned some noteworthy individual research and literary achievements. Joseph Tenenbaum's *In Search of a Lost People* (New York, 1948) attempts to give a comprehensive picture of the tragedy of Polish Jewry. Leo W. Schwarz's carefully edited *The Root and the Bough* (New York, 1949) is an anthology of firsthand material from survivors of almost all the European countries, some of it previously unpublished. Also based on the life-history idea are *We Survived,* the stories of fourteen Nazi victims, edited by Eric H. Boehm (New Haven, 1949); and *I Did Not Interview the Dead,* by David P. Boder (Urbana, 1949), who introduces a new, more exacting psychological method of interviewing and recording. In Yiddish two noteworthy autobiographical volumes have been published: *Ikh bin der korbn un der eydes* (I Am the Victim and the Witness), by Aharon Twersky (New York, 1947); and *Mir viln lebn* (We Want to Live), by Jacob Rassen (New York, 1949).

Apart from the United States, the most important publications that have appeared in the Western Hemisphere have come from the Association of Polish Jews in Argentina, in the huge series edited by Mark Turkow and published by A. Mittelberg. From 1946 to the end of 1950, more than seventy volumes have been issued dealing with the history and culture of Polish Jewry. Over twenty of these volumes are concerned with the fate of Polish Jewry during and after World War II.[5] Scattered publications in Yiddish, Spanish, and German have appeared from the presses of other Jewish publications in Argentina, as well as in Mexico and Canada.

## Projects in Progress

Several important research projects underway are deserving of mention. Most of these have been initiated by the YIVO or assisted by it. Among these are "The Extermination of the Jews in the Reichskommissariat Ostland" by J. Guttmann; a statistical study of German Jewry by Bruno Blau,[6] and a psychological analysis of the accounts by children on World War II, by M. Kligsberg. In 1948 I undertook the preparation of an extensive annotated bibliography of the literature on the Jewish catastrophe of 1939–1945. The bibliography (sponsored by the Research Council in the Social Sciences of Columbia University) is now nearing completion and will contain approximately 18,000 entries.[7] A series of studies on the Jews in the East European countries after World War II has been prepared under the auspices of the American Jewish Committee, and some of the material is soon to be published. These studies contain a great deal of material on the Holocaust.

## Conclusions

The United States will in all probability remain the center for research on the catastrophe of the Jewish population in World War II. The Jewish community in the U.S. has, for the time being, the most favorable conditions and facilities for this kind of research. Here are centered the greatest agglomerations of Jews in the world and the largest Jewish research and publishing centers. The steady flow of materials and archives from Europe enables Jewish and non-Jewish institutions to bring their libraries and archives to a leading position in this field. The recent immigration of DPs has brought great numbers of survivors and Nazi victims, the living source of information and a moving permanent incentive for research in the field of the Holocaust. A vital interest in this kind of activity has developed in the *landsmanshaftn* and in the more recently established associations of former inmates of Nazi concentration camps. Some of the newcomers to this country have brought with them their collections of materials, in some instances substantial and precious.

Nevertheless, not all the requisite conditions for leadership in this field exist in the United States today. Even if we concede that much has been accomplished, we must admit that much more should have been achieved. Let us frankly acknowledge that Jewish leadership in the United States has not yet fully realized the paramount importance of giving Jewish research institutions the necessary financial means for their share in this field of research. It goes without saying that, as our research activities expand and develop, our association with the Israeli and European scholars, both Jewish and non-Jewish, in this field of research will become even closer. This will be of great importance to us, as well as to our partners. Just as the Jewish catastrophe in the Nazi era can be studied only in the broader context of worldwide events, so the general European history of that period cannot be adequately interpreted without a full understanding of the German war against the Jewish people. Consequently, the establishment of close cooperation between the vital Israeli, American, and European centers of this research, whether of universal, national, or denominational allegiance, is one of our most important tasks and a paramount objective for all future scholarly activities.

[In 1954, a Joint Documentary Project of the Yad Vashem Martyrs' and Heroes' Memorial Authority in Jerusalem and YIVO Institute for Jewish Research in New York was established, with Philip Friedman heading the division for the Bibliography of the Jewish History under Nazi Impact, until his death in 1960. Up to 1973 (when the bibliographical project was discontinued), thirteen volumes of this series appeared. It is regrettable that Philip Friedman, who laid the foundation of this work, was deprived of the joy of seeing any of the volumes in print.—*Ed.*]

⟨ This essay is based on the second part of a paper prepared for the First International Conference on World War II in the West, held in Amsterdam on September 5–9, 1950, under the auspices of the Rijksinstituut voor Oorlogsdokumentatie (The Netherlands State Institute for War Documentation). It was published in *Jewish Social Studies*, 13 (1951), 235–50, under the title "American Jewish Research and Literature on the Jewish Catastrophe of 1939–1945."

# Notes

1. For a more detailed discussion and survey of the European research and literature on the Holocaust, see the preceding essay; also see my "Research and Literature on the Recent Jewish Tragedy" in *JSS*, 12 (1950), 17–26; and "Our Hurbn-Literature," in *YK*, 31 (1950), 87–91 The pursuit of these studies was made possible by the grant-in-aid allotted to me by the Council for Research in the Social Sciences of Columbia University.

2. The aims, collections, and activities of the institute are exhaustively described in two mimeographed reports, "Institute of Jewish Affairs: Its Aims and Methods" (New York, 1942), and "Report of the Institute of Jewish Affairs for the Period February 1, 1941–April 30, 1947" (New York, 1947).

3. Zorach Wahrhaftig and Boris Shub, *Starvation over Europe* (New York, 1943); a collective study, *Hitler's Ten-Year War on the Jews* (New York, 1943); Arieh Tartakower and Kurt R. Grossmann, *The Jewish Refugees* (New York, 1944); Gerhard Jacoby, *The Racial State: The German Nationality's Policy in the Protectorate of Bohemia-Moravia* (New York, 1944); Jacob Lestschinsky, *Di yidishe katastrofe* (The Jewish Catastrophe) (New York, 1944).

4. Published in *JSS* as Supplements to vol. 8, nos. 1 and 3 (1946), vol. 9 (1947), and vol. 10 (1948).

5. Among the more important are V. Grosman and J. Wiernik, *Treblinka* (Buenos Aires, 1946); S. Polakiewicz, *A tog in Treblinka* (A Day in Treblinka) (Buenos Aires, 1948); N. Grüss, ed., *Kinder martyrologie* (Children Martyrs) (Buenos Aires, 1947); S. Kaczerginski, *Partizaner gayen* (Partisans on the Move) (Buenos Aires, 1947); Mark Turkow, *Malka Owsiany dertsaylt* (Malka Owsiany Tells the Story) (Buenos Aires, 1946); I. Tabaksblat, *Hurbn Lodz* (Destruction of Lodz) (Buenos Aires, 1946); S. Waga, *Hurbn Czenstochov* (Destruction of Częstochowa) (Buenos Aires, 1949); J. Kermisz, *Der oyfshtand in varshever geto* (The Warsaw Ghetto Uprising) (Buenos Aires, 1948); my *Oshwientsim* (Auschwitz) (Buenos Aires, 1950); and the diaries of Hillel Seidman, M. Strigler, J. Hirshaut, Tanya Fuchs, Jonas Turkow, Freda Zerubavel, and others. A number of these books were reviewed by Koppel S. Pinson and myself in "Some Books on the Jewish Catastrophe," *JSS*, 12 (1950), 83–94.

6. Portions of this study have appeared in *ibid.*, pp. 161–72; and in *Judaica*, 4 (1948), 45–57; and 5 (1949), 272–88.

7. Smaller segments of this bibliography have been published in *JBA*, 8 (1949–1950), 122–32; and 9 (1950–1951), 80–92; *Bleter far yidisher dertsiyung*, vol. 2 (1949) and vol. 3 (1950); *Kultur un dertsiyung*, 20 (1950), nos. 4, 5; *Bialystoker shtime*, vol. 30 (1950), nos. 259, 260.

# 22

# PRELIMINARY AND
# METHODOLOGICAL ASPECTS
# OF RESEARCH ON THE JUDENRAT

In this essay I shall discuss the methodological problems and prolegomena of research on the Judenräte and shall try to determine by what means we may achieve some clarification of the many and complicated issues involved. Let it be stated at the very outset, that there is a plethora of raw material on this subject, both in the prolific Yizkor literature and in the many autobiographical and memorialist works of that era. But this material is scattered in thousands of books and articles, often in the form of casual remarks, subjective appraisals, or partisan arguments. It has never been systematically collected, arranged, and studied, and there has as yet been no scholarly research, let alone a comprehensive scholarly publication, on this topic.[1]

In a number of works dealing with the period of the European Jewish Catastrophe, Gerald Reitlinger, Leon Poliakov, Joseph Tenenbaum, and others have viewed the problem from the outside, as it were. They see what their oppressors did to Jews; what the Jews suffered. But they have not looked within, they have not observed what really happened inside.[2]

And a Jewish life existed within! Whatever it was, the ghetto teemed with activity; there were constant changes and developments in its life. There were sudden metamorphoses and developments in the social and economic fabric. The changes were rapid and far-reaching. There were processes of social declassment and degradation, of changing social stratification, of real or pseudo-proletarization. There were other aspects of the day-to-day life in the ghetto. The development of Jewish self-government was bound up with those processes. When one immerses oneself in the complex problems of the Judenrat, one must deal with all these social, economic, ethical, and psychological phenomena, as well as with all the organizational problems of the ghetto. It is only against such a background that events and developments can be understood. And another factor of paramount importance should not be overlooked; namely, to what extent the success of the Nazi strategy depended upon Jewish "representation" or Jewish "autonomy."

## *Varieties of Jewish "Self-Government" Under Nazi Rule*

There are two aspects to the problem of the Judenrat. First of all we must deal with the morphology, if we may use the term, of the Judenrat, in its diverse organizational forms. The history of the Judenrat is closely bound up with the Nazi policy that created it. Secondly, we must understand the internal story of the Judenrat. I shall endeavor to enumerate the problems in this order. I am making things easier for myself when I use the term *Judenrat* to refer to all forms of Jewish "self-government" in the Nazi era; strictly speaking, this usage is etymologically and historically inaccurate. In some places, the organ of Jewish self-government was known as the Ältestenrat (Council of Jewish Elders); in other places, as the Reichsvereinigung (German Federation); elsewhere, as the Union Générale des Israélites de France (UGIF, in France), the Center of Jewish Communities (Upper Silesia), the Jewish Central Body (Rumania), and so forth. After the war, however, the term Judenrat came to symbolize all forms of the quasi-autonomous bodies imposed by the Nazis on the Jewish community. I therefore use the term generically. These "autonomous" governing bodies in various countries did not differ in name only. There were also more substantial differences between them. For instance, the Judenrat in Poland differed fundamentally in internal structure and functions from the Reichsvereinigung in Germany, the Union of Communities in Hungary, and to a certain extent, the UGIF in France. Thus the Nazis, who were so eager to enforce *Gleichschaltung* (uniformity) elsewhere, were not so keen to do so in this particular sphere. Perhaps one reason was their knowledge that in any case these institutions were only temporary. Perhaps there were other reasons, too; this is one problem that must be investigated. The experiments conducted by the Nazis with Jewish self-government in Germany,

Austria after the *Anschluss,* in the so-called Protectorate of Bohemia-Moravia, and other countries, indicate that there was no unified policy in the field.

## Genesis of the Judenrat

A number of problems pertaining to the Nazi policy on the Judenrat have not yet been properly investigated. We know about the ultimate goal of the Nazis, but we still have no precise knowledge of 'their strategy, nor do we know the source of their inspiration. Not only do we not know the man or men responsible; we do not know where they got the idea (though we do know that Reinhard Heydrich was the first to implement the idea; see below). This problem must be dealt with. I suspect that in everything pertaining to the internal organization of the Judenrat the source of the Nazis' inspiration was their own *Judenwissenschaft.* They possessed a number of "Jewish experts," such as Peter-Heinz Seraphim, Wilhelm Grau, Joseph Sommerfeldt, and others,[3] whose knowledge they utilized for their nefarious purposes and to deceive the Jews. We have certain evidence that they were adept in exploiting the idea of Jewish autonomy. Knowing that many Jews venerated the idea of self-government, they used it to hoodwink them. Many Jews, both in the ghettos and in the free countries, welcomed the fact that Jewish communities enjoyed internal autonomy. It was indeed a great thing! The Jews received at the hands of the Nazis a degree of self-government they had never before enjoyed. The dream of full autonomy had taken on flesh and sinew—in Theresienstadt and elsewhere. At all events there were people who believed so.[4]

That the Nazis tried to exploit Jewish ideologies for their own ends finds particular confirmation when we consider the Nazis' Madagascar "colonization project," which deliberately exploited the ideals of Jewish settlement and pioneering. It will be recalled that the plan envisaged primarily the dispatch of pioneers to Madagascar, but was never implemented.[5] The same ideas were exploited in Theresienstadt, on a smaller scale; the first people to come there were pioneers, Zionists, idealists, who undertook their task in a spirit of enthusiasm. They hoped to save the Jews of Bohemia and Moravia in this fashion, and also considered the Theresienstadt venture a challenge to their Zionist ideology, a first step toward setting up a *hakhsharah,* a training and vocational education center for Jewish pioneers for Palestine.[6]

That the Nazis' intent was to deceive the Jews in regard to their ultimate purpose, is indicated by the well-known *Schnellbrief* of Reinhard Heydrich of September 21, 1939, where the intention is evident to use the

Judenrat as an instrument to control the Jews and to get them ready for the "Final Solution."[7]

## The Führer Principle

I have already remarked on the fact that there was no *Gleichschaltung* in this sphere, contrary to what might have been expected from the Nazis. Nevertheless, certain features are common to all the Judenräte. One common feature is the Nazis' distaste for representational administrative bodies emanating from any kind of popular and free election. In 1939, for instance, they changed the name of the *Reichsvertretung* (Reich representation) of the Jews in Germany to the *Reichsvereinigung* (Reich union) of Jews, thereby emphasizing that it was to be not a representative but an appointed body, with a designated leadership. (The *Führerprinzip* can also be discerned in the appointments of leaders known as *der Älteste der Juden, der Leiter,* and the like.) In most places the Nazis did not appoint all the members of the Judenrat; they appointed only the "head," the Führer, although Jews were of course forbidden to use this term and were confined to such titles as those mentioned above. This "leader" appointed his council (*der Beirat, der Ältestenrat,* or other names were used). The members of the council acted in an advisory capacity.

## Decentralization vs. Centralization

Another common feature was the desire of the Nazis to confine Jewish self-government to local communities, although there were, in some countries, exceptions in the direction of centralization, because it suited the Nazis' goals. But not so in Poland, where attempts, for regional centralization only, were made in but a few provinces, such as Upper Silesia, which was incorporated into the Reich. There, however, the step was most likely due to the policy of the local German authorities, not the central authorities in Berlin. A short-lived experiment in this direction was also made in the district of Radom in Poland (Government General). Attempts at centralization of Jewish self-government on a national level occurred chiefly in the countries of Western and Central Europe (for instance, in France, the Netherlands, the Protectorate of Bohemia-Moravia). Why the Nazis insisted on centralization in just those areas is an unsolved question. As far as the satellite countries were concerned, there was no overall centralization in Hungary, where the two traditional Jewish congregational unions were left in operation. There was some sort of centralization in both Rumania and Slovakia. Again there is no explanation as to why they followed a different policy in those countries, except that the puppet governments in the satellite countries still had a shadow of "independence" in arranging some of their domestic affairs, including those pertaining to the "Jewish question" (of course, only until the moment of the Final Solution arrived).

The Nazis even made a number of attempts to organize "conferences" of the representatives of the Jewish communities from various countries. Adolf Eichmann convened a conference of this kind at the beginning of the war—we have information on this—in which representatives of the communities of Vienna, Bohemia-Moravia, Cracow, and one district in Poland (the Upper Silesian super community) participated.[8] Apparently the question of emigration was raised. This was in the period when the Nazis were still interested in Jewish emigration. It seems that the matter of a Jewish Reservation in Nisko (on the River San in Poland) or in Lublin was also discussed, but we have no definite, satisfactorily documented information on the agenda of this conference. Data on this aspect are scattered, and new material must be sought.

We have considerable, though not precise, information regarding another Jewish conference, referred to ironically as the *Drei Kaiser-Konferenz* (Three Emperors' Conference), attended by Mordechai Chaim Rumkowski, Adam Czerniakow, and Moses Merin.[9] The *Book of Lublin* and the *Yizkor Book of Chełm* contain the minutes of two other conferences, of the communities in the district of Lublin and the county of Chełm respectively. The purpose and result of these gatherings, which seem to have been sporadic rather than regular, is not clear, however.

## Exchange of "Experts"

It is of interest to recall that from time to time the Nazis dispatched experts from one country to another to advise the new Judenräte. We know that two Jewish experts were sent from Vienna to counsel French Jews in the establishment of the Jewish Council in that country. We know that Jakob Edelstein was sent from Czechoslovakia (the Protectorate) to Holland, where he established clandestine contacts with the Jewish underground and warned them of the Nazis' intentions. At that time he had already attained the status of an expert, having participated in the establishment of the Jewish Reservation in Nisko, and the Theresienstadt ghetto. It is interesting to know that the Nazis not only delegated Jewish experts but sometimes sent their own people to serve as experts on ghetto affairs. For example, Hans Biebow, head of the Lodz *Ghetto-Verwaltung* (administration), was sent in this capacity from Lodz to Warsaw for a short period of time.

## *"Representation" and the Political Parties*

As I have already stated, the Judenrat did not constitute a representative body in the true sense of the word. In the occupied territories and the satellite countries, the Nazis permitted some of the surviving members of the community councils of the pre-occupation period to stay on in office. At no time did all the representatives of the prewar Jewish community remain in office. A few were retained and were ordered to coopt others, or the Nazis themselves appointed the other officers. This was clearly not true representation.

At first, it is true, various parties and factions were represented in the makeup of the Judenrat, and a semblance of the system that had existed before the German occupation was retained. A number of grave questions arise here. Were all Jewish parties represented in the earliest Judenräte? If some parties were not represented, what was the reason for their nonparticipation? In the first months of the Nazi regime, all sorts of illusions might be cherished that the Judenrat could serve as an instrument of salvation— as a means of negotiating with the Germans. For that reason, most of the parties were not yet opposed to participation. The Communists did not take part in the Judenrat, however. One reason was that they had not participated, on principle, in the prewar *kehillot,* which were in most countries religious institutions. Other reasons for Communist opposition to the Judenräte (which were no longer religious in character and had become a national or, more exactly, a "racial" institution) are more complex and also involve attitudes toward the problems of resistance and rebellion.[10] We must not forget, however, that the period in which the Judenräte were set up in Poland and Western Europe was the period of the Stalin-Hitler pact. The Communists obeyed the commands of Stalin, not the dictates of judgment or conscience. After the war, they were able to claim that they were not responsible for the actions of the Judenräte.

Baptized Jews who lived in the ghettos did not participate in the Judenräte either, until the Germans appointed them—mainly to administrative posts, rather than the Judenrat councils per se. Many members of diverse political groups were of the opinion that participation in the Judenräte was a necessary evil to save a remnant of the Jewish population. They felt a responsibility for the life of the community. Those who were not imbued with such a sense of responsibility remained "innocent of all guilt," for they took no part in the Judenrat's activities.

## *Effect of Population Transfers on the Composition of the Judenräte*

Whom did the Judenrat represent? Did it represent the population of the ghetto? If so, which population? The residents of the ghetto changed daily.

One day, the Riga ghetto was inhabited only by local Jews; the next day their number was augmented by Jews brought from Germany or elsewhere. Similar changes occurred in the ghettos of Minsk and other cities. In the Riga ghetto, there were initially two Judenräte, one of Riga Jews, the other of Jews deported from Germany. One day the Nazis said that the Jews of Riga were evildoers who had killed Germans; so they executed the members of the Judenrat of Latvian Jews in Riga and placed the ghetto under the authority of the German-Jewish Judenrat. In other towns, the Germans used other pretexts for applying a similar technique in changing the composition of the Judenrat or its organ, the Jewish militia. For instance, in the small Polish town of Izbica, where both Polish Jews and Jewish refugees from Germany were crowded together in a ghetto, the Germans appointed a Jewish refugee from Stettin as head of the Judenrat, despite the fact that he did not know the people of the town. The Nazis declared that the local Jews did not know the German language sufficiently, and there was need of persons who would be able to receive their orders in German. In Minsk, the capital of Byelorussia, the Germans appointed Karl Löwenstein, a Protestant of Jewish descent (a "racial Jew" according to Nazi definition) and a former Prussian army officer, head of the Jewish militia. In the ghetto of Theresienstadt, where Jews deported from Germany, Austria, Czechoslovakia, Holland, Denmark, and other countries lived together, the Germans appointed an executive body of three men, each of whom "represented" a different nationality: an Austrian (Benjamin Murmelstein), a Czech (Jakob Edelstein), and a German (Paul Eppstein). In the larger advisory council, the Ältestenrat, Jews of various nationalities were also represented.

One may generalize and say that all three episodes typify the Nazi strategy of divide and rule. Both the roots and the consequences of these phenomena went much deeper, however. At the root of the estrangement between the Jewish population and its Judenrat lay, among other causes, the constant dislocations of the Jewish population in the Nazi era. As everybody knows, large-scale population movements are nothing new in Jewish history. But in the past, years, decades, and sometimes even centuries were required for a large-scale movement to be completed. What happened under the Nazi regime was quite different. Large-scale movements of the Jewish population were consummated in very little time, mostly preceding total extermination. In some ghettos and towns, the brutal process of deportation and dislocation was carried out by the Nazis within a few days, sometimes even a few hours. After such a displacement, one could walk through a ghetto and hardly recognize anybody. The old residents would have disappeared, and instead one met new people, expelled from other towns or countries, who even spoke another language.

The constant fluctuation of the ghetto populations was of course attended with severe economic consequences.[11] People suddenly uprooted from their homes and occupations became impoverished, and totally dependent on charity. It was not a purely economic phenomenon, however, but the outcome of a ruthless, premeditated strategy. The Nazis would send new residents to a city either as a distinct group endowed with special privileges (such as the German Jews in Riga or Minsk or the Danish Jews in Theresienstadt) or as a group deprived of all privileges—refugees, deportees, and expellees who would live in ruined buildings, depots, abandoned synagogues, and the terribly overcrowded and dirty "death houses" (refugee centers with a very high mortality rate) as, for instance, in Warsaw. (These tragic circumstances have been described in many eyewitness records and diaries.) In this way the Germans created grave social conflicts between the newcomers and the "native" population of the ghetto. The already intolerable economic and social situation in the ghetto was further aggravated. This question should be investigated to determine to what extent the Nazis deliberately sought to create or intensify anarchy.[12] It is well known that over 100,000 refugees and expellees were brought to Warsaw; that 20,000 Jews from Western Poland, Germany, Austria, Czechoslovakia, and other countries were deported to Lodz. Converts, too—many of whom regarded Jews with hatred—were deported to the ghettos, thereby adding new conflicts. The Nazis made every effort to appoint certain converts to high offices—for example, Józéf Szeryński, the commandant of the Warsaw Jewish militia; and Karl Löwenstein, the commandant of the militia in Minsk and later in Theresienstadt. Moreover, totally non-Jewish groups were sent to the ghettos. There were 5,000 Gypsies in the Lodz ghetto, obviously as a satanic gesture of contempt toward Mordechai Chaim Rumkowski's "empire." Gypsies were also sent to the ghettos of Siedlce, Warsaw, and other localities.

Thus, neither the population of the ghetto nor the Judenrat was static. There were many cases of internal changes in the composition of the Judenrat, under pressure from the Nazis. Also, many members of the Judenrat were killed by the Nazis under some pretext or for some petty or trumped-up "transgression." People appointed to the Judenrat hoped to save themselves and the members of their families, but many soon discovered that they would be the first to die—though I do not say this to justify the members of the Judenrat. I have in my possession material relating to Poland and other countries, testifying to repeated dismissals, deportations, and executions of members of the Judenräte by the Nazis. In one town, Bełchatów near Lodz, the members of the Judenrat changed eight times, in a "negative selection," as it were. The Germans sought weak, corrupt characters, and continued their search until they found the suitable persons. Among the members of the first Judenrat of Bełchatów, there were a number of persons guided by a sense of social responsibility; consequently, they were executed. The same thing happened with other persons in other places. Let us cite only one case out of many: Dr. Joseph Parnas, chairman of the Lwów Judenrat. In Lwów, too, the first Judenrat was followed by a second and a third.

Sometimes, the undesirable members were only dismissed but not executed, or were deported to a concentration camp, as in the case of Bieberstein of Cracow. Of course, the significance of deportation to a concentration camp is well known. The Germans continued with this policy until by a "negative selection" they achieved the results they sought.

## Jewish Opposition

Not only were there regular changes in the composition of the Judenräte, there were also intrigues and disputes within the Judenrat, as well as outside opposition from the various political parties that went underground. In addition, various gangs and cliques put all sorts of pressure on the Judenrat, sometimes through the Nazis, in order to achieve their narrowly selfish objectives. When we speak of the internal opposition to the Judenrat, we must take care not to confuse the diverse motives of the opposition. For instance, the various political parties who fought Chaim Rumkowski's dictatorship in Lodz must not be lumped together with the self-interested rivalry of David Gertler, commandant of the Sonderkommando of the militia (see above, essay 12). Another instructive case is the dispute between Jacob Gens and Josef Glazman, both of them Revisionists, with views of their own on questions of Judenrat policy. Glazman was among the leaders of the underground, while Gens was a notorious collaborator. It is another question whether he hoped to save some of the ghetto Jews from extermination.[13] There were also attempts to replace the dictatorship of the Judenrat with the dictatorship of the Jewish militia. When Karl Löwenstein was appointed commandant of the militia in Theresienstadt, he sought to impose the domination of the militia, in order to "weed out corruption" in the Ältestenrat.[14]

There was also an opposition made up not of the parties or the underground but of the general population. The Judenrat was hated, despised, and reviled by the Jewish populace in a great many places. The war waged by the "house committees" against the Judenrat in Warsaw was one expression of this feeling. Another was the war waged against the Judenrat by various cliques such as that of Abraham Gancwajch and his organization "to control prices and combat usury" in the Warsaw ghetto, the so-called

*Draitsentl* (the Thirteen), which was linked with the Gestapo.[15] Kaspi-Srebrovitch in Kaunas was another case in point. In Budapest there existed a dual authority: on the one hand, there was the representation of the Jewish communities; and on the other, the Jewish Rescue Committee, the chairman of which, Rudolf (Reszö) Kasztner, conducted negotiations with Eichmann. This tangled skein is well known because of the Grünwald-Kasztner trial. In this sphere, we have little other material at our disposal. Generally speaking, the material must be brought to light by people directly connected with the events. But these people prefer to keep to themselves their knowledge of these sometimes shameful episodes.

## The Marxist Interpretation

I now revert to the matter of whom and what the Judenrat represented. Some individuals like to see things in clear, unambiguous outline and have a natural tendency toward simplification. For example, some writers propose that the question of the Judenrat members can be solved very simply by orthodox Marxist analysis: for them, the Judenrat represented the plutocracy and the Jewish bourgeoisie, and collaboration with the Nazis was aimed at one goal—to save the bourgeoisie and strengthen its hegemony over the poorer classes. It is all so simple!

The reality of the situation was far more complex, however, than this simplistic Marxist interpretation. Frequent and radical changes occurred in the social structure of the ghetto and affected almost all classes. Entire strata were declassed. Many of the capitalists who had possessed money, buildings, estates, factories, and stores lost all they had. In Lwów in 1942, I saw a man with a broom in his hand, who had once owned many buildings. When I asked what had happened, he replied: "Have you not heard? I have become a happy man. I am now the doorkeeper of the same buildings I once owned. I am now considered a 'useful worker,' guaranteed against forced labor and deportation." This was pseudo-proletarization.

There was a terrible declassing of the bourgeoisie, particularly of the members of the liberal professions and the upper-middle subgroups, which included former managers, teachers, officials, and lawyers. On the other hand there was the rise of the *lumpenproletariat*. There was also a new *lumpenbourgeoisie*—blackmailers, smugglers, toughs, all the underworld. Sometimes they became the true rulers of the ghetto.[16]

Under such unstable circumstances, it is rather difficult to determine which group represented whom or what. Indeed, it is impossible to tell from this complex picture which class was the ruler and which the ruled.

## The Moral Dilemma

Every man whom the Nazis ordered to join the Judenrat was faced with a moral dilemma: should he accept the appointment or should he decline? Should he somehow evade it, should he flee? Was it really desirable to establish a Judenrat? There was also the alternative of "passive resistance" or "noncooperation." All these questions are dealt with in the literature on the subject.

What were the main objectives and the moral countenance of the Judenrat members? What policy did they follow? In the early period, they apparently hoped to be able to do something to deceive the Germans, to bribe them, or win them over somehow. Numerous controversies raged over this question within the Judenräte, and Jacob Gens, Moses Merin, and others declared that they were "holding the wild beast off" by satisfying it with small sacrifices.

On the other hand, there were Judenräte which worked with the underground or at any rate maintained friendly relations with it. Did they do so in order to secure for themselves insurance on both sides of the fence? Why did Ephraim Barasz of Bialystok maintain contacts with the underground? Why did Gens keep in touch with the underground and then hand Yitzhak Wittenberg (leader of the Jewish Fighting Organization) over to the Gestapo and deport Josef Glazman? There are other questions, too. Was the suicide of Adam Czerniakow, head of the Warsaw Judenrat, morally justified? Should he not have warned the community first? Czerniakow's case was by no means unique. I have found more than ten other examples of members of Judenräte who did likewise, not only in Poland but in other areas too (for instance, in Trieste, Italy). Some of them left letters behind explaining the reasons for their action and warning the community. Thus Czerniakow's action, far from being purely and simply idiosyncratic, warrants further study as a social phenomenon.

## Transition from Judenrat to Dictatorship

Another question must be investigated: How did the Judenräte degenerate into virtual dictatorships, and what role was played by the "dictators"? How did they comport themselves? Was their underlying motive a thirst for power, or did they cherish a messianic illusion[17] that they were the chosen instruments for the redemption of their people? Without study of these questions, it is impossible to arrive at a historical appraisal of the role of the Judenrat—let alone enter into the sphere of political and moral judgment. We are still far from such a historical evaluation of the role of the Judenrat. One must not forget that the members of the Judenräte included such different figures as Benjamin Murmelstein (Theresienstadt), Ludwik Jaffe (Lwów), and Rabbi Zvi Koretz (Salonika). There were also leaders like Rabbi Leo Baeck; and still others like Rudolf (Reszö) Kasztner, who headed the Rescue Committee in Budapest (and was not a member of the Judenrat). They were diverse personalities with different attitudes. We are not yet prepared to form a detached picture of this phenomenon.

## Power and Jurisdiction

Within its original jurisdiction, the Judenrat was autonomous. This fact gave rise to optimism in certain circles, both among naïve people inside the ghettos and among far-away observers in neutral or Allied countries, who were not aware of the realities of the situation. The naïve reasoning behind the interpretation was as follows: With the ghettoization and isolation, the Jews were granted powers they had never before had. Nazi authorities were even going so far as to give Jewish names to formerly non-Jewish enclaves within some ghettos (Warsaw, Lodz, and others) and had, moreover, sent away all the non-Jewish inhabitants of one city (Theresienstadt). The only authority within the borders of the ghetto was the Judenrat and its militia, with a Jewish commander and Jewish officers. Never before had the Jews enjoyed so great a measure of self-government. During the Middle Ages they had exercised jurisdiction in civil law, but their authority in capital cases had never been unrestricted. Now, in many of the Nazi ghettos, they exercised full, untrammeled jurisdiction, even in capital cases.[18]

The real powers of the Judenräte were actually much greater. By preparing various lists for the Nazis, such as the list of candidates for *Übersiedlung* (deportation), the Judenräte had the power to decide who should live and who should die. Some Judenräte did not want to assume this responsibility. But others did assume power over life and death.[19] The powers of the Judenräte were still more pronounced in the economic sphere, particularly in those ghettos where there was an almost complete centralization of industry. (In Warsaw there was some private trade and industry, but in Theresienstadt, Lodz, and Vilna, centralization was almost complete.) By every means the Judenräte supervised economic life. Even private enterprise—with the exception of the smugglers—was under their control. In the economic sphere, too, the power exercised was one over life and death. Whoever was given food, lived; whoever was refused, died. Whoever obtained employment was granted a lease on life; he who did not, was sent by the Nazis to forced labor, or was deported, often to his death.

All these expanded economic and administrative activities called for a large apparatus and personnel. The Judenräte of the larger communities employed thousands of persons, besides the militia, which also had a large staff. The Judenrat personnel were to some degree protected from forced labor and/or deportation. This was another source of the power wielded over life and death by the Judenrat.

To naïve or distant observers, then, the Judenräte—at least in the early period—appeared quite impressive. They did not realize the internal weakness of the Judenrat, its internal conflicts, its instability, the constant pressure applied by the Nazis, who were using the Judenrat merely as an instrument to weaken and destroy the Jews. They did not realize the widespread distrust of it among the Jewish population or the often-justified opposition of the political parties and the underground. And, last but not least, they did not anticipate how the Judenrat, in the realities of life under the Nazi tyranny, would degenerate into a fatal oligarchy or dictatorship of men entirely unfit to assume any social responsibility. We have few detailed descriptions of the inner working of these bodies of Jewish "self-government."[20] A further study of this important problem is imperative.

## General Importance of the Judenrat Question

The question of the Judenrat and the internal development of the ghettos is of major importance, in the history not only of the Holocaust but of humankind in general. Here we have something in the nature of a vast psychosociological laboratory for human conduct without a parallel in previous historical experience. How did human beings comport themselves under the threat of death? How did they refuse to believe the fate that awaited them? Some people understood from the very first day that the Nazis planned to kill them, but others said that a mass slaughter was inconceivable. They refused to believe the evidence of their own eyes. I witnessed this myself firsthand, and others had the same experience. You think: "The Nazis do not really mean what they say, they are bluffing." Here is a broad field for psychosociological investigation into the reactions of people under extreme stress, under terror of imminent death.

❰ This essay is based on a paper read before the Yad Vashem Circle for the Study of the Problems of the European Catastrophe, Jerusalem, July 18, 1957. It was first published as Part One in a two-part essay, "Preliminary and Methodological Problems of the Research on the Jewish Catastrophe in the Nazi Period" (*Yad Vashem Studies on the European Jewish Catastrophe and Resistance,* 2 (1958), 95–131), which was the subject of two addresses delivered by Philip Friedman at Yad Vashem,

Jerusalem, on July 18 and 25, 1957. Part One, which is presented here, is entitled "Problems of Research in Jewish 'Self-Government' ('Judenrat') in the Nazi Period" (pp. 95–113). Part Two: "Jewish Resistance" (*ibid.*, pp. 114–31) was omitted, because the topic is covered in essay 16 above, "Jewish Resistance to Nazism."

Philip Friedman was preparing a comprehensive volume on "Jewish Communal Organization During the Nazi Era," when he died in 1960. His entire collection of primary sources on the Judenräte, which he started to amass as the director of the Jewish Historical Commission in Poland, was given by his widow to the "Joint Documentation Projects" of the YIVO-Yad Vashem in New York, where he served as Research Director from its inception. The collection was used as a basis for the comprehensive volume entitled *Judenrat: Jewish Councils in Eastern Europe Under Nazi Occupation,* prepared in the framework of the Joint Documentation Projects of the YIVO-Yad Vashem, and authored by Isaiah Trunk. The book shared the National Book Award for history in 1973.


## Notes

1. See also in this volume "Aspects of the Jewish Communal Crisis in Germany, Austria, and Czechoslovakia During the Nazi Period"; "Pseudo-Saviors in the Polish Ghettos: Mordechai Chaim Rumkowski of Lodz"; "The Messianic Complex of a Nazi Collaborator in a Ghetto: Moses Merin of Sosnowiec"; and "Jacob Gens: 'Commandant' of the Vilna Ghetto." A reader interested in the subject of the Judenrat will find in these essays some of the pertinent bibliography.

2. It should be noted that Joseph Tenenbaum is the only one among the authors of books on the Holocaust who has devoted a special volume, *Underground: The Story of a People* (New York, 1952), to the problems of Jewish life and the Jewish underground in Poland and has drawn generously on sources in Yiddish, Hebrew, and Polish.

3. Max Weinreich has gathered much material about these Nazi experts, in his *Hitler's Professors* (New York, 1946). See also Bernard D. Weinryb's "Jewish History Nazified," *CJR,* 4 (1941), 147–67; "Nazification of Jewish Learning," *The Jewish Review,* 3 (1945), 25–44, 107–37; "Nazification of Science and Research in Germany," *Journal of Central European Affairs,* 3 (1944), 373–400.

4. I make no mention of names here. We are, all of us, liable to err in our evaluation of historical events when we lack the necessary perspective.

5. On the Nazi plans for the Jewish colonization of Madagascar wherein the Nazis even utilized Zionist terminology and drew upon the experience of Jewish settlement in Palestine and the Halutz movement, see essay 2 above, "The Lublin Reservation and the Madagascar Plan."

6. On this subject, see particularly Zdenek Lederer, *Ghetto Theresien-stadt* (London, 1953); and H. G. Adler, *Theresienstadt, 1941–1945: Das Antlitz einer Zwangsgemeinschaft* (Tübingen, 1955).

7. *NCA,* VI, 97–101, Doc. PS–3363.

8. See above, essay on Merin; and "Aspects of the Jewish Communal Crisis."

9. See above, essays 12 and 13, respectively, on Rumkowski and Merin.

10. See essay 16, "Jewish Resistance to Nazism."

11. See above, essay 6, "Social Conflicts in the Ghetto."

12. *Ibid.,* and essay 3, "The Jewish Ghettos of the Nazi Era."

13. See above, essay 14 on Jacob Gens.

14. See above, essay 5, "Aspects of the Jewish Communal Crisis."

15. See essay 6, "Social Conflicts in the Ghetto."

16. *Ibid.*

17. See above, essays 12, 13, and 14 on Rumkowski, Merin, and Gens.

18. There was a debate on this question in the Lodz Judenrat. A number of members voiced their opposition to assuming this responsibility. We have information that the head of the Vilna ghetto, Jacob Gens, passed a death sentence which was carried out (cited above, essay 14).

19. In some ghettos this question, known in certain localities as the "Maimonides debate" (because of a relevant passage in Maimonides' *Mishneh Torah,* dealing with capital cases, *Hilkhot Avodah Zarah,* V, 5), was hotly disputed. See above in this volume, essay 13 on Merin (in particular note 2); and also essay 14 on Gens, and essay 12 on Rumkowski.

20. In this connection I must mention the excellent description by H. G. Adler in his book on Theresienstadt (cited in note 6). Detailed information is also available regarding Lodz and, to a lesser degree, Vilna. About Lodz, see Bendit Hershkovitch, "The Ghetto in Litzmannstadt," *YB,* 30 (1947), 21–58; about Vilna, see M. Dworzecki, *Yerushelayim delite in kamf un umkum* (Jerusalem of Lithuania in Struggle and in Destruction) (Paris, 1948). (See also, in this volume, notes to essays 12 and 14.)

# 23

# PROBLEMS OF RESEARCH ON
# THE HOLOCAUST: AN OVERVIEW

There is a saying that every generation creates its own historiosophical doctrine as well as research methods compatible with its spirit. This saying is certainly true with regard to periods of crisis necessitating the creation of new concepts and outlooks in the sociological sphere and philosophical viewpoint.

Recent events brought about the destruction of European Jewry which resulted from the Holocaust, the greatest crisis in the annals of the Jewish people. Though the rebirth of Israel, only a few years after the catastrophe,[1] stimulated the national spirit and rekindled a flame of hope in the hearts of the mourning people, we nevertheless cannot suppress the innermost urge and command to remember the Holocaust and to study its history.

We cannot as yet determine what impact this crisis will have upon the trends of thought and upon the spiritual physiognomy of our people in the years to come. It is quite unusual for philosophical and historiosophical systems to spring up overnight, or to develop after a holocaust, because they require a long perspective to come into being and crystalize. Nevertheless, the eye which as yet is gazing into semidarkness can discern the beginning of a reappraisal of historic events and of past and present problems. This means that the appraisal at which we have arrived to date is also subject to a process of constant change.

## Trends in the Collecting and Processing of Data

### THE PRACTICAL-POLITICAL TREND

Within the short period of twenty-five years[2] since the Nazi accession to power in Germany, research on the Holocaust has already undergone several changes. Up to the early 1940s, when the extent of the destruction and the evil devices of the Nazis were still unknown, what was needed was not an objective historiography, but the obtaining of data for a practical purpose; namely, to expose the nature of Nazi intentions, to point out the danger threatening the Jews, to shock public opinion all over the world into action, to urge the different political factors to intervene, and to conduct relief and rescue work on behalf of the victims of Nazism. As a result, the collection of this data, which at that time served the main purpose of disseminating information about Nazism and denouncing it, produced a vast quantity of historical material that had to be filed, processed, and published by various institutions.

### THE PRACTICAL-JURIDICAL TREND

As the war drew to its end, and during the first postwar years, the work of documentation entered a new stage of development, and a new purpose became evident: to collect data that would be instrumental in establishing the guilt of the Nazi war criminals. In this connection, cooperation developed between the Jewish institutions and the tribunals set up by the Allied powers, both on an international scale, and in each country separately. Naturally, the preparation of material for war crimes tribunals requires a system of work different than the compilation of literature for information only, that is, great exactitude and minute analyses of the facts. On the other hand, it must be borne in mind that the selection of the data made from the prosecutor's point of view must necessarily be one-sided, so that the attention of the compilers was focused mainly on documents relevant to Nazi crimes, rather than on other features of the period.

### THE TREND OF HISTORICAL RETROSPECT

Simultaneously with the activities of the war crimes tribunals, the Jewish historical committees in various countries began their work. Within a short time, institutes, centers, and commissions for the study of the Holocaust were established in France, Poland, Hungary, Slovakia, Bohemia, Italy, Austria, Germany, and in neutral countries such as Sweden and Switzerland. Some of these carried on activities initiated by the underground during the Nazi occupation, as was the case in France, for instance. In some cases it was possible to recover buried or hidden archives of organizations that had been secretly active during the Nazi reign of terror, as happened with the "Oneg Shabbat" archives in Warsaw that had been established by Emanuel Ringelblum. Among others, mention should also be made of remnants of the archives of the Bund, of the Labor-Zionist underground movement, of the Judenräte councils of Vilna, Bialystok, Częstochowa, Lodz, Lublin, Theresienstadt, and elsewhere. Even in the concentration camps, as in Vittel in France, in the camp on Janowska Street in Lwów, or in the death camp in Auschwitz, attempts had been made by the inmates to put down in writing the sufferings of the Jews. We are today in possession of remnants of these statements and testimonies which were hidden away at the time and later recovered.

The appearance of the Jewish historical institutes opens a new chapter in the study of the Holocaust. The aim now is historical documentation per se, documentation to embrace all historical features during the Nazi regime, including the internal life of the Jewish community at that time, its social, cultural, religious, artistic, and literary activities. Yet here, too, the spirit of contemporary events influenced the work and its character. During the first postwar years, the employees of these historical institutes were unable to restrain their feelings, to suppress the memories of pain and injury sustained during the Nazi outrage. The first reaction of the survivors after their liberation was a passionate desire to dramatize the impact of the past experience. This was done by producing memoirs, diaries, testimonies, stories, poetry, and emotional accounts of what happened during the Nazi horror period. The description of the suffering and acts of cruelty inflicted by the Nazis ranked first and foremost in the literature. Nor were the people working on behalf of historical institutes unimpressed by the strong tide of this emotional trend.

In the late 1940s, a number of new institutions in the State of Israel were added to those mentioned above: Yad Vashem and Bet Lohamei Hagetaot named for Itzhak Katzenelson, as well as, more recently, the Leo Baeck Institute (which has centers in Israel, London, and New York), part of whose activities is concerned with problems of the Holocaust in Nazi Germany. A number of non-Jewish institutions and committees for the study of the Nazi era were also established and have succeeded in amassing considerable data on the European Jewish catastrophe. They are the Central Commission for Investigation of German Crimes in Poland, the State Institute for War Documentation in Amsterdam, the Comité d'Histoire de la Deuxième Guerre Mondiale in France. To this list should be added the recently established Institut für Zeitgeschichte in Munich, as well as the Hoover Institute and Library in California.

It is not accidental that of the dozen or so Jewish historical committees mentioned above, only a few are still extant. In some countries, the historical committees were dissolved because of mass Jewish emigration as well as for other reasons. This happened in Germany, Austria, Slovakia, Hungary, Bulgaria, Switzerland, Sweden, and the USSR. In a majority of cases, their material was transferred to institutions in Israel. In this connection it should be pointed out that nothing is known about the fate of the material in the possession of the disbanded Jewish Anti-Fascist Committee in Moscow. At present, there are only a few research institutes extant in Israel, France, Poland, and the U.S.A.

On the one hand, this may be a healthy process. As this natural selection has left only the most qualified, and in place of a great number of weakly established institutions, a few consolidated centers have been developed. On the other hand, there is ground to fear that this tendency of dispersion and dismantling will continue and that additional institutions will be liquidated for various external reasons. It should also be borne in mind that a number of rather important institutions either have abandoned the study of the Holocaust altogether or are devoting to it only part of their resources and time.

In the beginning all the historical committees acted separately, though there were attempts at coordination. In July 1947, the First World Congress of Jewish Studies was held in Jerusalem, and problems connected with the study of the Holocaust were aired on that occasion. A second attempt of this sort was the convention of committees for the study of the Holocaust, held in Paris in December 1947, on the initiative of Itzhak Schneersohn. It should be added that in February 1949 a convention for the study of the Holocaust was held in New York, under the joint auspices of YIVO and the Conference on Jewish Relations. In conclusion, and by way of a brief summary, it may be said that all these conventions did not, regrettably, yield any tangible results. Of all attempts at cooperation, only a single project has so far crystalized, the Joint Documentation Projects in the fields of archives and bibliography of Yad Vashem and YIVO.[3]

### THE RESULT OF THE THREE TRENDS IN RESEARCH

The question may thus be asked, what have we left today of all the efforts made in the past? It has already been pointed out that a great deal of material had been compiled and concentrated in the various institutions. What concerns the student of the period, however, is to know the nature of the species of material represented in great concentration in each of those institutions. Official German documents are available in the different institutions in more or less equal quantities. On the other hand, the assembling of documents relevant to the Jewish underground and to Jewish warfare was mainly undertaken by the Jewish Historical Institute in Warsaw (formerly the Central Jewish Historical Commission in Poland),

Yad Vashem, and Bet Lohamei Hagetaot. The collecting of eyewitness records was principally carried out by the Warsaw Institute, Yad Vashem, and YIVO. Documents and minutes of many trials held after the war are found in substantial quantities in the offices of the Centre de Documentation Juive Contemporaine in Paris, in the files of YIVO, and in some non-Jewish institutions in various countries, mainly the U.S.A., Germany, Poland, and the USSR. We do not know and cannot even imagine the extent of this collection of countless records, as we have not yet reached the stage where a general census of this multitude of documents appears to be practical.[4] In my view, Yad Vashem is the only institution in this field which has pursued the right track by systematically preparing microfilm reproductions of records kept in other institutions (such as the International Tracing Service, in Arolsen, Germany).

Finally, we must not lose sight of the Nazi press and literature compiled at the Wiener Library, Yad Vashem, YIVO, and the Institute of Jewish Affairs.

Although the great job of accumulating this copious material is still in progress and far from being completed, it may be asked what actually has been done till now by way of sorting out, cataloguing, and publishing in various forms the multitude of documents already assembled in the archives of the Jewish institutions. There is no room for a statistical review of these publications within the scope of this survey. Suffice it to say that the most intensive activity in this sphere has been carried out by the Centre de Documentation Juive Contemporaine in Paris, the Historical Institute in Warsaw, and YIVO. Of late, Bet Lohamei Hagetaot and Yad Vashem have joined in this work. Besides, other institutions have published, or are in the process of publishing, bulletins and periodicals devoted to the study of the Holocaust.

## *Private Research and* Landsmanshaftn *Publications*

More material than that published by these institutions has been published by private initiative. The institutions have, generally, been reluctant to publish research treatises and books of synthesis and have rather concentrated on publishing documents and monographs on limited subjects, while scholars and publishers have made attempts at producing comprehensive and synthetic books privately.

Speaking of publications, we must not leave out the great efforts and wide-ranging activities of the *landsmanshaften* (associations of fellow countrymen) or locality associations abroad. Whatever our view may be, from a scholarly standpoint, of the intrinsic value of the memorial volumes, which by now already amount to a few hundred in number, we must not take this sort of literary effort too lightly. For, do they not contain a great many eyewitness accounts of a unique nature? And as for the less valuable material included in those volumes, is it not the historian's business to tell the wheat from the chaff? As we know, it is only in rare cases that the publication of memorial volumes was undertaken by experienced editors and expert scholars. Organized research institutions should, therefore, find the ways to these *landsmanshaftn* with a view to assisting them.

## Schools of Thought on the Holocaust

### THE MARTYROLOGICAL CONCEPTION

At the outset of this essay, I pointed out that by now a certain development has already taken place in the historical concept of the Holocaust. Following the first two stages of this development—emphasizing publicity and legal claims—the third stage opened with the appearance of the institutes and committees for the study of the Holocaust. We are still in the third stage, in which historical documentation was started as a purpose in itself. As a matter of fact, this documentation should have embraced the historical background during the Nazi regime in all its aspects, which means the inclusion of the internal history of the Jewish people at that time. But here, too, the spirit of our times has exerted a one-sided influence. What I mean is that the spirit of martyrology emanating from our literature on the Holocaust prevents a clear-cut view from a historical perspective. True, the sympathizing heart beats in harmony with those of the scholars and authors who could not suppress their emotions roused by the impact of the tragedy. We are dealing here with an outbreak of emotionalism that has had no precedent in our literature. As a result of this phenomenon the material at the disposal of the scholars consisted mainly of one kind, namely of descriptions of the suffering inflicted and the atrocities committed by the Nazis. Thus we were reverting again to the historiographical system of the *Leidensgeschichte* (martyrology), which had become obsolete a long time ago. Even a man of Elias Tcherikover's caliber, who was certainly a long way from the school of thought of Leopold Zunz and Heinrich Graetz, has given prominence to the martyrological idea as the central theme in laying down the fundamental points of reference for a study of the Holocaust. Likewise, the first authors of comprehensive studies, such as Leon Poliakov, Gerald Reitlinger, and Joseph Tenenbaum, were consciously or subconsciously drawn to the martyrological conception. Only one of them, Joseph Tenenbaum, burst these narrow confines in one of his earlier studies,

*Underground,* in which he describes an important aspect of Jewish life in the Nazi era—the story of Jewish resistance in occupied Poland.

## EMPHASIS ON THE RESISTANCE
## AS A HISTORICAL PHENOMENON

Concurrent with this conception was the development of another school of thought, particularly among surviving members of the underground and of Jewish youth organizations, which laid emphasis on the acts of resistance during the Holocaust. This school of thought was again subdivided into two different trends. The first, represented by the Zionists, the Bundists, and the Orthodox Jews, underlined—in spite of differences of opinion reflected in the descriptions and interpretations of the Holocaust and resistance—the unity and cooperation of the Jewish organizations and of the Jewish people in their struggle against the Nazi foe. The second trend, represented by the Communists and their fellow-travelers, approached the study of the Holocaust from the background of an alleged class struggle within the ghetto; that is to say, an accentuation of the discord and disunity, in direct contrast to the former trend. In their own language: "The bourgeois circles and the Judenrat councils betrayed the common people." According to this view, the expressions of Jewish resistance were but one link in the chain of general anti-Fascist uprisings organized irrespective of national affiliation, by the proletariat against the Nazi invader. It must be admitted, by the way, that these historians devoted greater efforts to the study of the internal history of the Holocaust than did the representatives of the national trend. But the one-sided, categorical tendency that lavishly hurls accusations, including those without foundation, impairs the scholarly value of these treatises.

Finally, it should be pointed out that both camps, the nationalists and Communists alike, sinned against the principles of scholarly research by adopting a romantic approach and accepting apocryphal stories—such as are always likely to be invented and diffused in times of crisis—at their face value, without checking their authenticity. It will, therefore, be a difficult task for the scholar in years to come, to free himself of the new myth that has already struck deep roots in our historical consciousness.

## AMALGAMATION OF THE
## TWO FORMER CONCEPTIONS

A certain development in the study of the Holocaust has been noticeable in Israel for several years: the broadening of the historical picture through a particular combination of the subjects represented by the two schools of thought—Holocaust and Resistance. Yet this approach, too, is incomplete. I should like to draw attention here to Benzion Dinur's article published in the first issue of *Yad Vashem Studies* in which he said that it was not enough to deal "with the whole pattern of Catastrophe and Heroism," but that it was also our duty to conduct research in the sphere of "all processes that come to light in everyday life" as well as of events that took place "in the biological and sociological cells of Jewish society."

## The Jewish People as a Subject for Research on the Holocaust

In my opinion, the crux of the problem is how to effect a radical change in the field of research relating to the Holocaust and in our methods of work. We cannot rest content with a study of the persecutions and the reactions they provoked. In fact, most of the works published so far are solely concerned with the subject of anti-Jewish hostility and its effects. What we need is a history of the Jewish people during the period of Nazi rule in which the central role is to be played by the Jewish people, not only as tragic victims but as bearers of a communal existence with all the manifold and numerous aspects involved. Our approach must be definitely "Judeocentric" as opposed to "Nazi-centric."

### THE NECESSITY TO CONCENTRATE ON THE INTERNAL HISTORY OF OUR PEOPLE

It is now opportune to begin to concentrate and elaborate on the material for the internal history of our people during the Holocaust. Some may ask, what possible position can the internal history occupy within the framework of so short an episode as the Holocaust which was over in a matter of years, and which came to its conclusion in mass extermination? This objection is ill-founded, for a number of reasons.

Firstly, the importance of any period is not measured by the number of years it comprises. The French Revolution, for instance, has been the subject of more studies and treatises than many other periods in history, which stretched over a much longer span of time. Furthermore, during the few years of the period of the Holocaust, the events taking place in the life of our nation, in the ghettos and in concentration camps, were so rapid in succession and by way of impact, and so far-reaching in their consequences, that they were unprecedented.

Secondly, those who maintain that mass extermination was the closing stage of the process, are wrong. The six million victims (though no longer among us) have influenced, are influencing, and will continue to influence the fate of our nation. The reestablishment of the State of Israel immediately following the Holocaust is a striking proof of the correctness of this premise. Another example: the Jewish consciousness of the great masses of our people in the lands of the Diaspora during and following the Holocaust took on new tangible forms which are already beginning to find expression in literature, philosophy, and communal affairs.

Thirdly, the study of the internal life during the Holocaust is of particular significance not only from a Jewish, but also from a universal point of view. For the first time in the history of human civilization, a concentrated group of people of a comprehensive social structure and with a highly developed cultural and social standard found themselves compelled to live under the shadow of death, yet managed to leave to posterity survivors to tell the story and a significant amount of information on what had taken place. Thus, the internal history of the ghettos and the camps emerges before the eye of the student of the period as though inside a test tube of a vast psychosociological laboratory such as had never been set up before.

### THE UNIVERSAL ELEMENTS OF JEWISH HISTORY DURING THE HOLOCAUST

Some circles hold that the universal value of Jewish history is to be found in the annals of persecution rather than in those of our nation's internal life. Mankind, the proponents of this theory assert, is not concerned with the internal life of the Jewish people. This theory is unacceptable for a variety of reasons. (a) It is the Jewish historian's task to facilitate an understanding of Jewish ways of life, and of Jewish internal development rather than stress points of interest to the gentiles. (b) What is "universal history"? Every individual and every community is part of universal history by the modes of life peculiar to it. Why then should we, the Jewish people, with all our special and complicated problems, not be at least as important a part of universal history as are other communities? (c) Jewish history is universal even in a technical sense, because it embraces almost all countries and all periods. Thus Simon Dubnow called his history *Weltgeschichte des jüdischen Volkes* (World History of the Jewish People). (d) The main thing in a truly universal history of mankind is not necessarily the compilation of historical facts pertaining to ethnic or linguistic groups but the universal spirit permeating such a historical conception, that is, the presumption that there should be no bias in favor of, or against, any nation, or religious, philosophical, or social system. Mankind has as yet not reached such a high degree of perfection. A universal history capable of overcoming all ideological and internal difficulties in appraising historical facts and processes is as yet a Utopian dream. It is known that UNESCO is trying to lay the foundations for a universal history of mankind on such an international, intermovemental, and nondogmatic level. To what extent this effort will succeed, only the future will show.

It may be noted here that in the early history of the Jewish people, our prophets made attempts at forging a universal historiosophic outlook based on the recognition of international moral values. Much of this universal outlook was lost to us during the Diaspora in the isolated ghetto life we led in the Middle Ages. Perhaps the time has now come for a renewal of these attempts at forming a universal conception of historiography, especially in the study of the period of the Holocaust, the revelations and expressions of which are almost wholly of general concern to all mankind. For the problems arising, such as segregation, isolation, ghettoization, relations between Jews and gentiles, the reaction of individuals and the persecutions and attempts at extermination, the extent of suffering and its potential, the desire and ability for self-defense and resistance, the problems connected with deportations, the displaced persons phenomenon, survivors and their adjustment to normal conditions—all these are historical experiences to which not only the Jews were subjected, and their description and interpretation is important not only to us alone. Another universally human problem of a philosophical nature is the question of crime and punishment, the question of the responsibility of the community for the acts of its leaders and of the political organizations serving them, the questions of private, political, public, moral, and metaphysical responsibility, as defined by the German philosopher Karl Jaspers. The theory of responsibility for war crimes against civilian populations, especially the crime of exterminating whole peoples (now known as "genocide," a term coined by the Jewish savant Rafael Lemkin), has been worked out in international law. No doubt, this theory is a worthy expression of the Jewish moral tradition, but on the other hand, there can be no doubt that the fundamental stimulus that induced its originator to develop this theory and to fight for its adoption on the international stage for many years in a heroic struggle of one against many, was the great Jewish tragedy during the Nazi rule in Europe.

It also goes without saying that the mass extermination of Jews would have been impossible if the populations of many countries and nationalities had not for generations been imbued with anti-Semitism, particularly in Germany and in Eastern Europe. Benzion Dinur is right in saying (in (*Yad Vashem Studies* I) that it is impossible to penetrate into the structure of the Nazi plot without first unearthing the historical roots of anti-Jewish sentiment, at least during the modern era. In this regard, a study of anti-

Semitism in each country separately, on a local basis only, will not suffice. The study of anti-Semitism is again a classic example of the need for a universal approach, as regards both the material and a historic-sociological interpretation and appraisal. It is clear that anti-Semitism is not only a matter pertaining to Jewish historiography, but a universal moral and social matter, and the study of this problem is important from a universal point of view.

## Historical Problems Requiring Elucidation

In order to avoid dealing with abstract notions only, I will enumerate and describe briefly a number of questions which have hardly been studied so far and which require thorough and fundamental elucidation.

1. The Ghetto and the Judenrat: We are confronted with some form of Jewish self-government, but as a matter of fact, this home rule is nothing but a travesty of the term as a result of the misuse and abuse by the Nazis of ideas of Jewish autonomy and territorialism, for the purpose of misleading and deceiving. Further problems are: the external and the internal ghetto arrangements; the differences between the medieval ghetto and the Nazi ghetto in layout and purpose; the role of such creations as the Sammelghetto (central ghetto), Transitghetto, and others. Naturally, the external and internal aspects of ghetto life should be considered as well.

We must further consider the composition of the Judenrat, its system of work, its terms of reference and authority within the framework of the duties assigned to it by the Nazis.

From this subject of investigation many sub-subjects branch off, some of which are enumerated here:

(a) The attitude of the Jewish population toward the Judenrat.

(b) The Judenrat's cooperation with the enemy, and on the other hand, the Judenrat's contact and negotiations with the Jewish and non-Jewish underground.

(c) The ambivalence of the Judenrat's actions and purposes.

(d) The imposition of the *Führerprinzip,* the leadership principle, in the organizational structure of the Judenrat, and the influence of the latter upon the course of communal life.

(e) The problem of the moral attitude imposed upon the members of the Judenrat and the personal dilemma and complexes entailed thereby.[5]

2. The economic and social life with all its dynamic components. In short:

(a) The revolutionary upheavals taking place between the classes and their acute expressions, such as the social and economic restratification and displacement, the reversal of the class pyramid.

(b) The process of real and fictitious productivization and proletarization.

(c) The destruction of family life and the disintegration of other social cells, and on the other hand, the setting up of new social cells, especially in the underground movement.

3. The moral revolution as a result of purposeful corruption by the Nazis; the reappraisals of values and the unceasing conflict between moral values inherited from the forebears and values of distorted moral notions imposed by the Nazis. In short, the relation between man and God, man and his neighbor, and man and society.

4. The Jewish resistance movement against the background of outside factors and its integration into the same. This problem should be also studied against the wider background of international politics and the theory and practice of partisan warfare as expounded by the various theoreticians, such as Mao Tse-tung in China, the Soviet underground, and others. The success and advantages of Soviet planning in this field based on the experiences of others, and the Soviet efforts to spread its influence not only on underground activities in Eastern Europe but on those in Western and Southern Europe as well, have to be explained.

5. Intergroup relations between Jews and gentiles. In this field we have committed many sins by being drawn into acceptance of simplified formulas known to everyone. Our evaluation of the attitude of the Christian neighbors to the Jewish tragedy should be one of differentiation and the finest distinction. The blurred and deficient picture we have in general— and unjustly so—of the gentile friends, helpers, and rescuers of Jews during the Nazi era will also be decisively amended thereby.

6. Rescue and relief actions within Jewish society and outside it, on a local and international scale.


## *Summary of Practical Proposals*

In conclusion, I should like to summarize a number of proposals which have as their purpose laying down lines of action for the future.

1. We have, of course, to continue compiling documentary material, which means:

(a) Concentration of the ample material which is still dispersed in the archives of the various institutions, in different countries, as well as in the possession of private individuals. I have in mind not only documents from archives but also rare books, periodicals, manuscripts, photographs, films, reports, and the like.

(b) The unearthing of hidden sources (those not yet discovered).

(c) The creation of new material by organized recording of evidence from Jewish survivors and gentile eyewitnesses by means of questionnaires, interviews, the registration of material available in the archives of war crimes tribunals, civil courts.

While the material under (a) and (b) can be collected in the course of many years to come, proposal (c) must be translated into action as speedily as possible, as many eyewitnesses of the Holocaust are old and sickly people.

2. Furthermore, the cataloguing and bibliographical sorting of documents in the archives and libraries must be continued. Other institutions, thus far standing aside, should be made to join in such activity.

3. The coordination of the work of the various institutions is of the utmost importance. For this purpose, extensive planning is required: exchange of material, of students, research scholars, and lecturers; the holding of seminars, panels, and conventions.

4. The publication of a central periodical on a worldwide scale is urgently called for.

5. Only the training of students in universities and a crop of young research scholars can ensure the continuation of research. If not, the program may be paralyzed and die a painless death.

6. I have already touched on the necessity to include the *landsmanshaften,* and steps should be taken to this effect.

❧ This essay is based on an extended and revised version of a lecture delivered by Philip Friedman at the Second World Congress of Jewish Studies, Jerusalem, August 4, 1957. It was published under the title "Problems of the Research on the European Jewish Catastrophe," in *Yad Vashem Studies on the European Jewish Catastrophe and Resistance,* 3 (1959), 25–39; and in *From Hatred to Extermination. Seven Lectures Delivered at the Second World Congress for Jewish Studies, The Section for the History of the Jewish People, August 4, 1957* (Jerusalem, 1959), pp. 25–39. It was reprinted by Yad Vashem in *The Catastrophe of European Jewry. Antecedents–History–Reflections.* Selected papers. Ed. by Yisrael Gutman and Livia Rothkirchen (Jerusalem, 1976), pp. 633–50 (with additional notes).

The author has expressed his appreciation to Dr. Baruch Ophir, Jerusalem, and Dr. Jacob Robinson, New York, for their suggestions and assistance in preparing the final draft of the lecture.

# Notes

1. For consistency with other essays the term "Jewish Catastrophe" was for the most part replaced in the text by the term "Holocaust." [*Ed.*]

2. Refers to the time of the writing. [*Ed.*]

3. Since the time the author presented this lecture, several new institutions of research and documentation on the Holocaust have been set up, for example, *Moreshet*. In addition, research projects have been undertaken at various institutions attached to the universities in Israel, and international seminars have been held under the auspices of Yad Vashem.

4. It should be noted that under the initiative of the Institute of Contemporary Jewry at the Hebrew University of Jerusalem a project has been begun to publish a *Guide to Unpublished Materials of the Holocaust Period.* To date two volumes have appeared, containing material from several important archives located in Israel. At the moment, a third volume is in preparation, which will be published jointly with Yad Vashem, and which will contain material located in the Yad Vashem archives.

5. The cases of suicide among the members of the Judenräte and their officials are not only a purely personal phenomenon, as is widely believed, but one that should be interpreted from a social point of view.

(Notes 3, 4, and 5 are reprinted from *The Catastrophe of European Jewry.*)

# APPENDIX

*Outline of Program*
*for Holocaust Research*

# OUTLINE OF PROGRAM
# FOR HOLOCAUST RESEARCH

This program was first formulated by the author in 1945 during the formative stages of research on the great catastrophe. It was later revised and submitted by him to the First International Conference on World War II in the West (Section IV, subsection 4b), which was held in Amsterdam on September 5 to 9, 1950, under the auspices of the Rijksinstituut voor Oorlogsdokumentatie (The Netherlands State Institute for War Documentation); that paper was distributed in mimeographed form by the Rijksinstituut and is here published for the first time.

The problems involved in recording the history of the Jewish people during World War II are quite different from the problems in the overall history of that war. For a general history of the war, the most important subjects are the strategic and military course of the war; economic hardships; activities of the governments-in-exile and of the collaborationist puppet governments in the occupied countries; diplomatic activities; resistance and underground activities. Of rather secondary importance to a general history of the war, but of primary importance to the Jewish history of that period, are such topics as the persecution of the civilian populations; forced labor; the compulsory transfers in wartime; concentration camps and atrocities; reactions of the civilian population; and other facets of research. As became clear early in the war, the principal goal for the Allied countries was a political one, the victory of democracy; but for European Jewry the problem was more crucial—survival. The main topics of research on the Holocaust, therefore, relate to the sufferings of the Jewish population and the struggle for life. These topics may be outlined as follows:

*I. The Nazi Philosophy and Strategy of Annihilating the Jews*
   A. Antecedents of the Holocaust
      1. Growth of German anti-Semitism in the Wilhelminian era

2. Political, social, and ideological background of Nazism in the era of the Weimar Republic
3. Development of the Nazi anti-Jewish program from the time of Hitler's seizure of power in 1933 to the outbreak of World War II
4. Theory of "Lebensraum"; program for annihilating the indigenous peoples; implications for the Jewish question

B. Phases of the Nazi anti-Jewish policy during the years 1939–1942
1. Plan for deportation, transfer, and concentration of the Jewish population; resettlement program (the Lublin Reservation and the Madagascar plans)—a camouflaging device or a serious design for a non-bloody solution which failed?
2. Decision to annihilate the Jews in the "Soviet-contaminated" areas; elaborate plans for extermination; establishment of "special tasks" squads in cooperation with military and police forces
3. Decision to annihilate Jews in all Axis-occupied and satellite countries; real and alleged reasons for decision; discussions around the problem; the decisive conference in Berlin-Wannsee in January 1942; plan for the "Final Solution of the Jewish Question"; successive orders and instructions; propaganda and indoctrination
4. Execution of the "Final Solution" (1942–1944); conflict between high Nazi officials (NSDAP and SS) and representatives of army and big business regarding means of extermination of the Jews and exploitation of Jewish slave laborers in concentration camps
5. Influence of military and political situation on the Nazi extermination program; attempts of neutral mediators to bargain with Nazis about the remnants of the Jewish population; Swiss and Swedish attempts at mediation; negotiations in Hungary and elsewhere
6. The German people and the extermination policy; attitudes of rank-and-file bureaucrats, the administration and the army, the "man in the street"; attitude of anti-Nazi circles to the slaughter of the Jews; protests of German émigrés
7. Postwar discussions in German society on the question of responsibility for Nazi crimes against the Jews; about the collective moral, criminal, and "metaphysic" responsibility of the German nation; appraisal of the Nuremberg Trials and other war crimes trials in Germany; German literature and research on the Holocaust

*II. Legislative and Economic Action Affecting the Jews in 1939–1945*
A. Legal philosophy of the Third Reich with respect to the Jews
B. Abrogation of civil rights and franchise
C. Restriction of liberty of movement and communication
D. Identification and isolation of Jews
E. The ghetto; its establishment and motivations; types of Jewish ghettos
F. Forced labor; labor camps; labor brigades; Jewish labor in industrial plants; ghetto factories; and shops
G. Methods of confiscation of Jewish property: personal, real, and communal assets
H. Elimination from economic, national, and cultural life
I. Legislation pertinent to Jewish autonomous bodies, social welfare and self-help activities; destruction of Jewish communal and religious life

    J. Economic warfare: penalties, collective fines, "contributions," taxes and duties, reparations, "redemption of Jewish hostages," and so forth

    K. Biological warfare: food rationing and other supply restrictions; regulations aimed at undermining the health of the Jewish population; disruption of medical care

    L. Legislation prohibiting the protection and hiding of Jews by non-Jews

*III. Acts of Terrorism and Extermination*

    A. Pogroms: how they were carried out; role of army and various German officials and of the native populations; police raids, arrests, and "exemplary" executions

    B. Destruction and burning of Jewish institutions

    C. Exhibition of atrocities for "educational" purposes

    D. Nazi strategy of extermination

        1. Camouflaging measures

        2. Principles of selection: "priorities" in the extermination schedule (aged and sick persons, children, and women)

        3. Methods of extermination: "special treatment" (*Sonderbehandlung*); the death camps

        4. "West to East" movement for extermination; local deportations

    E. The perpetrators

        1. Social, educational, and psychological background

        2. Training for extermination

        3. Morale and philosophy

        4. Sadism and mental aberration

        5. Financial and material gains of the extermination program: for the Third Reich; for the NSDAP and the SS; for individuals

        6. Dehumanizing effects of extermination activities on the perpetrators; demoralizing effects on the German nation as a whole

*IV. Impact of Nazi Persecution on Jewish Life*

    A. Biological impact

        1. Decrease in birth rate

        2. Starvation

        3. Unsanitary conditions in the ghettos and concentration camps

        4. Ghetto and camp diseases

        5. Morbidity and mortality

        6. Statistics of biological destruction (breakdown by country, sex, age, social status, and so forth)

        7. Postwar medical and psychological examination of survivors

    B. Economic impact

        1. Destruction of the economic foundation

        2. Dispossession and pauperization

        3. Economic restratification

        4. Sham utilization of Jewish professionals in menial tasks and hard labor

        5. Proletarization

        6. Struggle for life through illegal occupations: black market, smuggling

        7. Material losses

    C. Social life

        1. General restratification and declassment

2. Degradation of the upper classes
3. Special persecution of intellectuals by the Nazis; peculiar predicament of the intellectual and white-collar workers
4. Plight of children and orphans
5. Rise of new social classes: new communal oligarchy (Jewish Council and militia); nouveaux riches (the corrupted outcasts of society, such as blackmailers, profiteers, speculators, doing service for the Germans, go-betweens, "snatchers," "fixers," and the like)
6. Attitude toward Judenrat oligarchy and nouveaux riches
7. Social antagonisms and conflicts in the ghetto
8. Disintegration of communal and social life
9. Disintegration of the family
10. Jewish self-help: organization; legal, quasi-legal, and illegal forms

D. Moral, spiritual, and cultural life
1. Influence of Nazi "morality" on some strata of the Jewish population
2. Collaborators: the philosophy of collaboration and cooperation with the Germans and their representatives
3. Moral appraisal of Jewish autonomous institutions and bodies; central and local councils
4. Rise and fall of Jewish ghetto dictators
5. Jewish militia
6. Jewish *"Kapos"* in the concentration camps
7. Attitudes in Jewish society
    (a) "Surrenderism"
    (b) Quest for oblivion and nirvana
    (c) Escapism
    (d) Survivalism
    (e) Determination of resistance and armed revolt
8. Religious life and religious interpretation of the Holocaust
    (a) The "God's Punishment" philosophy
    (b) Messianic and mystic attitudes; Hasidism
    (c) The "Confidence" (*'Bitokhn'*) philosophy
9. Folkways, folksongs, and folklore under the Nazis
10. Satirical weapons against Nazis and Jewish collaborators
11. "Cassandras"—monitors and bards of the ghetto
12. Literature of anger and resistance
13. Literary activity in the ghettos and concentration camps: popular trend to write memoirs and chronicles; sociopsychological reason, evidenced in clandestine ghetto literature
    (a) *J'accuse* ("I accuse the world") motive
    (b) "Non omnis moriar" ("I shall not wholly die")
    (c) "Let us have evidence of what happened"
    (d) *De profundis* call to God and humanity
    (e) Credo of faith in humanity and belief in final justice
14. Illegal Jewish press in the ghetto
15. Legal and illegal education for children and adults in the ghetto
16. Attempts at cultural activity in the concentration camps

E. Resistance and fighting
1. Forms of resistance

      (a) Spiritual, moral, individual, collective, spontaneous, and organized

      (b) Sabotage in German war-production plants

      (c) Anti-German propaganda and espionage

      (d) Armed resistance

2. Hiding and escape

      (a) Forged identification cards and "Aryan" papers

      (b) Hideouts

      (c) Strategy in building bunkers

      (d) Escape into the woods and mountains

      (e) Escape across frontiers (to Hungary, Rumania, Switzerland, Spain)

3. Participation of Jews in the general resistance

4. Separate Jewish resistance groups; reason for their coming into being; their relations with the general organizations of resistance

      (a) Underground groups, combat organizations, and youth groups

      (b) Urban underground and fighting

      (c) Field operations and guerrilla fighting

      (d) Geographic extent of Jewish underground and partisan movements (France, the Low Countries, Italy, Yugoslavia, Greece, Poland, Slovakia, Rumania, Lithuania, White Russia and Volhynia, North Africa)

## V. *The Outside World: External Factors*

A. Reaction in Allied and neutral countries; relief and rescue activities

1. International Red Cross

2. Western Europe

3. Rescue action by the Swedish people and government

4. Declarations by Allied governments and governments-in-exile

5. British government and the refugee problem

6. Palestinian issue and the infiltration of Jewish refugees

7. U.S. government and people

8. Jewish organizations in the U.S.

9. War Refugee Board in Washington

10. Palestinian Jewry: parachutists and the Jewish Brigade

B. German satellite countries

1. Changing attitudes and policies in Italy with respect to the Jewish question; Nazi-influenced racism of Farinacci and others; pro-Jewish attitude of the Italian people; the life-saving policy of the Italian authorities in the Italian zone of occupation in France

2. Gradual deterioration of the Jewish situation in Hungary under German pressure; destruction of Hungarian Jewry after March 1944

3. Rumanian policy on the Jewish question: tolerant attitude in the old country vs. extermination in the former Russian-occupied areas

4. Bulgaria: opposition to the extermination policy; severe legal and economic oppression of the Jewish population

5. Japanese administration in Shanghai, and the Jewish ghetto; racist philosophy in Japan.

6. Affiliation of extreme nationalistic Arab groups with the Nazi party; Grand Mufti's interference with the program of annihilation of the Jews

*VI. Relations Between Jews and non-Jews in the Nazi-Occupied Countries*

A. Rise and spread of anti-Semitism in Europe before the Nazi occupation

B. Reactions of various peoples to Nazi oppression of the Jews: assistance, protection, and sympathy in the Western and Scandinavian countries and Italy; callousness or hostility in other places; attitudes in various social milieus and classes

C. Christian churches and the Jewish question

1. Vatican

2. Position on Jewish converts and "racial Jews of Christian faith"; mixed marriages; *Mischlinge*

3. Nazi *Kulturkampf* against the churches and its connection with the Jewish question

D. Position of freedom movement and underground organizations on the Jewish question

E. Collaborationist and anti-Semitic organizations; their anti-Jewish actions in various countries

F. Fate of the Jews compared with that of other persecuted groups: the Karaites and the Gypsies; Nazi program of "depopulation" of the Slavonic nations

G. Cooperation between Jews and other persecuted groups—the "common destiny" philosophy

# INDEX